**W9-CMA-711**

British Novelists, 1890-1929: Modernists

Dictionary of Literary Biography

Dictionary of Literary Biography • Volume Thirty-six

British Novelists, 1890-1929: Modernists

Edited by
Thomas F. Staley
University of Tulsa

A Bruccoli Clark Book
Gale Research Company • Book Tower • Detroit, Michigan 48226

Manufactured by Edwards Brothers, Inc.
Ann Arbor, Michigan
Printed in the United States of America

Copyright © 1985
GALE RESEARCH COMPANY

Library of Congress Cataloging in Publication Data
Main entry under title:

British novelists, 1890-1929: modernists.

    (Dictionary of literary biography; v. 36)
    "A Bruccoli Clark book."
    Includes index.
    1. Novelists, English—19th century—Biography.
2. Novelists, English—20th century—Biography.
I. Staley, Thomas F. II. Series.
PR861.B73   1985   823'.912'09 [B]   84-28613
ISBN 0-8103-1714-1

To my Irish colleagues
Darcy O'Brien and Michael Whalon

Contents

Plan of the Series

. . . Almost the most prodigious asset of a country, and perhaps its most precious possession, is its native literary product—when that product is fine and noble and enduring.

Mark Twain*

The advisory board, the editors, and the publisher of the *Dictionary of Literary Biography* are joined in endorsing Mark Twain's declaration. The literature of a nation provides an inexhaustible resource of permanent worth. It is our expectation that this endeavor will make literature and its creators better understood and more accessible to students and the literate public, while satisfying the standards of teachers and scholars.

To meet these requirements, *literary biography* has been construed in terms of the author's achievement. The most important thing about a writer is his writing. Accordingly, the entries in *DLB* are career biographies, tracing the development of the author's canon and the evolution of his reputation.

The publication plan for *DLB* resulted from two years of preparation. The project was proposed to Bruccoli Clark by Frederick G. Ruffner, president of the Gale Research Company, in November 1975. After specimen entries were prepared and typeset, an advisory board was formed to refine the entry format and develop the series rationale. In meetings held during 1976, the publisher, series editors, and advisory board approved the scheme for a comprehensive biographical dictionary of persons who contributed to North American literature. Editorial work on the first volume began in January 1977, and it was published in 1978.

In order to make *DLB* more than a reference tool and to compile volumes that individually have claim to status as literary history, it was decided to organize volumes by topic or period or genre. Each of these freestanding volumes provides a biographical-bibliographical guide and overview for a particular area of literature. We are convinced that this organization—as opposed to a single alphabet method—constitutes a valuable innovation in the presentation of reference material. The volume plan necessarily requires many decisions for the placement and treatment of authors who might

properly be included in two or three volumes. In some instances a major figure will be included in separate volumes, but with different entries emphasizing the aspect of his career appropriate to each volume. Ernest Hemingway, for example, is represented in *American Writers in Paris, 1920-1939* by an entry focusing on his expatriate apprenticeship; he is also in *American Novelists, 1910-1945* with an entry surveying his entire career. Each volume includes a cumulative index of subject authors. The final *DLB* volume will be a comprehensive index to the entire series.

With volume ten in 1982 it was decided to enlarge the scope of *DLB* beyond the literature of the United States. By the end of 1983 twelve volumes treating British literature had been published, and volumes for Commonwealth and Modern European literature were in progress. The series has been further augmented by the *DLB Yearbooks* (since 1981) which update published entries and add new entries to keep the *DLB* current with contemporary activity. There have also been occasional *DLB Documentary Series* volumes which provide biographical and critical background source materials for figures whose work is judged to have particular interest for students. One of these companion volumes is entirely devoted to Tennessee Williams.

The purpose of *DLB* is not only to provide reliable information in a convenient format but also to place the figures in the larger perspective of literary history and to offer appraisals of their accomplishments by qualified scholars.

We define literature as the *intellectual commerce of a nation*: not merely as belles lettres, but as that ample and complex process by which ideas are generated, shaped, and transmitted. *DLB* entries are not limited to "creative writers" but extend to other figures who in this time and in this way influenced the mind of a people. Thus the series encompasses historians, journalists, publishers, and screenwriters. By this means readers of *DLB* may be aided to perceive literature not as cult scripture in the keeping of cultural high priests, but as at the center of a nation's life.

DLB includes the major writers appropriate to each volume and those standing in the ranks immediately behind them. Scholarly and critical counsel has been sought in deciding which minor figures to include and how full their entries should be.

---

*From an unpublished section of Mark Twain's autobiography, copyright © by the Mark Twain Company.

Wherever possible, useful references will be made to figures who do not warrant separate entries.

Each *DLB* volume has a volume editor responsible for planning the volume, selecting the figures for inclusion, and assigning the entries. Volume editors are also responsible for preparing, where appropriate, appendices surveying the major periodicals and literary and intellectual movements for their volumes, as well as lists of further readings. Work on the series as a whole is coordinated at the Bruccoli Clark editorial center in Columbia, South Carolina, where the editorial staff is responsible for the accuracy of the published volumes.

One feature that distinguishes *DLB* is the illustration policy—its concern with the iconography of literature. Just as an author is influenced by his surroundings, so is the reader's understanding of the author enhanced by a knowledge of his environment. Therefore *DLB* volumes include not only drawings, paintings, and photographs of authors, often depicting them at various stages in their careers, but also illustrations of their families and places where they lived. Title pages are regularly reproduced in facsimile along with dust jackets for modern authors. The dust jackets are a special fea-

ture of *DLB* because they often document better than anything else the way in which an author's work was launched in its own time. Specimens of the writers' manuscripts are included when feasible.

A supplement to *DLB*—tentatively titled *A Guide, Chronology, and Glossary for American Literature*—will outline the history of literature in North America and trace the influences that shaped it. This volume will provide a framework for the study of American literature by means of chronological tables, literary affiliation charts, glossarial entries, and concise surveys of the major movements. It has been planned to stand on its own as a vade mecum, providing a ready-reference guide to the study of American literature as well as a companion to the *DLB* volumes for American literature.

Samuel Johnson rightly decreed that "The chief glory of every people arises from its authors." The purpose of the *Dictionary of Literary Biography* is to compile literary history in the surest way available to us—by accurate and comprehensive treatment of the lives and work of those who contributed to it.

The *DLB* Advisory Board

Foreword

The foreword to *Dictionary of Literary Biography*, volume 34, *British Novelists, 1890-1929: Traditionalists*, discusses the fertility and diversity of the British novel during the forty-year period that bracketed the Great War and was marked by sweeping and revolutionary changes in the fabric of public and private life. These changes were so substantial and unalterable that Virginia Woolf proclaimed, "in or about December 1910 human character changed." This phrase is remembered more for its dramatic quality than its historical accuracy, but, nevertheless, it points with psychological accuracy to the profound changes in the way man was beginning to think about his universe, his social and governmental structures, and, most profoundly, about himself and his place in the world. In her choice of date, Woolf was referring specifically to the first postimpressionist exhibition in England, but her announcement serves as a summation of the developments that were to take place during the next twenty years. As novelists, both major and minor, sought to capture and give shape to these new developments, the novel became the most flexible and versatile of the literary genres.

The novelists in this volume form an interesting contrast to those covered in *DLB 34*. The realists had strong philosophical and aesthetic affinities to the novel as it had developed in the nineteenth century and were not preoccupied with experiments in form and structure. The modernists, while they were writing during the same period, relied less on the older order of the imagination. Their radical departure from tradition finds its distinct identity in what we have come to call *modernism*. Yet such terms as *realist* and *modernist* must be used to classify rather than define each group, to refer to general trends and impulses. For example, the works of Joseph Conrad contrasted with those of James Joyce demonstrate this division, but there are important similarities in their fiction as well, and among minor writers distinctions become blurred.

To a certain extent every generation of writers sees itself as being different from its predecessors, concerned as it is with its own problems and aesthetic demands, with new ways of ordering and defining experience. But in no recent artistic movement was the definition of the new so central as it was to modernism. Not confined to any one country, modernism pervaded Europe and later America and was manifest in all of the arts. Yet, because it was perceived in crucially different ways by its various practitioners, a precise definition of modernism is a challenge to literary critics and historians. It is difficult to find commonality in such diversity, even in one genre in a single country. Nevertheless, the diverse group of British novelists who may be classified as modernists, for all of their dissimilarities, reveal in their fiction those elements which literary critics identify with modernism. For all of the immediate differences among the modernists, as in the extreme example of Joyce and Lawrence, their sense of change and the range of their concerns set them apart from such traditionalists as Bennett or Galsworthy.

All of the vast and profound changes in British life affected the novel in a multiplicity of ways. Powerfully affected was, as Roland Barthes suggests, language itself. New forces and new awarenesses in society made past literary accountings seem incomplete, and, as the new was reflected in a multitude of innovative modes of writing, literary language ceased to be universal.

Modernism is characterized by its insistence on the autonomy of the work of art: a novel is not merely a reflection of the life it depicts but is its own enterprise; modernist fiction draws attention to itself, its codes, its forms, and its methods. Modernism is preoccupied with irony, and evinces an attitude of detachment and ambivalence, which is frequently expressed through experiments with point of view. The relativity of time is another preoccupation in the modernist novel, as in Virginia Woolf's *Mrs. Dalloway;* and myth is frequently used as an ordering device, as in Joyce's *Ulysses.* Finally, as Maurice Beebe has pointed out, there is in modernist fiction a reflexive quality, an insistence on the primacy of the individual consciousness. Yet, Joyce, Woolf, Lawrence, Dorothy Richardson, and the other novelists in this volume, as diverse as they are in their sensibilities and concerns, as different as they are in their choices of subject matter and form, have one major commonality and that is a profound commitment to recognize, capture, rearrange, and even reshape the perceptions of their contemporary world.

—Thomas F. Staley

Acknowledgments

This book was produced by BC Research. Karen L. Rood is senior editor for the *Dictionary of Literary Biography* series. The editorial staff includes Philip B. Dematteis, Jean W. Ross, and Margaret A. Van Antwerp.

Art supervisor is Claudia Ericson. Copyediting supervisor is Joycelyn R. Smith. Typesetting supervisor is Laura Ingram. The production staff includes Mary Betts, Rowena Betts, Kimberly Casey, Patricia Coate, Kathleen M. Flanagan, Joyce Fowler, Judith K. Ingle, Victoria Jakes, Vickie Lowers, Judith McCray, and Jane McPherson. Jean W. Ross is permissions editor. Joseph Caldwell, photography editor, did photographic copy work for the volume.

Walter W. Ross did the library research with the assistance of the staff at the Thomas Cooper Library of the University of South Carolina: Lynn Barron, Daniel Boice, Sue Collins, Michael Freeman, Gary Geer, Alexander M. Gilchrist, David L. Haggard, Jens Holley, David Lincove, Marcia Martin, Roger Mortimer, Jean Rhyne, Karen Rissling, Paula Swope, and Ellen Tillet.

The following booksellers provided invaluable assistance in providing illustrations for this volume: Bertram Rota Ltd., Clearwater Books, Guildhall Bookshop, Ian McKelvie Books, and Sylvester & Orphanos Booksellers & Publishers.

The editor also acknowledges with gratitude the significant contributions of Scott Simpkins, Charlotte Stewart, and Mary O'Toole.

British Novelists, 1890-1929:
Modernists

Dictionary of Literary Biography

Richard Aldington

(8 July 1892-27 July 1962)

Douglas M. Catron
Iowa State University

See also the Aldington entry in *DLB 20, British Poets, 1914-1945.*

SELECTED BOOKS: *Images (1910-1915)* (London: Poetry Bookshop, 1915); revised and enlarged as *Images Old and New* (Boston: Four Seas, 1916); enlarged again as *Images* (London: Egoist, 1919);

Reverie: A Little Book of Poems for H. D. (Cleveland: Clerk's Press, 1917);

The Love Poems of Myrrhine and Konallis, a Cycle of Prose Poems Written after the Greek Manner (Cleveland: Clerk's Press, 1917); enlarged as *The Love of Myrrhine and Konallis and Other Prose Poems* (Chicago: Covici, 1926);

Images of War: A Book of Poems (Westminster: C. W. Beaumont, 1919; enlarged edition, London: Allen & Unwin, 1919; Boston: Four Seas, 1920); enlarged as *War and Love (1915-1918)* (Boston: Four Seas, 1921);

Images of Desire (London: Elkin Mathews, 1919);

Exile and Other Poems (London: Allen & Unwin, 1923; Boston: Four Seas, 1924);

Literary Studies and Reviews (London: Allen & Unwin, 1924; New York: MacVeagh/Dial Press, 1924);

A Fool i' the Forest: A Phantasmagoria (London: Allen & Unwin, 1925; New York: MacVeagh/Dial Press, 1925);

Voltaire (London: Routledge, 1925; London: Routledge/New York: Dutton, 1925);

French Studies and Reviews (London: Allen & Unwin, 1926; New York: MacVeagh/Dial Press, 1926);

D. H. Lawrence: An Indiscretion (Seattle: University of Washington Book Store, 1927); republished as *D. H. Lawrence* (London: Chatto & Windus, 1930); revised and enlarged as *D. H. Lawrence: An Appreciation* (Harmondsworth: Penguin, 1950);

Remy de Gourmont: A Modern Man of Letters (Seattle: University of Washington Book Store, 1928);

Collected Poems (New York: Covici, Friede, 1928; London: Allen & Unwin, 1929);

Death of a Hero, A Novel (New York: Covici, Friede, 1929; London: Chatto & Windus, 1929; unexpurgated edition, 2 volumes, Paris: Babou & Kahane, 1930);

The Eaten Heart (Chapelle-Reanville: Hours Press, 1929; enlarged edition, London: Chatto & Windus, 1933);

At All Costs (London: Heinemann, 1930);

Last Straws (Paris: Hours Press, 1930);

Two Stories (London: Elkin Mathews & Marrot, 1930);

Love and the Luxembourg (New York: Covici, Friede, 1930); republished as *A Dream in the Luxembourg* (London: Chatto & Windus, 1930);

Roads to Glory (London: Chatto & Windus, 1930; Garden City: Doubleday, Doran, 1931);

The Colonel's Daughter, A Novel (London: Chatto & Windus, 1931; Garden City: Doubleday, Doran, 1931);

Stepping Heavenward: A Record (Florence: Orioli, 1931; London: Chatto & Windus, 1931; Garden City: Doubleday, Doran, 1932);

Soft Answers (London: Chatto & Windus, 1932; Garden City: Doubleday, Doran, 1932);

All Men Are Enemies, A Romance (London: Chatto & Windus, 1933; Garden City: Doubleday, Doran, 1933);

The Poems of Richard Aldington (Garden City: Doubleday, Doran, 1934);

Women Must Work, A Novel (London: Chatto & Windus, 1934; Garden City: Doubleday, Doran, 1934);

D. H. Lawrence: A Complete List of His Works, Together with a Critical Appreciation (London: Heinemann, 1935); republished as *D. H. Lawrence* (N.p.: Tobago, 1935);

Artifex: Sketches and Ideas (London: Chatto & Windus, 1935; Garden City: Doubleday, Doran, 1936);

Life Quest (London: Chatto & Windus, 1935; Garden City: Doubleday, Doran, 1935);

Life of a Lady: A Play, by Aldington and Derek Patmore (Garden City: Doubleday, Doran, 1936; London: Putnam's, 1936);

The Crystal World (London: Heinemann, 1937; Garden City: Doubleday, Doran, 1938);

Very Heaven (London & Toronto: Heinemann, 1937; Garden City: Doubleday, Doran, 1937);

Seven Against Reeves: A Comedy-Farce (London & Toronto: Heinemann, 1938; Garden City: Doubleday, Doran, 1938);

Rejected Guest, A Novel (New York: Viking, 1939; London & Toronto: Heinemann, 1939);

W. Somerset Maugham: An Appreciation (Garden City: Doubleday, Doran, 1939);

Life for Life's Sake: A Book of Reminiscences (New York: Viking, 1941; London: Cassell, 1968);

The Duke: Being an Account of the Life & Achievements of Arthur Wellesley, 1st Duke of Wellington (New York: Viking, 1943); republished as *Wellington: Being an Account of the Life & Achievements of Arthur Wellesley, 1st Duke of Wellington* (London & Toronto: Heinemann, 1946);

The Romance of Casanova, A Novel (New York: Duell, Sloan & Pearce, 1946; London & Toronto: Heinemann, 1947);

Four English Portraits, 1801-1851 (London: Evans, 1948);

The Complete Poems of Richard Aldington (London: Wingate, 1948);

Jane Austen (Pasadena: Ampersand Press, 1948);

The Strange Life of Charles Waterton, 1782-1865 (London: Evans, 1949; New York: Duell, Sloan & Pearce, 1949);

Portrait of a Genius But . . . The Life of D. H. Lawrence (London: Heinemann, 1950); republished as *D. H. Lawrence: Portrait of a Genius But . . .* (New York: Duell, Sloan & Pearce, 1950);

Pinorman: Personal Recollections of Norman Douglas, Pino Orioli, and Charles Prentice (London: Heinemann, 1954);

Ezra Pound and T. S. Eliot: A Lecture (Hurst, Berkshire: Peacocks Press, 1954);

Lawrence of Arabia: A Biographical Enquiry (London: Collins, 1955; Chicago: Regnery, 1955);

A. E. Housman and W. B. Yeats: Two Lectures (Hurst, Berkshire: Peacocks Press, 1955);

Introduction to Mistral (London: Heinemann, 1956; Carbondale: Southern Illinois University Press, 1960);

Frauds (London: Heinemann, 1957);

Portrait of a Rebel: The Life and Works of Robert Louis Stevenson (London: Evans, 1957);

Richard Aldington: Selected Critical Writings, 1928-1960, edited by Alister Kershaw (Carbondale: Southern Illinois University Press, 1970).

OTHER: *Letters of Madame De Sévigné to Her Daughter and Her Friends,* selected with an introductory essay by Aldington (London: Routledge, 1927; New York: Brentano's, 1927);

D. H. Lawrence, *Last Poems,* edited by Aldington and G. Orioli (New York: Viking, 1933; London: Secker, 1933);

D. H. Lawrence: Selected Poems, edited by Aldington (London: Secker, 1934);

The Spirit of Place: An Anthology Compiled from the Prose of D. H. Lawrence, edited with an introduction by Aldington (London: Heinemann, 1935);

The Viking Book of Poetry of the English-Speaking World, edited by Aldington (New York: Viking, 1941); republished as *Poetry of the English-Speaking World* (London: Heinemann, 1947);

The Portable Oscar Wilde, edited by Aldington (New York: Viking, 1946); republished as *Oscar Wilde: Selected Works* (London: Heinemann, 1946);

Walter Pater: Selected Works, edited by Aldington (London: Heinemann, 1948; New York: Duell, Sloan & Pearce, 1948).

TRANSLATIONS: *The Poems of Anyte of Tegea* (London: Egoist Press, 1915; Cleveland: Clerk's Press, 1917);

Feodor Sogolub (Feodor Teternikov), *The Little Demon,* translated by Aldington and John Cournos (New York: Knopf, 1916);

Greek Songs in the Manner of Anacreon (London: Egoist Press, 1919);

Medallions in Clay (New York: Knopf, 1921); republished as *Medallions from Anyte of Tegea, Meleager of Gadara, the Anacreontea: Latin Poets of the Renaissance* (London: Chatto & Windus, 1930);

French Comedies of the XVIIIth Century (London: Routledge, 1923; London: Routledge/New York: Dutton, 1923);

Cyrano de Bergerac, *Voyages to the Moon and the Sun* (London: Routledge/New York: Dutton, 1923; London: Routledge, 1927);

Choderlos de Laclos, *Dangerous Acquaintances (Les Liaisons Dangereuses)* (London: Routledge, 1924; London: Routledge/New York: Dutton, 1924);

The Mystery of the Nativity, Translated from the Liégeois of the XVth Century (London: Allen & Unwin, 1924);

Pierre Custot, *Sturly* (London: Cape, 1924; Boston: Houghton Mifflin, 1924);

The Fifteen Joys of Marriage, Ascribed to Antoine De La Sale, c. 1388-c. 1462 (London: Routledge, 1926; London: Routledge/New York: Dutton, 1926);

Voltaire, *Candide and Other Romances* (London: Routledge, 1927; London: Routledge/New York: Dutton, 1927);

Letters of Voltaire and Frederick the Great (London: Routledge, 1927; New York: Brentano's, 1927);

Remy de Gourmont: Selections from All His Works (Chicago: P. Covici, 1928; London: Chatto & Windus, 1932);

Julien Benda, *The Treason of the Intellectuals (La Trahison des clercs)* (New York: W. Morrow, 1928);

Euripides, *Alcestis* (London: Chatto & Windus, 1930);

The Decameron of Giovanni Boccaccio (New York: Covici, Friede, 1930; London: Putnam's, 1930);

Larousse Encyclopedia of Mythology, translated by Aldington and Delano Ames (New York: Prometheus Press, 1959).

Richard Aldington is perhaps best remembered among students of early twentieth-century poetry as a central figure in the imagist movement. His three poems published in *Poetry* (Chicago) in November 1912 were the first to be identified with the imagists. Aldington and Hilda Doolittle (H. D.), whom he married in 1913, were central contributors to the anthologies of poetry representing this new movement, among them *Des Imagistes* (1914), compiled by Ezra Pound. Later, Aldington

Richard Aldington, 1917

continued to represent the imagists in England, along with D. H. Lawrence and F. S. Flint, in the first three volumes of Amy Lowell's anthologies, *Some Imagist Poets,* published in 1915, 1916, and 1917. America was represented by H. D., John Gould Fletcher, and Lowell. Given Aldington's prominence in the most important poetic movement of the first half of this century, many critics have understandably paid little attention to his fiction. Nevertheless, Aldington did produce eight novels during a long and distinguished career as novelist, poet, translator, and critical biographer. At least two of these novels received considerable praise during his lifetime.

Aldington was born 8 July 1892 in Portsmouth, England, the eldest son of Albert Edward Aldington, a solicitor's clerk, and his wife, Jessie May Godfrey. The events of his early life are recorded in considerable detail in his autobiography, *Life for Life's Sake: A Book of Reminiscences* (1941). Here he recounts his boyhood in Dover and his early years at a private school, where he studied French and Latin. His early reading was broad. Beginning with his father's library, a surprisingly good collection of the best literature, Aldington continued to build on his knowledge of literature beyond the French and Latin classics. By the time he entered University College, London, in 1910, he was so well read he was able to pass a required reading examination with a "98 out of 100 on a special test paper." Sir Alec Randall, a close friend of Aldington's college days, describes him as "the centre of a group of admiring friends, of whom I was one."

In 1911, owing to his family's financial difficulties, Aldington left University College and began what would prove to be a distinguished career as a writer. His first efforts were as a part-time journalist covering sporting events and an occasional contributor to various poetry magazines. Later, because of the contacts he began to make among other young poets, particularly those of the imagist movement, he was able in 1914 to become assistant editor of the *Egoist,* a fortnightly review originally founded in June 1913 by Dora Marsden and Harriet Shaw Weaver as the *New Freewoman: An Individualist Review.* The title, Richard E. Smith notes, was "changed to *The Egoist: An Individualist Review* on the first of January of the following year." Even before the title change, however, the review became a vehicle for the emerging *Imagistes,* including Aldington. With the exception of the years of World War I, during which time Aldington served first as an enlisted man and later as a commissioned officer, Aldington devoted the next fifteen years to poetry and criticism, translations, and biographical work.

His first novel, *Death of a Hero* (1929), appeared at a point in his career when he was already well known and highly regarded as a poet and critic. Already the author of a dozen volumes, translator of as many more works, and veteran literary critic of the *Times Literary Supplement,* Aldington came to the novel with impressive credentials. He had been planning his first novel, *Death of a Hero,* for nearly a decade before he actually began the writing in 1928. Part of the novel was written at Port-Cros on the French Riviera during one of Aldington's twice-

yearly "escapes" to the Continent. Although he had been fortunate in finding employment with the *Times* and successful in placing his work for publication when he returned from the war, Aldington confessed to considerable difficulty readjusting to England and to his former acquaintances in literary circles. One might argue that *Death of a Hero* represents the story of its author's struggle and failure to readjust.

The novel opens with a prologue which reveals all. The novel should not be read, Aldington tells us in his autobiography, "for the trivial purpose of finding out what happened." The conclusion of the story is already known from the outset; George Winterbourne, a sensitive young painter-turned-soldier, is dead. Through the voice of a fellow officer, Aldington traces the causes of that death. What emerges from this narrative is a social indictment, a meticulous and unsparing satire of Victorian and contemporary England directed not only at George's parents and others of their generation but also at his fellow officers, his wife Elizabeth, his mistress Fanny, and assorted members of English literary society. Almost no one in the cast is spared. The Victorians, the author argues, were the architects of the war and the root cause of the death of George Winterbourne, a young man who stands as a symbol of the thousands who died needlessly.

Winterbourne might easily have been modeled on Wilfred Owen, another sensitive young artist-turned-soldier who died during some of the last action of the war, only a week before the Armistice. Indeed, Aldington has written a memorial to this fellow poet ("In Memory of Wilfred Owen"). Whatever the inspiration for Winterbourne, the novel stands as an important historical as well as literary document. It has been favorably and justifiably compared with Erich Maria Remarque's *All Quiet on the Western Front* and with Ernest Hemingway's *A Farewell to Arms* (1929).

By 1928, Aldington had given up trying to adjust to an England that was becoming increasingly alien to him. Like D. H. Lawrence, Aldington chose voluntary exile, first in Paris, then Italy, and later in America. His second novel, *The Colonel's Daughter* (1931), although inspired by the country folk he knew during his years at Chapel Farm Cottage in Berkshire, where he lived from 1919 to 1927, was written in Paris and Italy. At the center of the novel is Georgina Smithers, perhaps a spiritual sister of George Winterbourne of *Death of a Hero.* Georgina, the only child of a retired lieutenant colonel, is steeped in Victorian rules of conduct. Her conflict is a simple one; she wants a husband, but she is an unfortunate remnant of the old order, doomed to spinsterhood by a code which prevents her from seeking a husband among the few eligible bachelors with whom she comes in contact. Good Victorian that she is, she must wait to be selected by a proper mate; unfortunately, her station, her lack of talent, of wit, of beauty all legislate against her. This central plot seems thin, but it must have described a social reality for many young women in postwar England, when a whole generation of young men had been severely depleted.

The several subplots of *The Colonel's Daughter* exist mostly for satirical purposes. Yet beneath Aldington's satire one senses a genuine compassion. In his second novel Aldington allows his reader, less affected by the author's intrusions, to judge the characters. There is social condemnation, of course, but one could argue that Aldington's studies of Voltaire only a few years earlier had begun to take effect: he could now allow society to condemn itself. The satire of *The Colonel's Daughter* is tempered with many purely comic illustrations, revealing Aldington's efforts to depend more on dramatic or ironic presentation of his characters' foibles than on direct condemnation of them.

Richard Aldington, early 1930s

Aldington's domestic harmony during this period failed to match his professional success. Even before World War I ended and he returned to England to continue his writing career, Aldington's marriage to Hilda Doolittle was already crumbling. By 1919, their relationship all but finished, Aldington and Doolittle separated, although they were not divorced until 1938. Between 1919 and 1938, two women figured prominently in Aldington's life: Dorothy Yorke, an American art student whom he had met while on leave during the war and with whom he remained intimate after separating from Hilda Doolittle; and Brigit Patmore, a friend from the London days before the war and a member of the literary circle that included Violet Hunt, Ezra Pound, and Hilda Doolittle, among others. In 1938 Aldington married Netta McCulloch. Their daughter Catherine was born shortly thereafter.

Even with what might be considered an unquiet domestic life, Aldington produced during this period a score of critical works, six of his eight novels, and a dozen or more translations, not counting his poetry. His work in the novel, surprisingly, spans only about sixteen years or so of his career, from about 1929 through 1946. His third and fourth novels, *All Men Are Enemies* (1933) and *Women Must Work* (1934), are a continuation of the artistic direction he had established in his first two novels—social satire.

The first of these, *All Men Are Enemies,* traces the progress of Antony Clarendon, the protagonist, in his struggle toward what "he believes to be a finer and fuller life," as Aldington terms it in his prefatory note to the first American edition novel. Antony moves from despair, through spiritual death, and finally to rebirth in the course of the novel. Part one, which takes the reader from 1900-1914 through Clarendon's childhood and emergence into manhood, is stylistically pastoral. From the opening on Mount Olympus, where a council of the gods discusses Antony's birth and prophesies his struggle for a "life like unto our own," to the end of part one, Aldington strives to capture the atmosphere of prewar England through scenes reminiscent of several in D. H. Lawrence's early novels. Here time seems almost to stand still, keyed to nature's cycle of growth and harvest rather than to the more frenetic pace of a society dominated by the machine.

In part two, which begins in 1919, Aldington presents a stark contrast. Here, symbolically, may be seen the death of the old order. For Antony too the long nightmare of death, during which he is

Dust jacket for Aldington's 1933 novel, in which the protagonist struggles to recapture his prewar idealism in a society torn apart by World War I

haunted by phantom German soldiers, marks a new beginning. *All Men Are Enemies,* unlike *Death of a Hero,* is not a war novel; the war years are alluded to only by satirical bits of verse devoted to each intervening year between parts one and two. Rather, as Aldington reveals in his preface, it is a "Romance," the account of its protagonist's struggle to recapture his youthful idealism; to reclaim his first love, Katha, an Austrian girl he meets at the end of part one; to escape what for him has become a meaningless society. Parts three and four echo these goals, sometimes subtly, more often overtly. Yet because Aldington uses a council of gods to prophesy his end, the reader is left with few doubts about Clarendon's success.

Artistically the novel is uneven. Although Aldington shows considerable skill in part one in his description of pastoral England and in his depiction of the war's aftermath in part two, this level of skill is not maintained in parts three and four, where, as Richard E. Smith rightly observes, several parts are filled with "unnecessary details, dialogue, and commentary."

Aldington's next novel, *Women Must Work,* parallels *The Colonel's Daughter.* Unlike Georgina Smithers of the earlier novel, however, Etta Morison is bound by none of the conventions of Victorian society. She has been "emancipated" by the war; the character and extent of her emancipation is the theme of the novel. When Etta has an illegitimate child, for instance, she finds she must invent a husband; and even when she moves to London, she must maintain the illusion of having had a husband lost in the war. Although Etta achieves financial success, eventually marries, and manages to dominate her husband, Maurice, there are numerous hints through secondary characters in the novel that her success is less than it could have been. Ironically, Aldington makes clear, she has settled for a false ideal—emancipation and an empty sovereignty.

By 1935, after having lived briefly in both Spain and Portugal, Aldington decided that Europe

Richard Aldington, 1935 (photo by Robert Disraeli)

was becoming more and more an arena for political bickering, an atmosphere clearly unsuited to his temperament. With war apparently imminent, in Europe at least, Aldington resolved to leave Europe for good and make his home in the United States. For the next decade, except for several brief trips to Europe before the United States entered the war, Aldington lived in the United States. None of his four remaining novels was set in the United States, however.

Two of these novels contain thematic echoes of Aldington's previous fiction. In both *Very Heaven* (1937) and *Rejected Guest* (1939), the major characters (Chris Heylin and David Norris, respectively) are reminiscent of George Winterbourne of *Death of a Hero*. Though a generation younger than Winterbourne, they face many of the same conflicts: the growing sense of a gulf between themselves and the older generation, which blossoms into a deep cynicism, especially for Chris; and an impending war, which threatens their chances for any future at all, much less a happy one. Neither of these novels has the depth or impact of Aldington's earlier fiction, but there are passages in each that reveal Aldington's insight into character and his skill in handling description.

Between these rather similar novels Aldington produced one other set in the twentieth century, *Seven Against Reeves: A Comedy-Farce* (1938), in which he returns to a lighter satire rather like that of *The Colonel's Daughter*. John Mason Reeves, a successful London businessman, is beginning his retirement as the novel opens. To please his wife, Reeves embarks on a new, and brief, career as a socialite. The cast of characters (caricatures really) he encounters both in England and on the Continent is amusingly overdrawn. Reeves is the counterpoint to the absurd posturings of the would-be-artists, musicians, editors, and literati he meets during this brief whirl among another class of society to which he is totally unaccustomed. As one would expect, Reeves abandons the new life and returns to work to get, as he puts it, some "peace and quiet." *Seven Against Reeves*, a clever satire in the Horatian tradition, seems almost to have been written merely for fun, but such an assessment would ignore Reeves as counterpoint, his journey, and Aldington's previous satire. Even comic satire has its end: to laugh us out of folly.

Aldington's last novel not only ignores the war but abandons the twentieth century altogether. *The Romance of Casanova* (1946), as its title suggests, is set in eighteenth-century Italy. Several episodes in the novel parallel those in Casanova's own *Memoires* (1822, German edition; an unexpurgated French edition in twelve volumes was published between 1826 and 1838). The standard English edition, translated by Arthur Machen, appeared only a year before *The Romance of Casanova*. In Aldington's version, Casanova recounts his pursuit of Henriette, as well as a number of other affairs, intrigues, adventures, and narrow escapes. The portrait of this in-

Aldington with his daughter Catherine in Montpellier, France, 1955 (courtesy of Frédéric-Jacques Temple)

famous adventurer is both sensitive and entertaining.

Aldington's reasons for abandoning the novel after *The Romance of Casanova* are unknown, but as the bibliography of his works indicates, he was never idle. A biography of the Duke of Wellington, for which he received the James Tait Black Memorial Prize, appeared in 1943. Over the next twelve years he added biographies of D. H. Lawrence and T. E. Lawrence, as well as several critical editions and translations. As a result of his unsparing treatment of T. E. Lawrence, Aldington was either attacked or abandoned by most British critics, which perhaps accounts for his relative obscurity today. Even so, his reputation was undimmed in France, where he lived from 1946 until his death in 1962, and especially in the Soviet Union. Shortly before his death, Aldington was honored by the Soviet Writers' Union at a reception in Moscow.

Few writers of this century have been as prolific as Aldington. Fewer still have had the wealth of literary knowledge and historical insight to be at home with such diverse figures as Anacreon, Vol-

taire, Jane Austen, and Robert Louis Stevenson. And even though his reputation has suffered in the past two decades, Richard Aldington, whether studied as translator and critic or as poet and novelist, is well worth rediscovering.

Letters:

A Passionate Prodigality: Letters to Alan Bird from Richard Aldington, 1949-1962, edited by Miriam J. Benkovitz (New York: New York Public Library, 1976);

Literary Lifelines: the Richard Aldington-Lawrence Durrell Correspondence, edited by Ian S. MacNiven and Harry T. Moore (New York: Viking, 1981).

Bibliographies:

Alister Kershaw, *A Bibliography of the Works of Richard Aldington from 1915 to 1948* (Burlingame, Cal.: William Wredon, 1950);

Norman T. Gates, "The Richard Aldington Collection at the Morris Library," *ICarbS,* 3 (1976): 61-68;

Gates, *A Checklist of the Letters of Richard Aldington* (Carbondale: Southern Illinois University Press, 1977).

References:

H. D. (Hilda Doolittle), *Bid Me to Live* (New York: Grove, 1960);

Keath Fraser, "A Note on Aldington and Free Verse," *Four Decades of Poetry,* 1 (January 1977): 222-225;

Norman T. Gates, "*Images of War* and *Death of a Hero:* Aldington's Twice-Used Images," *Modern British Literature,* 4 (Fall 1979): 120-127;

Gates, *The Poetry of Richard Aldington: A Critical Evaluation and an Anthology of Uncollected Poems* (University Park: Pennsylvania State University Press, 1974);

Gates, "Richard Aldington and the Clerk's Press," *Ohio Review,* 13 (Fall 1971): 21-27;

Alister Kershaw and Frédéric-Jacques Temple, eds., *Richard Aldington: An Intimate Portrait* (Carbondale: Southern Illinois University Press, 1965);

Selwyn Burnett Kittredge, "The Literary Career of Richard Aldington," Ph.D. dissertation, New York University, 1976;

Kittredge, "Richard Aldington's Challenge to T. S. Eliot: The Background of Their James Joyce Controversy," *James Joyce Quarterly,* 10 (Spring 1973): 339-341;

Phillip Knightley, "Aldington's Enquiry Concerning T. E. Lawrence," *Texas Quarterly,* 16 (Winter 1973): 98-105;

Thomas McGreevy, *Richard Aldington: An Englishman* (London: Chatto & Windus, 1931);

John Morris, "Richard Aldington and *Death of a Hero* —Or Life of an Anti-Hero?," in *The First World War in Fiction: A Collection of Critical Essays,* edited by Holger Klein (London: Macmillan, 1976), pp. 183-192;

Richard Eugene Smith, *Richard Aldington* (Boston: Twayne, 1977).

Papers:

The largest collection of Aldington's papers is at Southern Illinois University. Other important collections of letters are at Harvard, Yale, UCLA, and the University of Texas.

Michael Arlen

(16 November 1895-23 June 1956)

Harry Keyishian
Fairleigh Dickinson University

BOOKS: *The London Venture* (London: Heinemann, 1920; New York: Doran, 1920);

The Romantic Lady (London: Collins, 1921; New York: Dodd, Mead, 1921);

"Piracy" (London: Collins, 1922; New York: Doran, 1923);

These Charming People (London: Collins, 1923; New York: Doran, 1924);

The Green Hat (London: Collins, 1924; New York: Doran, 1924);

May Fair (London: Collins, 1925; New York: Doran, 1925);

The Acting Version of the Green Hat (New York: Doran, 1925);

Young Men in Love (London: Hutchinson, 1927; New York: Doran, 1927);

The Zoo: A Comedy in Three Acts, by Arlen and Winchell Smith (New York & London: French, 1927);

Lily Christine (Garden City: Doubleday, Doran, 1928; London: Hutchinson, 1929);

Babes in the Wood (London: Hutchinson, 1929; Garden City: Doubleday, Doran, 1929);

Men Dislike Women (London: Heinemann, 1931; Garden City: Doubleday, Doran, 1931);

Man's Mortality (London: Heinemann, 1933; Garden City: Doubleday, Doran, 1933);

Good Losers, by Arlen and Walter Hackett (London: French, 1934);

Hell! Said the Duchess (London: Heinemann, 1934; Garden City: Doubleday, Doran, 1934);

The Crooked Coronet (London & Toronto: Heinemann, 1937; Garden City: Doubleday, Doran, 1937);

Atalanta and Michael Arlen

The Flying Dutchman (London & Toronto: Heinemann, 1939; Garden City: Doubleday, Doran, 1939).

PLAYS: *Dear Father,* London, New Scala Theatre, 30 November 1924; revised as *These Charming People,* New York, Gaiety Theatre, 6 October 1925;
The Green Hat, London, Adelphi Theatre, 2 September 1925; New York, Broadhurst Theatre, 15 September 1925;
Why She Was Late for Dinner, London, Everyman Theatre, 27 November 1926;
The Zoo, by Arlen and Winchell Smith, London, 1927;
Good Losers, by Arlen and Walter Hackett, London, Whitehall Theatre, 16 February 1931.

SCREENPLAY: *The Heavenly Body,* by Arlen and Walter Reisch, M-G-M, 1944.

Michael Arlen's name will always be associated most strongly with his most popular work, *The Green Hat* (1924), a romantic novel about a passionate, promiscuous woman whose true nobility of soul is only revealed at the novel's sensational ending. His play version, produced in 1925, provided popular vehicles for Tallulah Bankhead (in London) and Katherine Cornell (in New York); a film version, *A Woman of Affairs* (1928), with a scenario by Bess Meredyth, starred Greta Garbo. This great success brought Arlen fame on both sides of the Atlantic: as he put it years later, "I was a flash in the pan in my twenties. I had a hell of a good time being flashy and there was, by the grace of God, a good deal of gold dust in the pan." When the vogue for his work more or less collapsed shortly after, he continued to write for a smaller but appreciative audience and, to his credit, to extend his range as writer.

Although he became known for his portraits of English society figures, Arlen's origins were quite "foreign." Born into an Armenian family in Bulgaria, where his father, Sarkis Kouyoumdjian, had brought them to avoid persecution by the Turks, Dikran Kouyoumdjian arrived in England in 1901, studied at Malvern College, dropped out of the University of Edinburgh after a short time as a medical student, and in 1913 moved to London. By 1916 and during the years after he was traveling in the company of D. H. Lawrence (who used Arlen as the model for the popular playwright Michaelis in the third version of *Lady Chatterley's Lover*), George Moore, and the Café Royal group, and he had begun writing articles for an Armenian periodical, *Ararat,* and for A. R. Orage's journal of opinion and economics, *New Age*. Writing at first as a polemicist for the Armenian cause (in the aftermath of the infamous deportations of Armenians from Turkey in 1915), Kouyoumdjian gradually evolved a more romantic style and subject matter. In 1920 he collected his later *New Age* pieces—tales of love gone wrong told to a sympathetic narrator by sad and sophisticated women—and published them as *The London Venture,* under the name Michael Arlen.

In his first novel, *"Piracy"* (1922), and in three books of short stories—*The Romantic Lady* (1921), *These Charming People* (1923), and *May Fair* (1925)—Arlen developed a repertory company of elegant men and women whose affairs and intrigues he wittily chronicled after the manner of Saki, G. K. Chesterton, and O. Henry. More unruly characters—such as the rakish Michael Wagstaff in "The Cavalier of the Streets" (*These Charming People*), a con man who lives by his wits on the follies of establishment figures—would on occasion intrude, but the tone is always that of genial satire.

The Green Hat, on the other hand, is romantic melodrama. Its narrator describes his long friendship with Iris March. A woman of strong sexuality whose one true love was thwarted by class snobbery, Iris had married, on the rebound, a young man idolized by his generation. When her husband commits suicide on their wedding night, it is assumed that the cause was his disgust at her revelations about her sex life. In the end, however, it is revealed that she has secretly been preserving his reputation: her husband killed himself because he had a venereal disease. The knowledge of her sacrifice restores her first love to her, but rather than take him from his young wife, Iris nobly and

Nancy Cunard, a model for Iris March in The Green Hat
(painting by Alvaro Guevara, 1919; Melbourne
National Gallery)

spectacularly kills herself, by smashing her car into a tree. Those who found the novel overheated and silly (like heiress and book publisher Nancy Cunard, on whom the character of Iris was largely modeled) were many in number, but the novel had a tremendous hold on the public's imagination, and green cloche hats became popular in the world of fashion.

Arlen apparently enjoyed his time of celebrity. He gave witty interviews and hobnobbed with the Algonquin crowd and with Hollywood notables such as Charles Chaplin and Pola Negri. However, his reputation underwent a swift decline. The fickle public came to agree with those who had felt right along that The Green Hat was no profound study of idealism and the "new" woman but merely an overheated melodrama. Arlen also seems to have been the victim of snobbery, in certain social circles, for being an "upstart" and pretender. D. H. Lawrence's portrait in Lady Chatterley's Lover of the resentful Irish playwright Michaelis, who had first been exalted and then dropped by the public, seems to describe his situation and mood well.

But as his reputation declined, Arlen, to his credit, struck out in new directions. Young Men in Love (1927) deals seriously—perhaps too much so—with a young writer's surrender to commercial pressures and the collapse of his love relationships. The heroine of Lily Christine (1928) is, like Iris March, a misunderstood woman, sacrificed to the egotism and insensitivity of the men in her life, but the portrait is more restrained and realistic. In this period Arlen also wrote a full-length comic play, These Charming People (produced in 1925), a one-act play, Why She Was Late for Dinner (1926), and collaborated on The Zoo (1927).

On 1 May 1928 Arlen married Countess Atalanta Mercati in Cannes and settled in the south of France. A son, Michael J. Arlen, now an author and critic, was born in 1930; a daughter, Venetia, was born in 1933. Arlen continued to produce romantic fiction during this period; Babes in the Wood (1929) is a collection of short stories that contains a lively and revealing autobiographical account of his early days in London ("Memoirs of a Naturalized Englishman"). In 1931 he collaborated on a melodrama, Good Losers, and produced a novel, Men Dislike Women, closely patterned on Fitzgerald's The Great Gatsby (1925).

Man's Mortality (1933), a novel of the future concerning the dangers of advanced technology in the hands of messianic egotists, is perhaps Arlen's best work, certainly the one he took and intended

Brigit Patmore and Michael Arlen, 1920s

most seriously. *Hell! Said the Duchess* (1934) is a brief horror novel with political overtones. *The Crooked Coronet* (1937), a collection of short stories that had appeared in the *Strand* magazine, is mostly in the vein of his early romantic fiction, though strongly laced with irony. His last novel, *The Flying Dutchman* (1939), is a thriller about international intrigue, in which the troubles plaguing Europe are ascribed to a secret society of anarchist terrorists bent on disrupting the social order.

With the outbreak of war in 1939 Arlen returned to England. He wrote a series of articles, some romantic, some thoughtful and patriotic, for the *Tatler,* and took the post of public relations officer for the Central Midlands. Unfortunately resistance developed in Parliament to having a Bulgarian national (as he was termed) and writer of scandalous fiction in such a "sensitive" post, and Arlen was forced to resign. In 1941 he sailed to the United States to join his family and went again to Hollywood, where he coscripted *The Heavenly Body*

(1944) with Walter Reisch and saw his story "Gay Falcon"—whose hero was an updated version of his character in "The Cavalier of the Streets"—become the basis of a successful series of B films between 1941 and 1949. He moved to elegant retirement in New York in 1945 and died there in 1956.

Though very much a writer of a particular time and circumstance, Arlen may still be recommended for his wit and charm. One of his finest achievements is the narrative persona he developed in his early fiction, a confidential, ingratiating voice capable of keen observation and self-mockery. He was, in life and in his fiction, supremely good company.

References:

Michael J. Arlen, *Exiles* (New York: Farrar, Straus & Giroux, 1970);
Harry Keyishian, *Michael Arlen* (Boston: Twayne, 1975).

Stella Benson

(6 January 1892-6 December 1933)

Kitti Carriker Eastman
University of Notre Dame

BOOKS: *I Pose* (London: Macmillan, 1915; New York: Macmillan, 1916);
This Is the End (London: Macmillan, 1917);
Twenty (London: Macmillan, 1918; New York: Macmillan, 1918);
Living Alone (London: Macmillan, 1919);
Kwan-Yin (San Francisco: Grabhorn, 1922);
The Poor Man (London: Macmillan, 1922; New York: Macmillan, 1923);
Pipers and a Dancer (London: Macmillan, 1924; New York: Macmillan, 1924);
The Little World (London: Macmillan, 1925; New York: Macmillan, 1925);
The Awakening: A Fantasy (San Francisco: Lantern Press, 1925);
Goodbye, Stranger (London: Macmillan, 1926; New York: Macmillan, 1926);
Worlds within Worlds (London: Macmillan, 1928; New York & London: Harper, 1929);
The Man Who Missed the 'Bus: A Story (London: Elkin Mathews & Marrot, 1928);
The Far-Away Bride (New York & London: Harper, 1930); republished as *Tobit Transplanted* (London: Macmillan, 1931);
Hope Against Hope and Other Stories (London: Macmillan, 1931);
Christmas Formula and Other Stories (London: Furnival Books, 1932);
Mundos: An Unfinished Novel (London: Macmillan, 1935);
Poems (London: Macmillan, 1935);
Collected Short Stories (London: Macmillan, 1936).

Stella Benson's novels capture a view of her time that is both critical and compassionate. She deals with serious issues—people's feelings about woman suffrage, imperial colonization, World War I—but always with imagination and sympathy. Though her commentary is occasionally a bit too pat and charming, these weaker moments are eclipsed by a trenchant insight into human behavior and by an irrefutable wit. She achieved popular success with her novel *The Far-Away Bride* (1930; published in Great Britain as *Tobit Transplanted*, 1931), for which she won the Femina Vie Heureuse

California, 1919

Prize and the A. C. Benson silver medal of the Royal Society of Literature in 1932.

Always frail and delicate, Stella Benson was born on 6 January 1892 at Lutwyche Hall, Shropshire, to Ralph Beaumont Benson and Caroline Essex Cholmondeley Benson, the younger sister of novelist Mary Cholmondeley. Virginia Woolf later described Stella Benson in her diary as "quiet, as controlled, white, drawn as usual, also deaf: with steady honest eyes . . . a very weak but persistent voice; she coughs; & then goes on with a mild persistent patience. She is bleached; even her blue eyes are bleached. But at the same time she's practical; realistic. . . . All this serious, weary, intent." Educated at home and in France, Germany, and Switzerland, Benson continued to travel widely throughout her life, transforming her experiences into essays and fiction.

In 1912 Benson visited the West Indies, accumulating material for her first book. Home from the voyage, she worked from 1913 to 1917 in the East End of London. After serving for a time in the Charity Organization Society, she became disillusioned with their methods and opened a small store in Hoxton with a local woman as partner, determined to help the poor in her own, more personal and practical, way. During this time she was active as a suffragette and, drawing on all her recent experiences, wrote her first two novels.

The first of these is *I Pose* (1915), the story of an unnamed gardener and an unnamed suffragette who find themselves sailing together for Trinity Island. A record of their dubious romance, their separation on the island, and their eventual reunion in England, the story is told by a self-conscious narrator informing the reader of each character's every pose. The suffragette and the gardener always interact within the framework of various roles. The gardener, for example, poses "luxuriously as an enigma," and the narrator predicts that "even on his deathbed the gardener will pose as a dying man." Benson effectively points out the many ramifications of role playing, finally asking, "How deep may a pose extend?"

Benson also deals with woman suffrage in *I Pose*. With biting irony the suffragette exclaims that women live in a sphere where "Oh, my dear, too killing" is the motto. This motto is a subtle foreshadowing of doom as the suffragette's conversations with various characters carry out the theme that women's lot may well be "too killing." The focus of the final chapters of the novel is on the suffragette's social work in Brown Borrough, no doubt based on Benson's experiences in the East End of London. The suffragette's profound love for women and her deep-seated concern for their emotional, political, and economic well-being are skillfully interwoven with the theme of posing in a novel which has not lost its relevance.

This Is the End (1917), Benson's second novel, is also set in Brown Borrough. A wealthy young woman, Jay, has moved into a small apartment there, disowned her wealth, and taken a job as conductor on a city bus. (Benson was fascinated by buses; humorous and philosophical references to both buses and bus conductors occur throughout her writing.) Jay's family (aside from her brother and confidant, Kew) do not know where she is, and they glean clues from her letters, which tell of a "House by the Sea" where she lives with a "Secret Friend." Not realizing that Jay is describing the secret world of her imagination, they set out in search of her.

Mr. Russell, a family friend who is much older than Jay, falls in love with her—and with her imagination. A man of some imagination himself, he recites Milton to his hound dog and asks him for the truth about Death and Immortality. (Benson took a particular delight in personifying dogs, and clever, witty dogs appear in almost all her works.) The novel's title refers both to the end of Mr. Russell's youthful hopes that Jay will return his love and to the destruction of Jay's secret world when news of Kew's death in France shatters her childhood memories. The novel contains a cross section of attitudes toward World War I, ranging from the condescension of a pretentious Brown Borrough social worker to the logic of a pacifist Quaker, to Kew's own nonchalance about his possible death.

In June 1918 Benson went to New York and visited there and in New England before going to California, a state her doctor had suggested for her poor lungs. In California she worked for a while on a ranch, and then, just before Christmas, with only five dollars, she went on to San Francisco, where she finished *Living Alone* (1919).

Like *This Is the End*, *Living Alone* is set in the Brown Borrough during World War I and draws on Benson's experiences with the Charity Organization Society. The novel opens with a witch's surprise visit to the Charity Society, where Sarah Brown serves as a social worker. Sarah's life begins to change from the moment that she witnesses the witch's magic. Finding her sensibilities too refined for the Charity Society, she moves into the House of Living Alone, run by the witch as a harbor for those who feel out of place in the London mainstream. A series of cleverly constructed confrontations between fantasy and reality suggest that social problems may be solved more efficiently and effectively by magic than by the efforts of charity committees. Yet, though magic triumphs, this novel is not a fairy tale, for Sarah Brown remains quite disconsolate, and the conclusion gives no promise of happiness for her. Benson's criticism is of a society which does not temper charity with common sense.

After finishing *Living Alone* in December

"White Mountain Moonlight," "Tiger-Tiger . . . ," "Spanish Moss," "Sajuaro," "Angels in the Red Sea," "Tribeswoman, Yunnanfu,"
"Tribeswoman, Mengtsz," and "The Parvenu": illustrations by Benson for the second edition of The Little World

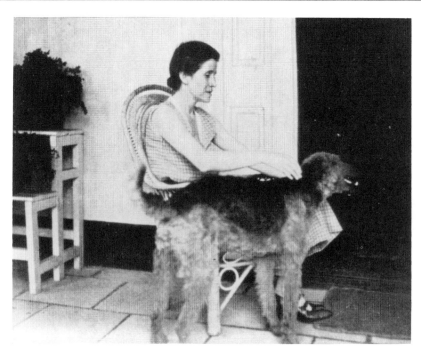

A 1933 photograph of Stella Benson in Pakhoi, China, the last post to which she accompanied her husband

1918, Benson moved to Berkeley, where she lived in a tiny room and did a variety of odd jobs. In January 1920 she made another adventurous journey, an eighteen-month voyage to England by way of India and China. In China she met James O'Gorman Anderson, a customs officer; they were married in London in September 1921. Their honeymoon was a trip to America, crossing the continent from east to west in a Ford car.

Many of her experiences in the United States and in the Far East are captured in *The Little World* (1925), a collection of essays which are as enjoyable as her fiction. She also drew on these experiences in her fourth novel, *The Poor Man* (1922), the story of Edward Williams, a luckless character who, despite his good intentions, is a victim of his own weak will. In vain pursuit of love, he sets out on a voyage which in some ways resembles Benson's own. For example, while in Hong Kong, he earns money to go on to Peking by teaching a class of fifty Eurasian and Chinese boys, just as Benson herself, while in Hong Kong, had taught a class of fifty Chinese boys in a mission school. Benson creates a main character who is not only a symbol, but a multidimensional human being, making *The Poor Man* a sympathetic psychological study.

Except for occasional trips, the remainder of Stella Benson's life, until her death from pneumonia in a hospital at Honkai, Tonkin, in December 1933, was spent in the various regions of China where her husband was stationed. One of these places was Manchuria, the setting for her last-completed and best-known novel, *The Far-Away Bride* (1930). This unusual novel follows the outline of the legend of Tobit in the Old Testament Apocrypha, replacing the exiled families of ancient Israel with two families of White Russian refugees in Manchuria and Korea during the 1920s. Russians once held a privileged position in Kanto, Manchuria, where the novel is partly set, but after the Russo-Japanese War and the Russian Revolution of 1917, they became isolated exiles. The imaginary Malinin and Ostapenko families of *The Far-Away Bride* are among the many White Russians from Siberia who joined the Russians in Manchuria. They have no political identity; their passports are invalid; and they are in Manchuria on sufferance only.

Benson writes of this Manchurian community and the array of cultures it encompasses with characteristic insight and vivid description, as she weaves a tale of love and family conflicts that parallels the story of Tobit. Seryozha Malinin, a young, rather simple adventurer, who sets forth from his Manchurian village to recover a small treasure which his father has in a Seoul bank, meets Wilfred Chew, a young Chinese man newly graduated from a London law school. While serving as Seryozha's guardian angel and his guide to Seoul, Chew, think-

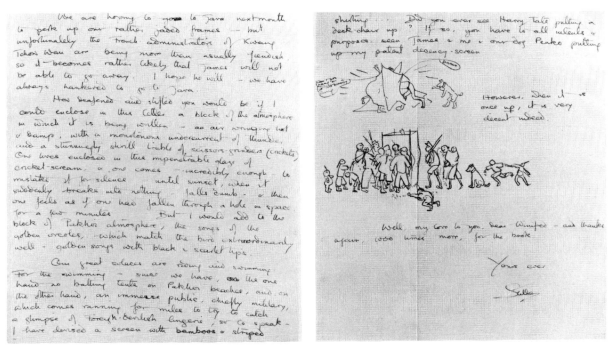

Pages from a letter Benson wrote to Winifred Holtby from Pakhoi, 1933 (R. Ellis Roberts, Portrait of Stella Benson, *1939)*

ing that the Russians will pay him well for his services, masterminds the union of Seryozha and Tatiana Ostapenko, the complex, withdrawn young woman who becomes Seryozha's bride. Despite the novel's allegorical aspects, Benson creates a realistic environment in which these complex and realistic characters interact.

Benson's last novel, *Mundos* (published posthumously in 1935), is unfinished: thirteen chapters were completed and revised; four, perhaps five, chapters remained unwritten. Set in Rhodatown, the capital of Mundos Island, the story revolves around Sir Victor Cole, governor of the island, and his discontented wife and son. As it observes the attendant ills and conflicts of what Benson ironically calls "liberal imperialistic thought," the novel delineates the complex network of relationships between the English civil servants and the native islanders, and the social unrest and disruption of Rhodatown provide a framework for the author's commentary on colonialism and human nature.

From the beginning of her career, Stella Benson, who also wrote essays, short stories, and poetry,

was hailed for her fresh and original wit. An expert observer of human motives and instincts, she achieved a fine balance between fantasy and reality in her early novels, where fanciful characters symbolize her feelings about serious social problems. In her later novels thorough characterization takes over, and her characters function in undeniably realistic settings. All her novels are sensitive studies of what people want and how they feel.

References:

R. Meredith Zehner Bedell, "The Novels of Stella Benson," Ph.D. dissertation, Florida State University, 1976;

Joseph Collins, "Two Lesser Literary Ladies of London: Stella Benson and Virginia Woolf," in his *The Doctor Looks at Literature* (New York: Doran, 1923);

S. P. B. Mais, "Stella Benson," in his *Some Modern Authors* (New York: Dodd, Mead, 1923);

R. Ellis Roberts, *Portrait of Stella Benson* (London: Macmillan, 1939).

Catherine Carswell

(March 1879-18 February 1946)

Charles Kemnitz
University of Tulsa
and
David Farmer
University of Texas

BOOKS: *Open the Door!* (London: Melrose, 1920; New York: Harcourt, Brace & Howe, 1920);

The Camomile: An Invention (London: Chatto & Windus, 1922; New York: Harcourt, 1922);

The Life of Robert Burns (London: Chatto & Windus, 1930; New York: Harcourt, Brace, 1931);

The Savage Pilgrimage: A Narrative of D. H. Lawrence (London: Secker, 1932; New York: Harcourt, Brace, 1932);

The Tranquil Heart: Portrait of Giovanni Boccaccio (London: Lawrence & Wishart, 1937);

Lying Awake: An Unfinished Autobiography and Other Posthumous Papers, edited by John Carswell (London: Secker & Warburg, 1950).

OTHER: *A National Gallery: Being a Collection of English Characters,* edited by Carswell and Daniel George (London: Secker, 1933);

The English in Love: A Museum of Illustrative Verse and Prose Pieces from the 14th Century to the 20th, edited by Carswell and George (London: Secker, 1934);

The Fays of the Abbey Theatre: An Autobiographical Record, edited by Carswell and W. G. Fay (London: Rich & Cowen, 1935; New York: Harcourt, 1935);

The Scots Weekend and Caledonian Vade-Mecum for Host, edited by Carswell and John Carswell (London: Routledge, 1936).

Catherine Carswell

Catherine MacFarlane Jackson Carswell began her career as a musician who enjoyed writing and literature, interests she claimed to have inherited from her mother. Her early music training became a central motif in both her novels: *Open the Door!* (1920) and *The Camomile* (1922). But two years of study in Frankfurt (around 1897-1899) convinced her to pursue a career in literature. She felt, as does her protagonist Joanna in *Open the Door!,* that her music did not "live" and she wanted, above all, an art that was alive. After the annulment of her

first marriage in 1903, Carswell returned to Glasgow with her daughter and became an "informal" literature student at Glasgow University. In 1907 she became a reviewer and critic for the *Glasgow Herald.* She was fired from the *Herald* for favorably reviewing D. H. Lawrence's *The Rainbow.*

Carswell wrote reviews for the *Herald* and later the London *Observer* late at night during bouts of insomnia. Her writing habits gave rise to the title of her posthumously published autobiographical writings, *Lying Awake* (1950), and formed the memorable characteristic of Juley Bannerman, the mother in *Open the Door!* Carswell was a frank critic, both of her own work and the work of others, particularly when it contained "too many thoughts and not enough thought." Successful writing, she believed, avoided "intellectualizing" but demanded a history of "thought, effort, secret failure, and experience." She found all these traits in the novels of D. H. Lawrence early in his career.

With Lawrence's help and encouragement Carswell was able to finish her first novel, *Open the Door!* His correspondence with Carswell from 1914 to 1920 reveals that he read and commented upon each draft, at first condemning its style but later saying the novel was "like Jane Austen on a deeper level." This praise reflects two aspects of *Open the Door!*; its autobiographical source and what the *Times* reviewer called its "successful analysis of motives." *Open the Door!* won the Melrose Prize for a first novel in 1920. It is a Bildungsroman that follows a young girl's break from her parents' demanding religion to her successful and passionate reunion with "the man she never knew she loved." Joanna Bannerman is left fatherless at the age of twelve when her father, a Presbyterian missionary, dies while on a speaking tour in America. After dreaming that she slams the front door in terror on her father's ghost, she forces herself to kiss a blind woman begging on the street corner. This "pious act," as she sees it, is expiation for the hate she felt in her dreams. But it is also the first in an accumulation of romantic actions that make Joanna "a fugitive from the realities surrounding her."

Joanna's first infatuation, at the age of twelve, is a romantic fantasy for an older boy, Lawrence Urquhart, who practices taxidermy on small birds. Psychological symbolism develops during an idyllic country scene. While watching Lawrence skin a bird Joanna imagines she is the bird as he slips his penknife painlessly into her breast. The fantasy is acted out when Lawrence playfully pins her against himself and holds the bloodied knife against her white blouse. This action prompts the first instance of what becomes Joanna's typical sexual response to rape: "She wished then he would not hesitate to plunge the blade into her breast so that she might gladly give herself to him and the cleansing pain."

Joanna dreams of becoming a great violinist and searches for an instructor who can make her music "live." But even German instructors fail her, and she returns to Edinburgh at the age of nineteen to become an art student. By chance she meets a fallen Italian Catholic who researches manned flight and motorcycles. She falls passionately (a synonym in the novel for *lustfully*) in love with him. A short engagement leads to a sadomasochistic marriage in which Joanna feels that she is a

Catherine Carswell, circa 1910

"trapped bird in a cage," even though she glories in Mario Rasponi's brutality toward her. The marriage ends after two or three months when Mario is killed in a motorcycling accident. Mario is the atavistic lover from Joanna's dreams. He possesses her body but not her hidden soul, figuratively and literally forcing her to submit. Joanna admires these qualities in her men, while fulfilling the romantic promise of the caged, passionate woman who can submit only in a love symbolic of rape.

Mario's death inspires Joanna to visit and then live for a time with her Aunt Perdy, her mother's sister who has lived in Italy for years (a biographical detail lifted from Carswell's own life). Aunt Perdy is an attractive but "mannish" woman who barely conceals her latent lesbianism. She teaches Joanna the gospel of free love, filled with such catch phrases as the Father-Motherhood of God, the Central Sphere of the Senses, the Divinity of Sex, the Man-Woman Creator, and the Duality of the Soul.

Again Joanna retreats to the safety of Edinburgh to languish on her inheritance and consider her aunt's philosophy, which she begins to accept, not as an end in itself but as a means to a greater self-ethic. She tries halfheartedly to become an artist and achieves a kind of success by becoming a designer of drapery patterns. She meets a middle-aged fan painter named Louis Pender, whom she seduces into an "affair complete in every way but that final passion." Despite the fact that his marriage is shaky and he and Joanna both seek consummation, Joanna once again looks for escape from the reality surrounding her. This time escape takes the form of her old friend Lawrence Urquhart, whom she tricks into an engagement. But when she confronts Louis with this engagement, his powerful personality, in a symbolic rape scene, convinces her to leave Lawrence and move to London as his mistress.

After a three-and-a-half-year affair, the lovers having consummated their passion in a rented flat above a mortuary, Joanna hits upon the plan to bind Louis to her forever by bearing his child. But no conception takes place, and Louis suddenly decides to end the affair because Joanna has become too "predictable." The accusation of predictability comes as a shock to her, but she then realizes that she is bound by society's expectations and codes of conduct, a situation she finds abhorrent. In a paragraph suggestive of D. H. Lawrence's influence on the novel, Carswell describes Joanna's cleansing epiphany: "Joanna's discovery was that 'evil' (in the Christian sense of the word) quite as much as 'good' had made her alive, that 'evil' quite as much as 'good' had made her an individual, a human being, a divine creation herself capable of creative life."

She felt that she had experienced an awakening similar to what her landlord's son felt while dying: the boy was in a coma from which he periodically awakened to reality, until finally he awakened to the ultimate reality of death and rebirth in a "better world." She escapes from the mortuary flat and again returns to Edinburgh, where she meets her old art instructor who takes her back to Duntarvie, the one place where she always felt free and at home and rejuvenated. There she accidentally meets Lawrence and they share "a new beginning, as if reborn."

Carswell's second novel, *The Camomile,* was not so well received as was *Open the Door!*, probably because the novel essentially expands upon the period of German music instruction alluded to in her first novel. *The Camomile* concerns the daily rounds of a young music teacher recently returned from Frankfurt to Glasgow. She has inferior musical talent, but has inherited a "tormenting desire to express herself in writing" from her mother, an "unsuccessful and worthless author." No amount of

discouragement from circumstances or from a famous author with whom she corresponds can eradicate her desire to write; it is, in fact, symbolized by the camomile, which grows faster the more it is trampled down. The flowering of her literary ability is retarded by the narrow minds of her circle of friends. Music and passion for a student distract her from her writing, but writing proves stronger than any of her other passions. In the end she pushes aside all that stands in her way, and sets out alone to reach her goal, leaving the novel open-ended, as the reader never learns whether or not her goal is achieved.

The epistolary structure of *The Camomile* lends the story of youthful revolt and search for individual ethics a sense of informality and intimacy. But Carswell fails here to endow her central character with an active, creative mind. This problem is compounded by Carswell's analytical attempt to expand the philosophy of a self-ethic first postulated in *Open the Door!*; here she achieves only a flimsy synthesis of character and philosophy.

As with Carswell's novels, which reflect a quest for individual ethics, the ideas of quest and ethic are a theme in her three major critical biographies: *The Life of Robert Burns* (1930), *The Savage Pilgrimage* (1932), and *The Tranquil Heart* (1937). In each of these works Carswell stresses the artist's ability to break from the cultural mold and develop an individual genius.

Though she was not by academic standards the person best suited to reassess Burns, Carswell does manage to make the reader aware that the popular legend encouraged by former biographers gave an idealized and emasculated hero. Encouraged by Lawrence, who read each draft of the Burns biography during its five-year gestation, Carswell determined to show Burns as a man striving after an individual goal. Her view of Burns as a poet "astute to see his chance and with the daring to seize and the energy to carry it through to fruition" has been sustained by later academicians. But in 1931 *The Life of Robert Burns* caused an explosion of anger among the more orthodox Burnsites who failed to realize that in characterizing him as opportunistic and immodest she praised Burns rather than condemned him.

About the time her Burns biography was published, the friendship Carswell valued above all others ended with Lawrence's death. Today, if she is remembered at all, it is as the author of a single critical work: *The Savage Pilgrimage: A Narrative of D. H. Lawrence.* With this book she separated herself from friends and critics who claimed to have exclu-

Jim Wybrow and Catherine Carswell at Toppesfield, 1942

sive understanding of Lawrence. *The Savage Pilgrimage* was originally published by Martin Secker, but such a controversy arose over its content that Secker withdrew the book. It was reissued later the same year by Chatto and Windus and continues to provide some of the most valuable insights into D. H. Lawrence's work and personality. The book made Carswell some bitter enemies, and their attacks, added to the brutality she suffered at the hands of certain Burnsites (one sent her a bullet and suggested she blow her brains out in a quiet corner to make the world a cleaner place), prompted her to leave England for Berlin. After a month she returned to Scotland and rented a house near Toppesfield. To this period belong her anthologies and editorial collaborations: *A National Gallery* (1933) and *The English in Love* (1934) edited with Daniel George; *The Fays of the Abbey Theatre* (1935) edited with W. G. Fay; and *The Scots Weekend* (1936) edited with her husband, John.

In her biography of Boccaccio, *The Tranquil Heart,* she commended Boccaccio's "admirable

foolhardiness" in undertaking a translation of Homer, though he knew no Greek, with no better a collaborator than a mendicant Orthodox monk who knew almost no Italian. She was adept at biography, bringing to each one the same phenomenological spirit that shaped the philosophy of her novels. In all her books she reiterated the ideal first articulated in her novels, especially in her satiric descriptions of James Bridie in her postscript to *The Fays*: "He is not only a busy man, but a godlike one, combining in himself the functions of the dramatist and the healer and therefore moving in a doubly mysterious way." That phrase—dramatist and healer—effectively sums up her ideal of the artist and literature. They should, at their best, dramatize life and heal the rifts between fantasy and reality, author and text, individual and cultural ethics. As she says of her Burns biography: "For some reason . . . this Burns book has turned out more than a mere book for me and has been definitely life-giving in the strangest ways."

Ivy Compton-Burnett

Shari Benstock
University of Tulsa

BIRTH: Pinner (Middlesex), England, 5 June 1884 (?) to James Compton Burnett, M.D., and Katharine Rees Compton-Burnett.

EDUCATION: B.A., Royal Holloway College (London University), Egham, Surrey, 1907.

AWARDS AND HONORS: Founders Scholarship, Royal Holloway College, 1906; Commander of the Order of the British Empire (C.B.E.), 1951; James Tait Black Memorial Prize, 1956; Honorary Doctorate of Letters, University of Leeds, 1960; Dame Commander of the Order of the British Empire (D.B.E.), 1967.

DEATH: London, 29 August 1969.

SELECTED BOOKS: *Dolores* (Edinburgh: Blackwood, 1911);
Pastors and Masters (London: Heath Cranton, 1925);
Brothers and Sisters (London: Heath Cranton, 1929; New York: Harcourt, Brace, 1929);
Men and Wives (London: Heinemann, 1931; New York: Harcourt, Brace, 1931);
More Women Than Men (London: Heinemann, 1933);
A House and Its Head (London: Heinemann, 1935);
Daughters and Sons (London: Gollancz, 1937; New York: Norton, 1938);
A Family and a Fortune (London: Gollancz, 1939);
Parents and Children (London: Gollancz, 1941);
Elders and Betters (London: Gollancz, 1944);
Manservant and Maidservant (London: Gollancz, 1947); republished as *Bullivant and the Lambs* (New York: Knopf, 1948);
Two Worlds and Their Ways (London: Gollancz, 1949; New York: Knopf, 1949);
Darkness and Day (London: Gollancz, 1951; New York: Knopf, 1951);
The Present and the Past (London: Gollancz, 1953; New York: Messner, 1953);
Mother and Son (London: Gollancz, 1955; New York: Messner, 1955);
A Father and His Fate (London: Gollancz, 1957; New York: Messner, 1958);

Ivy Compton-Burnett, 1960s (photo by John Vere Brown)

A Heritage and its History (London: Gollancz, 1959);
The Mighty and Their Fall (London: Gollancz, 1961; New York: Simon & Schuster, 1962);
A God and His Gifts (London: Gollancz, 1963; New York: Simon & Schuster, 1964);
The Last and the First (London: Gollancz, 1971);
Collected Works (London: Gollancz, 1972).

One of the most prolific writers of this century, I. Compton-Burnett (as she signed her works) produced twenty novels during a fifty-year writing career that extended from 1911 (with the publication of *Dolores,* a youthful novel that she later disclaimed) to 1971, with the posthumous publication of *The Last and the First,* which she was writing at the time of her death. Regarded during her lifetime as one of the most original writers of fiction in England, Ivy Compton-Burnett attracted a small but devoted coterie of readers who followed her epigrammatic prose style with all the attention to nuance it required, accepted her anachronistic interest in late-Victorian English family life, and delighted in plot structures that were more often than not outrageously complex. Her novels lay bare various characters' efforts to attain and maintain power in the family, dissect the artificiality of the society they examine in an equally artificial speech, and reveal the secret passions of family members through acts of theft, murder, blackmail, incest, and violence.

Difficult to classify, either in terms of genre or historical period, Compton-Burnett's works are both modern and outdated, both typical and atypical of the English novel tradition in which she wrote. Pamela Hansford Johnson has suggested that it is the very impossibility of classifying her work that has insured a continuing interest in it: "To refer to anyone so essentially uncontemporaneous as a great contemporary novelist seems to beg the question; she is contemporary with ourselves only because she happens to be writing while we exist, herself insulated entirely from any world save the one inside her own head. . . . Miss Compton-Burnett's great strength lies in the fact that we cannot place her; and so also does her weakness." Ivy Compton-Burnett shared nothing with other novelists of her time (with the sole exception, perhaps, of Henry Greene, who treats a similar set of eccentric characters in novels of equal wit, elegance and arch comedy), remaining as highly individualistic and anachronistic as her fictional subjects.

Indeed, the link between biography and fiction is crucial to an understanding of Compton-Burnett's work. The eldest daughter of her father's second marriage, Ivy Compton-Burnett was reared in a Victorian household of twelve children that included the numerous household staff (nursemaids, governesses, cooks, parlor maids, and other domestics) who so often constitute the dramatis personae of her novels. Her father was a successful homeopathic physician whose second wife, a beautiful woman fifteen years his junior, was socially conscious and competitive (particularly because her husband's defense of homeopathy over allopathic medicine placed her on the social margin of the professional class), proud, urbane, jealously protective of her children without being "at all maternal." To mark her own status, and that of her children, she introduced the hyphen into the

Compton-Burnett name, thus distinguishing herself from her husband and his children by a previous marriage. James Compton Burnett's medical practice in London (at 26 Wimpole Street, around the corner from the offices of Conan Doyle, whom he knew) kept him away from the family home in Hove during the week. It was easy for his wife to instill on a daily basis a sense of double family life, to privilege her own children over those of her husband's previous marriage, to create the atmosphere of family tension and to encourage the sibling rivalries and secret alliances that were later to be analyzed with such clinical precision in her daughter's fiction. Ivy Compton-Burnett's own family life was itself almost the clichéd existence offered in a Victorian novel: it included an adoring but absent father, a neurotic and jealous mother, a beloved nurse who reared all twelve children and cared for the parents in their old age, a constantly changing set of family domestics, a thirteen-bedroom house that confined a heterogeneous family behind the closed doors of political conservatism and social

Ivy Compton-Burnett (center) with her friends Daisy Harvey (far left) and Isabel Bremner (far right) during her first term at Royal Holloway College. Throughout her life, Compton-Burnett was proud of having received a university education (courtesy of Royal Holloway College, London University).

propriety. From the materials of her upbringing, Ivy Compton-Burnett would recreate this world, inverting and subverting its values.

Except for the years spent at Howard College and at Royal Holloway College, Compton-Burnett spent her life within the confines of this family group until she was thirty years old. The children from her father's first marriage left home as early as possible; after their father's sudden death in 1901, the children of the second marriage were left in the care of their mother, whose mental and physical health degenerated so severely in the period leading up to her own death in 1911 that Compton-Burnett was called upon to take increasing responsibilities in the rearing of her younger siblings. These responsibilities suited neither her interests nor her natural abilities. Like her mother, she was "not at all maternal." Between the death of Dr. James Compton Burnett in 1901 and the eventual breakup of the family home in Hove in 1915 (when Compton-Burnett's four youngest sisters moved to London, in large part to escape the tyranny that she had established over the house), the entire family lived "under the shadow of death." They passed

A 1914 photograph of Ivy Compton-Burnett's brother Noel, who was killed in the Battle of the Somme, 1916

Ivy Compton-Burnett, 1912

these years in mourning, first for their father and later for their brother Guy (next in age to Ivy), who died of pneumonia in 1905. Her other adored brother, Noel, was killed in the battle of the Somme in 1916, and two younger sisters, Topsy and Baby, committed suicide in 1917. During these difficult years Compton-Burnett became increasingly withdrawn, retreating behind a mask of reserve, watching carefully the behavior of those around her, her jovial spirits made bitter by the circumstances of her private life.

In 1911, the year of her mother's death from cancer, Compton-Burnett published her first novel, *Dolores,* a lugubrious and extended account of a young woman's self-sacrifice in the service of her family, a story whose tone and subject matter drew directly from her own experience. The novel opens over "an open grave with its mourners" at the funeral of Reverend Hutton's wife, whose daughter—Dolores—will be forced to sacrifice her university scholarship in order to serve as governess for her father's three children (the product of a second marriage that followed close upon the death of the first wife). This return to the family means that Dolores must abandon her work with the near-blind writer of classical dramas, Claverhouse, with whom she has fallen in love. Later she is able to return to her studies, but discovers that Claverhouse has fallen hopelessly in love with her beautiful friend Perdita. Despite Dolores's passion for both Claverhouse and Perdita (there is a hint of bisexuality in her affections), Dolores fosters the marriage, and endures with Perdita her pregnancy and the stillbirth that kills her. Just as Dolores returns to assist Claverhouse (now totally blind), her stepmother dies, leaving the entire family in Dolores's charge, and Soulsby—a kind don who urges Dolores to marry him to solve her problems—runs off with her beautiful half sister.

Although Compton-Burnett was later to disown *Dolores* as a piece of juvenilia, the novel presents major themes of her mature work (the tyranny of families, ill-conceived marriages, latent homosexuality, religious and educational constraints on women). Suffering under the burden of similar responsibilities in her own family, Compton-Burnett lacked the objectivity and irony that mark her later treatment of these themes. She had not yet learned to mask her feelings behind icy wit; she had not pruned her prose style; she had not developed the technical discipline that characterizes her later writings.

Between the publication of *Dolores* and *Pastors and Masters* (1925) there was a fourteen-year silence, during which Compton-Burnett recuperated from the psychological and physiological traumas she suffered because of the deaths of her parents and four siblings, and also tried—unsuccessfully by her own account—to recover from the effects of the Great War, which, she said, "quite smashed my life up." During these years she did not write (although she read voraciously while lying on a divan, eating chocolates). After her sisters left the house in Hove, she lived with various women (including the widow of her brother Noel), eventually meeting Margaret Jourdain, a strong, independent professional writer whose expertise was English antiques and period furniture. The two women began to live together when Jourdain was forty-three and Compton-Burnett thirty-five; Jourdain was in large part responsible for Compton-Burnett's return to health and her renewed interest in writing.

About this time Compton-Burnett discovered the writings of Samuel Butler, whose philosophy and prose style heavily influenced her works. Among the various passages she underlined from Butler's *Note-Books,* the following paragraph most succinctly describes her attitude toward the tyranni-

A 1910 photograph of Margaret Jourdain, the writer with whom Compton-Burnett went to live in 1919

cal and claustrophobic aspects of family life that constitute her artistic subject matter:

The Family

I believe that more unhappiness comes from this source than from any other—I mean from the attempt to prolong family connection unduly and to make people hang together artificially who would never naturally do so. The mischief among the lower classes is not so great, but among the middle and upper classes it is killing a large number daily. And the old people do not really like it much better than the young.

Here Compton-Burnett found the great theme of the nineteen novels that were to follow *Dolores*. She also discovered in Butler's work a succinct and skeletal prose style that she would imitate, refining it to an elegance previously unknown in the English novel.

In *Pastors and Masters*, the first of Compton-Burnett's novels to follow what was to become the classic pattern of her fiction, exploiting the tensions of family life through a fast-paced plot that relies almost solely on dialogue, the tyranny of family is extended to the public school, where deception and dishonesty are the subject of analysis. Although the *New Statesman* review of the book acclaimed it a "work of genius," the reviewer admitted that there was "nothing of which to take hold" in the work: *Pastors and Masters* concerns the duplicity involved in a literary prize-giving and the questionable authorship of a book; there is virtually no "story" in the novel. Despite the huge cast of characters and complex plot, one feels at the novel's close that nothing much seems to have happened. The events at Dotheboys Hall involve sexual attraction between members of the same sex, the thwarted ambitions of dons, the anxieties of a rather nasty headmaster, and the disharmony of a family. Although the setting of the novel is prewar Cambridge, the attitudes and tone of the novel are postwar.

Brothers and Sisters (1929) restricts its subject to family life and draws heavily on events from Compton-Burnett's own personal life. A character study of Dr. James Compton Burnett, the novel has as its central drama the death of Christian Stace. The character of Miss Patmore, the family nurse, is a tribute to Ivy's own nurse, Ellen Smith, the beloved "Minnie." The tyrannical guilt and grief of Sophia Stace following her husband's sudden death is reminiscent of Katharine Compton-Burnett's reactions to the death of her husband, and Sophia's self-indulgent remorse brutalizes the Stace children in the same ways the young Compton-Burnetts were destroyed by their mother's oppressive melancholy. Compton-Burnett directly traces here the last year of her father's life (1901) and her mother's death ten years later. There are recognizable portraits of Compton-Burnett, her brothers and parents, and her mother's father.

While the first two Compton-Burnett classics restrict wrongdoing to the level of plagiarism and suppression of wills, *Men and Wives* (1931) introduces the more heinous crimes central to Compton-Burnett's fiction—matricide, fratricide, and infanticide—demonstrating that while such crimes may never result in retribution (no Compton-Burnett criminal is ever brought to court; such secrets are kept within the family), crime never succeeds in significantly altering the balance of power. Compton-Burnett introduces here the first of a long series of charming baronets (Sir Godfrey Haslam) and the first of her articulate, comic, and irrepressible butlers (Buttermere). Buttermere begins the long line of servants whose pungent obser-

Ivy Compton-Burnett, early 1920s

vations on events and ability to "manage" their managers constitute a second level of Compton-Burnett comedy. Lady Haslam dominates a large number of characters throughout a highly complex plot and tyrannizes her family to such a degree that she is assisted in a suicide attempt by her physician son. The real villain of the piece, however, is not this "murderer," but the family solicitor, Dominic Spong (a comic type to reappear many times over in Compton-Burnett's fiction), who, having access to the knowledge of Lady Haslam's will (which prevents her husband from remarrying without sacrificing his fortune), uses this knowledge to benefit himself and to manipulate others.

Men and Wives is the most complicated of the early novels, and critical response reflected the strains that Compton-Burnett placed on her readers: many reviewers found the incessant dialogue, the rapid-paced action, the complicated net of interrelationships, and the absence of expected narrative structures too demanding. Every critic, however, acknowledged the originality of Compton-Burnett's enterprise, recognizing that the restrictions of period and setting, of social class and political conservatism, and the repetition of dialogue and plot were uniquely Compton-Burnett. Writing about her almost fifty years later, Mary McCarthy commented:

> She produces Compton-Burnetts, as someone might produce ball-bearings.... Hence the uniformity of labelling in her titles and the open-stock patterns of her incidents and dialogue. The author, like all reliable old firms, is stressing the *sameness* of the formula; senior service. She has no imitators. The formula is a trade secret.

In *More Women Than Men* (1933), Compton-Burnett again uses the setting of a school, this time a girls' school whose headmistress (Josephine Napier) is a tyrant. Although there is a murder and an element of the macabre, the novel is perhaps lighter hearted than any of the previous ones. The comic touch is provided by Felix, an absurd, witty homosexual who, when not in motion, is seated on the knees of Josephine's brother. Unlike *Pastors and Masters,* which concerned literary intrigues within the academic setting, *More Women Than Men* openly examines the struggle for authority and control of Miss Napier's school. The plot twists and turns around a series of complex relationships (primarily homosexual ones), confused identities, illegitimate births, deaths, and various economic and personal disasters.

As in Compton-Burnett's earlier novels, there seems to be no easily extractable "moral" from the story; indeed, the inversion of moral values is perhaps the central theme of her work. Rather than providing solutions to moral dilemmas, she merely sets in motion events that lead to such dilemmas, allowing the reader to juggle and balance ethical distinctions. Instead of ignoring or displacing legal and religious strictures that would ordinarily be placed upon the actions of characters like those she creates, she pushes the moral questions of her novels *beyond* the limits imposed on human action by church and state. Her novels complicate the ethical issues they treat, making it impossible to find easy solutions to the problems posed by her characters' efforts to establish power and dominion over other human beings. A reviewer in the *Observer* commented that "gradually it appears that the style disinfects and makes almost tolerable the squalid ugliness which has engaged the writer's attention. Curious relations between the sexes, strange cruelty and even murder do not confront the mind with their native brutality but, like characters in a Restoration Comedy, by virtue of their style acquire a curious, if not pleasant, artistic significance."

In *A House and Its Head* (1935) Compton-Burnett's fiction reaches a complexity of theme and purity of style characteristic of the middle period of her writing which reaches its summit with the publication of *Manservant and Maidservant* in 1947. Here she returns to the family, this one headed by Duncan Edgeworth. The novel opens on Christmas morning 1885 and is perhaps the most historically circumscribed of all of Compton-Burnett's stories: it is an analysis of a Victorian family divided against itself. When Ellen Edgeworth dies, Duncan Edgeworth is forced to evaluate his role in the premature death of his wife whose deteriorating illness may well have been affected—if not actually brought on—by his tyrannical behavior. Before he can actually make any progress toward reform, however, he has fallen in love with Alison, whom he marries and who produces a son, Richard. Richard's existence displaces the claim to the family fortune of Duncan's favorite nephew, Grant, a notorious seducer of women, including Alison. Richard is later found dead in his crib under suspicious circumstances, but by this time Alison and Duncan are divorced and Duncan has taken a third wife. Murder is tied to rights of primogeniture; illicit passion and illegitimate birth are part of a complex web of intrigue that eventually foils Duncan's control of the family he has founded. By the close of the novel there are at least three potential blackmailers (all women) who could publicly ruin Duncan Edgeworth; yet Compton-Burnett, like an auto mechanic who "might strip an engine," can "take a family apart, and then, often in the face of wild improbability, reassemble the machine so that such families as the Edgeworths can continue their progress," as Violet Powell commented. The status quo is successfully maintained.

Between the publication of *Men and Wives* and *More Women Than Men,* Compton-Burnett and Margaret Jourdain moved to a spacious first-floor flat at 5 Braemar Mansions in South Kensington—the residence they would occupy until their respective deaths. It remained as it was originally decorated by Jourdain, retaining both the charm and the inconvenience of its late-Victorian architecture. Although Compton-Burnett's relationship with Jourdain would be the closest personal friendship of her life, the dynamics of it had changed subtly but definitely since their first years together. When they met, it was Jourdain who was well known, to readers of *Country Life,* where she was a regular contributor on English furniture and decoration. Compton-Burnett, who had spent the years since her mother's death coping with family matters, then had few friends, was forgotten by the reading public who had greeted the publication of *Dolores,* and was physically and emotionally frail. In the early years of their friendship, Jourdain dominated, especially in social situations. Guests invited to their flat in Leinster Square and later in Linden Gardens remember Compton-Burnett as an inconspicuous hostess who would do embroidery while listening to Jourdain's conversation with her friends. Although there seems to have been no admission of an overtly homosexual relationship between the two women (Compton-Burnett described herself and Jourdain as "neuters"), one is nevertheless reminded that Alice B. Toklas played a similarly self-effacing role when entertaining the friends of Gertrude Stein. In the later years of her relationship with Margaret Jourdain, Compton-Burnett came more into her own: increasingly the visitors to the flat were her guests and it was Margaret Jourdain's contribution to the scholarship on nineteenth-century art and English antiques that was forgotten. The two women apparently adjusted to these shifts rather well; Jourdain is reported to have said to a friend: "It's odd when someone you know very well suddenly becomes famous."

As Compton-Burnett discovered that she was becoming well known as a novelist and well reviewed as a writer, she began to worry about the sales of her books. The discrepancy in physical and psychological strength between Jourdain and Compton-Burnett in the early years was reflected in their financial worth as well. Jourdain earned very good money with her writings during the years when Compton-Burnett was living on the small inheritance she had received from her parents. Compton-Burnett later grew concerned about her earning power as a novelist, becoming dissatisfied with more than one publisher because her novels, though they sold steadily, continued to sell in only a small market. After publishing three novels with Heinemann, she returned to Victor Gollancz. Gollancz addressed the problem of sales in its advertising campaign for *Daughters and Sons:*

> For years the cognoscenti have considered Miss Compton-Burnett one of the finest of living novelists, but 'the public' has appeared to prefer——— and ————. Will 'the public' now show that it is not without taste and discrimination?
> Probably not.

Daughters and Sons (1937) combines analysis of family tyranny with literary creativity: two of the family members are novelists. The ruling tyrant is Sabine Ponsonby, whose dominion extends over three generations. She takes special delight in tormenting her granddaughter, France, who writes in part to have an outlet from Sabine's matriarchy. France's father, John, is a successful writer of popular Victorian fiction whose daughter resolves that her own novels will not pander to popular taste. When John Ponsonby discovers that the dramatic presentation planned by the local vicar, Dr. Chaucer, is based on his daughter's writing, he becomes nervously jealous. He is afraid that her success may undermine further his already diminishing sales. France, therefore, submits her novel under a nom de plume (that of Edith Hallam, the governess for France's sister Muriel, the first of Compton-Burnett's comically irrepressible children). When the novel wins a prize, the secret is out and the multiple deceits of the story turn on the financial gain from this literary achievement. *Daughters and Sons* is unusual among Compton-Burnett novels in that no criminal action takes place and the sexual irregularities are confined to John Ponsonby's near-incestuous relationship with his sister, Hetta. And, in perhaps an ironic aside on her own concern about the sales of her novels, Compton-Burnett has France Ponsonby comment about her father's writing: "He would have written better if he had written for fewer and earned less."

The cover of the Penguin edition of *A Family and a Fortune* (1939) described it as the "kindliest" of Compton-Burnett's works. Elizabeth Sprigge, one of Compton-Burnett's biographers, comments that "this comparative mildness of climate is due to the absence of power in action. There is a frustrated invalid aunt who craves for it and a maddeningly officious niece who attempts it, but there is no tyrant." This novel, the first of Compton-Burnett's to be translated into another language (German), shows the effect on a family when a large sum of money is left to one of its members. *A Family and a Fortune* opens with one of the author's brilliant breakfast-table scenes. Here Blanche Gaveston presides over three children, her husband, Edgar, who is unusually forbearing by Compton-Burnett standards, and Edgar's younger brother, Dudley, who will come into a large fortune through the death of his godfather. With the ancestral home falling into ruins, Edgar Gaveston is having a difficult time supporting his family (he has even taken to letting part of the house to Blanche's father and an unmarried sister) when Dudley falls into his

Ivy Compton-Burnett at Bettiscomb, 1942

fortune and begins living like a man of means. The ensuing tensions are at last resolved when familial love overcomes greed and selfishness, allowing for a happier than usual ending in a Compton-Burnett novel.

Parents and Children (1941) has one of the strangest of all Compton-Burnett plots. Fulbert Sullivan, father of nine children and believed to have died in America, returns home at the precise moment his wife, Eleanor, is about to marry a neighbor, Ridley Cranmer. Though the situation demands a complex resolution, the novel's "real strength" and beauty, in Violet Powell's assessment, lie "in the growth of the personalities of the younger Sullivans," who represent the first large-scale effort by Compton-Burnett to examine the condition of childhood from remembered incidents and impressions of her own childhood.

Between *Parents and Children* and *Elders and Betters* (1944) there is a gap in Compton-Burnett's writing brought about by England's involvement in World War II. To escape the bombing of London, Compton-Burnett and Jourdain went to Hartley Court, near Reading, for the duration of the war. *Elders and Betters,* her only novel of the war period, is one of her darkest and most evil, featuring Compton-Burnett's best-remembered villainess, Anna Donne, and her most extraordinary children, the young Calderons. The novel explores again the

situation of a family bereaved by the loss of a parent (here a mother). The question posed by the novel is: who will care for the children? The Calderon siblings attempt to bear emotional pressures they cannot support, but the adult characters in *Elders and Betters* exist at the same infantile rank. Elizabeth Bowen, one of Compton-Burnett's most perceptive readers, commented that the ironic title of the novel (there are none who are either "elder" or "better") confirms its "Victorianness": "With the Victorians, we are in a world of dreadful empowered children. The rule of the seniors only is not questioned because, so visibly, they can enforce it; meanwhile, their juniors queue up, more or less impatiently waiting for their turn for power." Anna Donne awaits her turn less patiently than others, substituting a fake will for a genuine one, and helping her aunt Sukey toward death. This is a particularly bleak novel in which every character but one (Jenney) is marred by selfishness and greed, and every action tends to deceit and cruelty.

It may well have been anxiety over the war and its possible outcome that produced this unusually cynical work. Writing in 1941, Elizabeth Bowen employed the images of this conflict in her now-famous evaluation of Compton-Burnett's prose style, likening it to "the sound of glass being swept up, one of these mornings after a blitz." But it was Bowen who accurately placed Compton-Burnett with the Victorians rather than the Edwardians (where Compton-Burnett might herself have placed her own work) or the moderns. In a *Daily Telegraph* review of *Elders and Betters,* Bowen posed this question: "Have we, today, any serious novelist who has taken up or even attempted to take up, at the point where the Victorians left off?" She finds a "possible answer" in Compton-Burnett's work:

> She, like the Victorians, deals with English middle-class life—her concentration on it is even more frankly narrow. In form, it is true, her novels are ultra-Edwardian; their pages present an attractive lightness, through all the weight being thrown on elliptical dialogue; but, beyond that, their unlikeness to the Edwardians is infinite—to begin and end, they allow for no illusion. . . . Her avoidance of faked, or outward, Victorianism, however, is marked: we find ourselves with this, and more, guarantees that Miss Compton-Burnett is not merely copying but actually continuing the Victorian novel.

Manservant and Maidservant (1947) proves a brighter fictional landscape, this work representing the zenith of Compton-Burnett's career as a writer of comic fiction. The novel includes her most memorable opening scene (the fire smoking in the cold breakfast room of the Lamb house) and her best-known family retainer, Bullivant the butler. The novel openly exploits the discrepancy in viewpoint and attitude between "upstairs" and "downstairs" in a dignified, if uncomfortable, country house populated by a variety of near and far relations, each making a claim on Horace Lamb's decreasing ability to support this ménage. Horace's personality is marked by avariciousness in his defeated efforts to economize. The novel has a chilly air about it, most of its activity being devoted to vain efforts to produce adequate heat to keep the various family members warm. The setting is decidedly Victorian (the date of the novel's events is fixed at 1892), and it explores a theme common to most of Compton-Burnett's fiction: the apparent ability of the obviously unlovable person (here Horace Lamb) to be deeply loved by others (in particular, his cousin Mortimer). When, after complicated sexual and financial affairs, Mortimer returns to share Horace's cold and inhospitable hearth, it is with the comfort of already knowing the worst about Horace Lamb's personality and the situation in the household. Compton-Burnett said that of all her novels she liked this the best and enjoyed writing it. *Manservant and Maidservant* was her best-

selling book; under the title *Bullivant and the Lambs,* it was very well received in America.

In contrast to the lack of family warmth in *Manservant and Maidservant, Two Worlds and Their Ways* (1949) explores the effects of too much maternal love. The family includes Sir Roderick and Lady Shelley and their two children, Clemence and Sefton. Lady Shelley bears a certain resemblance to Katharine Compton-Burnett, being also a second wife fiercely protective of her own children's interests. She finds Oliver (the son of the first Lady Shelley) an unhappy reminder of her predecessor's continuing presence in the house, especially since Oliver blocks the right of succession for Lady Shelley's own son. The contrast of "worlds" encompasses not only successive marriages but types of education; the governess is contrasted to the headmistress, Miss Lesbia Firebrace (a lesbian, as her name suggests), who, like Josephine Napier of *More Women Than Men,* represents a kind of female firebrand. Young Clemence Shelley is caught in the grip of tensions existing between school and home and, not unlike Ivy Compton-Burnett herself fifty years earlier, learns to don the protective mask that keeps her true self outside the bounds of family and school tyranny.

Darkness and Day (1951) was published ten days after Margaret Jourdain's death from a lung ailment, marking the moment when Ivy Compton-Burnett's life again returned to the shadow of loneliness, recalling the years of despair that followed the breakup of her own family. (The subject of *Darkness and Day* is the mysterious ways of parentage, the plot involving a series of secret and denied parentages that result in a confusion of inheritances and the dissolution of family relationships.) *The Present and the Past,* the first book written after Jourdain's death, was published in 1953, the year before Compton-Burnett's seventieth birthday. It is a very slim volume with a large cast of characters. The tyrant, Cassius Clare, is a rather inadequate tyrant who is allowed to die by his own hand because those closest to him assume that this action is yet another faked suicide attempt. The ironic thrust of the novel is directed at marriage: Clare's present wife and his first wife, now divorced from him, become closest friends. Perhaps the most delightful members of the cast are the Clare children, who reenact scenes from Compton-Burnett's own childhood.

Just prior to the publication of her next book, *Mother and Son* (1955), Compton-Burnett again concerned herself with the marketing of her novels. The appearance of her fifteenth novel coincided with the publication of Robert Liddell's critical as-

MOTHER AND SON

a
new
novel
by

I.
COMPTON-
BURNETT

Dust jacket for Compton-Burnett's 1955 novel, for which she was awarded a James Tait Black Memorial Prize in 1956

sessment of her work *The Novels of I. Compton-Burnett,* its cover adorned with a Cecil Beaton photograph of Compton-Burnett, but she pressed hard her claim with Victor Gollancz for a more comprehensive advertising campaign. About this time, Arthur Calder Marshall devoted one of his BBC home-service programs, "Talking of Books," to *Mother and Son,* describing Compton-Burnett as "the strangest, the most bewildering, the wittiest and in the opinion of Robert Liddell the greatest living English novelist." *Mother and Son,* whose matriarch, Miranda Hume, is the last in Compton-Burnett's books, won a James Tait Black Memorial Prize, awarded to the year's best work of fiction. Several of Compton-Burnett's friends had already won the award (L. P. Hartley for *Eustace and Hilda* and Graham Greene for *The Heart of the Matter*), and she was very pleased by this recognition of her work.

Perhaps more than any other critic, Robert

Liddell was responsible for bringing Compton-Burnett's work to a larger reading public. In his 1953 study, *Some Principles of Fiction,* he returns again to her writing, addressing the problem of "pastness" in her novels, the necessity of their historical place in the transition years between the Victorian and Edwardian periods:

> She is . . . able to depict a world unshaken by modern warfare, a community rooted in a single place, and lives still ruled, and even laid waste, by family tyranny. She can do this, because she need only take a period of fifty years ago, when she was herself already alive—therefore she can recreate this age without the artificiality and falsity of the historical novelist.
>
> Already this device causes some readers to make the mistake of dismissing her novels as "Quaint"—but in time their date of publication may cease to be relevant, and they may come to seem novels of English life between 1888 and 1910, which might have been written at any time.

Compton-Burnett's personal life as well as her fictional world was rooted in these years before the twentieth century became "modern." She made no effort to become contemporary with her contemporaries. As the years separated her from the time period of her fiction, her thoughts turned almost obsessively to her youth, the years in the house in Hove, her experiences growing up in a Victorian family. She reexamined the events that had caused her wounds whose scars she carried into old age.

By the 1950s the brilliant middle period of her creativity had passed. Although she continued to write in these late years of her life, and in fact seemed to write even more quickly than before, the late novels lack the technical audacity and complexity of the earlier works. The last five novels all concern the power and authority of fatherhood, investigating again the concept of heritage. *A Father and His Fate* (1957) begins the five-novel sequence about paternity. A particularly bitter study of fatherhood, this novel creates a modern King Lear in the person of Michael Mowbray, who not only chooses his Cordelia (Verena Gray), but seduces her. Relationships between fathers and daughters become relationships between fathers and sons in *A Heritage and its History* (1959), as Simon Challoner waits impatiently for his inheritance; once secured, it makes a bitter, disagreeable, and domineering person of him. Implicit sexual attraction between fathers and offspring is treated directly in the next novel, *The*

*Ivy Compton-Burnett (third from right) on 19 May 1960, after receiving an honorary doctorate from the University of Leeds.
With her is the Princess Royal (fourth from left), who was chancellor of the university.*

Mighty and Their Fall (1961), as Agnes Middleton, a fourteen-year-old girl, serves nearly as wife to her widowed father. In *A God and His Gifts* (1963) Hereward Egerton, a man of strong sexual needs, seduces (and fathers children by) nearly every female member of the cast, producing children at about the same rate he produces novels. Violet Powell called the novel "a pyrotechnical display, bursting with literary energy and originality of imagination."

It was in these later years of her life that Compton-Burnett was discovered and appreciated by other writers; Natalie Sarraute's highly intellectual analysis of the Compton-Burnett writing style, which places it "somewhere on the fluctuating frontier that separates conversation from subconversation," brought her work to the attention of the French avant-garde, the writers of the *nouveau roman*.

The 1960s marked a decade of national and international recognition of her work, beginning

with the awarding of an honorary doctorate at the University of Leeds, 19 May 1960, and including the honorific title Dame Commander of the Order of the British Empire in 1967. Perhaps the award that gave Ivy Compton-Burnett the greatest pleasure, as indicated in Elizabeth Sprigge's biography, was her entitlement by the Royal Society of Literature as "the dignity of Companion of Literature" in 1968. In this year, too, Julia Mitchell's dramatization of *A Heritage and its History* was produced for British television.

Ivy Compton-Burnett spent the last years of her life with only the closest of friends—Herman Schrijver, Sprigge, and Charles Burkhart (who edited a collection of reviews and critical writings about her work). She suffered from a weak heart and two broken hips, the effects of several bad falls that made entertaining and traveling nearly impossible. In her last weeks she seemed particularly aware that her life was nearing its end, with one of her letters beginning: "You must be fearing I had

Chapter, 2.

"Osbert, you ought to know how to cut a ham."

"Then I do know, Grannie. I only dare to do what I ought."

"Do you expect other people to eat the fat ~~that~~ you have left?"

"Is it any good to expect it? Do you ~~think~~ they would?"

"The fat of ham is quite different from other fat."

"That hardly seems worth while, when it all has the same end."

"You should cut the fat and lean together, and leave what you can't eat."

"I knew waste was not wicked. That is what I will do."

"What good do you suppose the fat is by itself?"

"No good. Or with anything else. What good could it be?"

"A young man should ~~be able to~~ eat whatever is provided."

"The fat of ham is quite a wholesome food."

"How do you know? What means is there of knowing?"

"I know from my own experience."

"Grannie, what words are these? Pray do not go any further."

"Can't we forget the ham?" said Osbert's sister, "It ~~——— to the table.~~ It dominates the sideboard, but it need hardly do the same to our lives."

left the earth; and its binding forces hardly increase." She died of bronchitis on 29 August 1969, leaving unfinished the manuscript of her last novel, whose title suggests her keen awareness of its place in the canon of her writings: *The Last and the First*. Several of her friends helped to prepare this manuscript for its publication, Cicely Greig (who for many years had typed her manuscripts according to a precisely detailed system set out by Compton-Burnett) taking the major responsibility of its completion. Ivy Compton-Burnett left behind a large sum of money for the publication of a new collected edition of her works, which was completed by Victor Gollancz in 1972 and included the nineteen "mature" novels (omitting *Dolores*).

After Compton-Burnett's death, some of her friends wrote memoirs of her. One of the most fascinating is a collection of remembrances by Charles Burkhart and Herman Schrijver, *Herman and Nancy and Ivy*. Although Burkhart suggests that Ivy Compton-Burnett *was* her books, the remembrances collected in *Herman and Nancy and Ivy* give a clearer sense of her as a person than do either of the biographies. Burkhart describes her "tyrannical tea parties" as being "as formal as the innumerable meals taken in the twenty of her novels. It is hard to say which is more unreal, the breakfast which begins most of her books or tea with her in Braemar Mansions." Herman Schrijver describes her "total lack of interest in almost any subject except people and gossip, incest and money and servants, soft fruit and country flowers," and documents a life that was rigid, closed, and parochial. In particular, he analyzes the dynamics of the relationship between Compton-Burnett and Margaret Jourdain, distinguishing Compton-Burnett as the genius and Jourdain as the one who was erudite. He describes the relationship of the two women as a homosexual marriage and recounts hearing Compton-Burnett, on the day of Jourdain's funeral, repeating the phrase "I have lost my man" three times. (This peculiar habit of talking to herself and repeating sentences to herself is commented on by almost everyone who knew her as the most characteristic and also the most disconcerting of her habits.) Surrounded by homosexuals of both sexes, Compton-Burnett and Jourdain lived in a world where relationships like theirs were the rule rather than the exception. Schrijver writes in his memoir: "During the quarter of a century that I knew Margaret and Ivy together they behaved like any married couple who were bored with each other."

The presence of Margaret Jourdain in Ivy Compton-Burnett's life probably accounted for its division into two distinct parts: "Of course, if one has been miserable for thirty-five years, and wonderfully happy for thirty-five years, one cannot expect much from life for the remainder of the years to come," Compton-Burnett remarked in her last years. The first part of this life divided is the subject of Hilary Spurling's biography, *Ivy When Young*. It ends in the year 1919, when Compton-Burnett was thirty-five years old and the two women began living together. The most meticulously detailed of the biographies and remembrances of Compton-Burnett, Spurling's study searches for the explanation of her fictional subject matter and the pattern of her later life in the experiences of her young life, providing a carefully argued and psychologically powerful portrait of a woman whose personality, like the titles of her fictional works, was characterized by the juxtaposition of opposites:

> The life of Ivy Compton-Burnett falls into two parts sharply divided by the first world war. She was thirty when the war began; when it ended, her settled background, her home and occupation had all gone, and the last of the people who had mattered most to her was dead. After 1918 she drew a line beneath everything that had gone before, and drew it with a finality and force which had drastic repercussions on her life—"Ivy Compton-Burnett embodied in herself a quite unmodified pre-1914 personality," wrote Anthony Powell, describing his first meeting with her in the 1950s—as on her work.

Ivy Compton-Burnett made no concession to the present in which she lived or to the almost seventy years she spent in the twentieth century, remaining in her life as in her fiction a product of late-Victorian middle-class England.

Biographies:

Elizabeth Sprigge, *The Life of Ivy Compton-Burnett* (New York: Braziller, 1973);

Hilary Spurling, *Ivy When Young: The Early Life of I. Compton-Burnett* (London: Gollancz, 1974).

References:

Frank Baldanza, *Ivy Compton-Burnett* (New York: Twayne, 1964);

Charles Burkhart, *The Art of I. Compton-Burnett* (London: Gollancz, 1972);

Burkhart, *Herman and Nancy and Ivy: Three Lives in Art* (London: Gollancz, 1977), pp. 74-108;

Pamela Hansford Johnson, *I. Compton-Burnett*

(London: Longmans, Green, 1951);
Robert Liddell, *The Novels of I. Compton-Burnett*
    (London: Gollancz, 1955);
Violet Powell, *A Compton-Burnett Compendium* (London: Heinemann, 1973).

Papers:
Ivy Compton-Burnett's papers are at the Humanities Research Center, University of Texas, Austin, Texas.

Ronald Firbank
(17 January 1886-21 May 1926)

Charles Burkhart
Temple University

BOOKS: *Odette D'Antrevernes and A Study inTemperament* (London: Elkin Mathews, 1905); *Odette D'Antrevernes* revised as *Odette: A Fairy Tale for Weary People* (London: Grant Richards, 1916);
Vainglory (London: Grant Richards, 1915; New York: Brentano's, 1925);
Inclinations (London: Grant Richards, 1916);
Caprice (London: Grant Richards, 1917);
Valmouth: A Romantic Novel (London: Grant Richards, 1919; New York: New Directions, 1956);
The Princess Zoubaroff: A Comedy (London: Grant Richards, 1920);
Santal (London: Grant Richards, 1921; New York: Bonacio & Saul/Grove, 1955);
The Flower Beneath the Foot: Being a Record of the Early Life of St. Laura de Nazianzi and the Times in Which She Lived (London: Grant Richards, 1923; New York: Brentano's, 1924);
Prancing Nigger (New York: Brentano's, 1924); republished as *Sorrow in Sunlight* (London: Brentano's, 1924);
Concerning the Eccentricities of Cardinal Pirelli (London: Grant Richards, 1926);
The Artificial Princess (London: Duckworth, 1934);
The New Rhythm and Other Pieces (London: Duckworth, 1962).
Collections: *The Works of Ronald Firbank* (6 volumes, London: Duckworth, 1929, 1934; 5 volumes, New York: Brentano's, 1929);
The Complete Ronald Firbank (London: Duckworth, 1961; Norfolk, Conn.: New Directions, 1962).

Ronald Firbank has been called the last of the 1890s decadents, the first impressionist novelist, and a modernist like James Joyce, Virginia Woolf,

and D. H. Lawrence. Basically, however, he is an eccentric writer who belongs to no school. Though influenced by Maurice Maeterlinck, Joris Huysmans, Théophile Gautier, and Oscar Wilde, he remains independent of them. His uniqueness has attracted the admiration of many critics and novelists, from Arthur Waley to Edmund Wilson, from Evelyn Waugh to E. M. Forster to Osbert Sitwell. But despite their praise the number of his readers has remained small, and most of his books were published at his own expense.

It was an expense he could afford. His background, as Anthony Powell has pointed out in his introduction to *The Complete Ronald Firbank* (1961), is a very English story: his great-grandfather was an illiterate coal miner, his grandfather one of the most successful railway contractors of his day, his father (Joseph Thomas Firbank; married to Harriette Jane Garrett in 1883) an M.P., and Arthur Annesley Ronald Firbank himself, the well-to-do dandy and butterfly, a frequenter of first nights and collector of rare bibelots. In person he was as mannered as his prose style; he was vain, stuttering, effeminate, alcoholic, homosexual, shy to the point of writhing. His conversion to Roman Catholicism in 1907, which might to another writer have afforded theme and substance for his books, as it did, for example, to Evelyn Waugh and Graham Greene, in his case supplied him only with decorative details and sly humor about flagellation and the folly of choirboys; his attraction to the Church was ambiguous. He believed only in his own vision and probably would have denied that he had one; he might have shared the wish of Gustave Flaubert, another of his influences, to write "a book about nothing," sustained by style alone. Firbank's style

Ronald Firbank in the French Alps (courtesy of Miriam J. Benkovitz)

has been called mannered, precious, camp, arch, coarse, silly, and other more-or-less negative names, and they are all accurate. But it is also true that he is one of the great stylists of the novel and one of its great comedians, artificers, and wits.

After a private education and a few terms at Trinity Hall at Cambridge (1906-1909), he began a wandering life that included sojourns in Rome, Madrid, Algiers, Haiti, Havana, Barbados, places that supplied him with the exotic settings for his novels. He never remained too long away from his beloved mother, "Baba." He was a surprisingly expert traveler, as well as quite shrewd in the management of his money. A low period of his life was World War I, which cut him off from his pleasure resorts; much of it he spent in rooms on the High Street in Oxford; months passed, it is said, when he

spoke to no one but his charwoman and a guard on the train to London. Yet his isolation may have driven him into himself with beneficial results to his writing, for from this period come three of his best books: *Inclinations* (1916), *Caprice* (1917), and *Valmouth* (1919). His earliest work, *Odette D'Antrevernes and A Study in Temperament* (1905; *Odette D'Antrevernes* was revised and published as *Odette* in 1916), is a few pages of imitation Maeterlinck.

Vainglory (1915), his first mature work, concerns the desire of Mrs. Shamefoot to erect a memorial window to herself in a cathedral. It is a mélange of ecclesiastical politics and worldly prelates, of actresses and artists. The *Times* (London) complained of *Vainglory* that its "endless flow of scintillating nonsense is most exhausting," and the novelist Ada Leverson said that it was "restless and witty

Dust jacket by Albert Rutherston

Caprice is the story of the stagestruck Miss Sarah Sinquier, daughter of a cathedral dean, who steals the family silver in order to run off to London and pursue a theatrical career. The Café Royal, well-known as a literary hangout for Firbank and many other artists and writers, is one of the settings. With his typical cold and melancholy irony, Firbank ends the novel with the death of Miss Sinquier, who, dancing triumphantly on the stage of the theater she has hired to perform Juliet in, plunges to her death through a trapdoor.

A chapter of *Valmouth*, his next novel, was first published under the title of "Fantasia for Orchestra in A Sharp Minor," in the Spring 1919 issue of *Arts and Letters,* which Osbert Sitwell was editing. Much later *Valmouth* was made into a musical, performed first in Liverpool in 1958, then in London in 1959, and less successfully in New York in 1960. Valmouth is a watering place so salubrious that many of its inhabitants have lived to well over a hundred years. They enjoy patronizing a powerful black masseuse, Mrs. Yajñavalkya. Mrs. Yaj's niece, Niri-Esther, by her marriage to the dashing young Lieutenant Dick Whorwood, symbolizes the intrusion of more earthy forces into the desiccated nonagenarian aristocrats of Valmouth, and also marks Firbank's increasing interest in black people

and allusive enough to give anyone who understands it a nervous breakdown."

Inclinations, the first of the novels from Firbank's four years at Oxford, concerns the journey to Greece of Geraldine O'Brookomore, "the authoress of *Six Strange Sisters, Those Gonzagas,* etc.," and the youthful Miss Mabel Collins. The highlights of the novel are the accidental slaughter of one lady by another during a wild-duck shooting expedition; the worldwide search of an Australian named Miss Dawkins for her lost father—she is searching alphabetically (after Greece, she "proposes to do the I's . . . India, Italy, Ireland, Iceland. . . ."); and the singular chapter twenty which consists entirely of the exclamation "Mabel!" repeated eight times: these are the lamentations of Miss O'Brookomore after Mabel has left her for a young Italian count. As with his other early work, reviews of *Inclinations* were few in number, and patronizing, puzzled, or negative in tone.

Ronald Firbank, 1917 (photo by Elliott and Fry)

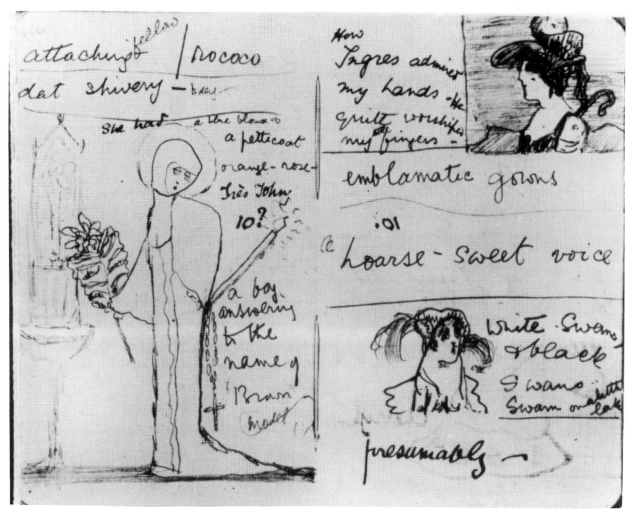

Page from the notebook Firbank kept while writing Valmouth *and* The Princess Zoubaroff *(Henry W. and Albert A. Berg Collection, the New York Public Library, Astor, Lenox and Tilden Foundations)*

and their, to him, more innocent vitality and charm.

This interest was to culminate in *Prancing Nigger* in 1924, but between it and *Valmouth* he published *The Flower Beneath the Foot* (1923), the life story of a fictional saint, Lady Laura de Nazianzi ("Some girls are born organically good; I wasn't") and her doomed love for His Weariness Prince Yousef, the son of King Willie and Her Dreaminess the Queen (for whom a royal visitor, Queen Thleeanouhee of the Land of Dates, conceives a tropical passion). For reasons of state Yousef must marry Princess Alice of England, and Laura enters a convent on her way to sainthood. The last scene, after the brittle and rococo wit that has preceded it, is moving: while cathedral chimes toll for the wedding of Yousef and Alice, Laura is beating her hands upon the broken glass ends atop the convent wall crying "Yousef, Yousef, Yousef. . . . "

Prancing Nigger (1924) is the title of Firbank's next novel in America, where he had a growing reputation and where it was first published; in England, where it appeared later in the same year, it was called *Sorrow in Sunlight*. A village family, the Mouths, migrate to the capital of their island (probably inspired by Haiti) to enter the great life of cities. Says Mrs. Almadou Mouth, "We leave Mediavilla for de education ob my daughters. . . . We go to Cuna-Cuna, for de finishing ob *mes filles*." It takes some adapting to clothing and plumbing, but the Mouths and their children, Miami, Edna, and Charlie, learn more worldly ways and have their social and sexual successes. *Prancing Nigger* is a part of the increasing consciousness in the 1920s of the black world by the white world, whether the passionate advocacy of African art by the Parisian surrealists and Picasso, of black political rights by

Dust jacket by C. R. W. Nevinson

Firbank's friend Nancy Cunard, or of Harlem and the black America of Firbank's admirer the American Carl Van Vechten. *Prancing Nigger* was successful both commercially and critically in the United States, receiving favorable reviews from Joseph Wood Krutch, Edmund Wilson, and others.

Firbank's final novel, published in 1926, the year of his death, was refused by Brentano's, the American publisher of *Prancing Nigger,* on "religious and moral grounds." A summary of the opening and closing scenes of the story may indicate why: *Concerning the Eccentricities of Cardinal Pirelli* begins with the cardinal baptizing a police puppy named Crack in the font of his Cathedral of Clemenza; it ends when the naked cardinal, who is to

leave for Rome the following morning to learn from the Pope his punishment for the baptism, drops dead while pursuing a boy named Chicklet around the same church. The novel has as little development as the rest of Firbank's books, but between the beginning and the ending are luxurious tableaux, redolent with Spanish life, or at least with Spanish life as Firbank fancied it, shining with preposterous wit and glowing with poetry and music.

Composition or coherence was not his gift; to try to summarize a plot of Firbank's is to break a butterfly. The life of his novels is a series of epigrams and polished paradoxes. His characters, with their mania for chic, are bisexual or lesbian or languidly gay; they spend their lives in little intensities. Thus his novels are meant to be dipped into, not pondered; too many minutes of a Firbank novel are like too many meringues. And for some, perhaps most, readers his books are not meant to be dipped into at all; his interests are too far from theirs; like his self-portrait, the poet Claud Harvester in *Vainglory,* his style is "brilliant and vicious." He is more a writer's writer than a reader's writer, and he has been dipped into, to their profit, by later writers as diverse as Ivy Compton-Burnett and Barbara Pym. He is not one of the staples, the beef and ale, of the English novel; instead he is caviar to the general; to change to an apter image, he is one of the rare eccentric flowers of the English romantic tradition.

Bibliography:
Miriam J. Benkovitz, *A Bibliography of Ronald Firbank* (London: Rupert Hart-Davis, 1962).

Biography:
Miriam J. Benkovitz, *Ronald Firbank* (New York: Knopf, 1969).

References:
Brigid Brophy, *Prancing Novelist* (New York: Harper & Row, 1973);
Mervyn Horder, ed., *Ronald Firbank: Memoirs and Critiques* (London: Duckworth, 1977).

Papers:
Some of Firbank's papers are in the Henry W. and Albert A. Berg Collection, New York Public Library.

William Gerhardie

(21 November 1895-15 July 1977)

Dido Davies

BOOKS: *Futility: A Novel on Russian Themes* (London: Cobden-Sanderson, 1922; New York: Duffield, 1922);

Anton Chehov: A Critical Study (London: Cobden-Sanderson, 1923; New York: Duffield, 1923);

The Polyglots (London: Cobden-Sanderson, 1925; New York: Duffield, 1925);

A Bad End (London: Ernest Benn, 1926);

The Vanity Bag (London: Ernest Benn, 1927);

Pretty Creatures (London: Ernest Benn, 1927; New York: Duffield, 1927);

Perfectly Scandalous; or, The Immorality Lady. A Comedy in Three Acts (London: Ernest Benn, 1927; New York: Duffield, 1928); republished as *Donna Quixote* (London: Duckworth, 1929);

Jazz and Jasper (London: Duckworth, 1928); republished as *Eva's Apples* (New York: Duffield, 1928); republished as *My Sinful Earth* (London: Macdonald, 1947); republished as *Doom* (London: Macdonald, 1974);

Pending Heaven (London: Duckworth, 1930; New York: Harper, 1930);

Memoirs of a Polyglot (London: Duckworth, 1931; New York: Knopf, 1931);

The Memoirs of Satan, by Gerhardie and Brian Lunn (London: Cassell, 1932; Garden City: Doubleday, Doran, 1933);

The Casanova Fable: A Satirical Revaluation, by Gerhardie and Hugh Kingsmill (London: Jarrolds, 1934; New York: Jarrolds, 1947);

Resurrection (London: Cassell, 1934; New York: Harcourt, Brace, 1934);

Meet Yourself as You Really Are, by Gerhardie and Prince Leopold Loewenstein (London: Faber & Faber, 1936; Philadelphia: Lippincott, 1936);

Of Mortal Love (London: Barker, 1936);

My Wife's the Least of It (London: Faber & Faber, 1938);

The Romanovs (New York: Putnam's, 1939; London: Rich & Cowan, 1940);

God's Fifth Column, a Biography of the Age: 1890-1940, edited by Michael Holroyd and Robert Skidelsky (London: Hodder & Stoughton, 1981; New York: Simon & Schuster, 1981).

Collections: *The Collected Uniform Edition of the*

William Gerhardie

Works of William Gerhardi (London: Macdonald, 1947-1949);

The Revised Definitive Edition of the Works of William Gerhardie (London: Macdonald, 1970-1974).

OTHER: Hugh Kingsmill, ed., *The English Genius: A Survey of the English Achievement and Character,* includes a contribution by Gerhardie (London: Eyre & Spottiswoode, 1938);

"My Literary Credo," in *Futility* (London: Macdonald, 1947);

"This Present Breath, a Tetralogy in One Volume," in *The Wind and the Rain,* edited by Neville

The Gerhardies' neobaroque mansion in St. Petersburg

Braybrooke (London: Secker & Warburg, 1962).

The achievement of William Alexander Gerhardie (originally Gerhardi) consists in seven fine novels and an engaging autobiography, which span only two decades, the 1920s and 1930s. His childhood in prerevolutionary Russia and hence his knowledge of Russian as well as German and French literature not only influenced the subject matter of many of his books but also shaped the ironic no-man's-land between tragedy and farce which his characters inhabit. Gerhardie had considerable success early in his career, but his general popularity has never matched the praise he received from eminent writers. He won the admiration of established literary figures of the day, including Arnold Bennett, H. G. Wells, Edith Wharton, and George Bernard Shaw, and influenced the generation younger than himself. Evelyn Waugh wrote to Gerhardie: "I learned a great deal of my trade from your own novels," and Graham Greene described *Futility* as having left "an indelible impression," explaining that "to those of my generation he

was the most important new novelist to appear in our young life." The critic Philip Toynbee considered him to be "of at least equivalent stature and achievement" to E. M. Forster.

Gerhardie was born in St. Petersburg of English parents, his father a second-generation expatriate who had prospered as a cotton manufacturer. Gerhardie's autobiography describes his background as "entirely Russian; and of the four languages taught me in childhood my knowledge of English was least and, until I was eighteen or so, quite abject." In 1914 he traveled to England (his first visit, save for a brief spell as a young child) with the intention of making a career of literature, but the outbreak of war caused him to volunteer for the army. After training with the Royal Scots Guards he was eventually posted to the staff of the British military attaché in Petrograd, where he remained until 1918, witnessing the revolution at close range. After the resulting ruin of his father, the family escaped to England, where Gerhardie joined them briefly at the end of the war before being posted to Siberia. He served for two years under General Sir Alfred Knox in the British Military Mission, Vladi-

William Gerhardie during cavalry training in York, 1916

vostok, remaining throughout a detached and skeptical observer of the efforts of the allied intervention. In 1920 Gerhardie left Russia forever and went up to Worcester College, Oxford, having already begun *Futility* (1922).

Gerhardie's first novel (originally written in both Russian and English) was published on the recommendation of Katherine Mansfield, who praised its "freshness and warmth and suppleness" and its avoidance of "that dreadful glaze of 'intellectuality' which is like a curse upon so many English writers." *Futility* is based upon Gerhardie's experiences and observations during the Russian Revolution. It tells of Andrei, a young English officer stationed in Petrograd, and his encounters with the Bursanov family, and in particular his love for the beguiling but infuriating daughter Nina. Against a background of momentous historical change the Bursanovs remain curiously and comically wrapped up in themselves, oblivious of Andrei's impatient insistence that they have all been "lifted out of Chehov." Nina's father, Nikolai, waits vainly for an improvement in his dwindling fortunes, while his dependents steadily increase. But as the story circles to its conclusion, Andrei is forced to realize that his own life has, in essence, been no less delusory. *Futility*'s striking originality lay in its suggestions of the absurd—the characters suffer from a constant in-

ability to communicate; repetitive utterances and protracted silences create an overwhelming sense of aimlessness, of perpetual waiting; tragic situations vacillate on the brink of the ridiculous.

John Middleton Murry praised *Futility* highly, but nonetheless took a narrow view that it illustrated "most admirably . . . the fantastic little microcosm of Russian life, the Russian spirit. . . ." In saying so, Murry was inadvertently articulating precisely those current English misconceptions about Russian literature that Gerhardie's polyglot predicament gave him the unique opportunity to portray. His critical work *Anton Chehov* (1923) was the first full-length study of this writer in any language. Its central thesis, advanced for its time, argued for the universal quality of Chekhov's work and demonstrated that far from being idiosyncratically Russian he "penetrates to a level immeasurably deeper than the superficial differences of men and race, to a bed-rock of common humanity." Gerhardie maintained that much of Chekhov's "high comedic quality" is lost in translation—an oblique criticism of the inadequacy of most contemporary renderings. To C. P. Snow he was "the first person in England actively to interpret Chekhov to his fellow writers," and this is as true of Gerhardie in his fiction as in his criticism. His second novel, *The Polyglots* (1925), set in Russia and the Far East after the revolution, describes the narrator's discovery of familial and romantic relations, and with *Futility* represents his most original work. All three of these first books were enthusiastically acclaimed. Wells found *Futility* "true, devastating. A wonderful book," and the American edition carried a laudatory preface by Edith Wharton. Anthony Powell called *The Polyglots* "a classic," and the *New York Times* praised *Anton Chehov* as "one of the ablest critical studies of recent years."

Success brought Gerhardie to the notice of Lord Beaverbrook, and they became close friends, Beaverbrook introducing Gerhardie to many celebrities of the day both literary and political. Gerhardie's satirical science-fiction novel *Jazz and Jasper* (1928), very different from his usual style, carried a portrait of Beaverbrook ("Lord Ottercove") which was, according to his biographer A. J. P. Taylor, the only convincing picture known to him of Beaverbrook in middle age. Bennett spoke of the book's "wild and brilliant originality," and it remained Waugh's favorite.

While working on a novel which "had for its theme immortality" Gerhardie found himself temporarily detached from his body—able to look down, apparently independent of space and time, upon his sleeping self. *Resurrection* (1934) describes this experience and, immediately after it is over, follows the narrator (Gerhardie) to a society ball, where he argues in defense of the immortality of the soul. In pursuance of the idea "Nothing is until it is over," he attempts to recreate a past year of his life, to conjure up a sense of himself independent of linear time, illustrating close affinities with Beckett in his appreciation of Proustian concerns with habit and time. Michael Holroyd considers this Gerhardie's masterpiece, and though Graham Greene shrewdly observed that he knew "no other writer with Mr. Gerhardi's ability to be creatively excited by himself," the complexity of ideas within the novel is also the perfect foil to his supreme gift: the ability to laugh at himself.

Written after more than fourteen years of gestation, *Of Mortal Love* (1936) explores the potential of the simple love story, "a charting of the development of human love, through succeeding stages, from the erotic to the imaginative." Gerhardie explained that as the chief character, Dinah, was based upon a close friend, the idea behind the book was the fusion of the novel form with "imaginative," "creative" biography based on personal knowledge, as distinct from "historical speculation and inferred knowledge in the old type of biography." Edwin Muir considered it "probably the best novel that he

has given us," and it was apparently the author's own favorite.

Gerhardie never married, and much of his earlier life was spent abroad. He lived in France, Austria, and North Africa; lectured in America and Canada; toured India. *The Romanovs* (1939), a biographical history of the dynasty, was his last book to appear in his lifetime. He spent his remaining thirty-seven years increasingly alone, an eccentric though amiable recluse in his London flat, working on a fictional tetralogy called "This Present Breath." Several chapters were anthologized in 1962 in *The Wind and the Rain*, but the whole has been found too fragmentary to publish. Macdonald began publishing a collected uniform edition of his works in 1947 and again in 1970. In 1981 Michael Holroyd and Robert Skidelsky edited *God's Fifth Column, a Biography of the Age: 1890-1940*, which met with a mixed critical reception. A richly detailed reflection upon the forces at work in the age through which Gerhardie lived, *God's Fifth Column* indicts politicians, monarchs, and statesmen for their tyrannical exercise of power, and historians for their justification of that power. God's fifth column is divine discontent, the "motive-power" of the age, which Gerhardie describes as "the natural resentment engendered by any person, class, nation, movement or religion attempting to justify its hegemony by identifying its interests with the supposed good of

William Gerhardie in Regent's Park, London

others." This divine discontent finds expression in the works of artists, who for Gerhardie are the true spokesmen for mankind.

While Gerhardie's most representative ideas on literature emerge in *Anton Chehov,* "My Literary Credo," published as the preface to a 1947 edition of *Futility,* expands his view that art should express experience on levels other than the purely rational: as T. S. Eliot wrote, "the poet is occupied with frontiers of consciousness beyond which words fail, though meanings still exist." The working out of his concerns with language, music, memory, and desire demonstrates his proximity to mainstream modernism. However, the increasing aloofness of Gerhardie's fiction from historical and ideological issues, in a world no longer recuperating from one war but rushing headlong into another, may account for the critical neglect he has suffered since the 1930s: the status of his oeuvre is still unsettled. Nonetheless his best novels, which successfully treat a diversity of subjects and are unified by his distinc-

tive ironic voice, constitute a significant contribution to modern writing.

References:

Walter Allen, *Tradition and Dream* (London: Phoenix House, 1964);

G. U. Ellis, *Twilight on Parnassus: a Survey of Post-War Fiction and Pre-War Criticism* (London: Michael Joseph, 1939), pp. 399-402;

Michael Holroyd, *Unreceived Opinions* (London: Heinemann, 1973), pp. 119-148;

Hugh Kingsmill, *The Progress of a Biographer* (London: Methuen, 1949), pp. 130-134;

Desmond MacCarthy, *Criticism* (London: Putnam's, 1932), pp. 119-125;

John Rothenstein, *Summer's Lease, Autobiography 1901-1938* (London: Hamish Hamilton, 1965), pp. 42-95.

Papers:

Gerhardie's literary papers are at the University Library, Cambridge, England.

Aldous Huxley

Jerry W. Carlson
De Paul University

BIRTH: Godalming, Surrey, 6 July 1894, to Leonard and Judith Arnold Huxley.

EDUCATION: B.A., Balliol College, Oxford University, 1916.

MARRIAGE: 10 July 1919 to Maria Nys; child: Matthew. 19 March 1956 to Laura Archera.

AWARDS AND HONORS: Award from the American Academy of Letters, 1959; elected Companion of Literature by the British Royal Society of Literature, 1962.

DEATH: Hollywood, California, 22 November 1963.

BOOKS: *The Burning Wheel* (Oxford: Blackwell, 1916);
Jonah (Oxford: Holywell, 1917);

The Defeat of Youth and Other Poems (Oxford: Blackwell, 1918);

Leda (London: Chatto & Windus, 1920; New York: Doran, 1920);

Limbo (London: Chatto & Windus, 1920; New York: Doran, 1920);

Crome Yellow (London: Chatto & Windus, 1921; New York: Doran, 1922);

Mortal Coils (London: Chatto & Windus, 1922; New York: Doran, 1922);

Antic Hay (London: Chatto & Windus, 1923; New York: Doran, 1923);

On the Margin: Notes and Essays (London: Chatto & Windus, 1923; New York: Doran, 1923);

Little Mexican & Other Stories (London: Chatto & Windus, 1924); republished as *Young Archimedes and Other Stories* (New York: Doran, 1924);

Those Barren Leaves (London: Chatto & Windus, 1925; New York: Doran, 1925);

Along the Road: Notes and Essays of a Tourist (London: Chatto & Windus, 1925; New York: Doran, 1925);

Selected Poems (Oxford: Blackwell, 1925; New York: Appleton, 1925);

Two or Three Graces and Other Stories (London: Chatto & Windus, 1926; New York: Doran, 1926);

Jesting Pilate (London: Chatto & Windus, 1926; New York: Doran, 1926);

Essays New and Old (London: Chatto & Windus, 1926; New York: Doran, 1927);

Proper Studies (London: Chatto & Windus, 1927; Garden City: Doubleday, Doran, 1928);

Point Counter Point (London: Chatto & Windus, 1928; Garden City: Doubleday, Doran, 1928);

Arabia Infelix and Other Poems (London: Chatto & Windus/New York: Fountain Press, 1929);

Holy Face and Other Essays (London: Fleuron, 1929);

Do What You Will: Essays (London: Chatto & Windus, 1929; Garden City: Doubleday, Doran, 1929);

Brief Candles: Stories (London: Chatto & Windus, 1930; Garden City: Doubleday, Doran, 1930);

Vulgarity in Literature: Digressions from a Theme (London: Chatto & Windus, 1930);

Apennine (Gaylordsville, Conn.: Slide Mountain Press, 1930);

Music at Night and Other Essays (London: Chatto & Windus, 1931; Garden City: Doubleday, Doran, 1931);

The World of Light: A Comedy in Three Acts (London: Chatto & Windus, 1931; Garden City: Doubleday, Doran, 1931);

The Cicadas and Other Poems (London: Chatto & Windus, 1931; Garden City: Doubleday, Doran, 1931);

Brave New World (London: Chatto & Windus, 1932; Garden City: Doubleday, Doran, 1932);

Texts and Pretexts: An Anthology with Commentaries (London: Chatto & Windus, 1932; New York: Harper, 1933);

Rotunda: A Selection from the Works of Aldous Huxley (London: Chatto & Windus, 1932);

Imperial College of Science and Technology: Huxley Memorial Lecture, 1932: T. H. Huxley as a Man of Letters (London: Macmillan, 1932);

Retrospect: An Omnibus of Aldous Huxley's Books (Garden City: Doubleday, Doran, 1933);

Beyond the Mexique Bay (London: Chatto & Windus, 1934; New York: Harper, 1934);

Eyeless in Gaza (London: Chatto & Windus, 1936; New York: Harper, 1936);

1936 . . . Peace? (London: Friends Peace Committee, 1936);

Aldous Huxley, 1920s

The Olive Tree and Other Essays (London: Chatto & Windus, 1936; New York: Harper, 1937);

What Are You Going to Do about It? The Case for Constructive Peace (London: Chatto & Windus, 1936; New York: Harper, 1937);

Ends and Means: An Enquiry into the Nature of Ideals and into the Methods Employed for Their Realization (London: Chatto & Windus, 1937; New York: Harper, 1937);

Stories, Essays, and Poems (London: Dent, 1937);

The Most Agreeable Vice (Los Angeles: Ward Ritchie, 1938);

The Gioconda Smile (London: Chatto & Windus, 1938);

After Many a Summer (London: Chatto & Windus, 1939); republished as *After Many a Summer Dies the Swan* (New York: Harper, 1939);

Words and Their Meanings (Los Angeles: Ward Ritchie, 1940);

Grey Eminence: A Study in Religion and Politics (London: Chatto & Windus, 1941; New York: Harper, 1941);

The Art of Seeing (New York: Harper, 1942; London: Chatto & Windus, 1943);

Time Must Have a Stop (New York: Harper, 1944; London: Chatto & Windus, 1945);

Twice Seven: Fourteen Selected Stories (London: Reprint Society, 1944);

The Perennial Philosophy (New York: Harper, 1945; London: Chatto & Windus, 1946);

Science, Liberty, and Peace (New York: Harper, 1946; London: Chatto & Windus, 1947);

Verses and a Comedy (London: Chatto & Windus, 1946);

The World of Aldous Huxley: An Omnibus of His Fiction and Non-Fiction over Three Decades, edited by Charles J. Rolo (New York: Harper, 1947);

Ape and Essence (New York: Harper, 1948; London: Chatto & Windus, 1949);

The Gioconda Smile: A Play (London: Chatto & Windus, 1948; New York: Harper, 1948);

Prisons, with the "Carceri" Etchings by G. B. Piranesi (London: Trianon, 1949; Los Angeles: Zeitlin & Ver Brugge, 1949);

Themes and Variations (London: Chatto & Windus, 1950; New York: Harper, 1950);

The Devils of Loudun (London: Chatto & Windus, 1952; New York: Harper, 1952);

Joyce, the Artificer: Two Studies of Joyce's Method, by Huxley and Stuart Gilbert (London: Privately printed, 1952);

A Day in Windsor, by Huxley and J. A. Kings (London: Britannicus Liber, 1953);

The Doors of Perception (London: Chatto & Windus, 1954; New York: Harper, 1954);

The French of Paris (New York: Harper, 1954);

The Genius and the Goddess (London: Chatto & Windus, 1955; New York: Harper, 1955);

Adonis and the Alphabet, and Other Essays (London: Chatto & Windus, 1956); republished as *Tomorrow and Tomorrow and Tomorrow, and Other Essays* (New York: Harper, 1956);

Heaven and Hell (London: Chatto & Windus, 1956; New York: Harper, 1956);

Collected Short Stories (London: Chatto & Windus, 1957; New York: Harper, 1957);

Brave New World Revisited (London: Chatto & Windus, 1958; New York: Harper, 1958);

Collected Essays (New York: Harper, 1959);

On Art and Artists, edited by Morris Philipson (London: Chatto & Windus, 1960; New York: Harper, 1960);

Island (London: Chatto & Windus, 1962; New York: Harper, 1962);

Literature and Science (London: Chatto & Windus, 1963; New York: Harper & Row, 1963);

The Crows of Pearlblossom (New York: Random House, 1967; London: Chatto & Windus, 1968);

The Collected Poetry of Aldous Huxley, edited by Donald Watt with an introduction by Richard Church (London: Chatto & Windus, 1971; New York: Harper & Row, 1971).

OTHER: Thomas Humphry Ward, ed., *The English Poets: Selections with Critical Introductions*, introductions to poetry of John Davidson, Ernest Dowson, and Richard Middleton by Huxley (London: Macmillan, 1918);

Rémy de Gourmont, *A Virgin Heart: A Novel*, translated by Huxley (New York: Brown, 1921; London: Allen & Unwin, 1926);

Mrs. Frances Sheridan, *The Discovery: A Comedy in Five Acts*, adapted by Huxley (London: Chatto & Windus, 1924; New York: Doran, 1925);

Oliver Simon and Jules Rodenberg, *Printing of Today*, introduction by Huxley (London: Davies, 1928; New York: Harper, 1928);

Maurice A. Pink, *A Realist Looks at Democracy*, preface by Huxley (London: Benn, 1930; New York: Stokes, 1931);

Douglas Goldering, *The Fortune*, preface by Huxley (London: Harmsworth, 1931);

The Letters of D. H. Lawrence, edited by Huxley (London: Heinemann, 1932; New York: Viking, 1932);

Samuel Butler, *Erewhon*, introduction by Huxley (New York: Limited Editions Club, 1934);

Alfred H. Mendes, *Pitch Lake: A Story from Trinidad*, introduction by Huxley (London: Duckworth, 1934);

Norman Haire, *Birth-Control Methods (Contraception, Abortion, Sterilization)*, foreword by Huxley (London: Allen & Unwin, 1936);

An Encyclopedia of Pacifism, edited by Huxley (London: Chatto & Windus, 1937; New York: Harper, 1937);

Barthélemy de Ligt, *The Conquest of Violence: An Essay on War and Revolution*, introduction by Huxley (London: Routledge, 1938; New York: Dutton, 1938);

Knud Merrild, *Knud Merrild, a Poet and Two Painters: A Memoir of D. H. Lawrence*, preface by Huxley (London: Routledge, 1938; New York: Viking, 1939);

Maxim Gorki, *A Book of Short Stories*, edited by Avram Yarmolinsky and Baroness Moura Budberg, foreword by Huxley (London:

Cape, 1939; New York: Holt, 1939);

Joseph Daniel Unwin, *Hopousia; or, The Sexual and Economic Foundations of a New Society*, introduction by Huxley (London: Allen & Unwin, 1940; New York: Piest, 1940);

Ashley Montagu, *Man's Most Dangerous Myth: The Fallacy of Race*, foreword by Huxley (London: Columbia University Press, 1942);

Bhagavadgita: The Song of God, translated by Swami Prabhavananda and Christopher Isherwood, introduction by Huxley (Hollywood, Cal.: Rodd, 1944; London: Phoenix House, 1947);

William Law, *Selected Mystical Writings*, edited by Stephen Hobhouse, foreword by Huxley (New York: Harper, 1948);

Ramakrishna, *Ramakrishna: Prophet of New India*, translated by Swami Nikhilananda, foreword by Huxley (New York: Harper, 1948; London: Rider, 1951);

Jiddu Krishnamurti, *The First and Last Freedom*, introduction by Huxley (New York: Harper, 1954; London: Gollancz, 1954);

Hubert Benoît, *The Supreme Doctrine: Psychological Studies in Zen Thought*, foreword by Huxley (London: Routledge & Kegan Paul, 1955; New York: Pantheon, 1955);

Frederick Mayer, *New Directions for the American University*, introduction by Huxley (Washington, D.C.: Public Affairs Press, 1957);

Alvah W. Sulloway, *Birth Control and Catholic Doctrine*, preface by Huxley (Boston: Beacon, 1959);

Danilo Dolci, *Report from Palermo*, introduction by Huxley (New York: Orion, 1959).

FILMS: *Pride and Prejudice*, scenario by Huxley and Jane Murfin, M-G-M, 1940;

Madame Curie, treatment by Huxley, M-G-M, 1943;

Jane Eyre, scenario by Huxley, 20th Century-Fox, 1944;

A Woman's Vengeance, adaptation by Huxley from his *The Giocanda Smile*, Universal-International, 1948.

Tall, witty, charismatic, conspicuously handsome, a polymath, Aldous Huxley was an intellectual lighthouse for over forty years. He wrote poetry; drama; screenplays; journalism; biography; social, scientific, and intellectual history; he was a distinguished essayist, but above all else, he was a novelist. Judged early by critics and by a large popular audience as an original lamp of modern fiction, Huxley's work is now best understood as a mirror that creatively distorts and reshapes two lines of the

narrative tradition. The dominant mode since Gustave Flaubert and Henry James has been the novel of selection, the novel that strives toward unity of effects, balance of parts, and realistic probability of story and its narration. Huxley's accomplishment does not lie in this line. Instead, his achievement has two sources: one in what Mikhail Bakhtin has called the "carnivalesque novel" and the other in what Sheldon Sacks has deemed the "apologue."

According to Bakhtin, carnivalesque narratives, which include Petronius's *Satyricon*, François Rabelais's *Gargantua and Pantagruel* (1534), and Miguel de Cervantes's *Don Quixote* (1615), emphasize inclusion rather than selection. Structured like "a plate of mixed fruit," such works enact, celebrate, and ridicule, but do not resolve the conflicts among different characters, ideologies, literary genres, and forms of language. Moreover, such narratives subordinate the linear development of plot and character to the interests of spatial juxtaposition. Indeed, if one takes the Flaubert-James mode as a norm for the novel, carnivalesque fictions may be seen as antinovels.

Apologues, by contrast, might be called "nonnovels" rather than antinovels. According to Sacks, apologues, which include Sir Thomas More's *Utopia* (1516), Voltaire's *Candide* (1759), and Dr. Samuel

Aldous Huxley at about the age of five

Johnson's *Rasselas* (1759), are organized as fictional illustrations of "the truth of a formulable statement or a series of such statements." Such fictions are structured as persuasive arguments and subordinate character and plot to the development and exploration of certain ideas. Agreement or disagreement about those ideas replaces feelings about characters and curiosity about events as the primary pleasures of the fiction. The greatest pleasures and interests of Huxley's fictions, and the greatest contributions of these fictions to the English novel, are mirrored from these lamps: the carnivalesque novel and the apologue.

The alliance in Huxley's work of modern ideas and vigorously rejuvenated, previously unfashionable forms of narrative has its origin in the rich intellectual heritage of his family, which could hardly be more distinguished. Leonard Huxley, his father, was teaching classics at Charterhouse when Huxley was born in July 1894. Somewhat later Leonard edited the influential *Cornhill* magazine, which attracted a bright constellation of contributors. With typically Victorian energy he also edited the letters of Jane Welsh Carlyle, Elizabeth Barrett Browning, and his own father, Thomas Henry Huxley, the noted orator, writer, and champion of Charles Darwin and his theories. Judith Arnold Huxley, Aldous's mother, was equally intelligent and talented. Granddaughter of Dr. Thomas Arnold of Rugby, niece of the poet Matthew Arnold, and sister of the admired, successful novelist Mrs. Humphry Ward, she was educated at Oxford and opened her own boarding school in 1902. Thus Huxley, who had two older brothers and a younger sister, was born into a family that had strong links with England's intellectual past yet had a tradition of leading the present and speculating seriously about the future.

For many children such a heritage would be an insufferable burden; for Huxley the family was a tonic, as it was for his eldest brother, Julian, who gained international recognition as a biologist. By the time Huxley was five or six, a cousin reports, "everybody knew that [he] was different," more gifted, more interesting than others. The pleasing emotional and intellectual symbiosis between Huxley and his family was severely threatened by his mother's sudden death in 1908.

In the next ten years other traumas followed. In 1911 Huxley developed difficulties with his eyes that left him blind for almost eighteen months; in 1914 his brother Trevenen committed suicide; and from 1914 to 1918 Huxley, who was disqualified from military service, watched as his generation was butchered in the trenches of western Europe. Yet a pattern was already set in his character that would prevail throughout his life. Huxley never ignored his difficulties, yet he never allowed them an upper hand. In later years he would criticize Freudian psychology for being exclusively "a study of the sick." For Huxley "other systems of psychology that concern themselves with the present state of the subject or his future potentialities" were "more realistic." In that sense, he was always "realistic" about his own psychology.

Huxley's persistence is nowhere clearer than in his academic, literary, and intellectual accomplishments during those ten troubled years. His masters at Eton, where he completed his secondary education, soon recognized and encouraged his brilliance, but they were also impressed by his friendliness, good humor, and lack of conceit. At Balliol College, Oxford, he graduated with a "First" in English and also won the Stanhope Historical Essay Prize. In addition, he had his first poetry published and helped edit several literary journals. According to L. P. Hartley, the novelist and a fellow Oxonian, "culture" had found in Huxley "a mortal envelope worthy of itself."

Yet much of what Huxley learned about modernity in those years was absorbed not at Oxford but at Garsington, the country estate of Philip Morrell, a member of Parliament, and of his wife, Lady Ottoline, who made her home a salon for England's finest minds. In 1915 a friend introduced Huxley to the Morrells, who were pleased to meet the grandson of Thomas Henry Huxley. At Garsington or through acquaintants he made there he met Virginia Woolf, T. S. Eliot, D. H. Lawrence, John Middleton Murry, John Maynard Keynes, Bertrand Russell, and many others. He also met a shy Belgian war refugee, Maria Nys, whom he would marry. Life at Garsington was socially unconventional, intellectually stimulating, and frequently downright silly. The experience of Garsington became an inspiration, direct or indirect, for Huxley's first four novels.

After leaving Oxford Huxley took a position at Eton, but soon relinquished it; from then on he would make his living by writing. In July 1919 he married Maria and took an editorial job on the *Athenaeum*, a distinguished journal edited by Middleton Murry. A year later Maria gave birth to a son, Matthew; and Huxley took two more jobs, dramatic critic for the *Westminster Gazette* and assistant at the Chelsea Book Club, to augment their income.

Amazingly enough, Huxley also found time to start writing fiction. Actually, he had done so once before: during his period of temporary blindness in 1911-1912 he had composed a novel of about 80,000 words—"a rather bitter novel," as he remembered it later, "about a young man and his relationship to two different kinds of women." His fiction would include many young men trapped between women, yet because the manuscript for this early work has been lost one cannot know how his initial treatment of male vulnerability bears relation to the later work. One can see, however, how his first published fiction, *Limbo* (1920), which includes six stories and a brief play, forecasts more important works.

The best and most representative selection is the novella "The Farcical History of Richard Grenow." Richard, an intellectually inclined Etonian and Oxonian, grows to realize that, as the critic Peter Firchow puts it, "he is at least a spiritual, if not biological hermaphrodite." Trapped in one body are two identities at war with one another. This, however, is no Dr. Jekyll and Mr. Hyde story. For one thing, the easy division between personalities, between sexes, and between points of view begins early to blur; for another, the tale's moral purposes are multiple and shifting. Clever psychological analysis turns to bold physical farce that then turns to scalpel-sharp satire. In this underrated novella Huxley's carnivalesque enterprise begins dramatizing the contradictions—sometimes appalling, sometimes hilarious, often both—of an increasingly fragmented world.

Huxley submitted his manuscript to Chatto and Windus. Frank Swinnerton, the novelist and critic, was the publisher's reader and recommended it for publication. The publisher's delight, however, at issuing a work by the grandson of Thomas Henry Huxley became fumes of irritation when the proofs arrived from the printer. At first, as Swinnerton tells it, the publisher "refused absolutely to publish anything so appallingly gross, blasphemous, and horrible." Eventually a few changes were made. Despite these difficulties, Huxley's first submission of prose fiction to a publisher initiated a mutually profitable arrangement that would last for the rest of his life.

Published in January 1920, *Limbo* sold a modest 1,600 copies. Nonetheless, many intellectuals and literate young people were "carried away," as Huxley's friend and biographer Sybille Bedford tells it, "by the cool bugle call of that new astringent voice expressing so essentially the coming post-war mood." Whatever tune the work played for its audience, it did not make enough money to free Huxley from his journalistic outpourings. Pressed for

Aldous Huxley, early 1920s

money and for space in their tiny flat, Huxley sent Maria and Matthew to live with her mother in Belgium. By April 1921 he had earned enough to join them on the Continent, where from May through August he wrote his first novel, *Crome Yellow* (1921).

Huxley told a friend that his next work would be "in the manner of" Thomas Love Peacock, whose *Nightmare Abbey* (1818) and other novels are composed largely of witty dialogues among eccentric characters who embody fashionable ideas. In manner *Crome Yellow*, which chronicles the visit of effete young poet Denis Stone to the country estate Crome Yellow, certainly resembles Peacock's work, as would Huxley's other novels of the 1920s. The novel's spirit, though, is another issue. For Peacock, ridicule shows deviance from a center that he knows; for Huxley, as for the poet Yeats, "the center cannot hold." In a 1922 article for *Vanity Fair* Huxley names eloquently the causes and inspiration of his art. "The social tragedy of these last years has gone too far and in its nature and origin is too profoundly stupid to be represented tragically. And the same is true of the equally complicated and devastating mental tragedy of the breakup of old traditions and values. The only possible synthesis is the enormous farcical buffoonery of a Rabelais or an Aristophanes—a buffoonery which, it is important to note, is capable of being as beautiful and grandiose as tragedy. For the great comics . . . are those who, almost miraculously, combine the hugely, the earthily grotesque with the delicately and imaginatively beautiful."

Like all his carnivalesque novels, *Crome Yellow* combines the grotesque and the beautiful, yet tips the balance toward the grotesque. Crome Yellow is a menagerie rather than a meeting place of a socially and intellectually cohesive set of friends. Henry Wimbush, the estate's owner, is more interested in writing the history of his property than in entertaining guests. His wife also avoids her guests, and spends her time predicting horse races by using horoscopes. She pays close attention to only one guest, Mr. Barbecue-Smith, whose talent is popularizing philosophy. "It's just a little book about the connection of the Subconscious with the Infinite," he says with transparent immodesty. Other characters misinterpret poetry, modern art, Freud, Catholicism, a myriad of other subjects, and—most persistently—each other's intentions. Denis distinguishes himself from his fellow solipsists not by changing his condition but by recognizing that he and the others *are* solipsists. "One had a philosophy and tried to make life fit into it," Denis discovers. "One should have lived first and then made one's philosophy to fit life," he concludes. "Parallel lines . . . meet only at infinity," he ruminates at another point. "We are all straight parallel lines."

Denis's conclusion is gloomy but the novel is not. Huxley guides his reader to do what no character can do: delight in the trajectories of the parallel lines. Here, for example, is Denis's conceit about the value of his time: "Oh, this journey! It was two hours cut clean of his time; two hours in which he might have done so much, so much—written the perfect poem, for example, or read the one illuminating book." Society may be a spectacle of human vanity, as Denis and his fellow guests show, but a carnivalesque artist like Huxley always reserves the right to emphasize the pleasures of the spectacle instead of the obvious futilities of vanity.

The novel was published in November 1921; Bedford reports that "people were dazzled"; Huxley had "made a name." The kind of name and its circulation were another issue. For the young who

had survived the war or who had just come of age, Huxley was exhilarating; his work embodied the moral instability and the pretension that constituted the new era. For their parents and others reared under Queen Victoria, Huxley was shocking, morally slack, perhaps even dangerous. None of these opinions, however, reached as yet into a wide popular audience. In its first year the book sold 2,500 copies, enough to give Huxley modest royalties, but not enough to free him from journalism or to mark him as more than a "coterie novelist."

The book's publication had a negative impact on many of Huxley's friends. Lady Ottoline, in particular, was offended: she took Crome Yellow to be Garsington. There was some truth to her belief. Nonetheless, her response is typical of a blindness about Huxley's working method that has characterized literary critics as well as his friends. Huxley's strength as an artist is in transforming materials for his use, not in inventing materials. He made the point clear in a late interview: "Of course I base my characters partly on people I know—one can't escape it—but fictional characters are oversimplified; they're much less complex than the people one knows. There is something of (John Middleton) Murry in several of my characters, but I wouldn't say I'd put Murry in a book." Huxley's works, then, do not reveal an interestingly autobiographical dialectic of his life and his works as do, say, the novels of his near contemporary, F. Scott Fitzgerald. Huxley wrote to portray the characteristics of his era, not the characters of his friends.

Huxley took an office job in London with Condé Nast, the magazine publishers, and continued his occasional writings. In May 1922 Chatto and Windus issued a new collection of his short stories, *Mortal Coils*. This set a pattern for the next eight years, during which Huxley published three novels. Each was followed by a collection of stories: *Antic Hay* (1923) by *Little Mexican* (1924); *Those Barren Leaves* (1925) by *Two or Three Graces* (1926); and *Point Counter Point* (1928) by *Brief Candles* (1930). Sales of the collections were modest, yet achieved the goal of keeping Huxley's name in the public eye between the occasions of his novels. In the long run, however, the stories have had little impact upon his reputation. They have not entered the canon of modern short fiction as have those of his fellow novelists James Joyce, D. H. Lawrence, and William Faulkner. Even so, Huxley's stories reveal the virtues of his novels. Frequently hilarious, always urbane and cleverly plotted, the stories give consistent delight; yet they seem to give their full pleasures upon a single reading. The novels do not

Aldous, Maria, and Matthew Huxley, 1920s

differ in use of narrative technique or in the "seriousness" of their subjects; rather, they achieve distinction by virtue of their structures. Units of the novels that could stand as stories or parts of stories intersect, collide, even molest one another. The result is a whole much richer than its parts, a narrative that is more a dynamic aggregate than a synthesized whole in the Flaubert-James tradition.

In 1922 Huxley received an offer of a new arrangement from Chatto and Windus. Under its terms Huxley would receive £500 per annum for three years in exchange for two volumes of fiction each year; he would also receive generous royalties from the sales of the books. The offer put Huxley under severe deadlines but promised freedom from the drudgery of reviewing and magazine work. In January 1923 Huxley signed the contract and thereby gained an autonomy that he would never relinquish.

At about the same time, Huxley had an affair with Nancy Cunard, a flamboyant, beautiful young poet and patroness of the arts. By the summer of 1923 Maria had had enough. She gave him an ultimatum, and the next day they moved to Italy, where they would stay for several years.

That summer he wrote his second carnivalesque novel, *Antic Hay,* whose protagonist, Theodore Gumbril, Jr., explores the selfish, sybaritic world of postwar London that Huxley had experienced with Nancy Cunard, the loose model for the novel's Myra Viveash. As the novel begins, Gumbril

decides to chuck his job as a public school teacher and seek his fortune in London, where he hopes to market his patented inflatable pants and to make himself a "Complete Man." What he finds instead is a portrait gallery of incomplete men and women, all of whom mistake their narcissistic monomanias for completeness.

Perhaps the most sympathetic character whom Gumbril encounters is his father, Theodore Gumbril, Sr. A recluse, he lives in a decaying eighteenth-century mansion, where he spends his time designing utopian architectural schemes for renewing London. There is little hope, of course, for his plans, but Gumbril, Sr., achieves a form of completeness on a smaller scale. When a friend is threatened by bankruptcy, Gumbril, Sr., sells one of his most prized possessions, an elaborate architectural model, to help. His love of the past and his plans for the future may be doomed, but he represents a standard of modesty, balance, maturity, and personal integrity that is lacking in his son's other acquaintances.

Those others are portrayed as the sum, ugly and corrupt if still amusing, of London life in the 1920s. Gumbril, Jr.'s commercial ambitions lead him to meet Bojanus and Boldero: the former is a tailor of interesting socialist views, who is not above helping Gumbril perfect the design of his inflatable pants; the latter is a ruthless marketing expert who devotes his time to exploiting "that painful sense of inferiority" that urges "ignorant and ingenuous" consumers to buy goods. Gumbril's other acquaintances in a world that seems incapable of nurturing true friendships include Shearwater, a physiologist whose study of kidneys holds no vital connection to physiology; Lypiatt, an older painter capable of misinterpreting cubism and abstract art; Mercaptan, a critic whose eighteenth-century sensibility renders him incapable of interpreting modern life; and, worst of all, Coleman, a pretentious, self-appointed prophet of despair, who devotes his time to corrupting others so that they may share his pessimism.

Gumbril's most important encounters, however, are in his romantic life. Seeking adventure, he dons a false beard in imitation of the successful seducer Coleman and soon beds a very willing, very bored sensualist and snob, Rose Shearwater, the physiologist's wife. Continuing his promiscuous quest, he finds himself caught between two women, neither of whom can be reduced to a satiric portrait. He tries to seduce Emily, another young married woman, but discovers her genuine sexual fears, drops his false beard to comfort her, and promises to meet her in the country, "a crystal world" where their attraction would be unmolested by the norms of London. In the meantime, he enters the ken of Myra Viveash, a beautiful, predatory seductress whose utter shallowness summarizes profoundly the moral void of her generation. An affected yet haunting presence, she moves from man to man on whim, as Gumbril wishes he could do with women. She is a serious version of Coleman, a version that satire cannot control. The weak Gumbril chooses her fashionable world and loses Emily.

The futility that Myra embodies echoes through the novel. In one particularly disturbing sequence Myra takes Gumbril on a long taxi ride through nighttime London. Ultimately, their journey is directionless; without a destination, they always return to the glittering promises of the advertisements above Piccadilly Circus. A similar image of futility ends the novel: in a sealed room Shearwater furiously peddles a bicycle in order to measure his perspiration. He is dancing the solipsistic modern version of "antic hay," an Elizabethan phrase meaning an idiotic or foolish ring dance that Huxley gleaned from Christopher Marlowe's *Edward II* (1593).

Published in November 1923, *Antic Hay* sold 5,000 copies within a year of publication. The novel confirmed Huxley's relationship with the postwar generation, or at least with the younger members of its privileged classes. Again, there was disapproval from other ranks, especially from Huxley's family.

He wrote a letter of explanation to his father that defended the book's premises against those of his father and his generation. *Antic Hay,* its author argues, "is a book written by a member of what I may call the war-generation. for others of his kind; and . . . it is intended to reflect—fantastically, of course, but none the less faithfully—the life and opinions of an age which has seen the violent disruption of almost all the standards, conventions, and values current in the previous epoch."

Huxley's ability to portray so vividly, so painfully, so amusingly, the disruptions of his generation was probably insured, ironically enough, by the security of his own domestic life and by the pleasures of living in Italy. Based in Florence, the Huxleys spent much time touring the country by automobile; Maria, in fact, was the first woman in Italy to receive a driver's license. These years set a pattern that would not alter greatly throughout Huxley's life: residence outside England punctuated by frequent travel and supported by near constant writing.

Huxley began his next novel, *Those Barren Leaves,* in March 1924. Although it is the third of his early carnivalesque novels, its origin seems to date from the completion of *Crome Yellow.* In a letter of August 1921 to his brother Julian he confided, "I have a plan to do a Peacock in an Italian scene . . . Here one has the essential Peacockian datum—a houseful of oddities . . . I am giving Realismus a little holiday: these descriptions of middle class homes are really too unspeakably boring." He confirmed his attitude toward realistic modes of writing when he wrote to his father in April 1924 while working on the novel, "which is to be, as much as anything, a discussion and fictional illustration of different views of life. The mere business of telling a story interests me less and less . . . When it was first done that sort of thing had a certain interest; I suppose it was Balzac who first exploited the curious subject. But it is a purely factitious interest. The only really and permanently absorbing things are attitudes towards life and the relation of man to the world." Huxley finished the novel in August, while on vacation in France. His enthusiasm for the work was still high in October, when he wrote his American publisher: "It cuts more ice, I think, than the others and is more explicit and to the point. The characters, too, are better, I think."

Critics have tended not to agree with Huxley that the third novel is superior to its predecessors, but have pointed out its debts to the earlier works. Here, in carnivalesque fashion as in the others, he achieves what he calls "a certain novelty . . . all the ordinarily separated categories—tragic, comic, fantastic, realistic—are combined . . . into a single entity, whose unfamiliar character makes it appear at first sight rather repulsive." From *Crome Yellow* and its Peacockian models he borrows the situation of a visit to a country villa, but by moving the action to Italy he liberates the already considerable eccentricities of his English characters and paints them against the sunny beauty of Italy and its vital, richly comic peasantry. From *Antic Hay* he adopts the device of a metaphorical title that suggests the essential thematic organization of the novel. The title comes from the last stanza of Wordsworth's "The Tables Turned":

> Enough of Science and of Art;
> Close up those barren leaves;
> Come forth, and bring with you a heart
> That watches and receives.

Science and art are "barren leaves" for Huxley not because they are false but because their secular truths are too often mistaken in the modern world for a singular absolute truth that believers inevitably use to justify their own self-serving ends. "The main theme," as Huxley puts it, "is the undercutting of everything by a sort of despairing scepticism and then the undercutting of that by mysticism." Again, Huxley creates a varied cast of venal characters to embody and test his hypotheses about the modern world.

The hostess at the Cybo Malaspina is Mrs. Aldwinkle. Obsessed with denying her middle age, she spends her time applying cosmetics, informing guests of the glorious history of her villa, and then pursuing them for seduction. For her the villa is not a refuge, for *refuge* acknowledges a relationship with another world that she wishes to disavow; for her the villa is a place unto itself. Her isolation is so complete that even her less-than-clever niece Irene needs to escape into the arms of a lisping Englishman.

A more complicated character, who suffers a similar self-delusion, is Mary Thriplow, a young, pretty, accomplished psychological novelist. Despite her modest success, she dislikes facing the world as herself. Just as Gumbril donned a beard before his adventures, she masks her personality and becomes an innocent, talkative, childlike woman. This triggers a sequence of farcical episodes that reveal that she is less than the sum of her masks.

While Mary Thriplow shifts uncomfortably between the demands of her art and her life, Mr.

Cardan, the novel's most despicably funny character, focuses on his material well-being. He claims other pursuits, such as scholarship, yet subordinates them all to his greed. This is clearest in his passionate pursuit of Grace Elver, an unmarried, very wealthy, yet mentally retarded woman. Huxley's description of this courtship is a minor masterpiece of comic writing that foreshadows the black comedies of Samuel Beckett and Eugene Ionesco. Alas, Miss Elver eats a bad fish and dies of food poisoning before Cardan can grab her money.

If Cardan's materialism forces him to plunder the world, the idealism of Francis Chelifer makes him reshape the world in his own distorted image. Appalled by the stupidity of the world, he retreats from it. A potentially gifted artist, he chooses to edit the *Rabbit Fancier's Gazette*. He can find no stable bridge between his mind and the material demands of society, which to him include the rabbitlike matings of his fellow guests.

The novel's most important character is Mr. Calamy. A traveler and connoisseur, Calamy bears some resemblance to Denis Stone and Gumbril. He is the youthful outsider whose arrival on the scene serves as the loose organizing principle for the various incidents. Like his predecessors, he feels a strong sexual attraction for an aggressive woman, in this case Mary Thriplow. Their affair dissatisfies her because she cannot escape her double consciousness, her need to record the materials for her novels even as she experiences those materials as the passions of her life. Calamy is equally dissatisfied, but for a different reason. Their brief affair, he understands, has only one ephemeral aspect, the physical. This contrasts with his larger insight about the world: "It's extraordinary . . . what a lot of different modes of existence a thing has, when you come to think about it. And the more you think, the more obscure and mysterious everything becomes. . . . It gives one a strange sense of insecurity, of being in the dark. But I still believe that, if one went on thinking long enough and hard enough, one might somehow come through, get out on the other side of the obscurity. But into what, precisely into what? That's the question."

To answer that question he retires to contemplation alone on a mountaintop. There he feels "somehow reassured," and on that note the novel ends. Although it offers no answer to Calamy's question, the ending marks a fundamental shift in Huxley's concept of the modern world and in his preference among narrative forms. Calamy is the first important young character to be granted an exit visa, however temporary, from the absurd iniquities of contemporary life. He embodies a set of questions worth pursuing rather than a set of ideas worth ridiculing. Amid the carnivalesque bumps and grinds of the many characters and their plots and subplots, Huxley introduces the promise of an apologue, a story that will embody a truth and whose lines of action could be resolved to demonstrate that truth. *Those Barren Leaves* remains a carnivalesque fiction, but Huxley's yearning for the prophetic stance afforded by the apologue form, which first manifests itself here, will return—once to brilliant advantage, many times to problematic disadvantage.

Published in January 1925, *Those Barren Leaves* again enhanced Huxley's reputation and sold 8,000 copies in the first year. Even so, Huxley was by then not so satisfied with the book. "I now feel jejune and shallow and off the point," he wrote to a friend. "All I've written so far has been off the point." This intellectual and artistic restlessness was given a shove by an unpleasant incident involving state security agents for Mussolini's Italy. In late June 1925 the Huxleys left Italy, traveled to London, and there made arrangements for a journey around the world.

After leaving Matthew with Maria's family, the Huxleys sailed from Genoa on 15 September 1925. Their journey lasted nine months and took them to India, Malaysia, the Philippines, Hong Kong, Japan, San Francisco, Los Angeles, Chicago, and New York. Huxley was immensely impressed with the vitality of America, although he remained ambivalent in his judgment of that vitality. During the trip he kept a travel diary which, as *Jesting Pilate*, was published in October 1926. Here another pattern emerges that would mark the rest of Huxley's career: although he never abandoned writing novels, he became more interested in using other narrative forms—travel chronicles, biographies, and histories—to complement his fiction.

In June 1926 Huxley made a second agreement with Chatto and Windus. He was to produce only one novel in the next three years, and possibly three other books. His royalties were increased, and his annual advance—the mainstay of the Huxleys' income—jumped from £500 to £650 per year.

The Huxleys returned to Italy in August, and in October he began his most panoramic, most ambitious, and most formally adventurous novel: *Point Counter Point*. In a letter to his father he described his thoughts about the project: "I am preparing for and doing bits of an ambitious novel, the aim of which will be to show a piece of life, not only from a good many individual points of view, but

also under its various aspects such as scientific, emotional, economic, political, aesthetic, etc. The same person is simultaneously a mass of atoms, a physiology, a mind, an object with a shape that can be painted, a cog in the economic machine, a voter, a lover etc. etc. I shall try to imply at any rate the existence of the other categories of existence behind the ordinary categories employed in judging everyday emotional life." In a letter to a friend a month later he summarized his approach as rendering "the synchronous portrait of different things an individual simultaneously is." The effort struck him as "very difficult," and in January or February 1927 he set it aside and devoted himself to a group of essays that would be published as *Proper Studies* in November 1927. Also during that time the Huxleys saw D. H. Lawrence and his wife, Frieda, for the first time in a decade. Lawrence's health was failing, and the Huxleys spent as much time as possible with them. Finally, in August 1927 Huxley took up the novel again and wrote for the next ten months as they traveled in Italy, Switzerland, and England. He completed the composing process in May 1928. In June the Huxleys moved to a suburb of Paris, where they entertained many fellow expatriates, including James Joyce, whom Huxley found "a very strange man."

The culmination of Huxley's carnivalesque enterprise, *Point Counter Point* is also his finest novel. However amusing, trenchant, and accomplished his earlier works may be, they stand as practice sketches for the full canvas of *Point Counter Point*. Virtually every idea, thought, attitude, character type, social class, and abrasive juxtaposition of style, genre, or narrative content that can be catalogued in the first three novels has a place in their successor. But there is more: because carnivalesque fictions convey meanings more by spatial juxtaposition than by linear sequence, the wealth of their narrative implications always exceeds the sum of their parts. Thus, *Point Counter Point* holds within itself the earlier works yet emerges as more complex than the total of their virtues. This invigorating complexity makes summary difficult, and has daunted some readers and more than a few professional critics.

Aware of the difficulties that the novel might present Huxley includes within it a guide to help the reader sort it out. The guide is a character, Philip Quarles, who wishes to write novels like the one in which he appears. Quarles wants to "musicalize" his fiction. Early in the novel Huxley describes Bach's B-minor suite, which is played at a party that many of the characters attend. "The parts live their separate lives; they touch, their paths cross, they combine for a moment to create a seemingly final and perfected harmony, only to break apart again. Each is always alone and separate and individual. 'I am I,' asserts the violin; 'the world revolves about me.' 'Round me,' the flute insists. And all are equally right and equally wrong; and none of them will listen to the others." As the novel unfolds, it becomes clear that the characters respond to each other as instrument does to instrument in the Bach suite.

Later in the novel Quarles tries to explain to his wife why he wants his new novel to be an excuse for a "new way of looking at things." Their conversation takes place on the deck of a ship and is juxtaposed with the remarks of other passengers: a Frenchwoman discussing clothes, a young Englishwoman reminiscing about a wonderful summer, and two women missionaries talking about internal church politics. All of these subjects, Quarles argues, "are really quite to the point. Because the essence of the new way of looking is multiplicity. Multiplicity of eyes and multiplicity of aspects seen. For instance, one person interprets events in terms of bishops; another in terms of the price of flannel camisoles . . . Each sees, professionally, a different aspect of the event, a different layer of reality. What I want to do is to look with all those eyes at once."

Quarles's proposition is a fine guide for reading Huxley's novel, but he might have gone on to say that such multiplicity makes summarizing the work nearly impossible. The cast of characters is vast, and their actions are rendered in short scenes that cut across wide gulfs of time and space. The critic Harold Watts indicates the novel's dense texture: "With masterly confidence, Huxley moves in this novel from one fragment of disparate human experience to another: from the mind of an old lecher artist fearful of waning powers and death to the complacent awareness of his still-vigorous mistress; from the mind of a socially irresponsible and 'pure' scientist to that of a socially committed one. He contrasts the whining thoughts of a neglected mistress to the guilty thoughts of her lover, whose sexuality requires the stronger lights and mad music that he finds with the shameless Lucy Tantamount." Each character, as even this brief summary begins to suggest, is placed in counterpoint to others and thus seen and heard with a multiplicity of eyes and ears. The importance of characters can be determined by the multiplicity of treatment they merit.

Aside from Quarles, the two most important characters are Mark Rampion and Maurice Spandrell. They are presented from many angles in many situations, and distinguish themselves from other characters by being able to articulate ideas about actions that others merely perform. They are the supreme examples of characters appropriate to Quarles's notion of the "Novel of Ideas": "The character of each personage must be implied, as far as possible, in the ideas of which he is a mouthpiece." Rampion and Spandrell represent polar opposite views of life and conduct, opposites that define the moral boundaries of the novel's world.

A painter whose works portray humans with monstrous features, Rampion is an outspoken critic of modern culture. He expresses visually what he senses morally: the egotism that leads people to various forms of perversion. He sees Quarles as an "intellectual-aesthetic pervert," another character as a "Jesus pervert," Spandrell as a "morality-philosophy pervert," and even himself as a "pedagogue pervert." Despite this self-condemnation, Rampion embodies and expresses values that the novel endorses. As Quarles puts it, Rampion "lives more satisfactorily, because he lives more realistically than other people. Rampion, it seems to me, takes into account all the facts (whereas other people hide from them or try to pretend that the ones they find unpleasant don't or shouldn't exist), and then proceeds to make his living fit the facts, and doesn't compel the facts to fit in with a preconceived idea of the right way of living (like these imbecile Christians and intellectuals and moralists and efficient business men)." Rampion's view of life is like Huxley's practice of carnivalesque fiction: inclusive rather than exclusive, it can contain a dynamic set of forces ranging from abstract thought to genuine sensuous pleasures.

Spandrell, too, experiences a wide range of human endeavors, but they remain futile because he can never understand the relations among them. Life, he believes, has been fully but inscrutably preordained by God. This divine order, paradoxically enough, enfranchises Spandrell to do whatever he wishes. His fondest hope is that some outrage will provoke God to show his hand. Spandrell arranges the murder of the Fascist leader Everard Webley not to achieve political justice but for the pleasure of plotting the crime. The list of Spandrell's outrages in the name of his nihilistic philosophy is long and leads to his ultimate gesture of provocation: suicide.

While the novel seems to endorse Rampion and condemn Spandrell, it does not suggest that the world will pay much attention to either. As Spandrell commits suicide, Huxley shows two other characters enjoying an erotic frolic in a bathtub. Rampion is himself an outsider, admired by Quarles but ignored or thought obnoxious by others. Rampion is unable to answer the question: how does one convince others that they must practice "integral living" when they think that they are already doing so?

Published in 1928, the novel sold over 10,000 copies in its first year and was a Literary Guild selection in the United States. Huxley had become a modestly best-selling author, and he would remain so for the rest of his life. Huxley himself was pleased with the book: "I have written a rather good, but also rather frightful novel," he wrote to an American friend. Even D. H. Lawrence, who knew he was the inspiration for Rampion and thought the character a "gas bag," read the novel with "rising admiration," despite his many differences with Huxley about the novel's portrayal of human nature. *Point Counter Point* is the peak of Huxley's novelistic career. In it he exhausted his interest in carnivalesque forms; in his next important work, *Brave New World,* he turned to the apologue. It was a decision that had profound consequences upon his novels and upon his critical reputation.

However, before Huxley wrote his next novel he occupied himself with minor writing projects and negotiated a third agreement with Chatto and Windus. The annual advance was raised to £1,000, and the publisher wished only two novels in three years and three other books "if possible." At about this time, Lawrence died in Huxley's presence in Vence, France, on 2 March 1930. Fourteen months later, at his new home in the south of France, Huxley started his new novel. He wrote rapidly and easily, and finished it in August.

In a 1961 interview Huxley explained his conception of *Brave New World.* The new forces of technology, pharmaceutics, and social conditioning can "iron" modern humans "into a kind of uniformity, if you were able to manipulate their genetic background . . . if you had a government unscrupulous enough you could do these things without any doubt . . . We are getting more and more into a position where these things *can* be achieved. And it's extremely important to realize this, and to take every possible precaution to see they shall *not* be achieved. This, I take it, was the message of the book—*This is possible: for heaven's sake be careful about it.*" Thus the book is not a prophetic novel about what will be but a cautionary tale about what could be.

In form *Brave New World* is an ironic apologue that demonstrates the falseness of a set of ideas held

Dust jacket for Huxley's anti-utopian satire

to be true by a number of characters and by the society in which they live. While only a few characters learn the depravity of their society's values, one of the novel's chief rhetorical strategies is to make all readers recognize what so few characters can comprehend: that preserving freedom and diversity is necessary to avoid suffering the repressions fostered by shallow ideas of progress.

Huxley makes his ironic stance clear from the beginning by contrasting the book's title with the action of its first scene. In Shakespeare's *The Tempest,* when Miranda, long sheltered by her father, first enters the company of men she declares:

> O, wonder!
> How many goodly creatures are there here!
> How beauteous mankind is! O brave new world
> That has such people in't!

Her effervescent, charmingly naive celebration of manhood is in ominous counterpoint to the novel's opening at the Central London Hatchery and Conditioning Centre, a factory that creates on a conveyor belt the citizens for this "brave new world."

It is no accident that Huxley begins by describing an institution rather than by focusing on the actions or attributes of a protagonist. *Brave New World* is a rare kind of novel: one more memorable and successful for its overall portrayal of a society than for its delineation of plot or psychologically individualized characters. In this world the method of "Bokanovsky budding" allows the creation of ninety-six persons from one sperm and ovum. Different classes exist—Alpha, Beta, Gamma, and so on—but their relations to each other and to society as a whole are stabilized by the painless technique of "sleep teaching" that demonstrates to each individual the manifest rightness of his or her place in the world. In adulthood citizens perform their tasks without complaint and are rewarded with material comforts, with leisure activities such as "Centrifugal Bumble Puppy" and "Obstacle Golf," and by guiltless group sex. If anxieties arise, they can be alleviated by a universally effective drug, "soma."

Presented by a class of "Controllers" to their underlings as a paradise, this world, Huxley bitterly demonstrates, is a malignant hell. There are two keys to Huxley's criticism: individualism and history. In his earlier, carnivalesque fictions Huxley used the comic extravagances of his characters to criticize individualism that is nothing more than narcissism; characters fail because they are incapable of connecting with others to form a community. In *Brave New World* Huxley explores the inverse, though no less dangerous, problem of how modern mass society could destroy the values of individualism by accepting a false belief in perfection by standardization. This becomes possible, he believes, when people misunderstand the relationship between progress and history. For Huxley, history gives mankind rich, fascinating access to human diversity and its webs of interconnectedness. Progress can be found in certain lines of development in certain places under certain diverse and retrospectively understandable, but not prophetically demonstrable, circumstances. The perversion of this "brave new world" comes, then, in its belief that humankind is on an unbending track of progress and that all other concepts of human destiny are the "bunk" of history. This concept of progress promises perfection but denies the freedom necessary for creativity.

The novel's main characters demonstrate the dangers of challenging or even merely deviating from the norms of perfection prescribed by the society. Bernard Marx shows himself unworthy of his Alpha class by desiring exclusive rather than communal sexual relations with Lenina Crowne, who is appalled by his antisocial impulses. His friends speculate that his strange desires may be the result of a chemical error in his early conditioning. No such simple excuse can explain or excuse the deviancy of the novel's central character, John the Savage, whom Bernard and Lenina meet on a visit to an Indian reservation. The son of Sir Mustafa Mond, the chief controller of the society, and of a mother who became lost on the reservation where she then raised her son, John is a horrible misfit: he shows the traits of humanity most denied by the society to which Bernard and Lenina bring him. Most telling is his love of Shakespeare, whose characters inspire him with a wealth of possibilities for thought, feeling, and action. His father, who knows Shakespeare's writings but keeps them from others, warns him that the Bard's work is very dangerous. "Because it's old; that's the chief reason. We haven't any use for old things here." Eventually, John turns from the society, focuses his attention on Lenina—whose sexuality ambivalently attracts and repulses him—and then commits suicide by self-flagellation, a brutal denial of the individualism that made him a "savage" in the "brave new world."

The novel was published in February 1932 and sold well in England: 13,000 copies in the first year and 10,000 copies in the second. Initial sales in the United States were only 3,000 in the first year. Even so, during the year Huxley negotiated a very handsome contract with the New York publishing firm of Harper and Brothers. At the same time he renegotiated his contract with Chatto and Windus to increase the yearly advance to £1,250 and initial royalties to twenty percent.

Although *Point Counter Point* may be Huxley's most ambitious and successful novel, *Brave New World* is certainly his most famous one. It has been in print ever since its publication, is taught widely, and remains a fount of reference for political scientists, editorialists, newscasters, and free-lance pundits. The book, to be sure, has many passages of intellectual interest; however, its enduring success is probably best explained by Huxley's mastery of the apologue form. Economical in structure and sure-handed in its treatment of scene and character, the novel is didactic but not essayistic. In later years Huxley saw the work's effectiveness as flawed by a simplification of issues. He regretted portraying the Savage as trapped between only two possible choices: nonindustrial primitivism or corrupt modernity. Ironically enough, this simplification, so uncharacteristic of Huxley's mind, may be another key to the work's lasting popularity and influence. Perhaps only George Orwell's *Nineteen Eighty-Four* (1949) rivals *Brave New World* in rendering as a story for millions of readers the enduring perplexities of technology, social development, and political enfranchisement.

Huxley's next novel, *Eyeless in Gaza,* was not published until 1936, and the intervening years marked several important changes in his life. The first was a definitive shift from notoriety to celebrity. For his remaining thirty years Huxley reigned in academic circles as well as in the popular press as an adventurous sage. As Huxley's generation came of age, so did his reputation. In summer 1932, for example, the king and queen of Belgium entertained the Huxleys at dinner. The second change was the financial security that grew with his celebrity. The Huxleys now leased a fashionable apartment in London while maintaining their home in France. This increased security allowed Huxley to pursue more widely the interests of his conscience, most notably by speaking for and actively supporting the Peace Pledge Union. The third change was directly related to these philanthropic concerns: his novels began to include more essayistic materials that propose his view of how people can alter their lot on earth. Passages of speculative prose in his last six novels assume, as Harold Watts puts it, "proportions that many readers do not regard as welcome." Indeed, all the novels after *Brave New World* remain problematic. All, to be sure, contain varying measures of Huxley's wit, invention, and intelligence. However, none return with success to carnivalesque organizing principles and none manage to repeat the economical brilliance of *Brave New World* as an apologue.

Eyeless in Gaza, which he composed between January 1934 and March 1936, illustrates well the mixed virtues and flaws that haunt the remaining novels. Bedford reports that as he composed the novel he considered its theme to be liberty: "What happens to someone who becomes really very free—materially first . . . and then mentally and emotionally. The rather awful vacuum that such freedom turns out to be. But I haven't yet worked out the whole of the fable—only its first part."

Nonetheless, Huxley did know how he wanted to arrange the events of the story. The novel begins with a section marked "August 30, 1933" and ends with another designated "February 23, 1935." The intervening months allow the protagonist, Anthony Beavis, a middle-aged academic, to work out his relationship with Helen Ledwidge, his lover of several years. The narrative units—chapters is not the right word—between the two dates number fifty-two and do not stay within the chronological progression of those seventeen months. Instead, the fragments, each carefully dated, jump with ease amid occasions as far distant as the funeral of Edward's mother on 6 November 1902. The novel's scrambled chronology is a point of controversy, although the events are much easier to follow than those in works by Huxley's near contemporaries Marcel Proust, William Faulkner, and Hermann Broch. One of the novel's most perceptive critics, Peter Firchow, explains that the mixed chronology is consistent with Huxley's nonlinear view of history. Meaning, for Huxley, is made by telling juxtapositions and associations, not by strict linear development. Thus Beavis's search for the meaning of his self requires the multitemporality that the scrambled structure allows.

Although the novel's method cannot be dismissed, its message—what Huxley calls "the whole fable"—has been questioned by many readers. Beavis is a representative twentieth-century intellectual, and his familial, intellectual, political, and erotic woes are portrayed with Huxley's usual candor and convincing detail. Unfortunately, late in the novel Huxley proposes an unconvincing remedy for Beavis's difficulties. In desperate straits in Mexico during a provincial revolution, Beavis meets an anthropologist named Miller whose help saves him in the short run and whose teachings and example save him for the long run. A doctor and a Quaker as well as an anthropologist, Miller demonstrates to Beavis the virtues of simplicity and directness. Equally important, he tells Beavis: "We're all of us what we are; and when it comes to turning ourselves into what we ought to be—well, it isn't easy." For some reason, this cliché is a revelation to Beavis, who alters his life accordingly. For most readers, the weight of problems felt by Beavis far exceeds the strength of the solutions proposed by Miller and endorsed by Huxley.

The novel's unbalanced rhetoric can be illustrated by contrasting Miller's boring homily with a scene early in the work. Anthony and Helen are making love on a beautiful Mediterranean rooftop when a passing airman shoves a dog from his cockpit. The dog lands on the roof, splattering blood over the lovers. No one who reads the novel will forget this scene and its connection with the troubled sexuality of the lovers. Most readers want to forget, by contrast, Miller's appearances as a mod-

Saturday Review, *11 July 1936*

ern saint. Huxley tries to portray Beavis as a Samson, to whom the title refers, who regains his sight after his defeat by the Philistines. Unfortunately, Huxley himself seems blind to the inadequacies of his protagonist's solution.

In April 1937 the Huxleys and their friend Gerald Heard, planning ultimately to travel to India, sailed for the United States to lecture promoting peace. The journey was not planned as an emigration. However, opportunity to work in Hollywood, and then the outbreak of World War II, conspired to keep the Huxleys in America. It would be a mistake, however, to believe either that Huxley rejected England or that he fully embraced southern California, where they settled and owned a series of pleasant homes. Huxley was that rare creature: a citizen of the world. An inveterate traveler and a passionate student of all cultures, he needed a base from which to chart his voyages and where he could rest his always delicate health. Southern California met these needs for the last twenty-five years of his life.

In 1938 and 1939 Huxley almost went blind again; his enormous intellectual curiosity, however, saved him. Frustrated by the normal methods of ophthalmology, he turned to the Bates Method, which prescribes vigorous physiological conditioning to build the natural strength of the eye. For Huxley the therapy worked very well, and he enjoyed his best eyesight in his later years.

The initial impact of settling in southern California was, despite Huxley's eye troubles, novelistic inspiration. Between October 1938 and July 1939 he wrote *After Many a Summer Dies the Swan*, a comic jeremiad about the California way of life. The title comes from a line in Tennyson's "Tithonus," whose protagonist is granted immortality but not eternal youth; and the novel explores the relations among time, aging, responsibility, and the temptations of California's seductive mass culture. The novel shows Huxley's inability to choose between the carnivalesque and apologue forms; it is an unresolved mixture of the two in which the carnivalesque sections recall the pleasures of the early fiction and the apologue sections continue to tax readers in the same way as *Eyeless in Gaza*.

Like much of the early fiction, *After Many a Summer Dies the Swan* (1939) uses a young Englishman—here, Jeremy Pordage—to explore a world of eccentric characters who represent modern foibles. The other main characters are Jo Stoyte, a California millionaire whose mansion is so stuffed with "culture" that a Vermeer hangs in his elevator;

Virginia Maunciple, his witless and childlike yet very sexy mistress; and Dr. Sigmund Obispo, a wacky scientist who researches how to retard the aging process. The early sections of the novel are a comic wonder as they show Pordage's initiation into the strange potpourri of California's mass culture, where the dreamy promises of advertising shape the real landscape of castles built by wealthy narcissists.

Hired to catalog some recent acquisitions for Stoyte's library, Pordage finds amid the papers evidence that the fifth earl of Haubeck, the nineteenth-century descendant of a noble English family, discovered a way of prolonging life by eating the entrails of carp. Eventually, Stoyte, his mistress, and Obispo go to England, where they find the earl still alive but devolved into animalhood. The earl still manages "a curious humming noise that was like a simian memory of the serenade in 'Don Giovanni' " before he copulates with an equally debased companion. This appalling scene leaves Stoyte shaken but undaunted: he will try the treatment. "Once you get over the first shock," he says, "well, they look like they were having a pretty good time." There the novel ends.

If the novel were structured solely by the adventures of Pordage and Stoyte, it would rank with Huxley's early carnivalesque fictions. Such is not the case. The novel also includes in a clumsy fashion the philosophizing of William Propter, who instructs anyone within earshot. His favorite topics are "time," "evil," "good," and other such concerns. In the early novels Propter would be a target for ridicule; here he is not. The novel, as Maria Huxley told a friend, is "everybody's cup of tea—in parts—but I can also see that it will be everybody's red rag in parts." Nonetheless, it sold 10,000 copies in its first year after publication in October 1939.

Huxley found many opportunities to work for Hollywood studios, most notably for M-G-M adapting Jane Austen's *Pride and Prejudice*. The Huxleys enjoyed a comfortable life punctuated by frequent travel within the United States and abroad. Their friends included some of Los Angeles's most gifted émigrés: Charlie Chaplin, Christopher Isherwood, Thomas Mann, and Igor Stravinsky.

Although Huxley's next novel did not appear until August 1944, the project itself went easily and was delayed by other duties, not by problems with the writing. Indeed, Huxley and his critics agree that *Time Must Have a Stop* has the most tightly structured, traditional plot of any of his novels after *Brave New World*. The title is derived from a speech by Hotspur in Shakespeare's *Henry IV, Part One* and, as is Huxley's habit, it suggests the novel's fundamental concerns:

> But thought's the slave of life, and life's time's fool;
> And time, that makes survey of all the world,
> Must have a stop.

Can one avoid slavery to time and can one exist outside time? These large questions animate the strong linear course of the story, which is set in London, Florence, and the afterlife. In 1929 the book's protagonist, Sebastian Barnack, is seventeen years old and sets for himself two goals: a new suit and a mistress. Even these fairly humble ambitions, he realizes, cannot be attained under the supervision of his politically liberal father or amid the mediocrity of London's professional class. Like so many young Englishmen before him, Huxley included, he goes to seek life in Italy, where his wealthy, self-indulgent Uncle Eustace lives. There he meets a typical Huxley menagerie that includes an old blind woman who shares Stoyte's desire to extend life; a young widow whose compulsion is seducing young men (Sebastian included); and a young American social idealist who wants to save the world with the money his family earned from manufacturing breakfast food. It seems that Sebastian will achieve his goals until his uncle dies in the downstairs toilet. This triggers a farcically logical sequence of events that ends in the arrest of a distant relative, Bruno Rottini, by Fascist officers. Meanwhile Uncle Eustace does not leave the novel. He hovers somewhere in an afterlife, where he can contemplate his relation to time but cannot effectively communicate it to his friends and relatives. In an epilogue set in 1945 Huxley shows the adult Sebastian making amends to Rottini, whom he never meant to harm and from whom he can learn much.

Much of the novel's strength lies in its tone, as Huxley understood when he told a friend that he "kept light" the events of the story. There is a nearly constant comic discrepancy between the weightiness of the questions at stake and the worth of the answers that can be given or understood by Sebastian or Uncle Eustace. Bruno Rottini, this novel's Propter character, engages the reader's attention because his observations are firmly grounded in his experience of Fascist Italy. Moreover, while the novel is full of allusions to Dante's *Divine Comedy* and *The Tibetan Book of the Dead*, the references are used to emphasize the difficulty of answering questions of time and death in the modern secular world.

Some of the novel's early critics faulted it for including the nonrealistic sections on Eustace's afterlife. The argument fails to understand Huxley's fundamental antipathy to realistic fiction. For him, the novel would have been a failure if it had been merely realistic. Still, one can find the Eustace sections troubling on other grounds. The problem is rhetorical and can be hidden but not resolved by Huxley's comedy. He shows the difficulty that Eustace has in passing his insights to his living friends, but there is no such problem for the readers of the novel, who do have access to Eustace's ruminations. Thus the ineffable becomes the everyday, and Huxley betrays his own position. This flaw does not overpower the work's considerable excellences and pleasures, which its audience quickly understood. The novel was first published in the United States (World War II delayed Huxley's correspondence with Chatto and Windus) and sold 40,000 copies in its first year.

For his next novel Huxley briefly considered a setting in fourteenth-century Italy but reversed his direction in time by writing an apologue of life in twenty-second century Los Angeles. *Ape and Essence*

Aldous Huxley, circa 1950 (courtesy of Matthew Huxley)

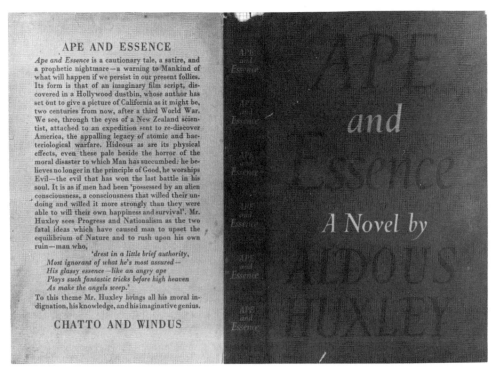

Dust jacket for British edition of Huxley's prophetic novel of life in the twenty-second century

(1948), whose title is taken from Shakespeare's *Measure for Measure,* reassesses the ground of *Brave New World.* However, there is a major difference between the works: *Brave New World* warns about what could happen; *Ape and Essence* proclaims what probably will happen.

Aware of the possible objections among novel readers to blatant prophecy, Huxley embodies his harangue in an unusual combination of old and new forms. The body of the text is a manuscript which the unnamed narrator claims to have found and which he prints "without change and without comment." Here Huxley uses a device common to the eighteenth-century novel. The narrator's position suggests: "Here is something worth saving; you should read it too." If this framing device is old, the manuscript's form—a rejected screenplay saved from the studio's incinerator—could not be more modern. The scenario form is, as Maria Huxley remarked in a letter to her son, "an excellent medium for cutting out all that he actually does not need and for getting in, via the narrator, all he needs to say." The cinema, Huxley recognized, has no tolerance for the longwindedness of Miller, Propter, or even Rampion.

The action of the scenario is set, as Huxley told a friend in a letter, in "a post-atomic society in which the chief effect of gamma radiations" has

been to alter the genetic structures of humans. Alfred Poole, a young biologist, arrives in Los Angeles on an exploratory mission from New Zealand, the only advanced society not destroyed by "the Thing," as Huxley calls the atomic bomb. Poole's party is killed by the primitive, animalistic inhabitants who live in a brutal theocracy administered by eunuch priests and worship the hedonistic god Belial. The civilized veneer of *Brave New World* is gone from this future. Faith in progress has led to outright regression, a state without even the arguable amenities of life of the earlier novel. Luckily for Poole, he finds a young woman, Loola, who is repelled by the commands of the priest caste. Because she and Poole cannot abide by the rule that forbids sexual contact except during a prescribed mating season, the two are "Hots," the label for sexual criminals. After Huxley has used Poole and Loola as a lens through which to view the atrocities of the future, he allows them to escape and seek asylum in a community of Hots. On their way they pass the tree under which William Tallis, the author of the screenplay in which they appear, is buried.

Ape and Essence, despite its clever form and economical presentation, is a distinctly minor work. It is uncharacteristically simple; a clever flourish here and there cannot hide the impression that most of the characters and ideas come from a dis-

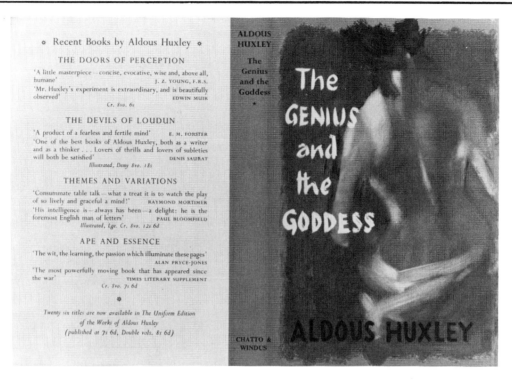

Recent Books by Aldous Huxley

THE DOORS OF PERCEPTION
'A little masterpiece—concise, evocative, wise and, above all,
humane'   J. Z. YOUNG, F.R.S.
'Mr. Huxley's experiment is extraordinary, and is beautifully
observed'   EDWIN MUIR
                        Cr. 8vo. 6s

THE DEVILS OF LOUDUN
'A product of a fearless and fertile mind'   E. M. FORSTER
'One of the best books of Aldous Huxley, both as a writer
and as a thinker . . . Lovers of thrills and lovers of subtleties
will both be satisfied'   DENIS SAURAT
               Illustrated, Demy 8vo. 18s

THEMES AND VARIATIONS
'Consummate table talk—what a treat it is to watch the play
of so lively and graceful a mind!'   RAYMOND MORTIMER
'His intelligence is—always has been—a delight: he is the
foremost English man of letters'   PAUL BLOOMFIELD
               Illustrated, Lge. Cr. 8vo. 12s 6d

APE AND ESSENCE
'The wit, the learning, the passion which illuminate these pages'
                                          ALAN PRYCE-JONES
'The most powerfully moving book that has appeared since
the war'   TIMES LITERARY SUPPLEMENT
                        Cr. 8vo. 7s 6d

Twenty six titles are now available in The Uniform Edition
of the Works of Aldous Huxley
(published at 7s 6d, Double vols. 8s 6d)

CHATTO &
WINDUS

ALDOUS
HUXLEY

The
Genius
and the
Goddess

The
GENIUS
and
the
GODDESS

ALDOUS HUXLEY

Dust jacket for British edition of Huxley's 1955 novel about a physicist and his wife

count Huxley warehouse. Perhaps more important, the novel is relentless. Bedford makes the case well: "Aldous strained to pile horror upon crass horror . . . the book, it always seemed to me, achieves a high degree of unbearableness."

In his next novel, *The Genius and the Goddess*, which he wrote between March and October 1954, Huxley once again borrows from the history of the novel in order to find an appropriate disguise for his apologue. This time he uses the memoir form, which Joseph Conrad, Marcel Proust, and Henry James had developed to exquisite complexity in the early twentieth century. Huxley's narrator is John Rivers, an aging American physicist who thinks back over his stay some thirty years before in the household of Henry Maartens, a Nobel Prize winner and the "genius" of the title.

The story that Rivers tells has the causal linkage among events that characterizes psychological fiction. Maartens, although a "genius," seems dependent upon the ministrations of his lovely wife Katy, the "goddess" of the title. Rivers understands their need to achieve wholeness by being together, and initially he shows some attraction to their daughter Ruth, although he enters their home a virgin at twenty-eight years old. However, as circumstances unfold, Rivers sees that Katy cannot sustain herself by exclusive devotion to her hus-

band. Rivers loses his virginity to her advances. His actions, he believes, are for the greater good and transcend the limits of conventional morality. Ruth takes a different view of matters, and she and her mother die in an auto accident as they argue about the situation. Maartens, ironically enough, not only survives the loss of his wife but marries twice again and contributes to the development of the atomic bomb.

While a summary of the novel suggests that it is written in the mode of psychological realism, the experience of reading the work itself denies that classification. Huxley's narrator differs significantly from those of Conrad, Proust, and James: they look back over events to investigate their meanings and their surprising filiations; Rivers, by contrast, seems to want to use his experience to address the world. In other words, one always suspects that he is Miller or Propter in disguise. Huxley's characters, too, deviate from the standards of psychological fiction. Maartens and his wife are deemed "the genius and the goddess," but why they deserve those titles remains undemonstrated. Their roles seem allegorical, as Peter Firchow observes: Maartens is "the archetype of modern man," the end point of false faith in science; his wife, "a primeval mother goddess." The narrator and his remembered characters seem suspended between being sensate personalities and being embodied examples of ideas. They cannot fully meet either demand. Nonetheless, the novel was briefly a best-seller.

During the last ten years of his life, Huxley engaged in experiments with the hallucinogenic drugs mescaline and LSD, under the supervision of a physician friend. In *The Doors of Perception* (1954), he wrote about the insights and heightened perceptions he experienced under the influence of the drugs. Huxley's skepticism about the claims made for the explanatory powers of modern scientific methods led him to investigate other possible modes of knowing: mysticism, Hindu philosophy, parapsychology, and hypnosis.

A victim of cancer, Maria Huxley died on 12 February 1955, with Aldous comforting her in her last hours. He wrote to a friend that he felt part of his life "amputated" by her death. Still, with the support of his son and a very busy schedule he came slowly back to his own full life. In March 1956 he married an old family friend, Laura Archera, twenty years his junior. Originally trained as a concert violinist, Miss Archera had worked as a film editor and was a practicing psychotherapist when they married.

In his later years Huxley's schedule included teaching or lecturing at Berkeley, Duke, MIT, and many other universities. [In 1959 he was given an award by the American Academy of Arts and Letters, and in 1962 he was elected a Companion of Literature by the Royal Society of Literature.] *Island*, Huxley's last completed novel, is his positive utopia, his picture of what a modern Eden would be and how it must fall. Huxley worked on the book from the summer of 1956 until June 1961; the manuscript was one of the few items the Huxleys saved when their home was destroyed by a brushfire on 12 May 1961. His troubles with the novel issued from his desire to avoid the rhetorical disguises for his apologue that he had used in *Ape and Essence* and *The Genius and the Goddess*. Still, he worried about his failure, as he called it in an interview, to be a "congenital novelist." In a letter to his son he confessed his worry about the static, essayistic nature of his work: "I am trying to lighten up the exposition by putting it in dialogue form; which I make as lively as possible." Given these problems, one may wonder why Huxley struggled to use the novel as his form of expression. The answer for Huxley was simple: the novel has an audience much larger and wider than any other potentially appropriate written form. Although he was never a popularizer, Huxley wanted to communicate the

Huxley with his second wife, Laura Archera Huxley, in 1958 (courtesy of Laura Huxley)

urgency of his ideas to as many potential thinkers as possible.

Huxley's intentions, however admirable, do not make a convincing novelistic apologue. Huxley's device for introducing his ideas is familiar. Will Farnaby, caught, as so many Huxley protagonists are, between two women, goes as a journalist and scout for an oil company to the island of Pala in the Indian Ocean. He finds a remarkably harmonious society that balances the technological advances of the West with the spiritual insights of the East. The island has evolved in accord with these influences since the nineteenth century when an enlightened Raj engaged the services of an equally open-minded Scottish doctor.

Much of the novel chronicles Farnaby's education about the island in conversations with his Palanese mentor, Dr. McPhail. As John the Savage was introduced to what-could-go-wrong in *Brave New World*, so Farnaby is instructed in what-goes-right-here. For agriculture, education, child rearing, law enforcement, and all other aspects of socie-

Huxley about 1960 (George Kramer, University of California, Los Angeles)

ty the Palanese have planning that maximizes their freedom and minimizes their conflicts. Dr. McPhail's instruction is complemented by Farnaby's amorous involvement with a beautiful Palanese woman, Susila, whose lovemaking teaches him to jettison the false guilts of his Western upbringing. Not surprisingly, all this bliss comes to an end. Paradise is lost when outside forces that cannot understand Palanese virtues want to control the island's resources. Still, some hope remains, in Huxley's view, if readers truly understand the most important Palanese aphorism: "We must dream in a pragmatic way."

Island was published in March 1962 to very mixed reviews and has not been highly regarded by critics since then. Perhaps in response to his own doubts about the book, perhaps in response to its mixed press, Huxley began, as he put it, "ruminating a long and complicated novel." He never finished it, but Laura Archera Huxley published the existing fragment in *This Timeless Moment* (1968), her memoir of her husband. The fragment reveals that Huxley was returning to the memoir form he used in *The Genius and the Goddess*. Autobiographical in outline but not in substance, the fragment includes a finely nuanced, sensory evocation of childhood in Edwardian England. In fact, the work seems more Proustian than Huxleyan. His

mental agility as an experimenter with novelistic forms was exercising itself, it seems, even as his physical powers were failing.

Huxley's health, which was never robust, took several turns for the worse in the early 1960s: he had a malignancy removed and suffered a bad fall while on a stroll. As he continued to work on a variety of projects, his strength continued to slip away. He died peacefully in his Los Angeles home on 22 November 1963.

Since his death Huxley's reputation, somewhat damaged by the late novels, has not risen but does seem to have stabilized. It is unlikely that he will ever be ranked with such Olympians as Joseph Conrad, James Joyce, Virginia Woolf, and his good friend D. H. Lawrence. His reputation, it seems, will be as a lesser master and will rest upon his carnivalesque masterpiece *Point Counter Point* and its delightful predecessors, and upon his great apologue *Brave New World*. In a sense, his reputation is a victim of his own chameleonlike genius. He never cultivated the mystique of being a novelist above all else. Although conspicuously modern in intellect, he may have been, in his diversity of talents, the last Victorian man of letters.

Letters:

Letters of Aldous Huxley, edited by Grover Smith

And all day long the hippopotami
Kept murmuring, "What am I? Oh, tell me what am I?"

The accompanying woodcut showed a young Hippo in the agonizing

act of self-interrogation. Standing on his hind legs and

dxx clothed all in black, like the Prince of Denmark

culture is a wardrobe of well worn costumes

school for performing animals he was

intently at his own distraught image in a cheval glass. "What

am I?" It was a funny picture and the rhyme was richly

comic. But, even as a child, I knew obscurely that

xxxxxxxxxxxxxxxxxxxxxxxxxxx beneath the nonsense lay plunging gulfs

of metaphysical darkness. Cxxxxxxxxxxxxxxxxxxxxxxxxxxxxxxxxxx-

xxxxxxxxxxxxxxxxxxxxxxxxxxxxxxxxxxxxxxxx "What am I?" asked the

soliloquizing Hippopotamus. "And what am I?

little boy I once was used to wonder, as he lay on his

stomach in the blue bedroom, poring over

Sibylline nonsense. Inside my skull The question has

gone on reverberating ever since. It asked It echoed there when

still echoing now that I am seventy-three.

What am I? Yes, what am I? And what, while we're on the subject

of identities, are you? You, my mother. You, my wife and

children and grandchildren: You, my transient bedfellows? You,

my German enemies doing your dutiful best to kill me:

And you, my bosses, and my subordinates -- what are you? And

what are you, my culture-heroes and exemplars -- my Dostoevskis

and Clerk Maxwells, my Gautamas and Wordsworths? And what are

the strangers? You, my fellow passengers in buses, fellow

listeners at concerts, fellow shoppers at Woolworth's and the

and the supermarket? xx What are you, the fascinating, inac-

cessible women glimpsed out of the windows of

(London: Chatto & Windus, 1969; New York: Harper & Row, 1969).

Bibliographies:

Percival H. Muir and B. van Thal, *Bibliographies of the First Editions of Books by Aldous Huxley and T. F. Powys* (London: Dulau, 1927);

Hanson R. Duval, *Aldous Huxley: A Bibliography* (New York: Arrow, 1939);

Claire John Eschelback and Joyce Lee Shober, *Aldous Huxley: A Bibliography 1916-1959* (Berkeley & Los Angeles: University of California Press, 1961; London: Cambridge University Press, 1961);

Thomas D. Clareson and Carolyn S. Andrews, "Aldous Huxley: A Bibliography 1960-1964," *Extrapolation*, 6 (December 1964): 2-21;

Dennis D. Davis, "Aldous Huxley: A Bibliography 1965-1973," *Bulletin of Bibliography*, 31 (April-June 1974): 67-70.

Biographies:

George Heard, "The Poignant Prophet," *Kenyon Review*, 27 (Winter 1965): 49-93;

Julian Huxley, ed., *Aldous Huxley, 1894-1963: A Memorial Volume* (London: Chatto & Windus, 1965; New York: Harper & Row, 1965);

Ronald W. Clark, *The Huxleys* (London: Heinemann, 1968; New York: McGraw, 1968);

Laura Archera Huxley, *This Timeless Moment: A Personal View of Aldous Huxley* (New York: Farrar, Straus & Giroux, 1968; London: Hogarth, 1969);

Philip Thody, *Aldous Huxley: A Bibliographical Introduction* (London: Studio Vista, 1973);

Sybille Bedford, *Aldous Huxley: A Biography*, 2 volumes (London: Chatto & Windus, 1973-1974);

Tom Dardis, *Some Time in the Sun: The Hollywood Years of Fitzgerald, Faulkner, Nathaniel West, Aldous Huxley, and James Agee* (New York: Scribners, 1976): 163-192.

References:

John Atkins, *Aldous Huxley: A Literary Study* (London: Calder, 1956; revised, New York: Orion, 1968);

Robert S. Baker, *The Dark Historic Page: Social Satire and Historicism in the Novels of Aldous Huxley 1921-1939* (Madison: University of Wisconsin Press, 1982);

Joseph Warren Beach, "Counterpoint: Aldous Huxley," in his *Twentieth Century Novel: Studies in Technique* (New York: Century, 1932), pp. 458-469;

Milton Birnbaum, *Aldous Huxley's Quest for Values* (Knoxville: University of Tennessee Press, 1971);

Peter Bowering, *Aldous Huxley: A Study of the Major Novels* (London: Athlone Press, 1969; New York: Oxford University Press, 1969);

Laurence Brander, *Aldous Huxley: A Critical Study* (Lewisburg, Pa.: Bucknell University Press, 1970);

Jocelyn Brooke, *Aldous Huxley*, British Book Council pamphlet "Writers and Their Work: No. 55" (London: Longmans, Green, 1954);

Philo M. Buck, Jr., *Directions in Contemporary Literature* (New York: Oxford University Press, 1942), pp. 169-191;

Richard V. Chase, "The Huxley-Heard Paradise," *Partisan Review*, 10 (March-April 1943): 143-158;

David Daiches, *The Novel and the Modern World* (Chicago: University of Chicago Press, 1939), pp. 188-210;

Peter E. Firchow, *Aldous Huxley, Satirist and Novelist* (Minneapolis: University of Minnesota Press, 1972);

Stephen Jay Greenblatt, *Three Modern Satirists: Waugh, Orwell, and Huxley* (New Haven: Yale University Press, 1965);

Charles M. Holmes, *Aldous Huxley and the Way to Reality* (Bloomington & London: Indiana University Press, 1969);

Bharathi Krisham, *Aspects of Structure, Technique and Quest in Aldous Huxley's Major Novels* (Stockholm: Almquist & Wiksell, 1977);

Robert E. Kuehn, ed., *Aldous Huxley: A Collection of Critical Essays* (Englewood Cliffs, N.J.: Prentice-Hall, 1974);

André Maurois, *Prophets and Poets*, translated by Hamish Miles (New York: Harper, 1935), pp. 287-312;

Keith M. May, *Aldous Huxley* (London: Elek, 1972);

Jerome Meckier, *Aldous Huxley: Satire and Structure* (London: Chatto & Windus, 1969; New York: Barnes & Noble, 1971);

Berthold Thiel, *Aldous Huxley's "Brave New World"* (Amsterdam: Gruner, 1980);

Harold H. Watts, *Aldous Huxley* (New York: Twayne, 1969);

George Woodcock, *Dawn and the Darkest Hour: A Study of Aldous Huxley* (London: Faber & Faber, 1972; New York: Viking, 1972).

Papers:
Most of the books, diaries, and papers Aldous Huxley had accumulated over a lifetime were destroyed when his house burned in 1961. The most substantial collection of the remaining papers is at the library of the University of California at Los Angeles. Some additional materials are at the Stanford University Library.

Storm Jameson
(8 January 1891-   )

Margaret B. McDowell
University of Iowa

BOOKS: *The Pot Boils* (London: Constable, 1919);

The Happy Highways (London: Heinemann, 1920; New York: Century, 1920);

Modern Drama in Europe (London: Collins, 1920; New York: Harcourt, Brace & Howe, 1920);

The Clash (London: Heinemann, 1922; Boston: Little, Brown, 1922);

The Pitiful Wife (London: Constable, 1923; New York: Knopf, 1924);

Lady Susan and Life: An Indiscretion (London: Chapman & Dodd, 1924);

Three Kingdoms (London: Constable, 1926; New York: Knopf, 1926);

The Lovely Ship (London: Heinemann, 1927; New York: Knopf, 1927);

Farewell to Youth (London: Heinemann, 1928; New York: Knopf, 1928);

Full Circle: A Play in One Act (Oxford: Blackwell, 1928);

The Georgian Novel and Mr. Robinson (London: Heinemann, 1929; New York: Morrow, 1929);

The Voyage Home (London: Heinemann, 1930; New York: Knopf, 1930);

The Decline of Merry England (London: Cassell, 1930; New York: Bobbs-Merrill, 1930);

A Richer Dust (London: Heinemann, 1931; New York: Knopf, 1931);

The Triumph of Time: A Trilogy (London: Heinemann, 1932)—includes *The Lovely Ship, The Voyage Home,* and *A Richer Dust;*

That Was Yesterday (London: Heinemann, 1932; New York: Knopf, 1932);

The Single Heart (London: Benn, 1932);

No Time Like the Present (London: Cassell, 1933; New York: Knopf, 1933);

A Day Off (London: Nicholson & Watson, 1933);

Women Against Men, includes *A Day Off, Delicate Monster,* and *The Single Heart* (New York: Knopf, 1933);

Company Parade (London: Cassell, 1934; New York: Knopf, 1934);

The Soul of Man in the Age of Leisure (London: Nott, 1935);

Love in Winter (London: Cassell, 1935; New York: Knopf, 1935);

In the Second Year (London: Cassell, 1936; New York: Macmillan, 1936);

None Turn Back (London: Cassell, 1936);

Delicate Monster (London: Nicholson & Watson, 1937);

The World Ends, as William Lamb (London: Dent, 1937);

Loving Memory, as James Hill (London: Collins, 1937; Boston: Little, Brown, 1937);

The Moon Is Making (London: Cassell, 1937; New York: Macmillan, 1938);

No Victory for the Soldier, as James Hill (London: Collins, 1938; New York: Doubleday, Doran, 1939);

Here Comes a Candle (London: Cassell, 1938; New York: Macmillan, 1939);

The Novel in Contemporary Life (Boston: Writer, 1938);

Farewell, Night; Welcome, Day (London: Cassell, 1939); republished as *The Captain's Wife* (New York: Macmillan, 1939);

Civil Journey (London: Cassell, 1939);

Europe to Let: The Memoirs of an Obscure Man (New York: Macmillan, 1940);

Cousin Honoré (London: Cassell, 1940; New York: Macmillan, 1941);

The End of This War (London: Allen & Unwin, 1941);

The Fort (London: Cassell, 1941; New York: Macmillan, 1941);

Then Shall We Hear Singing: A Fantasy in C Major (London: Cassell, 1942; New York: Macmillan, 1942);

Cloudless May (London: Macmillan, 1943; New York: Macmillan, 1944);

The Journal of Mary Hervey Russell (London: Macmillan, 1945; New York: Macmillan, 1945);

The Other Side (London: Macmillan, 1946; New York: Macmillan, 1946);

Before the Crossing (New York: Macmillan, 1947);

The Black Laurel (London: Macmillan, 1947; New York: Macmillan, 1948);

The Moment of Truth (New York: Macmillan, 1949);

The Writer's Situation and Other Essays (London: Macmillan, 1950);

The Green Man (London: Macmillan, 1952; New York: Harper, 1953);

The Hidden River (London: Macmillan, 1955; New York: Harper, 1955);

The Intruder (London: Macmillan, 1956; New York: St. Martin's, 1956);

A Cup of Tea for Mr. Thorgill (New York: Harper, 1957; London: Macmillan, 1965);

A Ulysses Too Many (London: Macmillan, 1958); republished as *One Ulysses Too Many* (New York: Harper, 1958);

Morley Roberts: The Last Eminent Victorian (London: Unicorn, 1961);

Last Score: Or, The Private Life of Sir Richard Ormston (London: Macmillan, 1961; New York: Harper, 1961);

The Road from the Monument (London: Macmillan, 1962; New York: St. Martin's, 1962);

A Month Soon Goes (London: Macmillan, 1963; New York: Harper & Row, 1963);

The Aristide Case (London: Macmillan, 1964); republished as *The Blind Heart* (New York: Harper & Row, 1964);

The Early Life of Stephen Hind (London: Macmillan, 1966; New York: Harper & Row, 1966);

The White Crow (London: Macmillan, 1968; New York: Harper & Row, 1968);

Journey from the North (2 volumes, London: Collins, 1969, 1970; 1 volume, New York: Harper & Row, 1970);

Parthian Words (London: Collins, 1970; New York; Harper & Row, 1971);

There Will Be A Short Interval (London: Harvill, 1973; New York: Harper & Row, 1973);

Storm Jameson, 1923

Speaking of Stendhal (London: Gollancz, 1979).

OTHER: Guy de Maupassant, *Yvette and Other Stories,* translated by Jameson (New York: Knopf, 1924);

de Maupassant, *Mont-Oriol,* translated by Jameson (New York: Knopf, 1924);

de Maupassant, *Eighty-Eight Short Stories,* translated by Jameson and Ernest Boyd (London: Knopf, 1930);

Lilo Linke, *Tale Without End,* introduction by Jameson (New York: Knopf, 1934);

Challenge to Death: A Symposium on War and Peace, edited by Jameson (London: Constable, 1934; New York: Dutton, 1935);

Rebecca West and others, *London Calling: A Salute to America,* edited by Jameson (New York & London: Harper, 1942);

de Maupassant, *88 More Stories,* translated by Jameson and Boyd (London: Cassell, 1950);

"William the Defeated," in *The Book of the P.E.N.,*

edited by Hermon Ould (London: Barker, 1950);

Guy Chapman, *A Kind of Survivor: The Autobiography of Guy Chapman,* edited by Jameson (London: Gollancz, 1975).

Since the end of World War I Storm Jameson has written more than forty novels, a play, television scripts, short stories, criticism, and autobiography.

Though she is best known as a novelist, Jameson's scholarly books are significant contributions to the study of literature and culture. Almost alone among British women novelists of her generation to earn a university graduate degree, she wrote sound books on drama and literature, such as *Modern Drama in Europe* (1920), *The Georgian Novel and Mr. Robinson* (1929), *The Novel in Contemporary Life* (1938), *The Writer's Situation and Other Essays* (1950), *Parthian Words* (1970), and *Speaking of Stendhal* (1979). Her historical and biographical works include *The Decline of Merry England* (1930), a study of Puritanism, and *Morley Roberts: The Last Eminent Victorian* (1961). Born in Whitby, Yorkshire, to William Storm Jameson, a sea captain, and Hannah Margaret Gallilee Jameson, Margaret Storm Jameson came from an extremely poor family. It was largely through her mother's determination that she learned of the competitive scholarship that enabled her to attend Leeds University, where she received the B.A. (first class honors) in 1912. She earned the M.A. in 1914 at King's College, London, where she held a research scholarship in modern drama. In 1948 she was awarded an honorary D.Litt. from Leeds University.

Jameson also influenced the world of literature as an administrator. In the mid-1920s she managed the British branch of Alfred Knopf publishing company and sought out both recognized authors and new writers of promise to submit their manuscripts for publication. She was president of the International P.E.N., English Centre, from 1938 to 1945 and then served on the executive board of International P.E.N. for several years. As a P.E.N. executive, she went to central Europe in the late 1930s, traveling to Austria, Czechoslovakia, Germany, Hungary, and Poland to aid writers. She strongly articulated her views as governments banned books and imprisoned writers; she moderated disputes among influential authors; and she helped to keep the International P.E.N. a strong political force. Although she shifted in the late 1930s from a determined pacifist stance to support of the British declaration of war, her reputation for honesty and her ability to write and speak persua-

sively enabled her to maintain her pacifist friends during this period. Continuing to grieve for her brother who was killed in World War I, her conflict over supporting World War II deepened when her youngest sister was killed in a London bombing. Because of her prominence in P.E.N. Jameson saw her books banned early by the Nazis, and she learned from a journalist in October 1950 that she was listed in a Soviet "Book of Death" with other so-called "monsters and cannibals."

In the decade following the end of World War II, she presided at tumultuous meetings of the annual P.E.N. International Congress. In Stockholm in 1946 delegations from several countries presented blacklists of writers who had collaborated with the Germans. In Zurich in 1947, over tremendous opposition, Jameson helped a few Germans get authorization to reestablish a P.E.N. center in Germany, after they had maintained their center in England since 1934 following the book burnings in Germany. She presided at meetings in Oslo, Paris, and Venice; and in the small foreign hotels she always wrote more easily than in her own household.

In her autobiographical books and some of her novels, Jameson seems preoccupied with her ambivalent attitudes toward her family and with a fictitious family she invented for "disguised autobiography." She wrote repeatedly of her parents, her grandfather, the landscape at Whitby on the North Sea, and her ill-considered and violent marriage in 1914. She was not divorced until 1924, but she and her husband lived together only for brief intervals. Her only son, C. W. Storm Clark, provided psychic stability during her early career, and she suffered when he had to be left in a boarding home in Whitby while she worked in London and wrote her first fiction, her poverty for a decade making her exist often near starvation. On 1 February 1926 she married Guy Patterson Chapman, and the two lived happily together for forty-eight years, until his death in 1972. In the 1960s, she was much involved with her two grandchildren and with her son's venturesome yachting expeditions—once as far as Australia with his wife and small baby and once across the Atlantic and back with only his wife and two young children for crew. She is proud of his success as an airplane pilot and seems to feel that his having grown up as a brave and confident adult was a miracle, given all of the mistakes she had made as his parent and her struggles to support him during his early childhood.

In her autobiography, Jameson explains that she had what she terms a "pathological hatred" for

A 1941 photograph of Jameson's second husband, Guy Chapman, during his service in the Army Educational Corps. After his death in 1972, Jameson edited his autobiography.

kitchen before daylight with strong tea and a piece of dry bread and feel again the pleasure of childhood.

Jameson has sought especially to interpret in her fiction the contemporary social scene and later in her career expressed a sober and cautionary outlook on the future of a world that had survived the cruelty of Nazism only to face probable annihilation in nuclear war. She linked her generation's determination to survive such odds with the strength her parents and grandparents derived through hardship and repression on the North Sea and in Yorkshire. Except for some of her novels written after World War II, her best books center on unresolved fragments of her own life and the lives of her parents and grandparents. The plots deal with families involved with shipbuilding or sailing, and they are set in Whitby or elsewhere in Yorkshire, the land Jameson both hated and loved. Her characters break away—they go to Liverpool, London, or even New Orleans—but they belong, in some way, to Yorkshire and to ships. Their memory of childhood and their last thoughts before they die are of the sea: "The curve of a coastline, of a gull's wing, the whiteness of a white petal, the sea, voyages."

Jameson's finest work may be her two-volume autobiography *Journey from the North* (1969, 1970). Writing when she was over seventy, she employed every aspect of the art of the novel in analyzing her life. The chronology of the first volume moves backward in a slow and intricate revelation of Jameson's growth. As in her fiction, no character in this autobiography exists alone; characters develop through family and community relationships—often in situations fraught with great conflict and ambivalent emotions. Her autobiography centers on herself as protagonist; but the stage is always full, and the emotional drama sometimes focuses on others in scenes where she is peripheral.

The energy of Jameson's first half-dozen novels, published from 1919 through 1926, caught the attention of reviewers. The books sold well, but they must be regarded as apprentice work. After Jameson's third novel, in 1922, Rebecca West wrote in the *New Statesman:* "Miss Jameson is a person of enormous horse-power. . . . It looks as if she was developing in this book a curious emotional clairvoyance." A reviewer in the *Saturday Review* described her work as "a volcano in eruption," and a writer in the *Spectator* heard her words as a "loud and discordant brassband." After her fourth novel, published in the following year, a reviewer in the *Times Literary Supplement* concluded that she was

domesticity. She avoids cooking, and she has said that, unless she was traveling or frequently changing apartments, she felt caged. Writing of her first marriage in her autobiography, she remarks casually: "One day I decided to sell the furniture." Her extreme restlessness also drove her to write compulsively—and to produce far too many books, according to her own assessment.

Jameson has attributed her fear of settled home life to her mother's similar feeling. Jameson's father, a sailor from age thirteen, worked as a sea captain on small vessels for more than sixty years, and her mother envied the captains' wives who had no children and no homes on shore and traveled all the time. When Jameson was the only child, she and her mother frequently met the father's boat at one port and traveled with him for days or weeks to another port; these times remained dominant memories. She has recalled with intensity the experience of sitting in the cold kitchen before dawn drinking strong tea and chewing a crust of bread before they left for a trip. At difficult times in her life she has found that she could sit in a darkened "now able to concentrate a natural exuberance . . . upon her immediate subject." Assessing Jameson's achievement and designating those elements which distinguished her later fiction, L. B. Hartley concluded in the *Saturday Review* in 1926 that her "power consists in seeing her characters in relation to one another. . . . The emotion is of a high quality, intense and sudden." She also learned early that unity can derive from the narrative voice, and she had begun to employ first-person narration in the novels she considered purely fiction and third-person narrative in those she called her "disguised autobiographies."

Jameson has written more than ten books involving four generations of interrelated Yorkshire families. John Galsworthy's wide embracing of families and generations in his fictional sagas makes his comment on the characteristic vitality of Jameson's early work interesting. He wrote in a letter to Charles Evans of Heinemann after he read her second novel: "This authoress has done what none of the other torrential novelists of the last ten years has achieved—given us a convincing . . . summary of the effervescence, discontent, revolt, and unrest of youth; the heartache and beating of wings. . . . She must have seen and felt things. . . . To an old-fashioned brute like me, of course, the lack of form [may] stick a little in the gizzard, but the stuff is undeniable."

The Triumph of Time trilogy focuses primarily on the life of Mary Hervey, head of a shipbuilding firm. Because she was born in 1841 and died in 1923, the books cover shipbuilding history from sailing vessels to steamships to carbine-engine ships. In *The Lovely Ship* (1927), the first novel of the trilogy, Mary Hansyke is born to Charlotte Garton Hansyke of the Garton shipbuilding family. Charlotte's unemotional husband, Richard Hansyke, is relieved when eight years later his unfaithful wife leaves him and he can send Mary to her uncle, Mark Henry Garton, head of the shipping company, where she is brought up with various Roxby and Garton cousins. At fifteen Mary feels ready to enter the shipbuilding business, but discovers Mark believes only men can join the enterprise. In disbelief, Mary goes back to her father, who—as businesslike as his child—arranges a marriage to the elderly and ailing Archibald Roxby. Archibald dies not long after their son, Richard Roxby, is born. Mary acquires for Richard most of his father's estate (against the claims of the Roxby brothers). She returns confidently to Mark Garton and enters the firm, which she can now subsidize in part. Her second marriage, to Hugh Hervey, is one of love, but

he becomes unfaithful soon after their daughters Clare and Sylvia are born. Mary lives many years with the understanding that Hugh is welcome whenever he chooses to return, and he eventually does. In the meantime, she takes over the company and it flourishes; she has an affair with her managerial assistant until his wife intervenes; and she brings up Richard, Clare, and Sylvia.

In *The Voyage Home* (1930), Sylvia, Mary's favorite daughter, runs away to marry Captain Russell, a man her mother had fired for irresponsibility. Because Mary refuses Sylvia's demand that she rehire Russell at a high level in the company, the two women become alienated for life. Clare marries her wealthy cousin Nicholas Roxby, the man Mary had hoped Sylvia would marry. Because both Mary's son and Clare's husband die, Mary's grandson, also named Nicholas Roxby, becomes heir to her shipping company and is her hope for the future. Nevertheless, by the end of the final volume of the trilogy, *A Richer Dust* (1931), it appears that Mary considers sharing that interest with the granddaughter she has never met, Sylvia's oldest child and her namesake, (Mary) Hervey Russell. Though she asks Nicholas to send for her granddaughter, when Hervey Russell arrives, her grandmother has slipped into a coma; and no reconciliation can occur.

Hervey is clearly identified with Jameson herself. She has been living for four years in London while her infant son has been boarded out with a woman near her mother's home in Whitby; she has an editorial job; and she has written two novels. Her husband has not made his home with her since returning from the military. Hervey appears in eight later books by Jameson, and she always appears in autobiographical context. Jameson seems to have been unable psychologically to separate herself from Hervey, and she wrote of her compulsively year after year, although it disturbed her that she was still writing of her unhappy first marriage a decade after her good second marriage began. In *That Was Yesterday* (1932) the depiction of the marriage of Hervey and Penn Russell follows closely the notes Jameson made after each quarrel with her first husband whenever he came for visits during the latter years of the marriage. In *The Captain's Wife* (1939), which first appeared as *Farewell, Night; Welcome, Day,* she wrote the story of Sylvia Hervey, Hervey Russell's mother. Again Jameson moved into autobiography by using her own mother as the model for the character, thus reinforcing the link between herself and the fictional Hervey Russell. In *The Journal of Mary Hervey Russell* (1945) Jameson

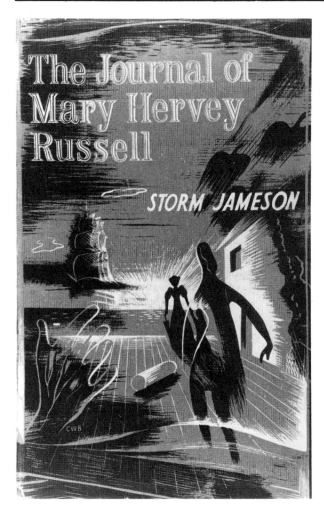

*Dust jacket for Jameson's 1945 book, one of the novels she calls
"disguised autobiography"*

employed the literary device of a diary, thus presenting Hervey's single point of view.

She considers neither *That Was Yesterday, The Captain's Wife,* nor *The Journal of Mary Hervey Russell* part of her projected saga, *The Mirror in Darkness,* designed as a continuation of *The Triumph of Time* trilogy. The five books in this saga of Hervey Russell's life were never published together under the proposed title, and they were written at irregular intervals. *Company Parade* (1934), the book Jameson identified as first in the series, quickly introduces a large number of characters and then parades them in later and somewhat independent sequences. It is 1923, and Hervey's situation is that described at the end of *A Richer Dust* as her grandmother dies in the presence of Hervey and the cousin she has just met, Nicholas Roxby. The most important of the new characters is David Renn, supervisor of Hervey's editorial work in the London publishing office. He

is a war veteran who suffers constant pain from a nearly fatal leg wound. In the last two books in the series, Renn is a principal figure. He is seen before World War II in *Before the Crossing* (1947) and after the war in *The Black Laurel* (1947). In the second book of *The Mirror in Darkness* saga, *Love in Winter* (1935), Nicholas Roxby and Hervey Russell have become lovers and live together.

Though the third book, *None Turn Back* (1936), received generally good reviews, Jameson felt great discouragement about the series and did not return to it until 1945, although she wrote two books connected with Hervey Russell in the interim. She felt that she was writing with neither the honesty of an autobiographer nor the imaginative vision of the novelist. She remained confused about her return in novels to her first marriage. She was also confused about her use of the "autobiographical disguise" in the novels in which she saw herself as an interpreter of the social world of her generation. This goal, in fact, did not please all her readers and critics—even those who gave her talent high praise. For example, Edwin Muir, reviewing *None Turn Back* in the *Listener,* praised Jameson's "passion and complete honesty," commenting further that "the writing is sometimes exquisite, and always has the directness and candor of good prose. . . . This is a novel which no contemporary can afford to neglect." But Muir also concluded that the novel failed in imagination, because Jameson treated the characters as ventriloquist's dummies, allowing society to dictate all their behavior. Jameson recognized that she, like her characters, had become caught in the political and social turmoil leading toward war. She felt her individuality threatened.

Significantly, when she interrupted *The Mirror in Darkness,* she wrote another political novel, *In the Second Year* (1936), a futuristic novel in which an English intellectual returns from a trip to Norway to find British citizens starving and fascists throwing them into concentration camps. Reviewers generally indicated that Jameson's fear and hatred of fascism had so subdued her imaginative genius that she had begun to write dull propaganda. Most thought she had attempted to repeat the success of Sinclair Lewis's *It Can't Happen Here.* A reviewer in the *Times Literary Supplement* expressed the general response: "We shall be glad when Miss Jameson returns to her Yorkshire shipyards, to real life, and real human beings again." But this book only prefigures Jameson's even more intense compulsion to make international politics the subject of most of her remaining novels.

Recognizing the problem of multiple iden-

Dust jacket for Jameson's 1955 novel, which questions the right of any individual to take upon himself the punishment of treachery

tities in her work, as well as that of excessively rapid writing, Jameson adopted a curious solution. She stopped writing as Storm Jameson and wrote three books under the pen names James Hill and William Lamb, using different publishers from those with whom she normally worked. However, in addition to these books—*The World Ends* (1937), *Loving Memory* (1937), and *No Victory for the Soldier* (1938)—she had two books published under her own name in 1937, *Delicate Monster* and *The Moon Is Making,* and *Here Comes a Candle* in 1938. Altogether, counting the novels written as James Hill and William Lamb, in the five years when she was supposedly dealing with the problem of writing too much, Jameson actually had ten novels and four novellas (in *Europe to Let,* 1940) published, and she wrote an unpublished dramatic version of *The Fort* (1941) before composing the novel.

Of these years of confusion, Jameson wrote more than thirty years later in *Journey from the North,* "I had an impulse to efface Storm Jameson altogether. . . . She was making a fool of herself. Instead of turning the poor animal round to find her right road, I left her. . . ." If writing under the pen names of two males did not decrease her problem with multiple identities, it may have made Jameson less concerned about critical reception of some of her books. However, it could not have mitigated the problem of rapid writing under stress.

Jameson was able to return to the writing of *The Mirror in Darkness* through becoming deeply engrossed in writing *The Journal of Mary Hervey Russell* (1945), with disciplined maintenance of the single point of view. Disturbed occasionally by the image of her young sister's recent death in a bombing raid, Jameson discovered image upon image rising from her unconscious as she wrote. She gained a renewal of imaginative power and an integration of self with her memories of her family. She thus experienced some resolution of her grief over her sister's death and the increasing devastation of the war. Several fortunate occurrences reinforced this experience. She felt it a miracle when a long-time friend, the historian R. W. Tawney, wrote a letter praising *The Journal of Mary Hervey Russell.* When asked for a manuscript to be auctioned for benefit of the American War Bond Committee, she found herself confidently choosing this latest work as her best book. In 1945 she went with three other British citizens sponsored by the Polish Embassy in London to Poland and Czechoslovakia. Seeing the courage of people in those countries renewed her own determination. Fortunately also, at this point of renewed creative energy and confidence, she discovered many forgotten boxes of notes for *The Mirror in Darkness,* the series she abandoned nine years before upon her completion of *None Turn Back.* The book she had projected as the fourth in the series now grew quickly into the two closely connected novels *Before the Crossing* and *The Black Laurel*. The two books unify the saga, in part, by emphasizing some of the characters Hervey Russell knew in her years in London after World War I, particularly David Renn, who was introduced in the first book of the series.

These last two books of *The Mirror in Darkness* were completed about the time of the bombing of Hiroshima. Jameson wrote in her autobiography of the reasoning through which she gradually came to terms with life in a world endangered by the discovery of nuclear fission: "Before Hiroshima, a writer who feared that civilization . . . was in danger could think of finding a monastery or could remove himself and his brain to another country, less immediately threatened by the barbarians. . . . Only the artist—a class of persons which includes the man who set a pot of geraniums outside his hotel in the ruins of Warsaw—can tell us how, in what conditions, men can survive as human beings. I mean a being who is not only human, not an existential animal, but a creature possessed of a divine instinct to create pleasure for himself and others. It was because he had lost his faith in this saving instinct that H. G. Wells died in despair. . . . Now that none of us is safe, we can really laugh, really mock our pedantic teachers, really live."

Jameson continued to write at her rapid, steady pace throughout the 1950s and 1960s. Now reviewers stressed her "intelligence" and her "satire." The works characteristic of these years are connected with World War II, international politics, and the danger of nuclear holocaust. All tend toward the didactic, but Jameson maintained her ability to create interesting characters and to crowd her books with them. She also maintained her ability to keep her plots intriguing, even in some extremely long novels.

Most of the later novels sold well and received favorable reviews. Among those she herself particularly likes are *Cousin Honoré* (1940), *Cloudless May* (1943), and *The Green Man* (1952). *Cousin Honoré*, a tale of an Alsatian village from 1918 to 1939, features unheroic characters. Honoré himself is a lusty, cunning egotist who owns a small foundry. The appeal of the characters lies in their love for France and their willingness to resist the threatened invasion by the German forces. Jameson ended the book with scenes of hope—her optimism based on the determined, though commonplace, village folk. France fell a few days after she submitted the manuscript to the publishers, but she refused to change a word of the novel to accommodate the event.

Storm Jameson, 1957

Cloudless May examines the complex relationships among the occupants of a village in the valley of the Loire. Placed slightly later in time than *Cousin Honoré*, this novel searches for the reasons for the fall of France. The "cloudless May" of 1940 leads in the book to the mid-June occupation that with apparent suddenness divides the characters into either collaborationists with the German invaders or members of the underground resistance.

The Green Man, considered by many to be excessively long, maintains interest through the techniques Jameson had used earlier in her two sagas and the related novels of Hervey Russell. All the people are connected with one English family, and all have roots in British tradition as well as in family pride and concern. She follows them slowly through the years 1930 to 1947, using her own understanding of the growth of Marxism in the 1930s and the mixture of confidence and defeatism that underlay the intellectual talk of the "Age of Anxiety." While the suspenseful intrigue that marks the gossip of the villagers in *Cousin Honoré* and

Cloudless May is missing here, the reader becomes gradually absorbed in the conflicting motivations of the family members who believe variously in power, in money, or in scholarly and artistic traditions. The single recurring negative criticism of this best-seller—other than its length—was made of many of Jameson's other books during this period: she had become oppressively didactic in her concern with international political problems. A critic writing in the *Times Literary Supplement* in 1953, for example, declared that her readers are "governessed into accepting her version" of the way things happen in the world.

When asked in recent years about her favorites among her books, she has usually mentioned her later works, but, significantly, she has included in several such responses a short novel that might otherwise be overlooked in a revival of interest in Jameson—*A Day Off* (1933). It is unlike any of her other work, and it merits rediscovery. In it, an aging prostitute spends a single day walking about Lon-

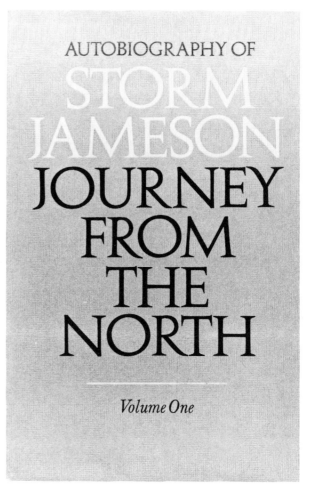

Jameson explained that her life "spans three distinct ages: the middle class heyday before 1914, the entre deux guerres, *and the present; three ages so disparate that to a person who knows only the third the others are unimaginable"; she promised to "excavate two finished stages in society."*

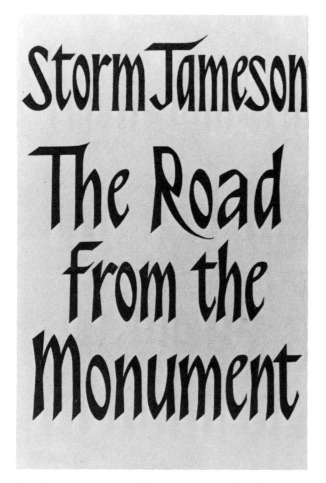

Dust jacket for Jameson's 1962 novel, the story of a religious man whose beliefs are shaken as he is forced to see himself with greater clarity

don and simultaneously journeys in her mind through her past life, notable for its hardships and suffering. Jameson's realistic characterization and sustained empathy with her unattractive and mean protagonist provide a fascinating imaginative experience.

Throughout the 1970s Jameson maintained her creative energy and retained her extensive reading public. *Speaking of Stendhal* satisfied her in a form far more concise than the ambitious book she had initially thought would result from her years of study. Her most recent novel, *There Will Be A Short Interval* (1973), was given the P.E.N. English Centre Award in 1974. After Guy Chapman's death she edited his autobiography (1975). She has had no books published since 1979.

So abundant are Jameson's writings that it is difficult to define her contribution to British literature. Most impressive are the two long sagas, *The Triumph of Time* trilogy and *The Mirror in Darkness* quintet, and the associated novels related to Hervey Russell. Her autobiography, *Journey From The North*, also remains impressive for her depiction of bitter parents and bitter marriages, for the recreation of the milieu of North Sea sailing fleets, for the vignettes of famous people whom Jameson knew from her stormy days with the International P.E.N., and for her unreserved self-disclosure. Few fiction writers or autobiographers have ever tried so agonizingly to be absolutely honest, but her intentions in this respect seem to have remained always stronger than her achievements. She probably reached the peak of her accomplishment as a realist in the characterization of the old woman in *A Day Off*. Although her reputation grew after World War II, the many novels related to that war and to international politics may prove to have been important primarily to people of her own day, rather than to later readers.

Papers:
Collections of Jameson's writings are at the University of Texas, Austin, and at Wellesley College, Wellesley, Massachusetts.

James Joyce

Bernard Benstock
University of Tulsa

See also the Joyce entries in *DLB 10, Modern British Dramatists, 1900-1945* and *DLB 19, British Poets, 1880-1914.*

BIRTH: Dublin, Ireland, 2 February 1882, to John Stanislaus and Mary Jane Murray Joyce.

EDUCATION: B.A., University College, Dublin, 1902.

MARRIAGE: 4 July 1931 to Nora Barnacle; children: Giorgio and Lucia.

DEATH: Zurich, Switzerland, 13 January 1941.

SELECTED BOOKS: *Two Essays: "A Forgotten Aspect of the University Question," by F. J. C. Skeffington, and "The Day of the Rabblement," by James Joyce* (Dublin: Privately printed, 1901);
Chamber Music (London: Elkin Mathews, 1907; Boston: Cornhill, 1918 [unauthorized]; New York: Huebsch, 1918 [authorized]);
Dubliners (London: Richards, 1914; New York: Huebsch, 1916);
A Portrait of the Artist as a Young Man (New York: Huebsch, 1916; London: Egoist, 1917);
Exiles (London: Richards, 1918; New York: Huebsch, 1918);

Ulysses (Paris: Shakespeare & Company, 1922; London: Egoist, 1922; New York: Random House, 1934);
Pomes Penyeach (Paris: Shakespeare & Company, 1927; Princeton: Sylvia Beach, 1931; London: Harmsworth, 1932);
Collected Poems (New York: Black Sun Press, 1936);
Finnegans Wake (London: Faber & Faber, 1939; New York: Viking, 1939);
Stephen Hero (London: Cape, 1944; New York: New Directions, 1944);
The Critical Writings of James Joyce, edited by Ellsworth Mason and Richard Ellmann (New York: Viking, 1959);
The Workshop of Dedalus: James Joyce and the Materials for a Portrait of the Artist as a Young Man, edited by Robert Scholes and Richard M. Kain (Evanston: Northwestern University Press, 1965);
Giacomo Joyce, edited by Ellmann (New York: Viking, 1968);
Ulysses: A Facsimile of the Manuscript, edited by Clive Driver (New York: Farrar, Straus & Giroux, 1975);
Ulysses Notebooks, edited by Phillip F. Herring (Charlottesville: University Press of Virginia, 1977);
The James Joyce Archive, 63 volumes, edited by

Michael Groden, Hans Walter Gabler, David Hayman, A. Walton Litz, and Danis Rose (New York & London: Garland, 1978).

Few writers have as secure a claim to be the major figure of the modernist period in literary history as James Joyce, a position that he prepared himself for with diligence and commitment. During his student days at University College in Dublin he prophetically envisioned his role as the major writer of his age, although he remained for a time undecided as to the form that his writing would take. Even before his twentieth birthday Joyce wrote and arranged to have published (with an essay by his friend F. J. C. Skeffington) an essay titled "The Day of the Rabblement" (1901), which concluded with a prophecy: "Elsewhere there are men who are worthy to carry on the tradition of the old master who is dying in Christiana. He has already found his successor in the writer of *Michael Kramer,* and a third minister will not be wanting when his hour comes. Even now that hour may be standing by the door." In placing himself immodestly in the succession of Henrik Ibsen and Gerhart Hauptmann, the young Joyce still visualized himself as a potential playwright (and may well have dedicated an early play to his own soul—no published work of his was ever dedicated to anyone), but of the three plays he presumably wrote, he allowed only the later *Exiles* (1918) to survive. During his youth he also persisted in composing lyric poetry—the basic literary medium of the age he lived in—and continued to write poems even after he settled into a career as a novelist. In *Ulysses* (1922) the boastful young poet Stephen Dedalus is deflated by his companion Lynch, who asserts, "those leaves . . . will adorn you more fitly when something more, and greatly more, than a capful of light odes can call your genius father." To make good on the claim (also attributed to Stephen in *Ulysses*) that he "is going to write something in ten years," Joyce turned to prose narrative, first in a series of short stories and a quasi-autobiographical novel. The publication of *Dubliners* (1914) and *A Portrait of the Artist as a Young Man* (1916) brought him to the attention of the literati, while the 1922 publication of *Ulysses* brought him to the attention of the world.

The year of Joyce's birth, 1882, was also the year in which several other contributors to modernism were born (Virginia Woolf, Wyndham Lewis, Igor Stravinsky, Georges Braque, Mina Loy, and futurist Umberto Boccioni), but the world into which he was born was light years away from the intimations of international modernism. Dublin was then still the second city of the British Empire, and the coincidental birth in 1882 of Eamon de Valera, who would eventually rule over an independent Ireland, is far more germane to the provincial Irish environment in which Joyce was reared. His family was Roman Catholic and his father, John Stanislaus Joyce, had property in his native city of Cork; but the family fortunes took a sharp turn for the worse during Joyce's childhood. John Joyce had allied himself politically with Charles Stewart Parnell, leader of the Irish Parliamentary party that sought home rule for Ireland, and the divorce scandal in 1881 that destroyed Parnell's career also cost Joyce's father his patronage job. The economic decline of the bourgeois Joyces is caustically traced in Stephen Dedalus's description in *A Portrait of the Artist as a Young Man* of his father as a "medical student, an oarsman, a tenor, an amateur actor, a shouting politician, a small landlord, a small investor, a drinker, a good fellow, a storyteller, somebody's secretary, something in a distillery, a taxgatherer, a bankrupt and at present a praiser of his own past." Mary Jane Murray, Joyce's mother, was a devout Catholic who had hoped for a clerical vocation for her oldest son, and her death when James Joyce was only twenty-one signaled the end of the disrupted and impoverished family, which included at least ten children who had survived infancy. In various ways Joyce wove the details of his own life into each of his novels, using these autobiographical materials as an imaginative fabric that he frequently rewove.

The intellectual climate during Joyce's youth also figures prominently in his works, especially *A Portrait of the Artist as a Young Man* and *Ulysses,* as he views the flourishing Irish literary revival from the sidelines with a mixture of anxiety and indifference. Both the strong nationalism, with its accentuation on the revived Gaelic language, and the accompanying mysticism were unacceptable to the young Joyce, and he was determined to establish himself in the European mainstream, referring contemptuously to Ireland as a "backwater," and "an afterthought of Europe." The emphasis on Ibsen and Hauptmann in the modern literary world paralleled his interest in the medieval Catholicism of Dante, as he sought an intellectual and spiritual heritage for his artistic commitment, a commitment that distanced him from William Butler Yeats and AE (George Russell) and the Celtic Twilight movement that he would later characterize in *Finnegans Wake* as the "cultic twalette." He was also sensitive to the major achievement of the English literary tradition which spanned the eight centuries in which Ireland was under English rule, and the ac-

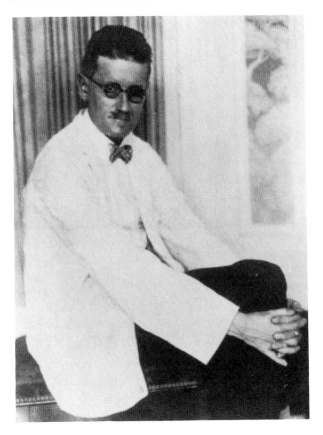

complishment of a William Shakespeare within that tradition. Whereas his friends in Gaelic League classes were attempting to return to the moribund Irish language, Joyce accepted with misgivings the necessity of writing in the tongue of the conquerors in order to broaden his intellectual perspectives, and, like his Stephen figure, he relied on "the only arms I allow myself to use—silence, exile, and cunning." His estrangement from Ireland became as necessary to him as detachment from family, friends, and religion; once he had finished his university education in 1902 (he had studied Romance languages), he made his way to the European continent. Tentative self-exile as a medical student in Paris actually found him at the Bibliothèque Nationale reading Ben Jonson, an influence on the delicate lyrics that he later published as *Chamber Music* (1907), but his mother's serious illness brought him back to Dublin for more than a year. When he left in October 1904 to become a teacher of English at a Berlitz school in Pola, 70 miles south of Trieste, Joyce took with him a young woman, Nora Barnacle, who would remain his wife for the rest of his life on the Continent,

although he refused to honor the sacrament of marriage and remained outside the Church as well. (They legalized their marriage in a civil ceremony on 4 July 1931.)

The history of Joyce's lifelong exile on the Continent is also the history of his artistic development and of his literary publications. He brought with him to Trieste, where he settled with Nora after a short period of teaching in Pola, the poems that would appear as *Chamber Music* in 1907, the stories that he began publishing in the *Irish Homestead* in 1904, and the completed chapters of a quasi-autobiographical novel he called *Stephen Hero* (posthumously published in 1944). The birth of a son, Giorgio (in 1905), and a daughter, Lucia (in 1907), extended the immediate family, but Joyce also managed to lure a brother, Stanislaus, and a sister, Eva, from Dublin—Stanislaus Joyce was his closest sibling and would prove to be his severest critic. By 1906 the short stories had been tentatively shaped into a volume titled *Dubliners,* and years of publication delays and cancellations resulted in anger and bitterness, so that his last visit to his native city in 1912 resulted in his determination never to return to Ireland. By 1907 he had scrapped some thousand pages of *Stephen Hero* and reconstituted the scheme into *A Portrait of the Artist as a Young Man,* which also ran into difficulties—his own delay in completing the book. Nonetheless, the Trieste years (which ended with the advent of World War I) determined Joyce's views of his own literary talents as a writer of prose fiction.

In 1915 the Joyces were granted permission to leave for neutral Zurich, Joyce, having completed *A Portrait of the Artist as a Young Man* and begun *Ulysses,* taking time away from fiction writing long enough to write *Exiles*. Most of *Ulysses* was written during the war years in Zurich, but the composition of that work is actually a tale of three cities: in 1920, after a short attempt to reestablish himself in Trieste, Joyce heeded the call of Ezra Pound to come to live in Paris, where *Ulysses* was published in book form in 1922. The Paris years lasted until the outbreak of World War II, during which fame as well as notoriety, and even financial largesse, were component factors in Joyce's life. He worked on *Finnegans Wake* (segments of which were published under the tentative title of *Work in Progress* in small limited editions and in little magazines such as *transition* and by esoteric presses between 1928 and 1937) and lived the life of a fairly affluent bourgeois. A long series of eye operations and Lucia Joyce's progressive development of mental illness, which Joyce insisted on hiding from himself, plagued these years of success.

No sooner was *Finnegans Wake* published in 1939 than the war broke out, and the Joyces were once again on the road to exile. A stay in the south of France eventually led to their being admitted into Switzerland again, once Lucia was hospitalized and the rumor that Joyce was a Jew was scotched. Three weeks after arriving in Zurich, James Joyce died on the operating table of peritonitis.

Joyce's reputation as a fiction writer rests on his three completed novels, although his innovative techniques in narrative prose allow his short-story collection *Dubliners* (1914) to be included into the novelistic scheme he created. Originally slight vignettes that earned him a few pounds, these stories were eventually fashioned into a coherent unity, a highly structured text in which each component element is balanced in support of the whole. By 1905 Joyce had decided on a format composed of twelve stories—three on childhood, three on young adults, three on mature adults, and three final, longer stories of public life. The publication delays that caused increasing frustrations for Joyce also allowed him to elaborate on the pattern, so that the two inner groups were expanded to four each, and "The Dead" was added as a cumulative coda story, a novella that was much longer than even the longest story of public life. That in 1906 Joyce toyed with the idea of adding another piece, a story to be titled "Ulysses," indicates the degree to which the larger narrative format began dominating his thinking. The collection of fifteen stories was finally published in 1914, and the idea for *Ulysses* took shape as a long novel instead.

The basic unit of Joyce's early prose work was what he called an "epiphany," a minute anecdote or observation, an overheard conversation, or a recorded dream sequence. Each first existed as a separate entity, but they were soon worked into the *Stephen Hero* manuscript. A definition of that minimal art form appears in the extant text of this early novel: "By epiphany he meant a sudden spiritual manifestation, whether in the vulgarity of speech or of gesture or in a memorable phrase of the mind itself. . . . the most delicate and evanescent of moments." Even as late a work as *Ulysses* contains one of the early epiphanies folded into the elaborate structure, and although epiphanies are not present as separate and discrete texts, the essence of the concept was retained throughout the novels, so that *Finnegans Wake* as well elaborates upon a progression of anecdotes and fables, extensions of the humble epiphany. The first stories that Joyce wrote for the *Irish Homestead* were hardly more than extended epiphanies, vignettes that were short, sim-

ple, straightforward, and easily comprehensible, upon which he would later build for the *Dubliners* collection, which in 1904 Joyce first conceived of as a series of ten pieces that he called "epicleti." As the volume grew in size Joyce announced his intended style as that of "scrupulous meanness," and although the stories retained their apparent aspect of simplicity, they were far from random selections of Dublin life, especially since Joyce advertised them to prospective publishers as a "moral chapter of the history" of Ireland, citing the city of Dublin as the "centre of paralysis."

Joyce's focus in *Dubliners* is almost exclusively on the middle-class Catholics known to himself and his family. Within the confines of that major element of the social structure of the city, however, he managed to determine numerous variations and combinations: among the Dublin Catholic bourgeoisie an occasional former Protestant can be seen backsliding in "Grace," and an acknowledged Protestant is present at the Christmastime festivities among his Catholic neighbors in "The Dead." "Grace" even alludes to a Dublin Jew, one of that very small community in the city at that time, which Joyce would explore further in *Ulysses*. As for the economic level of these middle-class citizens, Joyce's range is extensive: shop girl, law-office clerk, bank employee, the scion of a wealthy butcher, and the shiftless son of a police official, as well as those living on more meager incomes. The occasional workman is glimpsed in "Two Gallants," and the suggestion of wealth is apparent in "After the Race," but essentially *Dubliners* presents the common denominations of the petty bourgeoisie.

The first three stories, "The Sisters," "An Encounter," and "Araby," are not only concerned with childhood but each is also narrated through the first-person perspective of a young boy, either the same protagonist in the progression of three stories or a separate protagonist in each. Anonymous, of no specific age, and ostensibly parentless (he lives with an aunt and uncle in "The Sisters" and "Araby"), he undergoes a series of somewhat traumatic experiences, well within the framework of ordinary childhood occurrences: the death of a priest who had served as his mentor, a run-in with a menacing stranger when out on a day's truancy from school, and disappointment during a period of immature love when he arrives late at a church bazaar, where he had hoped to buy a gift for a girl. In each case the effect on the boy is measured by his own narrative, the immediacy recorded by the limited perception of an intelligent but nonetheless inexperienced and susceptible consciousness. As his

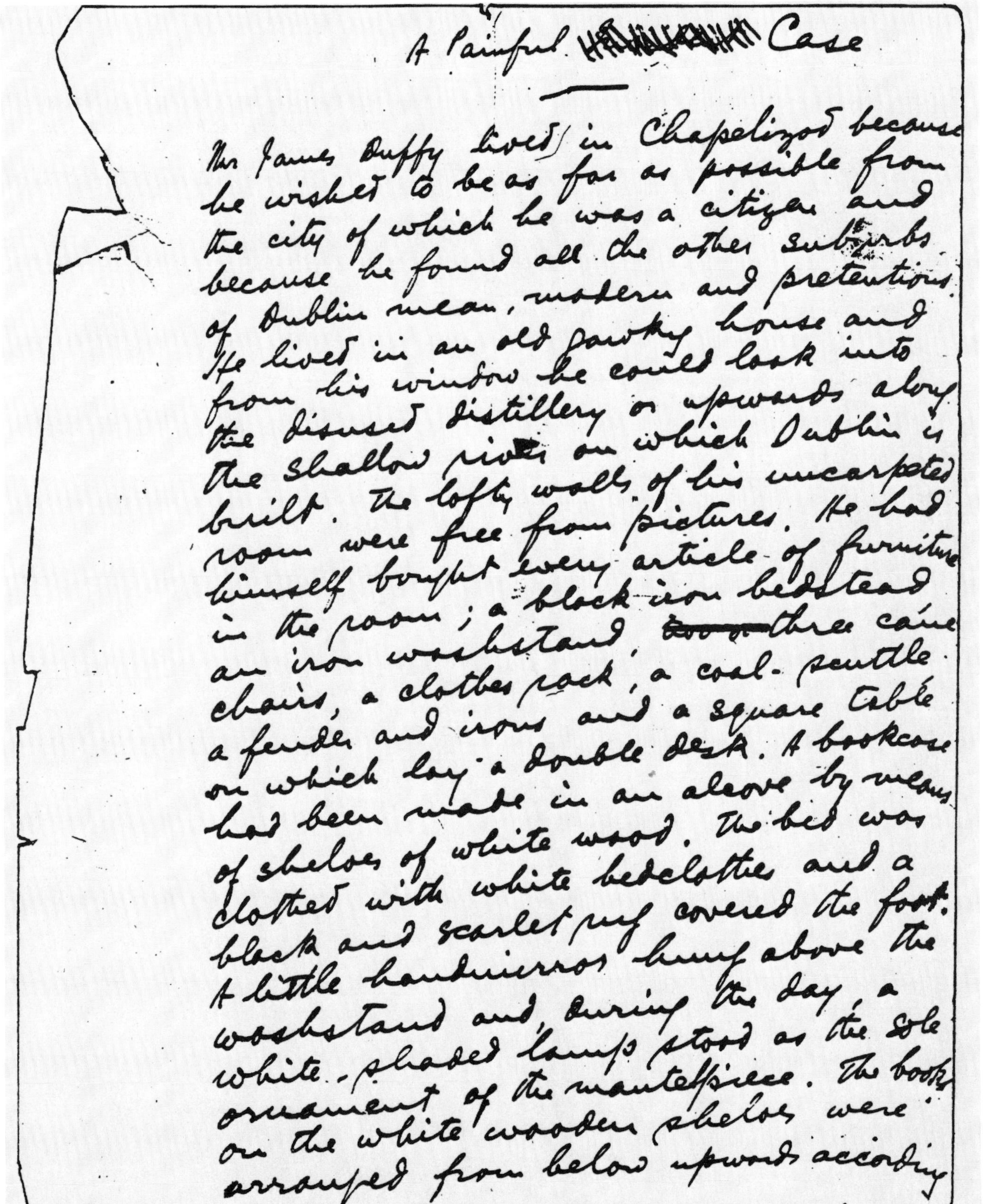

A Painful ~~HHHHHHHH~~ Case

Mr James Duffy lived in Chapelizod because
he wished to be as far as possible from
the city of which he was a citizen and
because he found all the other suburbs
of Dublin mean, modern and pretentious
He lived in an old gawky house and
from his window he could look into
the disused distillery or upwards along
the shallow river on which Dublin is
built. The lofty walls of his uncarpeted
room were free from pictures. He had
himself bought every article of furniture
in the room; a black iron bedstead
an iron washstand, ~~too~~ three cane
chairs, a clothes rack, a coal-scuttle
a fender and irons and a square table
on which lay a double desk. A bookcase
had been made in an alcove by means
of shelves of white wood. The bed was
clothed with white bedclothes and a
black and scarlet rug covered the foot.
A little handmirror hung above the
washstand and, during the day, a
white-shaded lamp stood as the sole
ornament of the mantelpiece. The books
on the white wooden shelves were
arranged from below upwards according

First page from a draft for one of the stories in Dubliners *(The James Joyce Archive)*

83

aunt gossips with the priest's sisters at the side of the coffin, the boy is expected to register betrayal and bewilderment about the cleric's presumed madness, but the method of narration only allows for the recording of the actual conversation without any registering of the boy's reactions. When encountering the pederast the boy attempts several childish ploys for his own protection against something he cannot really comprehend, but finds himself envious of his companion, a boy he considers his inferior, who nonetheless proves impervious to the danger. And when, in "Araby," he nurtures his pure and sacred affection for a slightly older girl, envisioning himself as a chivalric knight carrying his chalice through a corrupt world, the sordidly ordinary bazaar defeats him, and he views himself as "a creature driven and derided by vanity." His awareness and articulative powers increase as he moves through these events.

From the fourth story on, the method of narration in *Dubliners* changes to the impersonal third person as the focus changes from childhood to the adult world, a loss of the honest immediacy of the immature perceiver and a shift to the calculated responses of the adult, but fused through an "objective" reproduction of events. "Eveline," "After the Race," "Two Gallants," and "The Boarding House," however, deal with the inexperience of what Joyce called adolescence, the ages of the four protagonists ranging from nineteen to the early thirties. They are each trapped in the paralytic condition of the lives that they have fashioned around them, despite the numerous differences in their individual situations. Eveline Hill is already on the eve of her departure from Dublin with a sailor-lover who is presumably taking her to Argentina, yet her eagerness to leave her tyrannical father and depressing job fails to take account of the strength of her obligation to her dead mother to care for the young children of the family; and at the gate to the ship Eveline finds herself physically unable to take the important step to personal freedom. Her impoverished circumstances and her poverty of spirit contrast sharply with the wealth and élan of Jimmy Doyle, who in "After the Race" is involved in the exciting world of foreign auto racers, sophisticated drinkers and gamblers, quite unaware how much he is out of his element until the all-night carousal ends in his having lost a substantial sum of money, probably most of his patrimony. Few of Joyce's Dubliners begin with so great a financial advantage, and few fall from such exalted financial heights: in "Two Gallants" Lenehan and Corley are unemployed loungers, although Corley's father is a police in-

spector, and Corley's mysterious assignation with a servant girl leaves Lenehan wandering aimlessly and dejectedly through Dublin, until his friend's return with the profits from his adventure, a half-sovereign stolen by the slavey that will provide the gallants with drinking money. Their desultory lives are set against the seriousness of Bob Doran, gainfully employed and residing in a boardinghouse, where he has been seduced by the proprietor's daughter, is facing the distasteful prospect of marrying her against his will and better judgment, and is terrified lest he lose his job because of scandal.

The mature protagonists of the next quartet of narratives, "A Little Cloud," "Counterparts," "Clay," and "A Painful Case," extend the possibilities potential in the lives of the previous four, but with no further positive development. Thomas Chandler of "A Little Cloud" is basically the same age as Lenehan and Bob Doran, and apparently as securely employed as Doran, but he is already married and the father of an infant son. He dreams of being a poet and expanding his horizon, and on this particular evening he has drinks with an old acquaintance, a raffish journalist now on the London press. But Chandler's sensibilities are disquieted by Gallaher's coarse bragging, and he retreats home to read Byron, only to be defeated by his child's wailing and his wife's anger. His counterpart is a clerk named Farrington, a family man apparently unsuited to his sedentary job, who runs afoul of his employer because of his indolence and insolence. Pawning his watch for a night's carousal, Farrington is bested at hand wrestling by an English artiste and runs through his money, failing to get sufficiently drunk. Frustrated and resentful, he takes out his aggression on his son, after he arrives home to find that the kitchen fire has been allowed to go out. These two married men then are succeeded by two unmarried protagonists: in "Clay" Maria leaves the laundry where she is employed for a Hallow Eve visit to the family of Joe Donnelly, for whom she served as a surrogate mother years ago. Her innocence and simpleminded naiveté prevent her from sensing the hollowness and pathos of her empty life, as she is tricked by the neighbor's children into choosing the symbol of death in a game of divination. Her precarious existence is contrasted with the solid security of James Duffy in "A Painful Case," a bachelor who has insulated himself from all unpleasant contacts with other people by living alone and dependent only on his own resources. A casual friendship with a married woman, however, had almost disturbed that stability, and he had abruptly terminated it before emotional involvement set in.

Now he finds in a newspaper item that she has drunkenly been killed or killed herself, and the horror of her death becomes increasingly more obvious to him—along with the emptiness of his own life.

The shift to public life in the fuller narratives "Ivy Day in the Committee Room," "A Mother," and "Grace" expands the focus beyond concentration on a single protagonist, but in actuality a central character persists as dominant in at least the last two of the triad. More important, "Dubliners" in general prove to be communal protagonists, especially in "Ivy Day in the Committee Room," where a handful of political canvassers stroll into their headquarters on a cold rainy day, discussing the politics of the day, as well as of the past when Charles Stewart Parnell was their party leader and "uncrowned king" of Ireland—although the eleven years since his death have devastated their loyalties and enthusiasms. The ghost of Parnell hovers over the committee room, and all of the petty politicos present are viewed in relation to the dead leader. In "A Mother" music replaces politics as another public concern in Dublin, but disappointing attendance at a concert series necessitates cutting expenses by the officiating committee, which then attempts to renege on payment to the accompanist, a young woman whose career is being orchestrated by her mother. The ensuing tensions and flare-up result in Mrs. Kearney's whisking her daughter Kathleen out of the auditorium in mid-concert, seriously jeopardizing her musical future in Dublin. The degraded state of Irish politics and the depleted enthusiasm for culture in Dublin are then reflected in the condition of Irish Catholicism in "Grace," a tale of presumed spiritual redemption. When Tom Kernan, a backsliding Protestant who has married into the Catholic faith, drunkenly falls in a pub lavatory and bites off a tiny bit of his tongue, his Good-Samaritan Catholic friends quietly lure him into attending a retreat for worldly businessmen, at which a Jesuit preacher sets up a double-entry bookkeeping system for virtues and sins. This variant of simony is the most potent in *Dubliners,* where the selling of that which is sacred is an important theme, beginning with the desire of the paralytic Father Flynn in "The Sisters" to school the young boy for the priesthood in which he himself was disappointed. The boy, fascinated by portentous words, professes an interest in "paralysis," "gnomon," and "simony," words that have their thematic reverberations throughout the ensuing stories.

The placing of "The Dead" at the end of this progression of balanced stories is somewhat

anomalous in that it is a novella far longer than any of the other tales, and presumably outside the sequence. Joyce confessed, when the preexisting fourteen stories constituted the complete volume, that he found his stories rather harsh and that they failed to include the Irish talent for hospitality. "The Dead" is a Christmas story at which family and friends of the two spinster sisters, Julia and Kate Morkan, gather for music, dancing, feasting, and drinking. The "sudden spiritual manifestation" of an epiphany may have a literal understructure in "The Dead," since the festive soirée apparently takes place several days after the new year, probably on the Day of the Epiphany, and the protagonist, the old women's nephew Gabriel Conroy, is the logical recipient of that manifestation. A teacher and critic of literature, he considers himself intellectually superior to the other guests, as he prepares his after-dinner speech, and, as the husband of the "country-cute" Gretta, he fancies himself still an ardent lover after ten years of marriage. The conversation throughout is often about the past and the dead, of forgotten singers and monks sleeping in their coffins, and toward the end of the evening Gretta nostalgically succumbs to the singing of a ballad that reminds her of a young boy who many years before had loved her and died. As the Conroys settle into their hotel room for the night, Gretta confesses to her husband for the first time that Michael Furey had died "for her," a passion obviously far greater than any the stolidly bourgeois Gabriel has himself ever acknowledged. Gretta falls asleep while Gabriel broods quietly at the window, watching the snow fall and perhaps aware of his own limitations, his pomposity, and his comfortable complacency. At his aunts' he had had a slight unpleasantness with a young woman who was a fervent Irish nationalist and refused an invitation to take his holidays in the West of Ireland, despite Gretta's yearning to visit her native Galway. Now at the hotel window he muses over the snow falling on Michael Furey's grave, of the imminent death of his aged aunt, of snow falling on "all the living and the dead."

In the "style of scrupulous meanness" that Joyce adopted for *Dubliners* connectives, climaxes, and resolutions are often missing, attesting to the definition of *gnomon* in Euclidian geometry cited by the boy in "The Sisters": "the remainder of a parallelogram after the removal of a similar parallelogram containing one of its corners" (the word *gnomon* coming from the Greek for an interpreter, the pointer on a sundial). The stories in Joyce's collection are intended to be read by comprehending the substance from the shadow it casts or intimating the he had finished his recitation there was a silence and then a burst of clapping: even Mr Hynes clapped. The applause continued for a little time. When it had ceased all the auditors drank from their bottles in silence. Pok! the cork flew out of Mr Hynes's bottle but Mr Hynes remained sitting on the table as if he had not heard the invitation.

— Good man, Joe! said Mr O'Connor, taking out cigarette-papers and tobacco in order to conceal his emotion—

— What d'ye think of that, Crofton? said Mr Henchy. Isn't that fine — what?—

Mr Crofton said that it was a very fine piece of writing.

Jas A Joyce.
29 August 1905

Last page from the earlier of two fair-copy manuscripts for "Ivy Day in the Committee Room" (The James Joyce Archive) shadow from the substance. In the world of Joyce's Dubliners important plumcakes get left behind on trams, and corkscrews cannot be located; anticipated bazaars prove darkened and emptying; dust covers furniture although the room is dusted regularly; poets remain unread by would-be poets; and legal documents are not copied by clerks commissioned to copy them; political canvassers go unpaid, although the eventual appearance of a dozen bottles of stout soon makes them forget about the missing payment; musical accompanists go unpaid, although when half the promised four guineas is finally offered, even that payment is four shillings short, and the accompanist is removed by her mother with the concert only half over (Mrs. Kearney has brought her husband to help her negotiate the terms of her daughter's payment, but he proves ineffectual, almost as if he were not present). At a religious retreat the pews are filled with politicians and pawnbrokers and moneylenders, and chalices dropped by paralytic priests are reported to be empty. It is a world of absence and loss, smaller portions and smaller dividends, of interposing shadows and hollow substances, constricted by paralysis, shot through with simoniac practices, and gutted by gnomonic removals.

Joyce's scrupulously mean style also informed the new version of *Stephen Hero* when he began *A Portrait of the Artist as a Young Man* in 1907, practicing a style of stringent economy distinctly different from the rambling novel originally begun before leaving Dublin. *Stephen Hero* looked inward into a life, charting it meticulously and completely; and the title hero, Stephen Dedalus, was to be viewed by a literary process that moved from the first-person singular to the third person, subjective to objective. Joyce had worked simultaneously on the personal narrative of the artist himself and on the book of the "others," those Dubliners who gravitated in concentric circles around the consciousness of the artist. *Dubliners* and *A Portrait of the Artist as a Young Man* are best read as superimposed upon each other, as facing narratives of the two facets of the artist's consciousness of self and others. The boy in the opening triad of stories comes close to the Stephen of the opening chapters of the novel, sensitive and aware, observing without revealing his own thoughts. At the Christmas dinner that is the centerpiece of the first chapter, Stephen registers the impact of a disruptive political quarrel that stuns him into silence, much like his counterpart hearing the two sisters gossiping about the dead priest. A sensitivity to words also characterizes Stephen De-

dalus (Joyce for a while had considered demythologizing Daedalus to a common Daly but settled for dropping the digraph—he saved the Daly name for one of the aliases used by the Dedaluses in the last chapter when pawning their possessions), as at school he mulls over homonyms, onomatopoeia, nomenclature, and bilingual differences. The direction of the young Stephen toward the vocation of the literary artist determines the structure of *A Portrait of the Artist as a Young Man.* The selected portions of Stephen's life, from infancy to his departure from Ireland after his university education, contribute specifically to portraying the potentiality of the artist, and all other aspects of personal biography seem to have been stripped away.

Where *Stephen Hero* had the projected shape and girth of a nineteenth-century novel, *A Portrait of the Artist as a Young Man,* with jumps in chronology and tightly constructed vignettes, points toward the modernist narrative of the twentieth. The extant pages from the earlier version (published after Joyce's death) contain fully developed and elaborated incidents, some that Joyce later eliminated, some that he retained, others that he merely suggested in the succeeding novel. The economy Joyce practiced in his revision becomes all the more apparent in contrast to the remnants of *Stephen Hero*. As soon as he began the reconstitution of his material, Joyce envisioned a book in five long chapters, the first three of which he completed between October 1907 and early April 1908. The rhythmic rise and fall within each of the five parts controls the structuring of *A Portrait of the Artist,* as Stephen undergoes the traumatic instances of development and maturation between exploring the infant's world with the awakening of his five senses (the opening paragraphs of the text) and the suspended conclusion at which he prepares to embark for Paris. Chapter one concludes with schoolboy Stephen in triumph, lauded by his schoolmates for having bravely defied authority by having sought redress from the rector for being unfairly punished. Chapter two ends with the adolescent swooning in the arms of a prostitute for the first time, while chapter three ends with his return to piety, confessing his sins and being absolved. At the end of chapter four the potential artist undergoes an equally spiritual conversion, having encountered his muse and embraced his vocation, rejecting the possible vocation in the priesthood, and at the conclusion of chapter five he sets out for his new career and a new life, announcing, "I go to encounter for the millionth time the reality of experience and to

nations. They were held out to say:
We are alone — come: and the voices
said with them: We are your people:
and the air grew thick with their
company as they called to him their
kinsman, making ready to go,
shaking the wings of their exultant
and terrible youth.

Departure for Paris

From the Broadstone to Mullingar
is a journey of some fifty miles across
the midlands of Ireland. Mullingar, the
chief town of Westmeath, is the midland
capital and there is a great traffic of
peasants and cattle between it and
Dublin. This fifty-mile journey is made
by the train in about two hours and
you are therefore to conceive Stephen
Daedalus packed in the corner of a
third-class carriage and contributing
the thin fumes of his cigarettes to the
already reeking atmosphere. The carriage
was inhabited by a company of peasants,
nearly every one of whom had a bundle
tied in a spotted handkerchief. The
carriage smelt strongly of peasants
(an odour the debasing humanity of
which Stephen remembered to have

Page 447 from the manuscript for Stephen Hero. *This first surviving manuscript page, which predates* A Portrait of the Artist as a Young Man, *continues Stephen Dedalus's story from the point at which the later novel ends (The James Joyce Archive).*

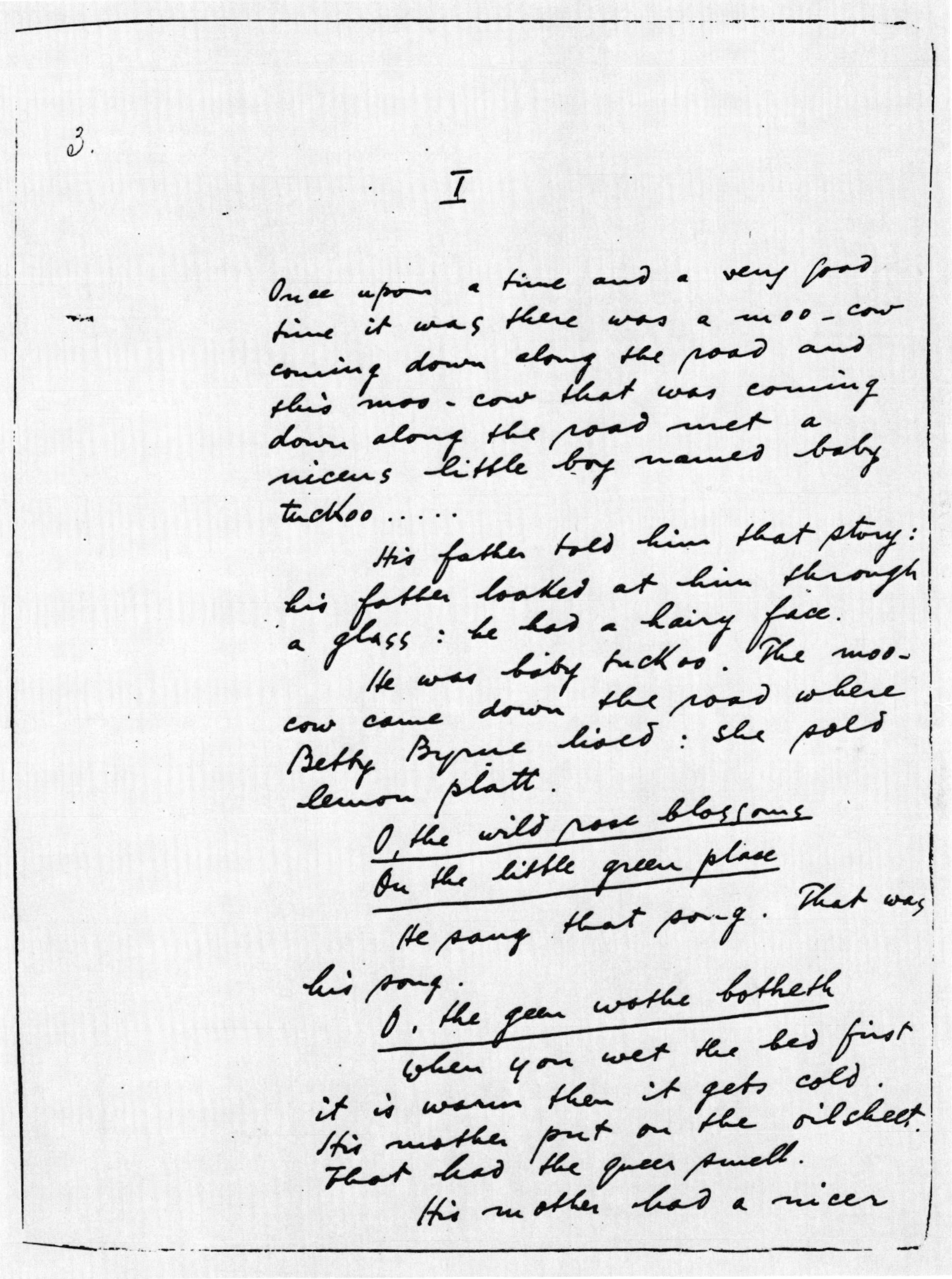

3.

I

Once upon a time and a very good time it was there was a moo-cow coming down along the road and this moo-cow that was coming down along the road met a nicens little boy named baby tuckoo . . . . . .

His father told him that story: his father looked at him through a glass: he had a hairy face.

He was baby tuckoo. The moo-cow came down the road where Betty Byrne lived: she sold lemon platt.

O, the wild rose blossoms
On the little green place

He sang that song. That was his song.

O, the geen wothe botheth

When you wet the bed first it is warm then it gets cold. His mother put on the oilsheet. That had the queer smell.

His mother had a nicer

First page of chapter one from the fair-copy manuscript for A Portrait of the Artist as a Young Man *(The James Joyce Archive)* forge in the smithy of my soul the uncreated conscience of my race."

The heightened curve of Stephen's emotions are inevitably countered by the realities of his youthful experiences, and each new chapter begins in sharp contrast to the exultations with which the previous one has been resolved. At the beginning of the second chapter Stephen is very much at loose ends: he has been withdrawn from the prestigious Jesuit boarding school because of the decline of his father's financial condition. As the third chapter opens, the ecstasy of sexual initiation has become a sordid commonplace, quickly developing into morbid guilt, and, although the spiritual cleansing evoked the ecstasy of virtue and grace, that new life at the start of the fourth chapter is already jejune, mechanical, and without spiritual enthusiasm. While the élan of his decision to become an artist is expected to carry through the entire last chapter, that section nonetheless begins in the most banal manner, as Stephen drags out his pathetic breakfast, his mother scrubbing his dirty neck, resentful that he chose the university in lieu of the seminary, and his father gratuitously cursing him. The aftermath of elation is invariably depression, and the triumph with which *A Portrait of the Artist* concludes is eventually undercut by the deflated opening of *Ulysses*.

The central focus of *A Portrait of the Artist* remains exclusively with Stephen throughout, and a narrative monologue tracks his perceptions and reactions, although at the early stages of his development those reactions that are traumatic are suspended, leaving meaningful gaps in the narrative process. An opening series of vignettes establishes the infant's perceiving his immediate world of parents and then other resident adults; his contained environment and then the road that runs outside his house; and eventually the child's contacts with neighboring elements, including the little girl who lives nearby. All five senses are employed in viewing his father's face, hearing his mother sing, differentiating her odor from that of his father, tasting candy, and experiencing the tactile sensations of wet, warm, cold. An infusion of literature (children's stories), music (songs), and dance leads to the child's own attempts to imitate and innovate; and when he is caught at a childish transgression, the voices of authority split between the palliative of apology and the insistence on punishment, so that Stephen creates from the dual demands a series of rhymed phrases in repetitive form. The extremely young artist begins to take shape almost immediately, and those factors that ultimately contribute to his potential as a literary artist provide the selective material for the mode of Joycean portraiture.

The threat that an eagle will "pull out" his eyes creates a web of leitmotivs that weave outward from the introductory node: at school the child with weak eyes fears the football that he views as a large and frightening bird, and, when he has his glasses accidentally broken and is unable to do his class work, the punishment meted out by the prefect of studies reinforces the threat of unjust authority: the instrument of punishment is a pandybat that one of the clerics refers to as a "turkey." A Christmas turkey, however, figures prominently at the dinner at home during the vacation from his Jesuit boarding school, longed-for respite that turns into an inexplicable trauma when political disagreement between members of the family and guests erupts into heated vituperation, and a blinding spit-in-the-eye accentuates the unpleasantness for Stephen. Just as his reaction to the threat of punishment goes unrecorded in the narrative elision, so now again he remains mute in the face of the painful dilemma. An awareness of a disrupted universe, however, stays with him, and even a ball of sweets can be pried into two halves. When he is unjustly pandied, Stephen undertakes to report the transgression to higher authority, a rash action that he would probably not have considered previously, especially since his father had once emphasized a gentlemanly code that legislated against such "peaching" on others. The split between religion and nationalist politics in post-Parnell Ireland mirrors the divided and decaying home life of the Dedaluses and will later accentuate conflicts between aesthetics and politics, between self and others, and various instances of divided loyalties. Stephen becomes progressively aware of claims made on him by his family, nation, religion, friends—all of which he eventually chooses to deny in an effort to forge for himself the role of an independent artist of lonely integrity.

The vague threats of eye-gouging eagles and pain-inflicting pandybats-dubbed-turkeys become specifically personified in a schoolmate named Heron during Stephen's adolescence at a Jesuit day school in Dublin. Stephen notes that Heron not only has a bird's name but that his face is like a bird's, and the association with previous "birds of prey" becomes apparent when Heron teases Stephen about the attentions of a young girl (Emma has replaced the Eileen of the childish transgression) and forces him to admit a relationship with her. By this time

Stephen has attained stature as a scholar and leader in his school, and he can parry the danger of the cane that Heron wields with a mocking replication of a religious confession; but the incident recalls a previous instance when Stephen was far more vulnerable, and Heron wielded a cabbage stump to force him to concede that Byron was immoral and consequently not worthy of poetic distinction. With Heron now more easily disarmed by Stephen's ironic tone and lofty demeanor, the image of the punishing bird is dispelled, and a new aspect of the heronlike bird appears to him in the form of a wading girl, whom he perceives as a crane, with dove-tailed skirts, arousing his erotic appreciation as well as his veneration of the madonna facets of her blue-and-white attire. His expression of joy is both sacred and profane, and the wading bird-girl assumes the balanced pose of the artist's muse for Stephen Dedalus, as he turns away from the possibility of a priestly vocation to that of the artist, "priest of eternal imagination."

The transition has not been an easy one for him, nor does the narrative give specific details of Stephen's changes of mind and heart: narrative progression moves from highlight to highlight, alighting at the moments of revelation and change, overpassing the transitional developments. Stephen's adolescent piety has brought him to the attention of the Jesuit director of studies, with whom Stephen has an audience regarding the intimations of an ecclesiastical vocation. Tempted by the image of himself as a Jesuit and the holder of vast powers as a priest, he is nonetheless put off by the communal living and the subservience of himself to a higher authority, as well as by the mundane matters of physical discomforts. The shrieking of a mad nun from a nearby asylum also filters into his consciousness, as does an image of the Virgin spread "fowlwise" on a pole in the nearby slums—bird imagery and the figure of the madonna combined—yet no actual process of thought invades the "objectified" narrative. The veneer of piety that had called his masters' attention to Stephen Dedalus had begun as an extreme reaction to his sexual guilt, but the pieties soon proved to be mechanical and superficial, and imperceptibly they faded into irrelevance. The Stephen Dedalus interviewed by the Jesuit director hovered between fixed points of direction, and the interview itself could have marked a point of departure. What the attentive youth may have observed with a high degree of concentration was the habit of the director in looping the curtain cord into a noose, as well as the shape

of his skull in the waning light outlined against the window as a death's head. A skull as a memento mori had graced the desk of the rector to whom Stephen as a child had appealed against the unfair pandying, and, although the rector had promised to honor Stephen's petition for redress, the boy later learned that the two priests laughed about the incident together; and the rector shared the joke with Stephen's father. Sensitive to betrayals of any sort, Stephen may well have superimposed the director's skull upon the rector's death's head and decided against joining the Society of Jesus. Whatever the subliminal process of decision-making operative within Stephen's consciousness, the narrative process reveals only the epiphanic moments.

Readers of *A Portrait of the Artist as a Young Man* have often been sensitive to a shift in narrative tone during the later portions of the book, despite the note of objectivity retained in the free indirect style of the narration. While Joyce had completed the first three chapters in 1908, at the age of twenty-six, it was not until 1914 that he was spurred into writing

A photo of Joyce taken in Zurich and inscribed to a pupil who had become a close friend

the two final chapters, after plans were made to serialize the novel in the London magazine, the *Egoist*. The extended distance of the author from his quasi-biographic protagonist in 1914 may account for elements of ironic treatment of the haughty university student present in the last chapter, or Joyce may quite consciously have planned the development of the treatment of Stephen to work outward from the "protected" handling of the delicate and sensitive child into the more objective dealing with a young adult capable of maintaining his own position. The Stephen tormented by the visions of damnation conjured up by his Jesuit mentors, resulting in nightmarish fits of vomiting and a desperate search for absolution, is indeed a sympathetic figure demanding the reader's compassion, yet even as he seeks salvation Stephen Dedalus goes far out of his way to find a chapel where he is not known. And the reader is at other times reminded that the sharpened focus on Stephen's egocentric concerns has on occasion been momentarily extended to reveal that although he was twice unfairly pandied, he also admits to having escaped various justifiable punishments, and that, although he defended his choice of Byron as the best poet, he had previously attempted to avoid confrontation with the safe choice of Cardinal Newman as the best writer of prose. Joyce's irony weaves its way through even the earlier sections of the novel, expanding considerably, however, in the last chapter.

The elaborate concluding chapter of *A Portrait of the Artist* concentrates on the closing months of Stephen's career at University College, and, as an extended narrative, it parallels the position of "The Dead" as the culminating novella of *Dubliners*. Stephen's gentlemanly father has been changed into a disgruntled tyrant, and his loving mother to a discontented woman, while a houseful of younger siblings share the poverty and squalor to which the Dedaluses have been reduced. The priests and schoolmates of the boarding school in the first chapter had given way to the priests and schoolmates of the day school in the middle chapters, and all of these have now been replaced by a completely new set of teachers and students at the university. Stephen Dedalus moves through the text as the single figure of concentration, all others existing temporarily only in relation to him. As he had his interviews with the rector and the director of studies at the previous schools, here he has an almost inadvertent conference with the dean of studies, but now as a self-sustained intellectual who politely masks his disdain for the lesser intellect of the En-

glish priest. His companions, among the various students who range from misguided idealists to prospective job seekers, are four in particular who in their own ways seek to enlist Stephen in their causes or influence his attitudes and opinions. Within the political arena one of them argues the case for Irish nationalism, but Stephen dismisses the cause as the limited one of priests and peasants; another argues for international socialism and world peace, but Stephen refuses to sign manifestos of any kind and allows himself to be considered antisocial. On a more subjective scale the friend to whom Stephen explains his aesthetic theories based on Aristotle and Aquinas instead holds out for the prospects of an eventual job and full belly, while the friend to whom he reveals his personal aspirations and fears suggests to Stephen a course of expedient hypocrisy and compromise. Stephen consequently announces his arrogantly individualist creed of "silence, exile, and cunning," insisting on flying by all nets flung at his soul and refusing, like Lucifer, to serve any communal creed or established authority. His image of himself is now that of a "hawklike man," an aloof bird of freedom, loneliness, and insecurity.

The emergence of Icarus (allied to Lucifer the fallen angel) as Stephen's symbolic totem echoes the use of an epigraph from Ovid's *Metamorphoses* for *A Portrait of the Artist* (*Et ignotas animum dimittit in artes*—"And he gave up his mind to obscure arts"), a reference to the myth of Daedalus and Icarus's metamorphosis into birdlike creatures escaping the confinement in Crete. The builder of the labyrinth stands for Stephen as a figure of the creative genius and a symbolic father to whom he makes his final appeal as he is about to leave Ireland and embark on his new life and new career. The closing portion of chapter five discards third-person narration to concentrate on Stephen's diary entries, a shift to first-person perspective in the ironic literary language of the involved protagonist, telegraphic, conversational, anecdotal, caustic, and in the end exaltational, yet on several occasions also compassionate, self-critical, and even self-lacerating. Stephen's own aesthetic theories had concentrated on the development from the subjective to the objective, from the lyrical mode to the epic to the dramatic mode; yet *A Portrait of the Artist* as a narrative text reverses the theoretical proposition in order to heighten the lyrical subjectivity of Stephen's voice, undercutting his theoretical base.

That Stephen Dedalus remains at stage center of the first three chapters of *Ulysses* increases the renewed emphasis on the lyrical mode and projects

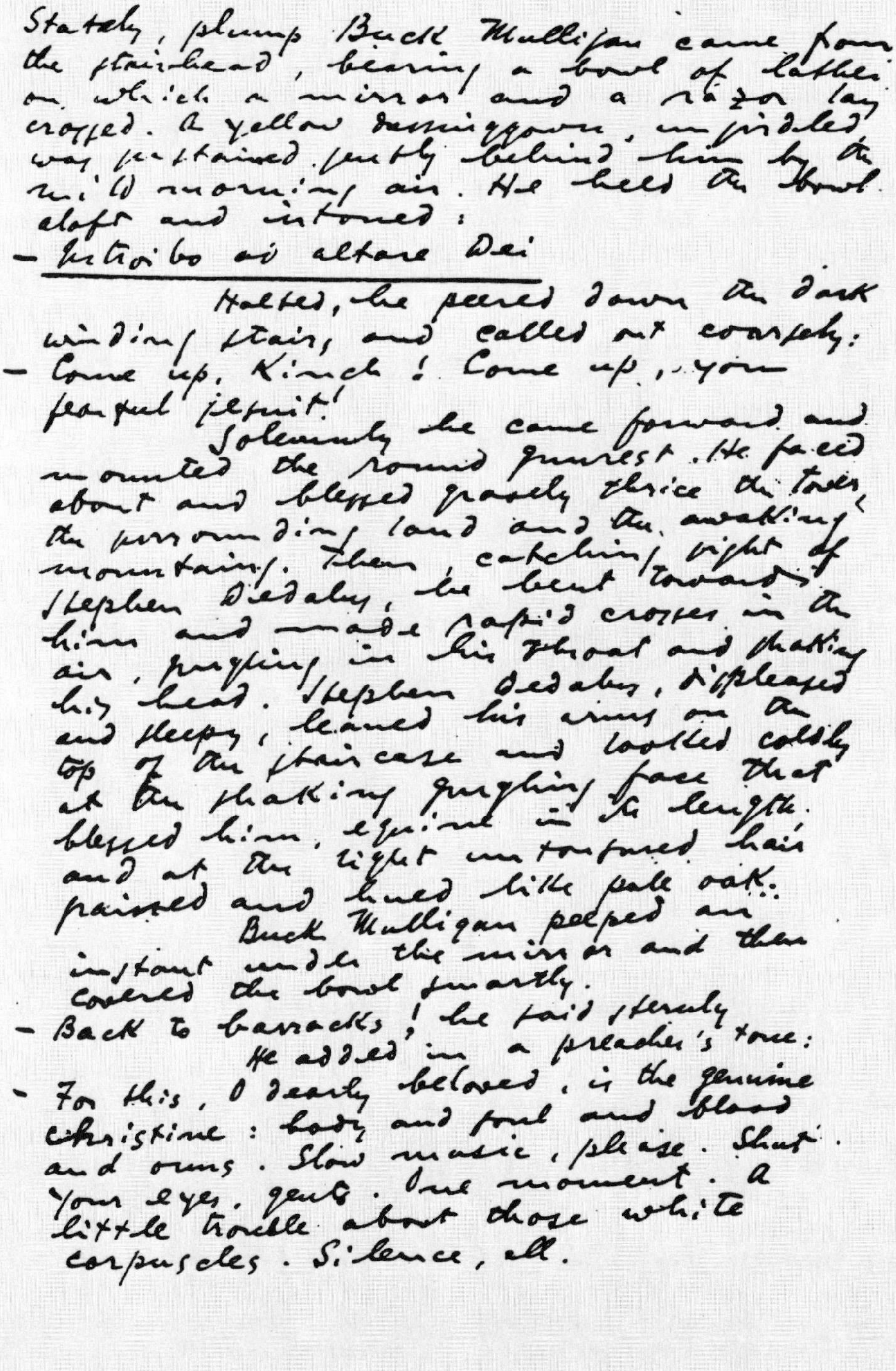

Stately, plump Buck Mulligan came from the stairhead, bearing a bowl of lather on which a mirror and a razor lay crossed. A yellow dressinggown, ungirdled was sustained gently behind him by the mild morning air. He held the bowl aloft and intoned:

— Introibo ad altare Dei

Halted, he peered down the dark winding stairs, and called out coarsely:

— Come up, Kinch! Come up, you fearful jesuit!

Solemnly he came forward and mounted the round gunrest. He faced about and blessed gravely thrice the tower, the surrounding land and the awaking mountains. Then, catching sight of Stephen Dedalus, he bent toward him and made rapid crosses in the air, gurgling in his throat and shaking his head. Stephen Dedalus, displeased and sleepy, leaned his arms on the top of the staircase and looked coldly at the shaking gurgling face that blessed him, equine in its length, and at the light untonsured hair, grained and hued like pale oak.

Buck Mulligan peeped an instant under the mirror and then covered the bowl smartly.

— Back to barracks! he said sternly.

He added in a preacher's tone:

— For this, O dearly beloved, is the genuine christine: body and soul and blood and ouns. Slow music, please. Shut your eyes, gents. One moment. A little trouble about those white corpuscles. Silence, all.

First page from the John Quinn manuscript for Ulysses *(Anderson Galleries, sale 1794, 14-16 January 1924)* an extension of the young artist, two years after his abortive flight from Ireland. Nonetheless, Joyce's first conception of the "Ulysses" story as a part of *Dubliners* attests to its position as a book about the extended world outside the artist-hero, and the shift to the Leopold Bloom protagonist in the fourth chapter of *Ulysses* signals the return to the larger universe, setting up the arena of interaction between the isolated artist and the mundane world. For James Joyce the year 1914 was the beginning of his success as a writer, with the publication of *Dubliners* and the completion of *A Portrait of the Artist as a Young Man* (already being serialized), as well as his beginning of work on *Ulysses.* Ironically, 1914 was also the year the lights went out in Europe with the beginning of World War I and the beginning of Joyce's precarious position as a British subject in the Italian city of Trieste under Austro-Hungarian rule.

For Joyce the transition into *Ulysses* went smoothly as he forged an amalgam between the world of *Dubliners* and the extended persona of Stephen Dedalus, and he needed one or two structural devices for the development of the new fiction. By this time, however, he envisioned a far more complex format in which to capture the modern world, and he compounded numerous structural devices for *Ulysses,* the most basic being the consolidation of his materials into a single day in the city of Dublin and its environs (Thursday, 16 June 1904), a day that had been facilely tagged "the dailiest day possible." The most elaborate structure was his use of Homer's *Odyssey* as an underlying grid for the depiction of a quite nonheroic day in an equally nonheroic world, with an "Odysseus" figure who was apparently very much an ordinary citizen. Despite the presence of Stephen Dedalus once again, it is Leopold Bloom—and his memorable wife, Molly—at the center of the Odyssean epic of Joyce's contemporary world. Joyce's use of formal structures, systematized in the schema that he prepared for his biographer and for analysts of the book, was nonetheless undercut by his imaginative virtuosity as a writer. Although Dublin is the focal center of the novel, four of the chapters (including the first three) take place outside the city, and the time frame is equally inexact: the morning hours with which *Ulysses* begins are duplicated for each of the two male protagonists, and only after noon does time flow chronologically and unduplicated, although with certain gaps, until the novel ends in the small hours of the next morning. The flow of time, like the firm situation in space, is subject to variations, disruptions, and faulty transitions, almost a

human variable introduced to dislocate the fixed patterns that control the tightly organized elements of the text. Human fallibility is invariably operative in Joyce's epic, which is also a mock-epic, but nonetheless epical.

The relationship between Joyce's *Ulysses* and Homer's *Odyssey* is signaled primarily by the book's title, and even that allows for a certain distancing—the use of the Roman name for the hero suggests a "translation" in language, culture, and geography from the original. Joyce reduced Homer's twenty-four books to eighteen chapters, and one of these focuses on an event that Homer's hero has specifically avoided, passage through the unpredictable "wandering rocks." The patterning of a three-part text follows the Homeric mold: the three opening chapters dealing exclusively with Stephen comprise the Telemachia; the central twelve chapters focusing primarily on Bloom but bringing Stephen into an eventual relationship to him form the Odyssey proper; and the last three chapters, which return Bloom home with Stephen in tow, parallel the Nostos. Joyce had originally designated a Homeric title for each of the eighteen chapters (and these were in actual use in 1918-1920, when *Ulysses* was being serialized in the *Little Review*), but they were deleted for the book, like scaffolding kicked away. Nonetheless, the titles are still employed as a critical convenience: Telemachus, Nestor, and Proteus (The Telemachia); Calypso, Lotus Eaters, Hades, Aeolus, Lestrygonians, Scylla and Charybdis, Wandering Rocks, Sirens, Cyclops, Nausicaa, Oxen of the Sun, and Circe (The Odyssey); Eumaeus, Ithaca, and Penelope (The Nostos). The centrality of Homer's text to that of Joyce's *Ulysses* has been strongly emphasized by some critics, the parody of a heroic epic in a novel of the mundane world by others, and the mere casualness of associations by still others. Odysseus's descent into the underworld allows (in the Hades chapter) for a funeral cortege through Dublin to bury an insignificant citizen in the Catholic cemetery, and numerous colloquialisms and clichés regarding death abound in the narrative. As Bloom hungrily wends his way toward lunch in the Lestrygonians chapter, hundreds of words suggesting food crop up in the oddest ways, his mind unable to ignore his stomach; the cannibalism of Homer's Lestrygonians is replicated in an unsanitary eatery, where Bloom looks in and retreats in revulsion. The Circe chapter introduces a brothel mistress who figuratively turns men into swine, and the Penelope chapter contains the night thoughts of Molly Bloom, whose unfaithfulness with her new lover on this day distinguishes

Sylvia Beach and James Joyce at Shakespeare and Company (Sylvia Beach Collection, Princeton University Library)

her from Odysseus's Penelope, although it may well prove to have been Molly's first infidelity ever. Parallel and parody, pastiche and travesty are all aspects of Joyce's handling of the Homeric materials in *Ulysses*.

Ulysses is at once a comic and a cosmic novel, and the *Odyssey* is not the only parallel text that tracks the life of Stephen Dedalus, the Blooms, and the other Dublin citizens. Leopold Bloom has his analogues in Moses, Christ, Elijah, the Wandering Jew, Sinbad the Sailor, as well as Odysseus, while Stephen is recognizable at times as playing the roles of Hamlet, Icarus, Lucifer, Siegfried, the Prodigal Son, as well as Telemachus (late in the book Stephen and Bloom will look into the same mirror and see the magical reflection of William Shakespeare). Molly is the Virgin Mary, the Daughter of the Regiment, Gea-Tellus the Earth Mother, and the Wife of Bath. Most of these associations are subtle and even tenuous, and in many ways the three principal characters in the novel are some of the most realistically drawn figures in literary fiction. *Ulysses* has its

primary existence on the literal—even the naturalistic—level, and the complex allusive system, and various other structural and stylistic innovations which distinguish the book as a revolutionary and modernistic work, are firmly established on that basic plot level. Although the modernist movement perfected the nearly plotless novel, *Ulysses* retains its fully proportioned (although antiheroic) story line. Glimpses into Stephen's thoughts and snatches of conversation throughout the novel recover the events between his having left for Paris to study medicine and his presence in Ireland, temporarily resident in a coastal tower which he shares with its renter, Malachi (Buck) Mulligan, and teaching in a genteel boy's school further down the coast. He has been called back because of his mother's illness and he has watched her die. The supposition that he refused her request that he pray at her bedside contributes to his guilt and the presence of his mother's "ghost" in his conscience. Moody and disgruntled, he plans to abandon his tenure at the tower and his friendship with Mulligan, and he finds himself almost as displeased with his ineffectual position as a teacher. Since it is Thursday, a half-day at the school, he wends his way into Dublin, where he tries to avoid Mulligan and their English guest, and, although he still considers himself a potential poet, he spends most of the day talking and drinking. His drunkenness results in a horrible vision of his dead mother that he exorcises by smashing a lamp in a brothel and in being knocked down by a British soldier in the streets of the red-light district. A worried and solicitous Bloom rescues Stephen and takes him home with him, but after a convivial talk and cup of cocoa Stephen refuses the offer of a night's lodgings, going off into the early morning homeless, friendless, and (by choice) jobless, once again on the verge of a new departure, still the proponent of silence, exile, and cunning.

The Leopold Bloom whose arc crosses Stephen's path on this day is a thirty-eight-year-old advertising canvasser, whose job allows him to voyage through the streets of Dublin most of the day, but who also assumes that he must keep away from home most of the afternoon and evening as well because of his wife's assignation with her concert manager, which he assumes is a lovers' tryst as well. The inevitability of Molly's infidelity intrudes on his thoughts, minimally in the morning as he prepares for attending the funeral, but more potently in the afternoon as he pursues an advertising agreement and seeks the comforts of lunch and an early dinner. At three instances during these wanderings his path crosses that of Stephen Dedalus (with whose father he shares a carriage in the funeral cortege), and on three occasions it crosses that of Blazes Boylan, Molly's prospective lover, whom he assiduously avoids until he sees him entering a pub at the exact time of the assignation with Molly. Fascinated by Boylan's being in the wrong place, Bloom spies upon him from the adjoining dining room and watches him depart for a late arrival at the Bloom residence. Mild-mannered and pacifistic Bloom has little connection with the Jewish heritage that his father had renounced before his birth (born Protestant, Bloom converted to Catholicism to marry Molly, but remains essentially agnostic), yet when confronted by virulent anti-Semitism later in the afternoon, Leopold Bloom vociferously stands his ground and denounces intolerance and hatred against a hostile pub group who have convinced themselves that Bloom (hardly ever a betting man) has won handsomely on a dark horse and still refuses to stand rounds of drinks.

Bloom's evening is spent as a good Samaritan

straightening out an insurance muddle for the widow of the recently buried man and inquiring at the maternity hospital about a woman who had been in labor for three days. In the hospital refectory he encounters a drinking party of medical students, among them the seriously drunk Stephen, whom he solicitously follows into the brothel district. When the revived Stephen leaves Bloom's house hours later, Leopold Bloom prepares for bed, surveying the damage to his life made by the intrusion of Boylan, but also the death in infancy of his son almost eleven years ago, the suicide of his father years before, and even the departure of his fifteen-year-old daughter, Milly, for an apprenticeship at a photographer's. The death of the boy has been haunting Bloom's thoughts, and the circumstances of his having been born deformed have convinced Bloom that he was responsible for that deformity. Consequently he avoided allowing Molly to conceive another child, as much as he has longed for a son and heir; and the sexual life of the Blooms has been erratic and insubstantial (Bloom has practiced interrupted coitus, apparently without Molly's comprehending his reasons). Aware of her dissatisfaction with their sexual cohabitation, Bloom has systematically arranged for Molly to meet Boylan and has sent Milly off to her apprenticeship so that the house might be free for the adulterous liaison. The reader's awareness of this complex rationale for the surface behavior of Leopold and Molly Bloom depends on perceiving and connecting isolated bits of information and buried inferences during the progress of this "dailiest day possible," as well as reading literal events and suggestions of motivation through the dense stylistics that progressively develop throughout *Ulysses*.

From 1914 until its publication in book form in 1922, *Ulysses* underwent a series of changes, as did the Europe that experienced the prolonged war and its aftermath of revolution and uneasy peace, and the Joyce family, as it moved from Trieste to Zurich and back, until Joyce agreed to Ezra Pound's suggestion that to live in Paris would mean living at the center of the cultural maelstrom. Despite the emergence of such revolutionary movements as futurism and dada, and the publication of the early poetry of Eliot and Pound, nothing quite prepared the English-reading world for the appearance of *Ulysses*, which, with the publication the same year of Eliot's *The Waste Land*, marked 1922 as the peak year of high modernism. The publication history in itself was constantly eventful: serialization in the *Little Review* was stopped by court action in America; copies were burned on the docks in England; a

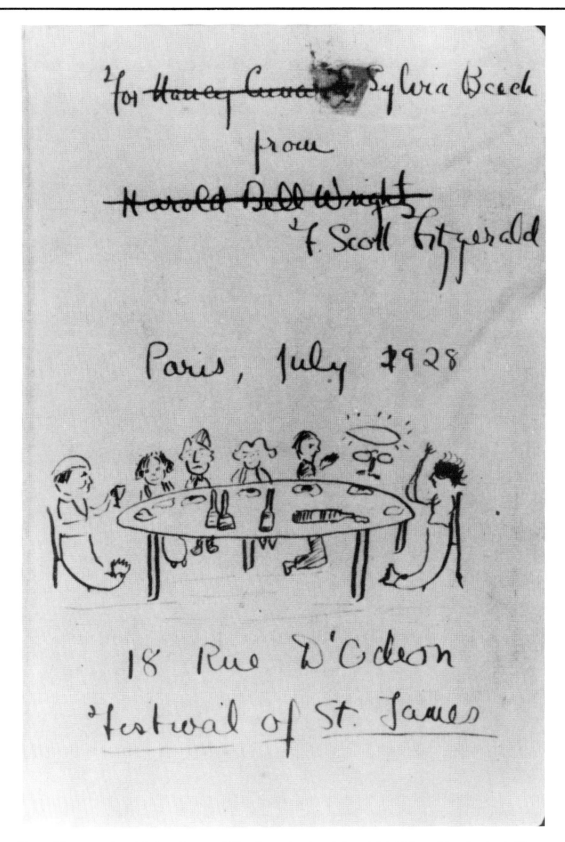

F. Scott Fitzgerald's cartoon in Sylvia Beach's copy of The Great Gatsby: *(left to right) Adrienne Monnier, Lucie Chamson, André Chamson, Zelda Fitzgerald, F. Scott Fitzgerald, James Joyce, and Sylvia Beach. The cartoon commemorates a dinner party that Beach gave to introduce Fitzgerald to Joyce (Sylvia Beach Collection, Princeton University Library).*

pirated serialization was protested by many of the world's intellectuals. It was not until a 1933 court decision declared that it was not obscene that *Ulysses* was published in the United States.

Salacious obscenity proved less of a hindrance thereafter than stylistic obscurity, although the first six chapters, despite Joyce's later revisions in the light of the later styles, still seem free from most of the difficulties of the succeeding chapters. The use of interior monologue intrudes almost immediately (actually with just a single word injected into one of the first paragraphs), and is easily assimilated into the narration and dialogue to form a triangularization of action, speech, and thought that remains relatively consistent for the first six chapters (what Joyce oversimplified in a letter to his patroness as "the initial style"), the first three chapters focusing exclusively on Stephen, the next three on Bloom. With the Aeolus chapter major changes become apparent as a series of sixty-three newspaper captions are intercalated into text, as befits the environment of a newspaper office, and the reader senses that the mechanical movement of the presses, inserting and withdrawing, complements the windy slamming of doors and the windy rhetoric of the hangers-on in the editorial offices. Stephen and Bloom share the arena, not only with each other but also with a larger segment of the general public, and, as the chapter opens with the approach and arrival of Bloom, it ends with the departure from the offices of Stephen, leading several others along with him as he narrates a recently conceived "parable." Organic structuring devices develop in every chapter on an individually conceived basis, a series of eighteen interlocked but discrete entities.

The two chapters that follow the Aeolus chapter seem to return to an established norm, the first concentrating wholly on Bloom, and the second on Stephen with Bloom intruding occasionally. Yet the Lestrygonians chapter allows for a few moments—as had the Hades chapter—for various Dubliners to gossip a bit about Bloom while he is out of earshot, the compilation of fragments of external data about him and Molly accumulating in the process of the narrative. The Scylla and Charybdis chapter, located in the National Library director's office, again features Stephen as public performer, holding forth on his theories about Shakespeare, with sudden stylistic changes deriving from the Shakespearean atmosphere: narrational prose broken into drama dialogue, stage directions, dramatis personae, as well as elided words and names moving to Elizabethan rhythms and dance steps. A dramatic

tension develops between Stephen's monologue and his private thoughts while extemporizing. Audience intrusions create still another area of tension, in a scene in which the Dublin intelligentsia of Joyce's day are physically present in the fictional resetting. More real people are mentioned in the library chapter than in any other in *Ulysses,* a dominance of the historical world over the fictional one but subsumed within the fiction that Stephen weaves around the life of William Shakespeare.

The remaining daylight chapters increase the degree of innovative changes and emphasize the individuated stylistic natures of each new segment. As the "central" divider of the chapters, the Wandering Rocks chapter calls attention to itself not only because it is segmented into nineteen separate units, each with its own cast of characters, but because both Stephen and Bloom are minor elements in a street scene featuring a cross section of Dublin humanity, four of whom are allowed the distinction of an individual monologue—a privilege hitherto enjoyed only by the two major figures. The distortions of the next chapter, however, are far more severe, as the Sirens determine the musicality of its language, even to the extent that broken bits of words and phrases introduce the chapter as incoherent sounds, later given coherence when found within their formulated contexts. Although compounded sound waves seem to warp the consistency of the narrative, a semblance of objective narration is sustained throughout the Sirens chapter, consistent with the rest of the text; but in Cyclops narrative responsibility is taken over by an anonymous character with a low-Dublin accent and a nasty tongue, speaking in the first person and focusing the perspective virulently against Bloom. Yet he in turns is interrupted at twenty-two instances in which outrageous parodies intrude as commentaries on the action, each taken from a literary form of sorts, including journalistic, folkloristic, legalistic, epical, and biblical. After a gap of several hours, as twilight falls, the Nausicaa chapter adds to the dislocation of narrative stance: a saccharine feminine voice deriving from Victorian women's magazines takes command in telling the story of the girls on the beach and the intrusive male presence, but it fades out with the exit of the women; and the familiar mode of Bloom's internal monologue returns after a long absence. In the ensuing darkness his thoughts become somber and somnolent, highly introspective and moody, paralleling those of Stephen Dedalus alone in the same area in the Proteus chapter.

The night world of *Ulysses* intensifies the

stylistic aberrations as each new chapter creates a world of its own. The random intrusions of parodic giganticism in the Cyclops chapter anticipate the systemized form of literary pastiche in the Oxen of the Sun chapter, with stylistic changes every paragraph or so, tracking the nine-hundred years of English prose styles, so that the fabricated voices of writers as diverse as Mandeville and Malory, Bunyan and Swift, Lamb and Pater, succeed each other in affecting the mode of narration. The density of styles mirrors the degrees of drunkenness in the hospital commons room, until the horde of medicals pours out of the building and into the nearest pub, and is characterized in the closing moments of the scene by the disintegration of language into vulgar colloquialisms and distorted dialects. The loss of a consistent narrative voice becomes complete in the Circe chapter where everything is presented totally in dramatic form as a distended psychodrama, dredging up ghostly figures from the past, projecting hypothetical characters and even inanimate objects, recapitulating the previous events in the lives of the protagonists through appearances and disappearances, entrances and exits, as hundreds of apparitions strut the hallucinatory stage. And just as the dramatic mode fixes the narrative locus in characterized voices, direct narration of a sort reenters through the convention of stage directions, undercutting the autonomy of the drama. In contradistinction, the style of the Eumaeus chapter affects an inflated literary pose full of overextended sentences, foreign language phrases, and clichés, reflecting Bloom's social gregariousness in the face of Stephen's sullenness, and yet the Ithaca chapter contains the most depersonalized style yet exhibited in *Ulysses*: a catechetical coupling of 309 questions and answers presented as disembodied information disclosing the events in Bloom's house upon his return with Stephen, their conversation and individual thoughts, as well as catalogues of facts and figures pertaining to their immediate environment. By contrast, Molly's night thoughts consume all of the concluding chapter, a feminine interior monologue of eight run-on sentences, devoid of punctuation but replete with her own expressive desires and past history, at once a corrective to the entire masculine text that precedes it and a mysterious departure into a private and unique consciousness. Through the multiple styles of the night chapters, the minimal plotline is carefully advanced, but the numerous suppositions that have threaded their way through *Ulysses* are either resolved or intensified, while numerous new possibilities and contingencies are introduced. Joyce

has added to the inconclusive endings of "The Dead" and *A Portrait of the Artist as a Young Man* a new stage of irresolution for *Ulysses*.

During the seventeen years he spent writing *Finnegans Wake* Joyce lived in a Paris well known for its avant-garde enthusiasms and excesses, for which Joyce served as a reluctant high priest, at once part of the constituent body of the magazine *transition,* in which seventeen segments of the then untitled *Work in Progress* appeared, and yet quietly aloof from all manifestos and movements. With the success of *Ulysses* and financial remunerations he established himself in Paris and vacationed yearly at various resorts, while the pattern of changing addresses continued as it had in Trieste and Zurich—as indeed it had in his father's residences in Dublin. Work on the work-in-progress was sporadic and desultory, delayed often enough by health problems that Joyce even considered handing over the incomplete project to Irish author James Stephens for completion. Begun in the year that Ireland was wrenching itself free from the British Empire and in the throes of wrenching itself apart, and as Mussolini was establishing fascism in Italy, *Finnegans Wake* was finally concluded, titled, and published on the eve of World War II. Whether a Chapelizod pubkeeper's dream or an erotic history of mankind or a pub yarn endlessly woven through a plethora of pub yarns, tall tales, and multifaceted narratives, *Finnegans Wake* obliquely subsumes the political events of the years of its composition, folding them away within a multitude of events from time immemorial.

The degree of innovation in *Finnegans Wake* is extraordinary, so much so that it remains the single most difficult text of the modernist period and is in a sense unreadable, although eminently suitable for analysis. The book challenges and changes our modes of reading, requiring on the one hand the explicative methods employed in reading poetry and on the other a suspension of disbelief that allows the reader to open and reopen constantly the possibilities and multiplicities of interpretation. Some sections were rewritten numerous times, each revision further elaborating and complicating the texture of the narrative; others in the later stages of composition emerged as thoroughly convoluted constructions ready to be fit into the completed pattern unchanged, as Joyce sought both to perfect a single unified work and constantly to alter the conditions of literary response with every segment of the text. Unlike *Ulysses,* it was written out of sequence, in bits and pieces and fixed set pieces, all of which Joyce eventually sewed together under a

A have flapped its southerly, kraaking of old bacckle to the kvarters up, that sky wherce Triboos answer. Wail! 'Tis well.

TRANSITION

done. Hit, hit, hit! This is the same white harse of the Willingdone. Culpenhelp, waggling his tailoscrupp with the half of a hat of lipoleums to insoult on the hinndoo seeboy Hney, hncy, hney! (Bullsrag! Foul!) This is the seeboy, madrashattaras, upjump and pumpim, cry to the Willingdone: Ap Pukkaru! Pukka Yurap! This is the Willingdone, bornstable ghentleman tinders his max-botch to the cursigan Shimar Shin. This is the doo-forhim seeboy blow the whole of the half of the hat of lipoleums off of the top of the tail on the back of his big wide harse. Tip. (Bullseye! Game!) How Copenhagen ended. This way the museyroom. Mind your boots goan out.

Phew!

What a warm ~~time we were~~ happiness childer everwas in there but how keling is here the airabouts! And such reasonable weather too! The wagrant wind's awalt'zaround the piltdowns and on every blasted knollyrock there's that gnarlybird ygathering, a runalittle, doalittle, preealittle, poura-little, wipealittle, kicksalittle, severalittle, eatalittle, whimealittle, kenalittle, helfalittle, pelfalittle gnarly-bird. She niver comes out when Thon's on shower or when Thon's flash with the Nixy girls or when Thon's blowing toomcracks down the gaels of Thon. Her would-be too moochy ~~breed~~ his. Of Burymeleg and Bindmeroll-ingeyes and all the deed in the woe. She jest does hopes till byes will be byes. Here, and it goes on to appear now, she comes, a peacefugle, a parody's bird, a peri pot-mother picking here, pecking there, pussypussy plunderpussy. But it's the armitides toonigh and toomourn we wish for a muddy kissmans to the minutia workers and there's to be a gorgeups truce for all the childers. She's burrowed the coacher's lamp the better to pry and all spoiled goods go into her nabsack: curtrages and rattlin buttins, nappy spattees and flasks of all nations, clavi-cures and scampulars, maps, keys and woodpiles of haypennies and moonled brooches with bloodstaned breeks in em and boaston nightgarters and masses of

t Under his seven16 wrothschields lies one, Lampacus. Our pigeons pair are flewn for northcliffs. the three of crows

Page from the first part of Finnegans Wake, *as it appeared in* transition, *no. 1 (April 1927), with Joyce's 1936 revisions*
(The James Joyce Archive)

Eugene Jolas and James Joyce, 1938. Jolas was editor of transition *magazine, which published seventeen fragments from the novel that Joyce eventually titled* Finnegans Wake *(photo by Gisèle Freund).*

title that he kept secret, insisting that he had a schematic plan in mind throughout. Serious critical attention has been focused on the assumption that nothing in *Finnegans Wake* is nonsense, yet it may be equally true that it is all pure nonsense, subsuming and perpetually violating the limitation of prosaic "sense." Readers and critics have attempted consistently to "translate" Joyce's language into what he had dismissed as "wideawake" language and have condemned some aspects of his tampering with language as trivial when something less than direct explication emerged from their frustrated efforts.

Joyce has been credited with and accused of destroying the English language, the language of the British conquerors of Ireland, and rebelling against everything bourgeois, even its esteemed language system; but Joyce himself claimed that what he destroyed in the writing of *Finnegans Wake* he also reconstructed, and the result is the creation of a language, what he called a night language, but commentators on occasion refer to it as dream language. From the closing passages of the Oxen of the Sun chapter through the four succeeding chapters,

various night languages were stylistically developed in *Ulysses* to contain the night world; and for *Finnegans Wake* a new night language, encompassing multiple variants, takes precedence. Joyce explained that he was turning away from "wideawake" day language, adding that he was also abandoning its "cutanddry" grammar. Many sentences in the text can still respond to the diagramming of a literal grammarian, but others defy artificial structuring, although the long, overly extended and complex "sentences" often give the impression of having a syntactical flow. Night language always "approximates" actual apprehension, a sense of an operative reality, a movement toward conceptualization and confinement, but always eludes the actual, the definite, the defined.

Just as early evaluations of *Ulysses* focused on its chaotic randomness, despite the highly schematized structures now apparent, so *Finnegans Wake* appears to be an uncharted minefield. The sense of a structure depends on the division into four parts, the final one a single chapter ending in an incomplete sentence. Joyce indicated that the four-part structure was intentional and implicated Giambattista Vico's cycles of history as germane to the pattern. Book one is viewed as corresponding to Vico's theocratic age (The Book of the Parents), book two to an heroic age (The Book of the Sons), and book three as a democratic age (The Book of the People), with book four as a Recorso. The pattern holds up marginally well: indeed the first four chapters seem to introduce an arriving hero in Humphrey Chimpden Earwicker, displacing vaguer heroic figures from a prehistoric past, who settles down, raises a family, and at a certain time in the recent past has committed an indiscretion of some sort that has volatile repercussions. The next four chapters apparently recapitulate these "events," but already in terms of his wife, Anna Livia Plurabelle, and his children, twin sons Shaun and Shem and a younger daughter Issy. Book two situates a particular evening during which the now much older children are at play and at their lessons before going to bed, and the pubkeeper Earwicker, at his bar with his customers, gets drunk and passes out, eventually finding his way upstairs to bed. Book three carries through the night, Earwicker's drunken dream reactivating his feelings of guilt, until an early morning scene reveals the parents in bed disturbed by an awakened child, time reverted to their early marriage days. Book four suggests a "real" dawn breaking on Chapelizod, and the flowing of the River Liffey out into Dublin Bay.

No plot summary, no matter how concise or how elaborately exhaustive, can capture the narrative condition in which there is no single narrative. On the one hand the digressions and interruptions return to the basic plot of one family of five, plus two servants of sorts (the charwoman a vaguely grandparental figure as well), and a dozen customers that may also include four old men; yet on the other hand the tale of Earwicker misbehaving with two girls in the park, overseen by three soldiers who spread the tale until a cad accosts Earwicker in the same park and manages some sort of accusation, never gets told despite the 600-odd pages of *Finnegans Wake* narration. All other tales participate in and diverge from the hint of a central narrative, and the multiplicity of characters with numerous tales to tell, on and off the subject, contribute to an oral history of the world, filtered through a universal language attempting to duplicate the nonverbal qualities of the world of dreams. The shift that Joyce made from the narrative method of *Stephen Hero* to *A Portrait of the Artist as a Young Man* was a shift from linear progression to a smaller series of compartmentalized packages of discrete units, a

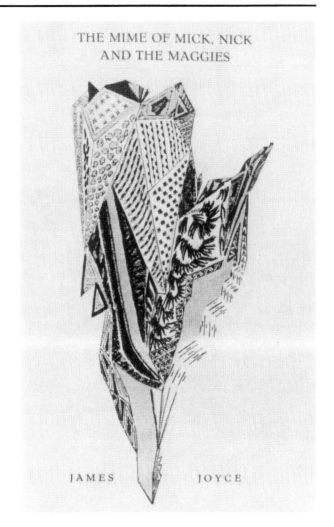

Dust jacket designed by Lucia Joyce for a fragment of Finnegans Wake *published by the Servire Press in June 1934 (McFarlin Library, University of Tulsa)*

method elaborated upon in *Ulysses* and perfected in *Finnegans Wake*. Rather than a continuous narrative, *Finnegans Wake* consists of packets of linked, blended, and interrupted tales, some no more complete than a single phrase, and a mélange of voices performing narrational services independent of any central intention. Not only does *Finnegans Wake* contain multitudes, but these multitudes interact and interconnect at junctures determined by accidental and coincidental factors, the net result of which is an almost seamless garment that the chapter separations only minimally affect. The four-part structuring implied by the segregation into books is both corroborated and belied by an "unseen" structuring that runs parallel with the more obvious one: instances of the word *silence* that serve as caesuras to the narratives and as bridges between them. They occur spaced out at four points in the text, the word never spelled the same way twice or positioned the same way twice in a sentence or paragraph, suggesting a lapse between eons, a new starting point between ages—and hence between tales told.

Reading *Finnegans Wake* has been likened to collecting sand in a sieve, and experienced readers have learned to read selectively, searching for specific threads or clusters at each reading. Some have persistently attempted to read the "plot" of *Finnegans Wake* and establish a chronology for the Earwicker family situation that straightens out the time warps of Joyce's method of presentation, to obtain cameo descriptions of the principal characters, and to determine the events of the Earwicker indiscretion and its reverberations. Others have sought major themes, which they find surfacing throughout: the endurance and flexibility of humankind; the comic foibles of human pretensions; the absurdity of feelings of guilt in a fallible universe; the monumental achievement of the building of cities or, conversely, the futility of man's accomplishments in the face of the relentless permanence of nature; the vying of brothers for rights of succession; the supplanting of fathers by sons; the woman as temptress, provoker of violence, healer and bringer of peace; the rivalry of mothers and nubile daughters; the eternal presence of man and woman in the natural landscape as mountain and river. Occasionally a reader decides that *Finnegans Wake* has a central theme or dominant message—that it is essentially about the Easter Passion or the Irish Civil War, the *Book of the Dead* or the "Ballad of Tim Finnegan": each of these interpretations tends to narrow the focus of an otherwise expansive universe contained in *Finnegans Wake*, yet every effort to capture the expansiveness can result in the loss of too many grains of Wakean sand.

All exigencies in *Finnegans Wake* remain continually operative: Earwicker guilty or innocent, captured or absconded, executed or exonerated; the crime a misdemeanor or felony, the sin venial or mortal. Whatever occurred may take the form of a civil disorder, a moral offense, a commercial manipulation, a tragedy—and yet only as a staged piece of dramatic literature, a story enacted—or only a rumor of scandal, a bruiting about of a bit of gossip, the echo of a fall in the Garden of Eden. Nor is there any real evidence that anything actually happened (or will happen) or that there is any actual narrative possible from the disjointed clues spread throughout the text. Instead of narrative events *Finnegans Wake* may essentially be a network of

thematic structures held together by narrative bits from preexisting texts, the cultural flotsam and jetsam of human civilization, its literary and oral storytelling traditions. The fall of Earwicker parallels the fall of Adam from grace in the Garden of Eden, the crucifixion of Christ at Calvary, the defeat of Napoleon at Waterloo, the fall of Humpty Dumpty from the wall. At ground level the motif involves the Irish-American ballad of the hodcarrier Tim Finnegan, whose fall from a ladder and subsequent death occasion a wake at which a bottle of whiskey—the water of life—is hurled during a fracas and smashes over the corpse, the spilled whiskey restoring him to life. To complement the mundane Finnegan there exists the Irish hero Finn MacCool, the buried giant whose form is the Dublin cityscape and whose anticipated resurrection is expected to signal the revival of the Irish nation. In the Wakean universe exalted things above are mirrored in the commonplace things below. *Finnegans Wake* constantly gives the impression of a rhythmic flow on infinite variation, of stylistic changes from section to section, from paragraph to paragraph, and even within individual sentences, areas of increased density and murkiness, relieved occasionally by pockets of near lucidity.

Whatever plans Joyce may have had for a work to follow *Finnegans Wake* remain a mystery, although some rumors persisted after his death in 1941: he is presumed to have commented that his next book would be a simple one, and also that, having written a book about a river in *Finnegans Wake,* his next project would be a book about the sea. Not as frequently quoted is a remark that he made during the valiant resistance of the Greeks to the invasion by Fascist Italy: that he was contemplating the writing of a Greek tragedy. In the year-and-a-half interval between the publication of *Finnegans Wake* and his death Joyce was a war refugee on the move, worried about hospitalization for his daughter and finding a neutral nation that would accept him and his family. He may well have assumed that he was terminally ill—a fear that he could not voice lest the Swiss refuse entry to a moribund refugee. Worried that the war was eclipsing the sales and fame of his new book, Joyce may also have been aware that *Finnegans Wake* would have no successor. As *A Portrait of the Artist as a Young Man* had established his reputation among a small circle of intellectuals, *Ulysses* had brought international fame and notoriety, a combination that proved effective in placing James Joyce in the primary role as the major modernist writer of his age; and in the four decades after his death that reputa-

*James Joyce in Switzerland (Dr. Giedion and
C. Giedion Welcker)*

tion has strengthened considerably. The first half of
the twentieth century produced such modernist
masters as Virginia Woolf, Gertrude Stein, Thomas
Mann, Marcel Proust, T. S. Eliot, Ezra Pound, Franz
Kafka, Federico García Lorca, Wallace Stevens, and
William Faulkner; yet just as the period in art persists as the Age of Picasso, so the period in literature
should be primarily recognized as the Age of Joyce.

Letters:
Letters of James Joyce, volume 1, edited by Stuart
    Gilbert (New York: Viking, 1957; revised,
    1965); volumes 2 and 3, edited by Richard
    Ellmann (New York: Viking, 1966).

Bibliographies:
John J. Slocum and Herbert Cahoon, *A Bibliography
    of James Joyce* (New Haven: Yale University
    Press, 1953);
Alan M. Cohn, "Supplementary James Joyce
    Checklist," *James Joyce Quarterly* (1959-   );
Robert Scholes, *The Cornell Joyce Collection: A

Catalogue* (Ithaca: Cornell University Press,
    1961);
Peter Spielberg, *James Joyce's Manuscripts and Letters
    at the University of Buffalo: A Catalogue* (Albany:
    State University of New York Press, 1962);
Cohn, "Joyce Bibliographies: A Survey," *American
    Book Collector,* 15 (Summer 1965): 11-16;
Maurice Beebe, Phillip F. Herring, and A. Walton
    Litz, "Criticism of James Joyce: A Selected
    Checklist," *Modern Fiction Studies,* 15 (Spring
    1969): 105-182;
Thomas F. Staley, "James Joyce," in *Anglo-Irish Lit-
    erature: A Review of Research,* edited by Richard
    J. Finneran (New York: Modern Language
    Association of America, 1976), pp. 366-435;
Robert H. Deming, *A Bibliography of James Joyce
    Studies,* revised and enlarged edition (Boston:
    G. K. Hall, 1977);
Staley, "James Joyce," in *Recent Research on Anglo-
    Irish Writers,* edited by Finneran (New York:
    Modern Language Association of America,
    1983), pp. 181-202.

Biographies:
Herbert Gorman, *James Joyce, His First Forty Years*
    (New York: Huebsch, 1924);
Frank Budgen, *James Joyce and the Making of Ulysses*
    (London: Grayson, 1934; revised edition,
    Bloomington: Indiana University Press,
    1960);
Gorman, *James Joyce* (New York: Rinehart, 1940;
    revised, 1948);
Stanislaus Joyce, *My Brother's Keeper: James Joyce's
    Early Years,* edited by Ellmann (New York:
    Viking, 1958);
Richard Ellmann, *James Joyce* (New York: Oxford
    University Press, 1959; revised, 1982);
Constantine Curran, *James Joyce Remembered* (New
    York: Oxford University Press, 1968);
Chester G. Anderson, *James Joyce and His World*
    (London: Thames & Hudson, 1968).

References:
James S. Atherton, *The Books at the Wake* (New York:
    Viking, 1959);
Samuel Beckett and others, *Our Exagmination Round
    his Factification for Incamination of Work in
    Progress* (Paris: Shakespeare & Company,
    1929);
Michael H. Bengal and Fritz Senn, *A Conceptual
    Guide to Finnegans Wake* (University Park:
    Pennsylvania State University Press, 1974);
Bernard Benstock, *James Joyce: The Undiscover'd

Country (Dublin: Gill & Macmillan, 1977);

Benstock, *Joyce-again's Wake* (Seattle: University of Washington Press, 1965);

Shari Benstock and Bernard Benstock, *Who's He When He's at Home: A James Joyce Directory* (Urbana: University of Illinois Press, 1980);

Robert R. Boyle, *James Joyce's Pauline Vision* (Carbondale: Southern Illinois University Press, 1978);

Joseph Campbell and Henry Morton Robinson, *A Skeleton Key to Finnegans Wake* (New York: Viking, 1944);

Richard Ellmann, *Ulysses on the Liffey* (New York: Oxford University Press, 1972);

Stuart Gilbert, *James Joyce's Ulysses* (London: Faber & Faber, 1930);

S. L. Goldberg, *The Classical Temper* (London: Chatto & Windus, 1961);

Arnold Goldman, *The Joyce Paradox* (Evanston: Northwestern University Press, 1968);

Roy K. Gottfried, *The Art of Joyce's Syntax in Ulysses* (Athens: University of Georgia Press, 1980);

Clive Hart, *Structure and Motif in Finnegans Wake* (Evanston: Northwestern University Press, 1963);

Hart, ed., *James Joyce's Dubliners* (London: Faber & Faber, 1969);

Hart and David Hayman, eds., *James Joyce's Ulysses* (Berkeley: University of California Press, 1974);

Hayman, *A First-Draft Version of Finnegans Wake* (Austin: University of Texas Press, 1963);

Hayman, *Ulysses: The Mechanics of Meaning* (Englewood Cliffs, N.J.: Prentice-Hall, 1970; revised, 1982);

Richard M. Kain, *Fabulous Voyager: James Joyce's Ulysses* (Chicago: University of Chicago Press, 1947);

Hugh Kenner, *Dublin's Joyce* (London: Chatto & Windus, 1955);

Kenner, *Joyce's Voices* (Berkeley: University of California Press, 1978);

Karen Lawrence, *The Odyssey of Style in Ulysses* (Princeton: Princeton University Press, 1981);

Harry Levin, *James Joyce* (New York: New Directions, 1941);

A. Walton Litz, *The Art of James Joyce* (New York: Oxford University Press, 1961);

Colin MacCabe, *James Joyce and the Revolution of the Word* (London: Macmillan, 1978);

Marvin Magalaner and Richard M. Kain, *Joyce: the Man, the Work, the Reputation* (New York: New York University Press, 1956);

Roland McHugh, *Annotations to Finnegans Wake* (Baltimore: Johns Hopkins University Press, 1980);

McHugh, *The Sigla of Finnegans Wake* (Austin: University of Texas Press, 1976);

William T. Noon, *Joyce and Aquinas* (New Haven: Yale University Press, 1957);

Margot Norris, *The Decentered Universe of Finnegans Wake* (Baltimore: Johns Hopkins University Press, 1976);

Charles H. Peake, *James Joyce: The Citizen and the Artist* (Stanford: Stanford University Press, 1977);

John Henry Raleigh, *The Chronicle of Leopold and Molly Bloom* (Berkeley: University of California Press, 1977);

John Paul Riquelme, *Teller and Tale in Joyce's Fiction* (Baltimore: Johns Hopkins University Press, 1983);

Danis Rose and John O'Hanlon, *Understanding Finnegans Wake* (New York: Garland, 1982);

Brook Thomas, *James Joyce's Ulysses: A Book of Many Happy Returns* (Baton Rouge: Louisiana State University Press, 1982);

William York Tindall, *James Joyce: His Way of Interpreting the Modern World* (New York: Scribners, 1950).

Papers:

The largest collections of Joyce's manuscripts may be found in the libraries of Cornell University and the State University of New York at Buffalo. Other notable collections of Joyce's papers are at the Beinecke Rare Book and Manuscript Library, Yale University; the National Library of Ireland, Dublin; the Rosenbach Foundation, Philadelphia; the British Library, London; and the libraries of Southern Illinois University at Carbondale, the University of Texas at Austin, and the University of Kansas.

Sheila Kaye-Smith

(4 February 1887-14 January 1956)

Paul A. Doyle
Nassau College, State University of New York

SELECTED BOOKS: *The Tramping Methodist* (London: Bell, 1908; New York: Dutton, 1922);

Starbrace (London: Bell, 1909; New York: Dutton, 1927);

Spell Land: The Story of a Sussex Farm (London: Bell, 1910; New York: Dutton, 1927);

Isle of Thorns (London: Constable, 1913; New York: Dutton, 1913);

Willow's Forge and Other Poems (London: Macdonald, 1914);

Three Against the World (London: Chapman & Hall, 1914); republished as *The Three Furlongers* (Philadelphia: Lippincott, 1914);

John Galsworthy (London: Nisbet, 1916; New York: Holt, 1916);

Sussex Gorse: The Story of a Fight (London: Nisbet, 1916; New York: Knopf, 1916);

The Challenge to Sirius (London: Nisbet, 1917; New York: Dutton, 1918);

Little England (London: Nisbet, 1918); republished as *The Four Roads* (New York: Doran, 1919);

Tamarisk Town (London: Cassell, 1919; New York: Dutton, 1920);

Green Apple Harvest (London: Cassell, 1920; New York: Dutton, 1921);

Joanna Godden (London: Cassell, 1921; New York: Dutton, 1922);

Saints in Sussex (Birmingham: Mathews, 1923; New York: Dutton, 1927);

The End of the House of Alard (London: Cassell, 1923; New York: Dutton, 1923);

The George and the Crown (New York: Dutton, 1924; London: Cassell, 1925);

Anglo-Catholicism (London: Chapman & Hall, 1925);

The Mirror of the Months (London: Mathews & Marrot, 1925; New York: Harper, 1931);

Iron and Smoke (London: Cassell, 1928; New York: Dutton, 1928);

The Village Doctor (London: Cassell, 1929; New York: Dutton, 1929);

Sin (London: Allan, 1929; Milwaukee: Morehouse, 1929);

Shepherds in Sackcloth (London: Cassell, 1930; New York: Harper, 1930);

Songs Late and Early (London: Hamilton, 1931);

The History of Susan Spray, the Female Preacher (London: Cassell, 1931); republished as *Susan Spray* (New York: Harper, 1931);

The Children's Summer (London: Cassell, 1932); republished as *Summer Holiday* (New York: Harper, 1932);

The Plowman's Progress (London: Cassell, 1933); republished as *Gipsy Wagon* (New York & London: Harper, 1933);

Superstition Corner (London: Cassell, 1934; New York: Harper, 1934);

Gallybird (London: Cassell, 1934; New York: Harper, 1934);

Selina Is Older (London: Cassell, 1935); republished as *Selina* (New York: Harper, 1935);

Rose Deeprose (London: Cassell, 1936; New York: Harper, 1936);

Three Ways Home (London: Cassell, 1937; New York: Harper, 1937);

Faithful Stranger and Other Stories (London: Cassell, 1938; New York: Harper, 1938);

The Valiant Woman (New York: Harper, 1938; London: Cassell, 1939);

Ember Lane (London: Cassell, 1940; New York: Harper, 1940);

The Hidden Son (London: Cassell, 1941); republished as *The Secret Son* (New York: Harper, 1942);

Talking of Jane Austen, with G. B. Stern (London: Cassell, 1943); republished as *Speaking of Jane Austen* (New York: Harper, 1944);

Tambourine, Trumpet and Drum (London: Cassell, 1943; New York: Harper, 1943);

Kitchen Fugue (London: Cassell, 1945; New York: Harper, 1945);

The Lardners and the Laurelwoods (New York: Harper, 1947; London: Cassell, 1948);

The Happy Tree (New York: Harper, 1949); republished as *The Treasure of the Snow* (London: Cassell, 1950);

More About Jane Austen, with G. B. Stern (New York: Harper, 1949); republished as *More Talk of Jane Austen* (London: Cassell, 1950);

Mrs. Gailey (London: Cassell, 1951; New York: Harper, 1951);

Quartet in Heaven (London: Cassell, 1952; New York: Harper, 1952);

Weald of Kent and Sussex (London: Hale, 1953);

The View from the Parsonage (London: Cassell, 1954; New York: Harper, 1954);

All the Books of My Life: A Bibliography (London: Cassell, 1956; New York: Harper, 1956).

Serious novel readers who grew up in the first half of this century were quite familiar with the writings of Sheila Kaye-Smith. She was designated by critics as the novelist of Sussex and often compared with Thomas Hardy ("the novelist of Wessex"). She was lauded for the "masculine" strength of her prose and "man-like" unsentimental approach to her material. After World War II, however, her popularity declined, and although she continued to write spellbinding tales until her death, only a few of her books are presently remembered and alluded to.

Born in St. Leonards-on-Sea, near Hastings, Sussex, she was a bright and imaginative child who was particularly devoted to her father, a country doctor. She loved to invent, relate, and write stories and early resolved to be a famous novelist. Her first work of fiction, *The Tramping Methodist* (1908), was published when she was only twenty-one. In two ways it contained basic aspects that were to mark much of her later writing. First, it was obvious that the reader was in the presence of a born storyteller who had a pronounced tendency to overplot in order to maintain suspense and narrative drive. Secondly, this first novel demonstrated that Kaye-Smith was a close, almost naturalistic observer of the sights and sounds she was describing. In her future writing she was to correct her overplotting in only her finest novels, but her ability as an intimate viewer of the land and its people was to improve constantly so that the later favorable comparisons of her writing to that of Hardy in this respect had considerable justification.

After her first novel she published several more books before achieving critical success with *Sussex Gorse* (1916), which remains her finest book. The narrative's protagonist, Reuben Backfield, is not content with a small successful farm. He wants to purchase and cultivate the seemingly unconquerable Boarzell Moor, which is contiguous to his property. The moor is composed of thickly gnarled, coarse shrubbery and roots as well as stony soil. To achieve his obsessive ambition Backfield becomes totally ruthless and spartan. His wives are used to bear children; his children are used to work the land. Intense industry and penurious thrift result in more money, which is used to buy acre after acre of the moor. During his quest Backfield either drives away or indirectly kills everyone in his large family. He is well into his eighties before all of Boarzell is his; and although he is separated from family and close friends, he is exultant and completely satisfied.

Boarzell Moor is a significant rival to Hardy's Egdon Heath. The haunting atmosphere and pervasiveness of the landscape are convincingly rendered. The cruelty, toughness, and oppressiveness of the moor are equalled by these qualities in Backfield. He insists that nature is "a thing for man to tread down and subdue." He cannot in the least understand those environmentalists who battle him in order to preserve some of nature in its wild, primitive state. He wants every bit of land in use: "I'd lik to see the whole of England grown over wud wheat from one end to the other." Kaye-Smith's searing portrayal of conscienceless ambition is a stirring and frightening recital of one human being's ruthlessness.

Tamarisk Town (1919) successfully continues

the theme of all-consuming ambition. Edward Monypenny seeks to develop the finest seaside resort in England. Unlike the protagonist of *Sussex Gorse,* Monypenny allows human love to distract him from his ambition and then to thwart it. He ultimately doubts his dreams and loses the single-minded determination necessary to bring them to fruition.

Monypenny is a much more complex character than Backfield. He is of a higher social class, well educated, and sensitive. Consequently, the very reckless, straightforward simplicity that drives him is tempered by a humanity that is nonexistent in Backfield. Nevertheless, when his sweetheart commits suicide, Monypenny uses his energy to destroy that which he had initially attempted to build. He sinks to a more primitive, animalistic level, uncaring of human feelings. The suffering he incurs from the deprivation of his beloved envelops his spirit. He becomes blind to the realization that humanitarianism should be paramount even in the face of soul-shaking disaster and disappointment. The theme is implicit and is reenforced symbolically at the end of the novel when the sightless statue of the now dead Monypenny broods over the desolate seashore.

Kaye-Smith continued her finest creative period (1916-1931) with *Joanna Godden* (1921), the saga of a resourceful and courageous woman who must, while in her early twenties, assume control of her father's farm after his unexpected death. She succeeds in making the homestead even more prosperous than it was under her father. In addition to the farm, she must care for her younger sister and also work out various romantic relationships which develop.

Up to this point in her career, Kaye-Smith had been chiefly interested in depicting men as the dominant figures in Sussex life. Now she portrays a strong, youthful woman who must not only direct a large, constantly growing and developing estate and compete with the other farmers in the area (all men), but also work out a satisfactory love relationship. No amount of career-woman achievement can compensate for her emotional needs for love and motherhood. Her pregnancy by a man she realizes she cannot marry forces her to give up her landholding and move away, but spiritual fulfillment is uppermost: "Broken, utterly done and finished as she was from the worldly point of view, there was in her heart a springing hope, a sweet softness—she could indeed go softly at last." Kaye-Smith shows, without sentimentality, that for some women emo-

tional, maternal instincts must take precedence over all else.

Joanna possesses a humanity that is both credible and moving. There is nothing wooden, false, or farfetched in her characterization. She is a much more sympathetic and understandable figure than either Reuben Backfield or Edward Monypenny. Like Monypenny, she is vulnerable in love, but unlike him she does not allow romantic heartbreak to thwart a basically affirmative and outgoing approach to existence. Sheila Kaye-Smith always depicts life as tragic, defeating, and frustrating; yet despite such oppressiveness, individual victories can be achieved through determination and/or love.

In 1918 Sheila Kaye-Smith was received into the Anglican Church. Her growing interest in religious themes is reflected in *The End of the House of Alard* (1923). The Alard estate, dating back before the Crusades, is one of the oldest in Sussex, but is now heavily mortgaged. Even though he loves Stella Mount, Peter Alard, the eldest son, marries a wealthy woman in order to save the family property. He discovers, however, that all his thoughts revolve around Stella, and he attempts to persuade her to be his mistress. Stella, a deeply religious Anglo-Catholic, rejects this proposal, and Peter commits suicide. Stella broods about his death and is emotionally torn between feelings of guilt and her religious faith.

Through her characters Kaye-Smith presents what she feels to be the limitations of Low Church Anglicanism and the superiority of Anglo-Catholicism. The Low Church seems to focus chiefly on humanitarian concerns, such as giving soup tickets to the poor, while the High Church centers more on the awesome mystical relationship to the Almighty, with people, inspired with God's reality, kneeling to pray before an altar. Several critics have censured the novel as religious propaganda, and it is true that in this narrative Kaye-Smith departs from her usually objective presentation of material and too obviously takes sides. Nevertheless, the characterizations are exceedingly well drawn and very credible in context.

In addition to the religious motif, there is a second and equally important theme emphasized in *The End of the House of Alard*. A quotation from G. K. Chesterton, printed on the title page, underscores this point: "We only know that the last sad squires ride slowly towards the sea/And a new people takes the land. . . ." Many of the old estates are deeply in debt, and the families increase their economic dif-

The house Sheila Kaye-Smith and her husband, Theodore Penrose Fry, built in Sussex, circa 1930 (photo © Eric Gray)

ficulties by living too lavishly. They tend to live in the past, supporting large numbers of servants and maintaining many buildings. Furthermore, the land is left untended. It is not being planted and harvested. The gentry are hence starting to pass from the countryside, and more realistic, energetic farmers from a lower social class are succeeding to the soil and bringing the land to new fulfillment.

Unlike her point of view on the interwoven religious theme, Kaye-Smith does not lament the departure of the gentry. She observes their deficiencies, the dry rot that has accumulated after centuries of living unrealistically. She notes how foolish family pride and tradition can thwart the happiness the Alard sons and daughters had come to expect. Only by breaking with false notions of family rights and arrogance can any of the Alards achieve balanced, healthy lives. The old ways of the squires will vanish more and more in the post World War I period. *The End of the House of Alard* is a good narrative with fascinating characters and perceptive insights into the social and economic changes taking place in England during that time.

In 1924 Kaye-Smith married the Reverend Theodore Penrose Fry, a High Church Anglican rector, and five years later they both converted to Roman Catholicism. Fry gave up his living as an Anglican clergyman, and he and his wife moved to a farm in Sussex and actually worked the soil. It is not unusual, therefore, that Kaye-Smith's last really significant novel should involve a minister.

The History of Susan Spray, the Female Preacher (1931) analyzes the life of a woman brought up in the Hur Colgate Brethren. Hur Colgate had seceded from High Calvinism and went about England preaching and establishing various chapels. Although he died before Susan was born, his beliefs were strongly embedded in her family. At a very young age Susan imagines that she hears God speaking to her in the thunder of a sudden storm.

Sheila Kaye-Smith, 1931 (photo © Eric Gray)

Theodore Penrose Fry and Sheila Kaye-Smith in their Sussex home, 1931 (photo © Eric Gray)

Actually, she invents this episode in order to avoid a beating for leaving her work in the fields. Nevertheless, being steeped in biblical readings and having a vivid imagination, she comes to rationalize the experience and to believe that she has special inspirations and revelations from the Almighty. She eventually becomes a speaker at the meetings of various groups of the sect and achieves considerable popularity among the largely uneducated Brethren.

Susan marries three times in her life; her first husband dies and her second is reported dead. Her second marriage enables her to live without having to preach the Gospel, but, unsatisfied without her work, she is impelled to return and spread the biblical message. She is always sustained by the belief that she is doing not only the will of the Lord but also the will of "His servant Hur Colgate . . . her friend in heaven."

The portrait of Susan Spray is drawn with realism and objectivity. At times it is evident that she is hypocritical, yet so closely is hypocrisy mingled with her genuine feelings of biblical inspiration and communion with heaven that she cannot be judged negatively. She is a woman with notable talent and imagination, haunted by spiritual awareness, a good example of Kaye-Smith's emphasizing the power of the spirit in the lives of particular individuals.

After her study of Susan Spray, Kaye-Smith

wrote other novels, but none that maintained the realism and power of her finest work. In addition to her novels (the most important phase of her career), she published poems, short stories, three autobiographical segments, and other works, including two charming studies of Jane Austen (in collaboration with G. B. Stern).

Kaye-Smith was a born storyteller and possessed a consummate command of rural Sussex — its people, its dialect, its customs, its landscape. Except for parts of *The End of the House of Alard* and *Superstition Corner* (1934), which focused on Roman Catholic themes relating to English history, she generally presented her material with extraordinary objectivity.

Kaye-Smith wrote more than forty books. Many of the characters in her lesser novels tend to be cardboard figures rather than flesh and blood; and there is an overly detailed, overfurnished, excessively documentary quality about much of her writing. Her best novels, however, present effective and arresting portrayals of humanity struggling in various ways with the problems of survival and achievement in a grim, tragic world.

Bibliographies:

Paul A. Doyle, "Sheila Kaye-Smith: An Annotated Bibliography of Writings About Her," *English Literature in Transition,* 15 (1972): 189-198;

Doyle, "Sheila Kaye-Smith," *English Literature in Transition,* 16 (1973): 152-153;

Doyle, "Sheila Kaye-Smith," *English Literature in Transition,* 17 (1974): 45-46;

Doyle, "Sheila Kaye-Smith," *English Literature in Transition,* 18 (1975): 62.

References:

Doris N. Dalglish, "Some Contemporary Women Novelists," *Contemporary Review,* 127 (January 1925): 79-85;

Elizabeth A. Drew, *The Modern Novel* (Port Washington, N.Y.: Kennikat, 1967), pp. 115-116, 124-132;

R. Thurston Hopkins, *Sheila Kaye-Smith and the Weald Country* (London: Cecil Palmer, 1925);

Margaret Mackenzie, "The House That Sheila Built," *Thought,* 6 (June 1931): 108-118;

Andrew E. Malone, "The Novelist of Sussex: Sheila Kaye-Smith," *Fortnightly Review,* new series 120 (2 August 1926): 199-209;

G. B. Stern, "The Heroines of Sheila Kaye-Smith," *Yale Review,* 15 (October 1925): 204-208;

Dorothea Walker, *Sheila Kaye-Smith* (Boston: Twayne, 1980).

Margaret Kennedy

(23 April 1896-31 July 1967)

Barbara Brothers
Youngstown State University

BOOKS: *A Century of Revolution, 1789-1920* (London: Methuen, 1922);

The Ladies of Lyndon (London: Heinemann, 1923; Garden City: Doubleday, Page, 1925);

The Constant Nymph (London: Heinemann, 1924; Garden City: Doubleday, Page, 1925);

The Constant Nymph: A Play in Three Acts, by Kennedy and Basil Dean (London: Heinemann, 1926; Garden City: Doubleday, Page, 1926);

A Long Week-End (London: Heinemann, 1927; Garden City: Doubleday, Page, 1927);

Red Sky at Morning (London: Heinemann, 1927; Garden City: Doubleday, Page, 1927);

Dewdrops (London: Heinemann, 1928);

The Game and the Candle (London: Heinemann, 1928);

Come With Me, by Kennedy and Dean (London: Heinemann, 1928);

The Fool of the Family (Garden City: Doubleday, Doran, 1930; London: Heinemann, 1936);

Return I Dare Not (London: Heinemann, 1931; Garden City: Doubleday, Doran, 1931);

A Long Time Ago (London: Heinemann, 1932; Garden City: Doubleday, Doran, 1932);

Escape Me Never! A Play in Three Acts (London: Heinemann, 1934; Garden City: Doubleday, Doran, 1935);

Together and Apart (London: Cassell, 1936; New York: Random House, 1937);

The Midas Touch (London: Cassell, 1938; New York: Random House, 1939);

Autumn, adapted by Kennedy and Gregory Ratoff from the book by Ilya Surguchev (London & New York: Nelson, 1940);

Where Stands a Winged Sentry (New Haven: Yale University Press, 1941);

The Mechanized Muse (London: Allen & Unwin, 1942);

Who Will Remember? (Chicago: Dramatic Publishing Company, 1946);

The Feast (London: Cassell, 1950; New York: Rinehart, 1950);

Jane Austen (London: Barker, 1950; Denver: Swallow, 1950);

Margaret Kennedy, 1930s

Lucy Carmichael (London: Macmillan, 1951; New York: Rinehart, 1951);

Troy Chimneys (New York: Rinehart, 1952; London: Macmillan, 1953);

Act of God (New York: Rinehart, 1955); published as *The Oracles* (London: Macmillan, 1955);

The Wild Swan (New York: Rinehart, 1957); published as *The Heroes of Clone* (London: Macmillan, 1957);

The Outlaws on Parnassus (London: Cresset, 1958; New York: Viking, 1960);

A Night in Cold Harbour (London: Macmillan, 1960; New York: St. Martin's, 1960);

The Forgotten Smile (London: Macmillan, 1961; New
York: Macmillan, 1962);
Not in the Calendar: The Story of a Friendship (London:
Macmillan, 1964; New York: Macmillan,
1964);
Women at Work (London: Macmillan, 1966).

Margaret Moore Kennedy demonstrated that
she had the ability to tell a story which could effectively capture the imaginations of large numbers of
the reading public with the publication of her second novel, *The Constant Nymph* (1924). Reprinted in
a number of editions both in America and Britain,
the latest of which was 1959, the novel was also
adapted by Kennedy and Basil Dean for the stage
and was successfully produced in both London and
New York. The appeal of the story is further apparent as film versions of the novel were produced in
1934 (Fox), 1935 (Gaumont), and 1943 (Warner
Brothers). Of the fifteen novels which Kennedy
wrote, three others received special recognition:
The Feast (1950) and *Lucy Carmichael* (1951), Literary
Guild and Book Society choices, and *Troy Chimneys*
(1952), recipient of the James Tait Black Memorial
Prize for 1953.

In her history of the craft of fiction, *The Outlaws on Parnassus* (1958), she defended pleasure and
entertainment as sources of value for the novel and
struck a sympathetic nerve in many critics, such as
Orville Prescott, who were less than sympathetic to
the claims being made for "serious" fiction, so
labeled either because of its moral content or technical virtuosity. In part, Kennedy's history is an
apology for her own fiction and an attack upon
critics and reviewers who would dismiss her as being
merely a popular writer. Kennedy also treated the
subject in "The Novelist and His Public," an address
given to the Royal Society of Literature, of which
she was a member. The irony is that Kennedy's
failure to be considered a novelist of significant
stature by reviewers can be attributed to their
judgment that she strove so to tell a good story that
she frequently overloaded her narratives, making
her characters appear thesis-ridden or pawns of an
overly complex action. The reviewers point to such
flaws as too many characters and melodramatic and
sensational events. Many of her novels do read like
soap operas.

Novelist, playwright, biographer, and critic,
Kennedy was born in London and educated at
Cheltenham Ladies' College and Somerville Col-
lege, Oxford, receiving a second class honors in
history in 1919. In 1925 she married Sir David
Davies, a barrister. She continued her career as a

professional writer while rearing a son and two
daughters, her last novel appearing in 1964, the
year of her husband's death. In addition to her
novels, she wrote *Escape Me Never!* (1934), a three-
act version of her novel *The Fool of the Family* (1930),
and two other plays as well as adapting Dickens's
"The Old Curiosity Shop" for the movies, an art
form she discussed in a monograph, *The Mechanized
Muse* (1942). Though she never used the war years
as a setting for any of her novels, she did publish a
journal of the months from May to September 1940
in which she recounts her experience in the Welsh
village to which she and her children had retreated.
Rather than using a specific historical event of the
twentieth century as the background for the action
of any of her novels, Kennedy drew upon her
knowledge and understanding of the historical
milieu of the whole twentieth century—its wars, its
Victorian heritage, its materialism, its economic and
social class discriminations—to delineate her
characters and their dilemmas. Only two of her
novels, *Troy Chimneys* and *A Night in Cold Harbour*
(1960), are set in the nineteenth century, and both
focus upon a character's struggle which results from
a specific social problem of that time, class distinctions in the former and the use of child labor in the
latter. Her novels also reflect her extensive interest
in the arts. She was herself an accomplished pianist,
according to her friend Richard Bennett, who wrote
of her for the *Dictionary of National Biography*.

Her first novel, *The Ladies of Lyndon* (1923), has
been ignored, only a few reviews appearing
after *The Constant Nymph* was so well received.
However, many contemporary readers, sensitized
by feminist criticism to examining the portrayal of
women and their lives in fiction, may find it one of
Kennedy's more substantive and sensitive narratives. In the novel Agatha Cocks has been reared to
be a "decorative" luxury, the very epitome of the
desirable wife for a man with an "assured, un-
earned income." She submits to the proper choice
of a husband, but her passion for a nobler man is
reawakened when her cousin returns after studying
nerve diseases in Paris. While she may have the
desire to be more than a showpiece, her upbringing
has subverted all the traits needed to fulfill the role
of helpmate. Integrated well into the personal and
family histories of Agatha and the man she marries,
Sir John Clewer, is an examination of the moral and
social values of the upper class, their understanding
and patronage of the arts, and their materialism. As
in most of Kennedy's novels, character development is accomplished partly through the use of
contrasting sets of characters.

In *The Constant Nymph* as in *The Ladies of Lyndon*, an unhappy love story is the vehicle for Kennedy's criticism of English society for its devotion to Victorian morality and convention, its inability to appreciate true artistic genius, and its failure to accept and value those who in their innocence do not conform to the mode of behavior considered proper. In *The Constant Nymph*, Tessa is one of the numerous offspring of the composer Albert Sanger, whose character was suggested to Kennedy, according to Bennett, when she saw a painting of Augustus John and his many wives. Tessa, pure and noble, is a victim of this society into which she is thrust when her father dies. Both Kennedy's depiction of Tessa and her portrayal of Tessa's love for an artist friend of her father's, Lewis Dodd, are excessively romantic.

In *Red Sky at Morning* (1927) Catherine Frobisher, a straitlaced Victorian housekeeper by looks and by mentality, devotes her life to furthering the reputation of her deceased husband, a second-rate writer, and to rearing her two children and their two cousins (they are offspring of a true artistic genius) according to the same values which have blinded her to artistic values and to an appreciation of human character. But heredity is stronger and the cousins turn out to be imaginative, sensitive creatures who, like Tessa, become the victims of a

society which is all too ready to use them for its own ends. The examination of social issues and of the interrelationships between temperament and family and social environments out of which character develops is unfortunately submerged by the demands of the tragic love relationships which govern the plot.

Kennedy returns to the Sanger family in *The Fool of the Family* to relate the lives and loves of two other of Albert's offspring. Caryl is the plodding, honest half brother of Sebastian, a brilliant artist but an irresponsible lover like his father. They are rivals for the hand of Fenella McClean, who cannot distinguish passion from love since passion was not what a proper woman should experience, and certainly not apart from love. At least one reviewer considered the portrayal of Fenella's predicament a "shockingly frank" comment on sex for a woman writer to make.

Return I Dare Not (1931) is a heavy-handed moral parable on the price of success for an artist, in this case a playwright by the name of Hugo Pott. The setting is a weekend house party. The marble-hearted, socially pretentious partygoers who inhabit the world of Evelyn Waugh's *Vile Bodies* are recognizable here, but the portrait of them and their antics is not as satirically or comically interesting as Waugh's.

Hendre Hall, Llwyngwril, Wales, where Kennedy and her family moved in 1937

Margaret Kennedy and Elizabeth Bowen on the pier at Southend, 1938

Kennedy seems to lack a sense of how the comic can serve a serious end, of how laughter, as Henri Bergson has pointed out, can "correct men's manners." *Together and Apart* (1936) opens with two mothers-in-law attempting to intervene in a divorce. The characters and the situation seem made for comedy; but instead of comedy Kennedy writes a banal, tragic melodrama: the teenage children run amuck and the spouses remarry only to find they have gained maturity at the cost of their true love for each other.

In *The Midas Touch* (1938), Corris Morgan, a wealthy financier, meets his spiritual son Evan, a salesman without a soul. An artistically more satisfying tale of corruption is provided by Kennedy in *The Feast*. She prepares the reader for a moral fable by the religious symbolism of the title and by the prologue: two clergymen come to meditate on the collapse of a North Cornwall cliff in which seven hotel residents, each symbolic of one of the Seven Deadly Sins, perish. The varying perspectives of the different characters through which the story is told make for rounded characters and build suspense.

In *Lucy Carmichael* Kennedy once again uses a love story to comment on the relationship of the arts

to society and to criticize men for their opportunism, naiveté, and lack of commitment to the social well-being of the communities of which they are a part. Less fantastic than her other novels, though still overromanticized, the novel relates Lucy's successful search for a man for whom she can be a helpmate.

Set in the 1800s, *Troy Chimneys* is a well-told tale of Miles Lufton, a man who leads a psychologically dual life. On the one hand, he enjoys the contemplative life of the arts, like his wealthy friend Ludovic. On the other hand, he must play the social circuit of the wealthy since he must make his way in the world. The novel examines the effects of social values and the wives men choose upon the lives they lead. *Act of God* (1955) is a less successful narration, the characters like cardboard, of a man who chooses a life of purpose and usefulness to a society which Kennedy has once again attacked for its materialism, phoniness—it cannot distinguish real art from a chair struck by lightning—and scientific illusions of progress.

In *The Wild Swan* (1957) Kennedy combines the story of Dorothea Harding, a Victorian poet and novelist whose creativity is stunted because she is made to accept the role of servant to her family, and a contemporary would-be director who nearly loses his chance to become the artist he desires to be because he believes he must play a social role game and prostitute his values to reach his goal.

After *A Night in Cold Harbour*, Kennedy chooses in *The Forgotten Smile* (1961) to juxtapose a mythical Grecian Island and England to attack an England she feels has lost the imaginative, poetic spirit. Overly ambitious here as she is in almost all her novels, she also tries to depict the predicament of a woman, Kate Benson, no longer needed by her children or husband, who seeks to find an identity for herself. Kennedy's last novel, *Not in the Calendar* (1964), is undone from the start by its large cast of characters and the author's attempts to tell what are after all two separate tales: that of a deaf-mute who becomes an artist and the other of the socially "un-

orthodox" young woman who once shared picture books with the deaf-mute.

Kennedy, who had known fame as a writer when she was only twenty-eight (with the success of both the novel and the stage version of *The Constant Nymph*), found that her reputation had faded following World War II. Though somewhat friendly with Elizabeth Bowen and L. P. Hartley, she was not involved in any particular intellectual or social circle. Instead she enjoyed long walks with her husband, held occasional dinner parties, and spent her life writing and running her household. Violet Powell published a biography of Kennedy in 1983, but except for reviews, Kennedy's work has not been the subject of any published critical studies.

Reference:
Violet Powell, *The Constant Novelist* (London: Heinemann, 1983).

D. H. Lawrence

Kingsley Widmer
San Diego State University

See also the Lawrence entries in *DLB 10, Modern British Dramatists, 1900-1945,* and *DLB 19, British Poets, 1880-1914.*

BIRTH: Eastwood, Nottinghamshire, 11 September 1885, to Arthur and Lydia Beardsall Lawrence.

EDUCATION: Teacher Training Certificate, Nottingham University College, 1908.

MARRIAGE: 13 July 1914 to Frieda von Richthofen Weekley.

AWARDS AND HONORS: James Tait Black Memorial Prize for *The Lost Girl,* 1921.

DEATH: Vence, France, 2 March 1930.

SELECTED BOOKS: *The White Peacock* (New York: Duffield, 1911; London: Heinemann, 1911);
The Trespasser (London: Duckworth, 1912; New York: Kennerley, 1912);
Love Poems and Others (London: Duckworth, 1913;

New York: Kennerley, 1913);
Sons and Lovers (London: Duckworth, 1913; New York: Kennerley, 1913);
The Widowing of Mrs. Holroyd (New York: Kennerley, 1914; London: Duckworth, 1914);
The Prussian Officer and Other Stories (London: Duckworth, 1914; New York: Huebsch, 1916);
The Rainbow (London: Methuen, 1915; expurgated, New York: Huebsch, 1915);
Twilight in Italy (London: Duckworth, 1916; New York: Huebsch, 1916);
Amores (London: Duckworth, 1916; New York: Huebsch, 1916);
Look! We Have Come Through! (London: Chatto & Windus, 1917; New York: Huebsch, 1917);
New Poems (London: Secker, 1918; New York: Huebsch, 1920);
Bay: A Book of Poems (London: Beaumont Press, 1919);
Touch and Go (London: Daniel, 1920; New York: Seltzer, 1920);
Women in Love (New York: Privately printed for

subscribers only, 1920; London: Secker, 1921);

The Lost Girl (London: Secker, 1920; New York: Seltzer, 1921);

Movements in European History, as Lawrence H. Davidson (London: Oxford University Press, 1921);

Psychoanalysis and the Unconscious (New York: Seltzer, 1921; London: Secker, 1923);

Tortoises (New York: Seltzer, 1921);

Sea and Sardinia (New York: Seltzer, 1921; London: Secker, 1923);

Aaron's Rod (New York: Seltzer, 1922; London: Secker, 1922);

Fantasia of the Unconscious (New York: Seltzer, 1922; London: Secker, 1923);

England, My England and Other Stories (New York: Seltzer, 1922; London: Secker, 1924);

The Ladybird, The Fox, The Captain's Doll (London: Secker, 1923); republished as *The Captain's Doll: Three Novelettes* (New York: Seltzer, 1923);

Studies in Classic American Literature (New York: Seltzer, 1923; London: Secker, 1924);

Kangaroo (London: Secker, 1923; New York: Seltzer, 1923);

Birds, Beasts and Flowers (New York: Seltzer, 1923; London: Secker, 1923);

The Boy in the Bush, by Lawrence and M. L. Skinner (London: Secker, 1924; New York: Seltzer, 1924);

St. Mawr: Together with The Princess (London: Secker, 1925);

St. Mawr (New York: Knopf, 1925);

Reflections on the Death of a Porcupine and Other Essays (Philadelphia: Centaur Press, 1925; London: Secker, 1934);

The Plumed Serpent (Quetzalcoatl) (London: Secker, 1926; New York: Knopf, 1926);

David (London: Secker, 1926; New York: Knopf, 1926);

Sun (expurgated, London: Archer, 1926; unexpurgated, Paris: Black Sun Press, 1928);

Glad Ghosts (London: Benn, 1926);

Mornings in Mexico (London: Secker, 1927; New York: Knopf, 1927);

Rawdon's Roof (London: Elkin Mathews & Marrot, 1928);

The Woman Who Rode Away and Other Stories (London: Secker, 1928; New York: Knopf, 1928);

Lady Chatterley's Lover (Florence: Privately printed, 1928; expurgated, London: Secker, 1932; New York: Knopf, 1932; unexpurgated, New

York: Grove, 1959; Harmondsworth, U.K.: Penguin, 1960);

The Collected Poems of D. H. Lawrence, 2 volumes (London: Secker, 1928; New York: Cape & Smith, 1929);

Pansies (London: Secker, 1929; New York: Knopf, 1929);

My Skirmish with Jolly Roger (New York: Random House, 1929); revised as *A Propos of Lady Chatterley's Lover* (London: Mandrake Press, 1930);

Pornography and Obscenity (London: Faber & Faber, 1929; New York: Knopf, 1930);

The Escaped Cock (Paris: Black Sun Press, 1929); republished as *The Man Who Died* (London: Secker, 1931; New York: Knopf, 1931);

Nettles (London: Faber & Faber, 1930);

Assorted Articles (London: Secker, 1930; New York: Knopf, 1930);

The Virgin and the Gipsy (Florence: Orioli, 1930; London: Secker, 1930; New York: Knopf, 1930);

Love Among the Haystacks and Other Pieces (London: Nonesuch Press, 1930; New York: Viking, 1933);

Apocalypse (Florence: Orioli, 1931; New York: Viking, 1931; London: Secker, 1932);

The Triumph of the Machine (London: Faber & Faber, 1931);

Etruscan Places (London: Secker, 1932; New York: Viking, 1932);

Last Poems, edited by Richard Aldington (Florence: Orioli, 1932; New York: Viking, 1933; London: Secker, 1933);

The Lovely Lady and Other Stories (London: Secker, 1933; New York: Viking, 1933);

A Modern Lover (London: Secker, 1934; New York: Viking, 1934);

Phoenix: The Posthumous Papers of D. H. Lawrence, edited by Edward D. McDonald (New York: Viking, 1936; London: Heinemann, 1936);

The First Lady Chatterley (New York: Dial, 1944);

The Complete Poems of D. H. Lawrence, edited by Vivian de Sola Pinto and Warren Roberts, 2 volumes (London: Heinemann, 1964; New York: Viking, 1964);

The Complete Plays of D. H. Lawrence (London: Heinemann, 1965; New York: Viking, 1966);

Phoenix II: Uncollected, Unpublished, and Other Prose Works, edited by Roberts and Harry T. Moore (New York: Viking, 1968; London: Heinemann, 1968);

John Thomas and Lady Jane (New York: Viking, 1972; London: Heinemann, 1972);

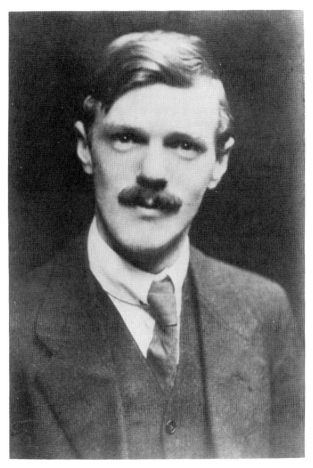

D. H. Lawrence, 26 June 1913 (photo by W. G. Parker)

Mr. Noon, edited by Lindeth Vasey (London & New York: Cambridge University Press, 1984).

Collection: *The Cambridge Edition of the Works of D. H. Lawrence,* general editors James T. Boulton and Warren Roberts, 34 volumes projected (Cambridge, London, New York, New Rochelle, Melbourne & Sydney: Cambridge University Press, 1980-   ).

One of the most widely discussed and renowned twentieth-century authors, D. H. Lawrence remains intriguing and problematic in terms of his biography, his writings, and his prophetic role. In his relatively short life, he was a prolific author of fictions, poetry, travel essays, speculative polemics, and other works. His writing, it is widely agreed, ranges from extremely good to extremely bad. He was, and continues to be, a provocative figure.

Lawrence's origins were unusual for a British writer of his time. Born into the working class in the industrial Midlands—his father was a lifelong coal miner—he was as a boy frail, hypersensitive, and bright. Physically and psychologically marred by his restricted background and by parental conflict, he gradually rebelled. In a strongly class-conscious society, the working-class youth became a schoolteacher and an aspiring writer. By his middle twenties he had been published and critically recognized as a lyric poet and prose fictionist. He soon abandoned teaching, middle-class aspirations, and the social-sexual decorums of his time. In a famous love affair, he fled to the Continent with another man's wife. Most of Lawrence's remaining years until his death in his early forties were marked by frequent travel, a socially marginal lifestyle, grave illness, and intense art and argument. Declassed and deracinated, he had become something of a bohemian-artist cynosure and an obsessive sexual and social critic-prophet against his times.

Much of Lawrence's writing is autobiographical, though some of his best works are not directly so. One of his earliest stories, "The White Stocking" (originally written about 1907 and revised for his first story collection, *The Prussian Officer and Other Stories,* 1914), shows some of his significant powers. This tale about a young lower-middle-class married couple probes, in a heightened realist manner, some of the emotional extremity underlying even a positive relationship. Though loving her young man, the young woman has erotically played with her sexually predatory middle-aged factory boss before her marriage—"perverse desire." He had once pocketed at a party a white stocking she had "mistakenly" taken with her for a handkerchief, a metaphor for her sexual flaunting. After her marriage, the roué sends her a gift on Valentine's Day, which she keeps secret from her husband. However, when she receives another the following year, she flauntingly confesses the gifts to her sedate husband. Enraged, he strikes her in "his lust to see her bleed, to break and destroy her." Chastened, she returns the roué's gifts, and she and her husband renew their tender love, with the now-tested male dominant. The extremes of erotic hungering and hatred, the warring polarities of male and female, have been briefly but acutely exposed. In Lawrence's uniquely uncondescending dramatization of passional struggle in ordinary life, the deep and complex "anguish of spirit" of otherwise apparently simple people is revealed.

This powerful tale is essential Lawrence. But his first novel, *The White Peacock* (1911), by contrast, is stilted and slight. This slow-paced account of the

The Lawrence family, 1897: (front) Lettice Ada, Lydia, David Herbert, and Arthur John; (back) Emily Una, George Arthur, and William Ernest (Nottingham Local History Library and George Roberts)

genteel romances of provincial adolescents—which shams indebtedness to early George Eliot and Thomas Hardy (and lesser late-Victorian fiction)—is narrated by an insufficiently characterized middle-class youth, Cyril Beardsal. It loosely centers on the decline of Cyril's farmer friend, George Saxon, who marries down (a pub girl) and within a few years becomes a depressive and defeated drunk. In the course of the narrative, an odd digressive concern with homoeroticism crops up. "I admired the noble white fruitfulness of his form," Cyril says of George and an obsessively remembered nude swim. He recalls how they rubbed each other dry: "the sweetness of touch of our naked bodies one against the other was superb." In "indecipherable yearning," Cyril always remembers that the young male "love was perfect for a moment, more perfect than any love I have known since, for man or woman." No more is done with it here, but homosexuality becomes an ambiguous issue through much of Lawrence's fiction.

Also striking, and inconsistent with the prevailing tone of the novel, is the brief tale of Annable, a local gamekeeper. This intellectual outsider is an educated ex-parson, once married to a noble lady and since become a misogynist and apocalyptic prophet. He provides the novel's entitling metaphor by describing a showy white peacock in a graveyard "perched on an angel . . . as if it were a pedestal for vanity. That's the soul of woman—or it's the devil." The peacock dirties the angel—"A woman to the end, I tell you, all vanity and screech and defilement." We learn from young Cyril that the embittered keeper "was a man of one idea— that all civilization was the painted fungus of rottenness." His counter to the falsity, in one of the earliest declarations of what was to be Lawrence's famous doctrine: "be a good animal, true to your animal instinct." He is also a first-run for Mellors, gamekeeper-lover of Lady Chatterley in Lawrence's final novel.

This early crude snapshot of the Lawrence prophet is cast aside with Annable's death in the middle of the book. The rest of *The White Peacock* consists mostly of sentimental adolescent posturings, florid descriptions of nature, and stilted cultural allusions from post-1890s fashions. The novel also reflects what were probably Lawrence's mother's lower-middle-class snobberies and hatred of drinking men. (Indeed, Lawrence rushed a pre-publication copy to his mother as she lay dying; she is reported not to have responded.) In his early twenties Lawrence was still trapped by the need to present his mother's puritanic-genteel values. Not surprisingly, then, women dominate all the relationships in the novel, with the males clearly defeated. Many critics have seen this slight fiction as a provincial exercise in late-Victorian quasi-eroticism, though a more essential Lawrence may be recognized in the touches of homoerotic misogyny and prophetic rage.

Lawrence's next novel, *The Trespasser* (1912), is also weak. He wrote most of it while a schoolteacher in the London suburb of Croydon (1908-1911), after pushing through to a teaching certificate at Nottingham (he had previously worked as a clerk in a surgical appliance factory and assisted in hometown schools). Perhaps some of the claustrophobic emotions in the novel should be related to the painfully slow dying of his mother in 1910 and to his own grave respiratory illness which followed. The book may have been further weakened by Lawrence's inappropriate desire to produce something for popular success. The basic materials for the novel came from an uninsightful schoolteacher friend, Helen Corke, who gave Lawrence her autobiographical manuscript recording a destructive love affair. His adaption covers a few days in the life of a near-middle-aged music teacher, Siegmund, whose adulterous affair with the semifrigid young-

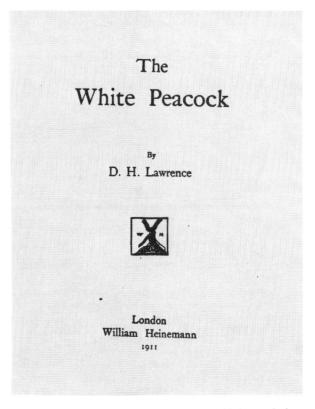

The White Peacock

By
D. H. Lawrence

London
William Heinemann
1911

Title page for Lawrence's first book. The publisher rushed an advance copy of the novel to Lawrence so that he could take it to his dying mother.

er Helen concludes with his guiltily hanging himself.

The writing is labored, burdened with poetically inflated statements ("their thoughts slept like butterflies on the flowers of delight"), and heavy with Wagnerian overtones of doomed love. More than half the narrative describes five days of a love tryst on the Isle of Wight, with drawn-out claustrophobic scenes of erotic rituals. These emphasize the resentful fluctuations in feelings between the lovers, mostly induced by the antisexual, willful, and sentimentally righteous woman. Though inadequately backgrounded and developed, these scenes do carry an essential Lawrence theme: the frigidly erotic woman "rejected the 'animal'" in her short-circuited sensuality, leaving the man feeling like a "balked animal." But the man, too, appears inadequate—narcissistic, priggish, and full of resentful self-pity. The scenes with Siegmund's embittered wife and rejecting children also lack dramatic depth, and the irony that Siegmund's wife is unaffected by her husband's death and takes a lover herself seems stock. Lawrence's insights do not rise here above the maudlin writing.

SONS AND LOVERS

THIS novel tells the story of two generations — men and women, boys and girls, and men and women again. It has the completeness and sincerity of a great novel, and it is written with the power and restraint of a great novelist. No book since "The Old Wives' Tale" has presented a life-drama so convincingly, or built up living characters with such intimate detail of conduct or such vivid realization of conditions. Father and mother, sons and daughters, sons and lovers of women, they live their lives and go their several ways, in their strength and their weakness, with their passions and sorrows and triumphs. It is a book of contrasts, with the inevitability of destiny itself, and the appeal both of the simple and the strange.

D. H. LAWRENCE

Dust jacket for the American edition of Lawrence's 1913 novel. He began the book as a tribute to his mother, but in the course of writing it, he came to see her differently.

Quite different is Lawrence's intensely realized third novel, *Sons and Lovers* (1913). Paul Morel in this novel provides Lawrence's first largely autobiographical character. The highly self-centered Lawrence only haltingly arrived at the autobiographical emphasis. Issues derived from his relations with his domineering mother and righteously willful girl friends usually took priority. Generally, Lawrence's fictional world, as well as his life, remained woman-dominated — and rebelled against. However, to center the issues of Lawrence and his fictions in the Oedipal, and especially in the reductive and self-insulating notions of psychoanalysis, seems needlessly narrow.

Sons and Lovers, the linear story of the Lawrence-like Paul Morel, moves from the early married life of Paul's parents, Gertrude and Walter, to Paul's desperate outcastness after the death of his mother when he is twenty-four. The novel is less about the mother and son than a whole way of life, although Lawrence does appear to have been influenced in his final (third) draft of the novel by the roughly Freudian views of the woman he then lived with, Frieda von Richthofen Weekley. He acknowledged some of that emphasis in a letter in which he speaks of many emotionally crippled mother-lovers, like his protagonist. However, he reasonably insisted that this was only a part-truth (and he flailingly attacked Freudianism in his later *Psychoanalysis and the Unconscious,* 1921, and *Fantasia of the Unconscious,* 1922 — two of his many syncretistic religious essays). Most essentially, *Sons and Lovers* is a novel of provincial family life — a major type of nineteenth-century fiction — with a lower-class and sexual emphasis. Its shape and texture insist on showing its characters as part if not parcel of a whole way of life and culture, not just as psychological cases.

Class ideology and repressions are at issue. No doubt speaking for Lawrence, Paul says of his social ambivalence: "from the middle classes one gets ideas, and from the common people, life itself, warmth." His mother, bitter in her marriage to an improvident coal miner, objects because she desperately wants her sons "to climb into the middle classes." The mother's social ambitions, as well as Paul's mother-fixation, provide much of the basic conflict. As a rising clerk for a surgical appliance firm, as a promising conventional designer, and as a priggish and "superior" young man shedding his social origins, traditional restrictions, friends, and girls, Paul follows his mother's aspirations. His creator had partly gone that route and then rebelled; after teaching, Lawrence turned toward declassed and deracinated bohemianism, becoming the adversary artist-prophet as dissident bourgeois — a role he maintained for the rest of his life.

Paul's rejection of his pit-working, beer-swilling, wife-beating father — who is presented as crude but sensuously and rebelliously immediate — is social as well as psychological. The mother-dominated, sickly, sensitive son chooses the genteel aspirations of his mother in opposition to much of the world in which he grew up. This petty bourgeois feminization causes Paul's alienation, and part of his desperation, at the novel's end.

The marriage between the ill-matched Gertrude and Walter had early turned into a "deadlock of passion" and produced an embittering social as well as psychological conflict. The puritanic daughter of an autocratic father, Gertrude had become dominant in her marriage — "she was her father now" — and undermined the working-class husband. She transfers her erotic and social passions to her sons. The eldest, William, an aspiring gentleman-clerk in London, trapped between his mother's sense of disciplined ambition and a love-hate relation with a frivolous girl, dies in his early twenties; then the guilty mother foists her devotion on her next son, Paul, engendering the same kind of emotional and social anxieties in him.

Walter's scenes, in spite of the antagonistic feminization of the author, suggest a harsh but warm masculine world, with the public house and its male camaraderie his chapel. The matey miner lives a life antithetical to that of his moralistic, chapel-going (Congregational) wife. Her Protestant ethos of self-denial, sexual repression, impersonal work, disciplined aspiration, guilt, and yearning for conversion-escape, not only defeats her already industrially victimized coal-miner husband but also contributes to the defeat of several of their sons. Understanding the social religious matrix seems crucial to understanding other aspects of *Sons and Lovers* as well. Too much of the critical discussion of Miriam Leivers, Paul's farm-girl love for seven late-adolescent years (derived from Lawrence's girl friend Jessie Chambers, a schoolteacher and later an embittered memoirist) focuses on her conflict with Gertrude for Paul's emotional allegiance. But Paul does not finally reject Miriam because of the disapproval of his jealous mother but because Miriam so totally represents the anxious Protestant sensibility. Acutely delineated as antisensual (see, for example, the fine graphic scenes with the swing and the pecking chickens), Miriam is too "fussy," too religiously earnest for "higher things," too burdened with puritan "proud humility" and a Christian "martyr" psychology. She thus quite lacks sexual passion, humor, irony, openness, and, as Paul repeatedly insists, the richer sense of life recognized in spontaneous feelings. Finally, driven in her twenties by Paul's overdue insistence, she gives herself sexually as a "sacrifice." Paul's tortuous break with the righteously suffering-demanding Miriam, who demonstrates Nietzschean "slave morality," cannot be defined by the Oedipal but by the provincial Protestant ethos, so dominant in Anglo-Saxon countries of the period.

Though sexually backward, Paul also has an affair—a profane love in contrast with his love for the sacral Miriam—with Clara, an older woman (a thirtyish feminist factory worker separated from her blacksmith husband Baxter Dawes). Partly delineated as an erotic "somnambule"—an early example of Lawrence's repeated Sleeping Beauty motif—Clara had never awakened into passional

A 1906 photograph of Jessie Chambers, the model for Miriam Leivers in Sons and Lovers *(University of Nottingham Library)*

life with her husband. She is aroused by Paul, who demands her submission in a different way. The eroticism becomes for him a conversion experience, "the baptism of fire in passion"—one of Lawrence's most obsessive themes. The erotic transformation is "the something big and intense that changes you when you really come together with somebody." Clara, as is usual with women in Lawrence, is appalled by "the impersonality of passion" and wants Paul to be more sentimentally personal. But the erotic transformation seems crucial for Paul, producing a heightened sense of immanent life. Thus, "having known the immensity of passion," they also know "their own nothingness" as part of a larger awareness of the impersonal flow of vital life. The desire-negation, eros-nihilism dialectic briefly adumbrated here becomes the central Lawrencean doctrine.

The break with Clara in part depends on Paul's emotional bond with his mother. Paul's mother slowly dies of cancer—her son finally aids in euthanasia—during the time of the love affair. However, the abrupt end of Paul's relationship with Clara also results partly from her demand for more security, her guilt toward her husband, Paul's self-centered social ambitions, and more obscure motives, including Paul's ambiguous relation to Clara's husband. A crude but pathetic character similar to Walter Morel, Baxter in frustration has brutalized his wife. He also thrashes Paul after the priggish youth has helped get him fired and taunted his manliness. Yet "they had met in an extremity of hate, and it was a bond." So Paul becomes a friend of the "sulking" Baxter, gives him money and help in finding a job, and finally insists on turning Clara back to him. This curious twist suggests guilt, homoeroticism, and a placation of the father-masculine world. It also allows Paul to again escape the female power.

Another power seems to be at work in *Sons and Lovers*. Paul is always "fretting" with himself, engaged in a never fully conceptualized internal warfare not adequately explainable by the social tensions and familial discord. Sickly from the start, he has long shown signs of "slow suicide." As more generally with Lawrence, Paul's death wish seems larger and deeper than any specific analysis, such as Oedipal despair, can account for. In "Derelict," the concluding chapter of *Sons and Lovers*, Paul's longing for annihilation goes beyond its ostensible cause in the death of his mother. Having turned Clara back to her husband and made a final rejection of the claustrophobic Christian Miriam, Paul "whimpers" for his dead mother and yearns for the final darkness. In a letter written after he had completed the novel, Lawrence characterized his protagonist as in a "drift toward death." Is this reversed in the concluding sentence of the novel when Paul turns away from the darkness represented (rather than caused) by his dead mother, "towards the faintly humming, glowing town, quickly"? Towns were usually negative images for anti-industrial Lawrence. But some readers ingeniously emphasize the older meaning of the novel's last word, *quickly* (that is, *lively*), to argue for the hopefulness of the conclusion. After all, Paul has achieved passional transformation and has perhaps partially transcended his Oedipal curse. Yet given the whole pattern of the novel, as well as the last chapter (and Lawrence's related works), the most sensible conclusion might be that Paul Morel has lost more than he has won.

Sons and Lovers may be viewed as considerably a story of defeat.

But the crucial experience of the story may be less Paul's progress or defeat than Lawrence's intense portrayal of the life of the lower-class provincials, executed with psychological complexity and without condescension. This portrayal includes not only the coal miner's conflict-ridden family but also life on the Leivers' farm, work in the factory, and the struggles of courtship. While the writing in *Sons and Lovers* is, typically for Lawrence, erratic because of instances of redundancy, inflated statements about feelings, and cursory handling of some important developments (such as Paul's loss of religion), the novel displays unusual sensitivity to the felt fabric of provincial life.

Some critics suggest that this power of the novel derives from its autobiographical basis, but Lawrence's too personal perspective also accounts for some evident weaknesses. The authorial persona is often described in embarrassingly narcissistic ways, while the other Morel children, though crucial to the family theme, are insufficiently developed. Also, there is little critical perspective on Paul's callow artistic views and antifeminist prejudices. Even the later Lawrence reportedly thought his treatment of Walter Morel too biased from the maternal perspective. *Sons and Lovers* falteringly records only part of Lawrence's struggle for a fuller critical consciousness of his background.

The writing of his third novel more or less coincided with drastic changes of consciousness in Lawrence's life. By 1912 he had given up the conventional and restricted life of a schoolteacher. He took a financial risk hoping to live on the income from his writing. (He had to have the help of patrons on several occasions.) After abortive relationships with several women, he ran off to the Continent the spring of 1912 with Frieda von Richthofen Weekley, the upper-class, German-born wife of a former college teacher of his. A combination of the maternal and bohemian, Frieda precipitously abandoned three children to go with Lawrence. The romance placed drastic demands on both. In what became a famous love affair, Lawrence personally dramatized several themes of his love stories, such as his belief that a deep passion requires a cross-class (and often a cross-ethnic and cross-cultural) mating. Does one thus escape some of the Oedipal-incest fears? One certainly thus engages in a relationship marked by considerable conflict, as was true of Lawrence and Frieda, whose marriage was formalized in 1914 and more or less

Frieda von Richthofen Weekley, 1912

maintained until his death. The two felt themselves to be, as Lawrence's lovers usually do, in self-exile from the staid communities they had violated and fled in their passion.

Because of his sense of personal liberation, as well as financial need, Lawrence was extremely productive in the following years. Staying first in Germany and then in remote places in Italy, he and Frieda returned to England before World War I. Though outraged at the war, which he saw as an expression of the death wish of Western civilization (and during which he sometimes had to endure police surveillance because of his German wife and his own antipatriotism), he unhappily remained in England for its duration. He completed a variety of essays, plays, sketches, poems, and stories. He had become an established literary figure, though his finances remained precarious and his way of life more or less that of a marginal bohemian.

Among his early writings, the novella *Daughters of the Vicar* (written in 1911) may be considered representative of Lawrence's strengths and weaknesses. Using what was to be one of his favorite

devices, he presents contrasting portraits of two sisters: Mary, the dutiful, repressed, and socially successful; Louise, the passional, unconventional, and erotically successful. The tale is an argument for personal liberation and harshly portrays the destructive middle-class Christian (High Church) milieu. With a mixture of realism and caricature, Lawrence savages the vicar's family in their snobbish, genteel poverty and repression. Mary pursues a cerebral clergyman, an Oxfordian with a church sinecure and other financial means, a cold and morally rigid "little abortion" of a man. Denying her erotic existence ("she *would* not feel"), Mary expediently marries him and produces the fussy little monster's children. She had "sold herself," "murdering" what was best in herself, and is filled with "general destruction" which will be directed "towards charity and high-minded living." Thus she commits the crimes of conventional and antipassional Christian moral love.

Sister Louise discovers herself rebelling against such morality in a commitment to passion and thus achieves purposeful character. She pursues, with difficulty, a sensitive, declassed coal miner, Alfred, who has bookish and musical proclivities and is "polarized" emotionally by his strong-willed, widowed mother, with whom he lives. Thanks to Louise, Alfred struggles, after his emotional collapse at his mother's death, from "great chaos" to a "wonderful" responsiveness, partly elaborated in Lawrence's heavy prose of passion ("lightening," "seared," "fiery anguish," "torment," "utter darkness," "agony of chaos," "glowing," "eternal," "kind of death," "swooning," etc.). Alfred's breakthrough is the emotional liberation of the repressed and requires a social-class violation. The story concludes with the snobbish and nasty rejection of the lovers by the vicar and his wife. The lovers plan to flee to the colonies; such are the social consequences of the realization of passion against the social-moral order. While *Daughters of the Vicar* is sometimes awkward in its caricatures and insistent abstract metaphors of the emotions, it is sharp in its contrasts of class and in its deployment of the dialectics of eroticism.

Another novella, *Love Among the Haystacks* (perhaps written shortly before *Daughters of the Vicar* but first published posthumously in 1930), shows one of Lawrence's simplest erotic patterns. Contrasting brothers, one a victim of "inflamed self-consciousness," the other a more confident mother's boy, discover themselves in a rural-ritualistic scene. They work the harvest haystack, respond intensely to the physical scenery (as is usual in Lawrence), jealously fight in a show of their erotic turmoil, and that night in the hayfield achieve sexual consummations—the confident brother with a "wildcat" foreign governess from a nearby vicarage, the emotionally tortured brother with the humble wife of a migrant worker ("both were at odds with the world"). Erotic realization required for each an alien partner. The brothers achieve not just coitus but also a sacramental heightening—what Lawrence here and elsewhere describes as the conversionlike experience of "wonder"—which gives a vibrant sense of inner and outer life.

More often, Lawrence's fictions present erotic recognition as anguished. In one of his best-known early short stories, "Odour of Chrysanthemums" (the materials and themes were also utilized in Lawrence's best play, *The Widowing of Mrs. Holroyd*, published in 1914), he combines a "realistic" study of working-class domesticity with a poetic heightening. The recurrent metaphor of the "wan flowers," along with Lawrence's usual fire and darkness imagery, reveals failed passion. The burdened and resentful pregnant wife ends up ritually preparing the corpse of her husband, killed in a mine accident. Her epiphany—"death restored the truth"—is that theirs had been an erotic failure and she had been "fighting a husband who did not exist." The righteously rigid wife had defeated the passional individuality of the man. The balancing forces of death and eros fuse in the haunting odor of failure.

The story might also be viewed as the compensatory other side—the woman's failure exposed—of the Walter-Gertrude conflict in *Sons and Lovers*. Additional variations on that autobiographical material appear in other pre-World War I stories of mining life. In the brief "A Sick Collier," a devoted and hardworking miner husband is properly "polarized"—a key Lawrence term for male-female passional balance—with his superior wife. But he is undermined by a painful and enduring injury. Desperate to join his mates in manly pursuits, he is restrained by his wife and breaks down into mad shouts that the pain is her fault and he wants to kill her. The story ends with his sobbing self-pity and his wife's fear that his sick pay may be stopped because of his derangement. Once the collier has lost his manly role, the balance of the marriage is destroyed. Lawrence often insisted on purposive maleness.

"Strike-Pay" loosely focuses on a miner who loses his money, witnesses the accidental death of a navvy, and goes "home vaguely impressed with the sense of death, and loss, and strife." Thus aware of the "greater" strife in life, he for once manages to win the lesser "battle" of domesticity, asserting his manhood against his mother-in-law and wife. The wife submits to the Adamic authority: "She attended to him. Not that she was really meek. But—he was *her* man. . . ."

In yet another of these early working-class stories, "A Miner at Home," Lawrence deploys his vivid sense of domestic reality to show the harsh disagreement between a husband and wife over his going on strike. In "Her Turn," a more comic version of the domestic battle of wills, a well-matched couple fights over whether he will share his strike compensation with his wife or use it only for masculine assertion. She counters by spending all their savings to fix up the home, thus forcing him to share his strike pay with her. From the same period, "Delilah and Mr. Bircumshow" concerns an unassertive bank clerk who has been defeated by his wife. She clipped "this ignoble Samson . . . from instinct," but by depriving her husband of his sense of masculine purpose, she has deprived herself of what passion they had. These minor stories are informed—perhaps overinformed, some might suspect—by the endless domestic conflict of Lawrence's Eastwood mining-family childhood. The sense of struggle between man and woman is at the center of much of Lawrence's work.

One of the most powerful of the early short stories is "The Christening." With a perception of family life alien to that of the sentimentalist, Lawrence reveals the kinship bond as one of proud hatred. The family of a retired and declining but still autocratic miner show their domestic scars: the painfully sensitive older daughter is a sickly schoolteacher; the son is a rough bully; the younger daughter resentfully mothers her bastard child by a man she despises. The ritual of baptism for the child certifies a larger bastardy as the legacy of disintegrating authority. The vague officiating clergyman feels overwhelmed by the patriarch—the New Testament by the Old (Lawrence's usual preference)—and the slobbering, self-willed wreck of a miner preaches to the preacher and names the bastard for himself while denying mere earthly fatherhood. His children harden themselves in emotional bastardy, finding his very blessing a curse. He concludes by joyously praising life—"The daisies light up the earth"—but his children sullenly shrink back. There has been generation without regeneration within the wrecked power of the old dispensation.

Nearly a dozen lesser early stories by Lawrence struggle with erotic torments. "The Shadow

Manuscript for a poem probably written in winter 1914-1915. The title echoes Christ's words on the cross from Matthew 27.46: "Eli, Eli, lama sabachthani? that is to say, My God, my God, why hast thou forsaken me?" (The Pierpont Morgan Library).

in the Rose Garden" plays bitter ironies on the traditional romance imagery of the rose. On her honeymoon, a woman unexpectedly meets her former lover in a rose garden. But he is now a lunatic incapable of even recognizing her. Her crude husband, now aware that his wife has been sexually possessed before, reacts with hatred. In the rather brittle "The Witch a la Mode" a guiltily adulterous young man is "accidentally" burned in his inflammatory love for a dangerous modern woman. In the slight "The Overtone" the issue is a woman's sexual revulsion for her husband. The fervid "New Eve and Old Adam" has a vaguely defined upper-class urban couple in conflict, with the old, Adamic male longing for a unity of the flesh and total commitment from the modern, willful Eve, who will not tolerate such subordination. In the mawkish "The Old Adam" a Georgian aesthete living in the home of a middle-class couple emotionally dallies with the wife, improbably wins a fistfight with the burly businessman husband—this drives the repentant wife back to the husband—and in a kind of homoerotic transfer becomes "close friends" with his rival. For Lawrence, modern love was indeed perplexed.

"A Modern Lover" is one of a group of stories which relate sexual repression to social class, with the woman defeating passion; Muriel and Cyril here are a version of Miriam and Paul in *Sons and Lovers*. Class more clearly dominates the archly heavy "The Shades of Spring," in which a superior young man, now married, visits his former love, who still longs for his intellectual companionship but has settled for a second-best lover, a gamekeeper. In the slight "Goose Fair" a middle-class young man is passingly tempted by a second-best, a goose girl, but ends in "bitter" submission to the "superior" girl. In the finest of these tales, "Second Best," a young woman desperately decides to settle in love for a man of lower social class. In an unconsciously symbolic act, she brings a dead mole—image of the blind unconscious—to the second-best swain. Throughout his work, Lawrence employs metaphoric animals to represent emotional issues. In "Second Best" social class disparity is overcome by the dark unconscious and ritualistic propitiation, though agony continues in the erotic submission.

After spending time in Germany with Frieda before World War I, Lawrence wrote four stories drawing on German military life, his first reach beyond provincial English materials. In "Once" (1913), a rather forced Maupassant-type erotic tale which may have had its origin in Frieda's experience (she was from a military family and had

numerous affairs), a demimondaine tells her current love of an exciting past escapade in which a stranger, a handsome aristocratic officer, came to her bed—a scene with crushed rose petals, gold chains, and other old-fashioned sexual fantasy decor. But the story's tone seems disapproving of the woman's sexual insatiability and search for "sensation." Lawrence, usually very serious about the erotic, frequently contrasts the search for sexual sensation with deeper passion. As he wrote in one of his polemics, "sex in the head, no real desire."

"The Mortal Coil," also brittle in manner, tells of an aristocratic young officer with gambling troubles who is brought to a sense of mortality by the accidental death of his mistress. A better story, "The Thorn in the Flesh," links the breakdown of authority with the breakthrough of passion. A young army recruit, driven to physical revolt against demeaning treatment, flees. He goes to his girl friend, a servant on an estate, and experiences for the first time a "furious flame of passion." Thus sexually liberated, in contrast to his military condition, he has a new sense of being. In the awkward ending, he is recaptured, but we are led to believe that a truer authority, the local baron (Frieda's father?) has responded with manly sympathy and will help the awakened youth.

No such easy escape weakens the most powerful of the stories drawing on German military life, "The Prussian Officer" (the original, and sardonically better, title, "Arms and Honour," was replaced by an editor). Again the story turns on a violent conflict between a harsh officer and an unconsciously rebellious soldier, but here the covert emotional bond appears homosexual, especially on the side of the cruel, aristocratic captain. (As Lawrence wrote in a letter of this period: "soldiers get their surplus sex and their frustration and dissatisfaction into their blood and *love* cruelty.") After much brutalization, the innocent youth strangles the tormenting officer, flees into the countryside, and wanders about deliriously until he dies. The concluding image of the captain and his orderly side by side in the mortuary emphasizes the irony of union in death for vicious authority and desperate rebel. But the dominant experiences of the story emphasize the obsessional intensification of love-hate feelings and suggest that the consequent alienation and guilt—repeatedly elaborated with scenic images— reveal the desire for annihilation. This, like several of Lawrence's best later fictions, explores the psychological dialectics of destructiveness. The violated innocent's intensification of desire becomes a death-longing.

Dust jacket for Lawrence's 1915 novel. The blurb on the spine was probably written by Lawrence.

In summary, of the early (pre-World War I) Lawrence fictions, one novel, *Sons and Lovers*, clearly stands out. The novella *Daughters of the Vicar* is not his best writing but displays some of his characteristic social and erotic insights against the milieu of Christian class morality. Although the early stories have a scattering of interesting descriptions and perceptions, especially around issues of erotic conflict, three tales particularly stand out: "The White Stocking," "The Christening," and "The Prussian Officer." These stories not only display the vivid intensity of scene and emotional conflict but also the erotic-nihilistic dialectics which characterize Lawrencean sensibility.

After finishing *Sons and Lovers*, one of Lawrence's many writing projects was an ambitious novel-saga of provincial life with such provisional titles as "The Sisters" and "The Wedding Ring." This project soon split into two loosely linked but quite different long narratives which became *The Rainbow* (published in 1915) and *Women in Love* (published in 1920). Because it was suppressed, partly by historical accidents, for obscenity in Britain and used in a morally tendentious way by several critics, *The Rainbow* has received more attention than it merits. Much of the writing is redundant and inflated; the story is often ragged and unrealized; the themes are frequently shifting and murky. An obvious failure of fictional craft, the novel may have been additionally defeated by its overly ambitious goal of explaining three generations in England as they pass through major changes in social values and passional relationships.

About half of *The Rainbow* centers on the adolescence of one third-generation, middle-class girl, Ursula. Her forbears were Midlands farmers of long heritage. The first detailed figure, Ursula's grandfather Tom, a youngest child, combines the sensual and transcendent in his "desire to find in a woman the embodiment of all his inarticulate, powerful religious impulses." In a language heavy with images of heat, flame, and other expressions of transfiguration, Lawrence presents some of Tom's struggle to break through his tormenting sexual repression. Finally he achieves a partial victory by means of his late marriage to Lydia, a mid-thirtyish Polish exile widow with a young daughter, Anna. Lydia's exotic foreignness (a trait that recurs in many Lawrence fictions and was important in his life) excites Tom but also makes for uncertain possession, which drives him to rages and drinking. In Lawrence's insistent (and sometimes unconsciously self-parodying) sanctification of the erotic, woman continues to represent for man the transcendent "unknown," part of the process for heightening passion to "eternal knowledge." Tom sees his marriage as "his Gethsemane and his Triumphal Entry in one" (the obscene puns may not be intentional), his sex with his wife as "blazing darkness" (among other oxymorons), and his intense subjectivity as his "transformation, glorification, admission" into a religious state. The actual sex is vague and the relationship apparently both impassioned and strained.

There are a few effective scenes: Tom's comforting stepdaughter Anna in the barn while her mother is giving birth; his drunken speech at Anna's wedding where the sacramental eroticism takes a seriocomic turn ("a married couple makes one Angel"); and other touches here and there. But Tom drops out of the narrative, ten years before his accidental death in a flood (to be answered by the rainbow?). Surprisingly, we then hear that he had been part of "the old brutal story of desire and offerings and deep, deep-hidden rage of unsatisfied men against women," which had not been dramatically developed.

The sexual burning and perplexity pass on to Anna, who has had to fight against her stepfather Tom to achieve sex and marriage with her cousin, Will Brangwen. Part of Anna's self-discovery occurs during the famous surrogate sexual scene in which she and Will shuck corn sheaves in the moonlight. This second generation's more self-conscious battle of male-female wills plays out in metaphors of heat, birds, unfolding plants, and arching cathedrals (further foreshadowing of the rainbow promise?). The marriage bed again becomes "the core of living eternity," but the passions turn into warfare in which "there could only be acquiescence and submission," temporarily salved by the "tremulous wonder of consummation." Anna overcomes Will

when she relinquishes "the adventure to the unknown" for compulsive breeding (nine pregnancies) and a "violent trance of motherhood." She forces Will into a resigned "darkness in which he could not unfold." His aspirations as a religious artist are reduced to a hobby of making church repairs while he earns a living doing mechanical design work (and later teaching crafts in the schools). He principally services the female will and family. We later learn that Anna and Will were never "quite defined as individuals."

The third generation engages in an even more perplexing, and certainly more self-conscious, struggle to relate the erotic to "a sense of the infinite." As an adolescent, the oldest child Ursula takes up with a maternal cousin, Anton, an on-and-off love for the rest of the novel. But Ursula does not really like Anton, except for the physical satisfaction he provides ("her sexual life flamed into a kind of disease"). Her dislike is not surprising, since Lawrence defines Anton as essentially conventional, a "conservative materialist" and statist who goes off to the Boer War as an engineering officer. "His soul lay in the tomb. His life lay in the established order of things."

With Anton away, Ursula works as a primary-school teacher for several years. In vivid scenes in the realistic mode (unlike much of the rest of the novel), Lawrence draws on his own teaching experience to show suppressed rage at the trivializing, regimented, and sometimes mean labors of doing a "collective inhuman thing"—compulsory schooling. Ursula finally escapes from teaching and takes her amorphous romantic yearnings to a university, where as a student she soon becomes disillusioned with that "apprentice shop" for "making money," that "commercial shrine" and "slovenly laboratory for the factory." She eventually flunks her exams.

While teaching, Ursula engages in a lesbian relationship with another teacher, Winifred Inger, taking up "the perverted life of the elder woman." (Lawrence uses *perverted* to describe any sexual situation he does not approve of.) But to Ursula's combined relief and disgust, Winifred calculatingly ends up marrying Ursula's uncle, Tom Brangwen, Jr. Though inadequately described, this coal-mine industrialist is presented as "perverted" in a larger sense, dehumanizing lives in his "putrescent" eagerness to serve "Moloch," the industrial machine. (Socially bad people almost always have bad sex in Lawrence's works.) Later Lawrence continues the ideologizing by having Ursula, rather improbably, make Nietzschean denouncements of bourgeois

Lawrence made this transcription of an English folk song for Catherine Carswell in summer 1919 (American Art Association / Anderson Galleries, sale 4283, 9-10 December 1936).

society as enslaved to "money-interest" and other false doctrines ("only degenerate races are democratic").

Returned from the war, Anton seems to Ursula an establishment degenerate. She lives with him for a brief time, searching through sexuality for a "consummation" which includes "the infinite." The sex seems to be good—Ursula "entered the dark fields of immortality"—but not good enough to bridge the split between "passion" and "the social self." Finally, Ursula finds Anton even sexually insufficient, and she becomes a predatory "harpy," insatiable and out to destroy his maleness. Anton, "his will broken," flees from her to a conventional marriage and a job as an Indian colonialist.

The final chapter of *The Rainbow* puts pregnant Ursula in a field with threatening horses (a semifantasy scene, the horses are apparently metaphors for masculinity). Frightened, she becomes ill and soon miscarries. Although now the modern experienced and alienated woman, she still

seeks a man "from the Infinite," though realizing that she dangles between the lost organic world of her forbears and an unacceptable present order which is disorder. "She grasped and groped to find the creation of the living God, instead of the old, hard barren form of bygone living." The concluding image of the Old Testament rainbow (repeatedly foreshadowed) gives an uncertain promise of a transcendent dimension and richer life.

The direction of *The Rainbow* may be summarized as an erratically desperate effort to sanctify the erotic in an increasingly anomic society. In spite of its provocative ideas, powerful moments, and intriguing issues, Lawrence's fourth novel stands as a largely failed work because of bad writing, indifferent dramatization, and fervent incoherences.

In the better-crafted *Women in Love* we still follow Ursula (and get a few details about Anna and Will, and even a casual reference to Anton), but the fifth novel is not in any important sense a continuation of the fourth. The materials of the narrative have drastically changed; so has Lawrence, his outlook altered by World War I into a new sophistication and hardness. The England at issue is no longer rural and marital but industrial and bohemian. In *Women in Love* even the old industrial ethic, as embodied by paternalistic mine owner Thomas Crich, is being replaced by the highly rationalized functionalism of his willful son Gerald; the patriarch is being replaced by the new "industrial magnate." Will Brangwen's religious art in *The Rainbow* has been replaced by his daughter Gudrun's modernist sculpture, by the modernist, antihumanist artist Loerke, by primitive art objects, and the like. In *Women in Love* social and sexual relations are also different and exacerbated. The "bitterness of the war," Lawrence wrote of the novel, though the story takes place prior to the war, provides a pervasive sense of personal and cultural "crisis" in the "passionate struggle into conscious being," which is the theme of the work.

Rupert Birkin, obviously the Lawrence persona, enters the Brangwen story as Ursula's lover and then husband. The narrative covers the love affairs of the sisters Ursula and Gudrun over a period of slightly less than two years, but their lovers, Birkin and Gerald, displace the sisters as the main focus. As Lawrence writes of his Birkin-self, "his way of seeing some things vividly and feverishly, and of his acting on this special sight" and his intense dialectical struggle with problems of consciousness give the fiction some of its power. But the novel also suffers from Birkin-Lawrence's tendency to make abstract statements about tortured subjectivity, a weakness compounded by the awkward conception of the character as a thirtyish, misanthropic school inspector with a substantial income. Birkin lacks solid personal background and social reality behind his upper-bohemian way of life.

Another difficulty with Birkin derives from the half-covert issue of bisexuality. *Women in Love* ends, after the suicide of Birkin's friend Gerald in the Tyrolean Alps while the two couples are on vacation, with Birkin promisingly married to Ursula yet still longing for an "eternal union with a man too." In a canceled opening section of the novel (first published in 1963 as "Prologue to *Women in Love*") Birkin's homosexual side is emphasized in overwrought prose about his "affinity for men," since he has "the hot, flushing aroused attraction" for alien males who "held the passion and the mystery to him." The partly obscured homosexuality dominates several scenes in the novel, especially the wrestling bout between Birkin and Gerald (in the chapter entitled "Gladiatorial"). Homosexuality

also explains some of the peculiarities of Birkin's ostensibly heterosexual conflicts with Ursula.

Such ambivalence may underlie such key doctrines of Lawrence's, here and elsewhere, as "Desire, in any shape or form, is primal, whereas the will is secondary, derived." The discovery, and maintenance, of passional desire—the main affirmation of life in a world of smashed values—requires one's protecting desire from the corruptions of willed behavior, be it industrial, social, intellectual, or artistic. *Women in Love* repeatedly focuses on conflicts, within a character and between characters, of desire against will.

Desire, it should be noted, takes some nastily extreme forms. Birkin, for example, emphatically tells Gerald that "a man who is murderable is a man who in a profound hidden lust desires to be murdered." What happens is what one desires. This absurd generality comes from Lawrence's turning "desire" into an all-encompassing absolute. It may be argued, as apparently the novel intends, that a variant of Birkin's statement applies to Gerald, whose final weakness of desire in his willful struggle with Gudrun becomes suicidal. Even here Lawrence claims larger application since Gerald is the "messenger" of the "universal dissolution into whiteness and snow," the modernist apocalypse without any rainbow promise.

Yet Lawrence's dogmatism with his vitalistic doctrines is not always simpleminded. For striking example, Lawrence gives the negative character Hermione, Birkin's mistress before Ursula (and the author's angry personal caricature of a cultured upper-class lady), some of his doctrinal gestures, such as an insistence on the "spontaneous" over the "self-conscious." Then he has Birkin attack this claim to vitalistic values as "the worst and last form of intellectualism, this love . . . for passion and the animal instincts." Ironically, Lawrence thus provides what was to be one of the major attacks on Lawrence's own doctrines.

Birkin nonetheless serves as spokesman for Lawrence's persistent recasting of the Nietzschean dialectic. This includes having a passionate "sensuality" (distinguished from the merely cerebral "sensuous" or "sensation") as the Dionysian necessity for true being and culture, the "great dark knowledge" (perhaps Lawrence's most notorious phrase). In *Women in Love,* various forms of the dark knowledge are presented in terms of a piece of African sculpture, responses to a modernist painting, several episodes with animals, and symbolic scenery. Lawrence's prophetic purpose pervades almost all.

Lawrence makes many of his points by antithesis, and much of the novel is less about desire than about nihilism. Birkin (and Lawrence, as we know from his other writings of the time), shows a raging misanthropy: "mankind is a dead tree"; his "dislike of mankind . . . amounted almost to a disease"; he "abhors humanity"; "Man is a mistake, he must go"; and on and on. Most of the characters are denounced as well as revealed as profoundly destructive (Hermione, Gudrun, Gerald, Loerke, et al.). Social scene after social scene—London bohemia, the colliers' Saturday night, the cultured wealthy at Hermione's country house, the Crich family wedding—is savaged. The dominant technological-commercial order, especially as represented by Gerald Crich, receives sweeping condemnation for its essence, not just its wrongs; it depends on a fundamentally inhumane will, the reduction of people to "instrumentality" and "the substitution of the mechanical principle for the organic." The resulting social order shows "pure organic disintegration and pure mechanical organization. This is the first and finest state of chaos." The only authentic alternative is individual awareness and flight.

Lawrence's erotic dialectic, in this argumentative fiction, develops out of, rather than in spite of,

Louie Burrows, one of the models for Ursula in The Rainbow *and* Women in Love *(University of Nottingham Library, Professor J. T. Boulton)*

this destructive ordering and the nihilistic conclusions. The Birkin-Ursula courtship becomes a "passion of opposition." Explicitly not a love ethic in any usual sense (like that which belongs to despised Christianity), the "strange conjunction" that Birkin demands is "not meeting and mingling . . . but an equilibrium, a pure balance of two single beings; as the stars balance each other." No doubt Birkin's individualist stance partly reflects a fear of merger with woman. Lawrence repeatedly and vehemently rejects usual sentimental courtship—elsewhere he scornfully calls it "adoration love"—and demands that passion be "stark and impersonal." Such love precariously intertwines with hostility.

While Lawrence's Birkin claims equality in the relationship, clearly one star is more powerful than the other; Ursula, reasonably enough, repeatedly characterizes her lover's demands as male bullying. Birkin's claim to go "beyond love" reveals considerable misogyny. Woman, as "man-to-man" lovers (Gerald and Birkin) know, "was always so horrible and clutching," full of "a greed of self-importance in love. She wanted to have, to own, to be dominant"—"the Great Mother of everything." Thus Birkin justifies the protective "conjunction between two men," such as the *Blutbruderschaft* he demands of Gerald. In the scene in which Birkin stones the reflection of the moon on a pond, he intends to shatter the nature goddess Cybele, "the accursed Syria Dea!" Ursula insists on interpreting his action as a demand for love. It is certainly a demand for submission. He wants "the surrender of her spirit," something even beyond the "phallic," for which she must forgo her "assertive *will*." The woman twists even that to her purposes: she "believed that love was *everything*. Man must render himself up to her. He must be quaffed to the dregs by her. Let him be *her man* utterly, and she in return would be his humble slave. . . ." In these conflicting erotic ideologies, mating becomes a kind of permanent warfare.

Curiously, Birkin grants of his transcendental passion that his "spirituality was concomitant of a process of depravity." In Ursula's affectionate surrender in the Sherwood Forest night scene Birkin's ambivalently domineering eroticism apparently takes the form of anal sexuality ("the darkest poles of the body" found "at the back and base of the loins"). How this relates to the "star-equilibrium" of Lawrencean love remains obscure. But the suggestive courtship, presented in intense and even witty scenes, remains provocative, as does the larger passional pathos in which the man desperately quests for "his resurrection" (part of an admitted "religious mania"). Whether the resurrection is momentarily achieved by the "bestial," by female submission, or by male-female warfare for heroic equilibrium, the consequences seem to be an asocial marriage with the couple in isolated flight.

By a not-always-clear antithesis, the Gudrun-Gerald love affair becomes a more deathly battle of wills as they struggle to master each other. Their passion becomes "disintegrating," driving Gerald to self-murder and Gudrun to a man-hating perversity. She takes up with Loerke, a gnomish and nasty German-Jewish modern artist whose "corruption" becomes hers as well. (Lawrence displays some conventional British anti-Semitism here and elsewhere.) For Lawrence, the talented Gudrun and Loerke represent modernist culture in its decadent subservience to the antihuman chaos brought on by industrialism and the war. Through them Lawrence mounts a modernist attack on modernism.

In *Women in Love* one sister finds an affirmative passion and the other a destructive twisting of passion, but neither achieves traditional marriage. The old world is dead in the most intimate as well as largest senses. The relationship of Ursula and Birkin depends on their being "disinherited"—deracinated, declassed, defamilied—though the protagonist, like Lawrence, retains wistful utopian longings for male bonding and even a new community ("I always imagine our being really happy with some few people"). Utopianism was the other side of Lawrence's nihilism. But the issues in *Women in Love*, as Lawrence's dialectics and overreaching metaphors suggest, can have little possible resolution. Erotic perplexity continues. And so does cosmic perplexity: as Birkin says near the novel's end, "Whatever the mystery which has brought forth man and the universe, it is a non-human mystery . . . man is not the criterion." So human efforts, erotic and other, provide only a momentary stay against the nothingness. This awareness is the deep modern disenchantment, but even so, it can intensify the possibilities of passional realization, which may be taken as the final moral of *Women in Love*.

This novel is Lawrence's most thoroughly wrought long fiction (though as balanced narrative it may not match *Sons and Lovers* and *Lady Chatterley's Lover*, and for perfection of craft and insight it does not equal the best of the short fictions). Its force comes from Lawrence's combination of perplexed dialectics and vivid metaphoric scenes. Among the latter: the fatal water party at the Crichs'; Gerald's willfully fighting his horse; Hermione's smashing Birkin; the stoning of the reflection of the moon; the rabbit's scoring Gudrun's arm; and Gerald's

death in the snow. The display of subterranean motives intensifies these scenes. The dialectics work similarly: Birkin's arguments with Gerald carry homoeroticism as well as anti-industrialism; the lovers' quarrels involve metapsychology as well as courtship; the erotic doctrines concern cultural nihilism as well as sexuality. Such intensification provides much of Lawrence's distinctive quality.

Lawrence's subsequent novels lack much of this force. *The Lost Girl* (published in 1920 but begun before the war) is a much less ambitious work than *Women in Love*. But though carelessly written, it is more interesting than the critics' neglect of it would suggest. Probably taking off from Arnold Bennett's *Anna of the Five Towns* (1902), Lawrence provides a study of shabby lower-middle-class provincial life, though the novel's railing tone suggests the author's distance from his parochial past.

In a perverse way, *The Lost Girl* is a "feminist" novel about the "liberation" of a Midlands spinster, Alvina Houghton, a failed shopkeeper's only child who frees herself to become a nurse, then a vaudeville piano player, then the wife of an Italian peasant. The rigid social system of the small Midlands colliery town where Alvina was born and reared produces the "Dead Sea fruit" of bitter old maids—the thirtyish virgin Alvina and the poignantly earnest viragos Miss Frost and Miss Pinnegar, who take care of her after her mother develops heart disease "as a result of nervous repressions." Other sad fruits of the old order include Alvina's father, a quasi-comic, always failing entrepreneur who finally becomes proprietor of a sleazy working-class vaudeville and cinema house. That entertainment center and the Congregational chapel Alvina attends encompass most of provincial culture, in all the oppressive narrowness Lawrence was forever fleeing.

Lawrence only thinly presents much of the material, including Alvina's fiancés: a rigid social-climbing colonial schoolteacher and a pompous older doctor—little boys with a domineering, manly veneer. No wonder that she prefers to have as a friend odd little Mr. May, her theater partner and a cryptotransvestite. Alvina loses social status playing piano for the vaudeville acts (as usual in Lawrence, one must break class for passional liberation) and falls in love with an "atavistic" Italian performer, Cicio, an image of alien, dark sensuality. Eventually Alvina and Cicio marry and move to his primitive family farm in central Italy.

The harshly different foreign scenes bring forth Lawrence's usual vibrancy in portraying such places without sentimentality, places which "resist us" and "have the power to overthrow our psychic being." As with his earlier Italian travel writings (*Twilight in Italy,* 1916), his later Sicilian and Sardinian descriptions (*Sea and Sardinia,* 1921) and sketches of Mexico (*Mornings in Mexico,* 1927), his scenes of the American Southwest in *St. Mawr* (1925), and his posthumously published account of an archaeological tour (*Etruscan Places,* 1932), the descriptions of the "spirit of place" in the alien scene of *The Lost Girl* are powerful. The place is not pretty: Lawrence evokes savage pagan gods, a "malevolent" spirit, dirt, crudeness, "venomous" inhabitants, and other repulsions. But the very harshness and differentness can liberate Alvina (and Lawrence) from the tight gray English scene and bring them into an expansive awareness of an indifferent universe and a nihilistic vitalism.

In *The Lost Girl* Lawrence's liberation of his heroine once again comes in her submission to the male. She had been seeking a "profound and dangerous inter-relationship," one which requires not just sexual arousal but flight from her social origins and culture as well. One cannot be lower-middle-class and liberated, nor can a passionate person exist within the routines of industrial-commercial society. No doubt Lawrence projects a traditional male fantasy in making this liberation require the woman's submission to a man. Even in Alvina's mind Cicio "made her his slave" with the power of his "dark flicker of ascendancy." Her sexual submission—"a paroxysm of unbearable sensation"—paradoxically becomes her individual completion. Alvina, "bewitched" and "submissive to his being," achieves the fulfillment of a richer sense of self.

Though the heroine fatalistically subordinates herself to her foreign demon lover, with whom she can hardly even converse (a traditional Italian male, he talks mostly to other men in public places), she reaches the "acquiescent passion" of the primordial feminine. But the transformation is not total, and the poor pregnant English girl, left on the harsh peasant farm when her husband is conscripted for World War I, remains "lost" in the simple sense as well. A pathetic old maid, the product of early twentieth-century provincial English repression, may have gone far, but her transformation still remains problematic. It is too bad that Lawrence wrote sloppily and jeeringly in his handling of this sometimes moving fiction of provincial rebellion, which was his as well as his heroine's.

Lawrence's shorter fictions of this period (World War I and the following couple of years) extend his range of subject and tone. Curiously, the war to which he so bitterly responded sometimes brought out a kind of bemusement in his writing. "Monkey-Nuts" wryly dramatizes a triangle consisting of a pair of soldiers—one naive and young, the other crassly cynical and old—and a "land girl" at a provincial commissary. The elder soldier intervenes in the developing relationship between his young cohort and the girl, pushing the youth to insult her and drive her away. The *senex* wins, not only defeating the sexual initiation of the youth and taking revenge on the female who scorned him but defeating the males' own sexuality.

"Tickets, Please," again with common folk, concerns another sexual reversal, done in mock-heroic manner. The conductors have been replaced in wartime tram service by young women with heroic esprit. The only male who remains in the service is the sexually predatory inspector, John Thomas (folklorish euphemism for the phallus, used several places by Lawrence). Annie, the last and toughest of the inspector's seven seduction victims, organizes revenge on the seducer in which the seven mock-vestals trap and beat him. The sardonic tale ends the reverse rape with a feeling of melancholy postcoital love-hate in which the defense of the sex has defeated sex.

Displaying little bemusement about the war is the long, awkward story "England, My England," which portrays an upper-class dilettante who goes to his death at the front. Like several of Lawrence's fictions, this partial roman à clef may be skewed by Lawrence's incompletely explained contempt for the novel's real-life source. We are told that the upper-class Georgian aesthete protagonist lacks "acrid courage, and a certain will-to-power"—a lack of purposefulness in Lawrence's neo-Nietzschean philosophy. After failing as a father and a man, he enlists in the wartime army, which Lawrence rages against as a "mechanism" of mass "insanity." As in "The Prussian Officer," Lawrence puts extended and vivid emphasis upon the man's death-longing. It is the self-destructive yearning of the old cultured England that provides much of the point of the tale.

"The Blind Man" takes a wounded victim of the war, Maurice, who has withdrawn with his devoted wife to a circumscribed farm existence. In one of Lawrence's many triangular parables, Maurice represents the "dark" values (sex and other touch, the organically unconscious, and the intuitive). The "light" values (rationality, cosmopolitan sophistication, conventional idealism) are represented by visiting Bertie, an antisexual and intellectual old friend of Maurice's wife. In a ritualistic scene of bonding in the dark sensate world of the barn, Maurice tries to explain to Bertie his passional sense of life and concludes with pressing the other man's hand against his facial scars. The two men return to Maurice's wife in the house—she has been feeling ambivalently caught between the dark and light values—and her blind husband now seems to her "like a strange colossus." Thus she affirms his dark values. Bertie, of the conventional light world, visibly shattered by the alien and primitive ritual of dark intimacy in the barn, "could not bear it that he had been touched by the blind man, his insane reserve broken in. He was like a mollusc whose shell is broken." The nerve-rubbing Lawrencean heightening lies in the repetitious extremity of language as well as in the striking and brief symbolic action and in the harsh irony that the blind Maurice deludes himself by believing that he has achieved intimate friendship when he has destroyed the other. The dark values may be richly positive, but they are also precarious.

The allures and dangers of the dark values are also at issue in the ornate novella *The Ladybird* (1923), an elaborate rewrite of the wartime story "The Thimble." As he was to do repeatedly in his later years, Lawrence here turned from the heightened realism which had been his prevailing manner to a synthetic allegorical mode, parallel to the attempts of many modernist writers to reinvent shattered mythic traditions. Lady Daphne (linked to Artemis, Atalanta, Astarte, Cybel, Isis, and other mythic figures), the bored wife of an idealist-Platonist, Lord Boris, brings to her home as a guest a middle-European officer wounded in the war, Count Dionys Pasnek (the outlaw deity Dionysius in the Nietzschean sense and also a dark Teutonic hero and ancient ritualist who possesses a scarab-snake symbolic jewel—the "ladybird" of the title). The ménage à trois seems to follow a Tristan-Iseult-Mark pattern of romance, with the count's strange wound, the husband's implicit encouragement of his wife's seduction, and death as the ultimate erotic consummation.

Apparently the lady is to be forever divided between the light values, her husband of the social world, and the dark values, the "dark flame" outsider with demonic power. *The Ladybird* displays the forced mythicizing and autocratic social-moral prejudices Lawrence was to feverishly poeticize in such work as *The Plumed Serpent*. The aristocratic fantasies of the coal miner's son seem to have encouraged some of his worst writing.

Usually recognized as more central to Lawrence are simpler stories of erotic regeneration such as "The Horse-Dealer's Daughter" (1916, originally entitled "The Miracle"). Mabel, a naive young

Poet Witter Bynner took this photograph of Frieda and D. H. Lawrence at Chapala, Mexico, in 1923

woman and a drudge in a collapsing marginal family, is fixated on her dead mother and tries to drown herself in a dank pond. A depressed young doctor saves her almost in spite of himself (he cannot even swim). But the real miracle comes from the characters' emotional change. Undressed and revived, desperately simple Mabel assumes that either the man wants her or she is dead. Confronted with such naked need, he "crossed the gulf over to her" and agonizingly assents to desire. The background of sexual repression against which this occurs is simply assumed. Such elemental courtship—one of Lawrence's variations on the Sleeping Beauty theme—not only shows a choice of passion over, and out of, death, but is also an inversion of Protestant conversion experience, casting desire as death of the old self and a rebirth.

Similar is the more complexly developed "You Touched Me" (1921). Hadrian, a young ex-colonialist and ex-soldier, returns to visit his dying foster father, a well-to-do retired brickmaker. The brickmaker's two dependent, virginal daughters fear the predatory young male, although the more responsive sister unconsciously dramatizes her sexual longings by "mistakenly" going at night to the young man's bed and touching him. The aroused Hadrian ruthlessly decides he must "possess" his foster sister as part of his inheritance. He convinces the father, who had a "strange desire, quite unreasonable, for revenge upon the women who had surrounded him for so long, and served him so carefully," to order the daughter to marry the foster son. The imminence of the father's death, the fairy-tale magic of the sleeper awakened by a strange touch, and the underlying psychodrama of covert incestuousness and misogyny inform the ritual succession of foster son replacing father as master of his money and sex. The tale culminates in the marriage of the genteel virgin and the amoral youth.

Even more harshly amoral is the related novella *The Fox* (1923), one of Lawrence's best-known fictions. The emotional triangle here includes another runaway-youth-returned-soldier, Henry, and a lesbian couple who have taken over the chicken farm where he once lived. The appearance of Henry is foreshadowed and then represented in a dream for the more vulnerable woman, March, by the sexual and demonic totemic image of the fox that preys upon the women's chickens. Henry struggles to conquer March. With animistic power, he kills the fox. Then, with diabolical propriety, he warns the other woman—the moralistic, anti-passional, selfishly dependent, and genteel Ban-

ford—that a tree he is cutting down could hit her. As he expects, in defiance of him she refuses to move and is killed. Henry and the freed March marry at Christmas. Every man must primitivistically transcend morality to achieve erotic destiny.

The Fox also exhibits some of the negative dimensions of Lawrence's eros: the extreme psychological drives of otherwise ordinary people, the attack on lesbians, the mastering male committing crimes. In form, too, the story violates limits in that Lawrence revised the early manuscript by adding a partially contradictory abstract-poetic code in which March remains unhappy after marriage with a "ghastly reaching, reaching for something that might be just beyond." Lawrence's evident condemnation of such romanticism undercuts the sense of erotic destiny in the marriage tale and suggests the insufficiency of passion for ordering life. Though fictionally awkward, this curious combination of passional intensity and harsh perplexity seems crucial to what Lawrence represents.

In a group of lesser stories of this middle period, Lawrence continues some of his earlier themes. "Fanny and Annie" provides a variation on the "second best" motif of some of the earlier stories. An attractive ladies' maid, Fanny, returns to her hometown with some money after having been disappointed in her ambitious love choice. She debates with herself about renewing her relationship with the socially inferior foundry worker who had been her first love. In chapel, she decides to accept the insouciant working man in spite of (or because of?) the scandalous denunciation of him by another woman, Annie, whom he had made pregnant. His very immorality, commonness, and indifference to conventional restraints and ambitions, guarantee—as so often in Lawrence—his passional being, a "physical attraction which she really hated but could not escape," and which would be her "doom." Such is the destined force of the erotic.

The ironically titled "Primrose Path" suffers from Lawrence's use of an unusual device, the priggish narrator (as in Henry James and Ford Madox Ford). This young man ponders the wayward life of his atheistic uncle. He has gone through various women, and he visits, with his nephew, an ex-wife dying of cancer. But the uncle's fear of death drives him not to piety but to sensuality with a young woman caught up in the "impersonal" power of passion. The story's revelation shows the uncle's "smile of passion, pushing away even the death-horror."

In "Wintry Peacock" Lawrence uses the negative image of the peacock to represent the soul of woman, as he did in his first novel. This peacock is the pet of the witchy wife of a sexually unfaithful returned soldier, who chases the bird away. Ironically, in his affair on the Continent the soldier had duplicated his relationship with the wife he is now battling—a female combination of malevolence and sexual submission which "makes a man lord of the earth." The primordial conflict of manly man and willful woman often provides Lawrence's norm of marriage. Hence in "Samson and Delilah" (which also repeats an earlier Lawrence motif), the woman, the pub-keeping wife of a wandering husband, has him brutally thrown out of the pub when he returns after an absence of some years. But she soon lets him back in and acknowledges him sexually. In the endless man-woman war, the woman fights to make her point, but, unless she is a modern destructive woman (the subject of several later stories) she submits finally to male purpose.

In the marriage novella *The Captain's Doll* (1923) Lawrence provides more sophisticated, affirmative variation on the male-female conflict in a rather ragged but charming comedy. The doll of the title is an image of the Scotch Captain Hepburn made by Hannele, his German mistress while he was serving in the occupation army. The doll, later replaced by a surrealist painting of itself, provides a metaphor for "adoration love" in which men are made into puppets. This subjection of men results from an idealized and feminized view of eros, which Lawrence so often attacks. The captain's "lardy-dardy" demanding wife, to whom he had played doll, fortuitously dies, and he goes in pursuit of his former mistress. The story includes sprightly descriptions of Austrian scenery and seriocomic arguments about the nature of love—variations on Birkin's speeches in *Women in Love* and probably quite autobiographical in terms of Lawrence's relations with Frieda. Hepburn defensively proposes marriage to the resisting Hannele: he wants "honour and obedience: and the proper physical feelings" expressing a "desire" that goes "very much deeper than love." To support this demand for traditional womanly submission, the man, Lawrence insists, must have an organically purposeful role. But the roles claimed by Hepburn seem mere gestures: he will write a book about the moon and go farm in Africa (Lawrence's usual yearning for pastoral flight from decadent industrial civilization). As Lawrence wrote in one of his essays, "there can be no successful [enduring] sexual union unless the greater hope of purposive, constructive activity fires the soul of the man all the time, or the hope of passionate, purposive *destructive* activity. . . ." De-

structive activity aimed at much of the modern order helped keep Lawrence going, though it is muted in this genial though not very probing tale of an antique marriage style.

We might, then, conclude this discussion of the middle period of Lawrence's fiction with a more destructive tale, and one, as he acknowledged, of his better pieces of writing, originally written as the introduction to Maurice Magnus's *Memoirs of the Foreign Legion* (1922) but also known by the title "Portrait of M. M." While formally not quite a novella, this work is a sharp and vivid account of Lawrence's friendship with Magnus, and it establishes an illuminating continuity with Lawrence's more intentionally artistic works. The characterizations, scenic descriptions, acute insights, and angry reflections are at one with those in the better fictions. From the opening ("On a dark wet wintry evening in November") through its lively descriptions of Mediterranean places, its staccato dialogues, its letters announcing M. M.'s suicide the following November, and Lawrence's mixed conclusions, it not only uses the techniques of the stories but also shows the responsiveness which fuses Lawrence with his art.

Lawrence felt a fascinated repulsion for M. M., the "superior" parasite, upper-bohemian con man, and marginal homosexual with literary and religious pretensions, whose final desperation suggested him as a persona of modern cultural decadence. Lawrence curses him, especially for his gentility and pretenses, yet notes that "he had his points, the courage of his terrors, quick-wittedness, sensitiveness to certain things in his surroundings. I prefer him, scamp as he is, to the ordinary respectable person."

In his reflections, as in his presentation of the wan rascal amid vibrant scenes, Lawrence suggests that M. M. had to die by his own hand, just as he had to be at odds with the world and in petty trouble with the police and live beyond his means (and leave a suicide note demanding that his ex-wife pay for a "first-class" burial). M. M., of course, was not a "good" person; he betrayed ordinary kindnesses and held disgustingly mannered views, including those of a narrowly aesthetic Catholicism. Yet he truly suffered in his finally fatal displacement from a dubious and false order. Understanding Magnus, this product of our counterfeit culture, leads not to a call for "charity" and "sloppy sentiment and cant" but to a knowledge which defines "the boundaries of human experience." The achievement of such awareness provides much of the purpose of Lawrence's art and life.

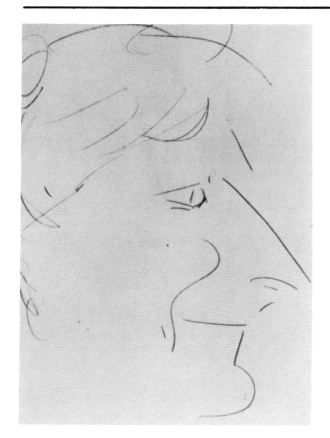 

Caricatures of Frieda and D. H. Lawrence drawn by Witter Bynner in New Mexico, 1923

Lawrence's novels of the early 1920s—*Aaron's Rod, Kangaroo,* and *The Plumed Serpent*—try to express extreme personal and ideological concerns, and, as is widely acknowledged, are poor fictions. Each is an authoritarian fantasy, sloppily conceived and hastily written, containing narcissistic projections of the author and often nasty caricatures of friends. Each is graced with some vivid scenic writing—Italy, Australia, and Mexico—reflecting his constant journeying for most of the decade following the war. Charitably, these books might be viewed as "thought experiments" often marred by an irascible ideological promiscuity.

Aaron's Rod (published in 1922, though part of it was written late in the war) loosely centers on a former coal miner and ex-teacher, who expertly plays the flute (his rod). Aaron abandons his bitterly resented wife and children and moves through marginal societies in London, Milan, and Florence. He also moves through unsatisfying relationships with women and through the postwar social-political turmoil to become the quasi-homosexual, intellectual sycophant of Lilly, Lawrence's persona in this more-or-less picaresque fiction. Lilly-

Lawrence has a "belief in himself as a savior" because he is a superior man of true "knowledge" whose "soul was against the whole world." His prophetic, megalomaniacal sermonizing—a posture Lawrence had intermittently assumed in his nonfictional writings since early in the war—includes racist ranting, misogynistic pseudoprofundities, raging condemnations of modern mass society, and near-mystical demands for "sacred" individualism to replace the dead absolute now that "there's no God outside." Lawrence's marital difficulties of the time are reflected in abstract summary in *Aaron's rod*: "Love was a battle in which each party strove for the mastery of the other's soul." The struggle is to be resolved finally by putting down willful females: "The woman must now submit," though in a way that goes beyond "slavery" to a "deep unfathomable free submission."

The submission is not altogether "unfathomable" since the subordination of eros to power is part of a larger Nietzschean subordination of "love," which includes *caritas* and much else that is traditional in Western morality. As Aaron says, "To hell with good-will. It was more hateful than ill-will." Or, as a more elaborate Lilly-Lawrence lecture puts it: "The ideal of love, the ideal that it is better to give than to receive, the ideal of liberty, the ideal of the brotherhood of man, the ideal of the sanctity of human life, the ideal of what we call goodness, charity, benevolence . . . all the whole bee-hive of ideals—has got the modern bee-disease, and gone putrid, stinking."

Developing his variant of Nietzscheanism, Lawrence posits Christian morality's leading to its "logical sequence in Socialism and equality." Lilly-Lawrence also insists, like Dostoevski's Grand Inquisitor, that, given their preference, the masses "will elect for themselves a proper and healthy and energetic slavery," "I mean a real committal of the life-issues of inferior beings to the responsibility of a superior being." However, Lawrence's dogmatism is no more consistently authoritarian here than in his related essays, such as those in *Reflections on the Death of a Porcupine* (1925). In one page, his demand for submission turns into his fervent espousal of the absolute of holy individualism, and he returns to his recurrent denunciation of the "bullying" of the individual as the most hateful vice, regardless of how often he rhetorically engages in such bullying himself. Much in Lawrence's polemics seems more symptomatic than serious.

The slight plot of *Aaron's Rod* runs down inconclusively amid the polemics. A bomb goes off in a café and destroys Aaron's flute. Interestingly, Lawrence seems to suggest that the social love-ethic may be a source of terrorism. "Religion and love—and all that. It's a disease now." So we must give up "love-whooshing" and magically "submit to some great soul." Lawrence may be rather desperately reflecting the European psychic conditions that were part of the rise of fascism during this period, as well as expressing his own sense of hopelessness.

He tried again to deify autocratic higher purpose and hero-worship in his next long novel-tract, *Kangaroo* (hastily written during a few weeks in 1922 and published the next year). This work also suffers from shapelessness and ranting. It includes some Australian tourist bits—he lived there only a few weeks—some of his customarily intense descriptive passages, and some digressive memories. One such memory is an angry account of his extreme revulsion at being examined for conscription during the war (he was eliminated for poor health). The Australian ramble also displays the Lawrences' continuing marital conflicts, which were exacerbated by the wandering, alienated Lawrence's yearning for homoerotic matiness and heroes,

which becomes part of the subject of *Kangaroo*.

The synthetic political issue that preoccupies touring essayist Somes, Lawrence's persona in *Kangaroo*, is the conflict between an ostensibly socialist group and a fascistic nationalist organization, "the diggers," led by a rich homosexual Jewish lawyer nicknamed Kangaroo. Lawrence-Somers ambivalently rejects the lawyer, who dies in a terrorist incident. But plot and narrative are slight. While much of Lawrence's political commentary comes out as ill-conceived bluster, he does display his intensifying demand for a passional-religious "new bond between men" to overcome the loss of community in modern disintegrative society. Though fond of spiteful calls for authoritarianism, the protagonist finds both the socialist and fascist forms false because they are still based on the dead ethic of the "will-to-love."

The political love-ethic is an expression of the "mob," and here Lawrence outdoes Nietzsche's attack on "herd morality," which consists of that "collection of all the weak souls . . . that lusts to glut itself with blind destructive power." Hysterical vituperation on this theme goes on for pages. In utter rage against the "compulsions" of World War I, Lawrence incoherently insists on even greater compulsions. Since the coercive war, and industrial-bourgeois society more generally, costume control and destruction in benevolence, traditional idealism provides the central evil: "For the idea, or ideal of Love, Self-Sacrifice, Humanity united in love, in brotherhood, in peace—all this is dead." While it is no doubt true that historically the great crimes of the modern state have usually laid claim to benevolence, Lawrence wishes to demystify Western civilization only to remystify it with "the great life-urge which we call God." By an old logic of mystagogy, Lawrence's cosmic vitalism displaces itself onto supposedly superior men, though the examples in *Kangaroo*, be they the imagined Australian demagogues of left and right, the Napoleon and Caesar invoked in Lawrence's political rhetoric, or the rather megalomaniacal author, undercut the argument. The ideas do not work in the novel and end up being ignored even by the protagonist. The intelligence of part of Lawrence's sensibility goes beyond his fervent dogmatizing and vituperation, which often makes him fascinating.

On yet another side, that of his overweening individualism ("the self is absolute"), Lawrence restates the positive meaning of the Nietzschean Will to Power: "It is a will-to-live in the further sense, a will-to-change, a will-to-evolve, a will towards the further creation of the self." By some creative "polarity" of agonistic conflict between the spiritual aristocrats who assert this Will to Power and the uncomprehending "mass," a new stage in civilized "evolution" will be reached and, hence, a new "*being.*" But this ontology remains abstract speculation, and in the novel (as he did in life), Lawrence rejects all actual social-political movements to hold on only "to one's own isolate being." Somers quickly flees Australia for America, as did his author. *Kangaroo* concludes not with affirmation of a saving ideology but with defiance of it, with explicit denial of "any meaning." Western idealistic nihilism comes full circle in the desperate ideological experimentation of a self-defined and self-outcast "last" individualist.

But for Lawrence the twentieth-century conflict between extreme individualism and the desperate yearning to escape from it was not over. He again tried to subordinate the individual to communion and community with the even more extreme political-religious mythology of *The Plumed Serpent,* which he completed in 1925 after a stay in Mexico. His most repulsive novel, written in the midst of physical and psychological illness, it draws, as the title indicates, on the Aztec myths of Quetzalcoatl (and probably on Nietzsche's forced philosophical myth in *Thus Spake Zarathustra*), to insist on the fusion of bird and snake, polarities of earth and sky, individual and cosmos. The myth serves as the overpowering background for the supposed regeneration of a middle-aged, middle-class Anglo-Irish widow, Kate Leslie. In a patronizing treatment of women, Lawrence declares that she must search for a conversion experience: "Ye must be born again. Out of the fight with the octopus of life, the dragon of degenerate or incomplete existence, one must win the soft bloom of being. . . ." This hectoring and muddled mixture of the archaic and abstract fairly represents much of the style. The jaded lady hungers "to be merged in desire beyond desire, to be gone in the body beyond the individualism" by becoming a "morning star" female goddess in submission to the dark sun of generic man. On a literal level, she self-hatingly makes "submission absolute" by succumbing to a sketchily characterized Indian reactionary military conspirator, Gen. Cipriano Viedma. Representing for Lawrence the rejection of Western bourgeois consciousness, this self-abnegation of the woman includes the denial not only of intelligence and decency but also of sexual gratification (described in the by-now notorious "Aphrodite of the foam" passage which rejects

direct female orgasm). Kate becomes Cipriano's servile sexual and religious mistress, subordinate partner in his militarized cult's taking over of chaotic Mexico.

The revivalist cult takes over the story as well as the country. The general and his pretentious stick-figure leader, Don Ramon Carrasco, turn out to be largely fanatical thugs. They peddle a made-up Aztec methodism incongruously mixed with European classical paganism, Christian demonology, marginal occultism, and the like, which they (and apparently Lawrence) grossly confuse with politics. Curiously mystagogic pastiche, some readers admire this, and even the ritualism developed at intolerable length and redundancy with a vulgar literalism in bad prose-poetry, but such readers tend to dislike Lawrence's best writing.

Lawrence once apologetically wrote in a letter: "one sheds one's sickness in books." Among the illnesses cast forth in *The Plumed Serpent:* Lawrence's anger at the repressive Christianity of his background; his resentment of women and their sexual demands, including his resentment of his then errant and unsubmissive wife; and his fantasies of powerful mystic males bonded in ecstatic theocracy, compensation for an alienated and deracinated literary bohemian in miserable health. *The Plumed Serpent* may serve to remind readers that new religions come out of old illnesses. Yet it should be granted that while Lawrence sometimes produced the ugly and outrageous, though rarely the trivial, even this bad book displays bits of the author's perceptiveness and descriptive power.

Many of the shorter fictions written during the same period as *The Plumed Serpent* show great violence, especially in Lawrence's obsessive concern with destructive women. In "None of That" (1924) Lawrence tells a brutal, melodramatic tale of a bored, rich, frigid American woman who rejects sex (hence the title) and egotistically asserts the power of the "imagination" to rise above anything, even rape. In a scheme to get his hands on her money, a shrewd brute of a Mexican bullfighter turns her over to half a dozen members of his entourage. Her spurious idealism—the sham belief in "imagination" and "will" overcoming all reality, including the body—collapses after the gang rape, and she commits suicide. This thinly textured story with its retrospective narration and shocker plot is not among Lawrence's best savagings of the willful, modern lady.

A richer version of the Eve corrupted by culture appears in the longer tale "The Princess"

(1924). Long indulged and overprotected by a doting father, the late-thirtyish, well-to-do woman protagonist lacks emotional responsiveness. Her test comes when she goes on a pack-trip in the heart of the Rockies with a Mexican guide, one of Lawrence's darkly passional demon lovers. She sleeps with him but frigidly denies response, thus turning the longing for eros into the act of rape. Outraged, he rapes her repeatedly, but her will triumphs. He dies in a shoot-out with a party searching for her. She obliterates the experience from her mind, marries an elderly man, and, having denied the demon of selfhood (elaborately developed in the story), the demon lover, and desire, continues her reign in the childish and sterile role of the modern "Princess" of Anglo-American culture.

In yet another variation on the destructive female theme, the novella *The Woman Who Rode Away* (written in 1924 and published in 1928), a well-to-do American wife and mother, bored and longing for "wonder" and "mystery," passively lets herself be taken prisoner by a "lost" tribe of primitive Indians in the mountains of northern Mexico. After elaborate ritual preparation, including hallucinatory mind-rinsing, she willingly goes to an altar on an icy mountain to be sacrificed with a stone dagger on the shortest day of the year, thus to renew "the mystery that man must hold." In *The Woman Who Rode Away* Lawrence again adapts the Aztec death cult to his woman hatred. The claim that the victim represents "the quivering nervous consciousness of the highly bred white women" is unsubstantiated in the novella. This regenerative sacrifice for male mastery of modern woman is, as contemporary feminist commentators have recognized, vehemently misogynistic.

However, Lawrence's misogyny was not simple. *Sun* (1926) gives the female the cultus power. The later Lawrence expressed in various statements in prose and poetry a sacramental view of the sun, in a view no doubt related to his yearning to be healed of his finally fatal tubercular condition as well as his yearning for a pagan religiousness. In *Sun* a New York businessman's depressed wife vacations with her young son in the Sicilian countryside, where she ritualistically engages in naked sunbathing. She thus achieves sexual heightening ("in the cosmic carnal sense") and the unitive experience ("something greater than herself") via natural mysticism. She also overcomes some ordinary anxieties, such as fear of snakes. With an initiate's double ethic, she looks toward impersonal adultery with a virile peasant. But her good gray man comes for a visit, wants his bit of the divine, and so she "would

feel her husband's futile penis in her once again." Lawrence portrays the partial regeneration of modern middle-class woman, without sadism this time, but retains the larger sense that she is also trapped by "the vast cold apparatus of civilization," including that of the conventional male.

A more complex exaltation of the questing twentieth-century heroine appears in *St. Mawr* (written in 1924 and published in 1925), a novel-length work often treated as a novella. Although one of Lawrence's more richly suggestive fictions, it raggedly shifts scene and emphasis (from London to New Mexico, from social satire to vitalistic fable). It also changes dominant metaphor, from the demonic horse St. Mawr to the awesome scenery around Taos, both representing regenerative vitalistic forces. Authorial intrusions include an apocalyptic declamation against over-population, over-mechanization, and consequent authoritarian ideologies, and a proclamation of vitalist cultural evolution. The story announces a search for "positive living," with the searcher a rich American woman, Lou Witt, unhappily married to a mannered invert, Rico Carrington, who is an English baronet. The lady eventually dumps her husband, who cruelly wants to castrate the rebellious symbolic horse, and flees to the American Southwest for the nontheistic religious condition Lawrence calls "wonder." Along the way, much is rejected, including the horse who raised the issue for the heroine by his passional responses, the comically treated willful matriarch, the nasty English high society, and the possibility of sexual submission to the primitive (partly represented by an Indian groom, Phoenix—Lawrence reversing one of his favorite late regenerative metaphors). Paradoxically, the search for "positive living" requires much defiance of the dying world as the heroine quests for authentic passional selfhood.

In the last section of *St. Mawr*, the small ranch north of Taos (obviously Lawrence's own place, given him by an American woman patron, Mable Dodge Luhan, where he happily lived for some months during the mid-1920s), represents vitalistic knowledge. Its history, as Lawrence recounts it, emphasizes a kind of demonic power, the *"ne plus ultra"* of the beautiful and enlivening, a godless "absolute" (*"Jesus and a God of Love"* and any other claim to universal goodness are *"nonsense"*). Only by defiance of a sordid civilization and acceptance of this cosmic negation can one achieve "life, intense bristling life." The ending, again, may be viewed as a pyrrhic victory, with the heroic woman withdrawn from the social world and left nearly isolated; but,

A 28 October 1926 photograph of Aldous Huxley and D. H. Lawrence at the Villa Mirenda, in the Tuscan Hills near Florence, where the Lawrences lived for about a year in 1926-1927 (photo by Maria Huxley)

as Lawrence views it, she has achieved through her vitalistic nihilism an intensely regenerative awareness and being.

Some of Lawrence's finest fictions are harshly sardonic fables written in the mid-1920s. One of his most famous, "The Rocking-Horse Winner" (1926), again utilizes a magical horse (only this one is a toy), the fairy-tale device of a whispering house ("There must be more money!"), a mockingly detached style, and the dramatic issue of a superior son trying to prove himself to his anxious, hard-hearted middle-class mother who lives beyond her means. The young son Paul (an allegorical version of the mother-placating Paul of *Sons and Lovers*) seeks his mother's love by frenziedly rocking his horse, a masturbatory version of the totem of passion, until he has a powerful hunch as to which horse will win an upcoming race. The servant who got him involved in betting on horses and a cynical uncle profitably handle the wagers and arrange for money to be given anonymously to the increasingly demanding mother. In his final mock race to intuit the Derby winner, Paul ends in fatal delirium,

though not before picking the big winner and reassuring his aggrandizing mother. He dies, lucky in money but not, in this paradigmatically bourgeois home, lucky in mothers or love.

Such polished, cutting fiction can also be found in another of Lawrence's fine fables, the longer and much less well-known "The Man Who Loved Islands" (1926). Its lean, sardonic prose presents Cathcart, a "superior" idealist Englishman (with many parallels to Lawrence) who loves islands and seeks escape from the modern world. The tale has three sections, three islands, three philosophic denouements: On the large first island Cathcart creates a utopian colony, a product of his willed benevolent rationalism, but his inadequate philosophy of life is defeated by the covert malignity of place, by his autocratic behavior, and by his subterranean self; he abandons the island, which is sold as a resort for honeymooners. He then moves to a middling-sized island seeking, with more modest desire, a "refuge," but here his very abeyance of will and purpose entraps him in a matriarchy—he was tricked into marriage when leaving the first island—and the retreat turns out to be a nauseating family "suburb." Again he flees to another island, forsaking family as well as utopian order for a small and isolated pastoral hermitage. But on the third island the solitary denial of life that underlies Cathcart's ostensible idealism results in his increasing dehumanization, until he finally ceases even "to register his own feelings." Losing all connection as the winter storms snow-blanket the last, isolated island, the frigid idealist smugly identifies with his own annihilation. "The Man Who Loved Islands" is a rigorous dialectic and a powerful parabolic fiction that mocks idealism for defeating the vital struggle for felt life. This may be the most essential Lawrence.

In 1926, Lawrence completed one of his best novellas of erotic regeneration, *The Virgin and the Gipsy*, published in 1930. This work partly recasts his early *Daughters of the Vicar*, with its repressed clergyman's children, willful obese matriarch, out-of-class lover, and savaging of Christian morality and middle-class gentility. The righteously antilife Rector Saywell has lost his impassioned wife to another man, leaving him, his daughters, and his spinster sister to the greedy moral dominance of his Victorian "fungoid" mother. He hates the unconventional and passional. Daughter Yvette mildly rebels, pursues a "resurrected" dark outsider and demon lover, a married older gipsy, and arrives at the Lawrencean doctrine of the primacy of impersonal "desire." Symbolically, a tunnel built in pagan times underlies a dam and causes a flood that damages the rectory and drowns the matriarch. The gipsy saves Yvette and warms her to life in bed. He then leaves, sending her an illiterate, kind note. The young woman has been initiated into eroticism and has gained selfhood and a new bravery. The genteel Christian family ethos has been overcome. *The Virgin and the Gipsy* displays some of Lawrence's common fictional difficulties: undramatized statements of feeling, editorializing, the uncertain yoking of mythic elements with harshly observed social and psychological realism, and the author's rage at middle-class Christian values. But this erotic-religious fable of regeneration avoids the overreach of some of his more purely mythic tales and thus achieves a poignantly humane intensity.

The late Lawrence's most sardonic fables, such as "The Rocking-Horse Winner" and "The Man Who Loved Islands," may be his best fictional art. At the other pole lie mythic tales such as "Glad Ghosts" (1925), written in the vein of the earlier *The Ladybird*. Though obfuscated by religious rhetoric, ghost-story devices, and layers of mixed metaphors,

"Glad Ghosts" is less about erotic regeneration that it is a sniggering manipulation of upper-class English characters who indulge in a weekend of group adultery. Perhaps Lawrence's lower-class and outclass resentments encouraged rather bad handling of such materials.

A somewhat better Gothic tale, "The Border Line" (1924), uses the pattern (as in "The Blind Man") of a woman divided between a cerebral, unmanly figure (in this case her second husband) and an *Übermensch* (her first husband, killed in Germany in the war). After the woman has a demonic vision in the border regions of post-war Germany, the ghost of the manly husband returns, possesses the woman, and the unmanly husband is magically killed off. The maliciousness of the tale may have been prompted by personal motives of compensation (Lawrence's partly justified fears of the motives of his friend Middleton Murry toward Frieda Lawrence). Closely related are several slight and murky anecdotal stories also using supernatural devices, "The Last Laugh" (1924) and "Smile" (1926). Also closely related, the biographers report, is the longer and better satiric comedy "Jimmy and the Desperate Woman" (1924). Jimmy, a contemptible and fashionable literary and sexual manipulator, pursues on impulse a primitive poet, Mrs. Pinnegar, who is also a willful miner's wife. With deftly mocking insights, Lawrence dramatizes literary gesture turning into reality as Jimmy perversely proposes to the miner's wife, for the subterranean appeal is sexual consubstantiation with the embittered, manly husband.

In his last period, Lawrence, now widely recognized, produced a variety of writings. The slight anecdote "Rawdon's Roof" mocks an upper-class male neuter who in fear flees a declaration of love; he allows no woman under his roof, but his more sensible man-servant does. "In Love" (1927; originally entitled "More Modern Love") is, like some of the little essays Lawrence wrote in his last years for popular publications (posthumously collected in *Assorted Articles*, 1930), a brittle parody of ersatz sexuality fashionable in the media of the time.

Heavy sarcasm also damages the sharp satire of some wealthy, cultured American friends in "Things" (1928), which focuses on the covertly avaricious motives of an aesthete couple as they collect beautiful things in their travels, all inappropriately impressive for Midwestern American academic life. Though he had a puritan prudence about money and was a good bread-baking and housecleaning mate, Lawrence had little of the materialist about him. The story catches the idea he summarized elsewhere: "your idealist alone is a perfect materialist." Supposedly spiritual motives are frequently called upon to mask acquisitive and manipulative ones. Or as he starts one of his mocking poems: "How beastly the bourgeoisie is—." Lawrence's writings, whether satiric, mythic, realistic, or speculative, need to be understood as almost always iconoclastic about the mainstream middle-class values of Anglo-American culture.

This satiric purpose is combined with the destructive-woman theme in another late mocking story, "The Lovely Lady" (1927). Wealthy, narcissistic Pauline (like the mothers of the Pauls in *Sons and Lovers* and "The Rocking-Horse Winner") cannibalizes her sons, having emotionally killed her elder and neutered her dependent younger, who still lives with her. Like the couple in "Things," her money-making specialty is objets d'art, and her high-fashion, seventyish, seductive self is her fanciest piece. The total but fragile artifice of the lovely lady is undercut by her plain, suppressed niece, who loves the dependent son, using a drainpipe to make ghostly guilt reminders of Pauline's lurid past. The exposure brings on her death. Instead of being free for marriage, the son and niece find that the lovely lady has disinherited them by leaving all of her possessions to a museum for her antiques. As Lawrence wrote elsewhere, "Monuments, museums, permanencies, and poderosities are all anathema." He always sought out places, people, cultures, which expressed the impermanent flow of vitality, not the monuments of fixity, repression, and power—cultural artifact versus cultural vitality.

Another mocking variation on the destructive-woman theme, "Mother and Daughter" (1928) plays on artful decor in several senses. While part of the issue forms about "a strange *female* power," one of Lawrence's favorite beasts, the materialistic, willful matriarch and her possessions here are secondary to the author's attack on the counterfeit "independent woman" who, the story insists, does not really exist beneath the artificial veneer. He scorns the career woman—here head of a government department but male-imitative and unhappy—because Lawrence grants only men creative purpose. He is prejudiced, of course, yet several of the satiric thrusts against certain types of women in a supposedly male world should be recognized as apt. The story's pat ironic ending is that the careerist daughter marries a "tribal father," a fat, old, crafty, sensual, and controlling Armenian businessman—a submission that the artificially independent woman always really longed for.

The antiheroine wife of a literary man in

"Two Blue Birds" (1926), an ironic play on the cliché of the bluebird of happiness, also insists on her independence and on the "vehement pursuit of enjoyment." At a tea party both the wife and the husband's devoted secretary show up in blue dresses, and the wife decides that two blue birds are too much; he can have the other blue bird and the fatuous happiness of her submission. The mode of the story and its resolution display the intellectual mocking intellectualism, as happens so often in the late Lawrence.

Blue for Lawrence was often a metaphor for cold northern intelligence, that passionally defeating superiority. He plays upon it again in "Blue Moccasins" (1928). The proud owner of the moccasins is another "independent woman" who late in life marries a younger man and then willfully puts him down, sexually and socially. He rebels and gives the wife's precious blue moccasins to a responsive widow in recognition of her liberating performance in a local theatrical production. In his defiance of his superior, frigid wife, the husband, a branch-bank manager, for once has gone beyond his usual submissive niceness. But his is, indeed, only a small gesture of the passional male. This story, and related late fictions—unlike the lower-class stories with which Lawrence began his literary career—can be seen as essentially patronizing the middle class.

However informed by misogynistic demands for erotically responsive and submissive women, these late tales should be seen as broadly mocking of middle-class sensibility. Lawrence, who variously identified with peasants, vestigial aristocrats, the working-class, mythic *übermenschen* primitives, and outcasts, hardly ever identifies with the beastly bourgeoisie. He never forgave the middle class, either for its sexual repression that extended into feminization and sentimental idealism—"Sentimentality covers viciousness, as greenness covers a bog"—or for its controlling order and lack of passional intensity and human richness. From the beginning, he had been at religious war with the dominant values of the society.

So with the dying Lawrence's final novella, *The Man Who Died* (1931; written in 1928 and originally titled *The Escaped Cock*). This work presents a mythic version of his death-and-erotic-regeneration theme. In an intentionally blasphemous retelling of the Christian postcrucifixion story, Lawrence turns to his own existential doctrine that "immortality is in the vividness of life." With an often heavily incantatory and repetitive poetic prose, the "death nausea" of the Christ-figure risen from the tomb is

Frontispiece by Lawrence for the 1929 Black Sun Press edition of The Escaped Cock *(later titled* The Man Who Died*)*

overcome by sexual arousal, partly represented by the obscene pun of the freed rooster. There is also tumescence as resurrection, a black-mass impersonal coition, on an altar, of the ex-messiah and a priestess of Isis, which shows ecstatic mystical qualities, and a regenerative sense heightening. But all larger traditional salvations, such as atonement, immortality, and the conversion of the masses, are emphatically renounced. The refugee Christ, who is also the ancient god Osiris and the modern D. H. Lawrence, rejects autocratic order (represented by a Roman matriarch), leaves the priestess, who is pregnant, and demonically flees in the night from the authorities to become the eternal divine vagabond in the recurrent ritual drama of springtime regeneration. In this tour de force, Christ has been reduced to the dark god of death and Dionysian sexuality in an individual rising that holds to the

socially outcast and defiant. In its overwrought, redundant prose of sex and death, *The Man Who Died* seems a poignant testament to Lawrence's personal obsessions. It is also curious in its synthesis of religious themes, so important in the modernist literary movement, which attempts to turn Protestant anguish into a pagan individualism. But it is hardly Lawrence's best fiction.

The exploration of passional regeneration is better crafted as well as related to social time and place in Lawrence's last novel, *Lady Chatterley's Lover*. In the two years preceding its first publication in 1928, Lawrence wrote three nearly complete versions of the novel; the first two were published as *The First Lady Chatterley* (1944) and *John Thomas and Lady Jane* (1972). While each version has its partisan readers, the development of authorial intention as the versions progress seems evident. Lawrence,

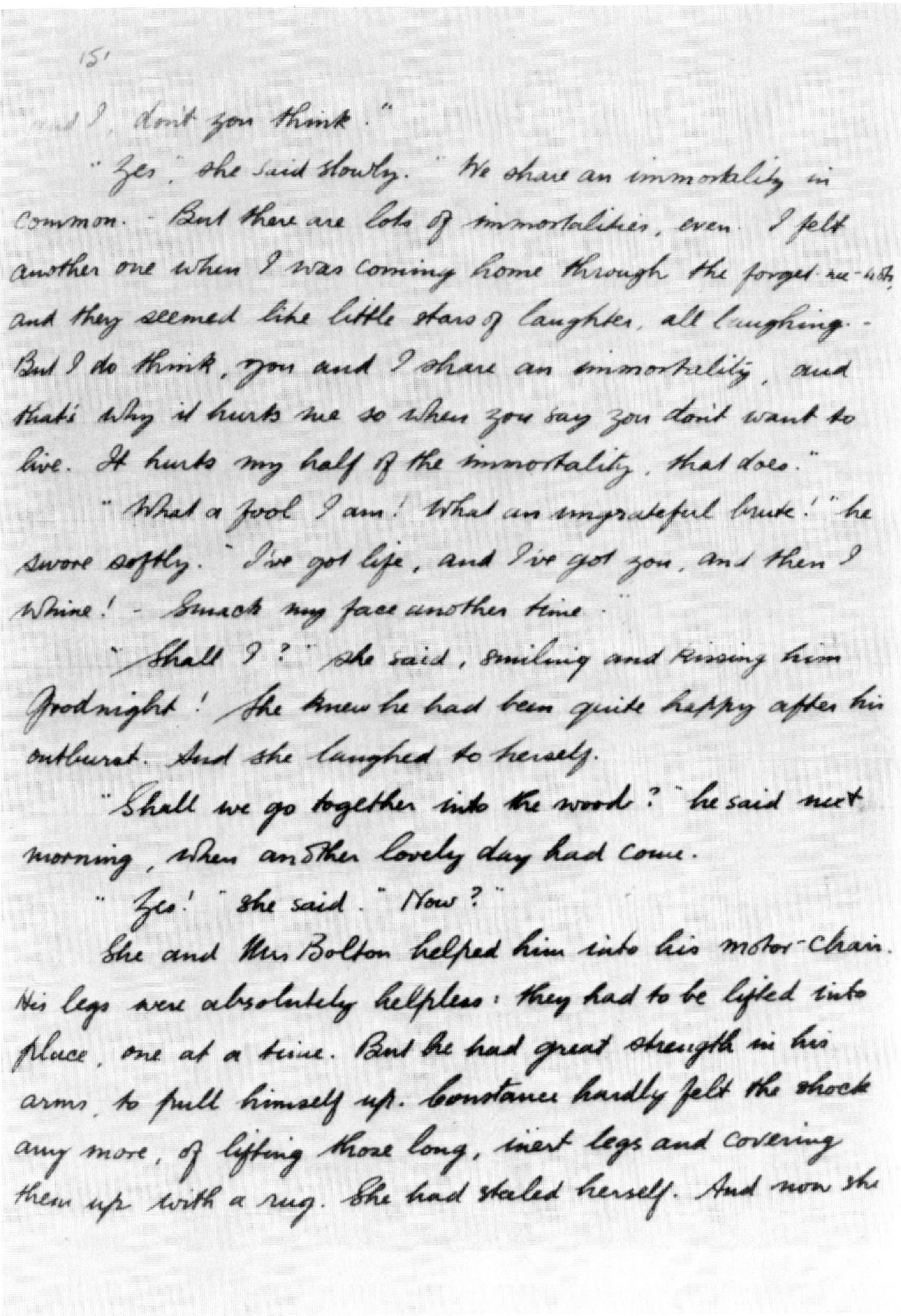

151

and I, don't you think."

"Yes," she said slowly. "We share an immortality in common. But there are lots of immortalities, even. I felt another one when I was coming home through the forget-me-nots, and they seemed like little stars of laughter, all laughing. But I do think, you and I share an immortality, and that's why it hurts me so when you say you don't want to live. It hurts my half of the immortality, that does."

"What a fool I am! What an ungrateful brute!" he swore softly. "I've got life, and I've got you, and then I whine! - Smack my face another time."

"Shall I?" she said, smiling and kissing him Goodnight! She knew he had been quite happy after his outburst. And she laughed to herself.

"Shall we go together into the wood?" he said next morning, when another lovely day had come.

"Yes!" she said. "Now?"

She and Mrs Bolton helped him into his motor-chair. His legs were absolutely helpless: they had to be lifted into place, one at a time. But he had great strength in his arms, to pull himself up. Constance hardly felt the shock any more, of lifting those long, inert legs and covering them up with a rug. She had steeled herself. And now she

Page from the manuscript for the first version of Lady Chatterley's Lover *(estate of Mrs. Frieda Lawrence Ravagli; courtesy of the Humanities Research Center, University of Texas at Austin)*

perhaps initially attempting to reconcile himself to the working-class world he had rejected earlier, gradually realized that his gamekeeper-lover (first Parkin, then Seivers, finally Mellors) had to go beyond the proletarian in this pastoral romance to be the forlorn utopian intellectual, like his creator. Although the myths of authoritarian social transformation in Lawrence's preceding novels are gone, in *Lady Chatterley's Lover* there is no reconciliation with industrial class society. The new wistful politics include—as a secondary authorial spokesman (Tommy Dukes) puts it—a call for a "democracy of touch, instead of pocket." There are also many, sometimes intrusive, denunciations of class and of "the Mammon of mechanized greed." The basic premise is that twentieth-century "civilized society is insane" and that therefore there must be at the edge of it regenerative human relationships. A few key passages propose a post-industrial pagan communalism.

But no such regeneration can come from the "mental lifer" attitude of Sir Clifford Chatterley and his order. The war-crippled, sexually impotent, wealthy upper-class husband of Lady Constance is an extreme version of the cold, cerebral side of Lawrence's recurrent erotic triangle. Though often perceptive, the portrayal of Clifford carries a heavy, multi-satiric burden since he represents not only class snobbery and antisensual idealism but also the Bloomsbury sort of clever writer and the willful, rationalizing, and modernizing industrialist. His wife Constance finally sees him as a "celluloid soul." Some of Clifford's scenes, such as his pompous speech in the woods about his power after which his motorized wheelchair and his humaneness break down, movingly make the points. He does develop in the novel, regressively—"the perverted man-child was now a *real* business-man"—in obscene dependence on his nurse-companion, Ivy Bolton. (This middle-aged and shrewdly manipulative working-class widow is probably the finest characterization in the novel.) Clifford and his kind mostly turn mean when confronted with human variety and need.

Constance Chatterley, though from a prewar bohemian background, took the role of an old-fashioned devoted wife and undeveloped person in another version of Lawrence's female somnambule ready for a "new awakening." Unlike most of the women in the late fictions, however, she is presented sympathetically. After a pathetic affair with a manipulative literary man, the frustrated wife, in her late twenties, offers herself to her husband's gamekeeper, Oliver Mellors, who is a decade older than she. In the third and final version of the novel, the gamekeeper, as he was in Lawrence's first novel, is a misanthropic declassed intellectual. Of working-class origins, he labored in the mines before enlisting in the army where he made junior officer in the colonies. His separation from his nasty "harpy" wife provides Lawrence yet another focus for angry commentary on willful and sexually aggrandizing females. Some readers find the declassed Mellors, in spite of several poignant scenes, unsettling because of his angry intelligence—he is misogynistic, misanthropic, and apocalyptic about the modern world. But, as usual in Lawrence, the quality of passion rests on such large negations.

Much of the experience of the novel is the exploration of the Mellors-Constance erotic relationship. As Lawrence knew when he arranged private publication and distribution of the book, the sexual explicitness, including the Anglo-Saxon physical terms, violated conventions of the time and would, obviously, serve *épater le bourgeois*. The novel was censored in English-speaking nations for a generation. Now the eroticism seems relatively mild, rather ritualistic and earnest, and, as intended, quite tender (one of Lawrence's working titles was "Tenderness"). Ironically, debate in the past several decades about the sex scenes (especially Constance's last night with Mellors in his cottage) has centered on the *lack* of explicitness about what seems to be anal intercourse and about its appropriateness to the theme of erotic tenderness.

Perhaps the more important issue for debate is that Constance "had to be a passive, consenting thing, like a slave." As in earlier fictions, in the relationship insisted upon the woman must be paradoxically submissive to the man in order to realize her full self. The notion that the female must be submissive to the male is variously and fully insisted upon by Lawrence. In *Lady Chatterley's Lover*, the erotic conflict is not only between man and woman and between the lovers and the dominating social order, but also within the woman, "tormented by her own double consciousness" (her superior critical self versus her submissive sexual self). Only when she "dared to let go everything, all herself, and be gone in the flood" is the sex good and the larger realization of passion achieved. If one wants Lawrence's "sexual message," besides the pervasive importance of the erotic, that is it.

The regeneration of Constance Chatterley, both at the level of personal response (for example, the physical world takes on new aliveness for her) and of moral vision (she can no longer accept Clifford and the mean order of domination he represents), may be convincing. But some of her didactic speeches about it seem intrusive expressions of Lawrence: "Give me the body. I believe the life of the body is a greater reality than the life of the mind: when the body is really awakened to life."

Yet, of course, a good passional relationship does not resolve social issues in Lawrence. At the end of *Lady Chatterley's Lover* the pregnant Constance and the unemployed gamekeeper remain separated, though with hopes of getting divorces from their spouses, of overcoming the gulf of hostilities caused because they belong to different social classes, and of reuniting on a farm in Scotland (to be provided by her money). In a concluding letter to Constance, Mellors provides a brief Lawrencean editorial on the need for a better, postindustrial society based upon warm, simple community. In Mellors's excoriating words in early sections of the novel—the masses' "living intuitive faculty was dead." He would revive the worship of "the great god Pan" in place of decadent Christianity. But though fundamental to the prophet Lawrence, this view seems but a yearning gesture in an apocalyptic context—"nothing lies in the future but death and destruction for these industrial masses." That is the harsh awareness shadowing the lovers' somewhat forlorn effort at regenerate eros in an unregenerate society.

This pastoral romance stands as one of Lawrence's better novels. If Mellors, the odd-man-out intellectual, remains problematic in his irascible misogyny and misanthropy, Constance and some of the lesser characters are handled with warm responsiveness. The detailing of many scenes shows vibrant Lawrence, and the commentary, in spite of some strident intrusion, is often serious and insightful. The combination of romance and satire, of tender eroticism and exacerbated denunciation, seems essential to Lawrence, however uncomfortable it may be for readers, for he was hardly ever just a writer of fiction but one of the gods' angry men.

When Lawrence died of his longtime tubercular condition in southern France at the age of forty-four, he had published ten novels and nearly sixty novellas and stories. While disagreement continues about the quality of Lawrence's works, three quite different novels do stand out: *Sons and Lovers*, *Women in Love*, and *Lady Chatterley's Lover*. Two long novellas, *St. Mawr* and *The Virgin and the Gipsy*, are the most interesting in their genre. A good selection of the stories, a form in which Lawrence produced much of his best-crafted writing, would contain "The White Stocking," "The Christening," "The

Prussian Officer," "Tickets, Please," "The Blind Man," "You Touched Me," "The Princess," "The Rocking-Horse Winner," "The Man Who Loved Islands," "The Lovely Lady," and the related writing "Portrait of M. M." But it should be emphasized that Lawrence was not just a fiction writer and that his novels and stories do not sufficiently define his work and significance.

Unlike most other fiction writers in the England of his time, Lawrence was a prolific and interesting poet. He also wrote half a dozen volumes of lively travel sketches, more than half a dozen volumes of psychological, social, and religious speculations, and some good personal essays. Some of his provocative works in literary criticism, especially *Studies in Classic American Literature* (1923), have had great influence. He also wrote plays and produced translations, a history text, and amateur paintings. His personal effect on a variety of people was considerable; his frequently lively and outrageous letters are expected to run eight substantial volumes in the definitive edition which has begun to appear. All of this was accomplished in two decades of incessant travel, grave illness, self-exacerbated public conflict (especially as a result of official censorship of several of his works), and considerable domestic turmoil. Because of his extreme and provocative personality, Lawrence's life has a persistent fascination, making him the subject of an immense number of memoirs and biographies for half a century. And, for complex reasons in a drastically changing Anglo-American culture, his obsessive concern with exploring erotic themes, social angers, and religious perplexities has put him in the role of bedeviled prophet. A full sense of Lawrence, then, cannot be limited to a specific group of literary artifacts. But his best fictions, however varied in form and style, do convey his harsh and vibrant intensity of perception, his radical erotic-nihilistic dialectics, and, simply, some of his exceptional passion.

Letters:

The Letters of D. H. Lawrence, edited by Aldous Huxley (London: Heinemann, 1932; New York: Viking, 1932);

The Collected Letters of D. H. Lawrence, 2 volumes, edited by Harry T. Moore (New York: Viking, 1962; London: Heinemann, 1962);

Lawrence in Love: Letters to Louie Burrows, edited by James T. Boulton (Nottingham: University of Nottingham Press, 1968);

The Quest for Rananim: D. H. Lawrence's Letters to S. S. Koteliansky, 1914-1930, edited by George J. Zytaruk (Montreal & London: McGill-

Queen's University Press, 1970);

Letters to Thomas and Adele Seltzer, edited by Gerald M. Lacy (Santa Barbara: Black Sparrow Press, 1976);

The Letters of D. H. Lawrence, Volume I, September 1901-May 1913, edited by James T. Boulton (Cambridge: Cambridge University Press, 1979).

Bibliographies:

E. W. Tedlock, Jr., *The Frieda Lawrence Collection of D. H. Lawrence Manuscripts: A Descriptive Bibliography* (Albuquerque: University of New Mexico Press, 1948);

F. Warren Roberts, *A Bibliography of D. H. Lawrence* (London: Hart-Davis, 1963);

Carole Ferrier, "D. H. Lawrence's Pre-1920 Poetry: A Descriptive Bibliography of Manuscripts, Typescripts, and Proofs," *D. H. Lawrence Review*, 6 (1973): 333-359;

John E. Stoll, *D. H. Lawrence: A Bibliography, 1911-1975* (New York: Whitson, 1977);

Ferrier, "D. H. Lawrence's Poetry, 1920-1928: A Descriptive Bibliography of Manuscripts, Typescripts, and Proofs," *D. H. Lawrence Review*, 12 (1979): 289-303;

James C. Cowan, *D. H. Lawrence: An Annotated Bibliography of Writings About Him* (De Kalb: Northern Illinois University Press, 1982).

Biographies:

Catherine Carswell, *The Savage Pilgrimage* (London: Secker, 1932; New York: Harcourt, Brace, 1932);

Mabel Dodge Luhan, *Lorenzo in Taos* (New York: Knopf, 1932);

John Middleton Murry, *Reminiscences of D. H. Lawrence* (London: Cape, 1933);

Earl and Achsah Brewster, *Reminiscences and Correspondence* (London: Secker, 1934);

Frieda Lawrence, *"Not I, but the Wind . . . "* (New York: Viking, 1934);

Jessie Chambers, as E.T., *D. H. Lawrence: A Personal Record* (1935; revised edition, New York: Barnes & Noble, 1965);

Richard Aldington, *Portrait of a Genius, But . . .* (London: Heinemann, 1950);

Harry T. Moore, *The Life and Works of D. H. Lawrence* (London: Allen & Unwin, 1951; New York: Twayne, 1951);

Moore, *The Intelligent Heart* (New York: Farrar, Straus & Young, 1954); revised as *The Priest of Love* (New York: Farrar, Straus & Giroux, 1974);

Helen Corke, *D. H. Lawrence: The Croydon Years* (Austin: University of Texas Press, 1957);

Edward Nehls, ed., *D. H. Lawrence: A Composite Biography*, 3 volumes (Madison: Wisconsin University Press, 1957-1959);

Paul Delany, *D. H. Lawrence's Nightmare: The Writer and His Circle During the Years of the Great War* (New York: Basic Books, 1978);

Keith Sagar, *The Life of D. H. Lawrence* (New York: Pantheon, 1980);

Norman Page, ed., *D. H. Lawrence: Interviews and Recollections* (Totowa, N.J.: Barnes & Noble, 1981).

References:

Colin C. Clarke, *River of Dissolution: D. H. Lawrence and English Romanticism* (London: Routledge, 1969);

Herman M. Daleski, *The Forked Flame, A Study of D. H. Lawrence* (Evanston, Ill.: Northwestern University Press, 1965);

George H. Ford, *Double Measure: A Study of the Novels and Stories of D. H. Lawrence* (New York: Holt, Rinehart & Winston, 1965);

Mary Freeman, *D. H. Lawrence, A Basic Study of His Ideas* (Gainesville: University of Florida Press, 1955);

David J. Gordon, *D. H. Lawrence as a Literary Critic* (New Haven: Yale University Press, 1966);

Martin B. Green, *The von Richthofen Sisters: The Triumphant and the Tragic Modes of Love* (New York: Basic Books, 1974);

Donald Gutierrez, *Lapsing Out: Embodiments of Death and Rebirth in the Last Writings of D. H. Lawrence* (London: Associated University Presses, 1980);

Graham G. Hough, *The Dark Sun: A Study of D. H. Lawrence* (London: Duckworth, 1956);

Marguerite B. Howe, *The Art of the Self in D. H. Lawrence* (Athens: Ohio University Press, 1977);

Martin Jarrett-Kerr, *D. H. Lawrence and Human Existence* (London: S. C. M., 1961);

F. R. Leavis, *D. H. Lawrence, Novelist* (New York: Knopf, 1955);

Leavis, *Thought, Words and Creativity: Art and Thought in Lawrence* (London: Chatto & Windus, 1976);

Jeffrey Meyers, ed., *D. H. Lawrence and Tradition* (Amherst: University of Massachusetts Press, forthcoming 1985);

Julian Moynahan, *The Deed of Life; The Novels and Tales of D. H. Lawrence* (Princeton: Princeton University Press, 1963);

Ronald E. Pritchard, *D. H. Lawrence: Body of Darkness* (London: Hutchinson, 1971);

Sylvia Sklar, *The Plays of D. H. Lawrence* (London: Vision, 1975);

Mark Spilka, *The Love Ethic of D. H. Lawrence* (Bloomington: Indiana University Press, 1955);

Ernest W. Tedlock, *D. H. Lawrence, Artist and Rebel* (Albuquerque: University of New Mexico Press, 1963);

Daniel Weiss, *Oedipus at Nottingham* (Seattle: University of Washington Press, 1962);

Kingsley Widmer, *The Art of Perversity: D. H. Lawrence's Shorter Fictions* (Seattle: University of Washington Press, 1962);

Widmer, "Dark Prophecy: The Nietzschean Matrix," in *D. H. Lawrence and Tradition*, edited by Jeffrey Meyers (Amherst: University of Massachusetts Press, forthcoming 1985);

Widmer, "The Dialectics of Passion in Lawrence's Fiction," in *D. H. Lawrence*, edited by Gamini Salgado and G. K. Das (London: Macmillan, forthcoming 1985);

Widmer, *Edges of Extremity: Some Problems of Literary Modernism* (Tulsa, Okla.: University of Tulsa, 1980).

Papers: Collections of Lawrence's manuscripts include those at the University of California at Berkeley, the University of California at Los Angeles, the University of Tulsa, the University of Chicago, the Berg Collection at the New York Public Library, the University of Nottingham, the Humanities Research Center at the University of Texas at Austin, the Houghton Library at Harvard University, the Lockwood Memorial Library at the State University of New York at Buffalo, and the University of New Mexico.

Rose Macaulay

(1 August 1881-30 October 1958)

J. V. Guerinot
University of Wisconsin

BOOKS: *Abbots Verney* (London: Murray, 1906);

The Furnace (London: Murray, 1907);

The Secret River (London: Murray, 1909);

The Valley Captives (New York: Holt, 1911);

Views and Vagabonds (London: Murray, 1912; New York: Holt, 1912);

The Lee Shore (New York: Hodder & Stoughton/Doran, 1912; London: Hodder & Stoughton, 1914);

The Two Blind Countries (London: Sidgwick & Jackson, 1914);

The Making of a Bigot (London: Hodder & Stoughton, 1914);

Non-combatants and Others (London: Hodder & Stoughton, 1916);

What Not: A Prophetic Comedy (London: Constable, 1919);

Three Days (London: Constable, 1919);

Potterism: A Tragi-farcical Tract (London: Collins, 1920; New York: Boni & Liveright, 1920);

Dangerous Ages (London: Collins, 1921; New York: Boni & Liveright, 1921);

Mystery at Geneva (London: Collins, 1922; New York: Boni & Liveright, 1923);

Told by an Idiot (London: Collins, 1923; New York: Boni & Liveright, 1923);

Orphan Island (London: Collins, 1924; New York: Boni & Liveright, 1925);

A Casual Commentary (London: Methuen, 1925; New York: Boni & Liveright, 1926);

Crewe Train (London: Collins, 1926; New York: Boni & Liveright, 1926);

Catchwords and Claptrap (London: Woolf, 1926);

Keeping Up Appearances (London: Collins, 1928); republished as *Daisy and Daphne* (New York: Boni & Liveright, 1928);

Staying with Relations (London: Collins, 1930; New York: Liveright, 1930);

Some Religious Elements in English Literature (London: Hogarth Press, 1931; New York: Harcourt, Brace, 1931);

The Shadow Flies (New York & London: Harper, 1932);

They Were Defeated (London: Collins, 1932);

Venice, 1957 (photo by Roloff Beny)

Going Abroad (London: Collins, 1934; New York: Harper, 1934);

Milton (London: Duckworth, 1934; New York: Harper, 1935);

Personal Pleasures (London: Gollancz, 1935; New York: Macmillan, 1936);

An Open Letter (London: Collins, 1937);

I Would Be Private (London: Collins, 1937; New York: Harper, 1937);

The Writings of E. M. Forster (London: Hogarth Press, 1938; New York: Harcourt, 1938);

And No Man's Wit (London: Collins, 1940);

Life Among the English (London: Collins, 1942);

They Went to Portugal (London: Cape, 1946);

Fabled Shore: From the Pyrenees to Portugal (London: Hamilton, 1949; New York: Farrar, Straus, 1951);

The World My Wilderness (London: Collins, 1950; Boston: Little, Brown, 1950);

Pleasure of Ruins (London: Weidenfeld & Nichol-

son, 1953; New York: Walker, 1966);

The Towers of Trebizond (London: Collins, 1956; New York: Farrar, Straus & Cudahy, 1957);

Letters to a Friend: 1950-1952, edited by Constance Babington Smith (London: Collins, 1961; New York: Atheneum, 1962);

Last Letters to a Friend: 1952-1958, edited by Constance Babington Smith (London: Collins, 1962; New York: Atheneum, 1963);

Letters to a Sister, edited by Constance Babington Smith (London: Collins, 1964; New York: Atheneum, 1964).

Emilie Rose Macaulay, whom Elizabeth Bowen called "one of the few writers of whom it may be said, she adorns our century," was born at Rugby, where her father was an assistant master. Descended on both sides from a long line of clerical ancestors, she felt Anglicanism was in her blood. Much of her childhood was spent in Varazze, near Genoa, and memories of Italy fill the early novels. The family returned to England in 1894 and settled in Oxford. She read history at Somerville, and on coming down lived with her family first in Wales, then near Cambridge, where her father had been appointed a lecturer in English. There she began a writing career which was to span fifty years with the publication of her first novel, *Abbots Verney*, in 1906. When her sixth novel, *The Lee Shore* (1912), won a literary prize, a gift from her uncle allowed her to rent a tiny flat in London, and she plunged happily into London literary life.

The early novels are unsatisfactory, and many years later Macaulay was thought to want to steal the London Library's copies. *The Making of a Bigot* (1914) is the first of her works to sound her characteristic note of high comedy. After the war she settled in a flat in Marylebone and began the witty, satiric novels for which she is remembered.

Potterism (1920) is directed against muddled thinking, cant, and sentimentality, of which the newspapers of Lord Potter are the dreadful illustration; the satire has not lost its point. *Told by an Idiot* (1923), a family chronicle, traces in the liveliest way the changes in British thought and life through the Victorian, fin de siècle, Edwardian, and Georgian periods. The clergyman father of the family is in the course of the novel successively converted to and then lapses from all of the churches from Roman Catholicism to the Higher Thought. The scholarly and loving interest in religion, the detached, ironic, and elegant prose, and the sheer sense of fun are typical of all her best work. *Orphan Island* (1924) takes us to an idyllic Pacific island

Rose Macaulay in her twenties

Devonshire and goes on to recreate one of her favorite historical moments, the spiritual and intellectual milieu of Cambridge just before the Civil War. The seventeenth century had been one of her abiding loves since Oxford (as her *Some Religious Elements in English Literature,* 1931, and *Milton,* 1934, also show), and her deep understanding of seventeenth-century poetry, the Anglicanism of the Laudian reform, and Cambridge Platonists has always won the book admirers, including such expert ones as the historian Cicely Veronica Wedgwood, with whom Macaulay used to indulge in long telephone conversations about seventeenth-century history.

Going Abroad (1934) is surely one of the best comic novels in the language. In it the Anglican bishop of Xanadu and his wife, now retired from missionary work and settled in Cambridge, are on holiday in the Basque country. The bishop is studying the survival of such early heresies as Collyridianism and Priscillianism among the Iraqui tribes, his wife the fauna and flora of the Garden of Eden, and also Basque grammar. They are kidnapped by bandits and held for ransom with the owners of Europe's largest chain of beauty parlors. There are as well some amiable young Buchmanites out to convert the Basques, a lovely and brainless girl of Byronic descent, and a simple Basque priest who is quite unable to understand the quotations from the *Eclogues* and Milton's *Defensio pro Populo Anglicano* with which the English, being unable to communicate with him in Basque, attempt to explain their plight.

I Would Be Private (1937) takes the deeply embarrassed parents of quintuplets to a remote island in the Caribbean with their offspring. *And No Man's Wit* (1940) visits Spain after the Spanish civil war. Both are minor works. The Second World War brought tragedy. Gerald O'Donovan, the married man with whom Rose Macauley had been in love for many years, died of an illness, and her valuable library was destroyed when her Marylebone flat was bombed. *The World My Wilderness* (1950), one of her most distinguished novels, reflects the sadness of these years. It is a somber and moving story of two children raised in southern France during the war. Transported abruptly to fashionable London after the war, they spend their time in the ruins of the city, playing in the bombed-out churches.

In 1950 Macaulay began her correspondence with a Cowly Father (a member of the Society of St. John the Evangelist), her cousin John Hamilton Cowper Johnson. Her letters to him were published after her death as *Letters to a Friend* (1961) and *Last*

where we are delighted to discover that the orphans marooned fifty years before have created a faithful replica of mid-nineteenth-century England complete with a matriarch who fancies herself Queen Victoria. The heroine of *Crewe Train* (1926) is typical of the girls Rose Macaulay was fond of portraying: they hope to grow up to be men and join the navy; they wish to spend their lives bathing and exploring; they see little point in books, pictures, and conversation. *Staying with Relations* (1930) offers a marvelously imagined rococo palace in the jungles of Guatemala, which Rose Macaulay had never visited, and a fine chase through Baja California, which she had, while recording the young novelist heroine's failure to penetrate human character. People must be like something, she broods, if one can only discover what.

The 1930s are marked by two of her finest achievements. *They Were Defeated* (1932), her only historical novel, opens with Robert Herrick in dull

Letters to a Friend (1962). Under his guidance she returned to the full sacramental life of the church, from which she had been absent for thirty years. The letters, erudite, funny, full of spiritual insight, were reviewed with admiration and respect and read with such enthusiasm that they were issued in paperback.

With a new serenity and renewed zest at the age of seventy-five, in full command of her powers, she published her most popular book, *The Towers of Trebizond* (1956). The poet and critic Sir John Betjeman, reviewing it for the *Daily Telegraph,* felt it was "the best book she has written, and that is saying a lot." It was also praised by Orville Prescott in the *New York Times* and Harold Hobson in the *Christian Science Monitor.*

The book begins, " 'Take my camel, dear,' said my aunt Dot, as she climbed down from this animal on her return from High Mass," goes on to explain that aunt Dot's Morris had recently been stolen from her by an Anglican bishop from outside the Athenaeum annex where she was dining with Professor Gilbert Murray and Archbishop David Mathew, and continues as surprisingly and engagingly. Laurie and her aunt go to Turkey to see about

the possibility of establishing an Anglican mission there, and with the camel and "an ancient bigot," Father Hugh Chantry-Pigg, visit the shores of the Black Sea, remembering fondly everywhere the Argonauts and Xenophon and the Trebizond, which had been for eight years the last outpost of Byzantium. Led by a desire to see more Armenian churches and to fish in the Caspian, aunt Dot and Father Chantry-Pigg disappear behind the Iron Curtain. Laurie, left alone with the camel, lingers in Trebizond, buys a potion from a local enchanter, and rides to Jerusalem.

The Towers of Trebizond is not only a brilliantly comic novel; it is a novel of religious belief and doubt, grace and sin. Laurie, in love adulterously with Vere, feels herself unable to give him up and reluctantly, bewilderedly, ceases to practice her religion. Trebizond becomes for her a symbol of the splendors of the courts of God, the church from which she is cut off, and when Vere dies in an automobile accident at the end, Laurie knows sadly that she is forever on the outside of "the Towers of Trebizond, the fabled city, gated and walled."

Macaulay's travels provided material not only for the settings of her novels, but also for her travel

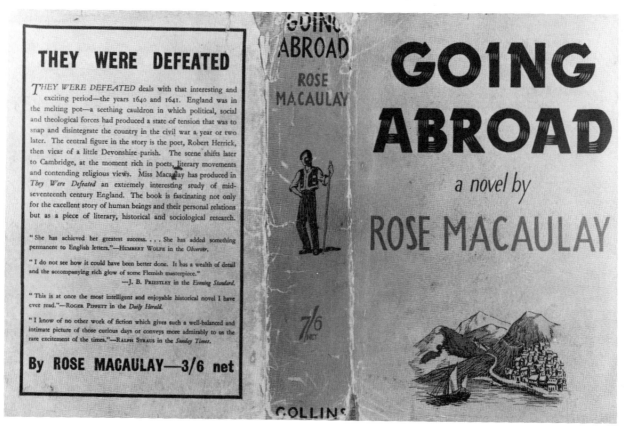

Dust jacket for Macaulay's 1934 comic novel, the story of a retired bishop and his wife who are kidnapped by the owners of a chain of beauty parlors

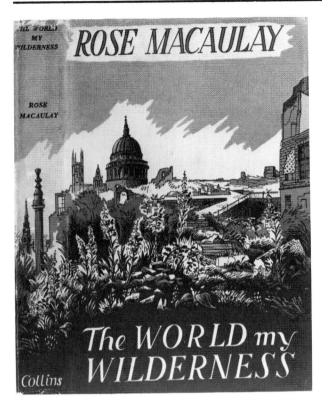

Dust jacket for Macaulay's 1950 novel. Set in southern France and London during World War II, the book reflects personal as well as world tragedies.

books. After the war she was able to visit Spain, and *Fabled Shore* (1949) is her account of her trip by car—she was famous as an intrepid and reckless driver—down the western coast of Spain, following the route of Avienus's fourth-century *Ora Maritima.*

It is the ideal travel book, full of sensitive descriptions of architecture and scenery, filled with classical and archaeological learning. But her gift for travel writing found its perfect expression in *Pleasure of Ruins* (1953), a long labor of love that surveys ruins from Central America to Cambodia. On Rome, on Alexandria, Palmyra, Greece she is predictably splendid. Never was her prose richer, more baroque, more filled with nostalgia, or her enthusiasm for travel more infectious than in this book.

She was for many years a prominent figure in London, attending every opening and literary luncheon. T. S. Eliot pleaded with her not to swim in the Serpentine in winter on her way home from mass at Grosvenor Chapel; Evelyn Waugh and Henry Green tried to repair her water cistern. She was given an Honorary Doctorate of Letters by the University of Cambridge in 1951 and was made a Dame Commander of the British Empire in 1958. She died in London on 30 October 1958.

There are some welcome signs of a revival of interest in Macaulay's writing. *The Towers of Trebizond* is now available in paperback in the United States, Oxford has reissued *They Were Defeated,* and Virago Press plans soon to republish several of the earlier novels. At her best Macaulay is a novelist of real distinction, and nothing that she wrote after the First World War is untouched by her urbanity and learned wit, her deeply civilized imagination.

Reference:

Constance Babington Smith, *Rose Macaulay* (London: Collins, 1972).

Arthur Llewelyn Jones Machen
(3 March 1863-15 December 1947)

Wesley D. Sweetser
State University of New York College At Oswego

SELECTED BOOKS: *Eleusinia, by a Former Member of H.C.S.* (Hereford: Privately printed, 1881);

The Anatomy of Tobacco (London: Redway, 1884; New York: Knopf, 1926);

The Chronicle of Clemendy (London: Privately printed, 1888; New York: Privately printed, 1923);

The Great God Pan and the Inmost Light (London: Lane, 1894; Boston: Roberts, 1894);

The Three Impostors (London: Lane, 1895; Boston: Roberts, 1895);

Hieroglyphics (London: Richards, 1902; New York: Kennerley, 1913);

The House of Souls (London: Richards, 1906; with different contents, New York: Knopf, 1922);

Dr. Stiggins: His Views and Principles (Westminster: Griffiths, 1906; New York: Knopf, 1925);

The Hill of Dreams (London: Richards, 1907; Boston: Estes, 1907);

The Angels of Mons (London: Simpkin, Marshall, Hamilton, Kent, 1915; New York: Putnam's, 1915);

The Great Return (London: Faith Press, 1915);

The Terror (London: Duckworth, 1917; New York: McBride, 1917);

War and the Christian Faith (London: Skeffington, 1918);

The Secret Glory (London: Secker, 1922; New York: Knopf, 1922);

Far Off Things (London: Secker, 1922; New York: Knopf, 1922);

Things Near and Far (London: Secker, 1923; New York: Knopf, 1923);

The Grand Trouvaille: A Legend of Pentonville (London: Privately printed, 1923);

The Shining Pyramid (Chicago: Covici-McGee, 1923; with different contents, London: Secker, 1925);

The Collector's Craft (London: Privately printed, 1923);

Strange Roads (London: Classic Press, 1923);

Dog and Duck (New York: Knopf, 1924; London: Cape, 1924);

The London Adventure (London: Secker, 1924; New York: Knopf, 1924);

Arthur Machen, 1910 (photo by E. O. Hoppé)

The Glorious Mystery, edited by Vincent Starrett (Chicago: Covici-McGee, 1924);

Precious Balms (London: Spurr & Swift, 1924);

Ornaments in Jade (New York: Knopf, 1924);

The Canning Wonder (London: Chatto & Windus, 1925; New York: Knopf, 1926);

Dreads and Drolls (London: Secker, 1926; New York: Knopf, 1927);

Notes and Queries (London: Spurr & Swift, 1926);

A Souvenir of Cadby Hall (London: Lyons, 1927);

Parish of Amersham (Amersham: Mason, 1930);

Tom O'Bedlam and His Song (Westport, Conn.: Appelicon, 1930);

A Few Letters from Arthur Machen (Cleveland: Rowfant Club, 1932);

The Glitter of the Brook (Dalton, Ga.: Postprandial, 1932);

The Green Round (London: Benn, 1933);

The Cosy Room and Other Stories (London: Rich & Cowan, 1936);

The Children of the Pool and Other Stories (London: Hutchinson, 1936);

Tales of Horror and the Supernatural, edited by Philip Van Doren Stern (New York: Knopf, 1948; London: Richards, 1949);

Bridles and Spurs (Cleveland: Rowfant Club, 1951);

A Critical Essay (Lakewood, Ohio: Privately printed, 1953);

A Note on Poetry (Wichita, Kans.: Four Ducks Press, 1959).

OTHER: Marguerite, Queen of Navarre, *The Heptameron,* translated by Machen (London: Dryden Press, 1886; New York: Scribner & Wellford, 1887);

Beroalde de Verville, *Fantastic Tales,* translated by Machen (London: Privately printed, 1890; Carbonnek, N.Y.: Boni & Liveright, 1923);

The Memoirs of Jacques Casanova, translated by Machen, 12 volumes (London: Privately printed, 1894); republished as *The Memoirs of Jacques Casanova de Seingalt* (New York: Aventuros, 1925).

Arthur Machen's works cannot be classified as novels in the usual sense. The greatest body of his canon consists of essays and supernatural tales. The common chord, however, that runs throughout is the spirit of romance. His position is made clear in *Hieroglyphics* (1902), his book of criticism, which attempts to establish the essential difference between great and ordinary literature, a distinction which he terms "ecstasy"—the creation of wonder, of withdrawal from common life, and of the sense of the unknown. These qualities are exemplified best, in his opinion, by *Pantagruel, Don Quixote, The Pickwick Papers,* and *The Odyssey,* works which he unceasingly and abortively attempted to emulate by creating the Great Romance. Though he knew Oscar Wilde slightly and though his Bodley Head publications of the 1890s were illustrated by Aubrey Beardsley, Machen claimed to have had no part in the aesthetic-decadent movement of that period, a contention belied by his belated romanticism and interest in the weird and occult.

Born in Caerleon-on-Usk—in Roman times the fort of the legion and later the site of the mythical court of King Arthur—and reared by a clergyman father, an invalid mother, and a maiden aunt,

Machen lived a lonely boyhood and found solace in the enchantment of nature, in the living legends of Wales, and in great books from his father's library. Imagination became his outlet. After a secondary education at Hereford Cathedral School, where he became versed in the classics and religion, he went to London to study for the surgeon's examination, which he failed because he spent his time reading and writing instead of studying mathematics. Subsequently, he studied shorthand for a career in journalism, did some tutoring, wrote his juvenilia—*Eleusinia* (1881), a poem, and *The Anatomy of Tobacco* (1884), a discourse in imitation of Burton—and completed a much more polished work, *The Chronicle of Clemendy* (1888), a collection of medieval tales. He then, as did many other aspiring authors, served his stint with Grub Street, first as editor of *Walford's Antiquarian* and next as a cataloguer of rare and occult books with Redway and with Robson and Karslake. From this work he derived his knowledge of esoterica and sub-rosa literature, a permeating influence on his own work.

When a providential legacy in 1887 enabled him to marry and to begin a career as a creative writer, his all-embracing theme became to transform the world of everyday reality into a world of magic and wonder, to convey to the reader the naked transcendental forces behind human existence. His materials were drawn from the occult and the supernatural: demonology and witchcraft; dwarfish, wizened, and malignant fairies; unintelligible languages; transformations and transmigrations; and the ineffable mystery. Almost all of his fictional works contain the elements of romanticism, mysticism and symbolism, and the weird and occult.

Machen's first work to receive attention was *The Great God Pan and the Inmost Light* (1894). The story "The Inmost Light" is simply filler, but it does introduce the character Dyson, a paleontologist and armchair sleuth. "The Great God Pan" is similarly a tale, but with a more complicated plot, opening with an experiment in brain surgery enabling the victim to see the great god Pan. She later gives birth to a daughter and then dies in a state of hopeless idiocy. The story is mainly concerned with the daughter, Helen Vaughan, who, wherever she lives, leaves behind the aura of evil and the hint of nameless infamies. Villiers, whose friend had been married to Helen and had committed suicide, learns her true nature, confronts her, and gives her a rope to hang herself. In the process of dying, she converts from sex to sex, beast to man, man to beast, and beast to hideous protoplasm—an atavistic conception of the

Front cover for the American edition of Machen's 1894 book. In the first story a brain surgeon's experiment with forces he does not understand ends with his concluding "that when the house of life is thus thrown open, there may enter in that for which we have no name, and human flesh may become the veil of a horror one dare not express."

reversion of evolution. The tale is largely sensational in effect, with a slight tinge of the pseudoscientific and some symbolism. Certainly, the theme of the attraction and repulsion of evil has some prominence, but Machen's Pan cannot be equated with pure diabolism. Machen was more concerned with imparting terror of the unknown, an idea suggested by the Sabbatic Goat, a mythical figure from Jewish folklore which is neither good nor evil. All events are told in retrospect through memoirs and papers, and the diction is well selected to create mood. The characters are merely vehicles without living qualities. The unique aspect of Machen's

work is the vagueness of his symbols which suggest the hidden, eternal forces at work in all ages, ages which interpenetrate each other.

The Three Impostors (1895) is imitative of Robert Louis Stevenson's *New Arabian Nights* in the framework device for linking together a disparate collection of weird tales. The linking device is Dyson, to whom the fantastic events are gradually revealed, with little detection on his part, and to whom members of Lipsius's gang spin irrelevant tales surrounding the search for a gold Tiberius, a unique coin celebrating excess. One of the tales in the first edition, "The Iron Maid," is not intrinsic to the work. Of the others, the predominant elements are demonism or omnipresent evil, symbolically conveyed; the superstitions of folklore—transmutation, dwarfed and cannibalistic fairies, and unintelligible language—treated as a living reality, as in "The Novel of the Black Seal"; pseudoscientific devices, such as the infernal chemical of the Witches' Sabbath, inadvertently taken by Wyn Leicester in "The Novel of the White Seal," causing him to revert to primordial slime; and the armchair detective, Dyson, whose main ability lies in decoding cyphers and listening to weird tales.

Machen considered his tales to be mere potboilers and, piqued at being called a second-rate imitator of Stevenson, began in 1895 an experimental novel initially published as a magazine serial entitled "The Garden of Avallaunius," later as a book, *The Hill of Dreams* (1907). It is almost esoterically preoccupied with symbols and the inner life, reflecting the workings of the soul of Lucian Taylor, a clergyman's son, who resides near the ruins of an old Roman fort. Lucian adopts a literary career and creates in his imagination a Roman villa, which becomes his garden of delight. His love for Annie Morgan, who marries another, takes on perverse and unnatural means of fulfillment. On receipt of a legacy, he removes to London, where amidst sordid surroundings, addicted to drugs and married to a prostitute, he dwells more and more frequently on the beauty of his "garden." The gradual decay of spirit ends in suicide. The work is both symbolic and mystical, the symbolism focusing on the struggle of the artist against crass materialism which deprives him of his integrity in his struggle for creativity. Spiritual death results from the realization of the necessity to compromise. In a mystical sense, the flagellation, asceticism, and renunciation achieve a spiritual beauty, a fragmentary glimpse of the ineffable mystery; and the sacramental view of nature calls forth the unseen. Unwittingly, Machen created in *The Hill of Dreams* both a monument and an

You may search, I think, from one end of
his books to the other, without finding any
evidence that he realised the mystery of things;
he was never for a moment aware of that
shadowy double, that strange companion
of man, who walks, as I said, foot to foot
with each one of us, & yet his paces are
in an unknown world. And (unless you
have got any fresh arguments) I think
we decided last week that the book which
lacks the sense of all this is not fine
literature.

I hope you don't think I am abusing
Thackeray: I am always reading him, & I chose
his "Vanity fair" because it strikes me
as such a supremely clever example of
its class. I suppose there is nothing more
amusing than the society of a brilliant

Page from the manuscript for Hieroglyphics *(American Art Association/Anderson Galleries, sale 4279, 24-25 November 1936)*

157

epitaph for the aesthetic-decadent period.

After the death of his first wife, Machen became a member of Frank Benson's Shakespeare Repertory Company and continued as an actor for several years. After his second marriage, he turned once more to his pen for a livelihood and wrote for numerous periodicals for nearly the remainder of his life, most notably the *Academy, T. P.'s Weekly, Vanity Fair, John O' London's Weekly,* the *Lyons Mail,* the *London Graphic,* and the *Independent.* From 1910 to 1921, he was a reporter on the (London) *Evening News* and contributed not only news stories but fiction as well. His famous story "The Bowmen" (in which a battle is won by supernatural means), later published in *The Angels of Mons* (1915), appeared there, as did his notable work *The Terror* (1917), a wartime mystery story which reveals in its denouement that all members of the animal kingdom have revolted against man when they sense that he is not king. This may have been the inspiration for Daphne du Maurier's *The Birds.*

By 1922, when his works were republished widely in both England and the United States, Machen's creative powers were severely on the wane. To commercialize on his fortuitous rediscovery, he dredged all the periodicals and had several volumes of collected essays published, the best of which are *Dog and Duck* (1924) and *Dreads and Drolls* (1926). He also resurrected a long work, written in 1908, called *The Secret Glory* (1922), a mystical novel on the attainment of sanctity and the Holy Grail by a character living amidst the mundanity of London. It contains a disproportionate amount of vituperative satire on the educational and commercial systems quite disparate to the main purpose of the work.

His last sustained work of note was *The Canning Wonder* (1925), a repetitive documentary of an eighteenth-century trial; but even in this documentary account of Elizabeth Canning's inexplicable disappearance, the mystery remains as profound and insoluble as in the original source material.

Machen's diverse talents and stylistic adeptness, which ranged from the standard translation of Casanova's *Memoirs* to lively and charming essays, were greatly admired by such dissimilar authors as H. P. Lovecraft, Ray Bradbury, and Henry Miller. Abhorring, as he did, realism and naturalism, he only skirted the novel form in his strangely original, experimental work *The Hill of Dreams;* but, in a sense, it foreshadowed the stream-of-consciousness school. Like Poe, whom he frequently extolled, his forte was short tales and the creation of atmosphere, not character creation and involved plot. Machen's work is unsurpassed in the area of the transcendental occult. His peculiar knowledge of demonology, witchcraft, folklore, particularly Celtic lore, and occult societies and religions combined with his unique talent for suggesting the indescribable to make him the spokesman without peer for sorcery and sanctity existing behind the veil.

References:

Adrian Goldstone and Wesley Sweetser, *A Bibliography of Arthur Machen* (Austin: University of Texas Press, 1965);

John Gunther, "The Truth about Arthur Machen," *Bookman,* 61 (July 1925): 571-574;

Robert Hillyer, "Arthur Machen," *Atlantic,* 179 (May 1947): 138-140;

H. P. Lovecraft, *The Outsider and Others* (Sauk City, Wis.: Arkham House, 1939);

George Redway, "Some Reminiscences of Publishing Fifty Years Ago," *Bookman* (London), 81 (December 1931): 186-187;

Aidan Reynolds and William Charlton, *Arthur Machen* (London: Richards, 1963);

R. Ellis Roberts, "Arthur Machen," *Bookman* (London), 62 (September 1922): 240-242;

Dorothy Scarborough, *The Supernatural in Modern British Fiction* (New York: Putnam's, 1917);

Wesley Sweetser, *Arthur Machen* (New York: Twayne, 1964).

W. Somerset Maugham

(25 January 1874-16 December 1965)

Scott Simpkins
University of Tulsa

See also the Maugham entry in *DLB 10, Modern British Dramatists, 1900-1945.*

BOOKS: *Liza of Lambeth* (London: Unwin, 1897; revised, 1904; New York: Doran, 1921);

The Making of a Saint (Boston: Page, 1898; London: Unwin, 1898);

Orientations (London: Unwin, 1899);

The Hero (London: Hutchinson, 1901);

Mrs. Craddock (London: Heinemann, 1902; New York: Doran, 1920);

A Man of Honour: A Play in Four Acts (London: Chapman & Hall, 1903; Chicago: Dramatic Publishing, 1912);

The Merry-Go-Round (London: Heinemann, 1904);

The Land of the Blessed Virgin: Sketches and Impressions in Andalusia (London: Heinemann, 1905; New York: Knopf, 1920);

The Bishop's Apron (London: Chapman & Hall, 1906);

The Explorer (London: Heinemann, 1907; New York: Baker & Taylor, 1909);

The Magician (London: Heinemann, 1908; New York: Duffield, 1909);

Lady Frederick: A Comedy in Three Acts (London: Heinemann, 1911; Chicago: Dramatic Publishing, 1912);

Jack Straw: A Farce in Three Acts (London: Heinemann, 1911; Chicago: Dramatic Publishing, 1912);

Mrs. Dot: A Farce in Three Acts (London: Heinemann, 1912; Chicago: Dramatic Publishing, 1912);

Penelope: A Comedy in Three Acts (London: Heinemann, 1912; Chicago: Dramatic Publishing, 1912);

The Explorer: A Melodrama in Four Acts (London: Heinemann, 1912; Chicago: Dramatic Publishing, 1912);

The Tenth Man: A Tragic Comedy in Three Acts (London: Heinemann, 1913; Chicago: Dramatic Publishing, 1913);

Landed Gentry: A Comedy in Four Acts (London: Heinemann, 1913; Chicago: Dramatic Publishing, 1913);

Balkin-Pix

Smith: A Comedy in Four Acts (London: Heinemann, 1913; Chicago: Dramatic Publishing, 1913);

Of Human Bondage (New York: Doran, 1915; London: Heinemann, 1915);

The Moon and Sixpence (London: Heinemann, 1919; New York: Doran, 1919);

The Unknown: A Play in Three Acts (London: Heinemann, 1920; New York: Doran, 1920);

The Circle: A Comedy in Three Acts (London: Heinemann, 1921; New York: Doran, 1921);

The Trembling of a Leaf: Little Stories of the South Sea Islands (New York: Doran, 1921; London:

Heinemann, 1921); republished as *Sadie Thompson: and Other Stories of the South Sea Islands* (London: Readers Library, 1928);

Caesar's Wife: A Comedy in Three Acts (London: Heinemann, 1922; New York: Doran, 1923);

East of Suez: A Play in Seven Scenes (London: Heinemann, 1922; New York: Doran, 1922);

The Land of Promise (London: Heinemann, 1922; New York: Doran, 1923);

On a Chinese Screen (New York: Doran, 1922; London: Heinemann, 1922);

Our Betters: A Comedy in Three Acts (London: Heinemann, 1923; New York: Doran, 1924);

Home and Beauty: A Farce in Three Acts (London: Heinemann, 1923);

The Unattainable: A Farce in Three Acts (London: Heinemann, 1923);

Loaves and Fishes: A Comedy in Four Acts (London: Heinemann, 1924);

The Painted Veil (New York: Doran, 1925; London: Heinemann, 1925);

The Casuarina Tree: Six Stories (London: Heinemann, 1926; New York: Doran, 1926); republished as *The Letter: Stories of Crime* (London: Detective Story Club/Collins, 1930);

The Constant Wife: A Comedy in Three Acts (New York: Doran, 1927; London: Heinemann, 1927);

The Letter: A Play in Three Acts (London: Heinemann, 1927; New York: Doran, 1927);

Ashenden: or The British Agent (London: Heinemann, 1928; Garden City: Doubleday, Doran, 1928);

The Sacred Flame: A Play in Three Acts (Garden City: Doubleday, Doran, 1928; London: Heinemann, 1929);

The Gentleman in the Parlour: A Record of a Journey from Rangoon to Haiphong (London: Heinemann, 1930; Garden City: Doubleday, Doran, 1930);

Cakes and Ale: Or the Skeleton in the Cupboard (London: Heinemann, 1930; Garden City: Doubleday, Doran, 1930);

The Bread-Winner: A Comedy in One Act (London: Heinemann, 1930; Garden City: Doubleday, Doran, 1931);

Six Stories Written in the First Person Singular (Garden City: Doubleday, Doran, 1931; London: Heinemann, 1931);

The Book-Bag (Florence: Orioli, 1932);

The Narrow Corner (London: Heinemann, 1932; Garden City: Doubleday, Doran, 1932);

For Services Rendered: A Play in Three Acts (London: Heinemann, 1932; Garden City: Doubleday, Doran, 1933);

Ah King: Six Stories (London: Heinemann, 1933;

Garden City: Doubleday, Doran, 1933);

Sheppey: A Play in Three Acts (London: Heinemann, 1933; Boston: Baker, 1949);

Don Fernando; or, Variations on Some Spanish Themes (London & Toronto: Heinemann, 1935; Garden City: Doubleday, Doran, 1935; revised edition, Melbourne, London & Toronto: Heinemann, 1950);

Cosmopolitans: Very Short Stories (Garden City: Doubleday, Doran, 1936; London & Toronto: Heinemann, 1936);

Six Comedies (New York: Garden City Publishing, 1937);

Theatre. A Novel (Garden City: Doubleday, Doran, 1937; London & Toronto: Heinemann, 1937);

The Summing Up (London & Toronto: Heinemann, 1938; Garden City: Doubleday, Doran, 1938);

Christmas Holiday (London & Toronto: Heinemann, 1939; Garden City: Doubleday, Doran, 1939);

France at War (London: Heinemann, 1940; New York: Doubleday, Doran, 1940);

Books and You (London & Toronto: Heinemann, 1940; New York: Doubleday, Doran, 1940);

The Mixture as Before (London & Toronto: Heinemann, 1940; New York: Doubleday, Doran, 1940);

Up at the Villa (New York: Doubleday, Doran, 1941; London & Toronto: Heinemann, 1941);

Strictly Personal (Garden City: Doubleday, Doran, 1941; London & Toronto: Heinemann, 1942);

The Hour Before the Dawn: A Novel (Garden City: Doubleday, Doran, 1942; Sydney & London: Angus & Robertson, 1945);

The Unconquered (New York: House of Books, 1944);

The Razor's Edge: A Novel (Garden City: Doubleday, Doran, 1944; London & Toronto: Heinemann, 1944);

Then and Now: A Novel (London & Toronto: Heinemann, 1946; Garden City: Doubleday, 1946);

Creatures of Circumstance (London & Toronto: Heinemann, 1947; Garden City: Doubleday, 1947);

Catalina: A Romance (Melbourne, London & Toronto: Heinemann, 1948; Garden City: Doubleday, 1948);

Great Novelists and Their Novels: Essays on the Ten Greatest Novels of the World, and the Men and Women Who Wrote Them (Philadelphia & Toronto: Winston, 1948); revised and enlarged as *Ten Novels and Their Authors* (Melbourne, London & Toronto: Heinemann,

1954); republished as *The Art of Fiction: An Introduction to Ten Novels and Their Authors* (Garden City: Doubleday, 1955);

A Writer's Notebook (Melbourne, London & Toronto: Heinemann, 1949; Garden City: Doubleday, 1949);

The Vagrant Mood: Six Essays (Melbourne, London & Toronto: Heinemann, 1952; Garden City: Doubleday, 1953);

The Noble Spaniard: A Comedy in Three Acts, adapted from Ernest Grenet-Dancourt's *Les Gaîtés du veuvage* (London: Evans Brothers, 1953);

Points of View (London, Melbourne & Toronto: Heinemann, 1958; Garden City: Doubleday, 1959);

Purely for My Pleasure (London, Melbourne & Toronto: Heinemann, 1962; Garden City: Doubleday, 1962).

Collection: Collected Edition, 35 volumes (London: Heinemann, 1931-1969).

In a career spanning more than sixty years, W. Somerset Maugham wrote a handful of novels which are still studied as modernist works. His ear for language, the use of actual—sometimes grim—experience transformed into fictional material, and a concern with varieties of "bondage" contribute to the modernist flavor which surfaces in varying degrees in most of his twenty novels. Maugham's highly successful excursions into the realm of popular drama (he wrote thirty-one plays) eventually brought him enough money to give him the leisure he needed to produce some of his finest modernist novels (*The Razor's Edge* being the prime example). Yet, Maugham always felt self-conscious about his novels, and he spent much of his career hounded by uncertainty and resentment: "I know just where I stand," he concluded in *The Summing Up* (1938). "In the very first row of the second-raters."

William Somerset Maugham was born in Paris at the British Embassy, on Faubourg Saint Honoré, the fourth son of Robert Ormond Maugham, an English lawyer who handled the embassy's legal matters, and Edith Mary Snell Maugham, whose father had served in the East India Company. The first ten years of his life were spent fairly pleasantly in France, and Maugham managed to develop a stoic reserve toward those misfortunes he did encounter. He was slightly less than average in height (5'7" at his tallest), felt himself to be ugly, was almost always in frail health, and both parents died within three years of each other. Edith Maugham was a picture of Victorian beauty (her obituary described her as a woman "whose startling beauty once lit up

our most elegant salons"), and her death from tuberculosis in January 1882, the day after the birth of her sixth child, was the greatest tragedy in Maugham's life. Maugham's father died in June 1884 from stomach cancer, leaving his four surviving sons an estate that had been depleted by the family's extravagant life-style. But Maugham's early belief in goodness (a theme often found in his work) enabled him to persevere with an experienced sense of reality, as Ted Morgan notes, "like one of Dickens' youthful heroes who are tempered by misfortune at an early age."

The death of his father necessitated Maugham's going to live, at the age of ten, with his father's clergyman brother, Henry MacDonald Maugham, at the vicarage in Whitstable. No longer able to communicate in French, as he was accustomed, and forced to adapt to new surroundings, he developed what proved to be a lifelong stammer, perhaps because of his uncertain English and feelings of alienation. (A similar theme arises in *Of Human Bondage* when Philip Carey experiences isolation and loneliness that he attributes primarily to his clubfoot.) But it was during this period that he discovered a convenient and thrilling escape through books. When he read, he could forget his loneliness and self-doubt at King's School in Canterbury, which he entered in May 1885 and left four miserable years later in July 1889. Maugham's uncle wanted him to go to Oxford and eventually to become a clergyman, but the temptation of returning to Europe prevailed and Maugham chose to study in Heidelberg, where he went in 1890. In addition to private tutoring in German, he attended lectures at Heidelberg University, where he came under the powerful influence of the then-current aesthetic thought and, perhaps more important, Schopenhauer's philosophical pessimism, a way of thinking that he maintained throughout his long life.

It was also at Heidelberg that Maugham had his first homosexual experience and realized he was not suited for the clergy. In 1892 he decided to study medicine at St. Thomas's Hospital in London, but his medical studies were primarily a guise for his real interest, writing: "I wrote steadily from the time I was 15," he later explained. "I became a medical student because I could not announce to my guardian that I wished to become a writer." Instead of preparing him for medical practice, his experiences as a medical student provided material for future books. From his first year at St. Thomas's to his departure five years later, Maugham took notes and practiced writing from various narrative stances, often opting for the detached, omniscient

Maugham as a young man

(and omnipotent) observer who describes his observations of "life in the raw" among the wards. In 1897, the year he qualified as a doctor, his first novel, *Liza of Lambeth*, was published.

This novel was written after two of his short stories were rejected in July 1896 by the publisher T. Fisher Unwin. He was told that his stories were too short, but that if he ever produced longer fiction he should submit it. Maugham, who had stuck to a rigorous schedule of writing at night, was undaunted, and, employing his experiences in the hospital's obstetric wards, he wrote a novel along the lines of the "new realism" of the latter part of the nineteenth century. In his story of a young unmarried woman who dies after suffering a miscarriage, Maugham's description of slum life in Lambeth, with the common recourse to violence, and his pressing concern with population control amid cramped quarters shocked a number of reviewers with its bluntness. But Maugham was writing about what he had seen himself. "I was forced to stick to the truth by the miserable poverty of my imagination," he admitted. Still, the mild success of the novel gave Maugham the driving force to continue his literary career. "I was determined to stamp myself upon the age," he wrote at the time.

But with this encouragement came new waves of self-doubt. The reviewer for the *Academy* accused him of plagiarizing from Arthur Morrison's *The Child of the Jago* (1896)—several times throughout his career charges that he "borrowed" from other writers surfaced—and he began to feel so uncertain about the merits of his own work that he was willing to compromise with editors to get his works published.

In a burst of fast writing, Maugham turned out three novels—*The Making of a Saint* (1898), *The Hero* (1901), and *Mrs. Craddock* (1902)—two plays, and a collection of short stories by 1903. With a trip to Spain in 1897, he had begun the travels in search of material that continued throughout his life. *The Making of a Saint* was Maugham's attempt to cash in on the historical novel market by writing a novel about Italy toward the conclusion of the fifteenth century, employing the description of the Forlì insurrection of 1487 in Machiavelli's *History of Florence*. Maugham tried again to exploit current literary trends by writing about the Boer War and its threat to British Imperialism in *The Hero*, showing the war's effect on the English through a veteran who returns home and finds his country's provincialism almost unbearable. The hero's despair and alienation suggest a parallel to Stephen Dedalus, Jake Barnes, and J. Alfred Prufrock in the modernist works of James Joyce, Ernest Hemingway, and T. S. Eliot that were to follow soon after.

Mrs. Craddock is Maugham's first novel of personal "bondage," the theme that was to characterize much of his work. Once Berthe Craddock becomes attached to the man she has so strongly desired before her marriage, she begins to realize that the strictures of marriage suffocate as much as they support. "Oh, when I think that I'm shackled to him for the rest of my life, I feel I could kill myself," she tells the vicar. Provincial society plays the role of antagonist to such an extent that some critics have called the novel an "English Bovary."

The three stories connected by one character in Maugham's next novel, *The Merry-Go-Round* (1904), continue his concern with societal codes and their influence on individuals. Maugham demonstrates a modernist concern with form in his juxtaposition of three narratives to create a kind of fragmented unity: "I was myself living in several sets that had no connection with one another, and it occurred to me that it might give a truer picture of life if one could carry on at the same time the various stories, of equal importance, that were enacted during a certain period in different circles," he wrote in *The Summing Up*. He also conceded that his experiment was a failure because the novel "lacks the continuous line that directs the reader's interest."

From 1907 to 1915 Maugham's main emphasis was on his work in the theater. Ted Morgan recounts that "Between 1905 and 1907 he wrote three out-and-out potboilers; his first stage success in 1907 saved him from hatching any more. He was too busy after that writing plays." In the potboilers—*The Bishop's Apron* (1906), *The Explorer* (1907), and *The Magician* (1908)—Maugham is indeed catering to the market for escapism. In the preface of the 1936 edition of *Liza of Lambeth* Maugham commented that, after the second of these three novels, even though he had worked with his usual great care, "To me it was all moonshine. I did not believe a word of it. It was a game I was playing. A book written under these conditions can have no life in it."

With the outbreak of World War I in August 1914, Maugham, who was too old to enlist, volunteered for the British ambulance corps and served for about five months at the front in Belgium and France, an experience which provided him with a great deal of material about war and suffering, which he employed in *Of Human Bondage* (1915).

Intensely autobiographical, the novel describes a process of psychological individuation closely paralleling Maugham's own. Philip Carey, who is orphaned at nine and has to move into his uncle's vicarage, has several painful relationships with women which make him come to a sense of

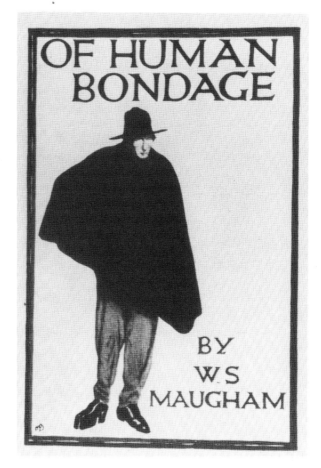

The original dust jacket for Maugham's 1915 novel. The jacket was replaced because, after a few copies were sent out, the publisher discovered that Philip Carey's clubfoot is on the wrong leg.

self-realization. (Maugham's first choice for a title had been "Beauty from Ashes.") Born with a clubfoot, Carey overcomes a life of harassment and isolation by becoming a doctor and satisfying himself by helping others. Maugham's persistent themes of misery, loneliness, alienation, loss of religious faith, and self-doubt reach a climax of sorts in *Of Human Bondage*. Early in the novel, for example, the narrator says that "Philip realized that he must live two years with a tormentor from whom there was no escape." More than 200 pages later, Philip still "could not understand himself. Would he always love only in absence and be prevented from enjoying anything when he had the chance by that deformity of vision which seemed to exaggerate the revolting?"

Of Human Bondage has never been out of print since its first publication, but when it came out, it met with a largely negative response. As Morgan

Page from the manuscript for Maugham's best-known short story

points out, "There was enough misery in British homes without [Maugham's] contribution, and it was hardly light reading for the men in the trenches." But a manuscript reader for Doran named Sinclair Lewis strongly urged that his company publish the novel in America, and Theodore Dreiser's enthusiastic review in the *New Republic* (25 December 1915) gave it the initial boost it needed. Dreiser called the novel a work of genius, saying that it was "the perfect thing which we love and cannot understand, but which we are compelled to confess a work of art." Dreiser added that "One feels as though one were sitting before a splendid Shiraz or Daghestan of priceless texture and intricate weave, admiring, feeling, responding sensually to its colours or tones. Or better yet, it is as though a symphony of great beauty by a master, Strauss and Beethoven, has just been completed, and the bud notes and flower tones were filling the air with their elusive message, fluttering and dying." Kingsley Amis later noted that Maugham's awareness of the influence of disfigurement (here both figurative and literal) added an element which reinforced the twentieth century's preoccupation with psychological influence—a distinctly modernist characteristic. The novel, Amis concluded, "shows how one barrier, in the shape of lameness, loneliness, puritanism or stupidity, will set up others: suspicion, overexclusive affection, vindictiveness, exhibitionism, obstinacy, intolerance, self-torture—the state of what a later generation has learned to call the injustice collector."

After leaving the ambulance corps in February 1915 Maugham went to work for the intelligence, going to Switzerland to replace an agent who had had a nervous breakdown. While there he wrote a play, *Caroline,* which opened in London in February 1916. He returned to London in summer 1916 with the intention of marrying Gwendolen Maud Syrie Wellcome, with whom he had been having an affair for almost six years and who had already given birth to his daughter, but her divorce had not yet become final. They were finally married in the United States on 26 May 1917 after Maugham had traveled to the United States and gone on to Hawaii, Tahiti, and American Samoa. On board the ship carrying them from Hawaii to Pago Pago were a prostitute, "Miss Thompson," and a medical missionary traveling with his wife. Maugham's speculations about what would happen if Miss Thompson and the missionary came together led to his writing the brief note that was the genesis for his short story "Rain" (first published as "Miss Thompson").

Not long after his marriage and still in the United States, Maugham was recruited by British Intelligence to go to Russia as a participant in an unsuccessful plan to prevent the Bolshevik takeover. Back in Britain after two and a half months in Russia, he discovered that he had contracted tuberculosis. He could not go to the more conventional treatment areas because of the war, so in November 1917 he went to a sanitorium in Scotland, where his treatment was successful.

Maugham based his next novel, *The Moon and Sixpence* (1919), on the life of Gauguin, a framework which allowed him to further discuss the interplay between life and art which he had focused upon in *Of Human Bondage.* In *The Moon and Sixpence* Charles Strickland, like Gauguin, abandons his family for the life of an artist in Tahiti. While the narrator, Ashenden, is disapproving, the author's sympathy for the artist is apparent; great art justifies ruthless behavior in breaking free of the bonds of society, especially those imposed by women.

Maugham continued traveling (going to Malaya, Borneo, the Pacific Islands, and Burma in 1922 and 1923) while his marriage gradually disintegrated. In fact, he had preferred homosexual relationships throughout his adult life and had never made much of an attempt to be a constant husband. "Maugham was blind to Syrie's good qualities," Morgan writes in his biography. "All he could see was that she had trapped him into marriage and become an emotional and financial drain."

In the years that followed, Maugham wrote

Dust jacket for Maugham's 1925 novel. While the novel was being serialized in Nash's Magazine, *Maugham was forced by threatened libel action to change the hero and heroine's last name. After 8,000 copies of the book had been printed, the Assistant Secretary of the Hong Kong Government protested the novel's having been set in Hong Kong. The publisher recalled all copies, and Maugham changed "Hong Kong" to "Tching-Yen."*

three more novels—*The Painted Veil* (1925), *Cakes and Ale* (1930), and *The Narrow Corner* (1932)—divorced Syrie (in 1929), and traveled to Spain in 1933. All three novels of this period deal with unfaithfulness, liberation from bondage, and the ravages of passion—themes which parallel the disruptive course his life was taking at that time.

In late 1935 he visited a penal colony in French Guiana to continue research on *Christmas Holiday* (1939), a novel he was writing about a French murderer whose trial he had observed. *Theatre,* Maugham's 1937 novel, once again relies upon personal observation, this time those of his years in the theatre, describing the schism between the public and private life of a well-known actress caught up in a bondage of sensation and human

First page from the manuscript for Cakes and Ale *(British Library)*

relationships. She pays a heavy price for creativity, which, however, eventually becomes the outlet which allows her to escape her bondage. The novel approaches journalism since so much of it is, typically, reality retold.

In fact, Maugham's lack of experience in India seems to have been the impetus behind his 1938 trip there. He had wanted to write about India for some time, but he felt his fiction would lack the authority of fiction, such as Kipling's, that had as its basis the author's firsthand experience in India. "I have never been able to write anything unless I had a solid and ample store of information for my wits to work upon," he said shortly before his departure.

It was not until 1944, however, that Maugham's novel based on his Indian experiences, *The Razor's Edge*, appeared. During the years between his trip and its publication, three other novels—*Christmas Holiday*, *Up at the Villa* (1941), and *The Hour Before the Dawn* (1942)—appeared. Maugham told his friend Edward Marsh that *Up at the Villa*, a novel of sexual intrigue and revenge, was written "to pass an idle hour," and many critics sensed Maugham's lack of commitment to it. "Hastily written, stilted, and implausible, *Up at the Villa* was scorched by the critics," Morgan notes. *The Hour Before Dawn* was commissioned by the British Ministry of Information to illustrate to America the

W. Somerset Maugham on his ninetieth birthday (Apis)

effects of the war on the average British family. At the same time Maugham was turning out second-rate books, however, he was doing some of his most rigorous writing.

If any novel could lift Maugham from the status of second-rate writer *The Razor's Edge* was the most likely candidate. Maugham's immensely popular novel proved his ability, once again, to produce a work that suited the tastes of the time. Dealing with popular religious issues and one man's search for genuine existence amid conformity and commercialized values, Maugham's first novel to include American characters also shows his willingness to experiment with narrative technique. The story is revealed through bits and pieces of reminiscences of a narrator named W. Somerset Maugham. Although Maugham appears in his works throughout his career in various autobiographical guises, in this novel, for the first time, he appears under his own name. This innovation allows the narrator-author to ask his characters questions and thus direct the outcome—a technique that exhibits decidedly modernist self-consciousness.

Drawing his title from the *Katha-Upanishad*: "The sharp edge of a razor is difficult to pass over; thus the wise say the path to Salvation is hard," Maugham tells the story of Larry Darrell, who, having been an aviator in World War I, finds it impossible to partake in the capitalistic recovery that seems to be the most convenient and comfortable way for a young man in his position to return to the real world. Like Philip Carey in *Of Human Bondage*, Darrell is uncomfortable with shallow postwar society and goes to India and then Paris in an attempt to come to peace with himself and live a life he can respect. Surprisingly, after Larry's quest leads him to intense self-introspection, meditation, and a time as a wandering scholar, he decides that the freest life is that of a taxi driver or a worker in a garage— employment which will pay him enough to live yet allow him to continue his studies of the great questions.

After the stunning success of *The Razor's Edge*, Maugham no longer had to concern himself about money, and he produced only two more novels before he died in 1965. *Then and Now* (1946) marked a return to the Renaissance Italy setting in

The Making of a Saint. The book was received as a lifeless historical novel written by a man in his seventies who was beginning to show the strains of his age. Edmund Wilson used his review of this novel in the *New Yorker* (8 June 1946) as a means of attacking Maugham's work in general. "It has happened to me from time to time to run into some person of taste who tells me that I ought to take Somerset Maugham seriously," he wrote, "yet I have never been able to convince myself that he was anything but second-rate." In his later years, Maugham's fears that he would never attain full mastery of his craft were reinforced by such attacks. Maugham's last novel, *Catalina* (1948), also met with harsh criticism. Set during the Spanish Inquisition, his story of a crippled girl who is healed by a miracle and goes on to become an actress was met with cries of "pathetic" and "feeble" by several critics. In a somewhat more sympathetic review in the *Times Literary Supplement* (21 August 1948), Anthony Powell, however, made an attempt to put these later works into the perspective of Maugham's entire body of novels. Powell concluded that "although we can be deeply grateful for the brilliance of the companionship that [Maugham] has provided in an increasingly prosy world, it may be wise to reserve judgment on the subject of his more didactic moods."

Despite the many assaults on the merits of Maugham's work, he often asserted that he did not care about such criticism, that he was content with his explorations of bondage, of the attainment of individuality, and of the complex relationships people go through in the course of their lives. "I have been highly praised and highly abused. On the whole I think I can truly say that I have not been unduly elated by one or unduly depressed by the other," he wrote. "You see, I have always written for my own pleasure."

Bibliographies:

Charles Saunders, *W. Somerset Maugham: An Annotated Bibliography of Writings about Him* (De Kalb: Northern Illinois University Press, 1970);

Raymond Toole Stott, *A Bibliography of the Works of W. Somerset Maugham,* revised and enlarged edition (London: Kay & Ward, 1973).

Biographies:

Karl G. Pfeiffer, *W. Somerset Maugham: A Candid*

Portrait (New York: Norton, 1959);

Garson Kanin, *Remembering Mr. Maugham* (New York: Atheneum, 1966);

Robin Maugham, *Somerset and All the Maughams* (London: Longmans/Heinemann, 1966);

Beverly Nichols, *A Case of Human Bondage* (London: Secker & Warburg, 1966);

Frederick Raphael, *W. Somerset Maugham and His World* (London: Thames & Hudson, 1976);

Anthony Curtis, *Somerset Maugham* (London: Weidenfeld & Nicolson, 1977);

Robin Maugham, *Conversations with Willie: Recollections of W. Somerset Maugham* (London: W. H. Allen, 1978);

Ted Morgan, *Maugham* (New York: Simon & Schuster, 1980).

References:

Laurence Brander, *Somerset Maugham: A Guide* (Edinburgh: Oliver & Boyd, 1963);

Ivor Brown, *W. Somerset Maugham* (London: International Textbook, 1970);

Robert Lorin Calder, *W. Somerset Maugham and the Quest for Freedom* (London: Heinemann, 1972);

Richard A. Cordell, *Somerset Maugham, A Writer for All Seasons: A Biographical and Critical Study,* revised edition (Bloomington: Indiana University Press, 1969);

Anthony Curtis, *The Pattern of Maugham: A Critical Portrait* (New York: Taplinger, 1974);

Klaus W. Jonas, *The World of Somerset Maugham* (New York: British Book Centre, 1959);

Wilmon Menard, *The Two Worlds of Somerset Maugham* (Los Angeles: Sherbourne Press, 1965);

M. K. Naik, *W. Somerset Maugham* (Norman: University of Oklahoma Press, 1966).

Papers:

Maugham's papers are at the Humanities Research Center, University of Texas at Austin; the Berg Collection, New York Public Library; the Lilly Library, Indiana University; Stanford University; the Houghton Library, Harvard University; the Fales Collection, New York University; the Butler Library, Columbia University; the Olin Library, Cornell University; Beaverbrook Papers, House of Lords Records Office, London; and the University of Arkansas Library.

Flora Macdonald Mayor

(20 October 1872-28 January 1932)

Rhonda Keith
University of Tulsa

BOOKS: *Mrs. Hammond's Children,* as Mary Strafford (London: R. B. Johnson, 1901);
The Third Miss Symons (London: Sidgwick & Jackson, 1913);
The Rector's Daughter (London: Leonard & Virginia Woolf at the Hogarth Press, 1924; New York: Coward-McCann, 1930);
The Squire's Daughter (London: Constable, 1929; New York: Coward-McCann, 1931);
The Room Opposite, and Other Tales of Mystery and Imagination (London, New York & Toronto: Longmans, Green, 1935).

Flora Macdonald Mayor has been compared as a novelist to Jane Austen because of her provincial settings and the uneventful lives of her characters but chiefly because of the obvious influence of Austen on her language and invention. Their true kinship lies in Mayor's capacity for acute observation of subtleties of personality, and in her ability to satirize character without reducing it. Like Austen; her scope and her output were small, but what she did was, for the most part, masterly. Mayor's work, however, has a different kind of complexity because of her willingness to delve into her subjects' emotional lives and because of her depiction of turn-of-the-century social changes and their disturbance of private and social relationships.

Mayor was one of twin daughters born 20 October 1872, at Montpelier Row, Twickenham. Her father, Joseph Bickersteth Mayor, was a clergyman and emeritus professor of classics at King's College, London, and wrote numerous scholarly books. He was undoubtedly the model, in some respects, for Canon Jocelyn in *The Rector's Daughter* (1924), as were Mayor's uncle J. E. B. Mayor, a clergyman also and professor of Latin at Cambridge, and Canon Robert Mayor of Frating, Essex. Her mother was the niece of philosopher John Grote of Cambridge and of George Grote, a philosophical radical, Greek historian, and cofounder of the University of London. One of her brothers, Robin Grote Mayor, also became a philosopher. Her other brother was Henry Bickersteth Mayor. And she had seven unmarried aunts—"U.F.s" (Unnecessary Females), who as a class of "surplus

F. M. Mayor at about the time she wrote
Mrs. Hammond's Children

women" became subjects for her writing. With this background, it is not surprising that in 1892 Flora Mayor entered Newnham College at Cambridge, where she read history, took part in student debates, and acted in student performances. What is surprising is that she should have pursued a professional stage career, after graduating in 1896, with the Ben Greet company. However, chronic ill health—bronchial asthma—forced her to give it up.

In 1901 Mayor's first book, *Mrs. Hammond's Children,* was published under the pseudonym Mary Strafford. It was a book about rather than for children. F. M. Stawell, among others, admired it for its unsentimental depiction of children's lives. Mayor herself seemed not to like it in later years, but Sybil Oldfield found it "a remarkable study in the antagonisms, emotional rivalry, and capacity for reconciliation in children."

Shortly after this book appeared, Mayor became engaged to a promising young architect, Ernest Shepherd. He died of typhoid in India on her thirty-second birthday. At this point her health worsened and she went abroad, where she observed the women who were to be her models for *The Third Miss Symons*—women of comfortable means who drift alone and without purpose up and down the Riviera. She originally planned to call the book "Not Wanted."

The Third Miss Symons was published in 1913 with an introduction by John Masefield. It was well reviewed, and the 12 April 1913 *New Statesman* compared Mayor to Austen and to Mrs. Gaskell, after which Mayor said, "Following the steps of Mrs. Gaskell is what I should most like to do." This short novel examines the life of an "unnecessary female," but it is not simply a social documentary. Miss Symons spends life alone and unloved, but to a great extent she is responsible for that life. And she becomes aware at last of how she has caused her own unhappiness. She has not been loved because she has not been lovable, and she has not been lovable because she gave way to sins of anger, envy, and so on. Mayor could not create true tragedy from this material, however, because she was a Christian, and she believed in moral choice and in redemption. *The Third Miss Symons* is a fine psychological portrait, and it also demonstrates Mayor's grounding in pre-twentieth-century values. Her revelations of emotional truths do not bloom in a vacuum.

Mayor did not publish again for eleven years, although her work was well received. Not only was her own health poor, but she also had to care for her octogenarian parents. From 1908 to 1910, some time prior to the 1924 publication of *The Rector's Daughter* by Virginia and Leonard Woolf, her twin sister, Alice, was secretary of the Friday Club, an "embryonic Bloomsbury" founded by Clive and Vanessa Bell. The Bloomsbury group was easy prey for Mayor's scathing portrait of literary society in *The Rector's Daughter*. Virginia Woolf seems to have disliked her personally; she made a snide remark about Mayor's looks (although—or perhaps because—Mayor had acted Ophelia and was to appear in *Vogue* magazine). In a letter to Pernel Strachey, Woolf wrote, "She hated us all, until I

wrote to her in praise of her novel, when she whipped round the other way, and now steps the world (it is said) like a stallion in the sun." Regardless of Woolf's praise, it seems unlikely that Mayor could have received much intellectual or other encouragement from "the set." Hogarth Press did, however, republish *The Rector's Daughter* in an inexpensive edition in 1935, probably because it had sold well in the first edition.

The Rector's Daughter is a story of unfulfilled love, but it is also about the frictions between the dying Victorian world and the modern world. Mary Jocelyn, the protagonist, has read John Stuart Mill's *Political Economy* and held a class on it for local working women, which her father, Canon Jocelyn, considers "a wild scheme"; he fears that the study of economics will replace mathematics at Cambridge. He disapproves of words such as *scientific* and *progressive*. He believes that one does not invite doctors to dinner. And yet, the time is past "when the clergy, as a matter of course, were accepted and pressed to the hard but faithful bosom of the county." Mary is pulled by the past and by the present, neither of which speaks to her, to the unique being that she is. Alienation is thought of as a twentieth-century theme in literature, but Mayor makes one feel that it is a timeless circumstance, not solely dependent upon culture. The young and the old alike are repelled by strong emotion, and Mary's passionate nature is perhaps not so much misunderstood as feared.

The revival of Mayor's novels can be attributed to the literary archaeology now being done on women's work, and there are decided strains of feminism in her books. Mary Jocelyn's lover confides to her, "When I was a young man I imagined reserve was a symptom of strength and manliness, whereas on the contrary, it is a weakness, which has cut me off from the best things in life." Nevertheless, though Mary is seeking a companion to love and to talk to, Mayor's characters, not even the women, do not waste their spirits in everlasting self-examination. Mayor demonstrates the folly of delving too skillfully into private consciousness as well as the grievous effects of insensitivity on human relations.

The Rector's Daughter was admired by the Woolfs, G. B. Stern, and Rebecca West, and a review by Sylvia Lynd (*Time and Tide*, 1924) noted that "Mary Jocelyn's 'nothing' was a full and rich state of being." Susan Hill has called Mayor's book a "novel of genius" since its republication by Penguin in 1973.

Mayor's last book published in her lifetime

F. M. Mayor at fifty-six

was *The Squire's Daughter,* which appeared in 1929. Its protagonist is Veronica "Ron" DeLacey, who resembles Kathy, Mary Jocelyn's rival. Unlike Mary, perhaps unlike Flora Mayor, she is young, strong, beautiful, and self-involved. Mayor wrote the book as she was dying, and the novel reflects a deep sense of change, change which cannot be stemmed by the past, by values, by tradition. The novel develops the theme of misunderstanding between adults and their parents. Not having married, Mayor would have known this relationship more intimately, perhaps, than any other. But as with the other kinds of relationships in her work, the causes of alienation are the same no matter what the personal connection.

The Squire's Daughter is written almost entirely in dialogue, an interesting contrast to experiments in stream-of-consciousness techniques with which she may have been familiar. Possibly Mayor was reacting against those techniques, suspecting that such tendencies would intensify the social and private alienation which became a hallmark theme of the modern novel. Her characters may have been—

or felt—disenfranchised from their cultures. But they could act only within their cultures and within their families. The difficulties of the younger generation of the 1920s, as depicted in *The Squire's Daughter,* may stem not only from an abstract sense of lost values and social structures ("the squirearchy") but from a concrete sense of the absence of clearly defined actions that accompany established social role functions. One way to compensate for this loss is to assume that to act purposefully is to be vulgar or ridiculous in some way. (The "U. F." in *The Rector's Daughter* is a Labour activist—"she will be terribly active.")

Rebecca West praised *The Squire's Daughter* in the *Bookman* as being better than John Galsworthy's *Forsyte Saga* in its portrayal of those members of the younger generation who still lived with their parents.

Mayor's collection of short stories entitled *The Room Opposite, and Other Tales of Mystery and Imagination* was published posthumously in 1935. Geoffrey Henderson said that one of the stories, " 'The Kind Action of Mr. Robinson'. . . must be one of the finest in the language." These stories demonstrate a marked ability to create mood, as well as basic, straightforward storytelling skills. Mystery and the supernatural are natural modes for the storyteller, but Mayor's sense of mystery or of otherworldliness probably also reflects her belief in "objective reality"—reality outside of human creation, certainly the very antithesis of the modernist trends.

Mayor died at Hampstead on 28 January 1932, having had a lung operation the previous summer. F. M. Stawell in a letter to the Newnham College *Roll* remembers that in spite of a lifetime of poor health, she retained a happy disposition and "wrote continually when the grip of disease would allow it."

Mayor is not a period writer, though there is historical interest in her portrayal of the social changes of the early twentieth century. The revived interest in her work stems from its intrinsic power and the skillful detachment of an author whose eyes were sharper than her heart.

References:

Susan Hill, Introduction to *The Third Miss Symons* (London: Virago, 1980);

Sybil Oldfield, *Spinsters of This Parish; The Life and Times of F. M. Mayor and Mary Sheepshanks* (London: Virago, 1984).

R. H. Mottram

(30 October 1883-16 April 1971)

Clark Thayer

Repose and Other Verses, as J. Marjoram (London: Rivers, 1907);

New Poems, as J. Marjoram (London: Duckworth, 1909);

The Spanish Farm (London: Chatto & Windus, 1924; New York: MacVeagh/Dial, 1924);

Sixty-four, Ninety-four! (London: Chatto & Windus, 1925; New York: MacVeagh/Dial, 1925);

The Crime at Vanderlynden's (London: Chatto & Windus, 1926; New York: MacVeagh/Dial, 1926);

The Spanish Farm Trilogy, 1914-1918 (New York: MacVeagh/Dial, 1927; London: Chatto & Windus, 1930);

Our Mr. Dormer (London: Chatto & Windus, 1927; New York: MacVeagh/Dial, 1927);

The Apple Disdained (London: Mathews & Marrot, 1928);

The English Miss (London: Chatto & Windus, 1928; New York: MacVeagh/Dial, 1928);

Ten Years Ago: Armistice, and Other Memories (London: Chatto & Windus, 1928); republished as *Armistice, and Other Memories* (New York: MacVeagh/Dial, 1929);

The Boroughmonger (London: Chatto & Windus, 1929; Boston: Little, Brown, 1929);

A History of Financial Speculation (London: Chatto & Windus, 1929; Boston: Little, Brown, 1929);

Three Personal Records of the War, by Mottram, John Easton, and Eric Partridge (London: Scholartis, 1929); republished as *Three Men's War* (New York & London: Harper, 1930);

Europa's Beast (London: Chatto & Windus, 1930); republished as *A Rich Man's Daughter* (New York & London: Harper, 1930);

Miniature Banking Histories (London: Chatto & Windus, 1930);

The New Providence (London: Chatto & Windus, 1930);

The Old Man of the Stones (London: Lindsey, 1930);

Poems, New and Old (London: Duckworth, 1930);

Castle Island (London: Chatto & Windus, 1931; New York & London: Harper, 1931);

The Headless Hound, and Other Stories (London: Chatto & Windus, 1931);

John Crome of Norwich (London: Lane, 1931);

The Lost Christmas Presents (London: Lindsey, 1931);

Home for the Holidays (London: Chatto & Windus, 1932);

Dazzle (London: Ward, Lock, 1932);

Through the Menin Gate (London: Chatto & Windus, 1932);

East Anglia: England's Eastern Province (London: Chapman & Hall, 1933);

A Good Old Fashioned Christmas (London: Lindsey, 1933);

The Lame Dog (London: Chatto & Windus, 1933); republished as *At the Sign of the Lame Dog* (Boston & New York: Houghton Mifflin, 1933);

Bumphrey's (London: Murray, 1934);

Strawberry Time and The Banquet (London: Golden Cockerel, 1934);

The Banquet, with Other Stories (London: Chatto & Windus, 1934);

Early Morning (London: Hutchinson, 1935);

Flower Pot End (London: Murray, 1935);

Journey to the Western Front Twenty Years After (London: Bell, 1936);

Portrait of an Unknown Victorian (London: Hale, 1936);

The Westminster Bank, 1836-1936 (London: Westminster Bank, 1936);

The Norwich Players (Norwich: Soman, 1937);

Noah (London: Rich & Cowan, 1937);

Old England: Illustrated by English Paintings of the 18th and Early 19th Centuries (London: Studio/New York: Studio Publications, 1937);

Success to the Mayor (London: Hale, 1937);

Time to Be Going (London: Hutchinson, 1937);

Autobiography with a Difference (London: Hale, 1938; New York: Appleton-Century, 1939);

There Was a Jolly Miller (London: Hutchinson, 1938);

Miss Lavington (London: Hutchinson, 1939);

Trader's Dream: The Romance of the East India Company (New York & London: Appleton-Century, 1939);

You Can't Have It Back! (London: Hutchinson, 1939);

Bowler Hat: A Last Glance at the Old Country Banking (London: Hutchinson, 1940);

The Ghost and the Maiden (London: Hutchinson, 1940);

The World Turns Slowly Round (London & New York: Hutchinson, 1942);

The Corbells at War (London & New York: Hutchinson, 1943);

Buxton the Liberator (London & New York: Hutchinson, 1946);

Visit of the Princess (London & New York: Hutchinson, 1946);

Hibbert Houses (London: Lindsey, 1947);

The Gentleman of Leisure (London: Hutchinson, 1948);

The Glories of Norwich Cathedral (London: Winchester, 1948);

Norfolk (London: Elek, 1948);

Come to the Bower (London: Hutchinson, 1949);

Through Five Generations: The History of the Butterley Company, by Mottram and Colin Coote (London: Faber & Faber, 1950);

One Hundred and Twenty-eight Witnesses (London & New York: Hutchinson, 1951);

The Broads (London: Hale, 1952);

The Part That Is Missing (London: Hutchinson, 1952);

If Stones Could Speak: An Introduction to an Almost Human Family (London: Museum Press, 1953);

John Galsworthy (London & New York: Longmans, Green, 1953);

The City of Norwich Museums, 1894-1954: A Diamond Jubilee Record (Norwich: Privately printed, 1954);

The Window Seat (London: Hutchinson, 1954);

Over the Wall (London: Hutchinson, 1955);

For Some We Loved: An Intimate Portrait of Ada and John Galsworthy (London: Hutchinson, 1956);

Scenes That Are Brightest (London: Hutchinson, 1956);

Another Window Seat (London: Hutchinson, 1957);

No One Will Ever Know, or The Hidden Life of Gregory Wantage (London: Hutchinson, 1958);

Vanities and Verities (London: Hutchinson, 1958);

Young Man's Fancies (London: Hutchinson, 1959);

Musetta (London: Hutchinson, 1960);

Time's Increase (London: Hutchinson, 1961);

To Hell, by Mottram and Crabb Robinson (London: Hutchinson, 1962);

Happy Birds (London: Hutchinson, 1964);

Maggie Mackenzie (London: Hutchinson, 1965);

The Speaking Likeness (London: Hutchinson, 1967);

Behind the Shutters (London: Hutchinson, 1968);

Twelve Poems (Stoke Ferry: Daedalus, 1968);

The Twentieth Century: A Personal Record (London: Hutchinson, 1969).

Ralph Hale Mottram wrote more than sixty books: novels, short stories, poetry, biography, autobiography, history, tour guides, topography, a study of banking—even this list is not exhaustive. However, he is usually remembered for his first three novels, *The Spanish Farm* (1924), *Sixty-four, Ninety-four!* (1925), and *The Crime at Vanderlynden's* (1926), which constitute *The Spanish Farm Trilogy, 1914-1918* (1927). In this trilogy the futility and waste of the First World War are depicted from the viewpoints of a young French peasant woman, a Norfolk bank clerk, and an obscure provincial architect—characters whose milieux and values are rarely examined with such depth and sympathy in British fiction.

Mottram's father, like his grandfather and great-grandfather before, was chief clerk of Gurney's Bank in Norwich. Born above the bank, Mottram himself held that position until 1927, when he was led by the success of his trilogy to trust writing as a career. His family was progressive, liberal, and committed to financial stability and what they considered permanent English values. Their influence and the city of Norwich, lovingly shown in Mot-

Ralph Mottram and his brother, Alfred, as young bank clerks in Norwich

followed the trilogy. The dominant theme and major concern of most of his books, whatever the genre, is a search for what is enduring in the English character, coupled with an attempt to define the nature, scope, and meaning of the changes in English life in the decades following the war.

The Spanish Farm and its sequels *Sixty-four, Ninety-four!* and *The Crime at Vanderlynden's* were, individually and collectively, immediate critical and popular successes. The first novel of the trilogy contained a preface by Galsworthy. It was awarded the Hawthornden Prize for 1924 and was made into a film, *Roses of Picardy*. The novel centers on Madeleine, a practical young Frenchwoman who struggles to keep her father's farm making a sharp profit despite the successive waves of British troops quartered there. She loses her aristocratic lover to the war and in her blind physical and emotional need has a brief and, for her, almost meaningless affair in Paris with a young officer from Norfolk. As they drift apart it becomes apparent that their inability to communicate has as much to do with their national differences as with their individual ones. Only the war could have brought them together. The farm itself, built by the Spanish centuries before to protect their holdings in Flanders, serves the soldiers as a physical and spiritual respite from the horrors of war, and the novel as an explicitly stated symbol of man's ability to survive.

Sixty-four, Ninety-Four! retells much of the story of the preceding novel from the point of view of Skene, the young British officer who loves Madeleine. Skene considers the war a senseless catastrophe that has befallen his generation. He joined because it was his duty and his destiny, and he sees it through to the end, dismayed by the organizational muddle and the waste of lives. Madeleine, for him, is all that is desirable in "normal" life but elusive in war. Still his English romanticism and her French practicality could never have come together except in the general disruption of war.

In *The Crime at Vanderlynden's*, Dormer, a Norwich bank clerk, is even more distressed than Skene by the muddle, disorder, bungling, and general bureaucratic mess of the war. He endures by working to insure efficiency in the small areas he can control. The plot centers around a typical foul-up. A wayward British soldier desecrates a previously ignored shrine to the Blessed Virgin on Madeleine Vanderlynden's farm by quartering animals there for the night. French authorities assume on the basis of her intentionally inflated but unintentionally ambiguous damage claim that it is Madeleine

tram's books as the archetypal provincial town, shaped and eventually sentimentalized his depiction of the changes in English living patterns after the war. His novel *Our Mr. Dormer* (1927) is a fictionalized history of his family from the eighteenth century to the early twentieth century.

In 1904 Mottram met John Galsworthy, who encouraged him to write. This meeting and the consequent close friendship with Galsworthy were decisive factors in his literary development. That Galsworthy became his mentor suggests something of the ambitions and limitations of Mottram's own work as the central characters of *The Spanish Farm Trilogy* reappear, aging and changing with England, in several subsequent novels. It is not totally unrealistic to think of Mottram as a minor Galsworthy.

World War I appears directly in much of Mottram's work, and its shadow is over much of the rest. Increasingly, as did so many men of his generation, he saw his prewar childhood as having taken place in a Golden Age. Nostalgia infuses his *Autobiography with a Difference* (1938) and many other books that

First page from the manuscript for the third novel in The Spanish Farm Trilogy *(Gilbert H. Fabes,* The First Editions of Ralph Hale Mottram, *1934)*

OUR MR. DORMER

The story of an East Anglican banking house in the nineteenth century. 'The book is a fine study in the peaceful evolution of men and things. It is like a portrait painted with a background of the events which made the man. *Our Mr. Dormer* is an excellent piece of dramatic storytelling.' Rt. Hon. J. Ramsay MacDonald in *The Banker*.
3rd Impression. 7s. 6d. net.

THE ENGLISH MISS

A portrait of an English girl. 'This book places Mr. Mottram in the front rank of contemporary novelists. We knew from Madeleine Vanderlynden that Mr. Mottram could particularize the universal. He has done it again, and nearer home. With the quietest of strokes he has drawn a soul and a civilization.' Gerald Gould in *The Observer*.

3rd Impression. 7s. 6d. net

*

'I regard R. H. Mottram as the most interesting novelist of his years in Britain to-day. And he is not a promising author; he is an author who has achieved large and mature work.' Arnold Bennett in *The Evening Standard*.

*

R. H. Mottram has also written a long preface to 'Joseph and his Brethren,' by H. W. Freeman (7s. 6d. net).

BOOKS
by
R. H. MOTTRAM

'His place in English fiction is securely established.' *Public Opinion* of '*The Spanish Farm Trilogy.*'

published by
CHATTO & WINDUS
97 & 99 ST. MARTIN'S LANE, W.C.2

THE
SPANISH FARM TRILOGY
1914-1918

Comprising: *The Spanish Farm, Sixty-Four, Ninety-Four!* and *The Crime at Vanderlynden's*, with some hitherto unpublished material.

'Centuries from now, perhaps, when the glamour of the flamboyant school of war literature has wholly faded, men and women who speak our language will still turn to *The Spanish Farm Trilogy* for a picture of reality all the more terrible because of the quietude of its tones and the sombre disillusion of its ultimate message.' *The Fortnightly Review*.

'The social historian of the future, looking back for evidence of the changes and struggles through which England passed in the first quarter of the twentieth century, will find *The Spanish Farm Trilogy* indispensable. It becomes a social document by being a work of genius. Already the moods, hopes, sufferings of English soldiers round that Spanish Farm on the French border are accepted, in Mr. Mottram's interpretation, as part of the national consciousness and heritage. The book is permanent.' Gerald Gould in *The Observer*.

800 pages. 4th Large Impression.

7s. 6d. net

TEN YEARS AGO
ARMISTICE AND OTHER MEMORIES
forming a pendant to
'The Spanish Farm Trilogy'

'Ten years. And, incredible as it would once have seemed, one begins to forget.' Mr. Mottram opens thus; and this book, which contains sketches and stories all immediately relating to the War, are not only a reminder and a commemoration of what is past, but show his writing at his finest. 5s. net

THE SPANISH FARM

With a preface by John Galsworthy. Awarded the *Hawthornden Prize* for 1924. 'By far the most distinguished novel which has come out of the War.' H. M. Tomlinson in *The Westminster Gazette*.
8th Impression. 2s. 6d. net

SIXTY-FOUR, NINETY-FOUR!

The civilian-turned soldier theme. 'A book to keep for the reading of future generations.' *Daily Chronicle*.
4th Impression. 2s. 6d. net

THE
CRIME AT VANDERLYNDEN'S

'It is a fine story, quite equal in brilliant achievement to the former two that preceded it.' *Daily Chronicle*.
3rd Impression. 2s. 6d. net

Publisher's brochure

herself who has been rudely used. Skene and Dormer share an attitude toward the war that the reader is made to feel is representative of their class and national heritage.

In *The Spanish Farm Trilogy*, Mottram depicts, with a sympathy that does not hide limitations of his characters, the damage done by the war to three noncombatants who survive because of their allegiance to their values. The style, direct and serviceable, seems right for its subject matter.

Geoffrey Skene, who becomes a municipal architect and genre painter, appears in several subsequent novels. *Europa's Beast* (1930) centers around the failing marriage of a young man who has been left an emotional adolescent by his war experiences and a young woman who seems to have stepped from an Evelyn Waugh novel leaving all the comedy behind. In *Come to the Bower* (1949), Skene and his second wife, Olive, adjust to post-World War II provincial life after losing a son and undergoing a temporary separation. The novel is marred by the presence of an American professor

studying the English character; he provides Skene with too many opportunities to talk about what has become his (and the reader suspects Mottram's) favorite subject, the English moral heritage. *Visit of the Princess* (1946) is a humorless comedy set in a future "socialist" England in which mundane economic and social advances are ultimately wed to the "enduring" English values. Mottram's work after the 1920s may be trying to readers not having the great good fortune to have been born English.

Mottram's prolific career was awarded with modest commercial success and recognition. He was a Fellow of the Royal Society of Literature and was made an honorary Doctor of Letters in 1966 by the University of East Anglia. In *Autobiography with a Difference* he described the skills of a family servant in terms of praise that could be used for his own work: "with much practice, no theory, some insight, . . . no panache, just plain hardiness. The English cook for all time." But *The Spanish Farm Trilogy* is something more than plain English cooking, and it is on this early work that his reputation stands.

Dust jacket for Mottram's 1929 novel, which centers on an election at the time of the 1832 Reform Bill

Dust jacket for Mottram's 1930 novel, dedicated to early mentors Ada and John Galsworthy

Liam O'Flaherty

(28 August 1896-7 September 1984)

Mary A. O'Toole
University of Tulsa

BOOKS: *Thy Neighbour's Wife* (London: Cape, 1923; New York: Boni & Liveright, 1924);

The Black Soul (London: Cape, 1924; New York: Boni & Liveright, 1925);

Spring Sowing (London: Cape, 1924; New York: Knopf, 1926);

The Informer (New York: Knopf, 1925; London: Cape, 1926);

Civil War (London: Archer, 1925);

The Terrorist (London: Archer, 1926);

Darkness: A Tragedy in Three Acts (London: Archer, 1926);

The Tent (London: Cape, 1926);

Mr. Gilhooley (London: Cape, 1926; New York: Harcourt, Brace, 1927);

The Child of God (London: Archer, 1926);

The Life of Tom Healy (London: Cape, 1926; New York: Harcourt, Brace, 1927);

The Fairy Goose, and Two Other Stories (New York: Gaige, 1927; London: Faber & Gwyer, 1927);

The Assassin (London: Cape, 1928; New York: Harcourt, Brace, 1928);

Red Barbara and Other Stories (New York: Gaige, 1928; London: Faber & Gwyer, 1928);

The Mountain Tavern and Other Stories (London: Cape, 1929; New York: Harcourt, Brace, 1929);

A Tourist's Guide to Ireland (London: Mandrake Press, 1929);

The House of Gold (London: Cape, 1929; New York: Harcourt, Brace, 1929);

The Return of the Brute (London: Mandrake Press, 1929; New York: Harcourt, Brace, 1930);

Joseph Conrad: An Appreciation (London: Lahr, 1930);

Two Years (London: Cape, 1930; New York: Harcourt, Brace, 1930);

The Ecstasy of Angus (London: Joiner & Steele, 1931);

A Cure for Unemployment (London: Lahr, 1931);

I Went to Russia (London: Cape, 1931; New York: Harcourt, Brace, 1931);

The Puritan (London: Cape, 1931; New York: Harcourt, Brace, 1932);

Liam O'Flaherty, early 1930s

The Wild Swan and Other Stories (London: Jackson, 1932);

Skerrett (London: Gollancz, 1932; New York: Long & Smith, 1932);

The Martyr (London: Gollancz, 1933; New York: Macmillan, 1933);

Shame the Devil (London: Grayson & Grayson, 1934);

Hollywood Cemetery (London: Gollancz, 1935);

Famine (London: Gollancz, 1937; New York: Random House, 1937);

The Short Stories of Liam O'Flaherty (London: Cape, 1937);

Land (London: Gollancz, 1946; New York: Random House, 1946);

Two Lovely Beasts and Other Stories (London: Gollancz, 1948; New York: Devin-Adair, 1950);

Insurrection (London: Gollancz, 1950; Boston: Little, Brown, 1951).

Liam O'Flaherty was born to Michael and Margaret Ganly O'Flaherty in the village of Gort na gCapall, Inishmore, the Aran Islands. The effects of extreme poverty, of the struggle against the elements, of isolation, and of an island mentality—that of the outsider—were ever apparent in his life and in his fiction. In order to get an education, O'Flaherty entered seminary. He studied first at Rockwell College of the Holy Ghost Fathers and in 1913 attended Blackrock College, where he organized a corps of Republican Volunteers among the schoolboys. He returned to seminary—this time Dublin Diocesan Seminary in Clonliffe—but left after a short while and attended University College, Dublin, for a few months before enlisting in the Irish Guards unit of the British Army. In September 1917, he was wounded by a shell explosion and, not completely recovered, was discharged in 1918.

For the next four years, O'Flaherty traveled extensively, almost compulsively—to London, to Brazil, and back to Liverpool. Deciding that he was still not ready to return to Ireland, he shipped out to the Mediterranean and then to Canada, where he worked as a laborer and was introduced to the Industrial Workers of the World. After this he went to Boston, where his brother was active in socialist movements, and his interest in communism increased. O'Flaherty then returned to Dublin, and in January 1922 he and a group of unemployed men captured and held the Rotunda, a public building, for a few days, flying the red flag from the top of the building and proclaiming an Irish socialist revolution. After this escapade, he fled to Cork and eventually to London. There he began writing and met Edward Garnett, who for the next ten years had a salutary effect upon him, encouraging his work and helping him get his books published.

O'Flaherty's first two novels, both written in England, are set in the Aran Islands. The first, *Thy Neighbour's Wife* (1923), has as its protagonist Father Hugh McMahon, an intellectual, a poet, and an outsider in the Islands. This character of the loner, the outcast, reappears in various manifestations throughout O'Flaherty's fiction. In his second

novel, *The Black Soul* (1924), a native Aran Islander returns as an outcast and finds a soul-healing sustenance in the Islands. In a review of the book, A. E. (George W. E. Russell) called it "the most elemental thing in modern Irish literature," saying that it recalled to him "the ancient sympathy between the spirit of man and the spirit of nature asserted in Irish legend." *The Black Soul* is probably the most autobiographical of O'Flaherty's novels. Its protagonist, Fergus O'Connor (usually called the Stranger), having been wounded in the war and having traveled the world as O'Flaherty did, returns home a physical and mental casualty. The novel begins in O'Connor's black winter of the soul and proceeds through the seasons to end, not in spring, the time of rebirth, but in autumn, the season of ripeness and serenity. There is a conflict in the novel between the instinctual and the cerebral life, and the island setting is an integral part of the novel—causal rather than merely descriptive. Unlike many of O'Flaherty's other novels, *The Black Soul* has a protagonist who survives.

The Informer (1925) is one of four novels that has as its protagonist the loner in Dublin. This is probably the best known, though not the best, of O'Flaherty's novels because it was made into an Academy Award-winning movie in 1935, directed by John Ford and starring Victor MacLaglen. That O'Flaherty is able to sustain reader interest and sympathy for a character who is only one level above an idiot, and who has committed what is regarded as the most heinous of crimes in Ireland, is quite an accomplishment in itself. Gypo Nolan is described as a man whose "mind was struggling along aimlessly in pursuit of his actions." He is impulsive and unreflective, and his nemesis, Frank Gallagher, appears at first glance to be his exact opposite. O'Flaherty, however, subtly undermines the Gallagher character by having him speak a socialist revolutionary jargon with the refrain "But I haven't worked that out fully yet." Gallagher's mind is, in its own way, as muddled as Gypo Nolan's.

The Informer is for the most part a naturalistic novel, but O'Flaherty superimposes Christian symbolism at the end as Gypo dies in a church, outstretched in cruciform position, after having been forgiven by the Sorrowful Mother, the Mary-like figure, for his betrayal of another man. Here, as in *The Black Soul*, the setting is causal and integral—the decaying slums of Dublin provide a sordid environment that both determines and reflects the characters' actions.

Mr. Gilhooley (1926), *The Assassin* (1928), and

179

The Puritan (1931) are also concerned with the isolated individual in the city. These are psychological novels with echoes of Crime and Punishment. In both The Assassin and The Puritan, the mentally unstable central character takes upon himself responsibility for changing and improving society, in both cases by committing a murder. There are in both novels a profusion and confusion of motives. In Mr. Gilhooley, the character is not mad until the end of the novel, when he too commits murder and suicide as the result of a complex set of motives and circumstances.

In the 1920s and 1930s, O'Flaherty was a part of the Dublin literary scene, associated with a group that included Cecil Salkeld and Francis Stuart and considered itself in opposition to the Yeats-A. E. establishment. In 1924, with Salkeld and Stuart, O'Flaherty published the short-lived (two issues) magazine To-Morrow, which carried the first appearance of Yeats's "Leda and the Swan." In 1926, O'Flaherty married Margaret Barrington. They had one daughter and separated in the early 1930s.

O'Flaherty was concerned for the poor and the working man, but he was never a doctrinaire Marxist-Leninist. Although he went to Russia in 1931 and wrote a book about the experience (I Went to Russia, 1931), the trip did not strengthen his dedication to communism; rather the reverse seems to have been the result. O'Flaherty turned against Catholicism, Republicanism, and communism, none of which satisfied his need for reform-making action. His personality was passionate, intense, and he had an aversion to passivity and apathy which is reflected in his novels. Accordingly, some critics consider his novels too melodramatic while others view them as powerful novels of existential angst.

Two of O'Flaherty's novels are set in provincial towns, one during the Civil War and the other during the years of the Free State. The first, The Martyr (1933), contains four character studies, and these characters represent four aspects of the problems of the Civil War years. They are the idealist who becomes the martyr at the end, the Free-Stater who places all his trust in the state, the anarchist who hopes for revolution and a workers' paradise, and the pragmatic middle-of-the-road character who functions as a mean in contrast to the other extremists. The novel is a parable of the state of Ireland and the Irish psyche, and O'Flaherty, with Crosbie's bizarre crucifixion and burning, loads the novel with more symbolic implications than it can accommodate, as he did at the end of The Informer. The House of Gold (1929) is also set in a provincial

Front cover for O'Flaherty's second autobiographical book

town, a cultural vacuum in the Free State. Here also attention is given to four characters, the most interesting of which is Ramon Mor, a gombeen man—one of the rising entrepreneurial class who, as Yeats lamented in "September, 1913," "fumble in a greasy till" when "Romantic Ireland's dead and gone." The characters in this novel represent the newly defined social classes in postrevolutionary Ireland. The title is ironically allusive to religion, country estates, the Protestant Ascendancy, and the new ascendancy of the gombeen men.

Skerrett (1932) and Famine (1937) are thought by most critics to be O'Flaherty's best novels. Both are set in the past in the west of Ireland, and both are based upon actual events. Skerrett derives from a real-life feud between a schoolmaster and a parish priest which resulted in a lawsuit, a trial, and the blowing up of the priest's house. In Skerrett, the peasant tradition is on the verge of breaking up. The hero reflects the economic and social changes taking place in the lives of the islanders, and Skerrett, having found his identity in the traditions of the past, tries to preserve those traditions. His idealism, in contrast to the worldly materialism of the priest, brings him to ruin, and in the end he breaks down and ends his days in mad defiance in an asylum. Skerrett is an intense, passionate hero in the mold of some of O'Flaherty's earlier heroes. He is strong-willed, but he meets his match in the priest who defeats him.

Famine begins around the mid-1840s and presents a fictionalized account of Ireland's Great Potato Famine and its tragic results. Probably the most realistic and the most traditional of O'Flaherty's novels, it chronicles the customs, rituals, crises, and eventually the death of a society. With an objectivity lacking in most of his other novels, O'Flaherty presents both sides of the case—the inertia, passivity, and acceptance of the peasants versus the need for action and revolution. These opposing beliefs are expounded through the characters of the two

Liam O'Flaherty, 1952

priests and the two generations of the Kilmartin family. The dialogue is authentic and the novel well paced. This is a communal rather than a personal drama as O'Flaherty presents the sad and inexorable catalogue of calamities leading to the depopulation of the valley. The near documentary approach, direct and unadorned, is marred only once or twice, most notably in the character of the landlord's agent, Chadwick. Making Chadwick a castrated sadomasochist is an unnecessarily lurid touch: the events depicted in the novel are grim enough without this obtrusive, artificial heightening. *Famine* is the first of a trilogy of historical novels, the second being *Land* (1946), set in 1879 at the time of the Land League battles, and the other being *Insurrection* (1950), which is about the Easter Rising in 1916. These two later novels are not noteworthy.

O'Flaherty's short stories are gems. Most have rural settings, some being animal stories which amount to little more than a descriptive sketch of simple beauty. "Spring Sowing" describes a newly married couple sowing seeds with the vague realization that they are to be forever tied to the land.

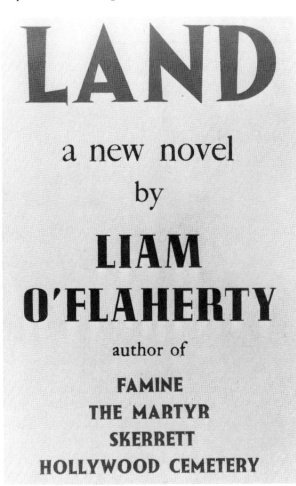

LAND

a new novel
by
LIAM O'FLAHERTY
author of
FAMINE
THE MARTYR
SKERRETT
HOLLYWOOD CEMETERY

Dust jacket for O'Flaherty's 1946 book, the novel in which he expresses most clearly his theories about life's meaning

Some of his best stories are fables, such as "Two Lovely Beasts" and "The Fairy Goose," both wonderfully capturing peasant custom and superstition. "Galway Bay" further depicts the diminution of the peasant class that was presented in some of the novels. In this story, the peasant has degenerated to the level of a mere curiosity to be gawked at by tourists. O'Flaherty also wrote a number of stories in Gaelic.

There are many passages of great beauty in O'Flaherty's writing, especially descriptive ones. There are great strength and power and strong passions, often in excess. The fiery subject matter and style of the earlier novels are counterbalanced by the restraint of a novel like *Famine*. His style is generally unpolished—O'Flaherty deliberately refused to develop and refine it. The short stories are perhaps his greatest accomplishment because of his descriptive powers and his ability to capture salient features of character and situation in a brief sketch, though he was unable to develop and sustain these in longer works.

During World War II, O'Flaherty traveled in North and South America. In the United States, he spoke in favor of Irish neutrality. On 7 September 1984 he died at St. Vincent's Hospital in Dublin.

References:
Paul A. Doyle, *Liam O'Flaherty* (New York: Twayne, 1971);

Benedict Kiely, *Modern Irish Fiction* (Dublin: Golden Eagle, 1950);

Vivian Mercier, "Man Against Nature: The Novels of Liam O'Flaherty," *Wascana Review,* 1 (1966): 37-46;

James H. O'Brien, *Liam O'Flaherty* (Lewisburg: Bucknell University Press, 1973);

Patrick F. Sheeran, *The Novels of Liam O'Flaherty: A Study in Romantic Realism* (Atlantic Highlands, N.J.: Humanities Press, 1976);

John Zneimer, *The Literary Vision of Liam O'Flaherty* (Syracuse: Syracuse University Press, 1970).

T. F. Powys
(20 December 1875-27 November 1953)

Kenneth Hopkins

BOOKS: *An Interpretation of Genesis* (N.p.: Privately printed, 1907; London: Chatto & Windus, 1929; New York: Viking Press, 1929);

The Soliloquy of a Hermit (New York: G. Arnold Shaw, 1916); republished as *Soliloquies of a Hermit* (London: Melrose, 1918);

The Left Leg (London: Chatto & Windus, 1923; New York: Knopf, 1923);

Black Bryony (London: Chatto & Windus, 1923; New York: Knopf, 1923);

Mark Only (London: Chatto & Windus, 1924; New York: Knopf, 1924);

Mr. Tasker's Gods (London: Chatto & Windus, 1925; New York: Knopf, 1925);

Mockery Gap (London: Chatto & Windus, 1925; New York: Knopf, 1925);

A Stubborn Tree (London: Archer, 1926);

Innocent Birds (London: Chatto & Windus, 1926; New York: Knopf, 1926);

Feed My Swine (London: Archer, 1926);

A Strong Girl and The Bride (London: Archer, 1926);

What Lack I Yet? (London: Archer, 1927; San Francisco: Gelber, Lilienthal, 1927);

Mr. Weston's Good Wine (London: Chatto & Windus, 1927; New York: Viking, 1928);

The Rival Pastors (London: Archer, 1927);

The House with the Echo (London: Chatto & Windus, 1928; New York: Viking, 1928);

The Dewpond (London: Mathews & Marrot, 1928);

Fables (New York: Viking, 1929; London: Chatto & Windus, 1929); republished as *No Painted Plumage* (London: Chatto & Windus, 1934);

Christ in the Cupboard (London: Lahr, 1930);

The Key of the Field (London: Jackson, 1930);

Kindness in a Corner (London: Chatto & Windus, 1930; New York: Viking, 1930);

The White Paternoster (London: Chatto & Windus, 1930; New York: Viking, 1931);

Uriah on the Hill (Cambridge: Minority Press, 1930);

Uncle Dottery: A Christmas Story (Bristol: Hill, 1930);

T. F. Powys

The Only Penitent (London: Chatto & Windus, 1931);

When Thou Wast Naked (Waltham: Golden Cockerel, 1931);

Unclay (London: Chatto & Windus, 1931; New York: Viking, 1932);

The Tithe Barn and The Dove and the Eagle (London: Bhat, 1932);

The Two Thieves (London: Chatto & Windus, 1932; New York: Viking, 1933);

Captain Patch: Twenty-One Stories (London: Chatto & Windus, 1935);

Make Thyself Many (London: Grayson & Grayson, 1935);

Goat Green, or The Better Gift (London: Golden Cockerel, 1937);

Bottle's Path (London: Chatto & Windus, 1946);

God's Eyes A-twinkle: An Anthology of the Stories of T. F. Powys (London: Chatto & Windus, 1947);

Rosie Plum (London: Chatto & Windus, 1966);

The Scapegoat, edited by Peter Riley (Hastings, Sussex: Brimmell, 1966);

Two Stories: Come and Dine, and Tadnol, edited by Peter Riley (Hastings, Sussex: Brimmell, 1967);

The Left Leg (London: Chatto & Windus, 1968; Freeport, N.Y.: Books for Libraries Press, 1970);

The Strong Wooer (London: Ward, 1970);

Three Short Stories (Loughton, Essex: Dud Norman Press, 1970).

T. F. Powys was a writer of short stories in that period between 1920 and 1940 when some of the finest short stories in English were written in England and the United States by such acknowledged masters as D. H. Lawrence, Katherine Mansfield, F. Scott Fitzgerald, Walter de la Mare, Ernest Hemingway, and A. E. Coppard. These writers—and Powys—extended the short story as an art form beyond the range even of Edgar Allen Poe, Rudyard Kipling, and Henry James. With the novels *Mr. Weston's Good Wine* (1927) and *Unclay* (1931), with the collection of stories called *Fables* (1929) (republished as *No Painted Plumage*), and with a dozen or so stories scattered through other collections, he produced a group of unassailable masterpieces of intrinsic excellence and unique character.

Powys was in Hardy country; indeed, he knew

The rectory in Shirley, birthplace of John Cowper and Theodore Francis Powys

The Powys brothers, circa 1901: John Cowper, Littleton, Theodore, Albert, Llewelyn, and William. John Cowper, Theodore, and Llewelyn were all to become well-known writers.

Hardy personally. The critic F. R. Leavis wrote of their literary connection, "We may take Mr. T. F. Powys today as the successor of Hardy: he is probably the last considerable artist of the old order (he seems to me to be a great one). It does not seem likely that it will ever again be possible for a distinguished mind to be formed, as Mr. Powys has been, on the rhythms, sanctioned by nature and time, of rural culture."

Theodore Francis Powys was born at Shirley, Derbyshire, England. He was at school briefly at Dorchester, Dorset (to which town his father, the Reverend C. F. Powys, had removed), and again briefly at Sherborne School, before being sent to a private school in Aldeburgh, Suffolk. He did not go on to university, but took up farming for some years, also in Suffolk. He then returned to Dorset and soon settled in the remote village of East Chaldon, where, in 1905, he married Violet Rosalie Dodds, by whom he had two sons, Theodore (who died young) and Francis. In 1932 he adopted a young child and brought her up as his daughter, Susan.

In 1939 Powys had a serious illness, from which he never completely recovered, and in 1940 he moved to another remote Dorset village, Map-

powder, where on 27 November 1953 he died. He was buried in the churchyard within a few yards of his cottage.

For many years after he gave up farming, Powys lived frugally on an allowance from his father and devoted much time to meditation and writing; but it was not until 1923 that he began to publish his stories and novels, although one small book, *The Soliloquy of a Hermit*, had appeared in New York in 1916. Accordingly, when he found a publisher in England he was able to bring out a number of books in quick succession, and this prompted him to write more freely, so that by 1936 he had had published eight novels, two volumes containing three novellas each, and four collections of short stories, together with seventeen pamphlets containing one or two short stories. The pamphlets were mainly in fine limited editions from the Golden Cockerel and other private presses, with illustrations by such artists as Robert Gibbings, Eric Gill, John Nash, Gilbert Spencer, and R. A. Garnett. Garnett also illustrated or provided decorations for several of the novels. About 1935 Powys ceased to write; two later collections of stories and two novellas represent work written earlier and either published in periodicals or never previously published.

Further uncollected work remains, including an "Interpretation of the Book of Job," announced in 1930 and never published, the text of which cannot now be found.

The original publisher's reader called *The Soliloquy of a Hermit* "clearly the work of a man of genius." This curious essay in spiritual autobiography might be subtitled, after *The Prelude,* as "the growth of a poet's mind," and within it may be found the seeds of the conflict between good and evil and the approach to God and to humanity which characterizes the subsequent stories and novels. The opening paragraph is a text, as for a sermon, from which all that follows is developed:

> Am I a fool? Is not a fool the best title for a good priest? And I am a good priest. Though not of the Church, I am of the Church. Though not of the faith, I am of the faith. Though not of the fold, I am of the fold; a priest in the cloud of God, beside the Altar of Stone. Near beside me is a flock of real sheep; above me a cloud of misty white embraces the noonday light of the Altar. I am without belief;—a belief is too easy a road to God.

With this text before him Powys proceeds here, and in his subsequent writings, to preach an eloquent and enduring sermon on Man, on Nature, and on Human Life—musing indeed in solitude, but publishing his conclusion that life is a pilgrimage toward death, the final good. The pilgrimage is beset at all times and in all places by the forces of lust, greed, poverty, ignorance, and all the other forms that evil takes; it is encountered and endured by love, humor, compassion, and a dogged, indefatigable obstinacy. Many of Powys's characters are engulfed, especially the innocent, the weak, and the forsaken; but at the last, for all humanity, the message is be "strong in will, to strive, to seek, to find, and not to yield."

The novel *Mr. Weston's Good Wine* is considered Powys's finest work (though some critics place *Fables* a little higher). It is a novel which does not yield up all its riches at one reading. It is set in Folly Down, a small rural settlement inhabited by brutal, greedy farmers and their dissolute sons; by sly village matrons exchanging malicious gossip; by undernourished, overworked laborers; by maidens with little chance of remaining so; by a harassed, ineffectual rector hopelessly in love with his own wife; and by a gravedigger who knows death from old acquaintance, and knows of nothing he likes better.

To Folly Down, late one afternoon, comes the wine merchant, Mr. Weston, driving his old Ford van with his assistant Michael for companion. Mr. Weston has only two kinds of wine, the light and the dark, and even these he will sell only to customers he approves of; nor is their ability to pay a condition of purchase. The light wine represents Love, and the dark, Death; there is no doubt which vintage Mr. Weston considers the finer.

As in any community, there are various threads of action already being woven among the villagers when Mr. Weston arrives—loves prospering or faltering, hatreds fermenting, lusts, envys, double-dealing. But when the wine merchant arrives the clocks stop, and over the timeless hours Mr. Weston distributes his wares, resolving a score of plots, hopes, and dilemmas, and irreversibly altering every life in the village. The supernatural rubs shoulders with the commonplace so easily that nobody notices the difference. Much of the action takes place in the village pub, and a long gallery of local characters passes in review against that familiar English background, talking their uncouth Dorset dialect, and some of them saying memorable things in it. Mr. Weston has written a book he is proud of; he is apt to refer to it with some complacency, not without justice, for it has had many readers and has exerted a wide influence. From his scattered remarks we can infer its title: it is the *Bible.*

There is a mordant, ironic humor in Powys's work. But except for certain stories written only for their humor and the novel *Kindness in a Corner* (1930), which is almost wholly comedy (apart from one chapter, "The Dirt of God," which some critics have considered the finest passage in the whole of T. F. Powys), the humor is closely linked to pathos and carries a burden of matters not in themselves humorous at all. An example is this passage from *Mr. Weston's Good Wine:*

> "But what were 'en John did take out 'is pick to do at this time o' night?"
>
> " 'E didn't tell I much," replied Mrs. Grunter. "Only there were the boot he did once bury wi' Ada Kiddle, and he mid be going to dig 'en up again."
>
> "Folk do want their own," observed Mrs. Meek.
>
> "So they do," replied her neighbour, "and Grunter bain't the man to allow any of 'is own property to rest in peace as 'tis said on stone, if so be 'is pick and spade will find 'en."
>
> " 'Tain't no madness that do want one's own," remarked Mrs. Meek.
>
> "But 'tis madness," replied Mrs. Grun-

ter, "that do tell a plain Christian woman that God Almighty be in Folly Down, and that two bloody suns be shining in sky."

"And what else did he say?" asked Mrs. Meek.

"Only this," replied her neighbour, "that I needn't hurry me frying of they kippers, for 'tis everlasting life that be come, and they fish mid cook for a thousand years before they be eaten."

"He'll tell a different story when supper-time be near," remarked Mrs. Meek.

Many of the *Mr. Weston* characters reappear in the novel *Unclay.* Characteristically, Powys takes his title (which means to kill someone) from a poem by Jeremy Taylor. (Although he read widely in the literature of all ages, he returned constantly to Bur-ton, Bunyan, Rabelais, Jane Austen, Baxter, Herbert, Browne, and such works as Southey's *Life of Wesley*; the *Bible* he seems to have known by heart.) *Unclay* begins with the arrival of John Death in Dodder—a village just along the way from Folly Down—with a job to do in pursuance of his trade, which is to "unclay." But he has forgotten the names of his victims, and has lost the bit of paper with this information written on it and signed by his Master. So time stands still in Dodder as it had in Folly Down, for until John Death discovers whom he must kill, nobody in Dodder can die. Death sits around sharpening his scythe and making love to the maidens. But Old Jar the Tinker is around, too, and Jar, like Mr. Weston, is not all that he seems. Powys employs the supernatural in many of his stories, and always so naturally that the reader's willing suspension of disbelief is never strained. In

FABLES

BY

T. F. POWYS

WITH FOUR DRAWINGS BY
GILBERT SPENCER

LONDON

CHATTO & WINDUS

1929

Frontispiece and title page for the British edition of one of T. F. Powys's finest books, which grew out of Llewelyn Powys's suggestion that his brother "write about anything—write about that log of wood and that old boot"

Unclay, as in *Mr. Weston,* various village problems and aspirations are sorted out before the story ends.

Although *Mr. Weston* is a more considerable work of art than *Unclay,* the later novel contains something close to a final statement of Powys's philosophy. The book suffers as a novel because the plot and the characters are sometimes overshadowed by the author as he expresses his own views, but it is rewarding to a reader who meets this fact halfway.

Fables comes between these two novels, and had its genesis in a remark by Powys's brother Llewelyn; they were discussing the raw material for plots and themes, and Llewelyn told him to "write about anything—write about that log of wood and that old boot." How far Theodore took him at his word the titles testify: "The Clout and the Pan," "The Seaweed and the Cuckoo-Clock," "The Corpse and the Flea," "The Bucket and the Rope," and so on. The conversations between these lowly characters show humanity in a novel light (not always a flattering one) and confirm that we may learn from the least of God's creatures, and even from the inanimate. There is an interesting parallel here between Powys's personifications of such objects as candles and lanterns and withered leaves and those of his brother John Cowper Powys in such works as *Atlantis* and his later fantasies like "Topsy Turvy." Indeed, although there could hardly be three more dissimilar writers than John Cowper, T. F., and Llewelyn Powys, a study of their works will reveal many surprising points of contact in theme, expression, and concept.

A small group of Powys's short stories may be considered as representative of the best: these are "Darkness and Nathaniel" and "John Pardy and the Waves" (in *Fables*), "The House with the Echo" (in *The House with the Echo,* 1928), and "The Only Penitent" and "The Key of the Field" (in *Bottle's Path,* 1946), all of which contain the special elements which are Powys's alone: his assured use of allegory, so that it seems natural and integral; his insight into the secrets of the human heart, his subtle and idiosyncratic dialogue, which always rings true; his individual and yet simple style, with the short words and short sentences which in his works rise to an eloquence associated more usually with the work of

more conscious stylists; and that vision of life, love, and death which is his alone.

Biographies:

Littleton Powys, *The Powys Family* (Cardiff: Privately printed, 1952);

Henry Coombes, *T. F. Powys* (London: Barry & Rockliff, 1960);

Kenneth Hopkins, *The Powys Brothers: A Biographical Appreciation* (London: Phoenix House, 1967; Rutherford, N.J.: Fairleigh Dickinson University Press, 1968);

Richard Perceval Graves, *The Brothers Powys* (London: Routledge, 1983; New York: Scribners, 1983).

References:

Gerald Brenan, *Personal Record, 1920-1972* (London: Cape, 1974; New York: Knopf, 1975);

Glen Cavaliero, *The Rural Tradition in the English Novel, 1900-1939* (London: Macmillan, 1977; Towota, N.J.: Rowan & Littlefield, 1977);

Reginald Charles Churchill, *The Powys Brothers* (London: Longmans, Green, 1962);

Belinda Humfrey, ed., *Recollections of the Powys Brothers* (London: Owen, 1980);

William Hunter, *The Novels and Stories of T. F. Powys* (Cambridge, England: Frazer, 1930);

Louis Marlow, *Swan's Milk* (London: Faber & Faber, 1934);

Marlow, *Welsh Ambassadors: Powys Lives and Letters* (London: Chapman & Hall, 1936; revised edition, London: Rota, 1971);

J. Lawrence Mitchell, *T. F. Powys* (Minneapolis: University of Minnesota, 1982);

John Cowper Powys, *Autobiography* (New York: Simon & Schuster, 1934; London: Bodley Head, 1934);

Littleton Powys, *The Joy of It* (London: Chapman & Hall, 1937);

Powys Review (St. David's University College, 1977-   );

Peter Riley, *A Bibliography of T. F. Powys* (Hastings: Brimmell, 1967);

Brocard Sewell, ed., *Theodore: Essays on T. F. Powys* (Aylesford: St. Albert's Press, 1964);

Richard Heron Ward, *The Powys Brothers* (London: Bodley Head, 1935).

Jean Rhys

(24 August 1890-14 May 1979)

Thomas F. Staley
University of Tulsa

BOOKS: *The Left Bank* (London: Cape, 1927; New York: Harper, 1927);

Postures (London: Chatto & Windus, 1928); republished as *Quartet* (New York: Simon & Schuster, 1929);

After Leaving Mr Mackenzie (London: Cape, 1931; New York: Knopf, 1931);

Voyage in the Dark (London: Constable, 1934; New York: Morrow, 1935);

Good Morning, Midnight (London: Constable, 1939; New York: Harper & Row, 1970);

Wide Sargasso Sea (London: Deutsch, 1966; New York: Norton, 1967);

Tigers Are Better-Looking (London: Deutsch, 1968; New York: Harper & Row, 1974);

My Day (New York: Frank Hallman, 1975);

Sleep It Off, Lady (London: Deutsch, 1976; New York: Harper & Row, 1976);

Smile Please (London: Deutsch, 1979; New York: Harper & Row, 1980).

OTHER: Francis Carco, *Perversity,* translated by Rhys but erroneously attributed to Ford Madox Ford (Chicago: Covici, 1928).

Jean Rhys claimed to have been born in 1894, but it is more probable that she was born on 24 August 1890. The daughter of Rhys Williams, a doctor, and Minna Lockhart, Ella Gwen Rhys Williams was born in Roseau, Dominica, an island in the Lesser Antilles. Her father was Welsh and her mother a third-generation Dominican Creole, and this Creole heritage was a strong influence in Jean Rhys's life and in her writing. Also strongly influential were the religious training she received in a convent school and the firsthand knowledge of Negro culture that she gained from servants. Her imagination was further shaped by her deep attraction to the black culture—the warmth, the color, the music—and the racial mixture of the islands; but the cultural contrasts between colonial and native life, as the intensely private Rhys experienced them, also contributed to the restless uncertainty of her identity.

Jean Rhys left this island of lush vegetation and color and went to England around 1907. Her sense of cultural rift and displacement in the alien climate and society of England created a curious racial identification with blacks and gave her a lifelong affinity for the exile. She lived with her aunt, Clarice Rhys Williams, and attended for a time the Perse School in Cambridge. In 1908 she entered the Trees School (now the Royal Academy of Dramatic Arts). Their records show that she was eighteen when she entered the school, which further substantiates the 1890 birthdate. Her father died soon after her arrival in England, and her mother came to England in poor health and soon died there.

After a term at the Royal Academy of Dramatic Arts, Jean began traveling with a musical-chorus troupe to the smaller provincial towns. Her experiences with the troupe were transformed into art later in her novel *Voyage in the Dark* (1934). After leaving the troupe, she took a number of theatrical jobs, playing a chorus girl in such light operas as *Maid of the Mountains* and *Count of Luxembourg*. She also posed as an artist's model, and her face was once used for a Pear's Soap advertisement. Like Rhys herself, many of the young women with whom she associated at this time were pretty, uneducated, poor, and a number of them became prostitutes and mistresses. The ignominy of their common plight reinforced Rhys's preoccupation with the themes of financial dependence and male domination, of the helplessness and passivity of the female, which later ran through all her writing. Specific experiences of this sort of life are depicted in *Voyage in the Dark*.

It was during these early days in England that Rhys had her first real love affair with a man whose name she never revealed. She was open and romantic; he was older, cautious, and soon tired of the relationship. At the end of the affair, Rhys began recording her experiences and feelings in a notebook which later became a source book for *Voyage in the Dark*. The man sent Rhys money until her marriage in 1919.

Near the end of World War I Rhys met Jean

Jean Rhys and a friend (probably Germaine Richelot) in Paris

Lenglet, who later wrote under the pen name Edouard de Nève. Lenglet had led an adventurous life, serving in the French Foreign Legion in Africa, later fighting on the Western Front, serving in the Deuxième Bureau, and traveling on secret diplomatic missions for the French. Rhys and Lenglet were married in Holland in 1919 and moved to Paris, and in the chaotic aftermath of the war, Lenglet worked for Japanese government officials who were representatives to the international mission charged with the administration of postwar Vienna. The couple moved constantly. A son, Owen, was born in 1919 but died three weeks after his birth. Feeling dislocated, fearful, and alone, Rhys exhibited in her despair an ironic sense of humor, which is reflected in her work, both relieving and deepening the bitter experiences of her heroines. The dark humor found in her novels has not received a great deal of attention by critics, but it is an important dimension to her themes. Rhys and Lenglet moved from Vienna to Budapest, to Prague, and then to Brussels, where their daughter, Maryvonne, was born in 1922. By this time Lenglet had left his post with the Allied Commission, and the couple soon returned to Paris. Some of the adventures of these

years appear in Rhys's works, especially in the short story "Vienne."

Putting Maryvonne into the care of others first in Brussels, then in Paris, Rhys worked in a Paris dress shop and occasionally as a mannequin. Pearl Adam, the wife of the *Times* Paris correspondent whom Jean had recently met, asked Rhys whether she ever wrote, and Rhys gave her some sketches which Mrs. Adam fashioned into "Triple Sec," a loose collection of narrative scenes and stories. Pearl Adam tended to romanticize Rhys's material, and the writing project collapsed, but Mrs. Adam introduced Rhys to Ford Madox Ford sometime in 1924. Around the time Rhys met Ford, she and Jean Lenglet were having acute financial problems, as usual, and Lenglet became involved in the buying and selling of objets d'art, the ownership of which was uncertain. He was arrested and imprisoned (in his 1932 novel *Barred* the character is imprisoned from January until June 1925, and these are possibly the exact dates of Lenglet's incarceration).

With her husband in jail, Rhys was nearly desperate when she met Ford and Stella Bowen, the Australian painter with whom he was then living.

Ford saw Rhys's potential and helped her with her writing. He helped her refine and publish *The Left Bank* (1927), for which he wrote a long and often self-serving preface. While the stories in this collection often lack subtlety or depth and are often merely fragments or impressions, they contain in embryo themes and ideas that dominate Rhys's later fiction. The Paris world depicted in these stories is not that of the literary circle of Hemingway and his fellow American expatriates. Instead, Rhys deals with the underside of the bohemian existence. She creates in these stories an entirely feminine world, a world where the feminine consciousness is not seen in the reflection of a masculine universe. The best of them—"Illusion," "Vienne," "La Grosse Fifi"— are harbingers of the more fully developed attitudes and characters that appear in her later novels. Rhys had a strong feeling for things French; and this affinity and her straightforward style, her gift for understatement and directness, appealed to Ford's literary taste.

In addition to helping her with her writing, Ford began to take a more personal, physical interest in Jean Rhys (the name, she says, that he suggested she use as an author). Stella Bowen apparently assisted Ford in seducing Rhys, feeling that both she and Rhys were required to serve the stronger male, to be his servants and handmaidens. The curious psychological forces, the twists and turns of this relationship, were fictionalized by Jean Rhys in her first novel, *Quartet* (first published by Chatto & Windus as *Postures*, 1928).

Although Rhys's work was never very closely attuned to the technical innovations of modernism, it does share with the modernist movement the problem of moral ambiguity and the relativism of the post-Freudian world. Her style, as demonstrated in *Quartet,* is sparse, understated, ironic, and the novel probes deeply the underlying relationships and conditions of the characters. *Quartet* also introduces the paradigmatic Rhys heroine, who with slight permutations and a more fully developed ironic humor, appears in all of her fiction of the 1930s.

Marya Zelli in *Quartet* lives a precarious life in Paris with her husband, Stephan. When he is arrested and imprisoned, she is alone and broke. Enter the Heidlers, H. J. and Lois, the "good Samaritans" ironically referred to in the epigraph to the novel. Marya is helpless, passive, and Heidler gives her comfort, reassurance, and protection. A strange menage à trois begins, with a variety of mixed motives and compromises. Lois thinks that a controlled affair under her aegis is a way to allow

Front cover for the American edition of Rhys's first novel, published in Great Britain as Postures

Heidler to stray only as far as Lois's leash will permit. Marya's compromise has to do with a certain abandonment of her will. She sees herself as a victim; Lois sees her as a child, a toy that she and Heidler can use to amuse themselves. But despite Marya's aimlessness and passivity, she is also an adversary to Lois. Both women are in different ways subservient to the male, and both get what they want—Lois a position in the art world of Paris, recognition; and Marya a fundamental, if temporary, protection and security. Marya is ready to settle for the present, whatever its ultimate cost, if it obscures temporarily the unpleasant contours of life, but she realizes at the same time that she will soon be discarded. She characterizes herself as a "naive sinner" and in this way justifies her own seduction, her own willingness to play the game. Both she and Lois are victims, and they distrust, indeed hate, each other for this very reason. After a trip to the country and a quarrel, Marya allows

Heidler to set her up in a hotel room. The narrative grows increasingly complex as it registers Marya's psychic descent through a series of interrelated images and extended metaphors, developing a structural rhythm that provides a special perspective on Marya's movement and reactions as events swarm around her. The realistic level of the earlier parts of the novel is blended with open-ended images and dreamlike flights that are, nevertheless, rigidly controlled by the direct and simple style. The imagery and rhythm of the second half of the novel render the dreamlike subtlety of Marya's consciousness, which breaks from the realistic strains of the narrative and marks the psychological dimensions of her entrapment. These passages reveal far more of Marya's subconscious motives and anxieties than she herself can realize, and thus they explore more profoundly the themes of the novel. On one level the force of the narrative seems to insist that Marya's inability to break away from those upon whom she is dependent is justified, but on a deeper level the consciousness revealed to the reader points to a broader framework of human culpability and to the underlying reasons for Marya's desperation, her flight from reality, and her amoral posturing.

Marya lies in her room, receives visits from Heidler, and goes to see Stephan in prison. Heidler has the money; Marya needs the money. She is torn between love and hate for Heidler, between loyalty to Stephan and despair at his situation. After his release and Marya's revelation that she has been Heidler's lover, Stephan violently flings her aside and leaves, ironically to be comforted by a stronger woman. The imagery which bears Marya's sense of her dilemma underscores her psychological vacillations and points to the inevitable consequences of her actions. The most persistent image in the novel is that of the caged animal with predatory overtones and depiction of human confinement, and it accommodates the various forms of conflict within *Quartet*. In the novel's earlier stages, the metaphor is not unpleasant—Marya thinks of herself "like some splendid caged animal," entrapped, but with resources for escape. Marya thus justifies the prospect of becoming Heidler's mistress as a chance for a new birth. The image, however, is transmuted as the complexity of the four-way relationship increases. Later, the sight of "a young fox in a cage" allows Marya again to entertain false hopes and justifications while at a deeper level intuiting the dire consequences of her actions.

This metaphor of entrapment is extended by the images accompanying the descriptions of the various hotel rooms in which Marya is "caged."

Although the narrative voice on the realistic level exposes Marya's feelings, stylistic alterations between direct exposition and metaphoric language subtly probe and reveal underlying conflicts of which Marya is only partially aware. The cage imagery soon gives way to grotesque, Kafkaesque images of claustrophobia and vertigo, reflecting Marya's horror, fear, and desperation. As Marya seeks refuge in drink and then in fantasies, the style takes on a nightmare quality that pervades the surface realism.

All the characters in *Quartet* prove to be victims of their own moral blindness, hatreds, illusions, and self-pity. The two men are blind and uncaring, and the women are no better because in their desire for protection they become accomplices to their own self-destruction in a life-denying battle. The enclosed world in which they all live is an amoral one. Marya has been reduced to an object and thus reaches an emotional state in which the exclusive object of her psychic energy is the self. Although *Quartet* has been called a morbid work, the directness of style and Rhys's clear narrative focus and technique relieve the novel's intense subjectivity and offer a dramatic, human portrait of the female consciousness in the modern world.

As Rhys's affair with Ford drew to its inevitable end, Jean Lenglet was finally released from prison. Rhys's revelation to Lenglet of the nature of her relationship with Ford spelled the end of their marriage, but a deep and lasting bond was to exist between them for years—a bond that was not solely related to their daughter, Maryvonne. Rhys's literary career in the late 1920s and early 1930s continued to show promise. Ford had gotten her the job of translating Francis Carco's *Perversity* (1928; erroneously attributed to Ford by the publisher), and *After Leaving Mr Mackenzie* and *Voyage in the Dark* were published in 1931 and 1934. Both novels received brief but favorable reviews, but sales were disappointing. Rhys's technique and form were praised, but her subject matter—the down-and-out female on the fringe of society—did not draw readers and both novels fell into obscurity.

Few writers before Jean Rhys in this century dealt sensitively with the unprotected woman in the contemporary world. The woman in the Rhys novel lives in a harsher, more-naked, less-sophisticated world than the women in the works of Virginia Woolf, Katherine Mansfield, or Dorothy Richardson. Rhys's women are without careers, ambitions, education, or particular talents. They move within a closed and essentially deterministic universe, and Rhys deals more directly with the sexual

Jean Lenglet sent Rhys this photograph of himself and their daughter, Maryvonne, after the couple separated

tensions and game playing that go on between a dominant male and a passive female. The subjects and themes of Rhy's fiction, however, were outside the mainstream of British fiction, and in her case originally did not lead to popular success.

After Leaving Mr Mackenzie and *Voyage in the Dark* amplify and enrich Rhys's vision of the feminine consciousness. *After Leaving Mr Mackenzie* deals with the Rhys woman long after youthful hopefulness and trust have vanished. The heroine, Julia Martin, is older, harder, more ravaged by the world than Anna Morgan of *Voyage in the Dark*. A precisely formed and structured novel, *After Leaving Mr Mackenzie* is compressed and relentless in its intimate portrayal of a woman fighting to delay her arrival at the nadir of her existence. Part one of the novel is set in Paris after Mr Mackenzie has disposed of Julia; the second and longest section is set in London, where Julia visits her sister, tries to attend to her dying mother, develops an abortive relationship with Mr Horsfield, and receives money from an old lover who makes it clear that this is the last time she can expect to be helped by him; the brief final section covers Julia's return to Paris.

While the novel traces Julia's search for money, it is, on a deeper level, concerned with her quest for some human engagement. The theme of failure is supported by images of ghostlike figures which emerge throughout, grim and foreboding, portents of a future where death is the only certainty.

Julia at the beginning of the novel inhabits the typically enclosed, restricted world of the Rhys heroine—in this case, the hotel room and strict schedule by which Julia has ordered her life, a controllable universe free from human intrusion, a world devoted exclusively to the self. It is a hiding place, a refuge created by Julia's defensive narcissism. Julia is bereft of those characteristics which give people identity—it is impossible to guess her age, nationality, or social background. She displays, however, a quality of self-respect, endurance, and an inherent resiliency. She has also developed a carelessness and restlessness which become an important defense in the inevitable sexual power relationships that men impose upon her.

The narrative distance is better handled and controlled in this novel than in *Quartet*. In addition to her sure handling of the feminine consciousness, Rhys in this novel makes an entry into the male consciousness, which gives further dimension to the heroine as other characters interpret her. Julia sets out to confront Mr Mackenzie, the man who has cast her off, and in so doing she confronts the whole social order. The scene between them is rendered from his point of view. Male motivation is revealed, and the external, social source of Julia's angst, the moral blindness of Mr Mackenzie, are also skillfully shown. His instinct for self-preservation underscores Julia's lack of a strong instinct of this kind. Ironically, the insincerity and cruelty of the Mackenzies of the world generate what little strength Julia has.

A more detailed and complicated analysis of male attitudes toward the female is presented in the character of Mr Horsfield. The preliminary scenes and the early meetings with Julia are rendered from Horsfield's point of view. Rhys's skillful handling of point of view deepens the reader's sense of what might otherwise be seen as a prosaic, if not merely melodramatic, relationship between Horsfield and Julia. Their first meeting is rendered exclusively through Horsfield's motivations and intellectual juggling. His footwork is quite humorous at times as he bounces back and forth between caution and recklessness, attraction to and revulsion for Julia. But for their second meeting the narratorial focus moves back and forth between the two, revealing the byplay and parrying beyond the dialogue. The shift between the two consciousnesses is effective here as it was not in *Quartet*, where Heidler, for example, was not convincing as a character because the narrator could not free herself from Marya's point of view. This failure in *Quartet* nearly reduced the novel to melodrama, but the shifting point of view in *After Leaving Mr Mackenzie* not only accommodates the unfolding of a relationship, it inaugurates and sustains the entire dramatic situation. When Julia finally acknowledges a need for him, Horsfield is able to indulge his sexual urges and at the same time maintain his self-image as the gallant protector. After sleeping with her, he silently leaves the room and feels an enormous "relief." He learns what Julia has learned but keeps forgetting—that self-protection is the rule of the jungle.

The third relationship depicted in this novel is that between Julia and her sister, Norah, who, while Julia (as Norah thinks) has been out living the gay life, has been tied to the home, taking care of their sick mother. Norah has accepted lower-middle-class life in all its drabness; outwardly stoic, she is inwardly embittered and self-pitying. She is, as Julia says, "fierce"—with a fierceness created out of hatred and self-pity. Julia is vulnerable where Norah is hard; Julia has retained some capacity for feeling while Norah has only coldness and self-righteous moral superiority. Norah's indifference to her awakes a forceful if temporary determination in Julia to keep up the fight. Here, as in other Rhys novels, the heroine fares no better in her relationships with women than she does with men. In Rhys, women are often betrayed by other women; and a natural feminine intimacy is no longer a part of the feminine consciousness.

After Leaving Mr Mackenzie is intimately concerned with the nature of human relationships at every level, the illusions and lies, self-deceptions, that exist for both sexes. The movement of the novel traces with shattering accuracy the desires and self-induced illusions of the male. It makes poignantly visible the male role in the sexual power struggle in which he must not only dominate but justify domination to himself. The results of this domination for the female are made very plain. The social and economic order is on the side of the male. As in *Quartet*, all four principals are victims to some extent. They are isolated; in each we see the impulse toward human companionship and, on the part of the men, the price they are unwilling to pay. The four are unwilling, incapable, or, in Julia's case, too broken down to find any meaningful human

bond. Each is fixed, either by choice or circumstances, in a world whose highest value is protection, not love. And the metaphysical weight of the novel exposes the vacuity of this hierarchy.

After the publication of *After Leaving Mr Mackenzie*, Rhys turned to her notebooks and began writing *Voyage in the Dark*, which she originally titled "Two Tunes." The novel is highly autobiographical, dealing with a young woman's life in England as an actress in a traveling musical troupe. The experiences are based upon Jean Rhys's own experiences, including her longing for the warmth and color of the Caribbean islands, her first love affair, and an abortion. Rhys is able to divorce the novel from events in her own life through her skillful use of first-person narration without endangering the necessary aesthetic distance. The novel enriches one's understanding of the two novels that precede it as well as the two novels that follow it in the Rhys canon. It gives more shape to the earlier heroines, and its Caribbean background anticipates the fully developed exoticism of *Wide Sargasso Sea* (1966). The special intimacy of the "I" narrator allows for an important structural feature of the novel, Anna Morgan's memories of her childhood in the West Indies.

We have in *Voyage in the Dark*, because of Rhys's structuring technique, a triple level of observation: first, the experiencing self, Anna's life in the present; second, the narrative self that is distant from the events; and third, the self of Anna's memory who is recalled in dream or conscious recollection and who experiences the events of childhood in the Caribbean. Without this element of memory and the dynamic resonance it creates, the novel would simply stand as a well-told but pathetic little tale of a young girl who through naiveté and lack of initiative falls into compromising circumstances. A series of beautifully constructed memory frames, however, blend into the narrative and set up a cumulative and complex process of awareness, giving depth, richness, and moral focus to the novel. The contrast between the two worlds is wonderfully achieved; the entire psychology, the deeper structures of civilization in the two cultures underscores their fundamental opposition, and Anna lives in both worlds. The style of the memory passages is clear and vibrant; the style of the England passages is often vague and dislocated. The development of these memory images gradually reveals a pattern and an accretive meaning. The narrative's dual focus on present and past invigorates the entire book as the two opposed worlds meet in Anna's experience, and the narrational self attempts to draw meaning from the personal struggle of the confrontation. It is in this matrix of both worlds that the deeper meaning of Anna's failure lies.

Anna seeks warmth, comfort, security. Her first lover, Walter, becomes for her a protector and comforter, a kind of surrogate father. She associates with him a kind of primal, noncarnal, human warmth. She is naive; he is skillful in seducing her. After her violation, the novel traces her downward path. The letter of dismissal inevitably arrives. Anna has been used and is now being disposed of when the male grows tired or fearful. She, in common with other Rhys heroines, has no real options; hers is a condition without recourse. Upon receiving the letter, Anna conflates in her mind images from the past and the present, an association of a prior rejection (by her uncle in the islands) with the present rejection. This fluctuation throughout the novel between Anna's childhood in the West Indies and her life in London is far more than a simple device to generate rhythm and set up contrasts. These earlier reflections by the "I" narrator create a fictional mode whereby the experiencing self of the novel is revealed beyond its contemporary context. Together present and past create a kind of dual passage or voyage which has, for Anna, merged into a dreamlike world that has left her unable to define experience. This fictional strategy provides the thematic resolution of the novel as we see Anna's oscillation between the world of reflected experience and present circumstances.

After being cast off by her lover, Anna is at loose ends. Seeking her lost security, false though it proved to be, Anna drifts from one male to another. She becomes pregnant, seeks out an abortionist, and at the end of the novel she has been seen by a doctor who tries to stop her hemorrhaging. She thinks about starting over again, going back to her childhood, "about being new and fresh." Starting over again becomes a central concern for the Rhys heroine, young and old, but the phrase carries a bitter irony. The doctor, while Anna is thinking of starting over again, says the same thing to Anna's roommate, but his meaning is entirely different from Anna's. He means that she will be able to start the same dangerous cycle over again: the search for money, the going from one man to another, in short, prostitution. The juxtaposition of this phrase as it is thought and spoken by the two characters, Anna and the doctor, completes the bitter irony of the novel. Anna is suspended between her dream world and reality. Hope will keep her going, to be

eventually replaced by the more natural, if less ennobling, instinct for survival. The will is gradually crushed, and survival, as she seeks the protection of another male, becomes a way of life. Anna represents the genesis of the Rhys heroine; most of the traits, including the tendency to drift into a netherworld of somnambulistic escape, are present in embryo in her.

The notices for *Voyage in the Dark* were favorable, but reviews continued to refer to the "dark subject matter" of Rhys's work, and the sales of both *Voyage in the Dark* and *After Leaving Mr Mackenzie* were disappointing. Since the early 1930s, after Rhys had separated from Lenglet, she had met Leslie Tilden Smith, a literary agent and publisher's reader. They began living together. Smith, associated as he was with the publishing industry, introduced Rhys to many of his literary acquaintances, but as with her life in Paris in the 1920s, she remained always on the fringes of the literary world rather than anywhere near the inner circle. She found literary people "alarming," and her natural shyness predisposed her to be more reclusive than many other writers of the period. She did mention later in life that she had met Rosamond Lehmann and others during the 1930s, but the acquaintances

Rhys's second husband, Leslie Tilden Smith

did not seem to develop into anything more substantial.

In the middle 1930s, Smith's father died, leaving Smith a sum of money, and Smith and Rhys were married. Smith had been divorced from his wife earlier but, although he lived with Rhys, he had not remarried, for fear of offending his father, a clergyman, and losing the inheritance. In 1936 Rhys and Smith made a trip to the West Indies stopping for a time in Dominica, where, of course, Rhys's relatives and the quality of life on the island fell far short of her romantic memories. She tried to write on the island, but was unable to get much accomplished. She never returned. Back in London she began to write *Good Morning, Midnight*. As Europe drew closer to war, Rhys's regular visits to the Continent were interrupted. Maryvonne, who lived with her father in the Netherlands, often visited her mother in England. The war also put an end to these visits, and during the war Maryvonne and her mother corresponded through friends in Portugal.

Good Morning, Midnight was published in 1939. In contrast with the socially conscious writings of others during this period, Rhys's writing seemed untouched by the military and political events of the day. Throughout the 1930s Rhys's heroines saw the world from the inside rather than the outside. Her aim was the perfection of rendering private consciousness through style, not the achievement of an enlarged vision of the contemporary world. *Good Morning, Midnight* advanced the major themes of her earlier work and deepened her portrait of women's emotional life. Although it contains no specific mention of contemporary events, the novel comes at the end of the Depression and near the start of World War II and lays an enormous emphasis on how much things cost, how much money one needs, how much protection money affords. These things always concerned the Rhys heroine, however. Set in Paris, the novel brings Rhys's fiction full circle and confirms that her real literary affinities are French rather than English.

Sasha Jansen bears the cumulative burdens of Rhys's earlier heroines; she is Julia Martin grown older, a bit more out of control, but for the present at least, less financially desperate. It takes more alcohol, more luminal, for her to keep things in place. Her attempts at self-control, the arrangement of her room, her daily rituals have become substitutes for meaning in a life that seems without purpose. Images of darkness, water, and drowning contrast with the heroine's tenuous, self-imposed hold on sanity, safety, dryness. The references to

Jean Rhys in Dominica, 1936, the only time she returned to the West Indies after her departure in about 1907

drowning and water set up a psychological pattern of sexual violation and fear which gradually reveals the depth of the heroine's consciousness and the entire range of her personality and feeling. All of her actions and reactions seem attempts to master the threats that the world imposes. The obsessional consciousness that the novel will explore is introduced through these images.

Past and present collide in this novel as they have in earlier Rhys novels. The major portion of part one carefully develops Sasha's earlier memories of her Paris failures. She confronts in memory the manager of the dress shop where she once worked. The malignancy of the faceless and nameless oppressor is seen more clearly by Sasha than by any of Rhys's other heroines. With this combination of paranoia and insight, Sasha recognizes those forces in society which turn her into a weak and helpless figure who simply cannot get on. We learn how her present attitudes and fears were formed, and this is important to our understanding of her later behavior.

Once again, images such as enclosing streets, threatening rows of houses, and small hotel rooms accommodate the consciousness of the heroine. Because, except for dialogue, *Good Morning, Midnight* is rendered entirely through Sasha's consciousness in first-person narration, her psychological states are necessarily well controlled by the style, which not only reflects her various immediate states of mind, but, as it orders her consciousness in language, offers further clues to the deeper, inner self. Brutally understated, the novel's style gives penetrating focus to Sasha's dreams, and the imagery with its sustained and continued tropes amplifies and expands meaning beyond the immediate rendering of consciousness.

What proves to be the most significant encounter in the novel occurs near the close of part one, when Sasha meets a man on the street as she is leaving a bar. He is the poor gigolo René, charming, hopeful, and clever, and in spite of herself, Sasha is attracted to him as an underdog like herself. She believes she is invulnerable and can shut the whole world out. Ironically, in this novel, René and two other impoverished male characters look to Sasha for comfort and protection because she has a bit more money than they do. After Sasha's meeting with the gigolo and others less fortunate than herself, the style of the novel becomes more open, the sentences longer, the images less grotesque, and Sasha's thought patterns less obsessive. The style softens as Sasha begins to look outside herself. She acquires a greater sympathy but still remains cynical and worldly in her ironic humor.

Again Sasha recalls the past and her marriage to Enno, who reminds us of Stephan Zelli in *Quartet*. They are young and hopeful, but their hopes are crushed and Enno leaves her because "you're too passive, you're lazy, you bore me." It is out of this past that Sasha's present has been formed. As the novel reaches its dramatic close, we become increasingly aware that Sasha's is an almost archetypal journey of return. It begins as an attempt to face the past by revisiting it in a most cautious way, but despite the caution it floods up and nearly engulfs the present.

Agitated and increasingly excited by René, Sasha feels that she still has a grip on herself. The water and drowning imagery is evoked by her in a different manifestation as she thinks that "Underneath there is always stagnant water, calm, indifferent." Her indifference, however, has begun to evaporate. René brings Sasha out of herself; amid

his gaiety and ebullience, she becomes witty, charming, clever, sarcastic—qualities she has always had but has never had the opportunity to reveal. This transformation is one of the novel's most important elements, and it is executed with brilliant narrative skill. Even Sasha's memories are transformed as she exchanges recollections with René; they grow warm and humorous in contrast to her dark memories reported earlier in the novel. When René and Sasha discover a mutual link, however (they had known the same person and stayed in the same house), Sasha is again on her guard. As René questions her, she becomes increasingly defensive and finally almost hysterical as she admits her fear of men. She sees her illusion crushed by the whole image of her life, past and present. The most striking feature of this entire scene is its economy of detail and the precision with which Sasha's whole life comes before her. The style acts to modulate every emotional phase which she goes through, and the reflexive quality of the images deepens our understanding of Sasha's despair. René persists, telling her that he wants to make love to her. The memory of vague, romantic yearnings from the past produces a profoundly complicated turmoil in Sasha in which her whole identity seems to give way. René is appealing to her sexual and romantic urges that have long been dormant.

The last section of the novel is a blur between dream and reality, hallucination and confrontation. The style never loses its sharp clarity, but in places it mounts to a lyric level as Sasha's mind absorbs a confusion between what she wants to believe and what is actually happening. With René in her room, she reaches an emotional pitch of joy and terror. She thinks of love, youth, spring, happiness, everything that she has lost, but suddenly the spell is broken and she grows cold and wary. Even her physical body signals the riot of her conflicting feelings: "My mouth hurts, my breasts hurt, because it hurts, when you have been dead to come alive." She insults René by telling him to take the money and forget the lovemaking. He leaves, and Sasha does not know whether she is the passionate woman seeking but unable to accept even a fleeting moment of human passion, or the aging, lonely female who has narrowly survived the advances of a gigolo. She is in a schizophrenic state, not knowing which self is the true self—the self that wants to reach outward and love or the self that wants to withdraw and defend and protect. René, she discovers, has taken only a bit of money when he could have taken it all. Again, dreams of romance and love refuse to die and rise up within her again as she imagines the gigolo returning. She lies in her bed waiting for him. Through the open door the man in the next room enters (a tension had been set up between him and Sasha throughout the novel); she reaches out to him, draws him down to her saying, "Yes—yes—yes," an ending with echoes of James Joyce's *Ulysses* (1922). It is a qualified affirmation, a hope for the possibility of union between man and woman in which each fulfills the other.

Theme and dramatic event have never been better wedded in Rhys's fiction than in *Good Morning, Midnight,* where they achieve artistic harmony and yield such telling insight into the consciousness of the heroine. Throughout the novel the reader is aware of the primary importance of style in all matters of form and expression. Its function here extends beyond the conventional expectations of prose. In the heroine's movements throughout the book and in her eventual illumination the style seems to form a biaxial movement understating, modulating, and finally overcoming the heroine's plight. The language itself becomes a mediating element between the heroine and the outside world. The style seems to contest the development of the novel. The architechtonics of *Good Morning, Midnight* emerge out of Sasha's obsessional preoccupations and the slender thread of events which take place during her brief visit to Paris, but it is the style which gives the full configuration of this interplay between the private consciousness and the outside world. As the style carries us through the mediations between the inner and outer selves, the images found in memory, topography, and dream struggle for what seems another destiny that is finally released in the last words of the novel.

The "yes" at the end is no more a grand affirmation of life than Molly Bloom's. Sasha's acceptance is weighted with full ironic implications. For Sasha, "yes" is not necessarily an acceptance of life but a recognition of its force. Rhys also gives vision in this conclusion to the narrow and restricted choice a woman has in this work.

However we may interpret the complex reverberations at the close of *Good Morning, Midnight,* they give the book a cohesion and intricacy beyond that of Rhys's earlier novels. The loneliness of the modern experience has been drawn into the rich vortex of the feminine self and accommodated with a vitality and an understanding of human nature few novels dealing with the feminine consciousness have achieved. In Sasha there is strength that confronts the terror—a strength at once fragile and human, but no longer merely defensive. The synthesis in *Good Morning, Midnight* is realized through

the character of Sasha. She is the most compelling and sympathetic of Rhys's heroines. Her bitter humor and sardonic wisdom provide us with abundant clues to her deeper nature. The women in Rhys's fiction have been crippled by life, but what we see—and nowhere more clearly than in this novel—is that there is a new consciousness forming, not one formed only from anger and despair, but one imbued with an awareness that women must share equally in life's promises and defeats, and if they do not, human life itself is lessened and even malformed. This revelation is nowhere better expressed in Rhys's fiction than in *Good Morning, Midnight.*

At the beginning of the war, Leslie Tilden Smith joined the air force. He was assigned to a radar station in Norfolk, where Rhys joined him temporarily, but she spent a great deal of time in London. Leslie died in Devon after the war ended, in October 1945. His cousin, Max Hamer, a family friend and solicitor, attended the funeral and soon became acquainted with Rhys. They were married two years later (1947), and lived in Beckenham, Kent. Rhys's writing career remained dormant during this time, and the few who had read and admired her work, which was now long out of print, believed she had died.

In 1949, the actress Selma Vaz Dias tried to find Rhys by putting an ad in the *New Statesman.* Rhys saw the ad, answered it, and this step became the first on the long road to a belated recognition of her novels and a certain measure of fame that had been denied her in her younger days. Selma Vaz Dias sent Rhys a dramatic adaptation of *Good Morning, Midnight,* and performed the work as a dramatic monologue at the Anglo-French Centre on 10 November 1949; it was later presented on BBC's Third Programme in 1957. Upon discovering that she and her works had not been totally forgotten, Rhys was encouraged to attempt writing again.

Rhys and Max Hamer visited London early in 1957 to have dinner with Selma Vaz Dias, and at this time they talked about Rhys's ideas for *Wide Sargasso Sea.* Selma Vaz Dias claimed ever after that the idea for the novel was born in her kitchen, and, obsessed with the idea that she and she alone had rediscovered Rhys, she laid claim to fees and royalties that Rhys earned at this time. In 1959 *Good Morning, Midnight* was broadcast in Bremen, while Rhys in England was saying that *Wide Sargasso Sea* just needed to be "pulled together." However, Rhys suffered a heart attack just before the novel was finished and was in poor health for years afterward. Publication was delayed for seven more years.

Dust jacket for Rhys's 1966 novel, which deals with the first marriage of Mr. Rochester, a character in Charlotte Brontë's Jane Eyre

After *Good Morning, Midnight* was broadcast on the BBC in 1957, Rhys became friends with Francis Wyndham, a longtime admirer of her work, and Diana Athill, who became her editor at Andre Deutsch and helped her re-enter the literary scene. A short story, "Till September Petronella," was published in the *London Magazine* in 1960, and another, "Let Them Call It Jazz," in the *London Magazine* in 1962. Movie rights to *Good Morning, Midnight* were discussed. In February 1966 part one of *Wide Sargasso Sea* was published in *Art and Literature*. The next month, Max Hamer died, and in October 1966 *Wide Sargasso Sea* was finally published. It was well received, and Rhys finally achieved the acclaim she had long deserved. Photographers and interviewers visited her cottage in Devon; she was given awards by the Royal Society for Literature and received public attention when she received the W. H. Smith Award.

Wide Sargasso Sea differs in time and setting from Rhys's other novels, but in its exploration of the male-female relationship, it has an affinity with the earlier works. In this novel, Rhys's characterization of Edward Rochester is the most complex and fully drawn of any of the male characters she had ever attempted.

The novel deals with the Rochester of Charlotte Brontë's *Jane Eyre* (1847) and his meeting with, marriage to, and early days with his first wife, Antoinette, who is known in *Jane Eyre* only as the madwoman in the attic. In the first section of the novel we learn of the child Antoinette and gain a view of the insular world in which she lived, both external and internal. As the reader understands the formation of the consciousness of Antoinette, he or she can understand her later behavior and her approaching madness. The first section provides a psycho-historical background for Antoinette's life. The setting is the West Indies after the emancipation of the slaves, a time bristling with resentment, hatred, vindictiveness. Rhys concentrates on the psychological, the personal traumas which larger historical events produce upon the individual. We come to understand the vast cultural gap separating the young Antoinette from her own surroundings and the completely unbridgeable gap that exists between her and the Englishman Edward Rochester.

Early dramatic events have a profound effect upon Antoinette. When blacks burn down neighboring estates, her family has to escape; as they flee, a black girl she had thought of as her friend throws a stone at her. Her attraction to the black culture is disrupted by the rebellion, and a disjunction in her personality results. Her brother's death and her mother's madness (and domination by a former slave) confirm Antoinette's complete isolation and seal her fate in a private schizophrenic world between two times, two races, two cultures.

Part two, which takes up nearly two-thirds of the novel, is largely Edward's account of the events following his marriage to Antoinette, a marriage arranged along financial terms rather than for love. Here Jean Rhys makes the Gothic mode an active element in the novel. This mode, of course, helps tie the novel to *Jane Eyre* and functions as a narrative idiom where the descriptions themselves, with their frequently elaborate portents, achieve a metaphysical relationship to the characters. Although part two is centered within Edward's intelligence, Rhys uses dialogue between Edward and Antoinette extensively. Her style in this section is triumphantly adapted to her narrative purpose. Its two qualities, which at first seem to conflict—an uncanny ability to describe an emotion completed and somehow resolved, and at the same time a rendering of feeling as much by implication as by statement—are fused by the close relationship she draws between the natural and psychological landscape.

Edward and Antoinette's honeymoon journey into the mountains is described in terms of the lush and exotic scenery through which they pass; it is an enclosed and intoxicating world, wild but menacing. The closeness and intimacy that Antoinette desires and needs is impossible for Edward, who is incapable of giving of himself. The whole exotic experience of the first few days at Granbois is a kind of initiation for Edward. There is a dominant sensual element—"too much blue, too much purple. . . . The flowers too red, etc."—he thinks. He finds this world at once seductive and hostile and goes on his guard after just a few short days and nights of abandon. Antoinette wants to draw him into her private world, to live naturally and passionately within the rhythms of the natural environment, but he is filled with deep foreboding. His thoughts and values have crystallized; he is egocentric, but not, perhaps, the conniving, malicious male he has been thought to be. He is blind rather than deliberately malicious, sad rather than vengeful.

The villainous Daniel Cosway informs him that Antoinette has had other men before her marriage to him. Edward, in typical Victorian fashion, is wounded and outraged. His inflated pride and imperious personality entrap him exclusively within himself, and any rapprochement with Antoinette becomes impossible. Two explicitly sexual scenes ensue. Antoinette, desperate to win him, asks the black Christophine for a potion. After drinking it, Edward indulges in the wildest sexual abandon. Antoinette has made the mistake of thinking that she can evoke and redeem his love through sexual passion. He, on the other hand, comes to hate her for causing him to lose control, to abandon his closely guarded self. Her attempt to bring them together through obeah, a Caribbean form of voodoo, causes him to despise her forever. He will not allow himself to become exposed and vulnerable. Antoinette, like her surroundings, becomes something alien and hostile to him, but his pathetic sense of honor endures. He does, however, plan a deliberate act of revenge which symbolizes his hostility and need to dominate. He takes the black servant girl Amelie to bed just behind the thin partition that separates his room from Antoinette's to ensure that she hears them. He thus demonstrates to himself the power of his maleness and shows that he has the power to destroy Antoinette. Near the close of part two Christophine points out to Edward his real sin, "nobody is to have any pride but you." He has not been able to fathom the life of the passions; he fears it and retaliates in this way, thereby driving Antoinette a little further down the road to madness.

Part three of the novel is a coda which confirms Antoinette's wretched destiny. As she and Edward leave Granbois, we recall the exuberance and hope with which Antoinette arrived there. At the end of the novel the groundwork has been laid for Antoinette's fate in Edward's country home.

The characterization of Antoinette is the major flaw in the novel. There is something hollow in her that is not covered over by the exotic and mysterious qualities Rhys gives to her. She has little understanding and never advances beyond the world of childhood. Her limitations as a character enforce certain limitations upon the novel and upon her relationship with Edward. A mature union would have been impossible given her limited capacity for understanding. The novel is, however, an extension of Rhys's basic themes; and Rhys's

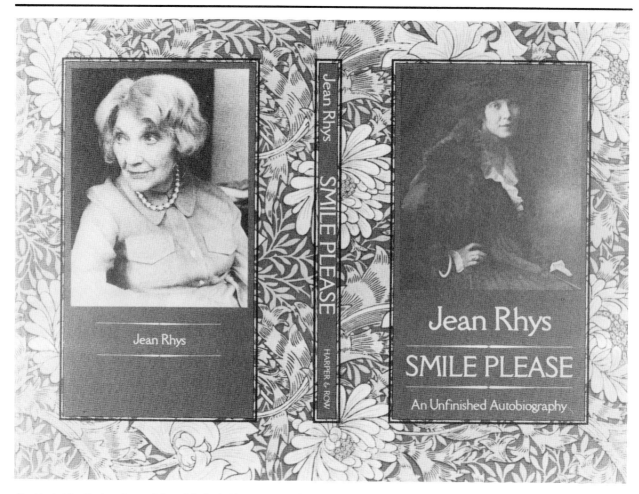

Dust jacket for the American edition of the book Rhys was at work on when she died. The photograph on the front of the jacket was taken in Vienna, circa 1920.

achievement is considerable, especially the way she captures with a lyrical intensity the rhythm between the physical and metaphysical worlds. *Wide Sargasso Sea* enriches one's rereading of *Jane Eyre*. However, whereas the nineteenth-century novel upon which it is based ends happily in matrimonial fulfillment, *Wide Sargasso Sea* is decidedly modern in that there is no fulfillment or reconciliation at the end.

After the publication of *Wide Sargasso Sea*, Andre Deutsch began republishing Rhys's earlier novels. *Good Morning, Midnight* and *Voyage in the Dark* were republished in 1967, and the other novels followed. Jean Rhys published three books after *Wide Sargasso Sea: Tigers Are Better-Looking* (1968), *Sleep It Off, Lady* (1976), and the privately printed autobiographical *My Day* (1975). *Smile Please*, the incomplete autobiography upon which she was working when she died, was published posthumously.

Tigers Are Better-Looking is a volume of short

fiction, including nine stories from *The Left Bank*, a segment of the original introduction by Ford, and eight additional stories, all of which had appeared in various periodicals through the 1960s. It includes "Till September Petronella," which proves that Rhys's talent for dramatizing the polarization of the sexes did not diminish with age. She does in this story something that she did not generally do in her fiction and that is to tie the story to an exact historical date, in this case July 1914, just one month before the beginning of World War I, thus linking her war between the sexes to a grander, more violent war.

Sleep It Off, Lady contains previously unpublished stories, many of which predate in initial composition the eight new stories in *Tigers Are Better-Looking*. The majority of stories in this collection confirm the clarity of focus that always marked Rhys's work as well as that certainty of feeling within the narrow world she draws upon for her subject

200

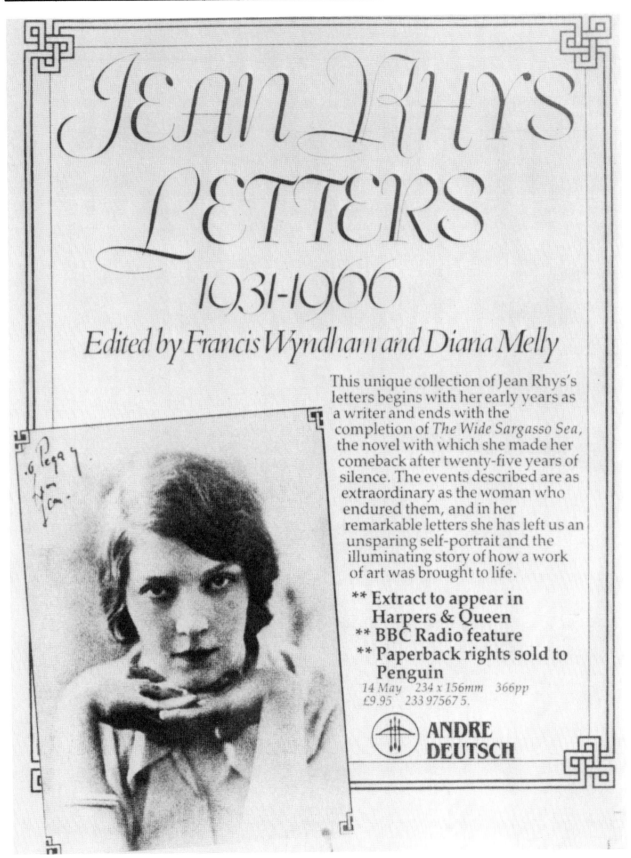

JEAN RHYS
LETTERS
1931-1966
Edited by Francis Wyndham and Diana Melly

This unique collection of Jean Rhys's letters begins with her early years as a writer and ends with the completion of *The Wide Sargasso Sea*, the novel with which she made her comeback after twenty-five years of silence. The events described are as extraordinary as the woman who endured them, and in her remarkable letters she has left us an unsparing self-portrait and the illuminating story of how a work of art was brought to life.

** Extract to appear in Harpers & Queen
** BBC Radio feature
** Paperback rights sold to Penguin

14 May   234 x 156mm   366pp
£9.95   233 97567 5.

ANDRE DEUTSCH

The Bookseller, *7 April 1984*

matter. She deals confidently with the very young and the very old in these stories, their vulnerability and their exclusion.

The publication of *Wide Sargasso Sea,* the new interest in Jean Rhys, and the republication of virtually all her earlier work had far-reaching effects upon Rhys's literary career and reputation. Her work became available to a whole new generation of readers. Her critical reputation has grown steadily. Critics have pointed primarily to her strong originality and her remarkable insight into the feminine psyche, and lying beneath most of the praise is the collective recognition that Rhys simply writes like nobody else; her talent and intelligence encompass dimensions not found elsewhere in the modern English novel. It is not only because readers are now more attuned to the feminine consciousness that Rhys has gained such wide attention, but, more significant, it has come to be recognized that her work explores with compassion and a rare intelligence the panic and emptiness of modern life. The range of her subject matter is never wide, but her understanding of what it is to have been a woman in this century is comprehensive. Written in a style that brings form and content into a harmonious whole rarely equaled in modern fiction, her work reveals in its humor, sympathy, and understanding a fully realized and significant portrait of the female consciousness in the modern world.

Smile Please, her unfinished autobiography, published posthumously in the fall of 1979, is especially revealing in its treatment of Rhys's early childhood in Dominica. The later portions of the autobiography are less finished, but her commentaries on writing and the relationship of art to life are interesting aesthetic statements in themselves. A selection of Rhys's letters was published in the spring of 1984.

In 1978 Jean Rhys was awarded a CBE for her services to literature. She died on 14 May 1979 in the Royal Devon and Exeter Hospital.

Letters:

Jean Rhys Letters 1931-1966, edited by Francis Wyndham and Diana Melly (London: Deutsch, 1984).

References:

Alfred Alvarez, "The Best Living English Novelist," *New York Times Book Review,* 17 March 1974, pp. 6-8;

Diana Athill, "Jean Rhys, and the Writing of *Wide Sargasso Sea,*" *Bookseller,* 3165 (20 August 1966): 1378-1379;

Hunter Davis, "Rip Van Rhys," *Sunday Times* (Atticus), 6 November 1966, p. 13;

Louis James, "Unconquerable Spirit," in *Essays in West Indian Literature,* edited by James (London: Oxford University Press, 1968), pp. 11-23;

Elgin Mellown, "Character and Theme in the Novels of Jean Rhys," *Contemporary Literature,* 13 (1972): 458-472;

Rosalind Miles, *The Fiction of Sex* (New York: Barnes & Noble, 1974), pp. 96-106;

Arthur Mizener, *The Saddest Story: A Biography of Ford Madox Ford* (New York: World, 1971), pp. 346-350;

Ellen Moers, *Literary Women* (Garden City: Doubleday, 1976);

Elaine Showalter, *A Literature of Their Own* (Princeton: Princeton University Press, 1977);

Thomas F. Staley, *Jean Rhys: A Critical Study* (London: Macmillan, 1979; Austin: University of Texas Press, 1979);

Michael Thorpe, " 'The Other Side': *Wide Sargasso Sea* and *Jane Eyre,*" *Ariel,* 8 (July 1977): 99-110;

Selma Vaz Dias, "In Quest of a Missing Author," *Radio Times,* 3 May 1957, p. 25;

Peter Wolfe, *Jean Rhys* (Boston: Twayne, 1980);

Francis Wyndham, "Introduction to Jean Rhys," *London Magazine,* 7 (January 1960): 15-18.

Papers:

The largest collection of Rhys's papers is at the University of Tulsa.

Dorothy M. Richardson

Gloria G. Fromm
University of Illinois at Chicago

BIRTH: Abingdon, Berkshire, 17 May 1873, to Charles and Mary Taylor Richardson.

MARRIAGE: 29 August 1917 to Alan Elsden Odle.

DEATH: Beckenham, Kent, 17 June 1957.

BOOKS: *The Quakers, Past and Present* (London: Constable, 1914; New York: Dodge, 1914);
Gleanings from the Works of George Fox (London: Headley, 1914);
Pointed Roofs (London: Duckworth, 1915; New York: Knopf, 1916);
Backwater (London: Duckworth, 1916; New York: Knopf, 1917);
Honeycomb (London: Duckworth, 1917; New York: Knopf, 1919);
The Tunnel (London: Duckworth, 1919; New York: Knopf, 1919);
Interim (London: Duckworth, 1919; New York: Knopf, 1920);
Deadlock (London: Duckworth, 1921; New York: Knopf, 1921);
Revolving Lights (London: Duckworth, 1923; New York: Knopf, 1923);
The Trap (London: Duckworth, 1925; New York: Knopf, 1925);
Oberland (London: Duckworth, 1927; New York: Knopf, 1928);
John Austen and the Inseparables (London: Jackson, 1930);
Dawn's Left Hand (London: Duckworth, 1931);
Clear Horizon (London: Dent & Cresset, 1935);
Pilgrimage, 4 volumes (London: Dent & Cresset, 1938; New York: Knopf, 1938)—includes *Dimple Hill*;
Pilgrimage, 4 volumes (London: Dent, 1967; New York: Knopf, 1967)—includes *March Moonlight*.

OTHER: "A few facts for you. . . ," in *Sylvia Beach (1887-1962)* (Paris: Mercure de France, 1963): 127-128.

TRANSLATIONS: Dr. Paul Carton, *Consumption Doomed*, Healthy Life Booklets, volume 7,

Dorothy Richardson, 1917

translated with a preface by Richardson (London: Daniel, 1913);
Carton, *Some Popular Foodstuffs Exposed*, Healthy Life Booklets, volume 11, translated with a preface by Richardson (London: Daniel, 1913);
Dr. Gustav Krüger, *Man's Best Food* (London: Daniel, 1914);
Karl von Schumacher, *The Dubarry* (London: Harrap, 1932);
Robert Neumann, *Mammon* (London: Davies, 1933);
Leon Pierre-Quint, *André Gide: His Life and His Works* (London: Cape, 1934);
Josef Kastein, *Jews in Germany*, translated with a foreword by Richardson (London: Cresset, 1934);

Robert de Traz, *Silent Hours* (London: Bell, 1934).

PERIODICAL PUBLICATIONS:
Fiction:
"Sunday," *Art & Letters,* new series 2 (Summer 1919): 113-115;

"Christmas Eve," *Art & Letters,* 3 (Winter 1920): 32-35;

"Death," *Weekly Westminster,* new series 1 (9 February 1924), reprinted in *Best British Stories of 1924,* edited by Edward J. O'Brien and John Cournos (Boston: Small, Maynard, 1924): 218-220;

"Ordeal," *Window,* 1 (October 1930); reprinted in *Best British Short Stories of 1931,* edited by O'Brien (Boston: Small, Maynard, 1931): 183-189;

"Beginnings: A Brief Sketch," in *Ten Contemporaries: Notes Toward Their Definitive Bibliography,* second series, edited by John Gawsworth (Terence Armstrong) (London: Joiner & Steele, 1933): pp. 195-198;

"Nook on Parnassus," *Life and Letters To-Day,* 13 (December 1935): 84-88;

"Tryst," *English Story,* second series (1941): 69-73;

"Haven," *Life and Letters To-Day,* 42 (August 1944): 97-105;

"Excursion," *English Story,* sixth series (1945): 107-112;

"Visitor," *Life and Letters,* 46 (September 1945): 167-172;

"Visit," *Life and Letters,* 46 (September 1945): 173-181;

"A Stranger About," *English Story,* ninth series (1949): 90-94.

Nonfiction:
"The Reality of Feminism," *Ploughshare,* new series 2 (September 1917): 241-246;

"Women in the Arts: Some Notes on the Eternally Conflicting Demands of Humanity and Art," *Vanity Fair,* 24 (May 1925): 47;

"Adventure for Readers," *Life and Letters To-Day,* 22 (July 1939): 45-52;

"Novels," *Life and Letters,* 56 (March 1948): 188-192;

"Seven Letters from Dorothy M. Richardson," edited by Joseph Prescott, *Yale University Library Gazette,* 33 (January 1959): 102-111;

"Data for Spanish Publisher," edited by Joseph Prescott, *London Magazine,* 6 (June 1959): 14-19.

Dorothy Richardson belongs among those singular novelists who do not fall easily into ready-made categories and who, because they are so resis-tant to labels, enjoy a relatively short-lived vogue as "originals"—often during their own lifetimes—and then become the property of literary historians, slipping out of range of the nonplussed critics.

The literary historians have credited Dorothy Richardson with being the first practitioner in English, if not the originator, of the stream-of-consciousness novel, a label for the novel which she herself rejected as imprecise and which, when applied to her own major work, the novels finally published together as *Pilgrimage,* had the effect of reducing it to a pale version of the more flamboyantly brilliant experimental fiction of her Irish contemporary James Joyce. The other writers with whom she was linked—Virginia Woolf and Marcel Proust—shared, with Richardson and Joyce, certain literary aims. They, too, not only looked for ways to render in fiction the very texture of consciousness but were also engaged in revolutionizing the subject matter of the novel, which in their hands was turning into consciousness itself—both as psychological process and content.

These four writers are acknowledged as the important experimentalists in early modernist prose fiction, but their critical reputations, for historically and culturally significant reasons, differ markedly. While the rank and estimate of Proust and Joyce have suffered the least fluctuation, Virginia Woolf's place in the literary pantheon has shifted radically since her death in 1941. Considered during the 1950s and 1960s as a gifted but precious and mannered minor writer, not until the 1970s did she achieve major status. Dorothy Richardson's position has remained consistently ambiguous. She was long regarded principally as a major innovator who had indeed invented a form but lacked the rich literary language that characterized the prose of her contemporaries. It is now possible to see that she presents to readers and critics profounder difficulties than any of the others, with the nature of these difficulties gradually coming to light through the action of the very same cultural forces involved in the revaluation of Virginia Woolf.

Woolf's gain in stature coincided with the fresh interest in women writers during the 1960s and 1970s, but it was not the result of any revision of esthetic criteria. Quite the contrary. Woolf was admitted into the company of the master prose stylists of the late nineteenth century—Henry James, John Ruskin, Walter Pater, Oscar Wilde, Robert Louis Stevenson—and with her highly developed political sense of herself as a disadvantaged woman in a family with strong literary and intellectual traditions, she became a potent feminist icon. Dorothy Richardson has not, in turn, been taken up by any special group, nor have the novels that constitute *Pilgrimage* been subjected, like Virginia Woolf's, to exhaustive literary analysis, in large measure because unlike Woolf's or Joyce's or Proust's novels, Dorothy Richardson's are sui generis in their materials as well as their form. Despite the fact that she has always had her share of distinguished admirers, even they have been hard pressed to find the language that would convey in general terms their particular, highly individualized, often personal response to her novelistic tones. John Cowper Powys, for example, writing about her in 1931, insisted she was a "Pythian soothsayer." He was trying to describe the special quality of the narrative presence she projected in *Pilgrimage*, ten volumes of which had by then appeared. Indeed, in his view, the creator of this large work taking shape over the years would deserve a place among the great writers of the Western world. While such praise may seem extravagant, it testifies nonetheless to a significant cultural phenomenon too often overlooked by students of literature—that the ears of a few readers are attuned to a different music, not heard by the rest of their generation.

The fact that Dorothy Richardson had set out to give her life an esthetic shape and character, to mythologize it, did not become evident immediately, largely because she did not wish it to be known. More important to her was *Pilgrimage* itself as a vessel of a woman's consciousness, from its first stirrings to an approximation of self-sufficiency. Hence very little was known about Dorothy Richardson as historical person until after her death in 1957 at the age of eighty-four, when she had already witnessed the failure of several generations of readers to extract from *Pilgrimage* what she had spent a lifetime putting into it.

Forty years old when she began to write *Pilgrimage,* she spent the rest of her life at work on it, a series of books about herself as Miriam Henderson from seventeen to forty. Every year—or two, or three—another chapter-volume appeared; and the distance in time grew between the writing self and the fictional self, between the events as they had actually occurred and her memory of them. Over the years, then, *Pilgrimage* developed into a complex, many-layered autobiographical fiction; yet the majority of its readers—unaware of its basis in fact—responded to Miriam Henderson as a character in a serial novel, more interesting initially for the method by which she was presented than in herself.

While Dorothy Richardson wanted *Pilgrimage* to be read as a novel, she was also convinced of the importance and value of her experience as a woman: it was *this* story she had committed herself to telling, in detail and with extraordinary faithfulness to states of mind and feeling. And it was precisely this story that met with the most resistance. Why she undertook to tell it in the first place, and why she devoted more than forty years—the second half of her life—to a work that remained, in the eyes of the world, unfinished, can be partially answered by her life history, the main outlines of which can be traced in *Pilgrimage* and confirmed in the records. Dorothy Richardson did not reveal very much about herself outside of her novel; she thought she had said quite enough inside it, and facts struck her as the least important data. But by means of various source-materials—her own letters and published statements as well as the testimony of relatives and friends—her life and personal history have been authoritatively reconstructed.

It is significant that Dorothy Miller Richardson grew up in the last quarter of Victoria's reign, served her apprenticeship as a writer in the decade known as Edwardian, and won a place for herself among the moderns. Just as all three eras are intertwined in her fiction, so in her life different worlds overlap and even blend indistinguishably; separate periods of time merge; fiction and fact are indivisible. Indeed, hybrids figure early in her life. She was the child of a man who tried to erase his past and establish a new identity for himself and his family, who had the instincts and the tastes of a member of the leisured class and the heritage of a tradesman. Dorothy was his third daughter, a disappointment at first—by her own account—because she was not a boy but soon tempting him by her behavior to refer to her as his "son." Shortly after the birth of a fourth daughter—his last child—Charles Richardson was enabled to turn his back on his tradesman past. His own father had built up a flourishing business in wines and provisions, and when he died in January 1874 Charles sold his inheritance in order to remove completely the taint of "trade" and set himself up as a gentleman.

Along with the family tradition in trade, Dorothy Richardson's father also rejected his family's nonconformism in religion. Most of the Richardsons in the Berkshire area where Dorothy was born appear to have been Baptists, but Charles Richardson took his wife and daughters to Anglican services in St. Helen's, the beautiful old church in Abingdon on the bank of the river Ock. Charles had

The class of 1890 at Miss Sandell's school, Putney. Dorothy Richardson is in the back row, far right; standing next to her is Amy Catherine Robbins, who later married H. G. Wells.

been married as an Anglican in 1866, in the tiny Somerset village of East Coker, the home of his bride, Mary Miller Taylor. Her family, however, was not Anglican by tradition, several members— including the sixteen-year-old Mary—having joined the church some years before.

Dorothy Richardson commented often on the differences—both temperamental and physical— between the two families. She described the Taylors, who were of West-country yeoman stock, as round-cheeked, ruddy, easygoing, prolific: her Taylor grandmother, she noted with astonishment, was one of twenty-two children; and her mother, she claimed, thought that life ought to be "jolly." The Richardsons, by contrast, were introspective and dour, tall, thin, bony. Charles, moreover, was an only son with but a single sister.

His marriage to Mary Taylor did not fare well. By all accounts, he was too exacting and domineering, more interested in culture and things of the mind than she—as well as more skeptical—and his young wife gradually withered beneath the burden

of her husband's patronizing, ironical manner. He was also investing his money unwisely, and the gentlemanly life so important to him became more and more precarious. When Dorothy was eight, Charles Richardson moved his family—mainly for economic reasons, it would appear—from idyllic Abingdon and the large comfortable house with the walled garden she never forgot to Worthington on the Sussex coast, which she remembered ever after, in all its aspects—from the rented house and the village school to the rough Channel sea—with utter loathing. These are strong feelings; and they suggest that Worthing was linked with more than mere unpleasantness, indeed that along with an evident need to economize the move was also occasioned by the first clear signs of Mary Richardson's unstable health. Coast air was routinely recommended for nervous ailments such as she seemed to suffer from, and at least twice more the same prescription would be followed, the second time with disastrous results.

Whether Mary Richardson's health improved in Worthing or not, her husband's fortunes took a decided turn for the better, and in the spring of 1883 the family settled into its most luxurious quarters—an imposing brick house in the fashionable London suburb of Putney, with easy access for Charles not only to his banker and stockbroker in the city but also to the music and art he craved. For six years the new Putney establishment prospered. The Richardson girls led middle-class suburban lives, boating on the Thames, playing lawn tennis outdoors and musical instruments in the drawing room, attending a school "for the daughters of gentlemen," and assuming that all this would be followed, in due course, by four appropriate marriages.

Dorothy and her younger sister Jessie were enrolled in a school in which both the curriculum and the teachers were relatively advanced for the time, where modern psychology, literature, and music were not minimized, and where girls were taken seriously as students. It was the only formal education Dorothy Richardson would have, for by the time she entered her last year at the Putney school, Charles Richardson had begun to suffer the financial reverses that would lead eventually to bankruptcy. To this situation she responded by secretly answering an advertisement in the *Times* for a pupil-teacher in a school in Hanover, Germany. Only when she had been offered the post and accepted it did she tell her family. For a seventeen-year-old girl in 1890, whose only accomplishments were a decided gift for playing the piano and a facility with languages, such an act required considerably more than courage. It bespoke an exceedingly strong will and a determination to direct her own life. Even when she returned from Hanover after six months and the expected bankruptcy of her father had not yet occurred, she did not remain at home. Her eldest and youngest sisters—Kate and Jessie—were engaged to be married; her older sister had taken a position as governess in a wealthy Wiltshire family; and Dorothy found a job teaching in a school in North London.

The experience in Germany, where everything breathed poetry and music, had been magical, but in North London life seemed gray and dreary. The little girls she taught, mostly from working-class families edging into the lower middle class, had only grayness to look forward to, no matter what they learned from her; and she could not bring herself to remain here for longer than a year and a half. But this time, the spring of 1895, her father was declared a bankrupt, the family possessions were sold at public auction, and the Putney household broken up at last. And toward the end of

In 1891 Richardson spent six months as a pupil-teacher at Fraulein Lily Pabst's school in Hanover, which later became the setting for her first novel

the year Mary Richardson killed herself, a victim of untreated, little-understood, classic depression.

Throughout 1895, in which the weddings of her two daughters took place as well as her husband's financial failure, Mary Richardson had grown steadily worse. In the autumn it was decided that the remedy of coast air should be applied again. Dorothy, who had taken a job as governess in a suburban family, was appointed to accompany her mother to Hastings. But the illness had progressed too far and the treatment was too genteel. One day, when Dorothy left their boardinghouse for a brief outing alone, her mother cut her throat with a kitchen knife. She was fifty-two years old; her daughter was twenty-two.

After her mother's death, her father went to live with his eldest daughter, Kate, and Dorothy took a job in London. She joined the ranks of London's "new women" who were emerging from the nineteenth century—not fully grown like Athena

The sitting room at the Harley Street dentists' offices where Dorothy Richardson went to work in 1896

from the head of Zeus, but more like a chrysalis from which either a moth or a butterfly might come. Freedom was what she had looked to London for—freedom from the burden of her mother's death and her father's guilt, freedom to follow up the instincts that had sent her to Hanover in the first place. She was interested, above all, in herself— that unmistakably English person with weak eyes and a perfect ear, who thought it simply extraordinary that anything whatever should exist, much less that she should be there to perceive it.

She lived in London on the modest salary of £1 a week, earned as a secretary-receptionist in the Harley Street offices of three dentists. Her room of her own was the attic of a boardinghouse on the fringe of Bloomsbury, but the whole of London was her home and soon her university as well. She described it as full of "secret societies" whose codes or language she wanted to learn. There were the Tolstoy Society, for instance, and the "simple-lifers," the vegetarians, the Fabian Socialists, the anarchists. And tutors appeared almost at once—among them

the young H. G. Wells, soon to marry (as his second wife) a former Putney schoolmate of Dorothy Richardson. He was also about to become famous. Already the author of *The Time Machine* and *The Wheels of Chance,* he would make a name for himself—and a fortune—with a brilliant series of "scientific romances" and realistic novels. When Dorothy met him, he was just thirty years old, already dogmatic, assertive, brash but also stimulating and challenging. With a scientific education as well as a remarkable facility with words and ideas, he was a formidable opponent in an argument. He was also the first writer she had ever met. Under his influence and tutelage during the next few years, she began to regard all her experiences—from her daily routine in the Harley Street dental surgery to a lecture on Dante and a roll and butter or an egg at an inexpensive restaurant—as more than nourishment for the developing self in which she placed such great store. Describing some of the things she did and saw to Wells, and noting with surprise that he not only liked her formulations but even praised her sharp eye, she found the link between self-expression and narration, indeed between interest in the self and the literary uses to which it might be put.

Over the years, as intellectual, social and literary attitudes formed, her life in London became an intricate network of relationships. Involved with Wells, with a Russian Jew named Benjamin Grad, who lived in her Bloomsbury boardinghouse and wanted to marry her, with a young woman-activist named Veronica Leslie-Jones, who wanted a soulmate, with medical men, editors, journalists, psychologists, she gradually realized that to preserve her precious independence she would have to cut loose. While this realization took shape, she was serving her apprenticeship as a writer, contributing reviews and essays to an unconventional monthly edited by one of her friends, Charles Daniel. These began to appear in 1906 on a range of subjects from Walt Whitman to the House of Lords. They indicate how widely and seriously she had been reading and forming opinions for ten years—about American literature and German philosophy as well as English politics and economic theory.

In 1908 she resigned her Harley Street position, having decided it was time to leave London, too, time to cut certain personal ties that threatened to bind. She and Wells had become lovers; there was a pregnancy and a miscarriage, a trip to Switzerland to recover, a need for still more time and solitude. Through her friend Benjamin Grad, she found the perfect retreat—a farm in Sussex, near Hailsham and Hurstmonceaux, run by a Quaker family. For the better part of the next three years, this was where she lived, among people from whom valuable lessons would be learned.

In the book she eventually wrote about the Quakers, the sources of their attraction for her are plain: their affirmative attitude to life, their belief in "the possibility here and now of complete freedom from sin," and their recognition of the "spiritual identity" of a woman. But perhaps most important of all, the Quakers seemed to her to be searching always for the "center of being" where one might remain, remote and impersonal, and yet "see freshly all the time." This was where she herself wanted to be, and in the process of finding her own way, she evolved a technique for art.

This technique can be traced through the sketches she had begun to write for the *Saturday Review*, descriptive pieces (called "middles") that appeared between 1908 and 1912 and allowed her to try out different means by which to establish a relationship with the reader. Already in some of her

reviews and essays she had created dramas and dialogues to draw in her readers. Now she began to experiment with more subtle effects, how to achieve both distance and closeness at the same time, implicating her reader by conveying a sense of immediacy, a sense of the experience taking place in the present, yet functioning as the agent of transmission. From the start, then, her creative impulse was autobiographical: to write of what she knew, as the person who knew, at the very moment of knowing.

Another significant characteristic of these sketches for the *Saturday Review* is the part that memory (or the past) played in them. One can see her testing her memory—by writing with vivid and sensuous detail about certain places (Vaud, in Switzerland, for one, and later Sussex) after she had left them, as if to prove, among other things, that the past—recalled—could have an even greater reality than the present. Paving the way to *Pilgrimage,* the majority of these sketches were written between 1909 and 1912. In 1911 she began to make use of her own experience in yet another form: essays about various aspects of dentistry, which appeared in the journal of the profession, the *Dental Record.* In fact, from 1915 to 1919, when the early volumes of *Pilgrimage* were already coming out, she also contributed an unsigned column, "Comments by a Layman." The "Layman" was apparently free to discuss any subject at all, so long as it could be brought into some relation to dentistry, which meant that she had the opportunity to air her latest views as well as to make capital of her years in Harley Street.

She had been living by her pen and her wits since resigning from the Harley Street position. By 1911 she was also ready to leave the Sussex farm; and for the next few years she made her home with one friend or another, with J. D. Beresford, for instance, whom she had recently met. Beresford provided her with the example of a man who supported himself and his wife solely by writing. He also introduced her to Cornwall, where one could live cheaply indeed. Here, on the southwest coast of England, more inaccessible in those days before automobiles and train service were taken for granted, writers and artists seeking remoteness, privacy, and economy rented rooms or cottages from the local inhabitants. Dorothy Richardson's first experience of Cornwall was in the fishing village of St. Ives, during the spring of 1912, where the Beresfords had rented a bungalow "with its knees on the rocks," she said. Beginning in summer, the Beresfords planned a stay further down the coast, in the less frequented, less picturesque

Padstow area. For £12 a year they had rented a stone cottage that was once a chapel and now belonged to a local farmer. It was in the tiny hamlet of Trehemborne, between Porthcothan Bay and St. Merryn, with a cottage next door, the farm across the road and another up the road. After spending the summer here with the Beresfords, Dorothy Richardson remained alone in the cottage for the winter. She and Beresford had agreed that in order to write the novel she had in mind she needed to be by herself.

The novel existed in a mass of false starts and discarded versions. Urged on by Beresford, by Wells, by the editors of the *Saturday Review*, she had not yet found the right way to present the only material that interested her and that she felt she knew—her own life. But in Cornwall, in the converted chapel she claimed was haunted, where her solitude was very nearly complete and the rest of the world "dropped away," yet everything took on a "terrific intensity," she had her vision. The girl named Miriam, the heroine of her novel who was also herself, had to meet her experience directly, without intermediary, without an author speaking for her. This would be the method of *Pilgrimage*—

the narrative seeming to proceed from a developing consciousness as the center of the novel's being.

She had learned the lesson of the Quakers and the lesson of her own experience but also—as *Pilgrimage* itself would testify—the lesson of Henry James in *The Ambassadors*. She had understood his use of point of view and had called it "the first completely satisfying way of writing a novel." Now in writing *Pilgrimage* as a third-person narrative that was nevertheless about herself and also had the effect of an inside story told in the first person, she demonstrated how thoroughly these lessons had been learned as well as the use to which they were being put. Her impersonal narrative, like discovery about oneself, would be highly personal, too; it would have both an objective existence and a subjective identity. Furthermore this subjective identity carried along with it the conviction on Dorothy Richardson's part that the sensibility—or consciousness—of her youthful heroine had an intrinsic value and interest. So she would not argue, she would not explain, she would not justify; rather she would present that sensibility in more and more detail, charting its education in the world at large as well as in the recesses of the psyche. *Pilgrimage* was

Mr. and Mrs. J. D. Beresford, a servant, and Dorothy Richardson outside the cottage in Trehemborne where Richardson wrote Pointed Roofs

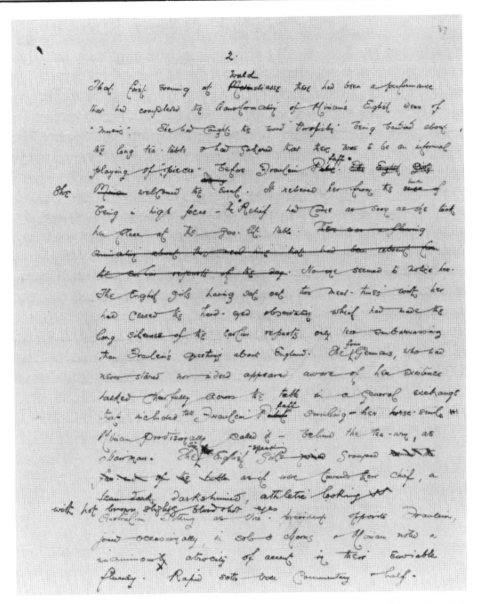

Page from the manuscript for Pointed Roofs *(Beinecke Rare Book and Manuscript Library, Yale University)*

to be, then, a historical document, a revolutionary fiction, and a philosophical statement about herself as a woman.

Pointed Roofs, the first volume of *Pilgrimage,* was finished by 1913 but not published until 1915, after Edward Garnett, reading for the publishing house of Gerald Duckworth, had recommended it. Dorothy Richardson was living in London again, in one of the residential districts frequented by artists and known as St. John's Wood. She had come here with the manuscript of her novel, aware that it was just the start of a large work for which she would need both time and support. Already, before beginning the second volume of *Pilgrimage,* she had con-

tracted to write a book about the Quakers and to put together an anthology from the works of the founder of the sect, George Fox. In addition, her editor-friend Charles Daniel, who was now publishing a magazine called *The Healthy Life* as well as a companion series of booklets, agreed to her proposal to translate for the series two French essays: Dr. Paul Carton's "Some Popular Foodstuffs Exposed" and "Consumption Doomed." Daniel also published her translation from the German of Dr. Gustav Krüger's *Man's Best Food.* All three of these appeared in 1913 and 1914.

Her two books about the Quakers were published in 1914, the second (*Gleanings from the Works of George Fox*) just three months before the outbreak of war in August. By the following September, when *Pointed Roofs* appeared and the hoped-for Allied victory had not materialized, such a novel as this one was bound to strike some impatient readers as belonging to a nineteenth-century world that had no relation to the present. But it also struck others not only as a most original book but also as remarkably fresh and radiant. In fact, the first reviewer (in the Sunday *Observer*) praised the book for its clarity and charm even though it "somehow read . . . as if the reader did not exist." He meant by this that allusions were not explained and information was not provided in the customary way, by a helpful author; yet he had not found this troubling, nor did the novel seem at all obscure. In contrast, the reviewer in the *Saturday Review* found *Pointed Roofs* full of "fevered fantasies," with evidence on every page of an "unsound mind" and a "sick imagination."

Such extremes of response would characterize the reviews of each volume of *Pilgrimage*. For Dorothy Richardson was a disconcerting writer, and *Pointed Roofs* a deceptively simple book that seemed straightforward in manner, yet did not add up in the familiar traditional ways. What was its subject? Or its point of view? Why, in spite of the girlish heroine and her inevitably feminine outlook, did the attitude toward women expressed in the novel seem hostile? In this context, how was one to understand the heroine's humiliating encounters with Hanover men and her loathing of the "masculine culture" of the Fatherland?

These were some of the questions *Pointed Roofs* raised without seeming to provide any answers. The truth was that the answers lay in the emotional experience and the cultural education of an autobiographical heroine who represented, at the same time, a generation and a class of women. She would grow up, in the course of *Pilgrimage*, to become its author, but in *Pointed Roofs* her future was painfully unclear. Indeed, she was also just beginning to make sense of her past.

One of the most remarkable qualities of *Pointed Roofs* was its fidelity to Dorothy Richardson's own experience as a seventeen-year-old girl in Hanover. Nearly forty, she had felt her way back to the anxious household in Putney and her own resolve to escape, to the foreign world of Hanover which had simultaneously enchanted and repelled her. She was able to recreate this experience for others because she virtually relived it for herself. One can see, in the manuscript of *Pointed Roofs* (the first draft and the revisions) that Dorothy Richard-son had almost total recall but also that it involved the senses even more than the mind. Indeed, when it is compared with the printed text, the manuscript shows that she first recorded, in their raw state and as she experienced them again, the inchoate feelings of the seventeen-year-old girl. Then, in the act of revision, she gave form to these feelings without refining (or falsifying) them, the author thus imposing her own maturity invisibly, in the service of art.

She had found the way to be someone else and herself at the same time, as well as how to live in both the past and the present at once. Committed to a multivolume, multilayered fiction that would establish her literary identity, she began to lead, in effect, two lives—one in the present and another life in *Pilgrimage* that conformed to her own youth and restored it to her. By the time *Backwater*, the second volume of *Pilgrimage*, appeared in 1916, Dorothy Richardson's name was beginning to be heard in advanced circles. In the famous Café Royal on Regent Street, for example, where artists and writers continued to congregate evenings in spite of the war, Dorothy Richardson's novel was one of the subjects of discussion among the habitués. One of these "regulars" was Alan Odle, illustrator of an edition of Oscar Wilde's poem *The Sphinx* and art-editor of *The Gypsy*, a magazine whose first issue had appeared in May 1915, during the first full year of the war, with a foreword that militantly declared the importance of Art over "the fate of nations."

Odle had been living for several years in St. John's Wood at 32 Queen's Terrace. This was the house into which Dorothy Richardson moved during the summer of 1915. She had an attic room, Alan Odle a studio bedroom; and all the tenants who wished to do so ate their breakfast in the basement. Alan Odle began to join them when the early closing of the Café Royal's Domino Room altered his daily routine. Instead of going to bed at breakfast time, he found himself talking about literature to Dorothy Richardson, whose name he had heard in the Café Royal. She, in turn, had known him only as the gentleman-artist in the house who kept unconventional hours and produced grotesque drawings.

Although his appearance was as strange as his pictures—he was extraordinarily tall and thin, with long hair wound about his head—his manners were exquisite and his literary tastes cultivated. Art, moreover, was the passion of his life. When Dorothy Richardson met him in 1915 he was twenty-seven years old and had been on his own in London for about six years, getting a small allowance from his banker-father in Kent and undermin-

Portrait of Alan Odle *by Ivy de Verley*

ing his not-too-sound constitution by drinking too much absinthe in the Café Royal. Even to the casual observer, he did not seem destined for old age and a long life. One had only to observe him for a short time to gather that survival meant nothing to him, that he would not lift a finger in his own material behalf. Dorothy Richardson saw this almost at once, and she found it confirmed as little by little she learned of his material circumstances, his history, and his uncompromising nature.

From an early age he had decided that Art mattered more to him than anything else and that those people to whom it did not matter at all were simply not worth his attention. He had also made it plain to his scandalized businessman-father that drawing for its own sake was his principal aim in life; furthermore that art supplies took precedence over food or clothing: hence, the monthly allowance. But absinthe cost money, too, and when Dorothy Richardson met Alan Odle, his shoes were thinly soled; his coat was in tatters; he had a chronic cough and complained of neuralgic pains.

During the winter of 1916-1917, his health was poor enough for her to suggest more than once

that he see a doctor, but he counted on being well again in the spring. Instead of relief, however, spring brought the notice that he was being conscripted into the army. When the time came for him to report, Dorothy Richardson was out of London, staying with the Beresfords in Cornwall and finishing the third volume of *Pilgrimage: Honeycomb*. Alan Odle wrote her regularly from London, still addressing her as "Miss Richardson" and reporting on the zeppelin raids then taking place with some regularity as well as on his own private affairs. He described the circumstances surrounding his appearance before the physical examiners, who finally pronounced him—not surprisingly—tubercular and who succeeded in frightening him into consulting a specialist. These letters make it abundantly clear that despite the lingering, formal mode of address, their relationship was not casual. He reported to her the inconclusive findings of the specialist—though the x-rays failed to show any definite lesion in either lung, the doctor was convinced there was something wrong; and he had recommended a number of what Alan Odle labeled "expensive cures." On her way back to London by slow stages, for she was still working on *Honeycomb,* Dorothy Richardson tried to persuade Alan Odle to follow the specialist's advice. Apparently she did not succeed, for a month after her return to London (at the end of July) they were married at a local registry office. Alan Odle was twenty-nine years old, Dorothy Richardson forty-four, but she listed her age as thirty-seven.

At the time of her marriage in August 1917, Dorothy Richardson had completed the first three chapter-volumes of *Pilgrimage,* bringing her heroine to the point of her mother's death by her own hand. It was an event that Dorothy Richardson turned into fiction only with great difficulty. And as it happened, she was moving into a new phase of her novel and her life simultaneously. *Pointed Roofs, Backwater,* and *Honeycomb* form a thematic as well as chronological unit, in which Dorothy Richardson's fictionalized self crosses the shadowline (in Joseph Conrad's term) between youth and adulthood. Indeed, each novel describes a different stage in this transition, with the tone and the imagery delicately modulated to convey those differences. Thus, the setting of each novel is counterpointed with the mental and emotional state of the central character, producing a distinctively characterized atmosphere of the mind. Among the early reviewers of *Pilgrimage,* it was often students of the Imagist Movement or poets who heard these changes in register. Randolph Bourne, for example, reviewing *Honeycomb* in the American magazine the *Dial,* described it as an "imagist novel," marveled at its "precision," and felt that it contained "the essence of quivering youth." Not long after, the young poet Babette Deutsch commented on the qualities of Dorothy Richardson's prose that appealed to her and how certain passages reminded her of T. S. Eliot in the "sensitiveness of their rhythms." For her the method of *Pilgrimage* was that of the poet—realizing an emotion not by analysis but rather, as she put it, by "inducing its systole and diastole."

For others, like May Sinclair, Dorothy Richardson was one of the daring experimental novelists who were trying to capture consciousness in its flow. A novelist herself as well as a student of philosophy, May Sinclair borrowed from William James the term "stream of consciousness" and applied it to Dorothy Richardson's *Pilgrimage* in an essay published in both the *Little Review* and the *Egoist.* Sinclair's essay appeared in April 1918, the month after the *Little Review* began to carry installments of *Ulysses,* the strange new work by James Joyce that everybody was also talking about and comparing with *Pilgrimage.* By the middle of 1919,

the fifth volume of Dorothy Richardson's novel, *Interim,* was being serialized along with *Ulysses* in the pages of the *Little Review.*

The fourth volume, *The Tunnel,* had been published in February 1919, launching in her London life Miriam Henderson, the counterpart of Dorothy Richardson nearly a quarter of a century before. In the present, her new life with Alan Odle had begun to assume its own distinctive shape. A few months after they were married, Dorothy Richardson introduced Alan Odle to Cornwall, which he could not help but recognize as a draftsman's country with its crooked coastline, its ragged crumbling cliffs against a moving sky, and all the tops of the spare trees sharply angled by the constant driving wind. The West country soon became as important a place in Alan Odle's life as London. His wife's plan for them was to spend only summers in their Queen's Terrace rooms and the rest of the year in Cornwall, where not only were accommodations cheap but the climate was relatively mild. The West country had few extremes of temperature, making it better suited, in Dorothy Richardson's opinion, to the uncertain state of Alan Odle's health. For his part, the only concession he appears to have made to the doctors who suspected TB was to stop drinking.

It may well be, as Dorothy Richardson was to claim long after their marriage, that she did not expect him to live more than a few years at most. But his health steadily improved. In fact, despite his bohemian appearance and dissolute life-style he was ready to adopt entirely different habits and abide by them religiously. He lived—and worked —by established rules that were turned into ritual almost at once, for nothing mattered in itself except Art.

His own art would never bring him either fame or a livelihood. There were always admirers among fellow artists (John Austen, for example) and writers (H. G. Wells and John Cowper Powys), but a taste for Odle *was* rather special. His drawings were brilliantly grotesque, uncompromising in their view of human beings as insatiably greedy and gross: he was the ideal illustrator of Swift's *Gulliver's Travels,* Voltaire's *Candide,* and Mark Twain's scurrilous *1601.* In fact, his commission to illustrate *Candide* came about as a result of the first exhibition of his work in 1919, at which the drawings he had amassed for *Gulliver* were shown. There were other commissions through the years as well as a second exhibition in 1925 (with three other artists). Certain magazines (*The Golden Hind,* the *Studio, Vanity Fair*) usually took his work; but he himself once re-

"The Illness of Candide in Paris," one of Alan Odle's illustrations for an edition of Voltaire's Candide

marked that it was "a wonder" anything of his had been published at all.

During the 1920s, however, his career as well as Dorothy Richardson's seemed to flourish. Volumes of *Pilgrimage* came out regularly (*Deadlock* in 1921, *Revolving Lights* in 1923, *The Trap* in 1925, *Oberland* in 1927); Alan Odle worked on various sets of drawings; and they both contributed to periodicals, even appearing on occasion in the same issue of *Vanity Fair*. Their life together—in Cornwall from October to June and in London for the summer months—scarcely varied until 1923. In that year, under the influence and with the help of their new friend, Winifred Ellerman (who wrote under the pen name of Bryher), Dorothy Richardson arranged for them to spend several months abroad—from November until May 1924—mainly in Switzerland, where Alan Odle had never been. The impact on him of the Swiss mountains was as dramatic as she had expected, but the Swiss air affected his lungs and set him coughing for the first time since their marriage. They stayed out their time, nevertheless, and on the way back to England stopped in Paris for ten days. This was Bryher's

special gift—introducing them to literary life on the Left Bank.

Married at the time to Robert McAlmon, the expatriate writer and energetic editor, Bryher entertained the Odles by gathering a group of bright young Montparnassites at one of the famous Paris cafés. Ernest Hemingway and his first wife were among them, as well as Mary Butts, Cecil Maitland, and Mina Loy. The entire visit was a grand occasion, an opportunity they would never have again, and they explored as much of Paris as they could—wandering about in the Louvre and Notre Dame, browsing among the bookstalls, ambling through the Bois de Boulogne. Dorothy Richardson said they found at least five Parises and loved them all, including the Paris of the tourist. For both of them it was the high point of the decade.

They led, after all, quiet frugal lives on a small combined income carefully husbanded. At the end of each summer, when they left London for Cornwall, their Queen's Terrace rooms had to be rented for the sake of economy, and sometimes the summer tenants turned out badly—making off with books or drawings, leaving without paying the rent.

During the fall and winter months—from October to April or May—they rented for nominal sums a succession of bungalows in one or another of the bays in the Padstow area, some of them only primitively equipped but providing splendid vistas for an artist's eye and often complete privacy. Every spring they rejoined the world, going into lodgings in one of the village houses for a period of relief from housekeeping (four to six weeks, depending on the state of their finances) before taking up their summer residence in London. All of which meant three moves a year, yet throughout the 1920s (except for the trip abroad) they followed this pattern and seemed to thrive on it.

The four volumes of *Pilgrimage* published between 1921 and 1927 continued the account of Miriam Henderson's London life that had begun in the two volumes of 1919 (*The Tunnel* and *Interim*). Faithful to the general outlines of Dorothy Richardson's own life in her attic room on Endsleigh Street (which became Tansley Street in *Pilgrimage*) and as a secretary-receptionist in the dental surgery in Harley Street (Wimpole Street in the novels), they are nevertheless works of fiction rather than autobiography and should not be treated as fact. In other words, the recollection of her past and the fictional arrangement of it in *Pilgrimage* provide Dorothy Richardson's biographer with psychological data but not necessarily with physical or material facts. The truth of *Pilgrimage* lies in the internal consistency of it, however closely it may sometimes correspond to the externals of Dorothy Richardson's life. Curiously enough, the contemporary readers of *Pilgrimage* scarcely questioned its fictive nature, responding as the author seemed to expect. Little was known about her. She did not grant an interview until 1931, and so few photographs of her existed that along with a review of *Oberland* in the *New York Times Book Review* the wrong likeness was printed. As it happened, an American writer had the same name, and a book by her, *The Book of Blanche*, was actually listed as the English Dorothy Richardson's in a biographical dictionary published in 1942, where the same incorrect photograph was also reprinted. Her features were not, like Arnold Bennett's, familiar to large numbers of readers, yet her name was on many lips throughout the 1920s.

Pilgrimage was vilified and praised in equal measure—vilified for seeming to be endless and static, praised for the very detail and precision that made it seem to stand still. There is no question that time moves slowly in these chapters of Miriam Henderson's introspective life. She finds a niche for herself in Mrs. Bailey's Bloomsbury house and among the dental surgeons in the West End; and in both *The Tunnel* and *Interim* she registers her feeling response to the "incomparable" city of London. Indeed, London virtually becomes a living character in all the novels that take place there. By the time of *Deadlock*, published in 1921, Miriam has not only settled into her beloved London but also established key relationships that will mold her experiences and educate her sensibility. Charting that education in the late-Victorian and Edwardian world in which she herself grew up was, after all, one of Richardson's principal aims in writing *Pilgrimage*. Its autobiographical basis, however, did not need to be known. She rightly felt that *Pilgrimage* had both integrity and coherence as fiction.

It had uniqueness as well. There was nothing like *Pilgrimage* in English literature, and periodically Dorothy Richardson's anomalous work—growing larger all the time—was accounted for in a slightly different way. If it were not exactly Proustian or Joycean, then perhaps it was Balzacian or Goethean. Virginia Woolf even suggested that Richardson had invented a new kind of prose sentence with a feminine gender. No one has associated *Pilgrimage* with Tanizaki's great novel of the forties, *The Makioka Sisters*, which celebrates ordinariness and the intimate minute details of daily life; yet the Japanese themselves discovered Dorothy Richardson, publishing a translation of *Pointed Roofs* in 1934.

At the same time, despite its author's evident wish that *Pilgrimage* be read only as a novel, there is a fascinating blend discernible—especially in the novels published during the 1920s—of fact and fiction, of historical and fictional reality. In *The Trap*, for example, which Dorothy Richardson worked on in Switzerland during her stay there in the winter of 1923-24, the stage is set for Miriam's first trip to the Alps, where the action of the next volume, *Oberland*, would take place. In fact, Miriam's involvement with Hypo Wilson takes up a good portion of *The Trap* while Dorothy Richardson is engaged in proofreading for Wilson's original, H. G. Wells. And in *The Trap*, to add to the already complicated blend, Richardson introduces—at a party sponsored by the Lycurgans, who are really the Fabians—Wells himself (along with George Bernard Shaw) as well as a recurrent character in several of his novels, Wilkins the author. In the midst of all this, Hypo Wilson's role in the novel continues unchanged. One is reminded of Christopher Isherwood's modulations of autobiography and fiction throughout his own writing life.

Oberland, nominated for the French Femina-Vie-Heureuse prize in 1928, signaled a shift in Miriam Henderson's London life. In the way that Dorothy Richardson had gone to Switzerland years before because of her uncertain health, Miriam takes a holiday in the Bernese Oberland with the understanding that on her return to London she will have decided whether to enter into an affair with Hypo Wilson. The interlude in the Oberland, then, is also a prelude to sex: and Miriam—never altogether free of the sense of Hypo Wilson—finds herself in a curiously suggestive atmosphere, where snow and ice and music and a small child's erotic attachment to a grown man provide the background for Miriam's preoccupations. It is not surprising that so richly textured a book as *Oberland* should have been the occasion for the American poet Conrad Aiken (who would produce his own strange autobiographical work, *Ushant*) to venture an assessment of *Pilgrimage* in the New York *Evening Post.*

Aiken suggested that *Pilgrimage* would earn for Dorothy Richardson "as precise and permanent a place in the history of literature as it is ever possible to predict for a living author." Yet, he went on to say, she was "curiously little known," and he offered as the most likely reason he could think of the exclusive presence in her novels of the mind of a woman. He himself had no objection to a feminine point of view per se, he claimed, but in Miriam's case (and by induction Dorothy Richardson's as well) he thought there was far too much "insistence on the superiority of her [own] mind—on its . . . richness and power and depth, as compared (frequently) with the minds of the men whom she meets." Without being certain how closely to identify author with character, Aiken tried to allow for the possibility that Dorothy Richardson had deliberately given her heroine unpleasant traits and was well aware, for example, how little Miriam really knew about men, but down deep he suspected Dorothy Richardson was as much of an "old maid" as Miriam Henderson and that to both of them "the whole dark, strange, horrible, fascinating, masculine mind remain[ed] an absolutely closed book."

Conrad Aiken did not know that Dorothy Richardson's heroine represented a version of herself nearly thirty years younger. At twenty-eight Dorothy Richardson thought she knew a great deal about life and men. Indeed, with the burden of her knowledge, she had lectured an amused H. G. Wells and had felt herself, as she approached thirty, climbing to the heights of the wisdom of middle age. But at fifty-five she was beginning to plumb the depths of middle age and the ironies of her youthful self-confidence.

After *Oberland* in 1927, Dorothy Richardson did not publish another volume of *Pilgrimage* until 1931. During this period she was still writing for periodicals (*Vanity Fair,* Charles Daniel's new magazine *Focus,* Bryher's film magazine *Close Up*) but also beginning to take up translation again as well as agreeing to contribute a foreword to a book about illustration by John Austen, one of Alan Odle's artist friends. The foreword, however, turned into a substantial essay which became her own small book, *John Austen and the Inseparables,* published in 1930. Although the Austen book had not been undertaken for money, there were financial difficulties in these years of the American Depression, so that when Harrap, the London publisher, asked her to translate a German monograph on the life of Madame Du Barry (the last mistress of Louis XV) she felt obliged to agree. Yet the volume of *Pilgrimage* promised to her own publisher, Duckworth, was not ready. The two books, however, *Dawn's Left Hand* and her translation for Harrap, appeared within a few months of each other, late in 1931 and early in 1932. About the same time, not only did the weekly *Everyman* print an interview with her, the first she had ever granted, but also the first book about her work appeared. It was by John Cowper Powys, already well-known as a writer and lecturer on literature, who had introduced himself to her in 1929 as an admirer of *Pilgrimage.*

Powys's *Dorothy M. Richardson* (1931), an extended essay full of praise for a novelist not sufficiently appreciated, in his opinion, and *Dawn's Left Hand* were both well-received, but Dorothy Richardson had not been able to persuade Duckworth to agree to slightly higher financial terms for her next novel, largely because over the years their advances to her exceeded their profits on the sale of her books. In fact, she owed Duckworth a considerable sum of money, a debt silently carried by the firm, but its existence cast a shadow on any negotiations Richardson attempted. In need of money, Dorothy Richardson felt she had no choice when, as a result of favorable reviews of her Du Barry, several more translations came her way. Between 1932 and 1934 she translated four books from French and German while also working on the next volume of *Pilgrimage.* The strain proved too great for her, and after the last translation (of Robert de Traz's *Les Heures de Silence*), in the fall of 1934, with only half of her *Pilgrimage* volume written, she fell seriously ill.

By then, however, she had come to know S. S.

Katherine Mansfield and S. S. Koteliansky, the reader-adviser for Cresset Press who arranged the 1935 publication of a four-volume edition of the first twelve parts of Pilgrimage

Koteliansky, a refugee from prerevolutionary Russia, who had made a place for himself in the London literary world through translations and collaborations as well as friendships—with D. H. Lawrence, for example, Katherine Mansfield, Middleton Murry, and Leonard Woolf. When Dorothy Richardson met him, he was serving as a reader-adviser for the newly formed Cresset Press. Koteliansky thought the time had come for a compact edition of *Pilgrimage,* bringing together the separately published chapter-volumes in an attractive, convenient format. He began to outline his plan to Dorothy Richardson late in 1933, but it was not until 1935 that anything came of it, for her illness (diagnosed as "acute neurasthenia") intervened.

Once she had recovered sufficiently to finish the eleventh volume of *Pilgrimage (Clear Horizon),* Koteliansky worked out a joint publishing agreement between the Cresset Press and J. M. Dent. *Clear Horizon* would appear separately, followed as soon as possible by a collected edition of all the novels, including the twelfth part, which Dorothy Richardson only gradually learned was expected to be the last. In other words, Dent and the Cresset Press planned to advertise their edition as the complete *Pilgrimage.* By the time Dorothy Richardson fully grasped the extent of their error it was too late for her to correct it.

The so-called "omnibus" edition of *Pilgrimage* in four volumes, which included *Dimple Hill* (pub-

lished for the first time) appeared late in 1938, when Europe was on the brink of war. The reviewers found that they were not reading a finished work, despite the advertisements, and some of them expressed irritation as well as confusion. Plainly, *Dimple Hill* was but another chapter in the life of Miriam Henderson, taking her into a new setting among Quakers in Sussex, exploring the qualities that seemed to set them apart and made them particularly attractive to a person like Miriam, who was bent on discovering and following the direction in which the inmost self, rather than another individual or group, would lead. In *Clear Horizon* she had freed herself from long-standing ties that by the time of *Dawn's Left Hand* (the novel preceding *Clear Horizon*) were threatening to overwhelm her. Interestingly enough, *Dawn's Left Hand* had been an unusually dramatic novel, filled with argument and dialogue, even containing a disquisition by Miriam on speech sounds. With the slate wiped clean, as it were, in *Clear Horizon, Dimple Hill* became a novel concerned with the nature of silence, with contemplative silence as a medium through which Quakers seemed able to approach themselves. Especially intriguing to Miriam was the impersonality Quakers managed to achieve, which she felt would provide her with a way to mediate between the demands of an importunate self and the desire to relate to others. It seemed to her that in learning from the Quakers the meaning of distance, she would also learn something about the nature of "human association."

A few critics, Richard Church among them, responded to the philosophic tones of *Dimple Hill* without quibbling over conventional endings or loose narrative structures, but Church himself had been involved in the publishing venture, representing Dent. Dorothy Richardson felt, with good reason, that *Pilgrimage* would only suffer from the misguided attempt to advertise the omnibus edition as a complete work.

Dorothy Richardson's life was bound up in her novel, and just when it seemed to her that events within the publishing world had conspired to close off *Pilgrimage* from potential readers, the world war threatened to ensure this result. She herself spent the war years immured in remote Cornwall. Realistically, it was the most sensible place for her to stay, especially since the London house in which she and Alan Odle had lived through so many summers was about to be torn down; but she was isolated more than ever from literary circles.

Distance and silence, rich subjects in *Dimple Hill*, took on new, ironic meanings for her between 1939 and 1945. Working on a successor to *Dimple Hill*, almost as if by force of habit, she was also finding it easier to get into touch with her child-self in the more distant past than with her older self projected as Miriam. Three short stories emerged about that child-self. Two of them were published in the magazine *Life and Letters* in 1945, to such favorable response that the editor asked Dorothy Richardson for more. At the end of the war she might well have seemed a new name in fiction. As a matter of fact, the last story she published, in the annual volume *English Story* (1949) was singled out as an example of the best work being done by current writers. Most ironic of all, when in 1946 the editor of *Life and Letters* published three installments of the thirteenth volume of *Pilgrimage* as "Work in Progress," very few readers were aware of the genealogy of these segments. The war had indeed changed the world.

Dorothy Richardson was seventy-two at the

Alan Odle and Dorothy Richardson in their Trevone cottage, painting by Adrian Allinson (collection of Thomas F. Staley)

end of the war, mindful that both she and Alan Odle preferred to remain in Cornwall rather than resume their annual trek to London. For the first time in years, they had something like a permanent home and it gave them an unexpected sense of security. Their quiet lives in the village of Trevone, near the bay and shops, were punctuated with letters and visits from friends. Alan Odle worked on a set of illustrations to Rabelais (never published), Dorothy Richardson on the thirteenth volume of *Pilgrimage* (not published, save for the excerpts in *Life and Letters*, until ten years after her death). When Alan Odle died suddenly in 1948, at the age of sixty, Dorothy Richardson stayed on in Cornwall, alone, until the early 1950s. The letters she wrote to friends and relatives in this last phase of her life seemed to matter more than *Pilgrimage*. They allowed her to express herself directly, to formulate intellectual positions and comment on the books she read. When her letters are published, they will surely round out the picture of Dorothy Richardson, revealing once and for all the coherence and integrity of a remarkable creative life that benefited and suffered in equal measure from spanning three distinctive periods of literary history.

When she died in 1957, in a nursing home near London, the world around her was still in its postwar state, with angry young men dominating the literary scene and angry young women waiting in the wings. Dorothy Richardson seemed, in such a scene, far too tame, her sensibility too Victorian and her style early-modern rather than high-modernist. But literary labels eventually come loose, and unique writers like Dorothy Richardson, whose work demonstrates the deep inadequacy, the irrelevance and the subversiveness of classification, find their audience.

Biographies:

John Rosenberg, *Dorothy Richardson: The Genius They Forgot* (London: Duckworth, 1973);

Gloria G. Fromm, *Dorothy Richardson: A Biography* (Urbana, Chicago & London: University of Illinois Press, 1977).

References:

Caesar R. Blake, *Dorothy M. Richardson* (Ann Arbor: University of Michigan Press, 1960);

Gloria G. Fromm, "What Are Men to Dorothy Richardson?," in *Men By Women*, edited by Janet Todd (New York: Holmes & Meier, 1981), pp. 168-188;

Horace Gregory, *Dorothy Richardson: An Adventure in Self-Discovery* (New York: Holt, Rinehart & Winston, 1967);

Gillian E. Hanscombe, *The Art of Life: Dorothy Richardson and the Development of Feminist Consciousness* (London: Owen, 1982; Athens: Ohio University Press, 1983);

Suzette Henke, "Male and Female Consciousness in Dorothy Richardson's *Pilgrimage*," *Journal of Women's Studies in Literature*, 1 (1979): 51-60;

Sydney Janet Kaplan, *Feminine Consciousness in the Modern British Novel* (Urbana, Chicago & London: University of Illinois Press, 1975);

Louise Morgan, "How Writers Work: Dorothy Richardson," *Everyman* (22 October 1931): 395;

John Cowper Powys, *Dorothy M. Richardson* (London: Joiner & Steele, 1931);

Shirley Rose, "The Unmoving Center: Consciousness in Dorothy Richardson's *Pilgrimage*," *Contemporary Literature*, 10 (Summer 1969): 366-382;

Elaine Showalter, *A Literature of Their Own: British Women Novelists from Brontë to Lessing* (Princeton: Princeton University Press, 1977);

Thomas F. Staley, *Dorothy Richardson* (Boston: G. K. Hall, 1976);

Doris Wallace, "The Fabric of Experience: A Psychological Study of Dorothy Richardson's *Pilgrimage*," Ph.D. dissertation, Rutgers University, Newark, 1982.

Papers:

The bulk of the Dorothy Richardson Papers (including the manuscript of *Pointed Roofs* and a portion of the manuscript of *March Moonlight*) are at the Beinecke Library of Yale University, with smaller collections of letters and papers at the New York Public Library (the Henry W. and Albert A. Berg Collection); the University of Texas at Austin; Princeton University (the Firestone Library); Rice University; Pennsylvania State University; and the British Library.

Dorothy L. Sayers

(13 June 1893-17 December 1957)

Bernard Benstock
University of Tulsa

See also the Sayers entry in *DLB 10, Modern British Dramatists, 1900-1945.*

BOOKS: *Op.I* (Oxford: Blackwell, 1916);

Catholic Tales and Christian Songs (Oxford: Blackwell, 1918);

Whose Body? (London: Unwin, 1923; New York: Boni & Liveright, 1923);

Clouds of Witness (London: Unwin, 1926; New York: Dial, 1927);

Unnatural Death (London: Benn, 1927); republished as *The Dawson Pedigree* (New York: Dial, 1928);

Lord Peter Views the Body (London: Gollancz, 1928; New York: Brewer & Warren, 1929);

The Unpleasantness at the Bellona Club (London: Benn, 1928; New York: Payson & Clarke, 1928);

The Documents in the Case, by Sayers and "Robert Eustace" (Dr. Eustace Robert Barton) (London: Benn, 1930; New York: Brewer & Warren, 1930);

Strong Poison (London: Gollancz, 1930; New York: Brewer & Warren, 1930);

The Five Red Herrings (London: Gollancz, 1931); republished as *Suspicious Characters* (New York: Brewer, Warren & Putnam, 1931);

The Floating Admiral, by Sayers and other members of the Detection Club (London: Hodder & Stoughton, 1931; New York: Doubleday, Doran, 1932);

Have His Carcase (London: Gollancz, 1932; New York: Brewer, Warren & Putnam, 1932);

Ask a Policeman, by Sayers, A. Berkeley, and others (London: Barker, 1933; New York: Morrow, 1933);

Hangman's Holiday (London: Gollancz, 1933; New York: Harcourt, Brace, 1933);

Murder Must Advertise: A Detective Story (London: Gollancz, 1933; New York: Harcourt, Brace, 1933);

The Nine Tailors: Changes Rung on an Old Theme in Two Short Touches and Two Full Peals (London: Gollancz, 1934; New York: Harcourt, Brace, 1934);

Dorothy L. Sayers

Gaudy Night (London: Gollancz, 1935; New York: Harcourt, Brace, 1936);

Papers Relating to the Family of Wimsey, by Sayers and C. W. Scott-Giles, as Matthew Wimsey (London: Privately printed, 1936);

Busman's Honeymoon [play], by Sayers and Muriel St. Clare Byrne (London: Gollancz, 1937; New York: Dramatists' Play Service, 1937);

Busman's Honeymoon: A Love Story with Detective Interruptions (London: Gollancz, 1937; New York: Harcourt, Brace, 1937);

The Zeal of Thy House (New York: Harcourt, Brace, 1937; London: Gollancz, 1937);

The Greatest Drama Ever Staged (London: Hodder & Stoughton, 1938);

221

He That Should Come: A Nativity Play in One Act (London: Gollancz, 1939);

The Devil to Pay: Being the Famous History of John Faustus, the Conjurer of Wittenberg in Germany: How He Sold His Immortal Soul to the Enemy of Mankind, and Was Served XXIV Years by Mephistopheles, and Obtained Helen of Troy to His Paramour, with Many Other Marvels; and How God Dealt with Him at the Last: A Stage Play (London: Gollancz, 1939; New York: Harcourt, Brace, 1939);

Double Death: A Murder Story, by Sayers and others (London: Gollancz, 1939);

In the Teeth of the Evidence and Other Stories (London: Gollancz, 1939; New York: Harcourt, Brace, 1940);

Strong Meat (London: Hodder & Stoughton, 1939);

Begin Here: A War-Time Essay (London: Gollancz, 1940; New York: Harcourt, Brace, 1941);

The Mysterious English (London: Macmillan, 1941);

The Mind of the Maker (London: Methuen, 1941; New York: Harcourt, Brace, 1941);

Why Work? (London: Methuen, 1942);

The Man Born to Be King: A Play-Cycle on the Life of Our Lord and Saviour Jesus Christ, Written for Broadcasting (London: Gollancz, 1943; New York: Harper, 1943);

The Other Six Deadly Sins (London: Methuen, 1943);

Even the Parrot: Exemplary Conversations for Enlightened Children (London: Methuen, 1944);

The Just Vengeance: The Litchfield Festival Play for 1946 (London: Gollancz, 1946);

Unpopular Opinions: Twenty-One Essays (London: Gollancz, 1946; New York: Harcourt, Brace, 1947);

Creed or Chaos? and Other Essays in Popular Theology (London: Methuen, 1947; New York: Harcourt, Brace, 1949);

The Lost Tools of Learning (London: Methuen, 1948);

The Emperor Constantine: A Chronicle (London: Gollancz, 1951; New York: Harper, 1951);

Introductory Papers on Dante (London: Methuen, 1954; New York: Harper, 1955);

Further Papers on Dante (London: Methuen, 1957; New York: Harper, 1957);

The Poetry of Search and the Poetry of Statement, and Other Posthumous Essays on Literature, Religion and Language (London: Gollancz, 1963);

Christian Letters to a Post-Christian World, edited by Roderick Jellema (Grand Rapids, Mich.: Eerdmans, 1969); republished as *The Whimsical Christian: 18 Essays* (New York: Macmillan, 1978);

Striding Folly, Including Three Final Lord Peter Wimsey Stories (London: New English Library, 1973);

Wilkie Collins, edited by E. R. Gregory (Toledo, Ohio: Friends of the University of Toledo Libraries, 1977).

OTHER: *Great Short Stories of Detection, Mystery and Horror,* edited by Sayers (London: Gollancz, 1928); republished as *The Omnibus of Crime* (New York: Payson & Clarke, 1929);

Tristan in Brittany, Being Fragments of the Romance of Tristan, Written in the XIIth Century by Thomas the Anglo-Norman, translated by Sayers (London: Benn, 1929; New York: Payson & Clarke, 1929);

Great Short Stories of Detection, Mystery and Horror, Second Series, edited by Sayers (London: Gollancz, 1931); republished as *The Second Omnibus of Crime* (New York: Coward-McCann, 1932);

Great Short Stories of Detection, Mystery and Horror, Third Series, edited by Sayers (London: Gollancz, 1934); republished as *The Third Omnibus of Crime* (New York: Coward-McCann, 1935);

Tales of Detection, edited by Sayers (London: Dent, 1936);

"The Murder of Julia Wallace," in *The Anatomy of Murder: Famous Crimes Considered by Members of the Detection Club* (London: Lane, 1936; New York: Macmillan, 1938);

Wilkie Collins, *The Moonstone,* introduction by Sayers (London: Dent, 1944; New York: Dutton, 1944);

Garet Garrett, *A Time Is Born,* introduction by Sayers (Oxford: Blackwell, 1945);

The Comedy of Dante Alighieri the Florentine, Cantica I: Hell, translated by Sayers (Harmondsworth, U.K.: Penguin, 1949);

The Comedy of Dante Alighieri the Florentine, Cantica II: Purgatory, translated by Sayers (Harmondsworth, U.K.: Penguin, 1955);

The Song of Roland, translated by Sayers (Harmondsworth, U.K.: Penguin, 1957);

The Comedy of Dante Alighieri the Florentine, Cantica III: Paradise, translated by Sayers, completed by Barbara Reynolds (Harmondsworth, U.K.: Penguin, 1962).

Although Dorothy L. Sayers (she always insisted on the use of her middle initial) later developed various writing careers, including religious stage and radio drama, essays, and translations of Dante, her reputation as a novelist rests exclusively on a dozen detective novels that established her as one of the finest practitioners of the genre. She was never quite comfortable with the stigma of writing what she termed "literature of escape," but her novels and stories—especially those that starred her detective, Lord Peter Wimsey—provided her with a large income and rescued her from work in an advertising agency so that she could eventually retire Wimsey (as Conan Doyle had retired Sherlock Holmes) and devote the last two decades of her life to the "literature of expression" of her strong religious concerns. Nonetheless, Sayers rescued detective fiction from a post-Conan Doyle slump, modernized it along her own lines, and imposed upon it a high literary standard. With Agatha Christie, who in contrast was overly prolific and continued producing mysteries for more than fifty years, Sayers shares the crown as "Queen of Detective Thrillers" in an era that has been dubbed the Golden Age of mystery fiction.

Dorothy Leigh Sayers was the only child of an Anglican clergyman and schoolmaster, the Reverend Henry Sayers, and Helen Leigh Sayers. When she was a child the family moved from Oxford to the bleak Fen country, where Henry Sayers had accepted a living. Dorothy Sayers later described the area powerfully in *The Nine Tailors* (1934); and it was there that she located the aristocratic Denver family, whose second son became her famous amateur sleuth, Lord Peter. Her education began at home with her father instructing her in Latin, followed by private tutoring in French and German. When she was fifteen she was sent to the Godolphin School at Salisbury, where she felt awkward and out of place and was not popular with the other girls. But she also discovered her gift for writing at this time and adopted a "corsage of defiance" to compensate for her insecurity. She went on to Somerville College, Oxford, where she took first-class honors in modern languages in 1915; in 1920, Oxford awarded her both the B.A. and M.A. degrees in the same ceremony (she was one of the first women to receive degrees there). Sayers immortalized Somerville as Shrewsbury College in *Gaudy Night* (1935), an unusual study of the world of female academics, disguised as a mystery thriller.

The necessity of earning her own living forced her into various odd jobs—mostly as a teacher, but also as a reader for Blackwell's, who published her early verse. Her longest tenure was at Benson's advertising agency in London, where she was employed in 1922. She was already at work on her first Wimsey novel at that time. Mary Brian Durkin describes Sayers's early novels, from 1923 to the end of the decade, as those dealing with "Murder and Mirth," an apt description of a group of novels

Dorothy L. Sayers, 1915

which follow the rules of fair play, supply the reader with clues necessary for detection, minimize the use of coincidence, and shy away from romantic entanglements. These novels also illustrate Sayers's concern with the telling of the story as well as the denouement—a fresh development in the sometimes formulaic genre of detective fiction.

Whose Body? (1923) introduces Lord Peter Wimsey, who unravels the puzzling dilemma surrounding two dead bodies—one which seems to be the result of foul play, and one which disappears. The Wimsey who appears in *Whose Body?* is already quite fully formed as the wit, the connoisseur, the collector of incunabula, and the accomplished pianist; and although he is something of the "silly ass" that his creator later called him and that his detractors emphasize, he is also a war hero with horrible nightmares of the trenches, where he was buried alive until rescued by his batman Bunter, now his valet assistant in detection. Later characteristics accumulate in slow sequence: his distinguished good looks (although delicate and not without comic aspects); his athletic prowess, especially as a skilled cricketer; and his charms as a deceiver of women, and later as an avid and romantic wooer

Panache

Whither goest thou, knight with the shining crest,
    "And the golden, gay habergeon?"
I am riding into the wondrous West,
    To the land where honour is sought & won.

. . . .

"Whence comest thou, knight with the bloody crest,
    "And the stained-shattered habergeon?"
Oh! I am returned from the weary West,
    Now that the battle is over & done.

'What were thy deeds in the far-off West,
    "Of derring-do & of chivalry?"
I fought all day, nor at night had rest,
    'gainst foes so many I could not see.

"What didst thou win in the wondrous West,
    'In the land of honour & high renown?'
Only the scars on my brow & breast,
    And the thought of those that my 'lance
                    struck down.

Dorothy Leigh Sayers. 1911.

Entry in the autograph album of Ivy Phillips, a classmate at Godolphin School (estate of Dorothy L. Sayers, courtesy of Miss Ivy Phillips) once he has fallen in love with Harriet Vane.

In *Clouds of Witness* (1926), Lord Peter attempts to refute murder charges against his brother Gerald, the duke of Denver. Evidence supporting Gerald disappears and some condemning circumstantial evidence surfaces, offering a rigorous test of Wimsey's analytical skills as he faces a seemingly airtight case. The duke's trial adds an element of urgency to the situation. In *Unnatural Death* (1927) Lord Peter investigates three murders that appear to be the result of the perpetrator's attempt to become the sole recipient of a fortune left in an oral will. Through a bizarre twist, the villain avoids punishment in a desperate final move. *The Unpleasantness at the Bellona Club* (1928) is set amid the stagnation of a conservative private club, which quickly provides an arena for Lord Peter's detective skills as he looks into what at first appears to be the natural death of an elderly general in his armchair at the club. Again, the stipulations of a will seem to be a determining factor in the case. Marking a move away from the Wimsey stories, a group of new characters in *The Documents in the Case* (1930) investigates a particularly nasty death to determine whether it was an accident, suicide, or murder. This epistolary novel was a new form for Sayers, who collaborated with Dr. Eustace Robert Barton on the project.

Never a particularly attractive woman physically—with thinning hair as a result of a childhood illness—Sayers ventured during the early 1920s into several love affairs, most of which were little more than flirtatious experiments; all of them ended unhappily for her, and one produced an illegitimate son to whom she gave birth secretly and passed on to her cousin, Ivy Shrimpton, for his upbringing, acknowledging him primarily by generous financial support. But she did visit the boy as he was growing up, and claimed to have adopted him later. In 1926 she married Capt. Oswald Atherton Fleming, a handsome man who was employed as a reporter when they met, a line of employment he continued until his health broke down. Although Fleming's drinking problem contributed to the deterioration of their marriage, they lived together until his death in 1950. He was apparently an excellent cook, and a cookbook—which Sayers may actually have ghostwritten—was published under his name.

In 1929 Sayers was able to quit her job at Benson's, and the Flemings moved to their own house in Witham, Essex. Although Sayers spent some time translating from the French, the next decade found her primarily immersed in writing her detective narratives, editing mystery anthologies, and participating in the founding of the Detection Club, with herself as *prima inter pares*. The club was formed upon the principle of writing stories in which the detective used his wits to solve crimes without relying upon deus ex machina of one form or another. Its members included Agatha Christie, Freeman Wills Croft, Anthony Berkeley, G. K. Chesterton, and Ronald A. Knox. Among the activities of the group were novels consisting of individual chapters written by various members.

The later Wimsey novels, those concerned with "Murder and Manners," herald a shift away from the established rules of the detective genre for Sayers. This move was criticized as diluting the genre's necessary elements, but Sayers contended that modification was needed to add sophistication and significance, which were greatly lacking. In these novels, unusual settings become more common, along with increasingly specialized knowledge and even elements of romance.

The second Wimsey series includes and features Harriet Vane, first in her role as the accused poisoner of her callous lover in *Strong Poison* (1930); she is saved from the hangman's noose by the determined detective work of Lord Peter. Although Lord Peter refuses to allow gratitude to affect her feelings toward him, he nonetheless declares his love and pursues her (for a long while from afar, as he travels widely as something of a diplomatic troubleshooter for His Majesty's Government). *Strong Poison* was intended to be the last work to feature Lord Peter, but his popularity persuaded Sayers to delay his retirement for seven years. *The Five Red Herrings* (1931) concerns a murder at an art colony and an investigation of six possible suspects—all of whom had substantial motivation to kill the victim. Five of the suspects' motives are revealed to be red herrings which impede Lord Peter's inquiry—and increase the reader's interest in the crafty sleuth's detective skills. "At last I really feel like Sherlock Holmes," says Lord Peter before he reveals his solution to the murder. No mention of Harriet graces *The Five Red Herrings*, but its successor, *Have His Carcase* (1932), finds her discovering a dead man on a beach with his throat slashed and attempting to put her skills as a writer of detective novels to work on the case. Complications arise when the tide carries off the body, but sufficient evidence has been gathered before this happens and the sleuthing continues anyway. It is Lord Peter who succeeds in solving the murder, but Harriet persists in refusing to marry him. The élan, tensions, and camaraderie of a London advertising

Front cover

concern are captured in *Murder Must Advertise* (1933). In this mystery Lord Peter, under the pseudonym of his two middle names (Death Bredon), works, as Sayers had, as an ad writer. He carries his burden of unrequited love for Harriet through the horrors and danger of *The Nine Tailors* (1934), in which new bodies begin to turn up after he takes on a twenty-year-old mystery.

Only after five years of supplication does he succeed, in the academic atmosphere of *Gaudy Night* (1935), called in by Harriet to solve vile acts of desecration at a college, in winning her during a plighting of troth conducted in Latin. *Busman's Honeymoon* (1937) records their first days of married life, during which they find a corpse in their honeymoon cottage; at the end, Lord Peter suffers

agonies over the hanging of the unrepentant murderer his powers of ratiocination have brought to justice. The dashing detective was then withdrawn by his creator from public view, and only during the first year of the Second World War did he make a brief reappearance as the father of three sons in a short story titled "Tallboys."

The Wimsey novels, supplemented by several volumes of short stories (some of which feature Montague Egg, a wine salesman with detective talents), are all of consistently high literary quality— perhaps overly so for the genre—displaying Sayers's penchant for witty repartee and erudite epigrams. Her personal involvements with Lord Peter and Harriet are apparent, as are her personal views and prejudices: highly moral (although allow-

Dorothy L. Sayers visiting the porcupines in the London Zoo, 1940 (photo by Wolf Suschitsky)

ber 1957 Sayers returned alone to her cottage in Witham after a Christmas shopping trip to London. She was found dead at the foot of the stairs the next morning, apparently the victim of a sudden stroke.

As she constructed her mysteries, Sayers was constantly searching for new and unusual methods of murder, tapping the knowledge of toxicologists and the medical profession so that the plots revolve around highly original—and often wildly improbable—modi operandi. After the first handful of novels, with a captured readership assured, she sharpened her talents within the format; the later volumes disclose exceptionally fine characteristics only hinted at in the earlier ones. *Murder Must Advertise* proves to be a comedy of manners and mores not unlike those of Evelyn Waugh, and *The Nine Tailors* is a grim and austerely atmospheric capturing of hardened people in a remote and somber country locale. Either of these two qualifies as her most accomplished piece of fiction, although *Gaudy Night* vies with them for honors, especially

ing for women in love to have illicit affairs); staunchly patriotic in defense of the traditional values of England and its ruling classes; caustic in her depiction of such "undesirables" as cads and communists, drug dealers and dizzy debutantes; and rather unsubtle in various intrusions of anti-Semitic sentiments. (It is quite likely that Lord Peter originally thought that the corpse in the bath in *Whose Body?* was not that of Sir Reuben Levy because it was uncircumsized—revealing a popularly held misconception that only Jews are circumcized. But that observation was apparently excised by the publisher.)

As the 1930s drew to a close, however, Sayers involved herself overwhelmingly with her religious plays, essays, and talks, and her translations, mainly of Dante. By then she also had become a celebrity—as well as an eccentric, famous for her pet pig "Francis Bacon," who shared her living quarters until he wound up in her frying pan during the austere war years. An honorary doctorate of letters was awarded to her by the University of Durham the year her husband died, and she later became a churchwarden at St. Thomas's in London, where she produced one of her religious plays. In Decem-

THE MAN BORN TO BE KING

by

Dorothy L. Sayers

THE TEXT of Miss Sayers' famous series of broadcast plays on the life of Christ: together with (1) notes on the action and characters as furnished by Miss Sayers to the producer, (2) a long introduction by Miss Sayers, covering the theology and dramatic structure of the plays, (3) a foreword by Dr. Welch of the B.B.C., giving the history of the controversy aroused, (5) a brief note on the production by Val Gielgud, and (6) the complete cast for each play.

Dust jacket for Sayers's radio plays broadcast by the BBC from December 1941 through October 1942

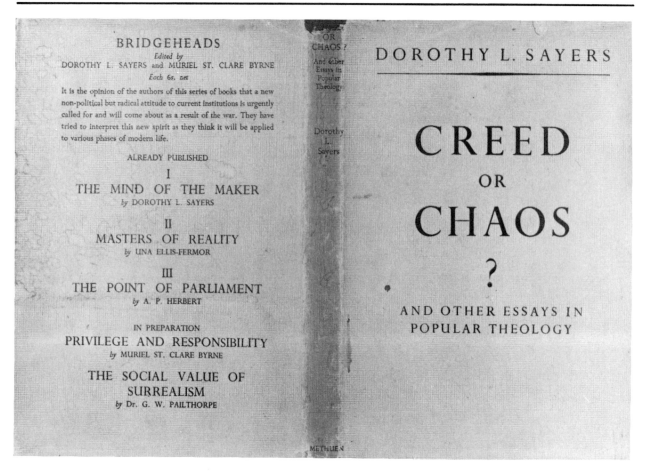

Dust jacket for the 1947 collection of Sayers's religious pamphlets

since it moves beyond the assumed constraints of the format: it is an overly long novel of careful characterizations, without the obligatory murder— only a series of disturbing hate messages and ugly acts of vandalism. It both celebrates the female academe and scrutinizes the limited lives of women cut off from "normal" contacts and concerns, and it strongly anticipates Sayers's interests outside the scope of detective fiction. Still, for every admirer of its literate excellence, there are dozens of aficionados of the detective story who find it an ineffective violator of the rules and norms of the genre.

Bibliographies:

Robert B. Harmon and Margaret A. Burger, *An Annotated Guide to the Works of Dorothy L. Sayers* (New York: Garland, 1977);

Colleen B. Gilbert, *A Bibliography of the Works of Dorothy L. Sayers* (London: Macmillan, 1978; Hamden, Conn.: Anchor, 1978).

Biographies:

Janet Hitchman, *Such a Strange Lady: An Introduction*

to Dorothy L. Sayers 1893-1957 (New York: Harper & Row, 1975);

Ralph E. Hone, *Dorothy L. Sayers: A Literary Biography* (Kent, Ohio: Kent State University Press, 1979);

James Brabazon, *Dorothy L. Sayers: A Biography* (New York: Scribners, 1981).

References:

Lionel Basney, "God and Peter Wimsey," *Christianity Today*, 17 (14 September 1973): 27-28;

John G. Cawelti, *Adventure, Mystery, and Romance* (Chicago: University of Chicago Press, 1976), pp. 120-125;

Alzina Stone Dale, *Maker and Craftsman: The Story of Dorothy L. Sayers* (Grand Rapids, Mich.: Eerdmans, 1978);

Mary Brian Durkin, *Dorothy L. Sayers* (Boston: Twayne, 1980);

Dawson Gaillard, *Dorothy L. Sayers* (New York: Ungar, 1981);

Martin Green, "The Detection of a Snob," *Listener*,

49 (14 March 1963): 461-464;

E. R. Gregory, "From Detective Stories to Dante: The Transitional Phase of Dorothy L. Sayers," *Christianity & Literature,* 26 (Winter 1977): 9-17;

George Grella, "Dorothy Sayers and Peter Wimsey," *University of Rochester Library Bulletin,* 28 (Summer 1974): 33-42;

Margaret P. Hannay, ed., *As Her Whimsey Took Her: Critical Essays on the work of Dorothy L. Sayers* (Kent, Ohio: Kent State University Press, 1979);

Barbara G. Harrison, "Dorothy L. Sayers and the Tidy Art of Detective Fiction," *Ms.,* 3 (November 1974): 66-69;

Howard Haycraft, *Murder for Pleasure* (New York: Appleton-Century, 1941), pp. 135-142;

Carolyn Heilbrun, "Sayers, Lord Peter and God," *American Scholar,* 37 (Spring 1968): 324-330;

Q. D. Leavis, "The Case of Miss Dorothy Sayers," *Scrutiny,* 6 (December 1937): 334-340;

G. A. Lee, *The Wimsey Saga: A Chronology* (Witham, U.K.: Dorothy L. Sayers Historical and Literary Society, 1980);

Nancy-Lou Patterson, "Images of Judaism and Anti-Semitism in the Novels of Dorothy L. Sayers," *Sayers Review,* 2 (June 1978): 17-24;

Barbara Reynolds, "The Origin of Lord Peter Wimsey," *Times Literary Supplement,* April 1977, p. 492;

H. P. Rickman, "From Detection to Theology: The Work of Dorothy Sayers," *Hibbert Journal,* 60 (July 1962): 290-296;

C. W. Scott-Giles, *The Wimsey Family* (New York: Harper & Row, 1977);

Julian Symons, *The Detective Story in Britain* (London: Longmans, 1962), pp. 26-28;

Colin Watson, *Snobbery with Violence: Crime Stories and Their Audience* (London: Eyre & Spottiswoode, 1971), pp. 146-148, 153-156, 160-162.

Papers:
The major repository of Dorothy L. Sayers's papers is at Wheaton College in Wheaton, Illinois.

May Sinclair

Margaret B. McDowell
University of Iowa

BIRTH: Rock Ferry, Cheshire, England, 24 August 1863, to William and Amelia Hind Sinclair.

EDUCATION: Cheltenham Ladies' College, 1881.

AWARD: Fellow, Royal Society of Literature, 1916.

DEATH: Bierton, Buckinghamshire, England, 14 November 1946.

BOOKS: *Nakiketas and Other Poems,* as Julian Sinclair (London: Kegan Paul, 1886);

Essays in Verse (London: Kegan Paul, Trench, Trübner, 1891);

Audrey Craven (Edinburgh: Blackwood, 1897; New York: Holt, 1906);

Mr. and Mrs. Nevill Tyson (Edinburgh & London: Blackwood, 1898); republished as *The Tysons* (New York: Dodge, 1906);

Two Sides of a Question (London: Constable, 1901; New York: Taylor, 1901);

The Divine Fire (London: Constable, 1904; New York: Holt, 1904);

The Helpmate (London: Constable, 1907; New York: Holt, 1907);

The Judgment of Eve (London & New York: Harper, 1908; New York & London: Harper, 1908);

Kitty Tailleur (London: Constable, 1908); republished as *The Immortal Moment: The Story of Kitty Tailleur* (New York: Doubleday, Page, 1908);

Fame (London: Elkin Mathews & Marrot, 1909);

The Creators: A Comedy (London: Constable, 1910; New York: Century, 1910);

The Flaw in the Crystal (London: *The English Review,* 1912; New York: Dutton, 1912);

The Three Brontës (London: Hutchinson, 1912; Boston & New York: Houghton Mifflin, 1912);

Feminism (London: Woman Writer's Suffrage League, 1912);

The Combined Maze (London: Hutchinson, 1913; New York & London: Harper, 1913);

The Judgment of Eve and Other Stories (London: Hutchinson, 1914);

The Return of the Prodigal (New York: Macmillan, 1914);

The Three Sisters (London: Hutchinson, 1914; New York: Macmillan, 1914);

A Journal of Impressions in Belgium (London: Hutchinson, 1915; New York: Macmillan, 1915);

America's Part in the War (New York: Commission for Relief in Belgium, 1915);

Tasker Jevons: The Real Story (London: Hutchinson, 1916); republished as *The Belfry* (New York: Macmillan, 1916);

The Tree of Heaven (London & New York: Cassell, 1917; New York: Macmillan, 1917);

A Defense of Idealism (London: Macmillan, 1917; New York: Macmillan, 1917);

Mary Olivier: A Life (London & New York: Cassell, 1919; New York: Macmillan, 1919);

The Romantic (London: Collins, 1920; New York: Macmillan, 1920);

Mr. Waddington of Wyck (London: Cassell, 1921; New York: Macmillan, 1921);

The New Idealism (London: Macmillan, 1922; New York: Macmillan, 1922);

Life and Death of Harriett Frean (London: Collins, 1922; New York: Macmillan, 1922);

Anne Severn and the Fieldings (London: Hutchinson, 1922; New York: Macmillan, 1922);

Uncanny Stories (London: Hutchinson, 1923; New York: Macmillan, 1923);

A Cure of Souls (London: Hutchinson, 1923; New York: Macmillan, 1924);

The Dark Night: A Novel in Verse (London: Cape, 1924; New York: Macmillan, 1924);

Arnold Waterlow: A Life (London: Hutchinson, 1924; New York: Macmillan, 1924);

The Rector of Wyck (London: Hutchinson, 1925; New York: Macmillan, 1925);

Far End (London: Hutchinson, 1926; New York: Macmillan, 1926);

The Allinghams (London: Hutchinson, 1927; New York: Macmillan, 1927);

History of Anthony Waring (London: Hutchinson, 1927; New York: Macmillan, 1927);

Tales Told by Simpson (London: Hutchinson, 1930; New York: Macmillan, 1930);

The Intercessor and Other Stories (London: Hutchinson, 1931; New York: Macmillan, 1932).

OTHER: Rudolf Sohm, *Outlines of Church History*, translated by Sinclair (London: Macmillan, 1895; Boston: Beacon Press, 1958);

Theodore von Sosnosky, *England's Danger, The Future of British Army Reform*, translated by Sinclair (London: Chapman & Hall, 1901);

Emily Brontë, *Wuthering Heights*, introduction by Sinclair (London: Dent, 1907);

Charlotte Brontë, *Jane Eyre*, introduction by Sinclair (London: Dent, 1908);

E. C. Gaskell, *The Life of Charlotte Brontë*, introduction by Sinclair (London: Dent, 1908);

Charlotte Brontë, *Shirley*, introduction by Sinclair (London: Dent, 1908);

Charlotte Brontë, *Villette*, introduction by Sinclair (London: Dent, 1909);

Charlotte Brontë, *The Professor*, introduction by Sinclair (London: Dent, 1910);

Anne Brontë, *The Tenant of Wildfell Hall*, introduction by Sinclair (London: Dent, 1914);

Jean de Bosschere, *The Closed Door*, introduction by Sinclair (London: John Lane, 1917);

Introduction to *Pilgrimage* (New York: Knopf, 1919).

PERIODICAL PUBLICATIONS: "Man and Superman: A Symposium," *New York Times*, Holiday Book Number, Literary Section, 1 December 1905, pp. 813, 814;

"Three American Poets of Today: Edward Arlington Robinson, William Vaughan Moody and Ridgely Torrence," *Atlantic Monthly*, 98 (September 1906): 325-335;

"The Novels of George Meredith," *Outlook*, 92 (June 1909): 413-418;

"The Gitanjali: or Song Offerings of Rabindra Nath Tagore," *North American Review*, 197 (May 1913): 659-676;

"The New Brontë Letters," *Dial*, 60 (November 1913): 343-346;

"Two Notes" I "On H. D." II "On Imagism," *Egoist*, 2 (June 1915): 88, 89;

"Prufrock: and Other Observations," *Little Review*, 4 (December 1917): 8-14;

"The Novels of Dorothy Richardson," *Egoist*, 5 (April 1918): 57-59; *Little Review*, 5 (April 1918): 3-11;

"The Reputation of Ezra Pound," *English Review*, 30 (April 1920): 326-335; *North American Review*, 211 (May 1920): 658-668;

"The Poems of F. S. Flint," *English Review*, 32 (January 1921): 6-18;

"The Future of the Novel," *Pall Mall Gazette*, 10 January 1921, p. 7;

"The Poems of Richard Aldington," *English Review*, 32 (May 1921): 397-410;

"The Novels of Violet Hunt," *English Review*, 34 (February 1922): 106-118;

"The Poems of H. D.," *Dial*, 72 (February 1922): 203-207;

"The Man From Main Street," *New York Times Book Review*, 24 September 1922, p. 1;

"Psychological Types," *English Review*, 36 (May 1923): 436-439;

"Primary and Secondary Consciousness," *Proceedings of the Aristotelian Society*, new series 23, no. 7 (1923): 111-120.

Mary Amelia St. Clair (May) Sinclair was born 24 August 1863, the child of William and Amelia Hind Sinclair. She was the youngest child and the only daughter among six children. Her father, the owner of a fairly sizeable fleet of small worldwide-transport ships, operated the business from Liverpool offices from 1850 to 1870, when the business failed and he became bankrupt. A heavy drinker, he died of cirrhosis of the liver and chronic nephritis in 1881. Her mother's oppressively harsh dominance of the family and fearful hatred of sexuality

and William Sinclair's alcoholism are frankly presented and perceptively analyzed in Sinclair's novels *The Helpmate* (1907) and *Mary Olivier* (1919). After the failure of the family business when May was seven, the parents separated. The children and their mother moved constantly from one part of London to another and from one relative's home to another. May Sinclair educated herself from books, except for a few piano lessons and a single year in 1881 at Cheltenham Ladies' College. All of her brothers died in early adulthood and her mother died in 1901. Consequently, the author was without family support almost from the beginning of her writing career and knew nothing of a secure and harmonious family as a child. Her love for two of her brothers was strong, and her emotional attachment for both of her parents was intense but extremely ambivalent.

May Sinclair became widely known with the publication of *The Divine Fire* (1904), and her popularity reached its peak between 1910 and 1920. In 1916 William Lyon Phelps called her "the foremost living writer among English-speaking women"; Thomas Moult in the *Critic* in 1920 referred to her as "the most widely known artist in the country and in America"; in 1924 the French illustrator and poet Jean de Bosschere thought her "the least conventional of women writers," and John Farrar declared her "the greatest psychological analyst in fiction." Although Bertrand Russell criticized Sinclair's *The New Idealism* (1922) for problems deriving from her relative unfamiliarity with mathematical logic, he termed that book "one of the best defenses of idealism that have appeared in recent years." Most critics would consider *The Three Sisters* (1914) and *Mary Olivier* Sinclair's strongest novels, but in *The Tree of Heaven* (1917) she probably achieved her greatest popular success (after *The Divine Fire*) when it reached second place among best-selling novels in America in the year of its publication.

Between 1897 and 1924, Sinclair published twenty-nine volumes of fiction (novels and collections of stories); three books of poetry, including the verse-novel, *The Dark Night;* two books on philosophy; and a book on the Brontë sisters. She also wrote many thoughtful essays and pamphlets, such as *Feminism* (1912) for the Women's Suffrage League and the short prose works in support of war relief: *A Journal of Impressions in Belgium* (1915) and *America's Part in the War* (1915) for the Commission for Relief in Belgium. Besides reviews and monographs on psychology and philosophy, her essays include considerable literary criticism of contemporary authors and the substantial introductions to

Thorncote, May Sinclair's birthplace in Rock Ferry, Cheshire

seven volumes in the Everyman Series (for the six novels by the Brontës and for Mrs. Gaskell's *Life of Charlotte Brontë*).

Like James Joyce, Dorothy Richardson, Rebecca West, D. H. Lawrence, Katherine Mansfield, and Virginia Woolf, Sinclair experimented with representing the free flow of fragmentary thought in fiction. She was more selective in choice of details and perhaps more conventional in shaping them than some of these authors; she also chose to follow chronological sequence more consistently in the development of her novels than did most of the others, who tended to use the flashback in memory or dream sequence more often. Like these other writers, her work revealed the influence of Freud and Jung in its rendering of the various levels of the unconscious and of the influence of childhood experience and traumas upon the adult psyche. More than most writers born in the 1860s, she emphasized the pervasive influence of sexual repression and sublimation upon the psyche, and she wrote frequently about sexual compulsions, frigidity, and hysterical illness. In several of her novels she chose to cover a birth-to-death span in the life of a character, and in *The Tree of Heaven* she was even more ambitious as she sought to cover three generations of an entire family.

Her stylistic experimentation—most notable in *Mary Olivier*—divided her readers and friends. She developed an impressionistic and random prose style in this and in some of her later novels which is different from the full characterization and expansive commentary of earlier books such as *The Divine Fire* or *The Three Sisters*. She substitutes a "telegraphic" fragment for conventional sentence structure, often omitting the subject of the sentence, most of the prepositions and conjunctions, and the transitions between sentences. *Mary Olivier* consists of an unusually large number of short vignettes grouped into chapters of greatly varying length. The earliest vignettes convey the perspective of the two-year-old Mary, and the latest vignettes reveal Mary's conscious thought and unconscious emotions and motivations at the age of forty-seven. While Sinclair felt sure this novel was her best and declared she would use only this style henceforth, she returned—perhaps because of the pleading of such friends as Edwin Arlington Robinson or the negative criticism of reviewers like Katherine Mansfield—to the more traditional style in some of her later novels.

Among Sinclair's friends who praised her work were older authors who had established themselves by the turn of the century: Sarah Orne Jewett, William Butler Yeats, William James, Henry James, John Galsworthy, Arnold Bennett, Thomas

Hardy, H. G. Wells, and George Gissing. More typically, however, she identified with new authors of her own age or younger and consistently encouraged, praised, and defended them: Ezra Pound, T. S. Eliot, Harriet Monroe, Hilda Doolittle (H. D.), T. E. Hulme, Richard Aldington, Ford Madox Hueffer (who later changed his name to Ford Madox Ford), Rebecca West, Violet Hunt, Hugh Walpole, Robert Frost, Wyndham Lewis, Charlotte Mew, Mary Webb, Rose Macaulay, Dorothy Richardson, Jack London, Sinclair Lewis, and Upton Sinclair. Important in literary history were her written defenses of several authors, including H. G. Wells, Ezra Pound, Hermann Sudermann, D. H. Lawrence, Robert Frost, and T. S. Eliot. From 1914 until the early 1920s, her home in St. John's Wood, London, provided a gathering place for writers. She began as a poet, and her interests remained strong in the new movements in poetry. She encouraged the young Vorticists and the Imagists, particularly Richard Aldington. In 1918 in a review essay on Dorothy Richardson, Sinclair notably used William James's term "stream of consciousness"— the first time this term was applied to literary technique.

Sinclair's interest in philosophy and psychology may have derived, in part, from her attempts to break away from the "gentle tyranny" of maternal pressure; she aligned herself with a conventional Christian theology that assumed an anthropomorphic conception of God and a resurrection of the body at some point after death. The principal of Cheltenham Ladies' College, Dorothy Beale, and Sinclair in the single year she attended the college (1881) shared interest in reading books in German and particularly in reading works on psychology and philosophy, and they then corresponded for several years. In 1893 Miss Beale advised her former pupil to read the mystical idealist Thomas Hill Green (who had influenced Mrs. Humphry Ward, as is evident in her best-selling *Robert Elsmere*, 1888). Evelyn Underhill, who wrote several books on mystical experience, also elicited Sinclair's mystical proclivities and remained her close friend for many years. Sinclair's interest in the psychology of depth consciousness intensified as she helped found, govern, and finance, with twelve other people, the first clinic in England to offer psychoanalytical therapy, the Medico-Psychological Clinic of London, in 1913 and as she became a member of the Society for Psychical Research.

In her avid interest in current intellectual and social movements, May Sinclair also supported the suffrage campaign between 1908 and 1910 by writing, marching, demonstrating, collecting donations, and drafting and circulating political petitions. She worked in the Women's Freedom League and the Women Writers Suffrage League, both nonmilitant groups; she collected money in December 1908 for the more radical Women's Social and Political Union; in 1910 she joined such writers as Shaw, Conrad, Bennett, and Galsworthy in a Writers' Memorial petition submitted to Prime Minister Asquith urging the passage of a Women's Suffrage Act. In 1910 she also joined Dr. Jessie Margaret Murray in a project to follow for a decade the medical history of women arrested or injured in the 18 November 1910 suffrage demonstration, in which two women, including Mrs. Pankhurst's sister, died.

Still further evidence of May Sinclair's involvement in causes appeared in the early weeks of World War I when, in September and October 1914, she served briefly with an ambulance unit led by Dr. Hector Munro, head of the London Medico-Psychological Clinic. He rejected her further ambulance work after she and another woman insisted, against his orders, on picking up two wounded Germans and providing first-aid care for them as well as for the British soldiers.

When she achieved her first success in fiction with *The Divine Fire*, May Sinclair was over forty, and in her fifties she was associating primarily with writers half her age. Some, like Rebecca West, wrote later that Sinclair remained old-fashioned in basic ideas and behavior. Writing to Sinclair's biographer, Theophilus Boll, in 1962, West commented on Sinclair's soft voice, primness, neatness, and unusual athletic energy and grace: "Her manners were of a forgotten age. All this fascinated me in contrast to her desire to be tough and masculine. . . . She was an anachronistic figure—in spite of her desire to be of the Enlightenment. She belonged to the age of the Lady. . . . She was at once La Princess de Cléves, and the Brontës—and wished to be D. H. Lawrence. On top of all this— and underneath it too—great, great sweetness. . . . She was extremely kind to young writers and particularly young women writers." With similar sense of Sinclair's being a woman caught between the old-fashioned and the modern in manner and attitude, Arnold Bennett said that he liked "this prim virgin," while Thomas Hardy invited her several times between 1910 and 1912 to his country home to enjoy bicycling trips with him.

In spite of her consistent athletic activity until her late fifties and her constant association with energetic young people and with revolutionary so-

May Sinclair (with sign) demonstrating for women's suffrage, Kensington, 1910

cial and intellectual movements, Sinclair aged prematurely. She was even by 1919 showing the first symptoms in her hands and in one leg of the neuro-muscular degenerative disease which debilitated her by the late 1920s. She was cared for in a rural nursing home for almost two decades. By the time of her death in 1946 the literary world had forgotten her, but in 1950 Joseph Warren Beach reminded historians of fiction that additional study of Sinclair would be appropriate, and in 1967 Walter Allen similarly saw her as an "unjustly neglected novelist." Probably most important in placing her in critical perspective has been Theophilus Boll's thorough biographical research and appreciative commentary on individual works in *Miss May Sinclair: Novelist* (1973), although he does not adequately separate her weak books from those that deserve serious study.

Both her books and her life provide insight into the transition period from the Victorian era through the Edwardian period—particularly as these years affected the attitudes of women and the attitudes about women. She was sympathetic certainly to the new and challenging influences of the time, and she was aware of the limitations of the traditional novel, but it is doubtful that she made more than a superficial use of the new ideas in her fiction or really influenced profoundly the form

and the direction the novel was to take. She was the forerunner of Dorothy Richardson and Virginia Woolf but by no means Woolf's equal in creativity, originality, or formative influence. She did illustrate the fact that a novelist of talent could no longer be comfortable in working within the intellectual and artistic tradition of the Victorian Age.

May Sinclair's *Nakiketas and Other Poems* (1886), published under the pseudonym Julian Sinclair, and *Essays in Verse* (1891) had infinitesimal sales and received no critical attention, but Sinclair's identification of herself as a poet later informed her characterization in *The Divine Fire* of Savage Keith Rickman, who struggles to become a poet. Like her, he at first writes sonnets. In the longest of the blank verse narratives in the *Nakiketas* volume, "Helen," Sinclair stresses the view that self-sacrifice is laudable in contrast with the view expressed in her later books. Helen is the victim of her husband's anger after his business fails, and although another man tempts her, she reconciles herself to her distasteful marriage. She has decided, in sentimental and masochistic fashion, that "love is not the whole of woman's life," and she can settle for "honor, faith, and self-sacrifice." Sinclair frequently explores religious doubt and the meaning of pain in the poems, and some of them celebrate literary figures such as Goethe, Shelley, and George Eliot.

Audrey Craven (1897) is a surprisingly well-structured and swiftly paced comedy of manners. Even in her first novel, Sinclair could maintain a detached asperity of tone as she recounted the episodic adventures of a flat character—the audacious and incorrigible Audrey Craven as she plays the game of courtship. She breaks the heart of her first admirer, her cousin Vincent, who has gone to the Canadian Rockies to write a book dedicated to her and to prove that he is stable enough for marriage. He returns to Audrey, who does not love him, and to Katherine, an artist who does secretly love him, and he dies. At that point, Audrey declares—to the heartbroken Katherine—that probably she really did love Vincent all the time. However, during his absence she has become engaged to Ted, an artist, who is Katherine's brother; she has had an affair, moreover, with the deceitful Wyndham Langley, a novelist who uses her as a recognizable model for the leading figure in a scandalous best-seller. Through his association with Audrey, Langley also wishes to make the woman who jilted him angry and jealous. Audrey, who feels most passion for this least worthy man, recovers from her wounded pride and in a year has interested the vicar, Flaxman Reed, in her, although Langley's novel has ruined her reputation. When she confesses to him that she was ready to yield to the sexual importunities of Langley and that only an accident had prevented her from doing so, Reed agrees with her that she has been guilty of lust. In his judging her, however, he suddenly realizes that he, too, lusts for her. Frightened by this self-realization he leaves her and joins the Catholic church to become a priest and protect his soul through celibacy. In the last few pages Audrey appears three years later, happy in her shallow existence. She has married Algernon Jackson, a "bore," "non-entity," and a successful goose-farmer. In this marriage she can dispense with love and moral integrity as irrelevancies. Jackson will never know that she is the chief character in Langley's lurid novel, because he reads no books. If she does not love him, it will not matter, because she would never think of telling him so.

George Gissing wrote Sinclair to praise the characterization and the construction of the novel, and he also said that he would never have guessed that *Audrey Craven* was a first novel. He commented sharply on a quality that often distinguishes Sinclair's best novels and saves them from a tendency toward the sentimental—"the taste of irony on this page and that." Unfortunately, Sinclair never repeated the kind of comedy she presented in this first novel. If the characters are shallow, the reader is yet aware that the book satirizes not only an immature woman's frivolity, but the demeaning and foolish nature of the game of love itself as played in modern society.

The tone of *Mr. and Mrs. Nevill Tyson* (1898) is bitter and harsh and suggests the influence of the naturalistic novel upon her. Sinclair lacks the sophistication to elucidate firmly the paradoxical conjoining of the tragic and the ridiculous that underlies her vision in this novel. Rather, it seems actually to be an experiment in the melodramatic. Near the end of the book the foolish Molly—who is sensuous, beautiful, and loving—tries to save her drunken husband from the flames of a lamp that he has tipped over, and she is severely burned. The villagers have already blamed her for the death of her infant, because she abruptly stopped nursing him. They do not know she simply acquiesced in Nevill's tyrannical demands, because her flowing breasts repelled him. Similarly, Tyson finds her burn-scarred body repellent and chooses to leave for the hardships and heroism of the distant battlefield, where he dies. The novel suggests possibilities that are never fully realized, such as Sinclair's attempt to contrast the hypothetical arrogant and clever woman, whom the villagers think appropriate for Tyson to marry, with the beautiful but silly Molly, whom he does actually bring home as his bride. In effect, Molly scorns their staid moralism and propriety with her impudence. Tyson appears at first to be a serious study. He evinces certain unusual qualities and a complex, if somewhat unintegrated, psyche. He is proud that he has impregnated a woman, quails at the violence of the birth process, rushes to buy a copy of a painting featuring an idealized madonna and child, and is jealous not of his friend who wants Molly but of his newborn son, whom he calls a beast and an animal. Unfortunately, the reviewers attacked the novel on the grounds of its unpleasant subject matter, instead of its lack of artistic control.

Two novellas, *Superseded* and *The Cosmopolitan*, appeared together in *Two Sides of a Question* (1901) but have little connection. All reviewers agreed that *Superseded* was the better of the two, and it alone was republished in later printings. In it, Juliana Quincey, a teacher who never has succeeded in her long career, loses her job to a younger woman. For a few months she finds excitement in her doctor's interest in her and weaves passionate fantasies about him. When she learns that he loves the teacher who has superseded her, she must come to terms with two losses that this woman has caused her—her career and her dream lover. Sinclair's presentation of

Juliana is sensitive and light enough to enable her to escape sentimentalism. Juliana's fantasy, Sinclair reveals, is from the beginning evanescent, and the figure of the little teacher becomes comic in the contrast between her commonplace existence and her lofty dreams. The strength of the short work lies in Sinclair's ability to convince the reader that everyone must inevitably face disenchantments similar to Juliana's. At some point, Sinclair suggests, figures of greater consequence than Juliana must yield to those who are younger, stronger, more efficient, and more attractive. Sinclair's lament is for the human race, not for the little teacher.

In *The Divine Fire* (1904) Sinclair studies the development of a poet by observing the tortuous development of a whole individual. Savage Keith Rickman, a Cockney shopkeeper's son, grows morally through self-denial for the sake of another. He grows spiritually through his fantasy of idealized passion, inspired by the intelligent Lucia Harden, and then through the actual experience of mutual love. He grows in his ability as a poet through the discipline of journalism, practiced with integrity, and through the sense of order he discovers in his study of Greek classical poetry and drama. The divine fire that makes him a poet is the flame engendered and sustained in him through experiences involving both his mind and his heart, through creative self-expression and greater concern for another than for himself. The book reflects Sinclair's own struggle to become a poet, her interest in T. H. Green's idealism based on self-denial, and her interest in the classics.

The focus throughout the novel is upon the development of Rickman, son of a secondhand bookshop owner, who begins in obscurity as his father's helper and becomes a poet of distinction and a verse dramatist of renown, thanks to the workings of "the divine fire" within him. This fire enables him to triumph over the limitations imposed upon him by his lower-class origins and background, though his progress from obscurity to distinction is not easy. At first, he passively accepts his position and circumstances, though even at this point his ambition to be a writer is firmly in place. At first he finds sexual release with Poppy Grace, a Jubilee Variety Theater song and dance entertainer, for whom he writes songs and poems reflecting his free and dissolute life, poems he would eventually collect under the title *Saturnalia*.

At this time, Keith spends several weeks appraising the library of Sir Frederick Harden, without knowledge that his father intends to use his appraisals unscrupulously to secure the books at a low price. (Harden has heavily mortgaged the library to cover gambling debts.) Before long, Rickman turns from the physical attraction of Poppy—and the *Saturnalia* poems—to a spiritual view of woman as inspiration and unattainable ideal, represented in the novel by Sir Frederick's daughter, Lucia Harden, with her beauty, moral insight, and classical education. Lucia, who is engaged to her cousin, Horace Jewdwine, an Oxford-educated editor of a journal, kindles in Rickman the "divine fire" that inspires him for several years to write sonnets emblematic of his adoration of her virtue.

When, at her father's death, Lucia loses the library and Isaac Rickman acquires most of the books for his shop, Keith Rickman angrily leaves his father's store and struggles for a livelihood as a Grub Street journalist, pursuing his chosen vocation as poet only in odd moments. At this time, he becomes engaged to Flossie Walker, a woman who lacks Poppy's sensuality and Lucia's idealized mind and spirit, but who would be a sensible though unexciting wife for Keith. She has no significant effect on his development as an artist, however, and their relationship ends without trauma for either of them when she finds a man with more financial stability; she settles for placid domesticity and has several babies before the end of the book.

As Rickman gradually begins to succeed as a poet, he loses one source of income when he refuses to continue selling his work to Horace Jewdwine's journal after he and Jewdwine quarrel about Keith's insistence on the literary integrity of reviewing books as he sees them. When his father dies, Keith inherits most of the books from the Harden library. He wants to give the books to Lucia, but first he must pay the unscrupulous solicitor who holds a lien against Harden's estate. In order to accumulate money to discharge this debt, he starves himself to the point of near-death and is hospitalized.

May Sinclair later said that she set aside the manuscript for an interval of seven years before adding the ending, although it appears to be the ending toward which the book moves inevitably. On the basis of the London success of his verse drama, "The Triumph of Life," Keith pays the debt and presents the library, almost intact, to Lucia, pretending it was simply his father's wish. Lucia, who has for years secretly loved him but has been inhibited by his remoteness and her aristocratic upbringing, now expresses her love for him. The implications of the ending are that Keith will revise and improve his drama for the competitive performances to open in Paris. Lucia—as partner in a mutual and passionate love affair, and no longer as

MISS MAY SINCLAIR

By May Sinclair

THE DIVINE FIRE

The story of the regeneration of a London poet and the degeneration of a London critic.   14th printing. $1.50.

"Certain it is that in all our new fiction I have found nothing worthy to compare with 'The Divine Fire,' nothing even remotely approaching the same class." — MARY MOSS, *in the Atlantic Monthly.*

"I find her book the most remarkable that I have read for many years." — OWEN SEAMAN, *in Punch* (London).

"A full-length study of the poetic temperament, framed in a varied and curiously interesting environment. . . . Moreover, a real distinction of style, besides being of absorbing interest from cover to cover." — *Dial.*

Atlantic Monthly Advertiser, *1904*

the literary personification of an ideal—has released him to move, as poet, from the formalized patterns and static effects of his sonnets to the forceful and dynamic poetic drama, inspired by the Greek classic dramatists who imposed order on chaos through their artistic powers.

Just as poems introduced into the text of this novel serve symbolic functions, so also does the library symbolize the cultural heritage Lucia can draw upon, which Rickman has never possessed as his birthright. Since she is the first woman heir to the library in twelve generations, her ownership suggests a changing conception of the status of women in Sinclair's generation. They must now be active intellectually, not mere passive assimilators of culture. Beethoven's sonata *Apassionata*, introduced at four crucial points in the novels, carries varying implications, but clearly functions as a unifying device to suggest Lucia's growing awareness of the sanctity of her passions. Lucia's earlier psychosomatic illness conveyed to the reader her inability to act decisively upon her emotions and intuitions and to express her feelings in a forthright manner to Rickman. She thus joins other characters created by Sinclair who experience hysterical illness related to sexual repression, as in *Superseded, Life and Death of Harriett Frean, The Three Sisters, The Tree of Heaven,* and *Mary Olivier;* Lucia, like some of the others, triumphs over such debility.

The stilted, formal style of this novel is unacceptable to the taste of most modern readers, but sales swelled at the time of publication. The book's eloquence, abundant imagery, lofty diction, and sometimes circuitous sentences suggested to Sinclair's contemporaries the author's sophistication or pseudosophistication. One has to read twice sentences such as these to be sure of the precise meaning: "Even more than for eminence he longed for power. He longed for it with the passion of a weak will governed despotically by a strong intellect." In this book, even casual conversation seems too formal, and Sinclair achieves intimacy with an artificial phrase such as "My dear fellow."

For Sinclair, November 1905 brought a triumphant journey to America, where *The Divine Fire* had attained a great reputation before it reached its peak of popularity in England. President Roosevelt, an admirer of Sinclair's, invited her to the White House; she met Sarah Orne Jewett; and she attended the Harper's celebration honoring Mark Twain on his seventieth birthday—where at Delmonico's she sat next to James MacArthur of *Harper's Weekly* and across from Emily Post. She shared with almost no one the news she had received short-

ly after her arrival in America that the last of her five brothers had died, leaving her with no immediate family. Ernest Rhys recalled the irony of Mark Twain's comment about the silently grieving woman whom he sat next to at a dinner: he said he had enjoyed in her company "a remarkably interesting silence." For Sinclair, the American trip marked her sudden initiation into the literary world, where editors and publishers besieged her with requests for her work. She now identified herself as a professional writer. But, unlike many who lauded her, she already had doubts about the greatness of *The Divine Fire,* particularly its form, and in later years a chief source of frustration for her was the opinion advanced by many of her readers that it was her best book.

When she was writing *The Helpmate* (1907), she confided to Morley Roberts, "You should see the opening of my new novel, where I've gone straight to the roots of the matter and cut preliminaries." This novel is more focused and tightly structured than *The Divine Fire* and reveals the degree to which Sinclair had broken with nineteenth-century notions about the relative unimportance of sexuality for women in marriage in comparison to loyalty. She also introduces her negative view about religion, where its easy availability makes it a substitute for human love. From the autobiographical revelations in *Mary Olivier,* one can assume that the dogmatism and intensity of Sinclair's mother's religiosity and her mother's fearful attitude toward sex contributed to Sinclair's characterization of Anne Majendie. Anne's rigid views on mingling of the classes also reflect anxieties that Sinclair's "holy little Mama," seen later in *Mary Olivier,* had often expressed—for example, that her husband's lack of status in the social world because he was a businessman was compensated for in the view of their affluent neighborhood by his ownership of a yacht. When Sinclair's father further lost status because of his bankruptcy in 1870, her mother used her own funds to arrange for each of their sons to own a yacht, in part to maintain their position as members of the upper-middle class, in spite of the financial disaster that had overtaken their father.

In *The Helpmate,* Sinclair studies Anne Majendie's destructive effect upon others when she identifies saintliness with celibacy. Sinclair suggests that Anne is, in part, to blame for the death of her small daughter, Peggy; for the stroke suffered by her husband, Walter; and for breaking up the affectionate relationship between her invalid sister-in-law and a lonely man. While one pities those hurt by Anne, Sinclair sympathetically presents her as a

Some of the guests at Mark Twain's seventieth-birthday party, 5 December 1905: (clockwise around table from left) unidentified woman, James MacArthur, May Sinclair, Hamilton W. Mabie, S. M. Gardenhire, Emily Post, and John A. Mitchell

deeply passionate woman, not as the stereotypical frigid wife. One of the earliest of British psychoanalytical novels, this book is distinguished by Sinclair's analysis of Anne's psychological orientation and her sexual behavior. Anne's ecstasy and passion on the fourth night of her honeymoon turn to disillusionment and physical rejection of Walter Majendie when she learns that he had a mistress, Lady Cayley, seven years earlier and paid the woman to leave town. Anne interprets this affair as unfaithfulness to her.

Sinclair clearly shows that Anne's anger and her intense religious asceticism ineffectively repress her sexual drive, particularly when her "high spiritual life died down in sleep." In her half-waking moments at night she reaches out her arms to enclose her husband; when she is in church and hears him sigh out of longing for her, she responds with a rush of desire. One day in the third year of their marriage, as she is walking in the woods with him, she sees a baby in the grass near a cottage and lifts it up. Feeling a great need to bear her husband's child, she allows her religiously sanctioned maternal aspirations to momentarily lessen her inhibi-

tions and hostility and impulsively gives herself to him when they stop to rest beneath a tree.

Anne's behavior implies that she continues to love Walter, although she continues to resist his physical advances. It is Walter's body—not his spirit—that has offended her. In this irrational division of the man into two halves—physical and mental—she clutches for support in the concept of the dichotomy of flesh and spirit in Christian orthodoxy. She further unconsciously transfers her hatred of Walter's body to hatred of her own body, and then feels insecure about her attractiveness as compared to that of Lady Cayley and later as compared to young Maggie, a flower-shop assistant, to whom Walter turns occasionally after four years of nearly celibate marriage. Anne compensates for her supposed physical unattractiveness through a compulsive search for spiritual perfection. When she becomes pregnant, Walter assumes that the child may rekindle their sexual life, but Anne perversely sees the infant as a more spiritual object of her love and rationalizes that the emotional energy which other women expend in sexual relations she will channel into overwhelming love for the baby, Peggy. Sinclair's complex interpretation is subtle and is naturally suggested wherever appropriate as the novel develops, so that the reader gradually sees Anne revealed as her behavior and meditations are interpreted by these Freudian or Jungian precepts.

In the seventh year of the marriage, Lady Cayley returns, but Walter refuses to resume their affair. Lady Cayley tells Anne of Maggie's affair with Walter, and Peggy—seeing her mother weep—assumes her father is dead and suffers a fatal heart attack. Walter, blamed by Anne for Peggy's death, suffers a stroke. At this point, Anne, as Walter's nurse, must concern herself primarily with Walter's body, which she has tried for seven years to ignore. In her tenderness in touching Walter, her inhibitions weaken. Unfortunately at this point—perhaps to accommodate readers who would be offended by the antireligious overtones of the novel, Sinclair presents the sweeping changes in Anne as religious revelation—that she has failed to love adequately and so God has punished her through the death of Peggy and the illness of Walter. In a long conversation Anne and Walter confess their sinfulness and beg each other's forgiveness. Such lip-service to orthodox religion did not protect the book from hostile reviews. Ezra Pound called the book "the finest, strongest," but few others recognized in it the impressive psychoanalytic characterization that also deepens the artistry of her best later books.

In the period of May Sinclair's greatest achievement as a writer, she wrote four novels which deserve serious discussion—*The Three Sisters* (1914), *Mary Olivier* (1919), *The Tree of Heaven* (1917), and *Life and Death of Harriett Frean* (1922).

In *The Three Sisters* Sinclair emphasized again the psychoanalytical interpretation of several characters, the pervasive effect upon them of the sexual drive and its various forms of expression and repression, and the ways in which heredity may be deterministic or may be altered by strong will. The questioning of self-denial as a positive ethical principle appears again in this novel, as in several of the later books that Sinclair wrote. Nearly all of the issues focused upon in *The Three Sisters* remain as preoccupations in *Mary Olivier*, *Life and Death of Harriett Frean*, and *History of Anthony Waring* (1927). Whereas in most of Sinclair's earlier books she did not stress nature as a positive force in the life of her characters, here, as in the earlier *The Flaw in the Crystal* (1912), the harmony to be found in the natural universe provides strength for Alice Carteret, Gwenda Carteret, and Jim Greatorex, as it did for Agatha Vorrall in the preceding novel.

If Sinclair as novelist continued to be a pioneer in her use of the new psychology, she also at this stage in her career attempted bolder experiments in technique. In *The Three Sisters* she develops her entire novel through a series of chronological episodes, vignettes, or brief conversations, often of only a few moments' duration. They appear as separate revelations of character, as separate events, or as separate thoughts. Since Sinclair offers few transitional statements, chronology provides the chief ordering device. A sustained mood, the use of detailed interiors of a few houses, and the power of the landscape on the characters provide for an intensification of emotional force and for aesthetic unity. The force of the brief scenes is stronger in this novel, in *Life and Death of Harriett Frean*, and in *History of Anthony Waring* than in *Mary Olivier*, where the number of vignettes reaches several hundred rather than a dozen or so and where some of the vignettes are only ten lines long and appear as a numbered series within a chapter. Since the order of the novel depends on chronology, only a few references to the past appear—specifically the explanations about the vicar's three wives, none of whom are present, and about Alice's "wildness," which made it necessary for the family five months before the opening of this novel to move from a well-to-do but conventionally oriented parish at the seashore to the isolated northern village of Garth, surrounded by moors and near only a single farm, that of Jim Greatorex. Consecutive episodes are sometimes separated by a leap of several years; at other times, the moment remains the same and the reader's view is abruptly shifted to another room in the vicarage, to another place in the village, or from the interior of Greatorex's farmhouse to his barn. A single scene or conversation is a chapter, making the chapters of varying lengths but nearly always unusually short; chapter five, for example, is half a page.

In *Mary Olivier* Sinclair pushes this technique further by the use of a "telegraphic" prose style in parts of the book to suggest the fragmentary nature of mental processes, and she employs fragments and phrases as well as full sentences. The controversial fictional technique of accumulating fragments that caught the attention of critics of *Mary Olivier* Sinclair had surely established five years earlier in her separate vignettes of *The Three Sisters*. That same technique was to appear again in modified form in the books on Harriett Frean and Anthony Waring.

In the first pages of *The Three Sisters* Sinclair masterfully and swiftly sets the mood of lethargy and vague anxiety that suffuses the novel, and she also introduces all the characters of consequence. In the dining room of the vicarage, Mary, Gwendolen (Gwenda), and Alice Carteret, the daughters of the vicar, await the prayer service conducted each night at ten o'clock by their father, with the assistance of the young servant, Essie, whose singing and praying are enthusiastic. Gwenda alone tries to be active and cheerful in this scene—although she has worn herself out walking fifteen miles across the moors that day. As they wait, they realize that the reason for their having to move to this poor and isolated parish had been a scandal involving Alice, the youngest daughter. After the prayers, they hear the horse of Dr. Steven Rowcliffe passing the vicarage, and they assume that the doctor is on his way to the bedside of the dying father of the young farmer, Jim Greatorex. All three women see the doctor as the village's only eligible bachelor. He later falls in love with Gwenda but, through a misunderstanding deliberately planned by Mary, he weds Mary instead. Jim Greatorex has already made Essie pregnant, but before long he becomes Alice's lover, makes her pregnant, and marries her. The vicar's indignation at Alice's marriage brings on a stroke which leaves him an invalid, cared for by his most independent, rebellious daughter—Gwenda.

In the opening scene where the daughters await the prayers that put an end to one more intolerable day of boredom for them, Sinclair reached a high point in her artistry. So heavy is the lethargy that the sisters seem drugged. Under the yellow lamplight, they appear to be statues fixed eternally in three different poses. They stare fixedly at some imaginary object in space but see nothing. Their hands hang empty—too heavy to lift. In the last two pages of the novel, Sinclair presents yet again the intolerable time of waiting for the night prayers. Gwenda, the partly paralyzed vicar, and the nagging young mother, Essie, once again await the striking of the hour of ten. At this point, Gwenda has that day lost her earlier verve and spontaneity after realizing that Steven no longer thinks of her. She seems to have joined the rest in their quiet despair and utter lethargy. The closing pages thus complete the frame for the novel projected in the early pages.

The Three Sisters develops as an ironic comedy of errors. The sisters speculate on the various measures they can take to meet Dr. Rowcliffe. Alice, looking out on the moors, shivers by the window in an attempt to get pneumonia so that they will call the doctor to attend her. In a few days she is ill from having half-starved herself, and malnutrition com-

plicates her chronic anemia. Dr. Rowcliffe diagnoses her condition as a neurosis caused by sexual frustration—particularly after he learns that the vicar and his daughters have left their former home because Alice had run after a man. Dr. Rowcliffe stresses the potentially fatal danger of a self-induced starvation and urges that the sisters help Alice marry soon. The vicar is bitter about marriage because he deeply resents the celibacy forced upon him by the desertion of his third wife (the first two wives died). In his frustration, he tyrannizes over his daughters, suspecting their sexuality of being too great and hiding from himself the sexual implications of the jealousy that he feels toward all of the men that his daughters like.

Gwenda, who already loves the doctor and has walked with him at night over the moors, slips away from home to live with her stepmother in London so that—according to Gwenda's naive projection—Alice can save her life by marrying the doctor. Gwenda has told only Mary why she has left for London, and Mary deceives Steven Rowcliffe by implying that Gwenda went there to see other men. Mary thus unscrupulously wins Rowcliffe for herself. Alice has, in the meantime, decided that she prefers the rough masculinity of Greatorex and marries him after she conceives his child. Gwenda returns home when her father suffers a stroke, and for a second time she martyrs herself, becoming this time the nurse for an invalid—the situation at the close of the novel.

Since Sinclair's central theme seems to be a questioning of the ethical value of self-denial, Gwenda's behavior is central to Sinclair's development of the novel. By going away, she did not help Alice; she brought only suffering to herself and Steven; she gave Steven cause to want to attempt adultery to be with her when he realizes that Mary tricked him. Later, when Gwenda thinks that Steven will help her by his presence in the village while she sacrifices herself to the care of her father, she asks him not to move to Liverpool with Mary and the children. He accedes to her request, and in turn engages in destructive self-denial for her sake. The results of this supposedly virtuous act are that he eventually loses his ambition to carry on medical research and he becomes increasingly smothered by Mary's excessive attention to his domestic comforts. At the end of the book when Gwenda recognizes how Steven has degenerated intellectually in Garth, she releases him from his promise to stay near her. She suffers mortifying emotion when she finds that it does not matter to him where he lives, so long as Mary keeps his life easy and comfortable. He has completely lost interest in Gwenda.

In the last pages of the book Gwenda succumbs to a despair and a lethargy as great as that experienced by anyone else in the book. The only hope for her lies in the suggestion that her "hidden" heart will revive whenever she hears the wind; she also still responds to the beauty of the flowering thorn tree. Nevertheless, she thinks now that nature will turn hostile and soon bring her more suffering than ecstasy.

The separate scenes in the book are strong and varied; the psychological analysis of the characters, particularly the women, is subtle and assured; the presentation of family life as unpleasant and debilitating serves as corrective to the idealistic accounts of it in Victorian fiction; and the discussions of sexual problems are refreshing by virtue of their frankness and insight into the feminine psychology.

For those readers who dislike Sinclair's experimentation with short vignettes, the best of Sinclair's later novels might be *The Tree of Heaven*. It was her record-breaking best-seller, and it appeared just in time to meet the popular demand for books about the war, especially books that offered an optimistic view of social and political change. Sinclair introduces the many members of an extended family—grandmothers, aunts, uncles, and cousins. Grannie Fleming, mother of Frances Harrison and mother-in-law of Anthony Harrison, is a tyrannical matriarch who holds antifeminist and antisuffrage views and still rules over the three Aunties, her unmarried daughters, as if they were children.

Trying to be less repressive to her children than her mother had been, Frances Harrison in the next generation encourages her sons and daughter to develop freely and imaginatively, but she unconsciously exercises more control over her daughter, Dorothea, than she does over her sons, Michael and Nicky. Dorothea becomes an economist and suffragist; Michael, a humanist studying art and literature; and Nicky, an engineer who designs military equipment for the war. The novel reflects the changing times in Anthony Harrison's business troubles with the Irish independence movement and with labor union strikes. His brother, Bartholomew, contends with a wife who is trying out the new sexual freedom and having extramarital affairs.

One must wonder about Sinclair's feminism when she has Dorothea express regret, after her lover is killed in the war, that she wasted time on feminist demonstrations when she could have spent time with him. This novel emphasizes patriotism, the privilege of serving one's country, and pride in the military. Sinclair competently handled the crowded stage and the multiple plots made necessary by the saga of the large Harrison family.

Mary Olivier was, for Sinclair, her best book, but many have felt that it is overly episodic and lacking in unity. The tremendous number of relatively unconnected short passages called for stronger characters or weightier themes to unify them. The incidents seem to have only one tonality and seem relatively undifferentiated from one another; and the disparate parts of the novel require a larger perspective than this novel provides. It is much longer than *The Three Sisters* and far more centered in the consciousness of one character. The problem of presenting the passing of time is great because Sinclair's new technique required that she maintain a chronological framework in a book featuring many unconnected episodes and few transitional statements. In this case, the Freudian background obtrudes so strongly that Sinclair becomes overinsistent on the necessary relationship between the Mary Olivier at forty-seven and the Mary Olivier at the age of two. H. G. Wells wrote Sinclair that the book was "delightful and wonderful," but it sold very poorly. Edwin Arlington Robinson, in telling her he liked the book, expressed his hope that she would return to her "more leisurely and discursive method." But Sinclair herself declared in 1924 that this book was her favorite. "I consider it my best book, and doubt if I shall ever be able to improve on it."

Sinclair in this novel uses many autobiographical details: the five brothers of Mary; the alcoholic Papa; the antisexual Mama, who expects her grown daughter to assume her mother's anthropomorphic concept of God; the favorite brother who succeeds in India and who was idealized by the possessive Mama; the brother who failed in America; and the long need for the grown daughter to nurse her mother. The several loves of Mary, however, appear to be fictional.

Mary Olivier today still has interest for the reader, beyond the autobiographical references. But a reader can best appreciate it, possibly, in sections, rather than as a whole novel. The telegraphic style, the attempt to write from the view of the two-year-old, or the confusion resulting from addressing the main character as "you" or "Mary" are experimental devices that sometimes seem successful and sometimes seem forced. *Mary Olivier* lacks the force and the impressive characters to be a

May Sinclair at her writing hut at Stow-on-the-Wold, circa 1920-1924. She began going there to write in 1919.

great novel, yet the reader admires the author for trying to do something unusual instead of repeating herself.

Generally speaking, except for *Life and Death of Harriett Frean*, the novels Sinclair published after 1920 are not her most distinguished and do not indicate any continuing development in her artistry. Her worsening illness necessitated her moving from London, and her physicians advised that she limit her social life. She thus lacked in these years the stimulation and encouragement of other writers to which she had become accustomed.

In *Life and Death of Harriett Frean* Sinclair, as in so many other books, considers the negative effects of supposedly altruistic self-denial. Like Gwenda in *The Three Sisters* and like Mary Olivier, Harriett remains close to her parents and then nurses her mother until her death, although mother and daughter have relatively little in common. If she gives herself to her parents in a self-sacrificing devotion, her parents have, even more significantly, denied themselves for her sake. One feels that Harriett is less motivated by self-sacrifice, even in rejecting her lover, than she is by immature dependence on her parents. She deliberately refuses to accept the proposal of Robin Lethbridge, the man she loves, because he had originally planned to marry Prissy, her best friend at school. Harriett's parents affirm the virtue of her decision made for Prissy's

well-being. However, it causes suffering for Robin to marry a woman he loved less than Harriett, and as Prissy senses his lack of love, she suffers a long-term paralysis induced mostly by an unconscious demand that her husband show his devotion to her.

As she ages, Harriett finds herself alone, and she now is forced to see the one great act of her life—giving up Robin— as negative. She becomes increasingly class-conscious and snobbish, assuming falsely that people are impressed when she tells them her father's name. As she becomes less happy, she recalls the haunting sense she had had as a child of playing mother to a doll who had become a dead baby—a baby she hid in a drawer-cemetery. All she has brought forth in her life has been dead, and she is barren. When her maid, Maggie, has a baby out of wedlock and needs to bring the infant to work with her, Harriett becomes increasingly tormented by the baby's presence and forbids Maggie to bring her to the house. As a result, the baby dies of neglect. In the final pages of the novel, Harriett feels pride and perverse joy that she is following her mother's example because she suffers from cancer, the disease her mother met with such dignity and courage. After her surgery, she reaches down and touches an ice bag placed between her legs and identifies it as the baby she has just borne as a result of such great pain. Again, what she has delivered has been lifeless and her effort futile. In her confusion, she calls out to the nurse, "Mama! . . ." She has again become her mother's baby.

Two years after she wrote *Life and Death of Harriett Frean*, Sinclair commented on its relationship to *Mary Olivier*: "I went with her over the road I had already gone with Mary Olivier and put her to similar tests. I think that I succeeded technically, and *Harriett Frean* is one of the best books I have done." Certainly, this is one of Sinclair's most effective explorations of the ethical value of self-denial, and probably a more successful book—if a less ambitious one—than *Mary Olivier*.

While *The Three Sisters, Mary Olivier, The Tree of Heaven,* and *Life and Death of Harriett Frean* stand above the rest of Sinclair's works in this major period of her achievement, several other novels that may never be revived sold moderately well in their time. More important, they enlarge our understanding of Sinclair's strong literary output at this time. They focus perceptively on changing attitudes toward marriage and, in several cases, also address the personal and artistic problems of a developing writer. These novels as a group reflect Sinclair's ambivalent views in a time of social and intellectual change, and they also reflect the taste of the popular reader in the years just before and after World War I. Most important for discussion are: *Kitty Tailleur* (1908), *The Creators* (1910), *The Flaw in the Crystal* (1912), *The Combined Maze* (1913), *Tasker Jevons* (1916), and *The Romantic* (1920).

In *Kitty Tailleur* (published in America as *The Immortal Moment*), Sinclair narrowly avoids making Kitty's portrayal that of the "noble prostitute," whose superior humanity contrasts with her sordid profession. Kitty honestly faces the problems involved in marrying the man she loves without telling him of her past. She understands why he rejects her as the stepmother for his little daughters. She also clearly recognizes that her former lover now proposes marriage only to get more permanent ownership of her. Nevertheless, Sinclair does not convince the reader that in 1908 suicide was the only answer for an apparently highly paid prostitute who wished to break away from her work. The book fails because of its sentimentality, although Kitty does become more than a stereotyped figure.

In *The Creators* and *Tasker Jevons* Sinclair considers several writers' struggles toward success in the literary world and also the effects of artistic ambition and of class difference on marriage. In *The Creators* she studies three married couples and a single woman. Her general conclusion would appear to be that an artist—male or female—cannot maintain "the double and divided flame" of marriage and artistic growth. George Tanqueray decides against marrying another novelist, who would expect intellectual companionship, and instead marries a servant girl. He insensitively fails to see his cruelty to her as he writes constantly for months, ignoring her and refusing to let her have the baby she wants because a child might interrupt his work. Jane Holland finds herself putting the needs of her husband's relatives and their children ahead of her own need for time for sustained work on her novels. She finally cries out that she will go mad if she cannot be fulfilled by the production of better novels each year, just as some women go mad when not fulfilled by pregnancy. Sinclair's probing inquiry may be broadened to the question of whether marriage and any significant career can be reconciled. She certainly doubts whether an artist should ever marry—a revolutionary issue in any age. Ezra Pound, disturbed after reading the first 163 pages of *The Creators*, wrote Sinclair that she must join him at once in Paris, because "The book is a perfect sign of the decadence which makes me stay out of London."

In *Tasker Jevons* she explores the weaknesses (and paradoxical strengths) of the marriage between the upper-class Viola Thesiger and Tasker "Jimmie" Jevons, novelist and son of a public registrar. When Viola leaves because she finds Jimmie's taste vulgar and his uninhibited behavior embarrassing, he becomes an ambulance driver. Wanting to remain near him, she volunteers also for battlefield work. Sinclair experiments for the first time with a narrator who is also developed as a character in a novel—in this case, a war correspondent. Jimmie saves Viola's favorite brother's life under fire, and thus is finally accepted by her snobbish family. When he and Viola are reunited, the reconciliation is not contrived or sentimental. Viola comments sensibly that "nobody but Jimmie knows how nice I *am*," and Jimmie recognizes the value—as well as the problem—connected with a marriage between people of different background and class when he remarks, "I'm the queer, unexpected thing she wants and will always want." Sinclair's treatment of Jimmie's methodical approach to success in fiction writing is lightly satiric. He calls himself "an engineer in literature." But the qualities Viola loves in him will make him a provocative novelist—he is surprising, unpredictable, honest, mysterious, and exciting.

The Flaw in the Crystal shows Sinclair's conventional belief that every attempt must be made to save an unsatisfactory marriage and that the happiness of the "other woman" must always be second to that of wife or husband. Agatha Verral, who meets Rodney Lanyon on weekends fifteen miles from London for their platonic affair, is ill, Sinclair makes clear, in part because her unconscious mind registers disapproval of her love for another woman's husband, even though she and Rodney do not have sexual intercourse. Rodney needs Agatha's company to provide relief from the tension of living with Bella, his wife, who suffers a long-term nervous illness. Agatha is a psychic with healing powers, but she knows that to tap the unlimited power implicit in the harmony of the universe she must be crystal pure—her vessel, to receive the healing spirit, must not be flawed by sexual desire nor wish for selfish gain through use of healing powers. If she becomes personally and emotionally involved with her patient, Rodney, she becomes vulnerable to the illness she drives out of the patient—she will have her own energy sucked away. The ominous process of self-destruction through selfish use of spiritual power is already evident to her in her slight sense of illness.

In a "flawless" healing she cures Bella by the power of her will—at a safe distance of fifteen miles. Rodney now will no longer need to come to Agatha for comfort. Not only does this tale draw on Sinclair's interest in psychoanalysis and psychic healing but also upon her interest in the ghost story as a literary form. This short novel Sinclair later included in *Uncanny Stories* (1923).

The Combined Maze recounts the entrapment in marriage of a twenty-three-year-old athlete who runs, swims, and performs gymnastics every night at the London Polytechnic Gymnasium and works as a clerk in a furnishing store by day. The "combined maze," an intricately designed footrace staged in the gymnasium demonstration each year, is the product of scores of men and women, assigned to be partners, running as fast as possible—linked together—through the long and intricate relay. It becomes the symbol for Ranny's marriage. He has been running joyfully at the gym with Winnie Dymond, a bookkeeper, who is the most engaging perhaps of all the women characters created by Sinclair. On impulse, he disastrously marries Violet Usher, who later abuses their children and then deserts Ranny and the children in order to run away with a lover. Ranny saves money for five years to get a divorce, and on the night that he and Winnie celebrate the filing for divorce, Violet returns to block the action. She tells of at least five lovers who have beaten and abandoned her; she has damaged lungs; and she persuades Ranny, who hates her, that he must out of pity take her back.

The conscientious and loving Winnie agrees that, if Ranny does not, Violet might become a "bad woman" on the streets. The disarming, detached comic tone of the narrative passages, the strong characterization of Ranny and Winnie, and the vivid day-by-day depiction of the fun and the pain of London's low-paid clerks and shop girls make the novel extremely moving and memorable, if not a great work of art.

In *The Romantic* Charlotte Redhead, recovering from a broken affair, is cautious about a sexual commitment to John Conway. Both are romantics. He seems particularly adventurous, though paradoxically fearful at times. Charlotte refuses to acknowledge even to herself that she is sexually attracted to John, and she convinces herself that she loves him primarily because he has a superb mind and personality. Such temporary repression—and hypocrisy—may be common in early attraction, but the shocking difference here lies both in Conway's psychosis (which Sinclair connects with impotence) and in Charlotte's long-continued refusal to admit that her interest in him sexually is stronger than her admiration of his mind. He pursues her with ardor and then suddenly acts as if he hates sex. Finally leaving Charlotte, Conway seeks romantic adventure on the battlefield but, as in sexual encounters, at the moment of great physical challenge he suddenly grows fearful of decisive action and retreats. Conway dies, but only after his cowardice at a crucial moment causes death to hundreds of Belgian soldiers.

For the first time, Sinclair includes psychiatrists as characters in a novel. Here one psychiatrist helps Charlotte recover from the grief and sense of guilt she has taken on herself by identifying with her lover and his destructive behavior. The other psychiatrist explains to her what he understands about John's personality (and this physician will become her lover once she is freed from her confused entanglement with John's memory). She is made to see that she invented John's "attractive mind" to repress her sexual desire for him and based an attachment on an illusion. She also is helped to understand that John's impotence caused his symptoms of sudden hatred at the moment of high desire and also his sudden fear and cowardice when faced with physical danger and challenge after having sought such adventure. May Sinclair wrote that earlier in her career she would have been unable to make Charlotte so sympathetic a character after describing her at the beginning of a novel as a woman who had had an extramarital affair.

By 1919 Sinclair's physical health had de-

May Sinclair, circa 1930

clined to the point that she had to give up her athletic activities and was unable to walk without some difficulty. The degenerative effects of the illness on her central nervous system were not dramatic at this stage. In spite of fatigue and pain, she was able to continue writing and did so with almost frantic speed. But, for the most part, the books she completed during her illness were of poorer quality, and only *Life and Death of Harriett Frean* increased her literary reputation. Two comic satires of ceremonious religiosity and egotism— *Mr. Waddington of Wyck* (1921) and *A Cure of Souls* (1923)—received favorable reviews and sold well to Sinclair's loyal readers. *The Rector of Wyck* (1925) was not equal to *Mr. Waddington of Wyck;* and *History of Anthony Waring* (1927), which Sinclair thought could be seen as a companion volume to her book on Harriett Frean, is far less effective—with loose organization of episodes, weak characterizations, and lack of unifying themes. Readers noticed that incidents or passages or characters from earlier books seemed to be appearing in the new books, and distracting repetitiousness within the late novels is evident. In *The Dark Night* (1924), *Arnold Waterlow* (1924), and *The Rector of Wyck* she returns

to her early themes—the importance of selflessness and the reward of mystical insight as spiritual compensation for self-sacrifice. Given the debilitating sickness from which she suffered, the weakness of these novels is less surprising than is the excellence of *Life and Death of Harriett Frean* in this period.

These late works lack the imaginative zest and the control of her craft that had distinguished her work in the dozen years that preceded them and that might have made her an even greater writer than she was in those years. The reason for her artistic regression can be understood now, but her reputation was hurt by contemporary reviews like Gertrude Atherton's in 1923: "There was a time when Miss Sinclair got down to the business of her story with as little delay as any expert. Now she meanders through chapters and chapters about nothing, devoting all her art and skill to describing insignificance in polished phrases."

As one considers May Sinclair's strong interest in the life and work of the Brontë sisters in relation to her own fiction, one can see her novels, like theirs, as departures from the staidness and propriety in much of Victorian art and morality. Sinclair evinces the keen sensibilities of the Brontës, but in her fiction she lacked their ability to convey passion as effectively as they did. She remains a most interesting writer of the first two decades of the twentieth century, but not a great writer nor one who changed the history of the British novel.

Bibliographies:

T. E. M. Boll, "May Sinclair: A Check List," *Bulletin of the New York Public Library*, 74 (September 1970): 459-467;

Kenneth Robb, "May Sinclair: An Annotated Bibliography of Writings About Her," *English Literature in Transition*, 16, no. 3 (1973): 177-231.

References:

T. E. M. Boll, *Miss May Sinclair: Novelist* (Rutherford, N.J.: Fairleigh Dickinson University Press, 1973);

Hrisey Zegger, *May Sinclair* (Boston: G. K. Hall, 1976).

Papers:

The University of Pennsylvania Library has a collection of Sinclair's papers. See T. E. M. Boll, "On the May Sinclair Collection," *Library Chronicle*, 27, no. 1 (Winter 1961): 1-15.

Bram Stoker

(8 November 1847-20 April 1912)

Daniel Farson and Philip B. Dematteis

BOOKS: *The Duties of Clerks of Petty Sessions in Ireland* (Dublin: Privately printed, 1879);

Under the Sunset (London: Low, Marston, Searle & Rivington, 1882);

A Glimpse of America: A Lecture Given at the London Institution, 28th December, 1885 (London: Low, Marston, Searle & Rivington, 1886);

The Snake's Pass (New York: Harper, 1890; London: Low, Marston, Searle & Rivington, 1891);

The Watter's Mou' (New York: De Vinne, 1894; London: Constable, 1895);

Crooken Sands (New York: De Vinne, 1894);

The Man from Shorrox's (New York: De Vinne, 1894);

The Shoulder of Shasta (London: Constable, 1895);

Dracula (London: Constable, 1897; Garden City: Grosset & Dunlap, 1897);

Miss Betty (London: Pearson, 1898);

Sir Henry Irving and Miss Ellen Terry in Robespierre, Merchant of Venice, The Bells, Nance Oldfield, The Amber Heart, Waterloo, *etc., Drawn by Pamela C. Smith* (New York: Doubleday & McClure, 1899);

The Mystery of the Sea: A Novel (New York: Doubleday, Page, 1902);

The Jewel of Seven Stars (London: Heinemann, 1903; New York: Harper, 1904);

The Man (London: Heinemann, 1905);

Personal Reminiscences of Henry Irving, 2 volumes (London: Heinemann, 1906; New York: Macmillan, 1906);

Snowbound: The Record of a Theatrical Touring Party (London: Collier, 1908);

Lady Athlyne (London: Macmillan, 1908; New York: Reynolds, 1908);

The Gates of Life (New York: Cupples & Leon, 1908);

The Lady of the Shroud (London: Heinemann, 1909);

Famous Impostors (London: Sidgwick & Jackson, 1910; New York: Sturgis & Walton, 1910);

The Lair of the White Worm (London: Rider, 1911);

Dracula's Guest, and Other Weird Stories (London: Routledge, 1914; New York: Hillman-Curl, 1937);

The Bram Stoker Bedside Companion: Ten Stories by the Author of Dracula, edited by Charles Osborne (London: Gollancz, 1973).

PERIODICAL PUBLICATION: "The Censorship of Stage Plays," *Nineteenth Century*, 66 (December 1909): 974-989.

Without *Dracula* (1897), Bram Stoker would be forgotten. As it is, he is one of the least-known authors of one of the best-known books. *Dracula* was his masterpiece, and a writer only needs one of those to achieve immortality; but Stoker was obscured by his creation of Count Dracula, just as Mary Shelley is hardly remembered though *Frankenstein* is a household word.

Stoker led a varied literary life which has been overshadowed by his most successful work. But Stoker's career ranged from rather strange children's stories to nonfiction to a handful of romances. Still, even *Dracula* is often relegated to the rank of second-rate literature, as a work which is of interest not as much for its literary merit as for its intriguingly macabre subject matter. As Anthony Boucher suggests, *Dracula* is "a masterpiece of a kind, if not a literary one."

Abraham ("Bram") Stoker was born on 8 November 1847 in Dublin, the third of the seven children of Abraham and Charlotte Thornley Stoker. The elder Abraham Stoker was a civil servant who worked as chief secretary at Dublin Castle. Charlotte Stoker, twenty years younger than her husband, was the stronger personality, and possessed a vaulting ambition for her five sons. When she was twenty-four, she had experienced the cholera epidemic which reached the town of Sligo in Western Ireland in 1832; the town became "a place of the dead." According to family legend, her house was bolted and secure, but one day she saw the hand of a looter reaching through a skylight, seized an axe, and chopped it off. She remembered an army sergeant who "died" from the plague and was so tall that the undertaker had to break his legs to squeeze him into the coffin; at the first blow, the man revived. Her accounts of the plague and of the narrowly averted premature burial became favorite bedtime stories during Bram's long childhood illness. This illness has never been explained; Stoker says of it in his *Personal Reminiscences of Henry Irving* (1906): "In my babyhood I used, I understand, to be often at the point of death. Certainly till I was about seven years old I never knew what it was to stand upright."

His recovery was remarkable, for by the time he entered Trinity College, Dublin, in 1864, he was a red-haired giant. As if to eradicate the feebleness of the boy and prove himself the man, he won his cap as footballer and numerous prizes for walking, and became the athletics champion of the university after two years.

It was while Stoker was at Trinity that he first saw Henry Irving, the actor whom he was to serve faithfully for twenty-seven years. On 28 August 1867 Irving appeared as Captain Absolute in a production of Richard Brinsley Sheridan's *The Rivals* at the Theatre Royal. Stoker was highly impressed by Irving's performance, but he was not to meet the actor for another ten years.

Stoker was still at Trinity in 1868 when Walt Whitman's *Leaves of Grass* was published in Britain and attacked as morally offensive. Stoker decided to read the controversial book for himself: "Very shortly my own opinion began to form; it was diametrically opposed to that which I had been hearing. From that hour I became a lover of Walt Whitman." Stoker defended Whitman's work and began a correspondence with the poet.

After graduating from Trinity with honors in mathematics in 1868, Stoker became a clerk in the Irish civil service at Dublin Castle, a position secured for him by his father. He found the job extremely boring and sought relaxation in reading Whitman, writing essays, and going to the theater.

In May 1871 Irving returned to Dublin in *Two Roses* by James Albery. Stoker went to see the play three times; then, incensed at seeing that the local newspapers made no mention of it, he offered his services to the Dublin *Mail* as unpaid drama critic. The offer was accepted, and Stoker held the position for the next six years. He also took on the job of tutoring students at Trinity to help his parents pay for their sons' education (his older brother, William, became a prominent surgeon and was knighted in 1895); gave speeches at the college; briefly edited a newspaper, the *Halfpenny Press*, in 1872; and wrote "The Chain of Destiny," a four-part serial about "a phantom fiend," for the *Shamrock* magazine in 1875.

In 1876 Irving returned to Dublin in *Hamlet*. Stoker was overwhelmed: "In his fits of passion there is a realism that no one but a genius can ever effect," he wrote in the *Mail*, and the young actor was so flattered that he invited Stoker to supper at his hotel; "and so began the close friendship between us which only terminated with his life—if indeed friendship, like any other form of love, can ever terminate." To please his new friend, Irving gave a private reading of Thomas Hood's poem *The Dream of Eugene Aram* and brought such power to the occasion that Stoker became hysterical when it was over, much to the surprise of his friends and himself. Irving staggered into his bedroom and emerged with a signed photograph, the ink of his inscription still wet: "My Dear Friend Stoker. God Bless You! God Bless You!! Henry Irving. Dublin, 3 Dec. 1876." The outwardly phlegmatic Stoker wrote later: "In those moments of mutual emotion he too had found a friend and knew it. Soul had looked into soul! From that hour began a friendship as profound, as close, as lasting as can be between two men."

Though he would have been appalled by the suggestion of anything physical, Stoker had fallen in love. Throughout his life he needed heroes—

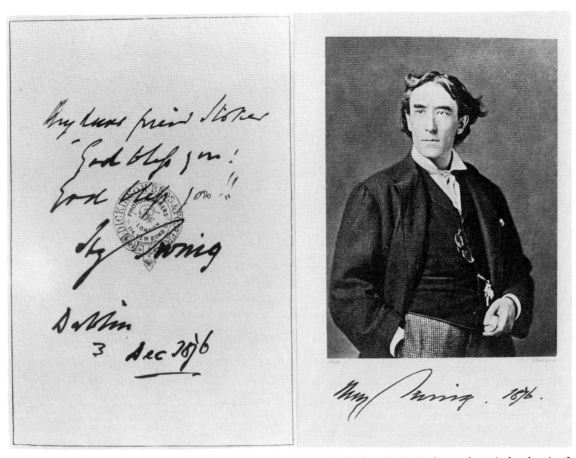

Photograph, with inscription on the back, that actor Henry Irving presented to Stoker after Stoker became hysterical on hearing Irving's dramatic recitation of The Dream of Eugene Aram *(Stoker,* Personal Reminiscences of Henry Irving, *1906)*

Whitman, Lord Tennyson—but his attachment to the actor, ten years older than himself and poised on the threshold of his career when they met, was the most enduring. Stoker was happy to stand in the wings applauding, while Irving stood in the spotlight receiving the applause.

Early in 1877 Stoker was promoted to the position of inspector of the courts of petty sessions, a more interesting job than his clerkship. He resigned as unpaid drama critic of the *Mail* to work on his first book, *The Duties of Clerks of Petty Sessions in Ireland* (1879).

During 1877 and 1878 Stoker and Irving met several times, both in Dublin and in London. Finally, in November 1878 Irving was able to secure a lease on the Lyceum Theatre in London, where he planned to form his own acting company. He offered Stoker the position of acting manager, and Stoker immediately accepted. Abandoning the civil service, Stoker moved up his planned marriage to his neighbor, the nineteen-year-old Florence Balcombe, to 4 December. He then sailed joyfully to

England with his bride—though his mother expressed her disapproval: "What a pity it is that my son has gone off to join a *strolling player*."

These were Stoker's happiest years. He was involved with the early triumphs of Irving and Ellen Terry and became a familiar figure himself, huge and red-bearded, as he stood by the Lyceum staircase on the first nights to welcome royalty, visiting celebrities, and the lions of London society. With an extraordinary capacity for work, he wrote several hundred letters a week on behalf of the theater; cultivated his friendships; looked after Irving; studied for the bar in his "spare time"; and started writing a succession of books.

The first was *Under the Sunset* (1882), a collection of highly unsuitable stories for children; one of them, "The Invisible Giant," about an impending plague, may have been inspired by his mother's experience in Sligo. It is dedicated to his only child, his son Noel, born on 29 December 1879.

In September 1882 Stoker saw a fellow passenger on a Thames steamer dive overboard in a suicide attempt. The burly Stoker jumped in after the man, overcame his struggles, and took him to his own home for medical treatment. The man died anyway, but Stoker was awarded a medal by the Royal Humane Society for his brave rescue attempt.

With Florence established in London as a successful hostess, everything seemed perfect; but appearances were deceptive. Florence was a considerable beauty and flirt: Oscar Wilde had thought himself in love with her before her marriage to Stoker and had made an excellent drawing of her; later in her life she encouraged a literary flirtation with W. S. Gilbert. But she was a cold woman, more interested in society than in her husband or son. Her frigidity has been confirmed by her granddaughter, Ann McCaw: "She was cursed with her great beauty and the need to maintain it. In my knowledge now, she was very anti-sex. After having my father in her early twenties, I think she was quite put off. I think it's highly probable that she refused to have sex with Bram after my father was born." If so, Stoker's sexual frustration forced him to go elsewhere, with disastrous results.

At least he was able to immerse himself in the affairs of the Lyceum. The annual American tours from 1883 until 1904 gave him the opportunity to meet his idol Walt Whitman and make new friends such as Mark Twain. One tour, however, was ruined by his rivalry with Irving's secretary, Louis Austin, who possessed a flippant sense of humor and seized every opportunity to bait and goad the stalwart Stoker, even making fun of the latter's literary efforts in front of Irving. In one letter, Austin—presumably referring to *Under the Sunset*—made a surprising revelation: "His first effort in literature, that marvellous book neither you nor I nor anybody else could understand, cost him seven hundred pounds, for which he has never had and never will have the smallest return." The fact that Stoker would invest such a sum, considerable in those days, reveals his new prosperity at the Lyceum and his faith in himself but also the lack of enthusiasm on the part of publishers.

Nonetheless, Stoker continued to write in his rare free moments. In 1889 his first full-length novel, *The Snake's Pass*, was serialized in several magazines and newspapers; it was published in book form in 1890 and was well received. Set on the wild, stormy coast of Ireland, it is a romantic novel involving a buried treasure, the rivalry of two men for a beautiful girl, and a villain who sinks into a bog.

At the Lyceum, Stoker lorded it behind the scenes and met the most interesting people of the

Bram Stoker, 1885

time when Irving entertained them in his private Beefsteak Club at the back of the theater. Guests such as Henry Morton Stanley and Sir Richard Francis Burton—who had translated *Vikram and the Vampire* (1870) from Hindi—were stimulating in their after-supper conversation; but the crucial inspiration came from a celebrity of the day, a Hungarian adventurer, traveler, and professor named Arminius Vambery, who recounted the legends of vampirism in Eastern Europe. Stoker met Vambery on 30 April 1890; in August he began work on *Dracula* while on vacation at Whitby, on the Yorkshire coast. It was apparently in the library at Whitby that Stoker first learned of Vlad, ruler of Wallachia—now part of Rumania—during the fifteenth century. Vlad successfully defended Wallachia against invasion by the Turks of the Ottoman Empire; but he was also an unspeakably cruel man who came to be called Vlad Tepes—Vlad the Impaler—for his favorite method of torture and execution. Vlad's father had the title of Dracul, having been invested with the Order of the Dragon by the Holy Roman Emperor; hence Vlad the Impaler was also known as the son of Dracul, or Dracula. Though he was reputed to have sometimes drunk the blood of his victims, the historical Dracula was never associated with vampirism; this connection was made by Stoker in his novel. Stoker also took the liberty of moving Dracula's castle from Wallachia to an adjacent Rumanian province with the more romantic and mysterious name of Transylvania—"the land beyond the forest."

Although he claimed that the idea for the novel came to him in a nightmare after a dinner of dressed crab, Stoker probably also derived inspiration for *Dracula* from at least two previous vampire tales: the novel *The Vampyre* (1819) by Lord Byron's friend, Dr. John Polidori; and the short story "Carmilla" (1871) by Stoker's fellow Dubliner, Joseph

Arminius Vambery, the Hungarian professor who introduced Stoker to the vampire legends of eastern Europe. In Dracula, *Professor Van Helsing refers to "my friend Arminius."*

Sheridan Le Fanu. The influence of Le Fanu's story can be found in Stoker's notes for *Dracula*, which show that Dracula's castle was originally to be located in Styria, the setting for "Carmilla." Stoker crossed out *Styria* and substituted *Transylvania*.

Although Leonard Wolf has called Stoker "a hasty writer with the habits of a hack," it is clear that a great deal of research and planning was done for *Dracula*. At Whitby, where the count first lands in England and where he attacks Lucy Westenra, Stoker made sketches of the town and its graveyard, consulted coast guard logs and weather manuals, and interviewed local people about shipwrecks. In London he gathered more information about vampire lore at the British Museum; he also asked his surgeon brother about the symptoms and treatment of a severe head injury such as the one that kills Renfield in chapter twenty-one. The early chapters describe Transylvania with such accuracy that the same landmarks can be found today, yet Stoker never set foot there. The complicated method of telling the story entirely by means of journals, diaries, letters, dictaphone recordings, memoranda, and newspaper clippings, and from several parallel points of view which ultimately converge, was also carefully worked out by Stoker. His notes for the novel, some of them on hotel stationery, indicate that he worked on it even during the Lyceum company's tours to America and the provinces.

The actual writing of *Dracula* was apparently done during three vacations: in 1892 at Bocastle and in 1893 and 1896 at Cruden Bay, Scotland. The book was finally published in 1897.

The year in which the action of the novel takes place is never given, but it is obviously supposed to be nearly contemporary with the date of the book's publication; a note by one of the characters at the end says that the events occurred "seven years ago." The first part of the novel is a series of extracts from the journal of Jonathan Harker, a young English solicitor who has been sent to Transylvania to help Count Dracula complete the purchase of a house in the suburbs of London. Peasants express alarm on hearing that his destination is Castle Dracula and warn him not to go; one woman even places a rosary around his neck. He dismisses their vaguely expressed fears as mere superstitions.

Count Dracula turns out to be "a tall old man, clean shaven save for a long white moustache, and clad in black from head to foot," with reddish eyes, sharp white teeth, and a pale complexion except for his full, red lips. During his stay of nearly two months at the castle, during which it gradually

The harbor at Whitby, on the Yorkshire coast, where Stoker began writing Dracula. *In the novel Whitby is Dracula's point of entry into England.*

dawns on him that he is being held prisoner, Harker has many weird and terrifying experiences. He notices that the count is never about during the daylight hours and never seems to eat or drink; he can speak of events hundreds of years in the past "as if he had been present at them all." Dracula casts no reflection in a mirror; and when Harker cuts himself while shaving, Dracula lunges for his throat— only to stop short when he touches the rosary. After disobeying Dracula's warning not to fall asleep anywhere in the castle except the guest room that has been provided for him, Harker awakes to find three beautiful women arguing over who is to be the first to "kiss" him. As he lies there with mingled feelings of fear and erotic anticipation, one of the women places her mouth to his throat; but the count bursts into the room and chases the women away, telling them: "This man belongs to me!" Harker passes out and wakes up in his own bed.

On several occasions he sees the count climb down the castle wall head first, like a lizard; he realizes that Dracula is stealing babies, which he brings back to the castle in a sack. When a distraught mother runs into the courtyard to plead for

her child's return, Dracula commands a pack of wolves to tear her to shreds. Harker finally discovers that the count sleeps in his coffin in a crypt beneath the castle during the day, and realizes that Dracula is preparing to have himself shipped to England. His journal breaks off with his decision to try to climb down the sheer castle wall and the precipice below, in order to escape or die in the attempt.

The scene then shifts to England, and back in time to the beginning of Harker's stay at Castle Dracula. In a letter to Mina Murray, Harker's fiancée, the beautiful Lucy Westenra tells of the three marriage proposals she has received in one day: from Dr. John Seward, the head of a lunatic asylum; from Quincey Morris, a Texan; and from Arthur Holmwood, the future Lord Godalming. She has accepted Holmwood's proposal. In an exchange of letters and telegrams, the three men— who are old friends—reaffirm their friendship, and the two rejected suitors commiserate with each other and congratulate Holmwood. Meanwhile, Dr. Seward confides his grief to the diary that he keeps on a phonograph and decides to throw himself into his work. He is particularly interested in a patient named R. M. Renfield, who has a proclivity for eating insects, birds, and rats for the "life" that is in them.

While waiting for Harker to return from Transylvania, Mina joins Lucy and her mother on vacation in Whitby; events there are described in her diary and in newspaper articles. One stormy night a Russian schooner runs aground in Whitby harbor. Aboard the ship is the body of the captain, lashed to the wheel; the ship's log, which tells of the disappearances of the crew members, one by one, during the voyage; a large black dog, which leaps ashore and disappears; and fifty boxes of earth, which are soon claimed by an agent and taken to London.

Almost immediately after the arrival of the mysterious ship, Lucy begins having nightmares and sleepwalking. When Mina awakes one night, Lucy is gone; Mina finds her in the churchyard, sitting on a bench on the grave of a suicide. A tall man with red eyes is bending over her, but he disappears when Mina's view is briefly blocked. Later, Mina notices two tiny holes in Lucy's neck, which she assumes she caused when she pinned Lucy's shawl around her in the churchyard. Back in London, Dr. Seward records in his phonographic diary that Renfield is growing increasingly restless and

A portrait of the real Dracula, Vlad the Impaler, who is believed to have had between 40,000 and 100,000 people put to death during his fifteenth-century reign in Wallachia

making enigmatic comments such as "The Master is here."

Lucy's sleepwalking continues; in addition, she seems to be getting progressively weaker and paler. Mina also notices a large bat hovering near the house. At this point, Mina receives a letter from a hospital in Budapest informing her that Jonathan has been there for six weeks suffering from "brain fever." She goes to join him, and they are married when he has recovered from his delirium.

In Whitby, Lucy—who has now begun keeping a diary—is growing worse. Holmwood writes to his friend and former rival, Seward, asking him to have a look at his fiancée. Seward, in turn, calls in his old professor, Abraham Van Helsing of Amsterdam. Van Helsing transfuses blood from Holmwood into the anemic Lucy, and she recovers temporarily; but a few mornings later the doctors find her paler than before, and this time she receives blood from Seward. Van Helsing also places a wreath of garlic flowers around her neck, and more garlic around her window. During the night, however, Lucy's mother removes the garlic and opens the window to let in some fresh air; and in the morning she is worse than before. Van Helsing gives her his own blood and replaces the garlic.

That night, Lucy and her mother are sitting up together when a monstrous wolf crashes its head through the window; Mrs. Westenra tears the garlic from Lucy's neck in her fright before dying of a heart attack, and Lucy faints. The next day the doctors discover her, weaker than ever; Quincey Morris shows up just in time to donate his blood. But it is too late, and Lucy dies two days later. She is buried in the family tomb in London.

The Harkers return to England with Jonathan believing that his experiences at Castle Dracula were a product of his delirium; but on their way home he is shocked to see the count on a London street, apparently much younger than he had been in Transylvania. Still not sure of his sanity, he says nothing to Mina. On their arrival at home, they receive a telegram from Van Helsing—who had heard of Mina from Lucy—informing them of Lucy's death.

Soon after Lucy's burial, the newspapers report that several small children have disappeared from the vicinity of the cemetery on successive evenings, only to be found the next morning in a weakened condition, with puncture marks in their throats. Each child tells of being lured away by an attractive "bloofer lady." Van Helsing comes to London to confer with Mina, who has read Jonathan's journal; when he learns the contents,

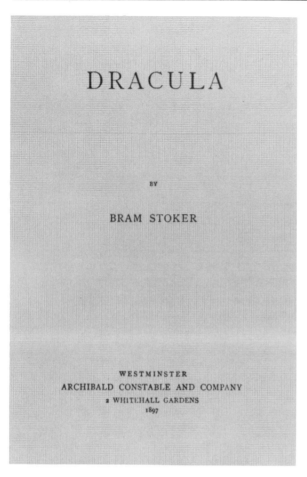

DRACULA

BY

BRAM STOKER

WESTMINSTER
ARCHIBALD CONSTABLE AND COMPANY
2 WHITEHALL GARDENS
1897

Title page for Stoker's masterpiece, which has never been out of print since it was first published

Van Helsing assures Jonathan that his experiences at the castle were not hallucinations.

On his way to the train, Van Helsing sees the newspaper accounts of the bloofer lady; he realizes that this is Lucy, risen from the dead. He takes Seward, Holmwood, and Morris into his confidence; at first they do not believe him, but he takes them to the cemetery that night, and they actually see Lucy walking—and in the process, they rescue another child. The next night the four men return to the tomb, where they drive a stake through Lucy's heart, cut off her head, and stuff her mouth with garlic, thereby saving her from the fate of the "Un-Dead."

Van Helsing, Seward, Holmwood, Morris, and the Harkers join forces to track down the count's boxes of earth and place holy wafers in them, thereby rendering them uninhabitable by him. They make their headquarters at Dr. Seward's hospital, which is next door to Carfax—the estate Jonathan Harker had gone to Transylvania to help

Dracula purchase. Van Helsing takes several pages to explain to the others—and to the reader—the various powers and limitations of the vampire. They discover only twenty-nine of the fifty boxes at Carfax, and Harker is sent to track down the others.

In the meantime, Dracula has been given access to the hospital by Renfield, who is in his power; one of the limitations of a vampire is that he can only enter a house if he is invited by one of the inhabitants. He has been drinking Mina's blood at night when everyone is asleep. Despite the fact that Mina is beginning to display the same symptoms as Lucy had, no one—not even the astute Van Helsing—realizes what is going on until it is almost too late. Matters come to a head one night when Renfield—who has tried to resist the count—is found in his cell with a broken back and a fractured skull. Before he dies he tells Van Helsing, Seward, Holmwood, and Morris about Dracula's nocturnal attacks on Mina. The men burst into the Harkers' bedroom, where they find Jonathan in a stupor and Mina, in a trance, sucking blood from the count's chest. Dracula flees before the sacred wafer Van Helsing brandishes at him. When Van Helsing touches the wafer to Mina's forehead for protection, it sears her flesh, leaving a vivid red mark.

They all realize that if the count is not destroyed soon, Mina will suffer Lucy's fate. They place the holy wafers in the boxes at Carfax. Through Harker's research, they have discovered that Dracula also purchased a house in Piccadilly. There they discover eight more boxes of earth, as well as papers that direct them to other refuges. After sanctifying the boxes in those places—leaving only one unaccounted for—they lie in wait for Dracula in the Piccadilly house. The count returns, but—even though a vampire's powers are at a low ebb in the daytime—he leaps through a window and escapes. Before he disappears, he calls back to his pursuers: "My revenge is just begun! I spread it over centuries, and time is on my side."

Dracula tries to return to the safety of his castle in his one remaining box of earth, but—guided by Mina, who is in telepathic communication with him—the men pursue him to the Continent. There Seward and Morris continue the chase by land, Harker and Holmwood hire a steamer to follow the count's boat up river, and Van Helsing and Mina go to the castle to head Dracula off. Van Helsing stakes the three vampire women in their caskets. Soon a band of Gypsies appears with a wagon bearing Dracula's coffin and Harker, Seward, Holmwood, and Morris in hot pursuit. In a fight with the Gypsies Morris is fatally wounded, but he and Harker pry the box open and—just as the sun begins to set—they cut off Dracula's head and plunge a knife into his heart. Before his body disintegrates, his face assumes an expression of peace. The mark disappears from Mina's forehead, showing that her soul has been saved.

Dracula is extremely effective as a horror novel. In part, this is probably due to the fact that it touches universal human fears that are expressed in the myths of vampires, werewolves, and zombies; but it is also due to Stoker's skill. Although *Dracula* is usually classified as a Gothic novel, it was a stroke of genius to bring the vampire up to date with references to such modern inventions as Kodak cameras and dictaphones. Placing the count in the mundane surroundings of fashionable Piccadilly makes him all the more alarming. Stoker also makes the vampire more fearsome by not keeping him on stage too much: Dracula is only physically present on 62 of the 390 pages of the original edition of the novel; in several of these instances he is only glimpsed briefly, and in some of them he is in the form of a dog or a bat.

Stoker is also able to make his characters vivid and real while the reader is caught up in the novel, even though, in retrospect, most of the human characters are even less believable than the vampires. Lucy and Mina are literally too good and pure to be true; it is also unlikely that three rivals for the same woman would remain as devoted to each other after two of them have been rejected by her as Seward, Morris, and Holmwood do. Morris comes across as something of a caricature—an Englishman's idea of what a stalwart, forthright Texan would be like. Van Helsing is a more realistic and complex personality, in spite of his ludicrous accent: "You have for many years trust me; you have believe me weeks past, when there be things so strange that you might have well doubt." (Stoker could handle accents well when he was familiar with them, though, as is shown in the conversations between Mina and the retired sailor, Mr. Swales, in the Whitby section of the novel.) Perhaps the most original and memorable character in the book is the insect-eating Renfield, with his wild swings from calm rationality to raving dementia.

The documentary format of *Dracula*, which has been lost in stage and film adaptations of the story, does much to add believability to the novel. Sometimes the same scene is described from different points of view, colored according to the personality of the character who is relating it. The juxtaposition of the various diaries, letters, newspaper clippings, and so forth enables the reader, for much of the novel, to know more than any character does, and so heightens the suspense.

Recent critics have penetrated the surface of the novel to find something much more complex than a rousing horror and adventure story. There are a number of instances of character doubling in the book: Lucy and Mina are so much alike as to be virtually the same person; Van Helsing and Dracula are both strong, dominant father figures, as well as both being foreigners; the young Jonathan Harker's travails have made him a haggard, white-haired man by the end of the book, as Dracula had been at the beginning, while Dracula has become younger.

Modern critics have also pointed out the strong, symbolic, and somewhat perverted sexual content of the novel. The heroines, Lucy and Mina, are totally pure and sexless; after her transformation into a vampire, Lucy—like the three vampire women at the castle—becomes "voluptuous" and sensual. The women are the sexual aggressors: the vampire women are about to "seduce" Harker when Dracula stops them; at Lucy's tomb, Holmwood is about to succumb to Lucy's deadly kiss when the other father figure, Van Helsing, intercedes. The only episode of vampirism explicitly described in the novel is the scene in which Mina sucks the blood from Dracula's chest—again, the female takes the active role. Blood appears to be a metaphor for semen in the novel: Van Helsing warns Seward and Morris not to let Holmwood know that they, too, have all given blood to his fiancée, as if that would be a betrayal of his trust; and Holmwood himself says that by virtue of giving his blood to Lucy, he feels that he is, in fact, married to her. The reaction of the males to the sexual aggression of the females is a mixture of excited anticipation and repulsion. The stake with which vampires are dispatched is an obvious phallic symbol, and it is noteworthy that the only stakings in the novel are of women by men: Lucy's "husband," Holmwood, drives one into her as she lies in her coffin; later, Van Helsing does the same to the three vampire women at Castle Dracula, after resisting their attraction. This violent metaphor for sexual intercourse seems to associate the sex act with pain and with punishment of the woman for her seductiveness. One can only speculate as to the connection of all this with Stoker's own sexual frustration. Other critics have claimed to find metaphors in the novel for sex role reversal, parricide, and the killing of children by their parents.

The book enjoyed a mild success on publication, but it was Stoker's mother who proved the most perceptive with her prediction: "My dear, it is splendid, a thousand miles beyond anything you have written before, and I feel certain will place you very high in the writers of the day. . . . No book since Mrs. Shelley's *Frankenstein* or indeed any other at all has come near yours in originality, or terror— Poe is nowhere. I have read much but I have never met a book like it at all. In its terrible excitement it should make a widespread reputation and much money for you." The last part of her prophecy was not to be, though *Dracula* is big business today and has made fortunes for others.

Being a man of the theater, it was only natural that Stoker would try to dramatize his novel. On 18 May 1897, at 10:15 A.M., his four-hour adaptation was presented on the Lyceum stage, with seats at deliberately high prices to *discourage* attendance. This performance was purely a read-through to establish copyright for the material, but Stoker may have hoped that Irving would play the part of the count in a full production. Any such hopes were dashed when Irving gave his one-word verdict on the play: "Dreadful!"

That was the last performance of Stoker's play, but Dracula has been portrayed countless times since then on stage and especially on film. The first film version was the 1922 German silent, *Nosferatu: eine Symphonie des Grauens (Nosferatu: A Symphony of Horror)*. This was an unauthorized adaptation, so the name Dracula was not used in it; *Nosferatu* is a Slavic word for vampire (Van Helsing mentions the word in the novel), and the count was renamed Orlok. Nevertheless, Stoker's widow successfully sued the company, Prana Films, for copyright infringement. Orlok was portrayed in the film by Max Schreck as a bald, bug-eyed, pointy-eared monster with fangs and long claws—not at all Stoker's conception of Dracula's appearance. The film is considered a horror classic and has some remarkable special effects. It was remade by another German company in 1979 with Klaus Kinski, made up in the same fashion as Schreck, as the vampire.

A successful theatrical adaptation of the novel, written by Hamilton Deane, opened in London in 1927; it was soon transferred to New York, where a young Hungarian actor named Bela Lugosi appeared as Dracula. Lugosi repeated the role in the 1931 motion picture version directed by Tod Browning. The clean-shaven Lugosi did not match Stoker's description of Dracula, but his darkly handsome features, suave manner, and Slavic accent (which was authentic, not assumed) fixed the image of the count in the public mind for years and has been endlessly burlesqued by comedians. Odd-

ly, the only other film in which Lugosi played Dracula was the 1948 comedy *Abbott and Costello Meet Frankenstein*, although he portrayed similar characters in *Mark of the Vampire* (1935) and *The Return of the Vampire* (1944). The other best-known movie Dracula is Christopher Lee, who has appeared in a series of British films—usually opposite Peter Cushing as Van Helsing—since 1958. Other Draculas on film and television have included Lon Chaney, Jr., John Carradine, Jack Palance, Louis Jourdan, and Frank Langella; in many of the more recent productions Dracula is depicted either as a romantic figure or as a pathetic victim of his condition, or both. The sympathetic portrayal of the count probably reached its climax in the 1979 comedy *Love at First Bite*, in which George Hamilton adopted Lugosi's cape and a travesty of his accent, and brought Dracula to modern-day New York City in search of love. What has to be termed "the Dracula industry" has continued to grow with comic books, toys, and Halloween disguises based on the count; there is also a worldwide group of enthusiasts of occult literature, the Count Dracula Society.

In spite of the success of his novel, Stoker remained loyally attached to Irving for another eight years, until the actor's death. They were eight years of declining fortunes. The high point of Irving's career had come in 1895, when he was knighted; at the end of 1896 he was incapacitated for ten weeks due to a fall after a party, and rumors circulated that he was a drunkard. His health began to fail at that time. In 1898 fire destroyed the warehouse where the Lyceum company's sets and props were stored, causing a loss of £30,000; shortly before the fire, Irving had had Stoker reduce the insurance on the property from £10,000 to £6,000.

Finally, due to intrigue and to bad business practices on Irving's part, they lost the Lyceum. Irving, weakened by illness, was forced to go on tour. He died in 1905 in the northern town of Bradford; Stoker arrived two minutes later, too late to do anything but close his friend's eyes. It was the end of a great friendship and collaboration. Even though the dry, sardonic actor had been inclined to take his friend for granted, he had brought the excitement of the Lyceum into Stoker's life and had given Stoker the chance to meet the most interesting people of their time on both sides of the Atlantic. In America they had been received like ambassadors, and in London they had entertained like ambassadors. Stoker had been happy in the actor's reflected glory, and now he was desolate. A slight stroke after—and probably because of—Irving's

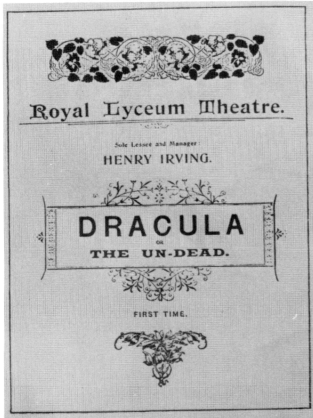

Royal Lyceum Theatre.

Sole Lessee and Manager:

HENRY IRVING.

DRACULA
OR
THE UN-DEAD.

FIRST TIME.

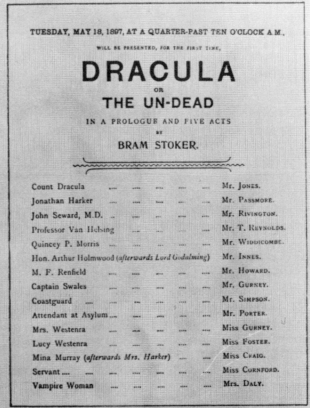

TUESDAY, MAY 18, 1897, AT A QUARTER-PAST TEN O'CLOCK A.M.

WILL BE PRESENTED, FOR THE FIRST TIME,

DRACULA
OR
THE UN-DEAD

IN A PROLOGUE AND FIVE ACTS

BY

BRAM STOKER.

Count Dracula	....	....	....	....	....	Mr. JONES.
Jonathan Harker	....	....	....	....	....	Mr. PASSMORE.
John Seward, M.D.	....	....	....	....	Mr. RIVINGTON.
Professor Van Helsing	....	....	....	....	Mr. T. REYNOLDS.
Quincey P. Morris	....	....	....	....	Mr. WIDDICOMBE.
Hon. Arthur Holmwood (*afterwards Lord Godalming*)				Mr. INNES.
M. F. Renfield	....	....	....	....	....	Mr. HOWARD.
Captain Swales	....	....	....	....	....	Mr. GURNEY.
Coastguard	....	....	....	....	....	Mr. SIMPSON.
Attendant at Asylum	....	....	....	....	Mr. PORTER.
Mrs. Westenra	....	....	....	....	....	Miss GURNEY.
Lucy Westenra	....	....	....	....	....	Miss FOSTER.
Mina Murray (*afterwards Mrs. Harker*)	....			Miss CRAIG.
Servant	....	....	....	....	....	Miss CORNFORD.
Vampire Woman	....	....	....	....	**Mrs. DALY.**

SYNOPSIS OF SCENERY.

Prologue: Transylvania.

SCENE 1.—Outside the Castle.
   ,, 2.—The Count's Room.
   ,, 3.—The same.
   ,, 4.—The Castle.
   ,, 5.—The Ladies' Hall.

SCENE 6.—The Count's Room.
   ,, 7.—The same.
   ,, 8.—The Chapel Vault.
   ,, 9.—The Count's Room.

Act I.

SCENE 1.—The Boudoir at Hillingham.
   ,, 2.—Dr. Seward's Study.
   ,, 3.—The Churchyard, Whitby.

SCENE 4.—The same—Night.
   ,, 5.—The same.

Act II.

SCENE 1.—The Boudoir—Hillingham.
   ,, 2.—The same.
   ,, 3.—The same.
   ,, 4.—The same.
   ,, 5.—Outside Hillingham.
   ,, 6.—Lucy's Room.
   ,, 7.—The same.

SCENE 8.—The same.
   ,, 9.—The same.
   ,, 10.—Mrs. Harker's Morning Room.
   ,, 11.—Room in the Berkeley Hotel.
   ,, 12.—Mrs. Harker's Drawing-Room.
   ,, 13.—The same.
   ,, 14.—Outside the North Hospital.

Act III.

SCENE 1.—Lucy's Tomb.
   ,, 2.—Room in the Berkeley Hotel.

SCENE 3.—Lucy's Tomb.
   ,, 4.—Outside the Tomb.

Act IV.

SCENE 1.—Room in the Berkeley Hotel.
   ,, 2.—Dr. Seward's Study.
   ,, 3.—The same.
   ,, 4.—Carfax.
   ,, 5.—Dr. Seward's Study.

SCENE 6.—Renfield's Room.
   ,, 7.—Mrs. Harker's Room.
   ,, 8.—Dr. Seward's Study.
   ,, 9.—Room in the Piccadilly House.
   ,, 10.—Dr. Seward's Study.

Act V.

SCENE 1.—Dr. Seward's Study.
   ,, 2.—Room in Hotel—Varna.
   ,, 3.—Room in Hotel—Galatz.

SCENE 4.—Outside the Castle—Night.
   ,, 5.—The same—Before Sunset.

Stage Manager	...	...	...	Mr. H. J. LOVEDAY.
Musical Director		...	...	Mr. MEREDITH BALL.
Acting Manager	...	...	...	Mr. BRAM STOKER.

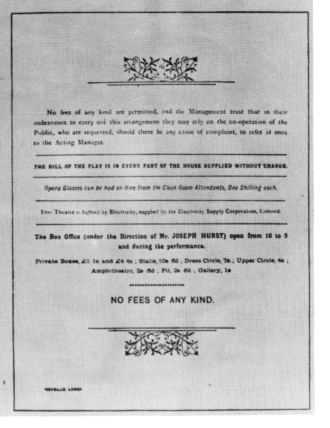

No fees of any kind are permitted, and the Management trust that in their endeavours to carry out this arrangement they may rely on the co-operation of the Public, who are requested, should there be any cause of complaint, to refer at once to the Acting Manager.

THE BILL OF THE PLAY IS IN EVERY PART OF THE HOUSE SUPPLIED WITHOUT CHARGE.

Opera Glasses can be had on Hire from the Cloak-Room Attendants, One Shilling each.

This Theatre is lighted by Electricity, supplied by the Electricity Supply Corporation, Limited.

The Box Office (under the Direction of Mr. JOSEPH HURST) open from 10 to 5 and during the performance.

Private Boxes, £1 1s. and £4 4s ; Stalls, 10s 6d ; Dress Circle, 7s.; Upper Circle, 4s ; Amphitheatre, 2s 6d ; Pit, 2s 6d ; Gallery, 1s

NO FEES OF ANY KIND.

NOVELLO, LONDON

Program for the reading of Stoker's theatrical version of Dracula. *The performance was held for copyright purposes only.*

Max Schreck as Count Orlok in the 1922 German film Nosferatu, *directed by F. W. Murnau. Although the name of the vampire was changed, Stoker's widow won a copyright infringement suit against the film company, which went bankrupt.*

death left his eyesight impaired; he became increasingly lame, though he returned to Cruden Bay, where he had written *Dracula*, every year for a holiday, striding across the sands with the support of a strong stick. But Bram and Florence could no longer afford the expense of the Kilmarnock Arms hotel; they rented a simple fisherman's cottage instead.

They were sufficiently poor to ask for assistance from the Literary Fund; Florence asked W. S. Gilbert for help (which does not seem to have been forthcoming), while Anne Ritchie, Thackeray's daughter, paid her three shillings and sixpence an evening for reading aloud. The most substantial assistance came from the best-selling novelist of the day, Hall Caine, the "Hommy-Beg" to whom *Dracula* is dedicated.

Stoker continued writing: *The Jewel of Seven Stars* (1903), about the resurrection of an Egyptian queen who ruled twenty-five centuries before Christ, is one of his most successful and popular books; *The Lady of the Shroud* (1909) has an echo of the masterpiece, with a Balkan princess who *pretends* to be a vampire, but it is unconvincing. A nonfiction study of dubious historical figures, *Famous Impostors* (1910) contains the intriguing theory that Queen

Elizabeth died as a baby and was replaced with a boy by her terrified guardians.

There are also a number of effective short stories, such as "The Judge's House," "The Burial of the Rats," and "The Squaw" (about the iron maiden in Nuremburg), all of which have Stoker's relish for horror; but his final novel, *The Lair of the White Worm* (1911), is a real literary curiosity. Hilarious throughout, without one line of intentional humor, it could still become a cult classic.

Adam Salton, a wealthy young Australian, has returned to his ancestral home in the Peak District. He notices something odd about his neighbor, Lady Arabella March, who has a sinuous figure, a low sibilant voice, and curious hands which wave gently to and fro. At their first encounter, he notices several black snakes on the ground and cries out a warning as she slips from her carriage with "a quick gliding motion," but the snakes seem more terrified of her and wriggle away. Later, when his mongoose attacks her, she whips out a revolver and shoots the animal, breaking its backbone; she pours in shot after shot, "her face transformed with hate." "Adam, not knowing exactly what to do, lifted his hat in apology and hurried on." Finally, his suspicions are confirmed: Lady Arabella is a monstrous white serpent who lives underground, and Adam rids the world of her by blowing up her lair: fragments of the "monstrous Worm" rise to the surface—"covered with insects, worms and vermin of all kinds. The sight was horrible enough, but, with the awful smell added, was simply unbearable. The Worm's hole appeared to breathe forth death in its most repulsive form."

With a landowner going mad in a turret, flying a great metal kite with a wire reel found in a chest which has no lock or key, the sexual symbols, as in *Dracula*, are rampant. Ironically, only three years previously Stoker had written bitterly in the *Nineteenth Century*, recommending censorship: "A close analysis will show that the only emotions which

Edward Van Sloan as Van Helsing and Bela Lugosi as the count in a publicity still for the 1931 film Dracula

in the long run harm are those arising from sex impulses, and when we have realised this we have put a finger on the actual point of danger."

Some of the defects of *The Lair of the White Worm* may be explained by the fact that Stoker was a seriously ill man when he wrote it. He died on 20 April 1912, at the age of sixty-four; the quiet funeral at Golders Green was attended by his widow, Hall Caine, and Henry Irving's son. Only the *Times* of London carried a brief obituary.

The exact cause of Stoker's death remained a mystery until 1975, when his grandnephew obtained the death certificate. The cause was given as locomotor ataxia and exhaustion; locomotor ataxia is equivalent to general paresis, the tertiary stage of syphilis. It can be conjectured that Florence Stoker's lack of interest in sex after the birth of their son drove Stoker to patronize prostitutes, from one of whom he may have contracted the disease. This might explain both his conscious, public antipathy toward sex, as expressed in the *Nineteenth Century* article on censorship, and the strange, unconscious sexual symbolism found in his novels.

Considerable merit can be found in Stoker's works, especially *Dracula*, in the skillful manipulation of narrative technique through multiple narrators, various narrative vehicles, and some masterful—if a touch *too* Gothic—pacing of suspense. As Leonard Wolf remarks, *Dracula* is "a complete masterpiece, flawed here and there, as the Chinese insist masterpieces should be, but, nevertheless, the real thing." Stoker did not live to see his most famous creation achieve worldwide fame through his numerous film incarnations, but he forecast the triumph to come when he had Dracula turn on his pursuers and say, "My revenge is just begun! I spread it over centuries, and time is on my side."

Biographies:

Harry Ludlam, *A Biography of Dracula: The Life Story of Bram Stoker* (London: Foulsham, 1962);

Daniel Farson, *The Man Who Wrote Dracula: A Biography of Bram Stoker* (New York: St. Martin's, 1976).

References:

C. F. Bentley, "The Monster in the Bedroom: Sexual Symbolism in Bram Stoker's *Dracula*," *Literature and Psychology*, 22 (1972): 27-33;

Joseph S. Bierman, "Dracula: Prolonged Childhood Illness and the Oral Triad," *American Imago*, 29 (1972): 186-198;

Bierman, "The Genesis and Dating of *Dracula* from

Bram Stoker's Working Notes," *Notes and Queries,* new series 24 (1977): 39-41;

Charles S. Blinderman, "Vampurella: Darwin and Count Dracula," *Massachusetts Review* (Summer 1980): 411-428;

M. M. Carlson, "What Stoker Saw: An Introduction to the History of the Literary Vampire," *Folklore Forum,* 10 (1977): 26-32;

Stephanie Demetrakopoulos, "Feminism, Sex Role Exchanges, and Other Subliminal Fantasies in Bram Stoker's *Dracula,*" *Frontiers,* 111 (1977): 104-113;

Radu Florescu and Raymond T. McNally, *Dracula: A Biography of Vlad the Impaler, 1431-1476* (New York: Hawthorn, 1973);

Florescu and McNally, *In Search of Dracula: A True History of Dracula and Vampire Legends* (New York: Warner, 1976);

Carrol L. Fry, "Fictional Conventions and Sexuality in *Dracula,*" *Victorian Newsletter,* 42 (Fali 1972): 20-22;

Mark M. Hennelly, Jr., "*Dracula:* The Gnostic Quest and Victorian Wasteland," *English Literature in Transition,* 20 (1977): 13-26;

Royce MacGillvray, "*Dracula:* Bram Stoker's Spoiled Masterpiece," *Queen's Quarterly,* 79 (1972): 518-527;

Grigor Nandris, "The History of Dracula: The Theme of His Legend in the Western and Eastern Literatures of Europe," *Comparative Literature Studies,* 3 (1966): 367-396;

Maurice Richardson, "The Psychoanalysis of Ghost Stories," *Twentieth Century,* 166 (December 1959): 419-431;

Phyllis A. Roth, *Bram Stoker* (Boston: Twayne, 1982);

Dorothy Scarborough, *The Supernatural in Modern English Fiction* (New York: Octagon, 1967);

Devendra P. Varma, *The Gothic Flame* (London: Baker, 1957);

Richard Wasson, "The Politics of *Dracula,*" *English Literature in Transition,* 9 (1966): 24-27;

Judith Weissman, "Women and Vampires: *Dracula* as a Victorian Novel," *Midwest Quarterly,* 18 (1977): 392-405;

Leonard Wolf, ed., *The Annotated Dracula* (New York: Ballantine, 1975);

Wolf, *A Dream of Dracula* (New York: Popular Library, 1972).

Papers:
Seventy-eight pages of Bram Stoker's diagrams, notes, and outlines for *Dracula* are held by the Rosenbach Museum and Library, Philadelphia.

Henry Major Tomlinson

(21 June 1873-5 February 1958)

Douglas M. Catron
Iowa State University

SELECTED BOOKS: *The Sea and the Jungle* (London: Duckworth, 1912; New York: Dutton, 1913);

The Tramp in a Gale, English Review, 12 (September 1912);

Old Junk (London: Melrose, 1918; New York: Knopf, 1920; revised edition, London: Cape, 1933);

London River (London & New York: Cassell, 1921; New York: Knopf, 1921; revised edition, London: Cassell, 1951);

Waiting for Daylight (London & New York: Cassell, 1922; New York: Knopf, 1922);

Tidemarks: Some Records of a Journey to the Beaches of the Moluccas and the Forest of Malaya in 1923 (London & New York: Cassell, 1924); republished as *Tide Marks: Being Some Records of a Journey to the Beaches of the Moluccas and the Forest of Malaya in 1923* (New York & London: Harper, 1924);

Under the Red Ensign (London: Williams & Norgate, 1926); republished as *The Foreshore of England: Or, Under the Red Ensign* (New York & London: Harper, 1927);

Gifts of Fortune: With Some Hints for Those about to Travel (London: Heinemann, 1926; New York & London: Harper, 1926);

Gallion's Reach: A Romance (London: Heinemann,

H. M. Tomlinson, 1949 (photo by H. Charles Tomlinson)

1927; New York & London: Harper, 1927);

Illusion, 1915 (New York: Harper, 1928; London: Heinemann, 1929);

Thomas Hardy (New York: Gaige, 1929);

Cote d'Or (London: Faber & Faber, 1929);

All Our Yesterdays (London: Heinemann, 1930; New York & London: Harper, 1930);

Between the Lines (Cambridge: Harvard University Press, 1930);

Norman Douglas (London: Chatto & Windus, 1931; New York & London: Harper, 1931; revised and enlarged edition, London: Hutchinson, 1952);

Out of Soundings (London: Heinemann, 1931; New York & London: Harper, 1931);

Easter MCMXXXII (London: Fanfare Press, 1932);

The Snows of Helicon (London: Heinemann, 1933; New York & London: Harper, 1933);

Below London Bridge (London: Cassell, 1934; New York & London: Harper, 1935);

South to Cadiz (London: Heinemann, 1934; New York & London: Harper, 1934);

Mars His Idiot (London: Heinemann, 1935; New York & London: Harper, 1935);

The Master (New York: New School for Social Research, 1935);

All Hands! (London & Toronto: Heinemann, 1937;

republished as *Pipe All Hands* (New York & London: Harper, 1937);

The Day Before: A Romantic Chronicle (New York: Putnam's, 1939; London: Heinemann, 1940);

The Wind is Rising (London: Hodder & Stoughton, 1941; Boston: Little, Brown, 1942);

The Turn of the Tide (London: Hodder & Stoughton, 1945; New York: Macmillan, 1947);

Morning Light: The Islanders in the Days of Oak and Hemp (London: Hodder & Stoughton, 1946; New York: Macmillan, 1947);

The Face of the Earth, With Some Hints for Those About to Travel (London: Duckworth, 1950; Indianapolis & New York: Bobbs-Merrill, 1951);

Malay Waters: The Story of Little Ships Coasting Out of Singapore and Penang in Peace and War (London: Hodder & Stoughton, 1950);

The Haunted Forest (London: Hodder & Stoughton, 1951);

A Mingled Yarn: Autobiographical Sketches (London: Duckworth, 1953; Indianapolis: Bobbs-Merrill, 1953);

The Trumpet Shall Sound (London: Hodder & Stoughton, 1957; New York: Random House, 1957).

OTHER: Edmund Blunden, *The Bonaventure: A Random Journal of an Atlantic Holiday*, introduction by Tomlinson (New York: Putnam's, 1923);

Christopher Morley, *Safety Pins and Other Essays*, introduction by Tomlinson (London: Cape, 1925);

"Robert Louis Stevenson," in *Great Names, Being an Anthology of English & American Literature from Chaucer to Francis Thompson*, edited by Walter J. Turner (New York: Dial, 1926);

David W. Bone, *Merchantmen at Arms: The British Merchants' Service in the War*, introduction by Tomlinson (London: Chatto & Windus, 1929);

Herman Melville, *Pierre or, The Ambiguities*, preface by Tomlinson (New York: Dutton, 1929);

Great Sea Stories of All Nations, edited with a foreword by Tomlinson (London: Harrap, 1930);

Samuel Butler, *Erewhon, or Over the Range*, introduction by Tomlinson (New York: Cheshire House, 1931);

Best Short Stories of the War: An Anthology, introduction by Tomlinson (New York & London: Harper, 1931);

"Preface and Prospect" and "The Upper Amazon," in *An Anthology of Modern Travel Writing*, edited by Tomlinson (London: Nelson, 1936).

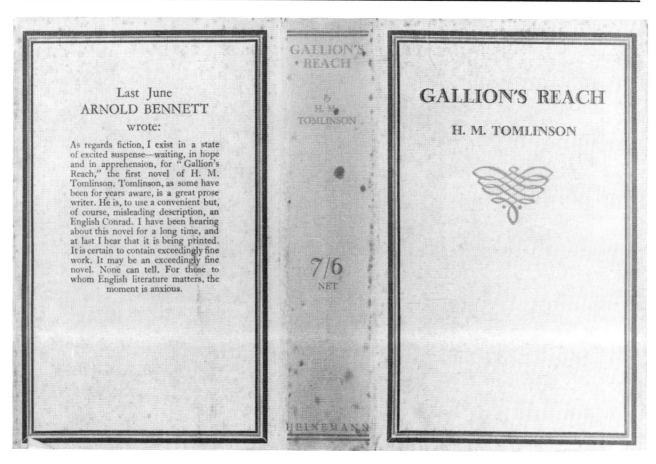

Dust jacket for Tomlinson's first novel, for which he was awarded the Femina-Vie Heureuse Prize

From his earliest publications, Henry Major Tomlinson has been cast by his critics as an adventure writer of seafaring novels. Four of his seven novels are either set on ships or strongly reflect life on sailing vessels. The remaining three are historical novels. Tomlinson's abiding fascination with the sea and with seafaring history, an interest traceable both to his family background and to his early work as clerk in a shipping office, dominates his nonfiction as well.

Tomlinson was born on 21 June 1873, in Wanstead, Essex, the eldest son of Henry and Emily Tomlinson. If anyone ever was born with the sea in his blood, it was Tomlinson. The son and grandson of seafaring men, Tomlinson absorbed the lore of the sea as much from the table talk in the home as from the docks at Poplar, a London shipping parish. He became a clerk at the offices of a shipping firm at the age of thirteen, shortly after the death of his father. As the eldest, Tomlinson was expected to go to work to help his mother and the younger children. One is only a bit surprised that he did not

go to sea. He would remain in this occupation for nearly twenty years, even after his marriage in 1898 to Florence Hammond.

Although Tomlinson's interest in writing developed early (he did, in fact, contribute several signed pieces to newspapers while he was still at the shipping firm), it was not until 1904 that his career as a journalist began in earnest on *The Morning Leader*. There he was able to develop his skill as an essayist, especially on several assignments involving excursions aboard ship, in 1904 on the *Windover*, a steam trawler, and in 1906 and 1909, respectively, on the *Celestine* bound for Algiers and the *Capella* on a trip up the Amazon. The latter trip resulted in his first book, *The Sea and the Jungle* (1912). And even though Tomlinson did not begin to experiment with the novel until after the war, he wrote several travel pieces and literary articles for little magazines between 1909 and 1927, including the *English Review*, the *Literary Digest*, the *New Republic*, and the *Nation and Athenaeum*. So successful was he in these early efforts and as a war correspondent, he was offered the position of associate editor of the *Nation* (later the *Nation and Athenaeum*) in 1917, a post he held until 1923.

By 1927, when his first novel, *Gallion's Reach,* was published, Tomlinson had already established a solid reputation as journalist, traveler, historical writer, and literary critic. Not surprisingly, the novel was well received. A year after its publication, Tomlinson was awarded the Femina-Vie Heureuse Prize, an honor awarded only a couple of years earlier to E. M. Forster for his *A Passage to India* (1924). Thus Tomlinson's third career, as novelist, began well.

The material for *Gallion's Reach* was drawn from Tomlinson's own experiences as a clerk and his longing for a different career. The novel traces the adventures of its protagonist, Jim Colet, from his desk at Perriam Limited, an importing firm, to the jungles of Malaya and back. As the novel opens, Jim is still a boy fascinated by the sea and by the romance of exotic place names: to the young Jim, even "London" is exotic. Immediately following this short opening chapter, however, we arrive at the present: Jim, now assistant to Mr. Perriam, argues with his employer over the dismissal of some dock workers. During the argument, Jim strikes Mr. Perriam and accidentally kills him. His voyage on the *Altair* is therefore as much an escape as an adventure. The novel traces Jim's voyage to Rangoon, to Malaya, and back to England. More than anything else, the novel reveals Tomlinson's skill in the description of the sea voyage and of Malaya. Most of the characters, excepting Jim and Sinclair, his confidant on the *Altair*, are rather sparsely drawn. The plot, too, seems arbitrary at times.

After he left the *Nation and Athenaeum*, Tomlinson began a series of travel works for various magazines, including a trip to the Far East from which much of the background for *Gallion's Reach* is derived. In 1927, he also toured part of the eastern United States, giving lectures at Harvard, Cornell, Princeton, Columbia, and Yale. The subject of these lectures was Tomlinson's theory of literature, later published as *Between the Lines* (1930).

That same year Tomlinson published his second novel, *All Our Yesterdays*, a historical account

ALL OUR YESTERDAYS

"I think that this is Tomlinson's finest book. When I say that I say that it is one of the finest books in modern English. I think it ranks with THE SEA AND THE JUNGLE and the best parts of GALLIONS REACH, but it is better than either because it is more creative than the first and much more evenly good than the second. The war parts of the book are, with Blunden's prose, the finest poetic realism yet given us in English about the war. This book will be a great and moving success in the year's literature, and I think it must last because of

1   Its lovely English
2   Its nobility
3   Its reality

This is Tomlinson's most *personal* book, and yet also his most *universal*."
—*HUGH WALPOLE.*

"This goes to the head of war books with a bang. It contains some of the best writing of the century—a book that is terribly, wonderfully alive."
—*J. B. PRIESTLEY.*

ALL OUR YESTERDAYS ❖ H.M.TOMLINSON ❖

ALL OUR YESTERDAYS ❖ H.M.TOMLINSON

HEINEMANN

Dust jacket for Tomlinson's second novel, an examination of British life from the last years of the Boer War to the beginning of 1919

of Britain from 1900 to 1919. The five sections of this novel form a calendar of the attitudes and aspirations of the British between the last years of the Boer War and the beginning of 1919. Tomlinson's own experiences as journalist and war correspondent through virtually all this period leading up to World War I gave him the materials he needed for the novel. Indeed, many of the descriptions in the novel echo those in previously published essays. One work, *Illusion, 1915*, published separately in a limited edition in 1928, is included in "War!," part four of the novel. Charley Bolt, the central figure of the narrative, is, like Tomlinson, bent on finding a new career. He leaves his teaching post to become a journalist and later submits the manuscript of a novel to an editor for consideration. Clearly, his career parallels Tomlinson's own aspirations and efforts during the early years of the century. Like Tomlinson, Charley Bolt, his younger brother Jack, and his friend and fellow journalist Jim Maynard all become involved in the war. Only Maynard returns.

While the novel is significant historically for its portraits of British society during the years leading up to World War I, it is still something of a hybrid—part exposition, part novel. Tomlinson it seems had some difficulty after he got into a subject remembering his characters. The novel is flawed by this frequent tendency toward didacticism and digression.

The Snows of Helicon (1933), Tomlinson's third novel, suffers from the same tendency. Like many of his novels, *The Snows of Helicon* is laced with criticism of contemporary society, but here Tomlinson's focus might be called a lament for lost art. The central figure, John Travers, a retired architect, craves classical beauty instead of the "great containers of concrete and steel" he sees all around him. In the course of the novel, he travels from New York to Liverpool, from the Bahamas to South America, all as part of a quest to save a temple to Apollo about to be destroyed in conjunction with a business venture of a certain Lord Snarge. Completely forgetting his wife Fannie, Travers goes off in search of the temple. As a vehicle for displaying Tomlinson's skill in description and as a reflection of his continuing argument against what he saw as a destructive "progress," *The Snows of Helicon* makes interesting reading. As a novel, however, it is far too implausible. Too many questions concerning the relationships between events in the novel and character motivation remain unanswered.

Several critics have noted Tomlinson's failure to provide logical connections in his novels. In a contemporary review, Arthur Colton argued that

The Snows of Helicon is flawed primarily because it is controlled by the mind of the author and, curiously, praised it for much the same reason: "it does not greatly matter what thread his mind follows, whether fiction, or travel, or a theme. He is a companion worth going with wherever he goes and as long as he chooses to go." Such a mixed criticism illustrates Tomlinson's major difficulty as a novelist: unable perhaps to distance himself from his characters and the emotions connected with his theme, Tomlinson is often too prominent in his fictions, the autobiographical elements too strong. In later works, he would depend more on history and less on his own experiences as traveler and journalist.

In the interval between wars, Tomlinson wrote numerous articles against war. As early as 1919 we find him arguing that the Treaty of Versailles would very likely lead to another war. Throughout the years leading to the next great war, Tomlinson continued to write antiwar pieces. Not until the very eve of World War II, when it became obvious that Germany under the Nazis was bent on total conquest of Europe, did Tomlinson shift the tone of his articles in the hope of encouraging

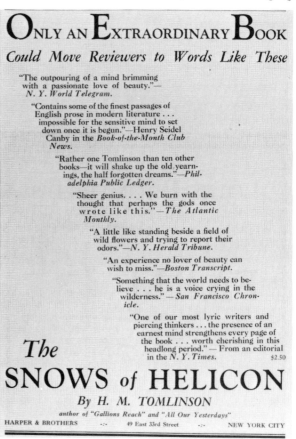

Saturday Review, *19 August 1933*

H. M. Tomlinson sitting for sculptor Sava Botzaris, circa 1934

America to enter the war. Several essays illustrating Tomlinson's antiwar pieces appear in *Waiting for Daylight* (1922); those characteristic of his later sentiments about World War II appear in *The Wind is Rising* (1941).

Tomlinson's fourth novel, *All Hands!* (1937), is perhaps one of his most successful works. Always at his best in his works about the sea and seafaring, Tomlinson is able to transform a historical event, the apparent loss of the *Rockingham* in an Atlantic storm, into a fictional one, the similar near loss of the *Hestia* in *All Hands!* The novel opens aboard the *Hestia* in Malaya where its crew awaits the arrival of the new captain, Jack Doughty. The previous captain is ashore and very near death. Tomlinson uses this early section of the novel to develop the personalities of Doughty and the officers and men who serve under him.

The *Hestia* and her crew are little more than a "parcel" to her owner, Sir John Dowland. But to those who serve aboard her, Tomlinson would surely say, she is a goddess, sometimes a rather cranky one who requires a bit of sacrifice. As we've learned from Joseph Conrad, Herman Melville, and Richard Henry Dana, ships are more than engines and a series of decks to the men confined to them for months at a time. Each ship has a kind of personality, and for Tomlinson, a ship is more than a vehicle of commerce.

The conflict then is set between the owner of the *Hestia*, Sir John Dowland, and Jack Doughty, captain of the ship. As Fred D. Crawford points out,

the name Doughty is probably drawn from Charles Montagu Doughty, a fellow British writer and traveler and author of *Travels in Arabia Deserta* (1888), a work which Tomlinson admired. In an essay written in 1927 and included in his autobiography, *A Mingled Yarn* (1953), Tomlinson writes, "But maybe the urgency of this mechanistic age will slow down. Some Doughty may explore its polished and efficient desert, and his word may begin to rust it; its impulse will falter and its wheels go not so fast." In *All Hands!*, Tomlinson himself becomes the voice of Doughty, exposing the conflict between owners and seamen. The near loss of the *Hestia* becomes the catalyst that will change Dowland's view of ships and the men aboard them.

Tomlinson's control of the historical materials and his ability to unify action and theme in *All Hands!* make it his most effective novel. Contemporary reviewers praised it highly, particularly because of Tomlinson's skill in describing the Atlantic storm and his effective use of a shifting point of view which allowed him to develop the conflict between owner and crew more dramatically.

During the next two decades, Tomlinson wrote three additional works, each of which would use historical materials in ways he had developed in *All Hands!*, none quite as effectively, however. In the first of this trio of novels, *The Day Before* (1939), Tomlinson returns to the years just prior to World War I. Building on his experiences as a journalist for the *Morning Leader* and the *Daily News*, Tomlinson creates a novel with many autobiographical elements but, nevertheless, the autobiography is filtered through the imagination. As he had done more broadly in *All Our Yesterdays*, he portrays in *The Day Before* English society from a few years before the war until the assassination of Archduke Francis Ferdinand, heir to the throne of Austria-Hungary, at Sarajevo, Bosnia, on 28 June 1914. By narrowing his scope and by limiting his third-person point of view almost entirely to a single character, Clem Venner, Tomlinson is considerably more successful in the later novel.

Clem Venner, the central figure, after being fired as supervisor in Davenant's shipping firm in Cheapside, begins a series of adventures as a journalist for the *Morning Echo* under the tutelage of a fellow journalist, Hankey Todd. It is Todd, in fact, who helps get Venner on the *Morning Echo*. Venner's assignments lead him to report on a strike and some sea maneuvers, among other incidents. After more than 200 pages, Tomlinson unites Venner with Julia Marshall, whom he had known at Davenant's shipping firm and who shares his sympathy for the working class. By the end of the novel, predictably, they are married. But such a bare sketch implies a greater unity than Tomlinson achieves in the novel. Several subplots complicate the relationships among characters, and Tomlinson's inability to depict passing time realistically makes even the bare sketch seem contrived.

Morning Light (1946) reflects Tomlinson's long-standing love affair with the history of seafaring. Set in the 1840s and 1850s, *Morning Light* is a study of the shipping industry when steam-powered ships were beginning to supplant sailing vessels in the merchant service. In addition to developing the conflict between owners and seamen he had introduced in *All Hands!*, Tomlinson creates in *Morning Light* a portrait of mid-Victorian ideals and attitudes. Although Tomlinson is not always precise about the passage of time, his few historical references allow the reader to place the action of the novel between about 1840 and 1854, the beginning of the Crimean War. These references become useful touchstones, as we follow the major character, David Gay, in his adventures in Branton, in London, and finally at sea. In the course of the novel, David rises from cabin boy aboard the *Star of Hope*, the ship on which he takes his first voyage to America, to a designer of engines for the new ships. As background to David's adventures, Tomlinson explores various social reforms in politics, in education, and in trade through such characters as David's Aunt Ruth, Lady Geraldine, and Mary Summers, a teacher at a school for the children of

Dust jacket for Tomlinson's 1946 novel, set in the 1840s and 1850s, when steamships were beginning to replace sailing ships in the merchant service

laborers. Thus *Morning Light* effectively combines two of Tomlinson's most prominent themes: a nostalgic interest in the era of the tall ships, and a recurring argument against a destructive progress.

Tomlinson's last novel, *The Trumpet Shall Sound* (1957), published shortly before his death, is set during the last few months of World War II. By limiting the scope of the novel and by restricting his focus to a single family, Tomlinson is able to depict the horror of war both historically and personally through the eyes of various members of the Gale family. As a result of the repeated bombing and the stress of the war, Sir Anthony Gale, an important official at Whitehall, his wife Lady Gale, and Uncle Nick do not survive the war. Both Lady Gale and Uncle Nick are killed as a bomb scores a direct hit on the family estate. Sir Anthony dies unexpectedly after returning from the front. The children,

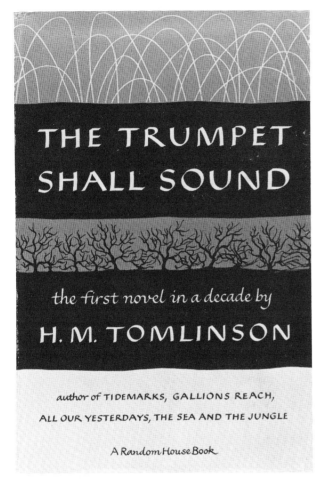

Dust jacket for the American edition of Tomlinson's last novel, set during the final months of World War II

Stephen and Lucy Gale, do survive, but their attitudes at the end of the novel reflect both hope for a new beginning and the hopelessness of those who have lost nearly everything.

For more than half a century, Tomlinson practiced his craft as journalist, travel writer, editor, and novelist. In more than twenty volumes, Tomlinson provides sympathetic and sensitive eyewitness accounts of life during these years, from London to the African Coast, from South America to Switzerland. And as the culmination of his distinguished career, Tomlinson's novels, particularly *All Hands!* and *The Trumpet Shall Sound*, reflect an equally sensitive creator of fictional characters.

References:

Helen Altick and Richard Altick, "Square-Rigger on a Modern Mission," *College English*, 5 (November 1943): 75-80;

David W. Bone, "Idle Tonnage," *Saturday Review of Literature*, 4 (11 February 1928): 587;

Henry Seidel Canby, "Life and Adventure," *Saturday Review of Literature*, 4 (3 September 1927): 83;

Arthur Colton, "Inconsequent Fate," *Saturday Review of Literature*, 10 (12 August 1933): 39;

Fred D. Crawford, *H. M. Tomlinson* (Boston: Twayne, 1981);

John Freeman, "Mr. H. M. Tomlinson," *London Mercury*, 16 (August 1927): 400-408;

Alva A. Gay, "H. M. Tomlinson, Essayist and Traveller," in *Studies in Honor of John Wilcox by Members of the English Department, Wayne State University*, edited by A. Dayle Wallace and Woodburn O. Ross (Detroit: Wayne State University Press, 1958), pp. 209-217;

J. Ashley Gibson, "H. M. Tomlinson," *Bookman* (London), 62 (April 1922): 6-7;

John Gunther, "The Tomlinson Legend," *Bookman*, 62 (February 1926): 686-689;

William Harlan Hale, "Mr. Tomlinson on War and Youth," *Saturday Review of Literature*, 13 (30 November 1935): 6;

"The Last of Tomlinson," *Newsweek*, 49 (8 April 1957): 116;

D. H. Lawrence, "*Gifts of Fortune*, by H. M. Tomlinson," in *Phoenix: The Posthumous Papers of D. H. Lawrence*, edited by Edward D. McDonald (New York: Viking, 1936), pp. 342-345;

"London River," *Frontier and Midland*, 6 (May 1926): 27-28;

Robert Lynd, *Books and Authors* (New York: Putnam's, 1923), pp. 252-259;

Frederick P. Mayer, "H. M. Tomlinson: The Eternal Youth," *Virginia Quarterly Review*, 4 (January 1928): 72-82;

J. B. Priestley, "H. M. Tomlinson," *Saturday Review of Literature*, 3 (1 January 1927): 477-478;

"The Sea and the Jungle," *Reviewer*, 1 (1 March 1921): 54-55;

Derek Severn, "A Minor Master: H. M. Tomlinson," *London Magazine*, new series 18 (February 1979): 47-58;

"Visit With the Author," *Newsweek*, 49 (8 April 1957): 116, 118;

"The Way Things Were," *Time*, 62 (13 July 1953): 102, 104;

Edward Weeks, "Authors and Aviators," *Atlantic Monthly*, 172 (November 1943): 58-59;

Weeks, "H. M. Tomlinson," *Atlantic Monthly*, 192 (August 1953): 82;

Rebecca West, "A London Letter," *Bookman*, 69 (July 1929): 519-520.

Allen Upward
(1863-12 November 1926)

Mary A. O'Toole
University of Tulsa

BOOKS: *Songs in Ziklag* (London: Sonnenschein, 1888);

The Queen Against Owen (London: Chatto & Windus, 1894);

The Prince of Balkistan (London: Chatto & Windus, 1895; Philadelphia: Lippincott, 1895);

A Crown of Straw (London: Chatto & Windus, 1896; New York: Dodd, Mead, 1896);

One of God's Dilemmas (London: Heinemann, 1896; New York: Arnold, 1896);

A Bride's Madness (Bristol: Arrowsmith, 1897);

Secrets of the Counts of Europe (Bristol: Arrowsmith, 1897);

'God Save the Queen!' A Tale of '37 (London: Chatto & Windus, 1897);

Athelstane Ford (London: Pearson, 1899);

Goldenhair and Curlyhead (London: Hurst & Blackett, 1900);

The Wonderful Career of Ebenezer Lobb, Related by Himself (London: Hurst, 1900);

The Accused Princess (London: Pearson, 1900);

The Wrongdoer (Bristol: Arrowsmith, 1900);

The Slaves of Society (New York & London: Harper, 1900);

The Ambassador's Adventure (London: Cassell, 1901);

High Treason (London: Primrose Press, 1903);

The Log of the "Folly" (London: Isbister, 1903);

On His Majesty's Service (London: Primrose Press, 1904);

The Fourth Conquest of England (London: Tyndale, 1904);

The Ordeal by Fire (London: Digby, Long, 1904);

The Romance of Politics (London: Tyndale, 1904);

The Secret History of Today, Being Revelations of a Diplomatic Spy (London: Chapman & Hall, 1904);

The Phantom Torpedo-Boats (London: Chatto & Windus, 1905);

The International Spy (New York: Dillingham, 1905);

The East End of Europe (London: Murray, 1908; New York: Dutton, 1909);

The New Word: An Open Letter Addressed to the Swedish Academy on the Meaning of the Word Idealist (London: Fifield, 1908; New York: Kennerley, 1910);

Allen Upward

Secrets of the Past (London: Owen, 1908; New York: Brentano, 1910);

Lord Alistair's Rebellion (London: Revere, 1909; New York: Kennerley, 1910);

The Discovery of the Dead (London: Fifield, 1910);

The Divine Mystery: A Reading of the History of Christianity Down to the Time of Christ (Letchworth: Garden City Press, 1913; Boston & New York: Houghton Mifflin, 1915);

Paradise Found; or, The Superman Found Out (Boston & New York: Houghton Mifflin, 1915);

Some Personalities (London: Murray, 1921; Boston: Cornhill, 1922);

The House of Sin (London: Faber & Gwyer, 1926; Philadelphia: Lippincott, 1927);

The Domino Club (London: Faber & Gwyer, 1926); republished as *The Club of Masks* (Philadelphia: Lippincott, 1926);

The Venetian Key (London: Faber & Gwyer, 1927; Philadelphia & London: Lippincott, 1927).

Allen Upward played many roles in his sixty-three years. He was poet, playwright, novelist, lawyer, teacher, journalist, adventurer, anthropologist, philologist, philosopher. The role he most desired, however—that of acknowledged genius and sage—always eluded him. Ezra Pound was one of the few who saw Upward as Upward saw himself—a neglected genius and victim of society.

Allen Upward was born in Worcester in 1863, into a family which belonged to the Plymouth Brethren congregation. His education was sporadic, eclectic, informal. His early life was one of constant movement and change—to the Five Towns, to Plymouth, to Camberwell, where he attended Great Yarmouth Grammar School in 1873, to London, and in 1882 to Dublin, where he attended the Royal University of Ireland. While working at the General Registry Office in Dublin, he wrote and published (anonymously) "The Truth About Ireland," a pamphlet advocating Home Rule. He also contributed some verses (again anonymously) to the nationalist paper, *United Ireland,* and gradually became friendly with the Fenians. At the age of twenty-four in 1887, Upward was called to the bar in Ireland.

His only published volume of poetry, *Songs in Ziklag,* came out in 1888. Later Upward said of it, "To the best of my recollection seventeen copies were sold of 'Songs in Ziklag.' I recently saw a pile of them on the floor of a second-hand bookseller in Charing Cross Road." Upward took part in the Bloody Sunday demonstration for the release from prison of the Irish M.P. William O'Brien. While in Ireland, he wrote his first play, *A Flash in the Pan,* which enjoyed limited success.

In the early 1890s Upward went to Cardiff and worked as a barrister on the South Wales circuit, and also as a journalist and politician. Apparently he was a natural orator (and in later life in London was a favorite after-dinner speaker). He was a barrister in Cardiff at the time of the awakening of Welsh nationalism and often defended labor leaders and farmers in court. He campaigned for the repeal of a law that kept workingmen off juries. All this activity, however, did not prevent his being defeated when he stood for Parliament in Wales. Upward wrote a humorous and often scandalous

column for the *South Wales Echo* under the pseudonym Ebenezer Lobb. He was an avid self-publicist who always seemed able to get his name into the newspapers, but in spite of this, he never received the recognition that he thought was his due.

In the 1890s, Upward says that he was "reduced to grind romances." He wrote them abundantly at this time: *The Queen Against Owen* (1894), *The Prince of Balkistan* (1895), *A Crown of Straw* (1896), *A Bride's Madness* (1897), *The Accused Princess* (1900), and *The Slaves of Society* (1900), along with several serials for popular magazines. Upward wrote these novels out of necessity and was embarrassed, at this time and throughout his life, by their commercial success.

In the late 1890s, Upward met L. Cranmer Byng, president of the Individualist Club. With Byng and others he attempted to found the "Order of Genius," for those who felt threatened by the surrounding mediocrity. This was to be a kind of cooperative society of poets and thinkers. It never materialized, but Upward remained in contact with Byng, who soon introduced him to James Legge's translations of Chinese poetry and philosophy. This was a felicitous discovery for Upward. These translations had an influence upon his future writings and were to be the basis of the rapport that developed between Upward and Ezra Pound.

Around the turn of the century, Upward spent two years in Torquay as deputy county court judge. Here, on the profit from his novels, Upward led a pleasurable life, but again the inequity of life became apparent to him. He believed that he had received only ingratitude in Cardiff when his social activism was at its height, whereas here in Torquay, while he was leading a comparatively selfish existence, they offered him the mayoralty.

In 1901 Upward went to Nigeria as proconsul. Here he aided the natives in setting up legal and administrative organizations, and he was able to observe them and their customs firsthand. He published an article about these customs in the *Journal of the African Society* (1903), and this became one of the bases for the anthropological and folkloric ideas in *The Divine Mystery* (1913), which Upward considered his master work. Upward did not remain in Africa long, however, staying there less than two years. He contracted malaria, and after a brief trip to Sweden to try to regain his health, he settled once again in London.

Upward and Cranmer Byng set up a publishing house in Fleet Street to launch "books of an idealist tendency," an idea influenced by the will of

THE NEW WORD.

"'The New Word' is Truth."—*Daily Chronicle.*

"'The New Word' is a book to add to the small store by the side of your bed. It is all good."—*Westminster Gazette.*

"One of those books which should be examined by a special committee of the people, so that they might advise the State how its suggestions might be carried out."—*Public Opinion.*

"Men of science will approve the spirit in which Mr. —— writes." *Nature.*

"The sort of writing that means stimulus to the well-grounded."—*Church Times.*

"Mr. —— ——'s previous record had not prepared the public for his appearance as a thinker of enormous power."—*The New Age.*

"Mr. —— has initiated, by means of 'The New Word,' a new school." —*Western Morning News.*

"The ordinary reader will peruse it with interest and pleasure; the man of letters and the thinker will study it with care as the possible spark of a new illumination."—*Publishers' Circular.*

"'The New Word' turns the world upside down.—*Chicago Tribune.*

"The first compelling book of the twentieth century."—*St. Louis Mirror.*

"He has given us at least a glimpse—and a very wonderful glimpse at that—of the 'Unknown God.'"—*Current Literature.*

"The book is an astonishing performance, a gigantic feat of spiritual engineering. Has never been approached in English literature except in 'Sartor Resartus.' Shakespeare might have done it."—*New York Times.*

"Darwin preached evolution; —— preaches evolution. This great idealist, whose greatness we scarcely dare to measure, regards the present volume merely as a prospectus; but we who read these chapters must feel that 'The New Word' is a relatively successful accomplishment in miniature.—*Boston Transcript.*

"In this book a man, who in the broader sense of both words is at once a scientist and a seer, has undertaken an inquiry into the sources of knowledge and the foundations of faith, a review of the jurisdiction of materialism and the credentials of the idealists, that has worked out into what he himself has admirably defined as a 'circumnavigation of hope.' Mr. ——'s equipment as a navigator of these reef-strewn and mirage-haunted seas is unequalled in our day. No controversial critic has had at his command so vitriolic a wit and used it so magnanimously; no ruthless iconoclast of intellectual idols has shown himself so conservative and yet so able an architect of intellectual optimism. Its prosecution is Socratic in its argumentative shrewdness, its unity of purpose, its unswerving directness and its triumphant simplicity."—*Life.*

Publisher's advertisement at the back of Some Personalities *(1921)*

Alfred Nobel, in which he proposed a prize for the "most distinguished work of an idealist tendency." At this time, Upward was working on his book *The New Word* (1908), which addresses the question of the meaning of the word *idealist*. In it, Upward delves into anthropology and etymology. He published this book at his own expense and in it tried to make a case for himself as Nobel's natural legatee. But at this time he was also producing books that were most definitely not of an idealist tendency— more popular novels such as *High Treason* (1903), several spy novels, *Lord Alistair's Rebellion* (1909), along with numerous articles and short stories.

Lord Alistair's Rebellion is a good representative novel. The fictional themes and Upward's real-life concerns are inseparable here as they are in many of his novels. There is a tendency toward the polemic, and the heroes are often misunderstood poets and freethinkers. *Lord Alistair's Rebellion* reflects Upward's concerns during the years when he was working on his major study, *The Divine Mystery*. Both works are concerned with the fate of genius in the unreceptive society. Lord Alistair, the outcast hero, is "the redeemer in whom the old vices and savage instincts in the blood of mankind are drained off and got rid of, for the salvation of the world." Lord Alistair, the man of genius, is the Christ, the sufferer and redeemer who permits society to continue functioning by his sacrifice.

Like Upward, Lord Alistair wants to set up a kind of sanatorium, a place of rest and refuge for the outcast geniuses of the world—a version of Upward's own "Order of Genius." But Lord Alistair will meet the same fate that Christ met and that genius must always meet. In contrast to the noble Lord Alistair, one of the unquestioning Christians in the novel is described as "the unconscious hypocrite whom the Gospel was written to make us loathe, and who has governed the church ever since the Gospel was written." In both fiction and nonfiction, Upward lamented the fate of genius throughout his life.

At some point early in the century, Upward met both A. R. Orage and Ezra Pound. He shared an interest in the occult with Orage and wrote many articles on occult subjects for Orage's *The New Age*. Pound was an admirer of Upward and reviewed favorably both of Upward's major works, *The New Word* and *The Divine Mystery*. Pound was responsible for getting Upward's poetry published by Harriet Monroe in *Poetry*. Upward's "Scented Leaves From a Chinese Jar" appeared in the September 1913 issue, and nine of Upward's thirty "Scented Leaves" appeared in Pound's *Des Imagistes* in 1914. The next year *The Catholic Anthology* appeared and in it some poems by Upward, but this represented Upward's second and last appearance in connection with Imagism. In May 1915, *The Egoist* published a "Special Imagist Number," but Upward was not included. He dashed off an autobiographical verse letter to *The Egoist* entitled "The Discarded Imagist," which was published in the next issue of *The Egoist* and again in *Poetry*, September 1915.

In this verse letter and in his autobiography, *Some Personalities* (1921), Upward seems to take a certain wry, self-deprecatory attitude toward the fact that he was always passed over when the literary recognition was being bestowed, but in fact this neglect hurt him deeply. He passed rather quickly in and out of the Imagist movement but continued for many years to write articles for *The New Age*, *The Egoist*, and other magazines, in addition to several more novels.

Ezra Pound never wavered in his high opinion of Upward's abilities. Pound mentions Upward in some of his letters and five times in *The Cantos*, and he mentions him generally in the context of the neglected, mistreated genius.

Allen Upward shot himself through the head in November 1926. Ezra Pound ten years later in a

SOME PERSONALITIES

By 20/1631

"*I will not be grieved because men do not know me; I will be grieved because I do not know men.*"—CONFUCIUS.

LONDON
JOHN MURRAY, ALBEMARLE STREET, W.
1921

Title page for Upward's autobiography. His pseudonym, the number assigned to him by the board of education during his school days, reflects his disappointment over his continued obscurity, even after the publication of The New Word, *for which he had hoped to win a Nobel Prize.*

letter to Eric Mesterton, commenting upon the comparative idealism of a number of turn-of-the-century writers, wrote: "Have always thought poor old Upward shot himself in discouragement on reading of award to Shaw. Feeling of utter hopelessness in struggle for values." This is speculation on Pound's part, of course. Upward hoped to win the Nobel Prize on the basis of *The New Word* and *The Divine Mystery*. The fact that the prize had been given to undeserving recipients (in Upward's opinion) over the years, and the fact that the 1925 award had been given to Shaw, self-publicist extraordinaire, may have been enough to push Upward over the edge.

Allen Upward is a curiosity. His novels were

extreme—either geared to the popular taste (like his romances and spy stories) or to the elitist and the snob (*Lord Alistair's Rebellion*). Upward knew many of the leading literary figures of the day, but he existed on the fringes rather than at the center of the literary world of London in the first quarter of the twentieth century. The modern reader's interest in him is more historical than literary.

References:

Kenneth Cox, "Allen Upward," *Agenda*, 16, nos. 3 and 4 (1978): 87-102;

Ezra Pound: Selected Prose, edited by William Cookson (New York: New Directions, 1973), pp. 403-412;

John Gould Fletcher, *Life is my Song* (New York: Farrar & Rinehart, 1937);

Bryant Knox, "Allen Upward and Ezra Pound," *Paideuma*, 3 (Spring 1974): 71-83;

The Letters of Ezra Pound, edited by D. D. Paige (New York: Harcourt, Brace, 1950);

A. D. Moody, "Pound's Allen Upward," *Paideuma*, 4 (Spring 1975): 55-70.

Rebecca West

Margaret B. McDowell
University of Iowa

See also the West entry in *DLB Yearbook: 1983*.

BIRTH: 21 December 1892, County Kerry, Ireland, to Charles and Isabella MacKenzie Fairfield.

EDUCATION: Royal Academy of Dramatic Art, 1909-1910.

MARRIAGE: 1 November 1930 to Henry Maxwell Andrews; child: Anthony West (by H. G. Wells).

AWARDS AND HONORS: Order of St. Sava, 1937; Fellow, Royal Society of Literature, 1947; Women's Press Club Award for Journalism, 1948; Commander of the Order of the British Empire, 1949; Chevalier of the Legion of Honor, 1957; Dame Commander of the Order of the British Empire, 1959; D.Litt., New York University, 1965; Benson Medal (Royal Society of Literature), 1966; Companion of Literature, 1968; Fellow of Saybrook College, Yale University, 1969; Honorary Member, American Academy of Arts and Letters, 1972; D.Litt. Literature, Edinburgh University, 1980.

DEATH: London, England, 15 March 1983.

BOOKS: *Henry James* (London: Nisbet, 1916; New York: Holt, 1916);

The Return of the Soldier (New York: Century, 1918; London: Nisbet, 1918);

The Judge (London: Hutchinson, 1922; New York: Doran, 1922);

The Strange Necessity: Essays and Reviews (London: Cape, 1928; Garden City: Doubleday, Doran, 1928);

Lions and Lambs, cartoons by David Low and text by West as Lynx (London: Cape, 1928; New York: Harcourt, Brace, 1929);

Harriet Hume, a London Fantasy (London: Hutchinson, 1929; Garden City: Doubleday, Doran, 1929);

War Nurse: The True Story of a Woman Who Lived, Loved, and Suffered on the Western Front, anonymous (New York: Cosmopolitan Book Corporation, 1930);

D. H. Lawrence (London: Secker, 1930); republished as *Elegy* (New York: Phoenix Book Shop, 1930);

Arnold Bennett Himself (New York: John Day, 1931);

Ending in Earnest: A Literary Log (Garden City: Doubleday, Doran, 1931);

A Letter to a Grandfather (London: Hogarth Press, 1933);

St. Augustine (London: Davies, 1933; New York: Appleton, 1933);

The Modern "Rake's Progress," paintings by Low and text by West (London: Hutchinson, 1934);

The Harsh Voice: Four Short Novels (London & Toronto: Cape, 1935; Garden City: Doubleday, Doran, 1935);

Rebecca West (Gale International Portrait Gallery)

ford University Press for the English Association, 1969);

Rebecca West—A Celebration: A Selection of Her Writing (London: Macmillan, 1977; New York: Viking, 1977);

The Young Rebecca: Writings of Rebecca West, 1911-1917, selected by Jane Marcus (New York: Viking, 1982; London: Virago, 1982);

1900 (New York: Viking, 1982; London: Weidenfeld & Nicolson, 1982).

OTHER: "My Religion," in *My Religion,* by Arnold Bennett and others (London: Hutchinson, 1925), pp. 19-24; (New York: Appleton, 1926), pp. 17-25;

"Divorce Is A Necessity," in *Divorce As I See It,* by Bertrand Russell and others (London: Noel Douglas, 1930); republished as *Divorce* (New York: John Day, 1930), pp. 61-71;

"Woman as Artist and Thinker," in *Woman's Coming of Age: A Symposium,* edited by Samuel D. Schmalhausen and V. F. Calverton (New York: Liveright, 1931), pp. 369-382;

"Mrs. Pankhurst," in *The Post-Victorians* (London: Ivor Nicholson & Watson, 1933), pp. 470-500;

"Elizabeth Montagu," in *From Anne to Victoria,* edited by Bonamy Dobrée (London: Cassell, 1937; New York: Scribners, 1937), pp. 164-187;

"I Believe," in *I Believe,* edited by Clifton Fadiman (New York: Simon & Schuster, 1939; London: Allen & Unwin, 1940), pp. 369-390.

The Thinking Reed (New York: Viking, 1936; London: Hutchinson, 1936);

Black Lamb and Grey Falcon, 2 volumes (New York: Viking, 1941; London: Macmillan, 1941);

The Meaning of Treason (New York: Viking, 1947; London: Macmillan, 1949; enlarged edition, London: Macmillan, 1952); revised and enlarged as *The New Meaning of Treason* (New York: Viking, 1964); republished as *The Meaning of Treason, revised edition* (London: Macmillan, 1965);

A Train of Powder (New York: Viking, 1955; London: Macmillan, 1955);

The Fountain Overflows (New York: Viking, 1956; London: Macmillan, 1957);

The Court and the Castle (New Haven: Yale University Press, 1957; London: Macmillan, 1958);

The Vassall Affair (London: *Sunday Telegraph,* 1963);

The Birds Fall Down (London & Melbourne: Macmillan, 1966; New York: Viking, 1966);

McLuhan and the Future of Literature (London: Ox-

Rebecca West's career as a writer of both fiction and of nonfiction spanned more than seventy years. She excelled in writing novels and short stories, literary theory and criticism, biography, political analysis, and persuasive rhetoric for various causes (socialist, feminist, antifascist, and anticommunist). Both her fiction and nonfiction are notable for their penetrating psychological analyses of motivation and behavior, and her nonfiction demonstrates her ability to research and to synthesize her findings on historical eras and sociological issues.

The parents of Cicily Isabel Fairfield, as Rebecca West was christened, came from families of some distinction. Her father, Charles Fairfield, had been an officer in the Rifle Brigade and was the son of a major in the Coldstream Guards. Her mother, Isabella MacKenzie Fairfield, a pianist, was the daughter of the regular conductor at the Theatre Royal in Edinburgh, whose early death limited the

Winifred Fairfield, two cousins, Letitia Fairfield, and Cicily Fairfield picking blackberries, circa 1898

income of his wife and children. Because the Fairfields could not turn to either of their families for income to supplement his army pay, Charles Fairfield left the military to pursue journalism. As an adult, Rebecca West eventually recognized her father's talent—his achievements as a scholar much interested in Herbert Spencer and as a writer—and the good influence of his keen mind and conversation on her life. She had, however, a much stronger identification with her mother and grieved over the waste of her musical talent and intelligence. When Cicily Fairfield was ten, her father, who had abandoned the family, died alone in a boardinghouse in Liverpool. Isabella Fairfield took Cicily, her fourteen-year-old sister, Winifred, and her seventeen-year-old sister, Letitia, from London, where they had been living, to her relatives in Edinburgh.

West's autobiographical novel, *The Fountain Overflows* (1956), a study of the ways in which genius is nurtured or destroyed, provides considerable insight into West's early life. Like her narrator, Rose, she was the third daughter in a family that lived in somewhat genteel poverty on the outskirts of London at the turn of the century, and, like Rose again, she was closest of the three daughters in sympathy with the mother. In the novel, as in life, all three daughters admire their father's handsome appearance and brilliant conversation, but they also see his failings—irresponsibility in keeping jobs, reckless

gambling in the stock market, and capricious abandonment of the family for many months at a time. They attempt seriously to follow their mother in becoming fine musicians, and they hope to go far beyond her to become financial and professional successes.

Cicily Fairfield's education was varied, if not systematic. At Edinburgh's George Watson Ladies' College, which she attended on a scholarship, she received the rudiments of an education, and, when she was in her late teens, she and her mother went to live again in London while she attended the Royal Academy of Dramatic Art to study acting for a year. After this year of study, her two sisters joined them, and Cicily Fairfield worked as an actress for about a year. Among other roles, she played the rebellious heroine Rebecca West in Ibsen's *Rosmersholm* and impulsively adopted that name to spare her family embarrassment when in 1911 she began to write for the *Freewoman,* a magazine she was not allowed to read at home because it condoned free love and radical activism. In September 1912 she also began writing for the *Clarion,* a socialist weekly with a larger circulation and a greater reputation. The paper published thirty-four of her articles over the next sixteen months, and between 1912 and 1916 she wrote for other newspapers as well. She continued to work for the *Freewoman* after it became the *New Freewoman* in June 1913. Founded by Harriet Shaw Weaver and Dora Marsden, the *Freewoman*

Students at George Watson Ladies' College, 1905. Cicily Fairfield is in the center of the last row.

and the *New Freewoman* were strongly feminist in emphasis, and Marsden, like West, did not want feminism limited to efforts on behalf of women's suffrage but thought the feminists should address all problems concerning social inequality. West continued for a time to write for the magazine after, having come under the influence of Ezra Pound, it became the *Egoist* in December 1913; but she regretted that Pound had moved the *Egoist* away from feminist issues.

The essays included in *The Young Rebecca* (1982), a selection by Jane Marcus of about half of the essays West published from 1911-1917, are impressive for their maturity of thought and style. During this early period Max Beerbohm called her "La Femme Shaw," and George Bernard Shaw himself remarked that she could "handle a pen as brilliantly as ever I could and much more savagely." In the essays written through 1917 West relied heavily on devices such as the strong opening statement, the witty turn of phrase, and the use of strenuous name-calling and insult. She is seldom overly subtle, but her complex thought is threaded with a wit that takes the casual reader by surprise. Her early essays include statements such as, "Writers on the subject of August Strindberg have hitherto omitted to mention that he could not write"; "Harold Owen is a natural slave, having no conception of liberty nor any use for it"; "when a socialist takes to being dull, he is much duller than anybody else"; and "Mr. J. M.

Kennedy is a bishop manque. He writes in the solemn yet hiccuppy style peculiar to bishops, with a 'however' or 'indeed,' or 'of course' interrupting every sentence."

In these early essays, for example, she calls the parliamentary orders for the force-feeding of arrested suffragists "Jack the Ripper" activities. She would complacently agree with an apparently innocuous statement made by her antagonist and then surprise the reader with an attack on a matter of more consequence. For instance, she once seemed to agree with a writer who complained of women entertainers who wore too little clothing, and then she passed on to complain rigorously of the indecency of a society that did not provide a mother with money enough to clothe her children. Her range of subjects was broad, although feminism and the economic problems of women and of lower-class people were the main preoccupations. Her book reviews were as notable as her articles on political figures or public issues. Her attacks on Mrs. Humphry Ward, Bernard Shaw, H. G. Wells, and Henrik Ibsen reveal little reverence for fame and reputation.

During these years before 1917 she also wrote *Henry James* (1916), the first book-length critical study of James to appear following his death. James's influence is clear not only in her novels but also in her nonfiction. Though she deplored what she considered his snobbishness, she wrote, "But we

A 1909 photograph of Cicily Fairfield in costume for a school play

mistress than by his many others—even without the addition of their child. His life had recently been disturbed by the birth of his daughter to the very young Amber Reeves, daughter of two of his fellow Fabians, who were significant figures among Wells's political and intellectual associates. Wells and his second wife, Jane Wells, who had been his mistress during his first marriage, maintained a genteel social life and a home for their two sons, aged ten and twelve; and their marriage had been, by agreement, without sexual relations since the birth of their second son. By agreement also, Wells informed his wife of each new mistress. In spite of such apparent openness, Wells—perhaps because of criticism of his portraying Amber Reeves recognizably in *Ann Veronica*—saw Rebecca West only furtively during her pregnancy and Anthony West's preschool years. She moved from one small village to another several times during her pregnancy and gave birth to her child without Wells or family members present. While Wells supplied some financial support and household assistance during his son's infancy, he visited infrequently, insisted that the son not be told the identity of his father, and agreed that Anthony should call him "Mr. Wells" and his mother "Aunty."

cannot do without him; he diagnosed the world's sickness. . . . A great, great genius."

In 1912 Rebecca West outrageously satirized H. G. Wells's *Marriage* and his "spinsterish" attitudes toward women in her review of his novel for the *Freewoman*. The sharp attack and lively style intrigued Wells and led to a meeting of the two authors in 1912; they became lovers in summer 1913, and she bore his son, Anthony West, in August 1914. During the ten years that she continued her relationship with the considerably older author, she frequently reviewed his books as negatively as in this first article. While their relationship was described by some as a friendship of "genius and laughter," Wells, attracted by West's fiery spirit, challenging ambition, and unusual intelligence, must have found his life more complicated by this

Rebecca West in 1912, the year she met H. G. Wells

H. G. Wells at about the time Rebecca West gave birth to his son Anthony West

Anthony West's *H. G. Wells: Aspects of a Life* (1984) presents Wells as the more caring parent, although he saw him infrequently. In his novel *Heritage* (1956) Anthony West portrays himself as a neglected and unwanted child, shunted off to boarding school too soon because his mother resented his existence and placed her career first. His introduction to a 1984 edition of the novel charges that his mother "was determined to do what hurt she could, and that she remained set in that determination as long as there was breath in her body to sustain her malice." While Rebecca West championed the right of unmarried women to bear children without censure, she never implied that single parenthood was advisable. Her views on motherhood for many young women are clearly expressed in "The World's Worst Failure: The Schoolmistress," published in the *New Republic* in 1916, when her son was two years old, and reprinted in that magazine on 11 April 1983. In this essay she contended that schools sentimentalized for students "the facts of motherhood. . . . that cruel failure of the human structure."

In spite of the urging of her family and friends that she end the relationship, Rebecca West remained one of Wells's mistresses for ten years. Living a life of isolation, characterized by overwork and social exclusion, she published essays regularly and maintained some of the reputation as a journalist which she had established when only eighteen. She suffered intellectually and emotionally from her relatively slight contact with the literary world. As the relationship deteriorated, it increasingly brought disorder to her life and interfered with her fulfillment through art at a crucial stage in her career. She had moved into the cycle of self-sacrifice which she always condemned on moral grounds. The basic premises of her enlightened feminism—the need to pursue order, freedom, knowledge, and art—helped her finally to end the affair in 1923, at which time she legally adopted Anthony West.

In the years after World War I, West became book critic for the British *New Statesman and Nation* and in 1923 was writing regularly for the *New Republic*. For this magazine she wrote features on travel covering her first trip to the United States and a trip to the Continent. In 1924 she became the first woman reporter in the House of Commons.

In her first two novels West used Jungian psychology to explore human behavior. *The Return of the Soldier* (1918) analyzes the vicissitudes of three women after the soldier of the title, Chris Baldry, returns shell-shocked from the front lines to his estate, Baldry Court. Because amnesia has wiped out his memory of the last fifteen years, he does not

Rebecca West (photo by Arnold Weissberger)

Ford Madox Ford and Rebecca West, circa 1914 (courtesy of University of Illinois)

recall his marriage to Kitty or recognize her on his return. Instead, his memory is fixed to a time fifteen years before, when he fell in love with Margaret Allington, a lower-class, middle-aged woman—who has now been married for more than a dozen years. Throughout the novel West plays ironically upon several connotations of the word *return*—he returns to his estate; he returns to a fixed moment in his past; he returns to his wife, Kitty; he returns to

sanity; and, at the end, he probably will return to the front lines and possibly to death. Chris finally recovers from his amnesia as a result of psychic shock, when a psychiatrist agrees with Margaret's suggestion that she show him the clothing and a photograph of his son, who had died at the age of two. Margaret knows his acknowledgment of his son's death and his own grief may lead Chris back not only to "reality" in the present time but to his traumatic recent memory of battle. She knows also that his return to the front as a result of his recovered sanity may lead finally to his death. At the close of the novel, he is reunited with the fact of his marriage. His recovery will ironically expose him to greater emotional and physical danger, but the naive Kitty simplistically cries, "He is cured!"

The Return of the Soldier shows the influence of West's study of James as she imitates some of his techniques, responds to many of his admonitions, and experiments imaginatively with his theories on point of view. For example, in the first pages, when Margaret—a stranger—calls to tell Kitty of the letter that she has received from Chris after a silence of fifteen years, Kitty and Chris's cousin, Jenny, the narrator, carry on a silent conversation with their eyes, as in James's fiction much is said by glances or slight facial changes. Action and time are limited as they tend to be in a James novel: all scenes in the novel take place within a few days and each scene is limited to three characters. The most significant success of the novel as a psychological exploration lies in West's control of the point of view, which consistently remains with Jenny. Jenny serves as a Jamesian central intelligence, but she is far less aloof and more spontaneous than a Jamesian narrator, because she is, in fact, the "third woman" in love with the soldier and has loved him since their childhood together. Jenny's implied presence thus complicates every scene between Margaret and Kitty, Kitty and Chris, and Margaret and Chris. While Kitty sits mute in her grief for her husband, Jenny moves from window to window to watch Chris and Margaret, and her intense jealousy is dramatically revealed to the reader.

Many readers have seen in this novel a psychological projection of West's inner conflicts over H. G. Wells's need for two women simultaneously—one woman complicating the other's life, but each complementing the other's ability to satisfy a man's need for happiness. While West denied that she consciously made Margaret and Kitty projections of herself and Wells's wife Jane Wells, she acknowledged that the idea may have been somewhere in her mind. A statement she made in 1957 suggested that Wells's need for mistresses as well as for a wife seemed linked with his guilt over leaving his warm but less intellectual first wife for his second, whose gentility frightened him. She speculated that his search for an ideal mistress— always one who would not interfere with his marriage to Jane Wells—may have been a search for a replacement for his first wife, for an ability to have both his first and second wives. Whether West con-

sciously or accurately reflected Wells's personal conflicts in this novel or not, the book shows considerable insight into human emotions and remarkably imaginative adaptation of Jamesian theory and example.

While she was writing *The Judge* (1922), West entered a period of personal loss. Her mother, to whom she remained close despite Isabella Fairfield's strong disapproval of West's affair with Wells, died of Graves' Disease in 1920 after West had nursed her for nearly three years during the acute stages of her disease. The "Edinburgh" half of *The Judge* closes with an extended scene in which Ellen Melville, the heroine, for a day and a night holds the hand of her mother who is dying from diphtheria. West's relationship with Wells had deteriorated, complicated by the presence of their son but also held together by him. Wells now railed against the impertinence of her reviews of his books, though her spirited writing had earlier intrigued him. He wrote that her praise of certain other authors showed how her friends (she had made very few in these isolated years) and her sister Letitia had corrupted her judgment and taste. (West's closeness to her oldest sister, a physician and important civil servant, had always annoyed Wells.) His letters also urged in 1920 and 1921 that she finish the book faster because it denied them time for companionship. Rebecca West must have recognized the effect of the relationship upon her initially brilliant entrance into a writing career in 1911 and realized that she had made relatively slow progress, in spite of hard work and absence of social life. When they finally parted in 1923, Wells was fifty-six, West was thirty, and Anthony was nine.

By the time *The Judge* appeared, it had grown to twice the length of most novels. Wells insisted in an angry letter that he must be honest about how much she had failed in this novel: "I've got no use for you at all as a hum-bugged pet woman. If I am going to have a female pet, I could get my number of prettier and more amusing pets than you." He went on to say that *The Judge* was "an ill conceived sprawl of a book with a faked hero and a faked climax, an aimless waste of your powers. . . ." Fortunately for West none of the published evaluations were as negative. Most of those in the prominent publications praised her writing (calling it splendid, rich, haunting, fine, forceful, or impressive), but they ended with reservations about the aesthetic value of the work. Its length, its slow pace, and the lack of unity between its two large sections clearly damaged the novel in the minds of the critics.

The book's unity depends on the lovers—

Rebecca West, circa 1923

Ellen Melville, a secretary in an Edinburgh loan office, and Richard Yaverland, a successful businessman just returned from Rio de Janeiro—and the events in which they are involved. Ellen may be West's strongest portrayal of a woman in any of her novels, but she seems misplaced in a book designed for heightened tragic effects, except in the scene where she silently holds her dying mother's hand for two days. Ellen's vitality enlivens every scene in the early part of the book; she marches for suffrage and writes rousing speeches which she is too shy to deliver before the crowds. She is simple, energetic, and comical—though conversely an intense and determined woman. Ellen's restless hopes and her humor dominate the first half of the book—some three hundred pages. She is innocent and joyous in her sudden love for Richard, an emotion which replaces her enthusiastic yearning for travel to remote and exotic places. The focus on her life-enhancing aspects is inconsistent with the tragic developments in the second part of the novel; and the presentation of Richard lacks ominous overtones to prepare the reader for the tragedy that emerges from his compulsive love for his mother

and his bitter envy and hatred of anyone who might rival him in that love.

In the second part of *The Judge,* West shifts abruptly from Edinburgh to the isolated, ancestral home of Richard near the mud flats of the Thames estuary, and from Ellen as the chief female character to Richard's mother, Marion Yaverland. On the journey Ellen and Marion make to Essex (Richard is to follow), Marion's intensity and secretiveness trouble Ellen, as does the bleak landscape with its barren fields, rutted muddy paths, congealed streams filled with debris, and the rocky gray cliffs. West gives haunting beauty and strangeness to the background that intensifies the impending tragedy.

In an excessively long review (one hundred pages) of Marion's past, one learns that she bore Richard illegitimately and that the man who impregnated her at the age of nineteen was the most prominent man in the area—the older and powerful squire. During her pregnancy she was attacked one day by angry villagers and stoned for her disgrace. Later, after Richard's birth, she was raped and, as a result, bore Roger, Richard's half brother, whom neither she nor Richard has been able to love adequately.

At the close of this review of Marion and her family's past, West moves ahead with astonishing speed to chronicle the violence that will tragically enclose the characters. Marion drowns herself to insure that Richard will no longer be distracted by her as he marries and loves another woman, Ellen. Roger makes a foolish remark upon hearing of his mother's drowning, and Richard impulsively stabs his brother to death. West's depiction of Richard's action suggests that his motivation actually comes from his subconscious desire to avenge his mother's rape, during which Roger had been conceived. It is as if Richard can now deny the reality of the rape of his beloved because he has destroyed the only remaining evidence. Like her suicide, his act simplifies his ability to love Ellen without the distraction of his conflicting feelings for others.

Some problems Rebecca West did not solve: the excessive length of book one, the failure to articulate the two sections of the novel to produce a closer aesthetic unity, and Ellen's absence from the action during the very long review of Marion's past that precedes the precipitous ending. Yet *The Judge* rises above its defects. West achieves power and originality in this haunting novel as she explores the themes of the Oedipal curse, maternal guilt, sibling rivalry, the cruelty of conventional individuals in judging sexual behavior, and the symbolic and mythic ramifications of various forms of sexual expression. Her understanding of character is profound, as is her knowledge of the hypocrisies of a society toward individuals who violate its taboos. She confronts squarely the abuses of power between individuals and between society and the individual and does so with a depth of insight that should assure *The Judge* a place among the notable novels of the twentieth century.

In *The Strange Necessity* (1928), a collection of eleven essays, West organizes the long title essay around a writer's observations during a single day's walk around Paris. Inspired by events or sights in the city, the writer muses about the books she has known, the arts as they appeal to her, and the meaning of the past. Critics have noted that in shaping her odyssey through the city West imaginatively orders a day's inner and outer experience, much as Marcel Proust, James Joyce, or Virginia Woolf do in their works. The ten shorter essays in the volume discuss incisively Willa Cather, D. H. Lawrence, Sinclair Lewis, and Sherwood Anderson. Her essay "Uncle Bennett" celebrates the influence of four "uncles" upon the life and writing of her generation—Arnold Bennett, H. G. Wells, Ber-

Anthony and Rebecca West, circa 1928

nard Shaw, and John Galsworthy.

In 1928 she produced the text for *Lions and Lambs,* a book of comic pictures by David Low, who introduced her to caricature as a technique that a prose writer as well as cartoonist might use. Low and West satirized many notable figures from the past and present—people of consequence in religion, government, literature, and science. In 1934 West and Low produced a second book, *The Modern "Rake's Progress,"* an imitation of Hogarth's series of paintings.

In *Harriet Hume* (1929), an experiment in fantasy, West also experiments with the form of the novel, producing the impression of a choreographed dance performance in which the separate sequences are highlighted as by shifting lights, rather than being firmly connected with one another. Harriet Hume and Arnold Condorex (his name negatively suggesting the condor or vulture) move through unspecified times and places, though the general background is London. She is a concert pianist; he is a politician. They meet in a drawing room, a garden, on a sidewalk, and on a stairway. In the series of encounters separated apparently by long intervals of time, West dramatizes a universal antagonism between male and female, which can either destroy or energize a love affair. In this case neither player in the game of sex rivalry is victorious. Arnold puts practical advancement ahead of his interest in Harriet and becomes involved with a more influential woman. His main advantage would be in his ability to dissemble, but Harriet, at times, has the gift of extrasensory perception which enables her to study his motivations and to apprehend his lies before they can influence her. She imposes a sense of order upon reality by providing artistic perspective. She is more concerned with public affairs and with art than he and is continuing to learn about these subjects. He has the public powers of government, law, and economy on his side—which West never disparages—but he lacks, in his intellectual equipment, the ordering influence of art, and his world at various times becomes surrealistic. Harriet has artistic talent, a commitment to social revolution, the drive to better herself, and an unwavering honesty and articulateness.

The tone of the book is melancholy for the most part, but West punctuates its slow pace with the lovers' animated quarrels and with comic repartee. The mannered movement is artificial but sometimes conducive to achieving comic effects. West apparently conceived the book as satirical allegory, but its subtlety and ambiguous nature make

Rebecca West, 1930

it difficult for the reader to decide exactly what is being satirized. Nevertheless, H. G. Wells wrote West a note of praise, stating that the love-antagonism of Harriet and Arnold illustrates Jung's "ideas about the persona, anima, and animus." The novel gained neither popular nor critical attention, but Wells could still be positive about this work, although his note implied disparagement of her other books: "It is just as though you were coming awake and alive after years in a sort of intellectual trance."

At the age of thirty-seven in 1930, after publication of her third novel, Rebecca West married Henry Maxwell Andrews, a banker and investment counselor, on 1 November 1930. They lived thirty-six miles south of London on an eighty-five-acre dairy farm, surrounded by eight acres of gardens. Because Andrews lost much of his money in the Depression, West continued to write for a living; but the farm operated at a profit. Her husband, a scholar as well as a businessman, frequently traveled with her. In 1939, she wrote in "I Believe" of her difficult early years and said that not until her late marriage "did I have one human being close to me who ever thought of saving me fatigue or pain or

responsibility" and that she was then "at last able to take pleasure in both my family and my work." From 1963 to 1968 she nursed Andrews in his last illness, and at his death she moved back to London, where she lived until her death.

Ending in Earnest: A Literary Log (1931) collects forty-two essays West wrote during her travels in Europe and originally had published in the *Bookman* during 1929 and 1930. In them she discusses such general subjects as censorship, the old and the new feminism, French culture and the French theater, and such writers as Edmund Gosse, André Gide, Virginia Woolf, Evelyn Waugh, and D. H. Lawrence. The "Ending" in the book's title probably refers to the final essay, "Regretfully," in which West says she is presenting her last work on a controversy which began with her attack on the neohumanists, whom she compared to modern French neoclassicists such as Julien Benda. These writers and intellectuals—whom she considered guilty of neglecting, at least to some degree, political responsibility—isolated themselves in ivory towers and then moaned in despair and self-pity about the end of the world. For example, although she praised T. S. Eliot's poetry, she found that his literary criticism exemplified the tenets of the effete and defeatist neohumanism that she was attacking. She distrusted conformity in intellectuals and sought writers who would respect tradition but be open to experimentation, writers who would respond to both romantic and classic influences rather than be single-minded in their emphasis. She advocated intellectual and artistic inclusiveness and deplored the compartmentalizing tendencies often present in literary movements that followed a well-defined program.

In the early 1930s West grew more interested in biography and wrote biographical pamphlets (*D. H. Lawrence*, 1930; *Arnold Bennett Himself*, 1931), biographical articles ("Mrs. Pankhurst" in *The Post-Victorians*, 1933; "Elizabeth Montagu" in Bonamy Dobrée's *From Anne to Victoria*, 1937), and a small book (*St. Augustine*, 1933). Her later work also reflects this interest in biography. In *Black Lamb and Grey Falcon* (1941), *The Meaning of Treason* (1947) and *A Train of Powder* (1955), she often proceeds by placing a character in the context of a certain time, place, or family, and by discovering the relationships between the individual and the people or events in his background. Whereas her experience as a fiction writer could have been responsible for such an approach in the nonfiction, her interest in biography as an art form undoubtedly stimulated her attempt at revealing the individual in relation to

"Miss Rebecca West," by Wyndham Lewis (published in his
Thirty Personalities and a Self-Portrait, *1932)*

economic depression. The wit of these novellas, their careful structure, and their depth of characterization motivated H. G. Wells to congratulate West, although he mistakenly supposed that she had intended to destroy her sister Letitia by her satire of a do-gooder in one of the short novels, *The Salt of the Earth.* Again he expressed approval of a current work through disparagement of her earlier achievement. He wrote that she had had to get beyond "such a spate of undisciplined imagination in *The Judge* before you got to the MASTERY of these stories."

The Thinking Reed (1936) was West's first notable success as a fiction writer, reaching the list of the top ten novels of 1936 compiled from weekly lists in *Publishers Weekly.* The list, headed by Margaret Mitchell's *Gone with the Wind,* also included Aldous Huxley's *Eyeless in Gaza,* Sinclair Lewis's *It Can't Happen Here,* and Walter Edwards's *Drums Along the Mohawk.*

The form of *The Thinking Reed* impressively manifests West's artistry in fiction in the way that *Black Lamb and Grey Falcon,* her next book, impressively manifests similar control of form in nonfiction. Writing of its artistic excellence, Elizabeth Bowen stated that *The Thinking Reed* seemed to her a book with "almost no imperfections. . . . It is impossible to think beyond it." In this and her two later novels, West stresses themes she emphasizes throughout her nonfiction, continuing to see the human being as inherently sinful and weak and to see that a hostile universe makes freedom of choice difficult. Anger and "strong hatred" directed against an impersonal universe help protect the reed-like human beings who inhabit it. A strength peculiar to the individual, she was convinced, lies in an ability to think abstractly about personal issues and to create order through art, imagination, law, and the knowledge of one's inevitable morality. Thinking individuals, though flawed and weak, can and should pursue their own happiness as the highest good and avoid ascetic self-denial as well as interference with the happiness of others.

In *The Thinking Reed* West explores these themes through Isabelle Tarry, who, as she loses her naiveté, her romantic expectations from life, and her arrogance, gains a degree of unselfishness, tolerance, and self-knowledge. Beginning to think, to question and to synthesize the fragments of her experience, and to discern abstract relationships more clearly than before, she recognizes that she must accept realities which she does not fully understand, such as the difference between the sexes. She perceives also the negative aspects of wealth without

his or her background. During the 1930s she had become a regular writer and board member for the feminist-oriented *Time and Tide,* and in 1935 she made a trip to Washington, D.C., to write about American politics in four essays for the magazine. As a result of her fascination with biography, these essays became sketches of Huey Long, Father Coughlin, and Franklin Delano Roosevelt as complex personalities as well as notable political figures. These sketches also reveal, of course, a novelist's insight into character and the exploration of motivations of individuals at significant points in their careers.

The four novellas in *The Harsh Voice* (1935) grew out of that same American trip, but they do not reveal an insider's grasp of the America that West saw that year. She is preoccupied in all four short novels with the importance of money-making in the upper-middle class. In the three set in America, she emphasizes the obsession of the characters with the materialistic "American Dream," failing to consider the irony of her preoccupation while the country was devastated by succumbing to a sentimental idealizing of poverty. West symbolically suggests Isabelle's longing for such an ordering of her life long before she thinks seriously of creating such order: She gazes at a large gold chandelier on which four eaglets, poised to fly in four different directions, are encircled by a gold ring which holds them in an aesthetically pleasing and significant pattern, as if the ring keeps the energy of the birds in perfect balance. Such harmony, of course, Isabelle desires for herself, and she speculates that the ring might be a symbol for the potential harmony possible in a happy marriage.

Isabelle's maturing occurs, in part, through her encounters with death: first, the death of her first husband, Roy Tarry, a famous daredevil pilot, just before the book begins, and later, the death of the unborn baby she has conceived in her second marriage, to Marc Sallafranque, a wealthy French automobile manufacturer. Near the close of the novel, after a traumatic miscarriage and a humiliating public scene with Marc, she decides on divorce. A few hours later, her growing capacity to think deeply—to become more than a wavering reed—enables her to recognize Marc's vitality and her own strong need for him as the energizing center for her life. In her assessment of him she now recognizes his faults as well as her own. She realizes the possibility that they will persist and that a strong marriage may result from the emotional and physical bond that remains between them. For the person who has become a "*thinking* reed," knowledge of the imminence of death can thus bring intense awareness of the potential for rebirth and renewal, as Pascal expressed in the passage from *Pensées* (1844) which West chose as epigraph for *The Thinking Reed*: "Man is but a reed, the most feeble thing in nature; but he is a thinking reed. . . . But if the universe were to crush him, man would still be more noble than that which killed him, because he knows that he dies and the advantage which the universe has over him; the universe knows nothing of this."

Peter Wolfe notes that D. H. Lawrence's work may have influenced the dynamics of the love that West portrays in this relationship between Isabelle and Marc. West had produced her short book on Lawrence only six years earlier, and his work may also have influenced her first two novels. Yet views on sex in these novels, as well as in *The Thinking Reed,* seem consistent with those in her essays, and they probably parallel, rather than derive from, those of Lawrence. The artifice and the intellectual ambience of West's novel, characteristic of a satiric comedy of manners, produce a tone unlike the intensity that suffuses most of Lawrence's work. The courtship rituals, a heroine who suddenly and gracefully regrets her destructive impulses in favor of "thinking," and the resilient characters who survive their follies, whether or not they achieve self-knowledge, suggest the influence of Jane Austen rather than that of Lawrence. Unlike Austen, however, West does not allow characters to achieve fully rational control of their lives, and she seldom allows them to amend fully their flaws and weaknesses. A *thinking* reed in a West novel remains a reed. The novel's most obvious parallel is to Henry James's *The Portrait of a Lady* (1881). Opulent hotels and casinos, wasteful luxury, and the snobbery of millionaires and aristocrats in *The Thinking Reed* recall James's novel, as does the figure of Isabelle Tarry, the single-view consciousness, limiting point of view. However, the two novels are fundamentally different because Isabelle Tarry remains a weak reed, while Isabel Archer develops into a strong individual. Yet both women are intelligent and sensitive, and both learn the value of self-knowledge. Isabelle Tarry's wildness, irrationality, and primitive selfishness, if present at all in James's Isabel Archer, are only latent and intermittent. Isabel Archer is always a lady, not a reed given to the expression of her passing emotions.

Black Lamb and Grey Falcon (1941), West's most massive book (1200 pages, two volumes), is both a travel book about Yugoslavia and an analysis of the historical and contemporary political dislocations of Europe in the 1930s. Diana Trilling termed it "surely one of the very greatest books of the last fifty years." It emerged from a lecture tour taken in 1936 and a second trip made with her husband the following year in which they toured the Balkans, particularly Yugoslavia. In this book, as in her other nonfiction and in her fiction, she suggests generalities through the use of abundant and significant particulars; and she has the novelist's eye for idiosyncrasies of personality and the novelist's sense of the psychological motivation of the individuals about whom she writes. Finding the country to be a unique combination of Western and Eastern influence, she began her journey in the section most Western in its characteristics. Volume one, related to her early months of travel in the northeastern section of the country, focuses on West European (largely Austrian) culture with its Christian characteristics. The wealth and provincialism of Belgrade impressed her, and at the close of volume one she speculates on the latent violence that she senses almost everywhere, in large part an opposition to the violence of authoritarianism but sometimes an expression of that authoritarianism itself. As she moves down the Dalmatian coast, the beauty of the Roman ruins captivates her, and she notes the still surviving influence of that ancient civilization.

By the beginning of volume two, she has moved into Macedonia, and she discusses the Greek and Eastern cultures that formed the country. Here the anti-Semitic, anti-Slavic attitudes of Gerda, the wife of the Slavic poet Constantine (who is traveling with them as guide and friend), disturb West and her husband. For Rebecca West, Gerda's views spoil Macedonia, "the most beautiful place that I had ever seen," and she senses in this marriage between German racist and Slavic poet-travel guide the pressures that are about to tear Europe apart.

Macedonians, she learns, sacrifice a black lamb in an annual fertility ritual, a practice she relates to a masochistic courting of violence, which only destroys a people. Representing a search for life through gratuitous destruction or death, she equates the black lamb ritual with cruelty and is repulsed by it as she was earlier by the theological interpretation of Christianity which centers on the crucifixion. Because she identifies the black lamb ritual with the violence which seems on the point of erupting at any time, she prophesies through implication the impending war in Europe, a war that had, in fact, begun by the time the book was published.

The grey falcon symbolizes a spiritual victory that can rise even in the midst of defeat. According to Serbian folk song and epic poetry, Prince Lazar had a vision of the grey falcon which assured him on the eve of the Battle of Kossovo, 28 June 1389 (St. Vitus Day), that if he died in the battle his soul would be saved. He died in the battle, which marked the beginning of five hundred years of Serbian subservience to the Turks. On the day of mourning each year over the defeat, the Serbs also remembered St. Vitus and the promise of the grey falcon.

The Meaning of Treason (1947) grew from West's commission by the *New Yorker* magazine to report the treason trials of the Englishmen who had broadcast for the Nazis on German radio during World War II—William Joyce (Lord Haw-Haw) and John Amery. To these reports she soon added an account of the trial of Dr. Allen Nunn May, who had more recently betrayed the secret of the atom bomb to a Russian agent and then confessed to the British police. In this book she develops the style she later uses in writing about other trials and about social issues: She considers the background of the accused and his motivation for the alleged treasonable or criminal activity, and then she puts within this context the arguments propounded in the

courtroom, without strongly siding with either the prosecution or the defendant.

At this point in her career, Rebecca West seemed less hostile to those accused of breach of national loyalty than she did later. She suggests, in fact, that the accused are much like their contemporaries, and equates treason with an expression of individualism and with an idealistic rebellion against outworn cultural and governmental institutions. Treason derives from loss of pride in one's country, she reasons, and all people should have, therefore, "a drop or two of treason in their veins." Her principal theme is that modern rationalism and secularism fail to recognize the existence of basic group loyalties, or else they fail to make these loyalties strong enough to withstand insidious pressures that may be destructive. The security of the state is important, she maintains, but so is the individual's right to rebel against tyrannies of any kind. The appearance of West's picture on the cover of the 8 December 1947 issue of *Time* magazine suggests the popular reputation of this book, as does the publication of a revised and enlarged edition of it, as *The New Meaning of Treason* (1964). Of great interest to West were the psychological adjustments that double agents had to make in enacting two separate roles while keeping their "actual" identity hidden as a secret "third self." The literary exploitation of the divided personality, which she used in her first two novels, she employed again almost thirty years later.

In 1953 West wrote a series of four articles for the London Sunday *Times,* which proved controversial in America as in England. In them she minimized the potential damaging effects of McCarthyism in the United States, that is, the persecution of individuals who had been identified as covert or former members of the Communist party on the assumption that such individuals were a threat to national security. Because she had in the past espoused liberal points of view and defended civil liberties, her failure to attack the activities of the House Un-American Activities Committee of the U.S. Congress disturbed many. The articles probably reflect her increasing concern about Russian strength and espionage activity in a nuclear age and her fears of the spread of totalitarianism.

It is not surprising, then, that in her next book, *A Train of Powder* (1955), she included not only three essays on the Nuremberg trials of World War II, looking back to the Nazi menace, but also "A Better Mousetrap," calling attention to Russian espionage in Britain. Her interpretation of the trial of a Russian spy in London is unresolved at the close of the essay, and a sense of the ominous prevails. In two essays unrelated to military or espionage activity, she covers murder trials, expressing her conviction that people on both sides of the Atlantic have become inured to violence and wanton destructiveness. "Mr. Settle and Mr. Hume" deals with the trial of Mr. Hume, a suburban London man convicted for murdering Mr. Settle and mutilating the body before throwing its parts in a stream. At the close of the essay West describes her visit to Mrs. Hume, who has sat with her infant quietly and apparently without emotion through the long court hearings and then divorced her husband after several dreary prison visits. West concludes that ironically in a few years life in the London suburbs will go on "as if it had never happened." "Opera in Greenville" describes how after days in a suffocatingly hot courtroom, she sees thirty-one men—nearly all cab drivers in the small city of Greenville, North Carolina—acquitted of the murder by lynching of a black youth. Yet, she reports, when the youth was taken from his cell to be lynched, fourteen cabs had been lined up at the door of the jail. She concludes again that an entire community can tolerate violence—and sometimes even sanction it. She extends her conclusion to prophesy acceptance of the ultimate violence of nuclear war.

The three essays on Nuremberg (dated 1946, 1949, and 1954) reflect changes in her thinking about the trials of the war criminals. All are collected under the title, "Greenhouse with Cyclamens," which refers to a visit she made to a greenhouse while she was attending the proceedings in 1946. There she saw a middle-aged amputee, who could hardly stoop or bend to tend the tiny cyclamen plants, but who insisted, nevertheless, upon growing quantities of them. At first a war veteran's effort to operate his greenhouse seemed to her symbolic of Europe's renewal of life through painful determination, but later his refusal to choose different work symbolized for her an obsessive, single-minded dwelling on the past and a waste of personal strength and effort for inadequate satisfaction. The question of "forgetting" injustice and adjusting to the present provided conflicts that could never be resolved by the Nuremberg trials. In the last of these three essays, she acknowledges that these trials failed to meet the hopes many had for justice. Nevertheless, she praises the brave men who sought to use the trials "to force a huge and sprawling historical event to become comprehensible. It is only by making such efforts that we survive."

All six essays in the book indicate West's lessening confidence in the relevance of existing legal systems for determining guilt, establishing justice,

Rebecca West, 1950s

and assigning appropriate punishment, although she still regarded the law as the only buttress against authoritarianism or fascism. The book's title, *A Train of Powder,* emphasizes West's primary aim: to warn her readers that violence begets violence and that greater destruction is ahead for the world than that experienced in World War II. The epigraph from John Donne provides the title and the warning: "Our God is not out of breath because he hath blown one Tempest, and swallowed a Navy; our God hath not burnt out his eyes, because he hath looked upon a Train of Powder." So the "god of violence" which modern society has enthroned, she would imply, has not spent its force: *A Train of Powder* is again building toward massive explosion.

The Fountain Overflows (1956), West's first novel in twenty years, reveals a remarkable richness of detail, character, and free expression of emotion—an abundant overflowing, as from a fountain, energy the narrator feels has come from her parents. The title derives from the line of William Blake's *The Marriage of Heaven and Hell* (1790) that West uses as epigraph: "The cistern contains; the fountain overflows." The novel sold well; it was serialized first in the *Ladies' Home Journal,* and it was a Literary Guild selection in the United States and a Book Club choice in England. West dedicated this novel to her eldest sister, Letitia. The fictitious Aubrey family also includes a brother, Richard Quin, although Rebecca West had no brother.

From the early pages of the novel the Aubrey family in 1900 suffers the privations of a harrowing genteel poverty. Piers and Clare Aubrey, who earlier had moved from South Africa to Edinburgh, move to the edge of London with their four children. They are "respectable"—owning an upright piano, books, and three valuable paintings—but they do not have enough to eat; the mother looks "wild" in her bad clothing, and the girls find the soles falling off their cheap shoes wherever they walk. Piers frequently changes jobs because he has a penchant for annoying people, and he leaves the family anxious and without money for months at a time. A gambler in the stock market, he at one point sells his wife's cherished furniture, and the family returns to find little more than the piano left in the house. Though Clare has buried her own musical ambitions, she strenuously prepares and inspires three of the children to become great—and well-to-do—pianists. She just as strenuously tries to keep the untalented Cordelia from playing her violin—at least in public and for money. Cordelia, the prettiest and most practical, possesses determination and a stubborn faith in her fallible judgment of her own powers that matches the intensity of her mother. At the close of the book Clare acknowledges that the family life has been adequate for the musically gifted children, in spite of their deprivations, but not for Cordelia, who needs freedom to get away from the artists in order to develop her own individuality. The novel thus illustrates the maturing of a family of artists even more than the survival of a poor family.

Besides the Aubrey family, West introduces a parallel family, who remain peripheral but who were to figure in a more important way in a projected trilogy, of which this novel would be the first volume. Though she wrote much of the second novel, "This Real Night," and included a portion of it, in which Rose continues to serve as narrator, in *Rebecca West—A Celebration* (1977), she abandoned the trilogy several years before her death.

In *The Fountain Overflows,* this second family lives in a shabby house where evil forces, Rose believes, throw the pots and pans across the kitchen when she and her mother go there to visit. The child narrator moves easily from the detailed documentation of reality to fantasy. This novel, thus, contains elements reminiscent of *Harriet Hume* in its use of the surreal and fantastic and the essentially threatening nature of such disordered phenomena.

Rose's precise presentation of vivid details in *The Fountain Overflows* creates a sense of the late Victorian and Edwardian period—gaslights, candles, chilly parlors, rose-colored flowers on worn carpets, Victorian wallpaper, feather boas, big hats, and tight skirts that make a woman seem like a pillar

to a child. Her excited curiosity sweeps material of great variety into the novel—concerts, encounters with unseen ghosts who move objects about, conversation about politics, a trial in which a schoolmate's mother is unjustly condemned for the murder of her husband, Christmas surprises, fights between Clare and Cordelia about the violin, Cordelia's attempted suicide, and a distressing illness of the little brother. Rose zestfully satirizes nearly all "outsiders" and introduces at least fifty characters, often for only a single scene or conversation. Dickensian eccentrics, evil individuals, fools, and a few saints crowd the novel as Rose's fountain overflows for page after page. At the same time, no one who is not part of the intensely related family and their music ever really matters to Rose. She identifies the source of her vitality and the fullness of the life she pours out in rapid anecdotal sequence when she speaks of the richly endowed sensibilities of her parents. She sees herself, near the end of the book while she awaits the beginning of her first concert with Mary, as part, though a lesser part, of these two fascinating people, so unlike anyone else's parents: "It was my father and mother who existed. I could see them as two springs, bursting from a stoney cliff, and rushing down a mountainside in torrent, and joining to flow through the world as a great river. . . . I was swept on by the strong flood of which I was a part."

West is able to unify the episodic novel by its persistent themes. Rose's effort to deduce inner being through observation of detail, an attempt West called "trying to make out what is inside the opaque human frame," is central. It allows her finally to understand her father and Cordelia—the two people who anger her most. Another unifying theme is the children's insatiable musical ambition. Because of the importance of this theme, the children's mother—though a tiny, wild-looking, nervous, and frightened woman—dominates Rose's imagination. She appears in almost every scene or is the subject of conversation when she is not present.

Emotions swing, as in Dickens, from ecstasy to heartbreak. Rose's intensity of spirit spills over in her depiction of the lavish abundance of the life of her family, her satirization of multitudinous minor characters, her descriptions of the varied events, and her obsession with perfecting her art so that it cannot be patterned or "contained" but will overflow the boundaries of her spirit and her understanding.

Some critics found the whimsicality and stylistic precision of Rose's narration lacking in artistic order and missed the shaping of more-traditional fiction, although the epigraph suggests that Rose

Dust jacket for the British edition of West's autobiographical novel about a London family living in genteel poverty

would liken such organization to water contained in a cistern. C. J. Rolo saw West's strengths in her "being possessed by her protagonists," her characterization, and her "group portraiture." Others praised her vivid and detailed portrayal of London in 1900, in spite of the sharp focus on the isolated microcosm of the Aubrey household. No static background descriptions establish the historical period as the reality builds through turmoil and constant talk. In what could have been a nostalgic autobiographical novel, young Rose's gusto and vitality sweep away all touches of sentimentality. It is surely West's best novel.

In *The Court and the Castle* (1957), consisting mainly of West's Terry Lectures at Yale University, she discusses literature in terms of the individual character (The Courtier), his or her society and its conventional demands (The Court), and the personal and spiritual aspirations of the individual (The Castle of God). Within this somewhat allegorical framework, she discusses character, theme, and plot in fiction and drama, beginning with Shake-

speare and devoting most of her attention to nineteenth-century novels.

The relationships among Courtier, Court, and Castle vary from one period of history to another and from one author to another and are infinite in their manifestations. No literature can be great, however, if the courtier avoids recognizing the reality and significance of the court on his way to the castle. The court, or society, may hinder as often as help a courtier on his way, but he or she must at some level come to terms with it, with its expectations from the individual and the power that it exerts over the individual. Should author or character ignore the court, the work of literature will be evasive, shallow, and chimerical. Both Shakespeare and Austen, West insisted, recognize that the individual character develops within a "court," not in solitude or in a realm of the Platonic ideal, where society is viewed only as a shadow on the wall of a cave.

As Rebecca West in her books on treason and criminality defended the law, in spite of its fallibility, in *The Court and the Castle* she also revealed a profound respect for the state and certain other systems of order, even though she knew that they sanction occasional inequities. In this light, she discussed with some degree of approbation Proust's resignation to the existence of a bureaucratic, often unjust, society. At least, she said, he recognized the nature of his political system and came to terms with it instead of evading political realities and refusing to bother with the institutions and demands of society. The social order, even when unjust in its workings, cannot be abrogated in literature if the writer is to possess significance or greatness. This volume, of course, shows that West did not end her discussion on neohumanists, and the tendency she saw in them to separate art and politics, in *Ending in Earnest* (1931).

West's writings on treason trials, her growing fascination with the complex psychology of the double agent's multiple personalities, her deepening anxiety about world violence and Russian espionage, and her literary criticism in *The Court and the Castle* all lent impetus to her turning again to fiction for the freedom to explore character and motivation beyond the limits of documentary nonfiction.

In *The Birds Fall Down* (1966) she created in Kamensky an attractive double agent and focuses on the people whose lives he has changed through his dehumanized espionage activity. Laura, age eighteen, provides, in particular, this focus. In several chapters Laura's beloved grandfather, Count Nikolai Diakanov, an exiled czarist, and Vassili Iulievitch Chubinov, an anarchist descended from a monarchist family, discourse on a train about political theory, philosophy, and religion. In the several chapters that follow, Count Diakanov rambles through a verbose farewell speech as he is slowly dying in a French hotel. He is dead by the middle of the novel, and Laura must adjust to life without her grandfather's affection and understanding of political intrigue. In spite of the wandering and lengthy discourse, the structure of the novel is surprisingly taut. The chief action takes place in two days; only the few consequential characters appear, and nearly all action is presented from the point of view of Laura Rowan, who matures markedly during the two days. The use of third-person narrator, who can appraise Laura, as well as record her views, allows West to avoid some of the naiveté and episodic looseness that resulted in *The Fountain Overflows* from the use of the young girl Rose as narrator.

One recurring theme in the book—that the victim of evil is forced into committing evil in order to survive—may be seen in Laura's becoming a conspirator in a murder because she, as the victim in the intrigue, has no choice if she is to survive. Self-sacrifice on her part would have been seen by West to be immoral in this situation. Human nature at its best is limited and possesses the capacity for evil. The relatively good young woman must call upon her ability to kill in order to avert the greater evil which will destroy her. Society will move from one polarity to its opposite and then may attain a position of strength and stability in the reconciling of the polarities. In killing her enemy Laura has been part of the process. West's point of view in this novel is pessimistic. The spy's double betrayal—of both extremist groups—may provide the vacuum into which a moderate government can move and gain power. West presents most strikingly in this novel the modern world's penchant for violence and hypocrisy. Symbolism intensifies the impact of *The Birds Fall Down,* unifies it, and tightens its structure beyond that of West's earlier fiction. Most pervasive of the recurrent images is that of the birds, whose fate suggests her pessimistic views of human potentialities. She sees the world hastening toward a cataclysm, in which the birds, which suggest ideal possibilities for mankind, will all fall down and be destroyed.

West's last book, *1900* (1982), provides a compact social history of a single year, as well as a perspective from which that year can be seen as pivotal between the nineteenth and the twentieth centuries. The book might be viewed as a nonfiction sequel to *The Fountain Overflows,* as if Rose had returned at the age of ninety to look back at her life in 1900. The episodic situation, the whimsical selection of anecdote, the swiftly sketched personalities, and the ranging interests of that novel all reappear, as does the vitality one identifies with the youthful narrator of that book and with the essays in *The Young Rebecca, 1911-1917* (1982). In *1900,* the substantial text is accompanied by excellent photographs.

The text and photographs cover an astonishingly encyclopedic range of subjects. The book recounts the natural disasters of that year (Vesuvius erupted; a pillar blew over at Stonehenge) and the milestone deaths occurring at about that time (in 1898 that of Gladstone and in 1901 that of Queen Victoria). The horrors of the Boer War fill the early pages. West then turns quickly to the exciting developments in turn-of-the-century British (and American) culture. She moves easily from art (Sargent, Matisse, Renoir, and Picasso) to music

(Mahler, Ravel, Sibelius, and Puccini) to philosophy (Bertrand Russell's study of Leibniz, Bergson's writings on laughter, and Freud's publication of *Interpretation of Dreams*) and to scientific theory (Einstein's latest theories, Planck's establishment of the quantum principle, and the new interest in genetics sparked by Mendel). She shows also a great interest in the practical applications of science: the caterpillar tractor invented that year; the Brownie camera coming on the market; subways beginning to be built in London, Paris, and New York; the cleaning out of the Danube estuaries; the explorations of polar regions; and the Wright brothers' gliders.

She writes less fully about literature (the publication that year of Conrad's *Lord Jim* and of *The Wizard of Oz;* Twain's popularity with British children; her views that Henry James fortunately avoided homosexuality in his books; and Proust's preoccupation with the Dreyfus case). She tends to dwell on the personal lives, problems, and backgrounds of prominent government figures and on the people with whom they associated (the harsh treatment of Edward VII as adolescent; his mistresses; Queen Alexander's being overburdened by the fertility of the royal couples related to her; and Alice Roosevelt's outspoken unconventionality). West's feminist interests surface in her discussion of the Gibson Girl (ironically, popular because she did nothing) and in her poignant comment after nine decades of life: "Men and women do not really like each other very much." (On her eightieth birthday she publicly endorsed the Equal Rights Amendment, saying, "It is much more fundamental than suffragism.")

West reveals some nostalgia for a world now gone, less chaotic than that which followed, but she emphasizes even more those exciting developments that heralded a new era. She does not disregard the militarism with which the British founded the empire and is critical of it; she cites the oppression of the poor and the repression of non-Caucasian races and of women, and she castigates class snobbery. Concurrent with these arresting new developments in science and the arts, the days of empire in Great Britain and of the frontier in America are drawing to a close. West's accomplishment lies in the perpetual appeal of *1900* to the reader's curiosity and in her unparalleled facility with language.

In her last years West remained articulate and thoughtful on public issues and figures. As in her comments upon individuals in her books on treason, she remarked in the late 1970s that Richard Nixon "was not stupid. He was an example of bad

form combined with Original Sin." Two years before her death, she appeared in the film *Reds,* commenting upon the Russian revolution. In May 1980 when the Iranian Embassy, adjacent to her home in Kensington, was under siege, she was reluctant to be evacuated. A month before her death her last article was published in *Vogue,* describing with sharp observation and gentlest wit the changes that age was producing in her sensory and mental processes— changes she found not only frustrating but sometimes intriguing. Because her eyesight caused stationary objects to move about, she could now enjoy a comedy of her own devising and watch such sights as church steeples dancing. She also described the preternatural intensity that age brought with it when one recalled past events, often out of context or apart from the ordered perspective of chronology: "One of the curious things about being ninety is that the power of memory is so strong that it often makes one feel as if one were several ages at the same time." Her final illness was brief. She remained alienated from her son and willed her estate, including her papers and copyrights, to her nephew, Professor Norman Mac Leod of the department of Engineering at Edinburgh University.

Rebecca West will be remembered in part for her early feminist and socialist essays, for *Henry James* (1916), and for creating a new genre of court reporting in which the writer speculates on the motivation and early psychological development or conditioning of criminals. She implies that criminals are more like average beings than different—all are limited by the presence of evil in human nature and human affairs. In the days after World War II, when Rebecca West had become known for her writing about trials and espionage, William Shirer sagaciously remarked that she had raised journalism to an art; Kenneth Tynan in this period declared that she was "the best journalist alive, the only one who can record both the facts and their flavor without loss of grace and vigor"; and Harry S. Truman, presenting her the Women's Press Club Award for Journalism, addressed her as "the world's best reporter."

While critics agree that Rebecca West may be the most consequential journalist of the twentieth century and one of the best modern essayists, one finds less agreement as to the permanence of her fiction in literary history. Most critics who have sought to generalize about her contribution to fiction since her death have stressed her style, wit, and facility with language, her tremendous intellectual powers, and her understanding of the intricacies of the human mind and emotions. William Shawn, editor of the *New Yorker,* speaking of her as "one of the giants" who would possess a lasting place in English literature, commented, "No one in this century wrote more dazzling prose, or had more wit, or looked at the intricacies of human character and the ways of the world more intelligently." Victoria Glendinning called her "the most interesting woman of this century . . . a major stylist, a major critical intelligence, a major commentator on public events and sexual politics, and a radical moralist." Diana Trilling judged her to be "one of the major literary figures of this century" and celebrated the rigor of an intellect that "was never taken in by any of the easy pieties of the literary or political culture." William F. Buckley, acknowledging her liberal persuasion as different from his own, acclaimed her as "a great literary figure," "the literary virtuoso of immense learning . . . who was . . . *forever* capable of marshalling her incomparable energies to make the case for human decency." Anne Tyler, with reference to *1900,* declared that West's incomparable use of the English language made her "one of treasures of the century" along with those heralded in her last book.

While some critics find her nonfiction more significant than her novels, West herself was reported to have said that, if she could live her life over again, she would write only fiction. Even in her nonfiction books she employed the techniques of fiction in order to produce a fuller truth. She augmented observation of behavior with speculation about the meaning, causes, and effects of that behavior. She examined relationships among people and events in order to answer questions that mere facts leave unexplained. *The Court and the Castle* indicates that she undertook serious study of, and theorizing about, the novel during the years when she herself was not writing in this genre.

If Rebecca West's varied and long career makes it difficult to generalize about her work, certain philosophical views do underlie and unify her writing. Though she claimed no Calvinist belief in original sin—in fact, she adhered to no creed or theological belief beyond mystical intuition—Rebecca West saw evil as inherent in the human being and in the universe, and she held no complacent assurance that good overcomes evil. The infant thrown from "the tideless womb" begins to cry in anger and to flail its arms at people it perceives as responsible for its discomfort. Such "strong hatred" becomes a weapon for survival in a hostile universe. (In one of West's early feminist essays, she wrote, "A strong hatred is the best lamp to bear in our hands as we go over the dark places of life, cutting away the

dead things men tell us to revere.")

Our hope, West says, lies in the fact that man is a "*thinking* reed." It is in the ability to think and to comprehend that the nobility of the weak, reedlike human being resides. One cannot avoid evil and suffering, but one should try to place them in perspective—to *know* reality. Through knowledge one can achieve some kind of harmony with the universe. This "process" of knowing reality allows the world of nature and the world of human beings to join, and the adaptation of the human being to his environment leads toward civilization. West obviously saw such attempts to attain order as superior to disorder; consequently in her radicalism she stopped short of certain measures which would lead, she thought, to violent change. Through the agency of art, one might move forward perceptibly toward order and mitigate the effects of evil. Art reflects reality at its fullest and thus becomes a means to the acquiring of fuller knowledge and to the ordering of chaotic experience.

Women, she felt, had particular difficulty in overcoming the obstacles that lay in the way of the "process" of harmonizing or ordering their universe. They lacked education. Conventional ideas about gender and appropriate roles for women limited their ability to mirror reality fully. They heard that self-sacrifice could be a particularly feminine virtue, rather than a conspiracy with evil and death. Women of privileged classes found themselves most debilitated or depleted, most powerless in reaching toward life, knowledge, and art as a result of being sheltered from reality, particularly in matters of economy and sex. They had learned to be frail reeds, not thinking reeds.

Rebecca West in her view of feminism saw suffrage as merely peripheral to the main struggle—the need for the affirmation of human life in its wholeness. Both men and women had to move beyond their traditional roles to perceive a full truth—to see without distortion. Women cannot attain knowledge and develop their artistic faculties until they are free to learn as much as they can and to express themselves fully through art. They too must become *thinking* reeds, made secure by knowledge and by responsiveness to art. In her involvement as an adolescent with the violence shown to feminists (including the force-feeding of them), in her concern with the struggles of workers in the trade-union movement, in her later hatred of fascism, and in her career as reporter on war crimes and treason trials, West never varied her basic conviction: she held to the view that one should not attack evil directly; one should rather pursue knowledge, art, and the pleasures of the mind and spirit in order to help humanity survive. The pleasure-principle (though not a passive hedonism) offered salvation; self-sacrifice and the pursuit of pain offered damnation. West's views were in direct conflict with Christian theology. While theologians interpret the crucifixion as an act of self-sacrifice on the part of Christ and God the Father that would redeem humanity from evil, to Rebecca West the crucifixion should have shamed humanity into virtue by providing the ultimate example of cruelty and evil in the victimization of the noblest of men. As the ultimate cruelty, the crucifixion became for West the ultimate evil.

Whatever the final critical judgments will be on Rebecca West's writing, she perpetually challenged her readers as she continued to interest them. The ability to do both so consistently may well be the hallmark of her genius.

Bibliography:
George Evelyn Hutchinson, *A Preliminary List of the*

Writings of Rebecca West: 1912-1951 (New Haven: Yale University Press, 1957).

References:
Motley F. Deakin, *Rebecca West* (Boston: G. K. Hall, 1980);

Gordon Ray, *H. G. Wells and Rebecca West* (New Haven: Yale University Press, 1974);

Anthony West, *H. G. Wells: Aspects of a Life* (New York: Random House, 1984);

West, Introduction to *Heritage* (New York: Washington Square Press, 1984);

Peter Wolfe, *Rebecca West, Artist and Thinker* (Carbondale: Southern Illinois University Press, 1971).

Papers:
There is a collection of West's papers in the Beinecke Library at Yale University.

Virginia Woolf

J. J. Wilson
Sonoma State University

BIRTH: London, 25 January 1882, to Leslie and Julia Prinsep Jackson Stephen.

MARRIAGE: 10 August 1912 to Leonard Woolf.

AWARDS: Femina/Vie Heureuse prize for *To the Lighthouse,* 1928.

DEATH: near Monks House, Rodmell, Sussex, 28 March 1941.

BOOKS: *The Voyage Out* (London: Duckworth, 1915; revised edition, New York: Doran, 1920; London: Duckworth, 1920);
Two Stories Written and Printed by Virginia Woolf and L. S. Woolf (Richmond: Hogarth Press, 1917); Virginia Woolf's story republished as *The Mark on the Wall* (Richmond: Hogarth Press, 1919);
Kew Gardens (Richmond: Hogarth Press, 1919; Folcroft, Pa.: Folcroft Press, 1969);

Night and Day (London: Duckworth, 1919; New York: Doran, 1920);
Monday or Tuesday (Richmond: Leonard & Virginia Woolf and the Hogarth Press, 1921; New York: Harcourt, Brace, 1921);
Jacob's Room (Richmond: Leonard & Virginia Woolf at the Hogarth Press, 1922; New York: Harcourt, Brace, 1923);
Mr. Bennett and Mrs. Brown (London: Leonard & Virginia Woolf at the Hogarth Press, 1924; Folcroft, Pa.: Folcroft Press, 1977);
The Common Reader (London: Leonard & Virginia Woolf at the Hogarth Press, 1925; New York: Harcourt, Brace, 1925);
Mrs. Dalloway (London: Leonard & Virginia Woolf at the Hogarth Press, 1925; New York: Harcourt, Brace, 1925);
To the Lighthouse (London: Leonard & Virginia Woolf at the Hogarth Press, 1927; New York: Harcourt, Brace, 1927);
Orlando: A Biography (New York: Crosby Gaige,

Virginia Woolf (Sotheby Parke Bernet, 15 December 1982)

1928; London: Leonard & Virginia Woolf at
the Hogarth Press, 1928);

A Room of One's Own (New York: Fountain Press/
London: Hogarth Press, 1929; London:
Leonard & Virginia Woolf at the Hogarth
Press, 1929; New York: Harcourt, Brace,
1929);

Street Haunting (San Francisco: Westgate Press,
1930);

On Being Ill (London: Leonard & Virginia Woolf at
the Hogarth Press, 1930);

Beau Brummell (New York: Rimington & Hooper,
1930);

The Waves (London: Leonard & Virginia Woolf at
the Hogarth Press, 1931; New York: Harcourt, Brace, 1931);

A Letter to a Young Poet (London: Leonard & Virginia Woolf at the Hogarth Press, 1932; Folcroft,
Pa.: Folcroft Press, 1975);

The Common Reader: Second Series (London: Leonard
& Virginia Woolf at the Hogarth Press, 1932);
republished as *The Second Common Reader*
(New York: Harcourt, Brace, 1932);

Flush: A Biography (London: Leonard & Virginia
Woolf at the Hogarth Press, 1933; New York:
Harcourt, Brace, 1933);

Walter Sickert: A Conversation (London: Leonard &

Virginia Woolf at the Hogarth Press, 1934;
Folcroft, Pa.: Folcroft Press, 1970);

The Roger Fry Memorial Exhibition: An Address (Bristol: Bristol Museum and Art Gallery, 1935);

The Years (London: Leonard & Virginia Woolf at
the Hogarth Press, 1937; New York: Harcourt, Brace, 1937);

Three Guineas (London: Hogarth Press, 1938; New
York: Harcourt, Brace, 1938);

Reviewing (London: Hogarth Press, 1939; Folcroft,
Pa.: Folcroft Press, 1969);

Roger Fry: A Biography (London: Hogarth Press,
1940; New York: Harcourt, Brace, 1940);

Between the Acts (London: Hogarth Press, 1941; New
York: Harcourt, Brace, 1941);

The Death of the Moth and Other Essays (London:
Hogarth Press, 1942; New York: Harcourt,
Brace, 1942);

A Haunted House and Other Short Stories (London:
Hogarth Press, 1943; New York: Harcourt,
Brace, 1944);

The Moment and Other Essays (London: Hogarth
Press, 1947; New York: Harcourt, Brace,
1948);

The Captain's Death Bed and Other Essays (New York:
Harcourt, Brace, 1950; London: Hogarth
Press, 1950);

*A Writer's Diary: Being Extracts from the Diary of Vir-
ginia Woolf,* edited by Leonard Woolf (London: Hogarth Press, 1953; New York: Harcourt, Brace, 1954);

Hours in a Library (New York: Harcourt, Brace,
1958);

Granite and Rainbow (London: Hogarth Press, 1958;
New York: Harcourt, Brace, 1958);

Contemporary Writers (London: Hogarth Press,
1965; New York: Harcourt, Brace & World,
1966);

Nurse Lugton's Golden Thimble (London: Hogarth
Press, 1966);

Stephen Versus Gladstone (Headington Quarry,
1967);

A Cockney's Farming Experiences, edited by Suzanne
Henig (San Diego: San Diego State University
Press, 1972);

Mrs. Dalloway's Party: A Short Story Sequence, edited
by Stella McNichol (London: Hogarth Press,
1973; New York: Harcourt Brace Jovanovich,
1975);

The London Scene: Five Essays (New York: Frank
Hallman, 1975);

The Waves: The Two Holograph Drafts, transcribed
and edited by John W. Graham (Toronto &
Buffalo: University of Toronto Press, 1976);

Moments of Being, edited by Jeanne Schulkind (Sussex: University Press, 1976; New York & London: Harcourt Brace Jovanovich, 1977);

Freshwater: A Comedy, edited by Lucio P. Ruotolo (New York & London: Harcourt Brace Jovanovich, 1976);

The Diary of Virginia Woolf, edited by Anne Olivier Bell, volume 1 (1915-1919) (London: Hogarth Press, 1977; New York & London: Harcourt Brace Jovanovich, 1979); volume 2 (1920-1924) (London: Hogarth Press, 1978; New York & London: Harcourt Brace Jovanovich, 1978); volume 3 (1925-1930) (London: Hogarth Press, 1980; New York: Harcourt Brace Jovanovich, 1980); volume 4 (1931-1935) (London: Hogarth Press, 1982; New York: Harcourt Brace Jovanovich, 1982);

Books and Portraits, edited by Mary Lyon (London: Hogarth Press, 1977; New York: Harcourt Brace Jovanovich, 1978);

The Pargiters, edited by Mitchell A. Leaska (New York: New York Public Library, 1977; London: Hogarth Press, 1978);

Virginia Woolf's Reading Notebooks, edited by Brenda R. Silver (Princeton, N.J. & Guildford, Surrey: Princeton University Press, 1982).

Collection: *Collected Essays*, 4 volumes (London: Hogarth Press, 1966-1967; New York: Harcourt, Brace & World, 1967).

The writings of Virginia Woolf have always been admired by discriminating readers, but her work has suffered, as has that of many other major authors, periods of neglect by the literary establishment. She was, as she herself put it, always a hare a long way ahead of "those hounds my critics." It was difficult to find copies of her books during the 1950s and 1960s, and they were rarely included on syllabuses for literature classes. However, even before 1972, when her nephew Quentin Bell's bestselling biography introduced her to a larger public, there were signs of quickening of scholarly interest. The extensive and serious treatment given Virginia Woolf's novel *To the Lighthouse* (1927) in Erich Auerbach's much-esteemed book *Mimesis* (translated into English in 1953), was a presage and perhaps one of the causes of the turnaround. Oddly enough, her very name has become a household word because of the catchy title of Edward Albee's 1962 play, *Who's Afraid of Virginia Woolf?*

Her many readers today would answer Albee's enigmatic question with a resounding no one. Her works seem much more accessible than they did to her contemporaries. Though there is now an enormous critical apparatus available, "common readers," as Virginia Woolf called them (borrowing the term from Samuel Johnson), need feel no fear in approaching her novels on their own. Secondary material should be used to enhance rather than impede or replace the reading of her work.

Nonetheless, the advantages of the recent critical and popular attention are manifold. Her novels are now in print again, in a variety of editions, often with introductions in homage by today's writers. They have been translated into more than fifty languages. Her essays, reviews, and short stories have been collected. Fragments of unpublished manuscripts have been pieced together and published, giving general readers access to valuable material such as Woolf's autobiographical writing, edited by Jeanne Schulkind in the collection *Moments of Being* (1976). And then there is the vast delight of the many volumes of letters and diaries, all scrupulously edited, copiously footnoted, and indexed. Even her reading notes are being published.

This new attention to Virginia Woolf has been paralleled by an increasing interest in the so-called Bloomsbury Group, which had its origins at Cambridge among some undergraduates who were under the influence of the philosopher G. E. Moore. At the instigation of Thoby Stephen, Virginia's brother, these college friends continued to meet in London, in Bloomsbury, and the group evolved to include Virginia, her sister Vanessa, and others.

For a reliable introduction to the memoirs and manifestos issuing from these fertile minds, see S.P. Rosenbaum's anthology, *The Bloomsbury Group* (1975). He includes a section called "Bloomsbury Criticisms and Controversies," which gives some perspective on how this group of intimates was perceived by such master controversialists as Wyndham Lewis, D. H. Lawrence, the Leavises, and others. His bibliography testifies to the enormous amount of Bloomsbury material now available. Noel Annan pointed out in a 1978 article in the *New York Review of Books*, "Virginia Woolf Fever," that we are witnessing "a documentation in detail of a kind never before seen in English letters: so that by the time it is completed we shall know more about the members of the Bloomsbury Group than of any other set of people in English literary history." Their lives and their work are revealed to have, as Virginia Woolf's has, special resonance for readers today.

From the turn of the century until World War

Vanessa Stephen, Stella Duckworth, and Virginia Stephen (photo by H. & R. Stiles; Sotheby Parke Bernet, 15 December 1982)

ll the members of Bloomsbury, as individuals and in various groupings, were grappling with many of the questions which still preoccupy us—for example: they sought to understand the complex relationships between freedom and form, between the object and its abstraction, between gender and sexual preference, between friendship and love; they studied the costs of imperialism, alternatives to war, the possibilities of socialism, the imperatives of feminism; they practiced, most of them, pacifism, and they mistrusted nationalism, patriotism, religionism, fanaticism of all kinds; they were proindividualism and prized personal relations above all other allegiances. Vanessa Bell, Duncan Grant, Roger Fry, and Clive Bell were active in the art world and in an artists' collective called the Omega Workshop. John Maynard Keynes was influential in the world of international politics and finance. Lytton Strachey applied Freud in his *Eminent Victorians* (1918), thereby revolutionizing the art of biography. These and other "members" of that elusive entity called the Bloomsbury Group were in the forefront of the progressive political and aesthetic thought of the time, and part of their importance was that they helped to provide Virginia Woolf the stimulating ambiance of candid exchange and support so valuable to an emerging writer.

Virginia Woolf's own story starts much ear-

lier, nineteen years before Queen Victoria's death, in the respectable purlieus of Kensington, at the household of Leslie Stephen, who was himself an exemplar of that Victorian phenomenon—a man of letters. It seems especially fitting to prepare an entry in this biographical series for Adeline Virginia Stephen Woolf, as her father was the primary editor of the prototype of all such reference books, the *Dictionary of National Biography*. Indeed, Virginia Woolf was always to claim that she had been cramped in the womb by the weight of those heavy volumes. While Leslie Stephen was eventually persuaded to give up this stressful task by his ever-solicitous wife, Julia, his interests in literary history continued, and it was he who encouraged his youngest daughter's omnivorous reading, giving her free access to his excellent library. She was to have very little formal education, but she described her father's influence in this way: "To read what one liked because one liked it, never to pretend to admire what one did not—that was his only lesson in the art of reading. To write in the fewest possible words, as clearly as possible, exactly what one meant—that was his only lesson in the art of writing. All the rest must be learnt for oneself." The young Virginia also benefited from the Who's Who of writers who came to call at 22 Hyde Park Gate: James Russell Lowell, George Meredith, Thomas

Virginia Stephen and her father, Sir Leslie Stephen, not long before Sir Leslie was operated on for cancer in December 1902 (photo by
G. C. Beresford; Sotheby Parke Bernet, 15 December 1982)

Hardy, Henry James, Aunt Anny (Anne Thackeray Ritchie, the novelist), and many others.

Virginia Stephen was the third of four children of Leslie and Julia Stephen—Vanessa, Thoby, Virginia, and Adrian; there were three other children from Julia Stephen's first marriage living in the house—George, Stella, and Gerald Duckworth—and, in the early days, Laura Stephen, the mentally deficient daughter of Leslie Stephen's first marriage, to Minnie Thackeray, who had died in 1875. The lives of this large family at Hyde Park Gate were filled with the usual Victorian comforts and discomforts. As a young don at Cambridge, Leslie Stephen had experienced a crisis of faith and as a result, refused to sign the Thirty-Nine articles of the Church of England, thus cutting himself off from what would have probably been a secure academic life. While this courageous stand eased his conscience in some ways (and according to Katherine C. Hill, set an example which "predisposed his daughters to cultural revolt"), the resultant financial worries preyed upon him, especially after his second wife's death in 1895.

The disastrous effects of the death of that "creator of felicity," as Julia Stephen was seen by her family, reverberated seismically throughout all seven floors of 22 Hyde Park Gate. As part of the aftershock, thirteen-year-old Virginia suffered her first nervous breakdown. The "cure" of rest, reading, milk, and long walks was to be the healing ritual used all of her life during recurrent bouts with what

she called madness; critics now quarrel over the terminology, the treatments, and the consequences of a too-general or incorrect diagnosis, but the alternating rhythms of well-being, collapse, convalescence became a pattern in her life.

During these early years, tragic event followed upon tragic event, testing Virginia's remarkable recuperative powers. First, Stella Duckworth, who had done her best to serve as a substitute mother, died, and then Sir Leslie (he had been knighted in 1902) in 1904, after a protracted illness. His death freed the younger generation to sell the Hyde Park Gate house; the Stephen contingent decided to move to the unfashionable but conveniently located area of Bloomsbury, with low rents, easy access to the British Museum, and, best of all, independence from hovering relatives.

At 46 Gordon Square, in a house that still stands today, by early 1905 the Bloomsbury Group, or groupings, can be said to have begun, with Thoby Stephen's "Thursday evenings." Virginia Stephen was teaching adult-education classes in English literature and history at Morley College. She was also, as she put it in a triumphant letter to her favorite correspondent at this time, Violet Dickinson, "realising the ambition of our youth, and actually making money" through writing reviews for such periodicals as the *Guardian* and the *Times Literary Supplement*.

In November 1906, Thoby Stephen, the young man of promise and the adored elder brother, died at twenty-six, of typhoid contracted on holiday in Greece. Again the repercussions were earthshaking. Two days after Thoby Stephen's death, Vanessa Stephen finally agreed to marry her brother's friend, Clive Bell; the marriage constituted for Virginia yet another loss. Leaving 46 Gordon Square to the newlyweds, Virginia and Adrian Stephen were reduced to housekeeping together at 29 Fitzroy Square. They were still living in Bloomsbury and still holding the Thursday-evening gatherings, but nothing was ever quite the same.

This precarious phase, marked by Virginia Stephen's beginning on her first novel and marred by illness, was to last for five years or so. Of the many events occurring during this relatively independent—and restless and reckless—time in her life, Virginia Stephen enjoyed retelling the story of the notorious *Dreadnought* Hoax. With her brother Adrian, Duncan Grant, and assorted other young pranksters, she had dressed up in full oriental regalia and blackface to pay a ceremonial visit to H.M.S. *Dreadnought*, the pride of the British Navy. They claimed to be emissaries from Abyssinia and, despite the incongruity of their physiognomies and dialects, were accepted as advertised, offered a twenty-one-gun salute, hospitality, and a complete tour of the so-secret ship. It was only later when the full story was leaked to the press that reproaches fell round the ears of the unrepentant participants and security was tightened on all British battleships. As Virginia Woolf said dryly, in an account she wrote of the incident years later, "I am glad to think that I too have been of help to my country." This escapade can be seen as a mock foray into the patriarchy's bastion, an emperor's-clothes fable, and the moral was not lost on the future author of *Three Guineas* (1938).

Marriage was one of the vexatious issues to be resolved during this period. Virginia Stephen's letters were full of complaints that ever since Thoby Stephen's death, her woman friends were after her to marry, but she too worried that she might never have a proposal and claimed to dread merely being "a virgin, an aunt, an authoress." Proposals did come, the most surprising, even to the suitor himself, being from Lytton Strachey, an avowed homosexual. The offer was quickly rescinded and this miscue did not damage their friendship. It was Strachey who first thought of Leonard Woolf as a likely prospect for Virginia Stephen, and it was to him that Virginia Stephen wrote a card with the single message "Ha! Ha!" when she finally overcame her own ambivalence and accepted Leonard Woolf's offer of marriage. She then triumphantly

announced her engagement, describing Leonard Woolf as "one of Thoby's greatest friends" and "a penniless Jew" and noting that "he wants to find out about labour and factories and to keep outside Government and do things on his own account"; "He has also written a novel, and means to write as well as be practical." Especially important to her was that "L. thinks my writing the best part of me." Later she was to write in her diary: "Had I married Lytton I should never have written anything. . . . He checks and inhibits in the most curious way. [Leonard] may be severe, but he stimulates. Anything is possible with him."

Leonard Woolf had been one of the original members of the Cambridge phase of Bloomsbury, but, after leaving Cambridge, he had accepted a post in the civil service. He served seven years in Ceylon, where he fulfilled his duties with distinction all the while formulating his strong anticolonial position. On leave and in love in 1912, his decision to resign from the service was in some ways analogous to Leslie Stephen's principled withdrawal

Leonard and Virginia Woolf, 1912 (Sotheby Parke Bernet, 15 December 1982)

The Daily Mirror

THE MORNING JOURNAL WITH THE SECOND LARGEST NET SALE.

WEDNESDAY, FEBRUARY 16, 1910

HOW THE OFFICERS OF H.M.S. DREADNOUGHT WERE HOAXED: PHOTOGRAPH OF THE "ABYSSINIAN PRINCES" WHO HAVE MADE ALL ENGLAND LAUGH.

Newspaper coverage of the Dreadnought *Hoax: Virginia Stephen as "Prince Sanganya," Guy Ridley as "Prince Mandok," Adrian Stephen as "Herr George Kauffmann, the German interpreter," Anthony Buxton as "Prince Makalen," Duncan Grant as "Prince Mikael Golen," and Horace de Vere Cole as "Mr. Horace Cholmondely, the Foreign Office attaché"* from the don's life. Leonard Woolf too became a freelance man of letters and found himself accepting onerous tasks to make ends meet. He helped Roger Fry with the controversial postimpressionist exhibit (which opened in November 1910), worked for the Labour party and for the Fabians, acted as literary editor of the *Nation* and later as editor of the *Political Quarterly,* among other things. This hardworking man would certainly never have foreseen at this turning point in his career in 1912 the two tasks for which he is now best-known—the nurturing of his wife's genius and the management of the Hogarth Press. It was Leonard Woolf's support of her writing and the publishing house itself that combined in the symbiotic relationship that allowed Virginia Woolf to exult in her diary in 1925: "I am the only woman in England free to write what I like."

How did the Woolfs get into the publishing business? "Almost in spite of ourselves," said Leonard Woolf, in an interview with Mary Gaither, on which she reports in her introduction to *A Checklist of the Hogarth Press* (1976). In 1917 they bought a small handpress, with a booklet of instructions, and set up shop on the dining-room table in Hogarth House, their lodgings in Richmond. They planned to print only some of their own writings and that of their talented friends. Leonard Woolf hoped the manual work would provide a relaxing diversion from the stress of writing for Virginia Woolf. Had either of them known then what this hobby was to turn into, probably even their courage would have failed them. It is a tribute to their combined business acumen and critical judgment that this small independent venture became, as Mary Gaither recounts, "a self-supporting business and a significant publishing voice in England between the wars." Lelia Luedeking adds: "Through the medium of the Hogarth Press she and Leonard made works available to the public in subjects highly controversial at the time. They published many writers whose works otherwise would have had difficulty seeing the light of day—Russians, socialists, labor organizers, women, experimental poets, psychoanalysts, and anti-imperialists." And, aside from publishing the works of Sigmund Freud, John Maynard Keynes, Harold Laski, Roger Fry, Robert Graves, H. G. Wells, T. S. Eliot, E. M. Forster, Katherine Mansfield and many others, the "dear old Press" (no longer small enough to sit on the dining-room table, but still housed with the Woolfs) published Virginia Woolf's own work and the reputations of her work and the publishing house enhanced one another. When we consider the effects of being a

co-owner of the Hogarth Press, combined with the literary tea parties at Hyde Park Gate and the Thursday evenings at Bloomsbury, along with the sustaining influence of her husband/publisher/ agent/nurse, we can begin to understand the special circumstances that made Virginia Woolf such a prolific and experimental writer.

While always a mixed blessing to the Woolfs, as is documented in Virginia Woolf's diaries, Leonard Woolf's autobiographies, John Lehmann's several accounts, and caricatured amusingly in Richard Kennedy's *A Boy at the Hogarth Press* (1972), the press did offer Virginia Woolf the immeasurable advantage of unlimited access to print. Also, being both a publisher and a publishing author meant that she could follow her books through all their stages, from the first ecstatic making them up in her head on long walks, to the actual tying them up in mailing packages. Reading piles of manuscript submitted for publication, though it took a great deal of her time, did help to keep her in touch with different intellectual and literary trends. It was through the press that the Woolfs made friends with T. S. Eliot and Katherine Mansfield. Virginia Woolf found with Mansfield, who was to die tragically young, "something in common which I shall never find in anyone else," and she always valued the "priceless talk" they had together, despite some rivalry and backbiting. The press imposed on both of the Woolfs a quasi-parental role, which they accepted conscientiously, as advice givers to the younger generation of aspiring authors. The quality of that advice can be seen in a letter Virginia Woolf wrote to Gerald Brenan on Christmas Day 1922 and in *A Letter to a Young Poet* (separately published in 1932 and collected in *The Death of the Moth,* 1942).

Still, the major advantage of the press to Virginia Woolf herself was that she was free to write and to publish what she liked. Certainly being one's own publisher made it much easier for Virginia Woolf to pursue her experimental bent. She had abhorred taking the manuscripts of even such relatively conventional novels as her first two, *The Voyage Out* (1915) and *Night and Day* (1919), to her half brother's publishing firm, Duckworth and Company. "I don't like the Clubman's view of literature," she recorded in her 1919 diary account of the experience. One wonders what Gerald Duckworth would have made of the antiwar portions of *Jacob's Room* (1922) or of Sally Seton's kissing Clarissa Dalloway in *Mrs. Dalloway* (1925), and he would have been puzzled indeed by the radical style of *To the Lighthouse* (1927) and *Orlando* (1928).

Fortunately for Virginia Woolf and for modern literature, she did not have to persuade someone to publish her experimental fiction. Each novel could therefore be an exploration of some uncharted territory of fiction, and each required the enormous effort that is involved in creating without direct models. The images used in her diaries to describe her daily writing task are always taken from the hyperbolic language of risk, making her seem a veritable Hotspur of pen and ink: "feeling each day's work like a fence which I have to ride at," "a quick and flourishing attack," "flogging my brain." She resisted all pressures to develop a formula for success for her novels, asserting early on, "They have to be new to be experiments."

What did new mean to the daughter of Leslie Stephen in the first part of the twentieth century? During this same period Ezra Pound had taken to wearing a scarf emblazoned with some Chinese calligraphy which, when translated, said: "Make it New!" The much-heralded move into the twentieth century made artists of all persuasions determined to do something different from what had been done in the past. They wanted to cast off what Harold Bloom has called "the anxiety of influence."

Virginia Woolf responded to this imperative directly in an often-reprinted essay called "Character in Fiction" (*Criterion,* July 1924; later that year published as a pamphlet, *Mr. Bennett and Mrs. Brown*), where she asserted that "on or about December, 1910 human character changed." The very arbitrariness of the date and the daringness of the overstatement show her mood—she is out, if not to kill the father, at least to prove him obsolete: "I think that after the creative activity of the Victorian age it was quite necessary, not only for literature but for life, that someone should write the books that Mr. Wells, Mr. Bennett, and Mr. Galsworthy have written. Yet what odd books they are! Sometimes I wonder if we are right to call them books at all. For they leave one with so strange a feeling of incompleteness and dissatisfaction." In this essay she is concentrating on demolishing Arnold Bennett's claim that the young novelists of the era cannot draw convincing characters. Using his novel, *Hilda Lessways* (1911), she demonstrates to her satisfaction at least that building up a complete material setting for the heroine no longer works: "One line of insight would have done more than all those lines of description." She warns that "the Edwardian tools are the wrong ones for us to use" and in a much-later fable, "The Shooting Party" (*A Haunted House,* 1943), she tumbles down the whole Edwardian house of fiction.

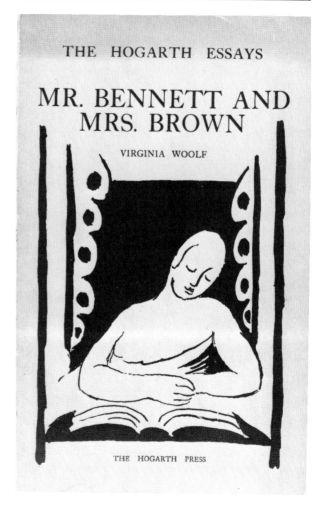

Front cover by Vanessa Bell for the first separate edition of Woolf's 1924 essay on modern fiction, published earlier the same year in the Criterion *as "Character in Fiction"*

As early as 1919, in an essay called "Modern Novels" (slightly revised as "Modern Fiction," *The Common Reader,* 1925), Virginia Woolf was designating Edwardian novelists as "materialists," certainly a more prejudicial label than "realists." It is in this essay that she asks the all important questions: "Is life like this? Must novels be like this?" For her the connections between fiction and life were vital, and for both to be "new," newly honest and free of illusions, fiction must, paradoxically, tell the truth. It must not promise in thirty-two perfectly balanced chapters that the material world is the real world, but it must give the sense of the internal world as well as the external. It must not end on a dominant tonic, "happily ever after." "Is life like this?" Its form must change too. Once the novelist—and the reader—escape the tyrannical demands of mere representation of reality and from the tyranny too of the plot, we are advised to: "Look within. . . . Examine for a moment an ordinary mind on an ordinary day. The mind receives a myriad impressions—trivial, fantastic, evanescent, or engraved with the sharpness of steel. From all sides they come, an incessant show of innumerable atoms; and as they fall, as they shape themselves into the life of Monday or Tuesday, the accent falls differently from of old; the moment of importance came not here but there; so that if a writer were a free man and not a slave, if he could write what he chose, not what he must, if he could base his work upon his own feeling and not upon convention, there would be no plot, no comedy, no tragedy, no love interest in the accepted style, and perhaps not a single button sewn on as the Bond Street tailors would have it. Life is not a series of gig lamps symmetrically arranged; but a luminous halo, a semi-transparent envelope surrounding us from the beginning of consciousness to the end."

Because Virginia Woolf was free to write what she chose and not what she must, she went on to enact many of the principles in this manifesto. Indeed, her first collection of short fiction, published by the Hogarth Press in 1921, was entitled *Monday or Tuesday*, and a close reading of these short pieces will show that she used them as a testing ground for her experiments with the novel form. The difficulty of character portrayal and the elusive nature of Mrs. Brown are considered in "An Unwritten Novel"; the internal life of a character, like Mrs. Brown, is taken into account, along with the principle of retaining in the narrative only those details that are essential. "Kew Gardens" works with point of view and with interior monologue, which has been misleadingly labeled her "stream of consciousness technique." Virginia Woolf is too much the consummate artist to trust to free association for her effects. She is seeking in this story, and in her later work too, a form to encompass "Silence . . . or the things people don't say," and while she sometimes simulates stream of consciousness, the results are quite different from those in the writings of Dorothy Richardson, James Joyce, Edouard Dujardin. "A Society" is a lively harbinger of *A Room of One's Own* (1929) and other such pieces. "A Haunted House" leads to the "Time Passes" section of *To the Lighthouse* and thence to the interludes in *The Waves* (1931). "String Quartet" contains elements later found in *Orlando* and *The Waves*. "The Mark on the Wall" is a *conte philosophique* which argues against generals and generalizations, men of action and housekeepers. Here too she describes her theory of history—"once a thing's done, no one ever knows how it happened"—thus proving the necessity for fictional recreations.

Aside from their connections with the novels, these short pieces are in themselves interesting, and other writers especially admire them. Curiously, despite all the attention Virginia Woolf's work now receives, the short fiction has yet to be "taken to heart," as she complained in an early diary. Most of these early stories, along with some important later ones, were republished in 1943 by Leonard Woolf in the collection *A Haunted House and Other Short Stories*, and interested readers can check to see if indeed *Jacob's Room*, her first novel not "in the accepted manner," is " 'Mark on the Wall,' 'K. G.' and 'Unwritten Novel' taking hands and dancing in unity," as she predicted. In general, these short stories seemed to serve the function of limbering up her style and giving her a respite from the elevation of spirits which she always felt when working on a novel.

The Voyage Out, first published in 1915 and a maiden voyage in every sense, did not show the full effect of this new theory of fiction, but when Virginia Woolf was revising it for publication in the United States five years later, she had written most of the *Monday or Tuesday* short stories. Perhaps some of that experimentation influenced the revision noticed by Louise DeSalvo and others in the description of her motherless heroine, Rachel. The first version sees Rachel as "a bride going forth to her husband, a virgin unknown of men . . . for as a ship she had a life of her own." In the version published in the United States, she is still a bride and a virgin, but the ship simile has been dropped and Rachel is herself "worshipped and felt as a symbol." A significant shift in poetic technique, certainly, though the outcome (Rachel's death) remains the same. The tragedy does not, however, overshadow the many Bildungsroman encounters that Rachel has, including some quite explicit conversations questioning the roles and education of young women in society of the time.

The same questions are taken up in *Night and Day*, and here there is a sympathetic spinster character who works for the suffrage movement. The focus, however, is on the conventionally inevitable young couples, all mismatched at the beginning of the book and reordered more successfully through the action of the novel. What is unconventional about the novel is the heroine, a sensitive young mathematician, with a passion for privacy, whose patience is tried by the tea table demands made upon her by her charming but scatterbrained mother, Mrs. Hilberry, in their excessively literary household. Katherine Mansfield reviewed this book as a regression to Jane Austen, and Virginia Woolf herself was to call it later "a book that taught me much, bad though it may be."

The next novel, *Jacob's Room,* is usually heralded as a major breakthrough and indeed Virginia Woolf so considered it, as we see from the following extract from her diary: "The day after my birthday; in fact I'm 38. Well, no doubt I'm a great deal happier than I was at 28; & happier today than I was yesterday having this afternoon arrived at some idea of a new form for a new novel . . . the approach will be entirely different this time: no scaffolding; scarcely a brick to be seen; all crepuscular, but the heart, the passion, humour, everything as bright as fire in the mist. . . ."

The approach may be different, but the theme is much like that of *The Voyage Out,* a failed "education of the young prince" novel—it is not the young prince that fails, but society which will fail him by its wars. Jacob's last name is, ominously, Flanders, and Virginia Woolf, in what we will come to see as a typical reversal, uses the Bildungsroman expectations to dramatize this wanton destruction of the carefully educated young man of promise. Thus Arnold Bennett and others who have regretted the lack of fullness in the hero's character are missing the point of the novel, which is an elegy to the missing heroes, the terrible loss of that World War I generation.

As we know from *Mr. Bennett and Mrs. Brown,* she did feel characters were elusive. She also felt that they deserved some privacy and, as her novelist persona says in *Jacob's Room:* "It is no use trying to sum people up. One must follow hints, not exactly what is said, nor yet entirely what is done. . . ."

If with *Night and Day* she had learned how to put it all in, with *Jacob's Room* she showed that she had learned the lesson in "An Unwritten Novel": "But this we'll skip . . . skip, skip. . . ." The transitions are agile, and the unity comes from the repetition of images, with ever-increasing resonance, until we feel the same sense of loss that we might from a more traditionally structured war novel; the end does not escape sentimentalism, and Virginia Woolf suffered the usual modern difficulty (as described by Frank Kermode in *The Sense of Ending*) with the endings of all her early novels.

Mrs. Dalloway, published in 1925, has often been compared to, and indeed said to have been influenced by, Joyce's *Ulysses* (1922), which the Woolfs were reading at T. S. Eliot's request in 1922, close to the time Virginia Woolf was writing "Mrs. Dalloway in Bond St." (*Dial,* July 1923), one of the stories which branched into the novel. It is true that the action of the book takes place in twenty-four hours and includes a walk about London reminiscent of Joyce's Leopold Bloom's stroll through Dublin, but the similarities seem at this distance due to what they had in common rather than to direct influences.

An original feature of this skillfully woven pattern of urban life is Septimus Smith, a tragic war-torn figure who acts as a counterpart or double to Clarissa Dalloway. This ingenious invention enabled Virginia Woolf to write of her own madness and suicide attempts in the novel while maintaining some psychical distance. Clarissa herself is not Virginia Woolf but the prototype of the society hostess figure which fascinated her. Virginia Woolf said in her diary that she wanted in this book to "show the despicableness of people like Ott" (Lady Ottoline Morrell) who invite poor embroideresses to her parties to be kind. In order to make Mrs. Dalloway less shallow and "tinselly," Virginia Woolf "invented her memories," and one of them is the vibrant Sally Seton scene in which Clarissa feels "only for a moment; but it was enough" what men felt, when Sally "picked a flower; kissed her on the lips."

In this novel Virginia Woolf said she wanted to give "life and death, sanity and insanity": "I want to criticise the social system, & to show it at work, at its most intense." Perhaps the press of "almost too many ideas" is what led her into allegory, a method she basically distrusted as lending itself to preaching. There are a Miss Kilman, a Hugh Whitbread, names suspiciously prejudicial, and also a long and passionate diatribe against doctors and all who "force the soul." In the elaborate party scene at the end Virginia Woolf hoped to "sum it all up" in the central figure who, "very white since her illness . . . very upright" has her own sort of gallantry in the face of death.

Brilliantly conceived and beautifully written, *Mrs. Dalloway* concentrates on the real feelings beneath the social surface, thus turning upside down the novel of manners. It was, and is, widely admired, but perhaps the compliment she appreciated the most was a backhanded one from her old antagonist, Arnold Bennett. He admitted that the book "beat" him: "I could not finish it, because I could not discover what it was really about, what was its direction, and what Mrs. Woolf intended to demonstrate by it. To express myself differently, I failed to discern what was its moral basis."

It was the next novel, however, *To the Lighthouse,* that established Virginia Woolf as a major novelist. Even her enemies liked this book. (The

(23)

Kennedy was supposed to have the charge of it, and then his

leg got so bad after he fell from the cart; and perhaps then

no one for a year; or the better part of one, and then Tommie

Curwen, and seeds might be sent, but who should say if they were

ever planted?

~~She hailed her son.~~ ~~He looked at her.~~ ~~He said nothing.~~

He was one of those quiet ones. / ~~He~~ *George* was a great one for work.

He was one of those quiet ones.

~~He turned to his scything again.~~ On he went, like a machine,

scything scything, wet or fine, ~~a~~ great one for work. Well,

they must be getting along with the cupboards, she supposed.

At last, after days of labour within, of cutting, raking

sweeping digging without, dusters were flicked out of the

windows; the windows were shut fast; keys were turned all over

the house; the front door was banged; it was finished.

And now, as if the cleaning and the scrubbing and the

scything and the mowing had drowned them, there rose that half

heard melody, that intermittent music which the ear half catches

but lets fall, a bark, a bleat, irregular, intermittent, yet

somehow related - the jar of an insect, the tremor of cut grass,

dissevered yet somehow belonging, the hum of a dor beetle, the

squeak of a wheel, loud, low, but mysteriously related, which

the ear strains to bring together and is always on the verge of

harmonising; but they are never quite heard, never fully

harmonised, and at last, in the evening, one after another the

one   died. & another died. ~   a the silence is ...

sounds ~~died out,~~ and the harmony faltered and fell into ~~complete~~

~~silence.~~ With the sunset sharpness was lost, and like mist

---

Page from the revised typescript for the "Time Passes" section of To the Lighthouse *that Virginia Woolf sent her French translator Charles Mauron. She made further revisions before the novel was published in English (courtesy of Quentin Bell and Alice Mauron).*

Leavises, in their anti-Bloomsbury journal, *Scrutiny*, pronounced it "the only good one in which her talent fulfills itself in a satisfactory achievement.") Why does it reach everyone so deeply? Because it is about the family? Actually, the genre is once again used to destroy itself; this is a family novel which reveals like an autopsy the painful cancers of family politics. And after the great dinner scene of communion over the steaming tureen of *boeuf en daube* ("a specially tender piece of eternity"), Virginia Woolf asks the difficult question: but can such moments endure? Answer: no, except in memory and in art. Are such moments then enough? Answer: that depends upon the person, but they are all we have.

Virginia Woolf felt that in writing this most obviously autobiographical of all her novels (it is set in a lightly disguised Tallant House, the St. Ives vacation place of her youth), she had laid to rest the ghosts of her parents. Perhaps that is what readers hope to achieve as well. But it is important when reading of Mr. and Mrs. Ramsay not to take sides. Virginia Woolf herself tried scrupulously to give both personalities their due, not to be partisan, and it is a misreading to impose one's biases on this account, of which her artist sister, Vanessa Bell, wrote: "as far as portrait painting goes you seem to me the supreme artist. . . ." Lily Briscoe is another memorable portrait in the book, providing the spinster-artist perspective so often found not only in Woolf's works but in other books by women. It is Lily who as the high priest, the artist, declares, using the last words of the mass, "It is finished."

The novel is consciously cast in the three-part, elegiac-ode form. Most people remember the first section when they think back on the novel, and that is the section so exhaustively analyzed by Auerbach. The "Time Passes" mid-section, in which no human figure appears on the stage for pages and pages and the haunted house begins its decay, should be read aloud to appreciate fully its power and its poetry and the *Lear*-like emphasis on nothingness. The last section has been variously interpreted. It satisfies some readers and puzzles others. An entire collection of critical interpretations of this one novel was edited in 1970 by Thomas Vogler. It is this novel of Woolf's which is the most frequently taught in college classes, and it is probably often misread. Though disguised as a Victorian family novel, it subtly subverts the solidity of the institution and the genre.

In *Orlando* the subversive use of genre is overt—Virginia Woolf subtitled this anomalous book "*A Biography*" to manifest all her criticism of conventional biography. It is the novel genre which best gives the "spirit of the times" and shows how a single human being can be the product of his or her past. These pronouns become especially slippery in this book, where the usual boundaries of gender, time, and tragic consequence are transcended in a light-hearted Ovidian skating over the same questions that will engulf the reader in the more Homeric *The Waves*. Sailing boats do not sink here as they do in so many of her other books. The mood is comic, and everything is to be mocked, as Woolf said in her plans, "even my own lyric vein." (Beware of that banana-peel preface upon which so many critics have slipped.) Certainly she is mocking the heavyhanded *Kulturegeshichte* critics, but just as certainly she is enjoying trying her hand at this kind of criticism herself, thus deriving a double kick from the parody. Her description of the coming of the Victorian Age has been often anthologized, as has The Great Frost scene, which has even been adapted as an animated cartoon for television. Androgyny, creativity, nationalism, metamorphoses, immortality, and more are skated around in *Orlando*.

Vita Sackville-West's life story and aristocratic lineage, which so fascinated Virginia Woolf, became the underlying myth upon which the other themes are woven. Indeed, the whole book is a kind of love letter tribute to Virginia and Vita's passionate friendship, which flourished from about 1925 to 1929. (It is certainly a tribute both to Vita and to her husband, Lord Harold Nicolson, that they never asked to see the book before publication.)

To read *Orlando* it does help to know something of the history of Knole, Vita Sackville-West's ancestral home, and there are some "in" jokes, as Elizabeth Bowen warns in her afterword to the Signet edition. But the lively pacing of the book, filled with surprising turns and twists, gives even the casual reader a treat. Like so many comic works, *Orlando* asks all the hard questions and, as Bowen suspected, it cleared the way by a kind of play therapy for *The Waves*, that "eyeless, mystical book," as Virginia Woolf called it.

While each of the novels has its adherents, most people agree with Leonard Woolf's early assessment that *The Waves* is her masterpiece. The hardest of all the books to summarize (as Virginia Woolf explained, "I am writing to a rhythm and not to a plot"), *The Waves* too asks the question "but what endures?" and answers, even more baldly than before: nothing but mutability and metamorphosis. Each human life is no more than a wave which, after arching its back and reaching forward, will break of them ought to be forcible. The idea has come to me that what I want now to do is to saturate every atom. I mean to eliminate all waste, deadness, superfluity: to give the moment whole; whatever it includes. Say that the moment is a combination of thought; sensation; the voice of the sea. Waste, deadness, come from the inclusion of things that don't belong to the moment; this appalling narrative business of the realist: getting on from lunch to dinner: it is false, unreal, merely conventional. Why admit anything to literature that is not poetry—by which I mean saturated? Is that not my grudge against novelists? *that they select nothing?* The poets succeeding by simplifying: practically everything is left out. I want to put practically everything in; yet to saturate. That is what I want to do in The Moths. It must include nonsense, fact, sordidity: but made transparent. I think I must read Ibsen, Shakespeare, & Racine. And I will write something about them: for that is the best spur, my mind, being whatever; then I read with fury & gusto. Otherwise I skip & skip: I am a lazy reader. But no: I am surprised & a little disquieted by the remorseless severity of my mind: that it never stops reading & writing; makes me write on Women—when it is too professional, too little any longer a dreamy amateur.

Page from Virginia Woolf's diary (28 November 1928) referring to the writing of "The Moths," published in 1931 as The Waves *(courtesy of Quentin Bell; Henry W. and Albert A. Berg Collection, The New York Public Library, Astor, Lenox and Tilden Foundations)* upon the shore and be dispersed back into the sea. The philosophical equilibrium of the book is extraordinary, balanced between defiance and acceptance, despair and exaltation. *The Waves* is beyond optimism and pessimism, a truly modern book. The compelling rhythm of the prose and the beauty of the form make reading the work a life-affirming experience, however stripped of illusions the message may be.

The form took her some time to find, a quest testified to in the holograph versions transcribed and edited by John W. Graham. Her long-felt objections to conventional dialogue are finally resolved into a series of soliloquies or interior monologues by six friends, three men and three women, all centered upon one heroic figure called, appropriately, Percival. He will, of course, disappear, as has the traditional concept of the hero in the twentieth century, and the friends are left to mourn and to discover what, if anything, holds them together after Percival's mock-heroic death. Again the message undercuts the genre, as Woolf uses epic form to describe the absence of the hero. In a series of dinner parties quite different from Mrs. Dalloway's carefully choreographed party or from the family table of the Ramsays, the members of the chorus see if they can take up the action in this epic of twentieth-century life. The wars are different from Homer's, but the stakes are similar—survival with honor.

The italicized interludes, like still-life paintings, which preface each "human" section, are reminiscent of the "Time Passes" section in *To the Lighthouse.* They interweave with the patterns in the rest of the book, reflecting different times of the day, a succession of seasons, and the movement from childhood to old age. Even those who have difficulty reading the novel, finding the characters' voices monotonous, acknowledge the remarkable precision and power of Woolf's observation of the natural and the social world. For example, Bernard, mid-monologue, notices his friend Neville: "You are making some protest, as you glide with an inexpressibly familiar gesture, your hand along your knee. By such signs we diagnose our friends' diseases. . . . 'Stop,' you say, 'Ask me what I suffer.' " And the lyric eye of the interludes observes at high noon: "The sun fell in sharp wedges inside the room. Whatever the light touched became dowered with a fanatical existence." The book, which opens in Eden, an Eden disturbed by the primal kiss, combines the double realities of the archetypal and the social (as do, to a lesser degree, *Mrs. Dalloway* and *To the Lighthouse*). Rhoda realizes at the end of

yet another painful party scene, "I am the foam that sweeps and fills the uttermost rims of the rocks with whiteness; I am also a girl, here in this room."

Critics have too often misread this book, as startled by its stark message as by its unusual form, so one must beware of the secondary sources. Virginia Woolf's essay called "The Narrow Bridge of Art," reprinted in *Granite and Rainbow*, serves almost as a self-interview about her intentions in *The Waves*, as does a letter she wrote to John Lehmann on 17 September 1931, reprinted in volume four of *The Letters of Virginia Woolf*. There is also an account she wrote to herself in her diary when she was putting her method to this stretch: "The idea has come to me that what I want now to do is to saturate every atom. I mean to eliminate all waste, deadness, superfluity: to give the moment whole; whatever it includes. Say that the moment is a combination of thought; sensation; the voice of the sea. Waste, deadness, come from the inclusion of things that don't belong to the moment; this appalling narrative business of the realist: getting on from lunch to dinner: it is false, unreal, merely conventional. Why admit any thing to literature that is not poetry—by which I mean saturated? Is that not my grudge against novel[ist]s—that they select nothing? The poets succeeding by simplifying: practically everything is left out. I want to put practically everything in; yet to saturate. This is what I want to do in The Moths [an earlier title for *The Waves*]. It must include nonsense, fact, sordidity: but made transparent." It is interesting to compare this private statement to her already-quoted manifesto from "Modern Fiction," of nearly ten years before. How consistent her struggle against mere realism, how committed she is to that intense moment of being, of vision, which has been called the modern epiphany. This combination of the senses and the liberation from narrative time which Woolf achieves in her moments of being are closely analogous to what the imagists hoped to achieve by their use of images in early twentieth-century poetry.

In her next novel, Virginia Woolf would seem to be eschewing these poetic techniques; indeed, she originally called *The Years* (1937) an "essay-novel." In this most extensively revised of all her books, she sought to juxtapose the inner and outer, the real and the symbolic: "But the Pargiters [working title of *The Years*]. I think this will be a terrific affair. I must be bold & adventurous. I want to give the whole of the present society—nothing less: facts, as well as the vision. And to combine them both. I mean, The waves going on simultaneously

9

head with no hair on it. *He turned.*

"Heel!" he bawled, "Heel, you brute!" And George turned;
and the nurses turned holding the furry bear; they all turned
to look at Sohrab the Afghan hound bounding and bouncing
among the flowers.

"Heel!" the old man bawled, as if he were commanding a
regiment . It was impressive, to the usrses, the way
an old boy of his age could still bawl and make a brute like
that obey him. Back came the Afghan hound, sidling, apologet¢
And as he cringed at the old man's feet, a string was slipped
over his collar; the noose that old Oliver always carried
with him.

"You wild beast...you bad beast" he grumbled, stooping.
George looked at the dog only. The hairy flanks were sucked
in and out; there was a blob of foam on its nostrils. He burst
out crying.

Old Oliver *raised* himself, his veins swollen, his cheeks
flushed; *he* was angry. His little game with the paper hadn't
worked. The boy was a cry baby. He nodded and sauntered on,
smoothing out the crumpled paper and muttering, as he tried
to find his line in the column, "A cry-baby--a cry-baby".
But the breeze blew the great sheet out; and over the edge
he surveyed the landscape-- flowing fields, heath and woods.
Framed, they became a picture. Had he been a painter, he would
have fixed his easel here, where the country, barred by
trees, looked like a picture. Then the breeze fell.

"M. Daladier" he read finding his place in the column,
"has been successful in pegging down the franc...."

Leave 2 lines white ⟶

Page from the final typescript for Between the Acts, *corrected by Virginia Woolf and edited by Leonard Woolf (courtesy of Quentin Bell;*
Henry W. and Albert A. Berg Collection, The New York Public Library, Astor, Lenox and Tilden Foundations)

307

with Night & Day. Is this possible? . . . And there are to be millions of ideas but no preaching—history, politics, feminism, art, literature—in short a summing up of all I know, feel, laugh at, despise, like, admire hate & so on."

A tall order—and though *The Years* was a publishing success, its goals have not been fully understood until recently, when thanks to the work of Mitchell Leaska, Grace Radin, and others, the book is coming into focus. Some of the excised manuscript portions have been published in a book of their own called *The Pargiters* (1977), and many of the social concerns present in her work since *The Voyage Out* are here developed in considerable detail.

The Years itself, building on the genre of the generation novel, moves from 1880 to the present day with the Pargiter family. While their tea table forms the center stage, bombs and other intrusions from the world's troubled history can be heard prophetically in the distance. The central figure, Eleanor, is a spinster who never breaks with her father or with her class but who manages nonetheless to live her life, to survive with honor. The servant figure, brilliantly described in her bitter obsolescence, the younger generation whose gains in freedom seem somehow unsatisfactory, and the war itself are all themes in this rich, mild-mannered book. At the last party everyone gathers for incomplete toasts and incomprehensible songs and interrupted conversations—all the advantages of modern civilization, in short. Yet at the end, Eleanor watches from the window (as so often the Pargiter women do) while an anonymous young couple get out of a cab and enter a house together: "The sun had risen, and the sky above the houses wore an air of extraordinary beauty, simplicity, and peace."

This peaceful moment does not endure, as we will see in the next novel, which was published posthumously without her usual last revisions. *Between the Acts* (1941) is a tough-minded book, with each character walled into his or her own territory. A village pageant of British history is trying to draw them together, but the record player gets stuck on the line "dispersed are we. . . ," and the last scene of the pageant features the cast holding up mirrors which reflect back the fragmented audience in an alienation device worthy of Brecht. Another of Woolf's frustrated artist figures, the dramatist Miss LaTrobe, in despair over the failure of her vision, goes off to a pub. The action then shifts back to the "real" people, again a couple. John Lehmann admits the last confrontation still has the power to "make *frissons* run through him." *Between the Acts*

shows the dynamics of Isa's and Giles's struggles as somehow related to the coming war. Virginia Woolf understood the connections between the personal and the political.

Indeed, it is as if the devastating losses of her life, "the erosion of life by death" as Leonard Woolf called it, were echoed by the bloody history of the twentieth century, confirming her preoccupation with the theme of the lost hero. It is chilling to realize that her first novel was published during World War I and the last, posthumously, during World War II. Like another great artist working in that period *"entre les deux guerres,"* Käthe Kollwitz, Virginia Woolf was able in her art to generalize her sense of personal loss into the universal. Like Käthe Kollwitz too, she, her family, and many of their friends were pacifists, not an easy position to maintain in England at any time, but especially during World War II, if one's husband was a Jew. Perhaps these contradictions contributed to her deep weariness, the problem of disembodiment which led her to take her own life in March 1941.

Her awareness of the risks the world was taking with its young men had been exacerbated by the death in the Spanish civil war of her nephew, Julian Bell, whose life and death seem to have been eerily foretold in *Jacob's Room*, written when Julian was just a boy. Certainly Vanessa Bell was the most affected, becoming a kind of pietà figure mourning this loss of her firstborn, but to the aunt goes the credit of discovering the archetype, of mourning for the holocaust that was ahead as well as for the blood sacrifice of Flanders field.

Virginia Woolf's understanding of the causes of war was political as well as symbolic, however, and in *Jacob's Room* she describes the horrors of modern technological warfare:

> The battleships ray out over the North Sea, keeping their stations accurately apart. At a given signal all the guns are trained on a target which (the master gunner counts the seconds, watch in hand—at the sixth he looks up) flames into splinters. With equal nonchalance a dozen young men in the prime of life descend with composed faces into the depths of the sea; and there impassively (though with perfect mastery of machinery) suffocate uncomplainingly together. Like blocks of tin soldiers the army covers the cornfield, moves up the hillside, stops, reels slightly this way and that, and falls flat, save that, through fieldglasses, it can be seen that one or two pieces still agitate up and down like fragments of broken match-stick.

These actions, together with the incessant commerce of banks, laboratories, chancellories, and houses of business, are the strokes which oar the world forward, they say.

"They" are all those who try to rationalize war as inevitable, and the irony in her tone deepens into anger as she ascribes the blame and sharpens the analysis in *A Room of One's Own* and *Three Guineas*. In these important nonfiction works, which continue to influence readers, despite those who try to discount them, Virginia Woolf recognizes the dangers of fascism, its origins and its appeal. Much of this material she may well have gleaned from conversations with Leonard Woolf, who had also written on the underlying causes of war. Their library contained many books on the subject. Much of the fire and the facts came from her own feminist analysis and from her identification with the outsiders of this world (in ways reminiscent of the twentieth-century philosopher and mystic Simone Weil). But at base the awareness seems intuitive, with the systematic argumentation built up later. She saw the fragility of the social contracts, the need and oppression and sorrow that await us.

In one of her last pieces, "Thoughts on Peace in an Air Raid" (*New Republic*, 21 October 1940), reprinted in the collection called *The Death of the Moth*, Woolf makes an impassioned plea for women to fight what Blake called "the mental fight," which means "thinking against the current, not with it." She wants women, by thinking, to free both men and women, both German and British, from the prison of war: "We can see shop windows blazing; and women gazing; painted women; dressed up women; women with crimson lips and crimson fingernails. They are slaves who are trying to enslave. If we could free ourselves from slavery we should free men from tyranny. Hitlers are bred by slaves."

In this deep concern, she takes her place with the writers and artists now studied under the rubric of modernism. But what separates her from many of her fellow modernists and what constitutes the triumph of her vision and of her style is that—even after accepting the nothingness, the loss of self, the eclipse of color and meaning, and the lack of benevolence in nature—the writer and her readers too emerge feeling not only the beauty of the world, so soon to perish, but also what Virginia Woolf calls again and again that "sense of effort" that prevails. Hermione Lee, in her determinedly balanced approach to the novels, has summed up as follows: "Virginia Woolf is often praised for sensitivity and lyricism and criticized for ineffectuality and pre-

ciousness. There is truth on both sides, but such praise and blame sidestep equally the determined pursuit of control and authenticity which invigorates even the slightest of her work, and makes her major achievements solid with integrity and rich with inventiveness." Professor Lee also says that even had Woolf written no novels, she would have "a place in the twentieth century letters as a considerable essayist." *A Room of One's Own* and *Three Guineas* are deft, witty, carefully thought-out polemics against what Woolf saw as the chief perils of the times. Indeed, Woolf's comic gift is never done full justice. Some of the scenes in the novels as well as in the essays are wonderfully humorous. Other essays along less serious lines, such as "Street Haunting" and "On Being Ill," are classics of their kind and reward reading and rereading.

Her literary essays and weekly reviews are still marvelously accessible, charming, and daring, adjectives not usually applied to the more academic critics. When read as a whole, these articles reveal an unorthodox, unified philosophy of criticism. Woolf was not ashamed to use biography and even gossip to help convey the spirit of the times. René Wellek speaks of Virginia Woolf as critic, admiring her "lively historical sense, a feeling for the color of England in different ages, and a feeling—rare at that time—for the changes in the audience of literature and the interplay between the author and reader, text and response." She was also a forerunner of the movement to look to the minor and often minority figures for intuitions about a period. Her essays "Lives of the Obscure" provide good examples of the rewards to be gained from resurrecting these marginal figures. Woolf's special attentiveness to all the women writers she could find, from the Pastons to Dorothy Richardson, continues to be consciousness-raising for students (and their teachers) reading mainly from the traditional canons. It was she who helped readers see Dorothy Wordsworth and Sara Coleridge as people and writers in their own right. Of course, she also speaks of Flush as a person in his own right (in her biography of Elizabeth Barrett Browning's cocker spaniel). Virginia Woolf, despite her deceptively light tone when referring to her nonfiction, intended her essays quite seriously, and they are now being taken seriously by such critics as René Wellek, Mark Goldman, and others.

Generally it can be said that the criticism of Woolf's work in all its aspects has improved in quality as well as quantity since the 1970s epidemic of "Virginia Woolf Fever." Her work attracts many different sorts of minds, from psychologists to

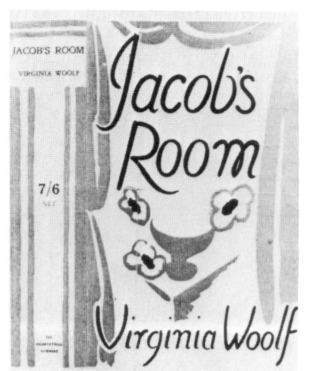

Dust jackets by Vanessa Bell

novelists to phenomenologists.

Many of the best critical essays on Woolf have been collected in useful series such as Twentieth Century Views and Contemporary Views, and anthologies of new essays are being edited by such longtime Woolf scholars as Ralph Freedman and by such lively new ones as Jane Marcus. The Critical Heritage Series volume on Woolf, edited by Majumdar and McLaurin, republishes for easy perusal contemporary critical reactions to her works as they appeared. There are concordances planned to all the major novels, tools now made feasible by computer technology. Beverly Ann Schlack has provided a treasury of Virginia Woolf's use of literary allusion. Extremely interesting too for specialists are the variant studies, looking at Woolf's creative process as revealed in the successive manuscript versions leading to her published works. There is much to be learned from this "following the footsteps in the author's mind," as Charles Abbott has called manuscript study. The serious sustained critical attention to her work has made us all better readers of Virginia Woolf and has raised the standards of criticism not only for Woolf's work but for that of other experimental twentieth-century writers as well.

One of the most vital impulses behind the revaluation of Virginia Woolf and her work has been provided by readers and scholars with feminist perspectives. There are some conflicts between these critics and those who feel she should be read as a universal rather than a woman writer, as there are between those who concentrate on the biography rather than on close stylistic scrutiny. The phenomenologists have one way of viewing Virginia Woolf's mental and physical condition and the family and friends another. There is probably an England/America split; France feels it understands her best; Japan finds in her work a literary affinity based on the pillow-book tradition and Lady Murasaki; India has a number of devoted Woolf scholars; Italy planned an impressive centennial conference in her honor. From being the most neglected major writer of her age, she has become now a prize to be fought over, and of course all this attention from so many different quarters is good for the critical dialogue. A newsletter called the *Virginia Woolf Miscellany* strives to keep all these different factions in touch with one another. Its mailing list includes many libraries and more than 1,000 names in thirty-two different countries. Journals devote special issues to her, scholarly meetings are held in her

honor, and there are *boeuf en daube* dinners, trips to lighthouses, and walks around Bloomsbury and Sussex held in celebration of what Woolf has given us. Her work has also stimulated creative efforts from artists in other media, and plays, concerts, and dance performances are being created in homage.

Thus we see how far her reputation has come from the Leavises' early "invalid lady of Bloomsbury" image as well as from the narrowly partisan readings of her enemies and friends, and from the 1960s when a French newspaper translated the title of Albee's play as "*qui a peur des loups de Virginie.*" Virginia Woolf now belongs securely to the world, and the influence of her life and of her work will continue to be felt in all future generations of "common readers."

Letters:

The Flight of the Mind, The Letters of Virginia Woolf, Volume I: 1888-1912, edited by Nigel Nicolson and Joanne Trautmann (London: Hogarth Press, 1975); republished as *The Letters of Virginia Woolf, Volume I: 1888-1912* (New York & London: Harcourt Brace Jovanovich, 1975);

The Question of Things Happening, The Letters of Virginia Woolf, Volume II: 1912-1922, edited by Nicolson and Trautmann (London: Hogarth Press, 1976); republished as *The Letters of Virginia Woolf, Volume II: 1912-1922* (New York & London: Harcourt Brace Jovanovich, 1976);

A Change of Perspective, The Letters of Virginia Woolf, Volume III: 1923-1928, edited by Nicolson and Trautmann (London: Hogarth Press, 1977); republished as *The Letters of Virginia Woolf, Volume III: 1923-1928* (New York & London: Harcourt Brace Jovanovich, 1978);

A Reflection of the Other Person, The Letters of Virginia Woolf, Volume IV: 1929-1931, edited by Nicolson and Trautmann (London: Hogarth Press, 1978); republished as *The Letters of Virginia Woolf, Volume IV: 1929-1931* (New York & London: Harcourt Brace Jovanovich, 1979);

The Sickle Side of the Moon, The Letters of Virginia Woolf, Volume V: 1932-1935, edited by Nicolson and Trautmann (London: Hogarth Press, 1979); republished as *The Letters of Virginia Woolf, Volume V: 1932-1935* (New York & London: Harcourt Brace Jovanovich, 1979);

Leave the Letters Till We're Dead, The Letters of Virginia Woolf, Volume VI: 1936-1941, edited by Nicolson and Trautmann (London: Hogarth Press,

1980); republished as *The Letters of Virginia Woolf, Volume VI: 1936-1941* (New York & London: Harcourt Brace Jovanovich, 1980).

Bibliography:

B. J. Kirkpatrick, *A Bibliography of Virginia Woolf*, third edition (Oxford: Clarendon Press, 1980).

Biographies:

Quentin Bell, *Virginia Woolf: A Biography*, 2 volumes (New York: Harcourt Brace Jovanovich, 1972);

John Lehmann, *Virginia Woolf and Her World* (New York: Harcourt Brace Jovanovich, 1975);

George Spater and Ian Parsons, *A Marriage of True Minds* (New York: Harcourt Brace Jovanovich, 1977);

Phyllis Rose, *Woman of Letters: A Life of Virginia Woolf* (New York: Oxford University Press, 1978).

References:

Noel Annan, "Virginia Woolf Fever," *New York Review of Books*, 25 (20 April 1978): 16-28;

Erich Auerbach, *Mimesis: The Representation of Reality in Western Literature*, translated by Willard R. Trask (Princeton: Princeton University Press, 1953);

Nancy Topping Bazin, *Virginia Woolf and the Androgynous Vision* (New Brunswick: Rutgers University Press, 1973);

Joan Bennett, *Virginia Woolf: Her Art as a Novelist* (Cambridge: Cambridge University Press, 1964);

Bulletin of the New York Public Library, special Virginia Woolf issue, 80 (Winter 1977);

Louise A. DeSalvo, *Virginia Woolf's First Voyage: A Novel in the Making* (Totowa, N. J.: Roman & Littlefield, 1980);

Leon Edel, *Bloomsbury: A House of Lions* (Philadelphia & New York: Lippincott, 1979);

Avrom Fleishman, *Virginia Woolf: A Critical Reading* (Baltimore: Johns Hopkins University Press, 1975);

Ralph Freedman, ed., *Virginia Woolf: Revaluation and Continuity* (Berkeley: University of California Press, 1980);

Mary Gaither, "A Short History of the Press," in *A Checklist of the Hogarth Press*, by J. Howard Woolmer (Andes, N. Y.: Woolmer/Brotherson, 1976);

Elaine K. Ginsberg and Laura Moss Gottlieb, eds.,

Virginia Woolf: Centennial Papers (Troy: N.Y.: Whitston, 1983);

Mark Goldman, *The Reader's Art: Virginia Woolf as Literary Critic* (The Hague: Mouton, 1976);

Susan Rubinow Gorsky, *Virginia Woolf* (Boston: Twayne, 1978);

Jean Guiguet, *Virginia Woolf and her Works*, translated by Jean Stewart (New York: Harcourt, Brace & World, 1965);

James M. Haule and Philip H. Smith, Jr., *Concordances to the Novels of Virginia Woolf*: volume 1, *A Concordance to The Waves* (Oxford: Oxford Microform Publications, 1981); volume 2, *A Concordance to Between the Acts* (Oxford: Oxford Microform Publications, 1982); volume 3, *A Concordance To the Lighthouse* (Oxford: Oxford Microform Publications, 1983);

Carolyn G. Heilbrun, *Toward a Recognition of Androgyny* (New York: Knopf, 1973);

Katherine C. Hill, "Virginia Woolf and Leslie Stephen: History and Literary Revolution," *PMLA*, 96 (May 1981);

Richard Kennedy, *A Boy at the Hogarth Press* (Harmondsworth: Penguin, 1972);

Jacqueline E. M. Latham, ed., *Critics on Virginia Woolf* (London: Allen & Unwin, 1970);

Mitchell A. Leaska, *The Novels of Virginia Woolf: From Beginning to End* (New York: John Jay Press, 1977);

Hermione Lee, *The Novels of Virginia Woolf* (New York: Holmes & Meier, 1977);

John Lehmann, *Thrown to the Woolfs* (New York: Holt, Rinehart & Winston, 1978);

Thomas S. W. Lewis, ed., *Virginia Woolf: A Collection of Criticism* (New York: McGraw-Hill, 1975);

Jean O. Love, *Worlds of Consciousness: Mythopoetic Thought in the Novels of Virginia Woolf* (Berkeley: University of California Press, 1970);

Robin Majumdar and Allen McLaurin, *Virginia Woolf: The Critical Heritage* (London: Routledge & Kegan Paul, 1975);

Jane Marcus, ed., *New Feminist Essays on Virginia Woolf* (Lincoln: University of Nebraska Press, 1981);

Herbert Marder, *Feminism and Art: A Study of Virginia Woolf* (Chicago: University of Chicago Press, 1968);

Allen McLaurin, *Virginia Woolf: The Echoes Enslaved* (Cambridge: Cambridge University Press, 1973);

Modern Fiction Studies, special Virginia Woolf issue, 18 (Autumn 1972);

James Naremore, *The World Without a Self: Virginia*

Woolf and the Novel (New Haven: Yale University Press, 1973);

Monique Nathan, *Virginia Woolf*, translated by Herma Briffault (New York: Evergreen Books, 1961);

Joan Russell Noble, ed., *Recollections of Virginia Woolf by Her Contemporaries* (New York: Morrow, 1972);

Jane Novak, *The Razor Edge of Balance: A Study of Virginia Woolf* (Coral Gables: University of Miami Press, 1975);

Roger Poole, *The Unknown Virginia Woolf* (Cambridge: Cambridge University Press, 1978);

Grace Radin, *Virginia Woolf's The Years: The Evolution of a Novel* (Knoxville: University of Tennessee Press, 1981);

Irma Rantavaara, *Virginia Woolf's "The Waves"* (Port Washington, N. Y.: Kennikat Press, 1969);

Harvena Richter, *Virginia Woolf: The Inward Voyage* (Princeton: Princeton University Press, 1970);

S. P. Rosenbaum, *The Bloomsbury Group: A Collection of Memoirs, Commentary and Criticism* (Toronto: University of Toronto Press, 1975);

Sonya Rudikoff, "How Many Lovers Had Virginia Woolf?," *Hudson Review*, 32 (Winter 1979-1980);

Beverly Ann Schlack, *Continuing Presences: Virginia Woolf's Use of Literary Allusion* (University Park: The Pennsylvania State University Press, 1979);

Stephen Spender, *The Struggle of the Modern* (Berkeley: University of California Press, 1963);

Claire Sprague, ed., *Virginia Woolf: A Collection of Critical Essays* (Englewood Cliffs, N.J.: Prentice-Hall, 1971);

Elizabeth Steele, *Virginia Woolf's Literary Sources and Allusions: A Guide to the Essays* (New York & London: Garland, 1983);

Stephen Trombley, *All that Summer She was Mad* (New York: Continuum, 1982);

Twentieth Century Literature, special Virginia Woolf issue, 25 (Fall/Winter 1979);

Virginia Woolf Miscellany, 1973- ;

Thomas A. Vogler, ed., *Twentieth Century Interpretations of To the Lighthouse* (Englewood Cliffs, N.J.: Prentice-Hall, 1970);

René Wellek, "Virginia Woolf as Critic," *Southern Review*, 13 (July 1977);

Leonard Woolf, *Beginning Again: An Autobiography of the Years 1911 to 1918* (New York: Harcourt, Brace & World, 1964);

Woolf, *Downhill All the Way: An Autobiography of the Years 1919 to 1939* (New York: Harcourt, Brace & World, 1967);

Woolf, *The Journey Not the Arrival Matters: An Autobiography of the Years 1939 to 1969* (New York: Harcourt Brace Jovanovich, 1970).

Papers:

See Quentin Bell's *Virginia Woolf: A Biography*, volume 1, pp. xi-xiii, for a general description of the three major collections: The Henry W. and Albert A. Berg Collection of English and American Literature, New York Public Library; The Charleston Papers, King's College, Cambridge; and the Monk's House Papers, University of Sussex Library. Washington State University's Library at Pullman, Washington, houses an extensive collection of books from Virginia and Leonard Woolf's libraries and other relevant materials. The University of Texas at Austin has Woolf material in its rich manuscript collection.

Appendix

The Consolidation of Opinion:
Critical Responses to the Modernists

Introduction

The immediate responses of the reading public to the "new," experimental fiction of the modernist writers were rejection by the general audience, bewilderment and dismay by the majority of reviewers, and celebration or condemnation by most other novelists of the period. We should not expect these reactions to be very objective or very helpful, if we are looking for a better grasp of the origins, nature, and significance of literary modernism. While the general reader has never warmed to the experimental writer, reviewers and critics (frequently novelists themselves) began the process of formulating and consolidating opinion as soon as the first shock waves of originality subsided. This process begins after the relatively gentle shock of the years 1913-1916, which saw the publication of Proust's *Swann's Way,* Richardson's *Pointed Roofs,* and Joyce's *A Portrait of the Artist as a Young Man,* the pronouncements of various radical literary movements (such as Imagism, Futurism, Vorticism), and the growing disillusionments of a world war. The epicenter of the modernist revolt in English literature, however, was the publication of Joyce's masterwork of experimental fiction, *Ulysses,* in 1922, contemporaneous with T. S. Eliot's equally masterful experimental poem, *The Waste Land,* both works provoking a storm of controversy. No longer could the critics and theorists point to the modernist novel as merely the expression of new psychological theories of consciousness in fiction; the assault on literary convention was too thorough, too radical, not to suggest some larger phenomenon in contemporary culture was taking place. Thus, throughout the 1920s and into the 1930s the novelists themselves, their reviewers and critics, theorists of fiction, and ultimately intellectual historians, psychologists, and sociologists attempted to define the nature of modernist fiction, describe its sources in our culture, and evaluate its influence and significance. They reached no consensus. Nor have more recent scholars and critics. Yet these early attempts at analysis and evaluation frequently anticipate the directions taken and the conclusions reached by later studies of the modernist novel.

The following essays and commentaries illustrate, in brief, this consolidation of opinion and movement toward evaluation. It is, however, a highly selective assemblage, making available discussions that are too little known, infrequently reprinted (and generally inaccessible), or rarely read as, in their present context, major statements in our culture's attempts to assimilate the revolutionary innovations of literary modernism.

The first four essays show some initial critical response to modernism. May Sinclair, praising Richardson's innovative presentation of the individual's fluid thought processes, is the first to apply William James's term "stream of consciousness" to this fictional technique, which is in fact more descriptive of Sinclair's own methods. An experimental novelist of the older generation, Ford Madox Hueffer (later known as Ford Madox Ford) assesses the experiments of the "haughty and proud" younger writers. The editor and man-of-letters John Middleton Murry searches for the roots of the "break-up" of the modern novel, between 1913 and 1922. And Wyndham Lewis, the artist, novelist, and self-styled "enemy" of the Bergsonian/Einsteinian preoccupation with time in modernist art (he championed "spatial" rather than "temporal" conceptions of art), launches an informed attack on his contemporaries in his ambitious philosophic analysis, *Time and Western Man.*

The next three extracts, from early critical studies, illustrate the growing academic interest in defining and describing the modernist novel, coinciding with the decline of the modernist movement itself. Both Elizabeth Drew and Joseph Warren Beach show a dominant concern for the innovative fictional techniques of the contemporary novelist, and most subsequent studies of literary modernism similarly focus on the writers' startling experimental techniques. Yet J. D. Beresford's neglected lecture, "Experiment in the Novel," raises the provocative possibility, only recently taken up again in critical discussion, that the modernist novel is questioning the very nature of perceived reality.

That the modernist movement has such larger implications for our understanding of contemporary culture is also the underlying assumption of Mary Colum's influential *From These Roots,* which begins the process of assimilating modernism into the intellectual history of our time by tracing its sources in the literary developments of the later nineteenth century.

For a fuller study of contemporary opinions on the sources, nature, and significance of the modernist novel, the following more generally available commentaries would be the places to start: Arnold Bennett's "Is the Novel Decaying?" (1923), "The Progress of the Novel" (1929), and reviews of works by Joyce and Woolf—collected in *The Author's Craft and Other Critical Writings of Arnold Bennett,* edited by Samuel Hynes (University of Nebraska Press, 1968)—E. M. Forster's *Aspects of the Novel* (1927), Henry James's "The New Novel, 1914," in his *Notes on Novelists* (1914), D. H. Lawrence's "Surgery for the Novel—or a Bomb" (1923; collected in his *Phoenix,* 1936), Rebecca West's "The Strange Necessity," in her *The Strange Necessity* (1928), and Virginia Woolf's "Mr. Bennett and Mrs. Brown" (1924) and "Modern Fiction" (1925), both reprinted in her *Collected Essays* (1966-1967).

—Thomas Jackson Rice

May Sinclair

"The Novels of Dorothy Richardson"

Pointed Roofs.
Backwater.
Honeycomb.

(Duckworth and company, London).

I have been asked to write—for this magazine which makes no compromise with the public taste—a criticism of the novels of Dorothy Richardson. The editors of the *Little Review* are committed to Dorothy Richardson by their declared intentions; for her works make no sort of compromise with the public taste. If they are not announced with the same proud challenge it is because the pride of the editors of the *Little Review* is no mate for the pride of Miss Richardson which ignores the very existence of the public and its taste.

I do not know whether this article is or is not going to be a criticism, for so soon as I begin to think what I shall say I find myself criticising criticism, wondering what is the matter with it and what, if anything, can be done to make it better, to make it alive. Only a live criticism can deal appropriately with a live art. And it seems to me that the first step towards life is to throw off the philosophic cant of the XIXth Century. I don't mean that there is no philosophy of Art, or that if there has been there is to be no more of it; I mean that it is absurd to go on talking about realism and idealism, or objective and subjective art, as if the philosophies were sticking where they stood in the eighties.

In those days the distinction between idealism and realism, between subjective and objective was important and precise. And so long as the ideas they stand for had importance and precision those words were lamps to the feet and lanterns to the path of the critic. Even after they had begun to lose precision and importance they still served him as useful labels for the bewildering phenomena of the arts.

But now they are beginning to give trouble; they obscure the issues. Mr. J. B. Beresford in his admirable introduction to *Pointed Roofs* confesses to having felt this trouble. When he read it in manuscript he decided that it "was realism, was objective." When he read it in typescript he thought: "this . . . is the most subjective thing I have ever read." It is evident that, when first faced with the startling "newness" of Miss Richardson's method and her form, the issues did seem a bit obscure to Mr. Beresford. It was as if up to one illuminating moment he had been obliged to think of methods and forms as definitely objective or definitely subjective. His illuminating moment came with the third reading when *Pointed Roofs* was a printed book. The book itself gave him the clue to his own trouble, which is my trouble, the first hint that criticism up till now has been content to think in clichés, missing the new trend of the philosophies of the XXth Century. All that we know of reality at first hand is given to us through contacts in which those interesting distinctions are lost. Reality is thick and deep, too thick and too deep and at the same time too fluid to be cut with any convenient carving knife. The novelist who would be close to reality must confine himself to this knowledge at first hand. He must, as Mr. Beresford says, simply "plunge in." Mr. Beresford also says that Miss Richardson is the first novelist who has plunged in. She has plunged so neatly and quietly that even admirers of her performance might remain unaware of what it is precisely that she has done. She has disappeared while they are still waiting for the splash. So that Mr. Beresford's introduction was needed.

When first I read *Pointed Roofs* and *Backwater* and *Honeycomb* I too thought, like Mr. Beresford, that Miss Richardson has been the first to plunge. But it seems to me rather that she has followed, independently, perhaps unconsciously, a growing tendency to plunge. As far back as the eighties the de Goncourts plunged completely, finally, in *Soeur Philomène, Germinie Lacerteux* and *Les Frères Zemganno.* Marguerite Audoux plunged in the best passages of *Marie Claire.* The best of every good novelist's best work is a more or less sustained immersion. The more modern the novelist the longer his capacity to stay under. Miss Richardson has not plunged deeper than Mr. James Joyce in his *Portrait of the Artist as a Young Man.*

By imposing very strict limitations on herself she has brought her art, her method, to a high pitch of perfection, so that her form seems to be newer than it perhaps is. She herself is unaware of the perfection of her method. She would probably deny that she has written with any deliberate method at all. She would say: "I only know there are certain things I mustn't do if I was to do what I wanted." Obviously, she must not interfere; she must not analyse or comment or explain. Rather less obviously, she must not tell a story, or handle a situation or set a scene; she must avoid drama as she avoids narration. And there are some things she must not be. She must not be the wise, all-knowing author. She must be Miriam Henderson: She must not know or divine anything that Miriam does not know or divine; she must not see anything that Miriam does not see. She has taken Miriam's nature upon her. She is not concerned, in the way that other novelists are concerned, with character. Of the persons who move through Miriam's world you know nothing but what Miriam knows. If Miriam is mistaken, well, she and not Miss Richardson is mistaken. Miriam is an acute observer, but she is very far from seeing the whole of these people. They are presented to us in the same vivid but fragmentary way in which they appeared to Miriam, the fragmentary way in which people appear to most of us. Miss Richardson has only imposed on herself the conditions that life imposes on all of us. And if you are going to quarrel with those conditions you will not find her novels satisfactory. But your satisfaction is not her concern.

And I find it impossible to reduce to intelligible terms this satisfaction that I feel. To me these three novels show an art and method and form carried to punctilious perfection. Yet I have heard other novelists say that they have no art and no method and no form, and that it is this formlessness that annoys them. They say that they have no beginning and no middle and no end, and that to have form a novel must have an end and a beginning and a middle. We have come to words that in more primitive times would have been blows on this subject. There is a certain plausibility in what they say, but it depends on what constitutes a beginning and a middle and an end. In this series there is no drama, no situation, no set scene. Nothing happens. It is just life going on and on. It is Miriam Henderson's stream of consciousness going on and on. And in neither is there any grossly discernible beginning or middle or end.

In identifying herself with this life which is Miriam's stream of consciousness Miss Richardson produces her effect of being the first, of getting closer to reality than any of our novelists who are trying so desperately to get close. No attitude or gesture of her own is allowed to come between her and her effect. Whatever her sources and her raw material, she is concerned and we ought to be con-

cerned solely with the finished result, the work of art. It is to Miriam's almost painfully acute senses that we owe what in any other novelist would be called the "portratis" of Miriam's mother, of her sister Harriet, of the Corries and Joey Banks in *Honeycomb,* of the Miss Pernes and Julia Doyle, and the north London schoolgirls in *Backwater,* of Fräulein Pfaff and Mademoiselle, of the Martins and Emma Bergmann and Ulrica and "the Australian" in *Pointed Roofs.* The mere "word painting" is masterly.

". . . Miriam noticed only the hoarse, hacking laugh of the Australian. Her eyes flew up the table and fixed her as she sat laughing, her chair drawn back, her knees crossed—tea was drawing to an end. The detail of her terrifyingly stylish ruddy-brown frieze dress with its Norfolk jacket bodice and its shiny leather belt was hardly distinguishable from the dark background made by the folding doors. But the dreadful outline of her shoulders was visible, the squarish oval of her face shone out—the wide forehead from which the wiry black hair was combed to a high puff, the red eyes, black now, the long, straight nose, the wide, laughing mouth with the enormous teeth."

And so on all round the school tea-table. It looks easy enough to "do" until you try it. There are thirteen figures round that table and each is drawn with the first few strokes and so well that you see them all and never afterwards can you mistake or confuse them.

You look at the outer world through Miriam's senses and it is as if you had never seen it so vividly before. Miriam in *Backwater* is on the top of a bus, driving from North London to Piccadilly:

"On the left a tall grey church was coming towards them, spindling up into the sky. It sailed by, showing Miriam a circle of little stone pillars built into its spire. Plumy trees streamed by, standing large and separate on moss-green grass railed from the roadway. Bright, white-faced houses with pillared porches shone through from behind them and blazed white above them against the blue sky. Wide side streets opened, showing high balconied houses. The side streets were feathered with trees and ended mistily.

"Away ahead were edges of clean, bright masonry in profile, soft, tufted heads of trees, bright green in the clear light. At the end of the vista the air was like pure saffron-tinted mother-of-pearl."

Or this "interior" from *Honeycomb:* . . . "the table like an island under the dome of the low-hanging rose-shaded lamp, the table-centre thickly embroidered with beetles' wings, the little dishes stuck about, sweets, curiously crusted brown almonds, sheeny grey-green olives; the misty beaded glass of the finger bowls—Venetian glass from that shop in Regent Street—the four various wine glasses at each right hand, one on a high thin stem, curved and fluted like a shallow tulip, filled with hock; and floating in the warmth amongst all these things the strange, exciting dry sweet fragrance coming from the mass of mimosa, a forest of little powdery blossoms, little stiff grey—the arms of railway signals at junctions—Japanese looking leaves—standing as if it were growing, in a shallow bowl under the rose-shaded lamp."

It is as if no other writers had ever used their senses so purely and with so intense a joy in their use.

This intensity is the effect of an extreme concentration on the thing seen or felt. Miss Richardson disdains every stroke that does not tell. Her novels are novels of an extraordinary compression and of an extenuation more extraordinary still. The moments of Miriam's consciousness pass one by one, or overlapping, moments tense with vibration, moments drawn out fine, almost to snapping point. On one page Miss Richardson seems to be accounting for every minute of Miriam's time. On another she passes over events that might be considered decisive with the merest slur of reference. She is not concerned with the strict order of events in time. Chapter Three of *Pointed Roofs* opens with an air of extreme decision and importance: "Miriam was practising on the piano in the larger of the two English bedrooms," as if something hung on her practising. But no, nothing hangs on it, and if you want to know on what day she is practising you have to read on and back again. It doesn't matter. It is Miriam's consciousness that is going backwards and forwards in time. The time it goes in is unimportant. On the hundredth page out of three hundred and twelve pages Miriam has been exactly two weeks in Hanover. Nothing has happened but the infinitely little affairs of the school, the practising, the "Vorspielen," the English lesson, the "raccommodage," the hair-washing. At the end of the book Fräulein Pfaff is on the station platform, gently propelling Miriam "up three steps into a compartment marked Damen-Coupé. It smelt of biscuits and wine." Miriam has been no more than six months in Hanover. We are not told, and Miriam is not told, but we know as Miriam knows that she is going because Pastor Lahmann has shown an interest in Miriam very disturbing to Fräulein Pfaff's interest in him. We are not invited to explore the tortuous

mind of the pious, sentimental, secretly hysterical Fräulein; but we know, as Miriam knows, that before she can bring herself to part with her English governess she must persuade herself that it is Miriam and not Mademoiselle who is dismissed because she is an unwholesome influence.

In this small world where nothing happens "that dreadful talk with Gertrude," and Fräulein's quarrel with the servant Anna, the sound of her laugh and her scream, "Ja, Sie Können Ihre paar Groschen haben! Ihre paar Groschen!," and Miriam's vision of Mademoiselle's unwholesomeness, stand out as significant and terrifying. They *are* terrifying; they are significant; through them we know Gertrude, we know Fräulein Pfaff, we know Mademoiselle as Miriam knows them, under their disguises.

At the end of the third volume, *Honeycomb,* there is, apparently, a break with the design. Something does happen. Something tragic and terrible. We are not told what it is; we know as Miriam knows, only by inference. Miriam is sleeping in her mother's room.

"Five o'clock. Three more hours before the day began. The other bed was still. 'It's going to be a magnificent day,' she murmured, pretending to stretch and yawn again. A sigh reached her. The stillness went on and she lay for an hour tense and listening. Someone else must know . . . At the end of the hour a descending darkness took her suddenly. She woke from it to the sound of violent language, furniture being roughly moved, a swift, angry splashing of water . . . something breaking out, breaking through the confinements of this little furniture-filled room . . . the best gentlest thing she knew openly despairing at last."

Here Miss Richardson "gets" you as she gets you all the time—she never misses once—by her devout adhesion to her method, by the sheer depth of her plunge. For this and this alone is the way things happen. What we used to call the "objective" method is a method of after-thought, of spectacular reflection. What has happened has happened in Miriam's bedroom, if you like; but only by reflection. The firsthand, intimate and intense reality of the happening is in Miriam's mind, and by presenting it thus and not otherwise Miss Richardson seizes reality alive. The intense rapidity of the seizure defies you to distinguish between what is objective and what is subjective either in the reality presented or the art that presents.

Nothing happens. In Miriam Henderson's life there is, apparently, nothing to justify living. Everything she ever wanted was either withheld or taken from her. She is reduced to the barest minimum on which it is possible to support the life of the senses and the emotions at all. And yet Miriam is happy. Her inexhaustible passion for life is fed. Nothing happens, and yet everything that really matters is happening; you are held breathless with the anticipation of its happening. What really matters is a state of mind, the interest or the ecstasy with which we close with life. It can't be explained. To quote Mr. Beresford again: "explanation in this connection would seem to imply knowledge that only the mystics can faintly realise." But Miss Richardson's is a mysticism apart. It is compatible with, it even encourages such dialogue as this:

" 'Tea' " smiled Eve serenely.

" 'All right, I'm coming, damn you, aren't I?'

" 'Oh, Mimmy!'

" 'Well, damn *me,* then. Somebody in the house must swear. I say, Eve!'

" 'What?'

" 'Nothing, only I *say.'*

" 'Um.' "

It is not wholly destroyed when Miriam eats bread and butter thus: "When she began at the hard thick edge there always seemed to be tender places on her gums, her three hollow teeth were uneasy and she had to get through worrying thoughts about them—they would get worse as the years went by, and the little places in the front would grow big and painful and disfiguring. After the first few mouthfuls of solid bread a sort of padding seemed to take place and she could go on forgetful."

This kind of thing annoys Kensington. I do not say that it really matters but that it is compatible with what really matters. Because of such passages it is a pity that Miss Richardson could not use the original title of her series: "Pilgrimage," for it shows what she is really after. Each book marks a stage in Miriam's pilgrimage. We get the first hint of where she is going to in the opening of the tenth chapter of *Pointed Roofs:* "Into all the gatherings at Waldstrasse the outside world came like a presence. It removed the sense of pressure, of being confronted and challenged. Everything that was said seemed to be incidental to it, like remarks dropped in a low tone between individuals at a great conference." In *Backwater* the author's intention becomes still clearer. In *Honeycomb* it is transparently clear:

"Her room was a great square of happy light . . . happy, happy. She gathered up all the sadness she had ever known and flung it from her. All the dark things of the past flashed with a strange beauty as she flung them out. The light had been there all the time; but she had known it only at moments. Now she knew what she wanted. Bright mornings, beautiful bright rooms, a wilderness of beauty all round her all the time—at any cost."

And yet not that:

"Something that was not touched, that sang far away down inside the gloom, that cared nothing for the creditors and could get away down and down into the twilight far away from the everlasting accusations of humanity. . . . Deeper down was something cool and fresh—endless—an endless garden. In happiness it came up and made everything in the world into a garden. Sorrow blotted it out; but it was always there, waiting and looking on. It had looked on in Germany and had loved the music and the words and the happiness of the German girls, and at Banbury Park, giving her no peace until she got away. '

"And now it had come to the surface and was with her all the time."

There are two essays of Rémy de Gourmont in *Promenades Littéraires,* one on "l'Originalité de Maeterlinck," one on "La Leçon de Saint-Antoine." Certain passages might have been written concerning the art of Dorothy Richardson:—

"Si la vie en soi est un bienfait, et il faut l'accepter comme telle ou la nier, le fait même de vivre le contient tout entier, et les grands mouvements de la sensibilité, loin de l'enrichir, l' appauvrissent au contraire, en concentrant sur quelques partis de nous-mêmes, envahis au hasard par la destinée l' effort d' attention qui serait plus uniformenent reparti sur l' ensemble de notre conscience vitale. De ce point de vue une vie où il semblerait ne rien se passer que d' élémentaire et quotidien serait mieux remplie qu'une autre vie riche en apparence d' incidents et d' aventures". . . . "Il y a peut-être un sentiment nouveau à créer, celui de l' amour de la vie pour la vie elle-même, abstraction faite des grandes joies qu'elle ne donne pas à tous, et qu' elle ne donne peut-être à personne . . . Notre paradis, c' est la journée qui passe, la minute qui s' envole, le moment qui n'est déjà plus. Telle est la leçon de Saint Antoine." ["If life itself is a benefit, and one must accept or deny it as such, the actual act of living is everything, and the large movements of sensibility, far from enriching life, on the contrary impoverish it, concentrating the effort of attention that could be more uniformly divided over the whole of our vital consciousness on some parts of ourselves which have been encroached upon at random by destiny. From this point of view a life where nothing would seem to happen except the elementary and day-today would be fuller than another life seemingly rich in incidents and adventures".... "There is perhaps a new feeling to be created, that of loving life for life itself, an abstraction made of the great joys that life does not give to all, and that it perhaps gives to no one.... Our paradise is the day that passes, the minute that evolves, the moment that is already no more. Such is the lesson of Saint Antoine."]

Reprinted from *Little Review*, 5 (April 1918): 3-11.

Ford Madox Hueffer

"A Haughty and Proud Generation"

It is easy to say who are our British novelists of the first flight: they are Mr. Conrad, Mr. Hardy, Mr. George Moore, Mr. W. H. Hudson—and possibly Mr. Bennett. That I regard as indisputable if we may take the novel as giving us something more than the tale—as being a tale with a projection of life, a philosophy, but not an obvious moral, or propagandist purpose. First-flight novelists, then, will be those who have perfected their methods and are resigned.

The second flight will be, in our literature, Pushkin's "haughty and proud generation: vigorous and free in their passions and adventures"; they are such writers as Norman Douglas, P. Wyndham Lewis, D. H. Lawrence, Frank Swinnerton, Katherine Mansfield, Clemence Dane, Dorothy Richardson, and James Joyce. Your first flight will be wise; your second, dogmatic. One likes to thank them for what it is worth, with one's note of applause. But they will not thank you much in return because they are going on to the new adventures, the new explorations of method.

Let us for a moment differentiate between the novel and the tale—or let us at least try to get at a working definition. The novel of to-day is probably the only intellectual, poetic, or spiritual exercise that humanity is engaged in performing. It is probably, too, the only work of exact and dispassionate science.

We may consider the tale first. Mr. Kipling, speaking at his reception at the Sorbonne, talked recently of "the literature of escape." I don't know whether this phrase is an accepted classification of academic criticism, or whether we owe it to the genius of Mr. Kipling. Mr. Arthur Symons said long ago that all art is an escape—but that is another matter. Anyhow, that is a very valuable phrase. For the literature of escape embraces whole century-

long ranges of effort from "The Golden Ass" of Apuleius to the last sadic rubbish of Miss Dash; all the works from the story of Morgiana and the Forty Thieves to "Treasure Island" or "Lorna Doone," reading which the tired city typewriter or the millionaire's office boy may escape from their environments and so recruit their vital forces.

The tale—even the novel of commerce—should not be despised. Mr. Gladstone sought refuge from the Irish Question in "John Inglesant"; Edward the Seventh read the nautical romances of Captain Marryat to solace himself whilst he was negotiating the *Entente Cordiale,* and thus we see the tale interlaced as it were with the greatest of international happenings. The King's taste was sounder than that of the Prime Minister—but King or Premier, *midinette* or millionaire, you must come at last to this: you must find escape from yourself in the artless tale—in the fiction of commerce. The late Mr. Meredith used to await with impatience the daily instalments of *feuilleton* in one of our ha'penny papers.

But when it comes to criticism of the tale one is, in England, thrown back almost entirely upon the "short story." The English long tale is practically always merely anodyne, without art, construction, presentation, or progressive effect. You read it and "escape," but you have no comment to make. It calls for none. And the short "short story" is a very old form. Told by story-tellers in bazaars, by mediaeval queens to their courts, or by anecdote-cappers round the fires of smoking-rooms, the tale was constrained by time to be short and by the exacting nature of audiences to be well told. For people who listen must be gripped more firmly than people who read.

And one may say that all the pure art of the English-writing peoples has until quite lately gone into the short story. You could cite Mr. Kipling, Mr. Wells, and even Mr. W. W. Jacobs without absolute shame against Continental writers of this one form. For the whole *art* of these three writers of genius has gone into their short stories—the whole, that is to say, of their senses of proportion, of narration, and of construction. The "Country of the Blind" volume of Mr. Wells, any volume of the Indian tales of Mr. Kipling, and any volume of Mr. Jacobs are products of sheer genius in narration. Naturally any volume of Maupassant in his greatest vein—say, the original "Yvette" collection—excels the English books because in addition to skill of narration Maupassant had a great, gloomy, philosophic outlook which transfused all his really representative writing. And when an artist has the temperament that will let his work be transfused by a profound or a lofty perception of the broader aspects of human vicissitudes, his work will have greater value to the republic than that of the most skilled constructors of anecdotes. Chekhov, though not so practised in elisions as Maupassant, was to all intents and purposes as skilled a narrator and so, for the matter of that you might say, is Schnitzler.

Let us then put it that, although the writing of good short stories is not an essentially English occupation, when English men of genius do turn their attention to that form, they not infrequently attain to high achievement in pure art. But as far as this country is concerned, the practice of that form seems to be in abeyance. I cannot, at any rate, think of any English writer who could be classed as in the second flight of writers of the short story. Mr. Kipling and Mr. Wells of the indisputable first flight have turned their attention to other things; I have seen nothing by Mr. Jacobs for a long time.

I ought perhaps to make a reservation in favor of Miss Katherine Mansfield. I have had for this lady for so long so considerable an admiration that, though dates are not my strong point, I think it possible that she stands chronologically with Mr. Lawrence, Mr. Joyce, and Mr. Lewis. Certainly in pre-war days—and that is probably the criterion for "second-flightness"—Miss Mansfield had arrived at a strong, severe, at an almost virulent skill in sheer elision: relevancy. I can still remember with precision some of her contributions to a journal called "Rhythm" that must have lived out its quite valuable life in 1913 or 1914; and certainly in her volume entitled "Bliss" Miss Mansfield has carried the methods of tight, hard, cold—I wish there were some translation for the Latin word *saeva*— selection further than it has ever been carried in English work. I wish she did more. Bulk is not a

quality for which one need feel any respect; but a number of instances is helpful when it is one's task to generalize. And anyhow there is not too much in the literature of escape that one can read, not only to get away from the remembrance of one's creditors, but also with the keen pleasure of appreciating the skill of chisel work. Miss Mansfield has spent a good deal of time, lately, in exercising a mordant pen on contemporary fiction. I wish she had not: we have so much more need of good stuff than of analysis of indifferent matter.

So we arrive at the novel and at the second generation of its practitioners. Compared with the short story which as an art form was certainly perfected in the day of the Parables—and who knows in how many generations of earlier Books of the Dead and on how many myriads of incised bricks?—the novel is still a babe in arms. Henry James was our first novelist; Mr. Conrad our next—and then we come to the second flight. Henry James was our first Anglo-Saxon writer to perceive that this life of ours is an affair of terminations and of embarrassments. Mr. Conrad was our next. He realized that the records of human lives cannot be set down as they are set down by the amiable, learned, and incompetent contributors to Dictionaries of National Biographies, as a straightforward "article" with dates but not too many references.

Of course, the great master of both these great men was Flaubert, and, if you read the account of the adulterous courtship of Emma Bovary by Rodolphe, you read the germ of "Ulysses," of "Tarr," of all the works of Miss Dorothy Richardson, of most of the stories of Mr. Lawrence. Rodolphe, the rather bounderish country gentleman is trying, at a cattle show, to seduce Emma Bovary, the wife of the country doctor. They are seated side by side on the seats of the tribune. Rodolphe says: "My love for you shall be eternal. We shall live as do the little birds in the sacred odor of Paradise." The Prefect cries out: "Trois boeufs; trois cochons; douze poules, et un coq!—Maitre Cornu!"—"Three oxen; three sows; twelve hens, and a rooster!—First Prize: Mr. Hornimann!" Rodolphe continues: "Gracious being! At the mere sight of your form my heart. . . ." The Prefect shouts: "Four onions; twelve potatoes; twelve turnips!—First Prize: Mr. Sprout!" It is something like that: the constant alternation of the romantic-heroic with the products of dung and sweat. And that is our life.

Mr. James must have known too many shrinkings, embarrassments, and fine shades to render them without remorse; Mr. Conrad, much coarser and much less shuddering in fibre than the Master from New England, has limited himself—as far as form goes—to registering how human lives, in a thousand devious, unconnected anecdotes, present themselves to the memory of the teller of a story. Mr. Conrad, in fact, is reconciled to, is tranquil in face of, his world of ships' captains and revolutionaries. Mr. James, much more akin in spirit to the Flaubert whom he could not bear—to the Flaubert who was really a good Christian horrified at the way in which Christian men mangled in their practice the precepts of Our Lord—Mr. James, then, never got over the crudities of merely living.

It has remained for our novelists of the second flight to unite, as best they could, the practices of Mr. James and of Mr. Conrad and to carry the process that one step further that art forever demands. The formula, the discovery, has trembled as it were on the lips of generations of novelists the world over. You find it in the banquet of Trimalchio; in the Sancho Panza of Cervantes; in Shakespeare's clowns; in Thackeray's comments on his characters—the sense of the gross, the ironic, or the merely smug world that surrounds and nullifies the hero. It has remained, let us repeat, for our novelists of the second flight to carry the conviction of the grinning, complex world into the consciousness, into the springs of action of their characters—to render it, not objectively, but from the inside.

Gissing had got so far as to emphasize that the gross, ironic, smug—and sordid!—world paralyzes the lives not only of heroes but of the least significant human beings. "New Grub Street" falls short of being a masterpiece of the first order only because, like Zola's "L'Oeuvre," it is perpetually harrowing—so ceaselessly harrowing that the mind cannot react against its protracted and heavy dragging. Still, "L'Oeuvre" and "New Grub Street" are serious studies of the hero as artist in process of strangulation by the drag of sordid material detail; just as "The Town Traveller" and "Demos" show the quite ordinary man's character being preyed upon by the mere sordidnesses of dirty table-cloths, greasy bacon, and frayed trouser-ends.

Gissing is little read to-day which is a pity, for he was a sound, industrious, and honest craftsman; and he has left practically no following. That is not so much to be regretted because his methods, as far as I can see, lead only into a *cul-de-sac*. And that brings me to Mr. Swinnerton.

To read Mr. Swinnerton at his best is to hear

all the time the cadences of Gissing; and even in such carefully psychologized work as the character called Jenny of "Nocturne" there is the perpetual undertone of the dirty table-cloth and the greasy bacon. The mental states of the girl are continually at the mercy of re-hashed mutton and wet hat trimmings—or of *bisque de homard* and peaches. Psychologically these are not *trouvailles*—only Mr. Swinnerton's neck of mutton and the bread pudding of the domestic hearth, as well as the Beaune in the glass of the seducer, are excellent renderings of still life.

But Mr. Swinnerton—and "Nocturne" is incomparably his best book—is not just doing the sordid surroundings plus the young woman's reaction into luxurious seduction on board a lordly yacht, that being the "plot" of this work stated unsympathetically. (And the plot of every work worth consideration should be capable of standing up against unsympathetic statement.) He has sufficient perception of the complexity of life to attempt to crowd into the story of five or six hours the whole mental history, the whole progression, of his young woman's "fall." And not only does he attempt this but he succeeds in the attempt. That is a very considerable achievement. It may or may not be merely a technical feat; but the effect is to convey some at least of the flicker and waver of the human soul in the life that we live.

Descending then from Gissing—though I am quite prepared to have Mr. Swinnerton or someone else write to the papers and declare that he has never felt the influence of the author of "Henry Ryecroft"—Mr. Swinnerton makes his assault upon the Modern Position. Descending from Henry James, Miss Clemence Dane makes hers—not quite so uncompromisingly. "Legend," which is Miss Dane's most interesting book, though "Regiment of Women" contains more harrowing stuff, is another attempt to work into a single evening the story of a whole life, the whole work of an artist, the complete love affairs, and the death of an unknown, problematic woman of letters. Without Mr. Swinnerton's courage or technical "chic," Miss Dane not only provides herself with a narrator, which of course is a necessity for her form, but provides the narrator with a humble, Jane Eyre-like psychology, vibrating sympathies, love affair, and marriage. Thus she carries the "story" on, though only in a "prologue," for months after the evening is over. Mr. Swinnerton just leaves the evening there as far as "Nocturne" is concerned: we do not get told whether the skipper of the lordly yacht marries the girl, or whether the young woman has a baby, or any of the other details that, rounding up endings, leave the voracious reader with a comfortable feeling of repletion.

Nevertheless, Miss Dane's attempt is an attempt—less to get at the complex impressionism of life than at the complexities of human judgments. A glamorous literary female figure is talked about from every point of view within the Jamesian-At-Home sphere of life, by almost every imaginable human type to be found in a South Kensington "highbrow at home." A nasty writing man thinks "She" does not love her husband; a nice painting man preserves discreet but illuminative silences; a "cattish" writing woman thinks "Her" second book a sentimental failure; a nice writing woman thinks it a monument of irony. So a curiously fussy image of the Figure is built up, the Figure herself dying in the distance whilst the "at home" proceeds. Miss Dane in short employs Mr. Conrad's method in unfolding her story and goes to the Henry James of "The Aspern Papers" and "The Real Thing" for her curiously provincial atmosphere.

The point, however, about both Mr. Swinnerton and Miss Dane is that they do have conceptions of life as a very complex affair of cross motives. Neither treats characters as simple beings whose story is a matter of straightforward achievement under one dominant passion—achievement of fame, fortune, automobiles, heroines, offspring. Nor does either of them seek to render the world a better place. Those are very good things.

We come, then, to the more obviously motive forces of the English novel of to-day. We may begin with Mr. Douglas—the Mr. Douglas of "South Wind" and "They Went"; though really you might just as well call "Alone" a novel with modern Italy as central character—modern Italy set down from as many angles, cut into as many-faceted a thing as the central figure of "Legend," and provided with even more wines and dishes than the central figure of "Nocturne."

In a sense Mr. Douglas is a writer of an older generation—of a generation infinitely old, critically. To come upon passages of appraisement in "Alone" is to be bewildered by the feeling that one's young, young youth has returned. You have Ouida and Mathilde Blind—Mathilde Blind of all people!—exalted at the expense of James; for all the world as if the late Mr. Watts-Dunton were still setting the standard of the late "Athenaeum." There is hardly anyone old enough to remember *that* literary point of view.

So that Mr. Douglas, as far as his gifts are concerned, must have sprung fully armed from some militant head. He does not descend from Gissing or Mr. Conrad; certainly James has not influenced him; it is impossible to imagine his having the patience to read "Education Sentimentale"; he has none of the swift attack of Maupassant. He is most like Anatole France—and yet he is very unlike Anatole France. He is like, that is to say, because at any moment he will illuminate a modern predicament with an anecdote from the depths of a most profound antiquity—only you feel that Mr. Douglas is quite capable of inventing his anecdote and conveying to it, with tremendous gusto and smacking of the lips, an almost too gorgeous patina. Not for nothing has he told us the story of the faun of Locri.

"South Wind" is the story, tremulous in surface and in treatment, of an affair—of, that is to say, an atmosphere. The bishop is nonsense; the duchess is nonsense; the millionaire, the boy, the count—they spring for moments into life that is more real than life and cast light, not on any humanity, but on a place that quivers in Mediterranean sunshine. Or let us put it that Mr. Douglas's central figure is the season of nineteen hundred and dash, in Taormina or Capri or some such place, and that Mr. Douglas's human dolls illuminate with their actions and illustrate with their disquisitions that period of fashionable time. I think this is the best way to put it: for this author's savage, mordant dislike for humanity would hardly let him make his central figure a bishop or any other created human being. The central figure of "They Went" is the Devil, who, I imagine, was not created; but even with his own devil Mr. Douglas has not very much patience, not enough to dwell very much or very often upon him. But here again his real hero is the fabulous city of the catastrophic end.

Loving the souls of places, not of men, Mr. Douglas can afford to write a great deal more than the human-centred novelist of to-day; so he can afford to be relatively personal too. For it matters very little if the personality of your writer sticks out in the foreground of places where the sunlight always quivers. It does matter a great deal if that personality intrudes on the always shadowy renderings of human interplay. That is the weak spot of "Tarr"—which Mr. Lewis wrote, not with as much aplomb, but quite as obtrusively as Mr. Douglas. That is no doubt because both these important writers began as essayists—a school that is exceedingly deleterious to the novelist-beginner. For your essayist learns to rely on his personality rather than on anything else of all the things there are under the sun. What, for instance, might not the Mr. Beerbohm of "Seven Men" be if he did not perpetually and for a living have to be Max—more *blasé,* more unpractical, more cynical, and less interested than any other man of London Town?

Mr. Douglas probably imposes his personality out of sheer damn-your-eyes don't-careness; but Mr. Lewis does it of set purpose—and sometimes he forgets to do it, out of sheer fatigue, one suspects. Then he writes the straightforward story of the tale-teller, as he does throughout the adventures of Kreisler in "Tarr," the Tarr episodes themselves being, except for the discussions, shadowy and unconvincing.

But in the discussions Mr. Lewis shows himself an extraordinarily great artist, not, heaven knows, in what his characters say, but in the rendering of their temperamental and physical reactions one upon the other. Mr. Lawrence is a great realist—except when he is recording conversations. Mr. Lewis is our greatest anti-realist; but when he is rendering conversations he is so great a realist that he makes you shiver. His characters writhe—over the marble table-tops of restaurants where the waiters rush about, harried, in the serving of "bocks," or over the gas cooking-stoves where they are making "lunches" out of the débris, the scraps from paper parcels purchased from an adjacent *crémerie.* They indulge in meaningless scraps of talk; but their personalities are set "one over against another," currents crossing, embarrassments, agonizing shynesses, remembrances—and nothing can be more bitter!—of points they might have made in their last speech but seven. That is very wonderful.

The characters of Mr. Lawrence, infinitely more real, infinitely more provided with ancestries, their feet infinitely more on the ground, sit about in punts, in fields of asphodels, and talk pathologic nonsense, every word of which Mr. Lawrence records as if he had been sitting on the other side of the hedge with a stenographer's tablet. But as for interplay of personality with personality, in the works of Mr. Lawrence there is none. Absolutely none. Lawrence's men and women discuss Love and discuss Liberty as if they were looking up those words in the "Encyclopaedia Britannica" and reading out what there they found, with a profound solemnity, an unwinking preposterousness.

On the other hand, the author of "Tarr" could never have written "Odor of Chrysanthemums," the descriptions of how a coal miner's widow washed the body of her husband, killed by a fall in a pit. The odor of chrysanthemums drifts in all the while, it being autumn.

That is Mr. Lawrence being almost greater than it is proper to be. For the Mr. Lawrence of "The White Peacock," of "Sons and Lovers," is a writer of genius. But he indulges his moods too much—at the expense of his subject. And self-indulgence is the last thing that a writer at all concerned with realism can allow himself. Temperament is, of course, necessary for the genius; but the genius who lets his books be nothing but temperament falls either into boredom or the ridiculous. And so, in "Women in Love," a recent novel, Mr. Lawrence gives us in all seriousness, during a discussion of Love-in-Liberty and Liberty-in-Love the most ridiculous sentence that was ever set down by the human pen. I regret that it is too indecent to be quoted in this context.

The fact is that sex discussion occupies—such is the idiocy of the repressive laws of Great Britain and the still more stupid laws of the United States—far too great a part in the public mind of the lands that border the Atlantic. It becomes an obsession; it ends as a nuisance. Sex is, I suppose, one phenomenon in a chain of the phenomena of growth and of reproduction. It has its importance along with eating and other physical processes. One should—the novelist, above all, should—regard it with composure. But so few do.

Indeed, I fancy that Mr. Joyce is the only artist we have to-day who with an utter composure regards processes of reproduction, of nourishment, and of physical renewal. But then Mr. Joyce, the supreme artist, regards with an equal composure—all things. That is why the law of the United States has persecuted his publishers. For law cannot—any more than the average of excitable humanity—contemplate composure with equanimity. It is in itself abhorrent. If we were all always composed, we should have no war, no crime, no daily journalism, no outcry, nothing contemptible, very little that was base. We should have nothing but the arts. What then would become of poor humanity—of *l'homme moyen sensuel,* of the preacher, the writer on morals and the always excited scientist? They must die! Some day they all will. But that time is not yet.

And Mr. Joyce is a writer of very beautiful, composed English. To read "The Portrait of the Artist as a Young Man" as against, say, "Interim" of Miss Dorothy Richardson is to recognize the difference between singularly fussy inclusiveness and absolutely aloof selection. There is really more enlightenment as to childhood and youth in the first three pages of Mr. Joyce's book—there is more light thrown on the nature of man—than in all Miss Richardson's volumes.

And that is not to belittle Miss Richardson; for to be infinitely little set over against Mr. Joyce, is to be yet considerable enough. But Mr. Joyce measures his effects by things immense and lasting, Miss Richardson by the passing standards of the lower middle-class boarding-house. It is as you might say Flaubert against Gissing.

Mr. Joyce's work is a voyaging on a much higher spiritual plane: the embarrassments and glories of Miss Richardson's young women are bound up in material details. You are embarrassed because of the fichu about your neck; you glory because, finding a restaurant open long after normal closing time, the Italian proprietor serves you himself, with an air of distinguished consideration, with a shiny roll and a cup of chocolate—at a table laid with the plates and cutlery for a party of four! Now, I am not decrying the rendering of that sort of glory or melancholy. A large part of the elation of our poor lives as now we live them may well come from the fact that with our insufficient means we have received at some restaurant more consideration than we had expected. Proprietors and waiters have some of the contempt of public officials for poor humanity, and some of the clairvoyance in appraising purses that belongs to the really successful tradesmen. To hoodwink such fearsome creatures is to achieve a feat such as seldom falls to our portion. But it is only a momentary pride. And the depression that comes with shabbiness of clothes, deep though it be, is not the essential depression of the healthy man.

That is why the school of Gissing is a lesser thing than the school of Joyce. You may put it medically. Doctors tell you that all your life you have in your throat seven million germs of the cold in the head: but it is only when your vitality is at a low ebb that those germs invade your system. For the Gissing of "New Grub Street" sordid table-cloths, monotonously passing lives, and material indigences were the fulcra, the essential motive powers, in the lives of heroes. But that is not true to life—or it so happens only when the system is in a state of low vitality. It is possible that the sudden perception of a dirty table-cloth, all other things being unbearable, might make a hero-poet rush out and sell his soul to an evening paper. But that would be an accidental culmination; a pathological state. The contemplation of mutton hash contributed largely to the

seduction of Mr. Swinnerton's Jenny—and that, given all the sordidnesses of her day, was true enough. But a whole procession of days of mutton hash, a whole Sahara of table-cloths stained with rings from the bottoms of stout glasses, would not turn Mr. Swinnerton's brave London Jenny into a prostitute by temperament or a real poet into a born journalist. In fact mere irritation at the sordidness of his surroundings will do no more than make a sound man or woman commit now and then a *lâcheté;* it will never change the essentials of a character.

It is the perception of that fact that gives such great value to Mr. Joyce—and to the whole movement of the second flight. The mind of every man is made up of several—three or four—currents all working side by side, all making their impress or getting their expression from separate and individual areas of the brain. It is not enough to say that every man is homo duplex; every man is homo x-plex. And this complexity pursues every man into the minutest transactions of his daily life. You go to a bookstall to ask the price of a certain publication. Yes! But part of your mind says to you very quickly: "This clerk has the nose of my uncle George!" Another part feels that you have plenty of time for your train; another that the fish you had for breakfast is disagreeing with you. Generally you are under a deep depression caused by the morning's international news, but you have a particular elation at some movement in the stock market. A lady passing leaves a scent of wallflowers; that calls up associations to which you hardly attend. Almost unknown to yourself, beneath your breath you are humming a tune that has yet other associations. It is this tenuous complexity of life that has its first artistic representation in the works of our second flight—and it is this that makes one feel hopeful in the general depression of the English literary world. It is true that it finds almost its sole appreciation in America; but America does at least keep it going. And as long as it keeps going—*les idées sont en marche.*

The "Portrait of the Artist as a Young Man" is a book of such beauty of writing, such clarity of perception, such a serene love of and interest in life, and such charity that, being the ungenerous creature man is, one was inclined to say: "This surely must be a peak! It is unlikely that this man will climb higher!" But even now that Mr. Joyce has published "Ulysses," it is too early to decide upon that. One can't arrive at one's valuation of a volume so loaded as "Ulysses" after a week of reading and two or three weeks of thought about it. Next year, or in twenty years, one may. For it is as if a new continent with new traditions had appeared, and demanded to be run through in a month. "Ulysses" contains the undiscovered mind of man; it is human consciousness analyzed as it has never before been analyzed. Certain books change the world. This, success or failure, "Ulysses" does: for no novelist with serious aims can henceforth set out upon a task of writing

before he has at least formed his own private estimate as to the rightness or wrongness of the methods of the author of "Ulysses." If it does not make an epoch—and it well may!—it will at least mark the ending of a period.

Reprinted from *Yale Review,* 11 (1922): 703-712.

John Middleton Murry

"The Break-Up of the Novel"

THE NOVEL? Perhaps it is almost as pure an abstraction as The Poem. And surely, if we were to attempt, by a process of induction, to discover the common element in all the works which have passed under that name during two centuries, we should be left with something which, though by no means an abstraction, would be far from satisfying the ideal demands of the name, The Novel. The residue in our hands would be The Story. A novel is a story in prose. The Novel should therefore be The Story. We are not much advanced.

And yet the simple change of the article has worked a minor miracle. Even if The Story is only the most delightful story, we find ourselves appealing to a new standard of judgment. For what is it delights us in a story? If we are children, its mere unexpectedness, no doubt, and in so far as we remain children in our later years, its power to afford us relaxation from the stress of practical life. To that attitude of mind a story is a game, a simple game or a game with intricate rules, hide-and-seek or a chess problem, fairy tale or detective story, but a thing whose import is completely closed within itself, a world which we enter, if we can, chiefly for the purpose of forgetting that acts have consequences. But a moment comes—it is the moment when we begin to talk of The Novel—when we make quite other demands upon it. We ask that the game should not be an interlude in our life but a significant part of it. We begin by asking that the story should, in the simplest fashion, teach us something, first perhaps that it should justify our notions of right and wrong, then that it should reveal to us exacter and more subtle ideas of good and evil. We ask that the story should be real and like-life, and we pass from demanding that the story should reflect

our own conception of life to an attitude of expectation that it will throw a new illumination on to life.

The story, which began as a game and remains a game for many, becomes for others a high and serious art. The two phases co-exist, and even to-day criticism hovers uneasily between the two conceptions. It is aware of two standards of judgment, and is uncertain which to apply. And there is some reason for the hesitation. For, though it seems that we can make a clean logical cut between the story-interest and the significance of the novel, as soon as we attempt to apply the knife we find we are operating upon a living and organic whole. The novel is something greater than its story indeed, but can the greater thing exist without the lesser? Is not the story the skeleton which holds the flesh and blood and tissue of the novel together? Revolving some such unanswered question in its mind, criticism confronts the novel to-day.

But, as usual, creation marches in advance of criticism. While the critic is trying to make up his mind about the terms of the ultimatum he will present to the novelist, the novelist takes the initiative and presents him with a *fait accompli.* He annihilates the story.

The beginning of the process which has ended in the abolition of the story may be traced back far into the nineteenth century. With the end of the early Romantic movement came the decay of the conception that the novelist is primarily a teller of tales. By the middle of the century the novelist who took himself seriously accepted, with individual interpretations, the principle that his art consisted in a faithful representation of life. The novelist was the scribe and life dictated to him. Though many of the realists—Flaubert in particular—felt uneasily that there was something inadequate in this mechanical conception, it was dominant in the West for a generation. The most original novelists endeavored to vary the monotony of their task by introducing intricate considerations of form. Flaubert and Henry James devised for themselves subtle problems concerning the angle of presentation and the identity of the hypothetical consciousness to which the events of the fiction were present. They made the writing of novels an infinitely subtle craft, and they increased its prestige and mystery. For many years, indeed to within the last decade, their principles and subtleties were regarded with an awful reverence. They were the *ne plus ultra* of the novel.

Suddenly—it is hard to say exactly when, but we can safely date the revolution within the present century—it began to be felt that, while most of the Western novelists had been circling in a technical labyrinth, in Russia had appeared two novelists at least whose work, composed with but the faintest attention to these problems of the craft, completely overshadowed that of their Western contemporaries. I well remember the appearance in "The English Review" in 1912 of Mr. Arnold Bennett's astonished confession on reading Mrs. Garnett's then new translation of "The Brothers Karamazov." With his usual honesty, Mr. Bennett, who had painfully formed himself in the school of Flaubert, acknowledged that Dostoevsky was a master "impatient of a minor perfection," and that it made not the slightest difference to his greatness. The confession that the technical perfection of a Flaubert or a James was, after all, only "a minor perfection" itself marked a minor revolution in the history of modern criticism of the novel. It began to be realized that the method of saying it was nothing compared to the significance of the thing said. Tolstoi and Dostoevsky had been saying tremendous things, while the novelists of the West had been busy with some private conception of "art." One immediate effect of this shock to accepted critical notions was that Mr. Thomas Hardy began to emerge from the comparative obscurity to which criticism had relegated him. After regarding him as an uncouth teller of country tragedies, artistically far less important than James or Meredith, and of course not to be named in a breath with Flaubert, the novelists and critics awoke from the technical spell to discover that he was the only English novelist of a magnitude remotely comparable with that of the Russians.

When the commotion had subsided a little and the attempt began to make instinctive feelings articulate, it was decided that there were two qualities which distinguished the "great" novelist. He ex-

pressed a philosophy of life; and he was formless. The first of these propositions, if carefully interpreted, is true; the second is not. The great Russian novelists have not the formal perfection of Flaubert and James, simply because it was of no conceivable use to them; but they have a form of their own. Nevertheless, the young novelists of the period, imagining that formlessness was in itself a virtue, poured volumes of diluted autobiography into the lap of a patient world. The philosophy of life was rather more difficult. The more enterprising put moral emblems on their title-pages and hoped for the best. The boldest introduced a little local color in the shape of perambulatory characters of no fixed abode, who uttered sentiments of nihilism and world weariness when nothing else was doing.

These manifestations of "the Russian influence" in English fiction have merely a local interest; but they serve to show into what a condition of ignorance and inanition our fiction fell when the constraining influence of Flaubert and James, of "style," was removed. After Mr. Wells, Mr. Conrad, and Mr. Bennett, there was nothing except Mr. D. H. Lawrence. It looked as though England might fall out of the running altogether. And France was in no better case. MM. Bourget and Barrès had become merely parochial; Anatole France alone remained. There was nothing after him. For in French literature a similar ignorant attempt to follow the lead of the Russians had been equally unfortunate. In France it was accepted (largely on the "expert" assurance of Melchior de Vogüé) that the secret of Russian literature was "the religion of pity." A whole school of young French novelists, with Romain Rolland and Charles-Louis Philippe at their head, began to be pitiful. This sentimental weakling expired shortly before the war. The ponderous epitaph "Unanimism" is written on its tomb.

At that moment the disorientation of the novel was complete. The Russians had ruined it by revealing its enormous potentialities. The vista was too big; instead of exhilarating, it terrified. Dostoevsky and Tolstoi had exploded the novel, and a whole generation of promising young souls in England and France lay buried under the ruins, whence they have emerged, wise and sad, to settle down to the respectable business of telling stories for library subscribers. The novel as a serious art had nothing more to hope or fear from them. Indeed, it would not be worth while to chronicle their history were it not that a historical retrospect of their failure gives the emphasis of contrast to a new vitality.

In the years 1913 and 1914 three significant

books, calling themselves novels, made an unobtrusive and independent appearance. In France Marcel Proust published "Du Côté de Chez Swann" (recently translated into English as "Swann's Way"); in America the Irishman James Joyce published "A Portrait of the Artist as a Young Man"; in England Dorothy Richardson published "Pointed Roofs." These books had points of outward resemblance. Each was in itself incomplete, a foretaste of sequels to come. Each was autobiographical and, within the necessary limits of individuality, autobiographical in the same new and peculiar fashion. They were attempts to record immediately the growth of a consciousness. Immediately; without any effort at mediation by means of an interposed plot or story. All three authors were trying to present the content of their consciousness as it was before it had been re-shaped in obedience to the demands of practical life; they were exploring the strange limbo where experiences once conscious fade into unconsciousness. The method of Marcel Proust was the most subtle, in that he established as the starting-point of his book the level of consciousness from which the exploration actually began. He presented the process as well as the results of his exploration of the unconscious memory. In the first pages of his book he described how he concentrated upon a vaguely remembered feeling of past malease, which he experienced in waking at night and trying to establish the identity of his room. It was a particular form of the familiar feeling: "I have felt this, been here, seen this, somewhere, somehow, before." We might almost say that Marcel Proust gave us an account of his technique in penetrating such a sentiment and gradually dragging up to the surface of full consciousness forgotten but decisive experiences.

This singularity of Marcel Proust's approach —implied in the general title "A la Recherche du Temps Perdu"—involving as it does a perpetual reference to the present adult consciousness of the author, is important. It gives a peculiarly French sense of control to his whole endeavor, and a valuable logical (or psychological) completeness to his work, in which is unfolded the process by which first a distinct and finally a supreme importance came to be attached to these sentiments of a previous experience. They are the precious moments of existence; they hold the secret of life. The growth of this conviction is the vital principle of Marcel Proust's book. The conviction becomes more immediate, the sense of obligation to devote himself to penetrating these moments more urgent, so that, even though the work is still unfinished, we can already see that the end will come when this necessity becomes fully

conscious and ineluctable—an end strictly and necessarily identical with the beginning. "A la Recherche du Temps Perdu" is at once a philosophical justification of its own existence and the history of its own creation.

That internal completeness is peculiar to Marcel Proust, and it gives him the position of conscious philosopher of a literary impulse which arose, quite independently, in two other minds at the same moment. Simply because it is the most conscious, Marcel Proust's effort subsumes those of James Joyce and Dorothy Richardson, though it is not for that reason more important than they. But common to them all is an insistence upon the immediate consciousness as reality. In Miss Richardson this insistence is probably instinctive and irrational; it has a distinctively feminine tinge. In James Joyce it is certainly deliberate, but less deliberate than in Marcel Proust. But the differences in conscious intention are unimportant compared with the similarity of the impulse.

To discover the origin of the impulse we should have to consider the history of the human consciousness, in its double form of sensibility and intelligence, from Rousseau through the nineteenth century. There we find the instinctive individualism of the artistic sensibility increasingly exacerbated by the sense that society in its new demo-plutocratic form had neither room nor respect for such an unprofitable activity of the human spirit as art. This increase of instinctive individualism received a rational reinforcement from the advance of science. The anthropocentric conception of the universe was finally abandoned, and an indifferent universe lent its weight to a hostile society in thrusting back the individual upon himself. The extremes of Romanticism receive a philosophical support from the doctrines of subjective idealism.

The extreme and deliberate subjectivism of the latest developments of fiction is the culmination of Rousseauism. Rousseau's social indifference allowed him to proclaim the intoxicating but misleading gospel that all men are spiritually equal, and the social consequences of that doctrine have made his descendants outlaws. They have accepted their destiny with a certain bravado, and have come to believe that social isolation is an eternal condition of artistic eminence. The conception of the artist as a superman is now more than a century old. The examples of Chateaubriand, Byron, Hugo, Baudelaire, Nietzsche, Dostoevsky, have given it the force of tradition, even of an absolute law. And science, by its necessary insistence on a fundamental materialism, has given the law a double sanction. It is not for us to lament over this evolution; at most we may have to consider whether a reaction against it is desirable, or possible, or probable. The important thing is to know where we are.

This movement towards artistic subjectivism has affected all the arts; but it is most obvious in prose fiction. The aim of the characteristic modern novelist—we are speaking only of those who consider the novel as a medium of expression which can satisfy the highest demands of the soul—is the presentation of his immediate consciousness. This alone is true, he believes; this alone is valuable or at any rate this alone has the chance of being of some permanent value. But the driving impulse is the demand for truth. A complete and fearless exploration of the self reduces the chance of self-deception to a minimum. To a generation before all things fearful of self-delusion the persuasion is of vital importance. And is it not merely carrying to a logical outcome the practice of all the great novelists of the past? They endure in so far as they have rendered their own consciousness of life. Not the stories they told but the comprehensive attitude to life embodied in their stories makes them important to us to-day. Then why not abolish the mechanism of the story completely, if the end to which it is a means can be achieved without it? And there is more than this. A story seems necessarily to involve a falsification, a distortion of the reality. Life does not shape itself into stories; much less does an individual and unique consciousness lend itself to complete expression by means of an invented plot. Let us do away with this illusory objectivity, this imposition of completeness and order upon the incomplete and chaotic. All that we can know is our own experience, and the closer we keep to the immediate quality of that experience, the nearer shall we be to truth.

Such are the arguments, conscious or unconscious, upon which the subjective movement in modern fiction depends. They are not final, but they are at least persuasive; and they are serious enough to show that the tendency which they support is more than a puerile esotericism. They remove all cause for wonder that many of the most gifted writers of the present generation have embraced it.

Nevertheless, the desire of the creative writer for objectivity cannot always be so easily suppressed. We have to take account of another movement, which may be described as an attempt, again no doubt not wholly conscious, to reconcile subjectivism with objectivity. To give it a label we may call

it the Chekhov tendency, although historically it seems to have originated with Baudelaire's "Prose Poems." But Baudelaire had no influence upon Chekhov, the direction of whose genius was finally determined, we believe, by the reading of Tolstoi's "Ivan Ilyitch." Like the subjectivists, Chekhov was obsessed by a passion for truth; like them he believed that the only reality was the individual consciousness; like them he had conceived a deep mistrust of the machine of story. But in a higher degree than they he possessed the purely creative genius of the writer, which is an instinct for objectivity and concreteness. He reconciled the two conflicting impulses in an individual creation. The short story of Chekhov was an innovation in literature. The immediate consciousness remains the criterion, and the method is based on a selection of those glimpses of the reality which in themselves possess a peculiar vividness, and by virtue of this vividness appear to have a peculiar significance. Baudeliare, who had practised the method, though on a simpler scale, with brilliant success in some of his "Prose Poems," defined the principle in words which are worth repeating. "Dans certains états de l'âme presque surnaturels," he said, "la profondeur de la vie se révéle toute entière dans le spectacle, si ordinaire qu'il soit, qu'on on a sous les yeux. Il en devient le symbole." ["In certain nearly supernatural states of the soul, the profundity of the life is revealed entirely in the scene, no matter how ordinary, that one has before his eyes. The scene becomes the symbol of the life."] This certainty that a fragment of experience is symbolic of the whole is subjective and immediate. The artist can attempt to present it without any misgivings about self-delusion or distortion. It was so; therefore it is true. Presented, the episode is objective, but its validity arises from an immediate intuition. To present such episodes with a minimum of rearrangement, as far as possible to eliminate the mechanism of invented story was Chekhov's aim. This is not to suggest that Chekhov invented nothing; but his constant effort was to reduce the part of invention. He strove rather to link moments of perception, than to expand the perception by invention. And certainly the impressive originality of his work lay in the closeness of his fidelity to immediate experience.

It was impossible for him, therefore, to write anything which could be reasonably given the name of a novel. Not, as some have said, because his constructive power was defective, but simply because the effort would have involved too wide a departure from the vivid moments of his own consciousness. He would have seemed to himself like the constructor of a metaphysical system, who leaves the solid ground of truth for cloudland. His feet once lifted from the firm earth, the very motive for flight would have failed him. What was the good of yet another attempt to impose finality upon the incessant?

But the method persists in advanced modern fiction as the internal antithesis to complete subjectivism. The most finished modern example is to be found in the short stories of Katherine Mansfield. The finest stories in "Bliss" and "The Garden Party" adhere closely to the Chekhov formula. But to speak of a formula is misleading. It is quite impossible to imitate, almost impossible to be influenced by, a method so completely intuitive as Chekhov's. It is simply that Miss Mansfield is a similar phenomenon: her work is of the same kind as Chekhov's, and precisely because it is of the same kind it is utterly different from his.

The two significant methods in the most modern fiction are, on the one hand, the presentation of a consciousness, on the other, the presentation of the vivid moments of a consciousness. Both are essentially subjective. They differ, however, in this important particular that, whereas the subjectivist novelists seem to be chiefly moved by a desire to express the truth, the story-writers aim at an art which is compatible with the truth. The most obvious consequence is that the second are much more easily comprehensible than the first, because they speak a universal language. A writer who presents a thing perceived, interests us immediately, because there is common ground between his perception and our own. It is also easier for us to appreciate the individual quality of his consciousness than to appreciate that quality in a writer who is engaged in insisting upon his consciousness. In a short story by Chekhov or Miss Mansfield it is as though an intense beam of peculiar light were cast upon a fragment of reality. By watching the objects revealed by it, we can far more easily tell the color of the light than we could if the color were described to us: above all, because we are made sensible of the light at the moment when it is, or is felt by the writer to be, most different from the ordinary light—"dans certains états de l'âme presque *surnaturels*."

On the other hand, an extreme subjectivism, without the control of this intuitive selection, tends to become incomprehensible. A consciousness is a flux, it needs to be crystallized about some foreign object to have an intelligible shape. Marcel Proust's historical and philosophical preoccupations supply such a thread; but even he can be excessively tedious when his grasp on the external world is slackened.

Miss Richardson can be as tiring as a twenty-four-hour cinematograph without interval or plot. And in "Ulysses" James Joyce at times carries his effort of analysis to such lengths as to become as difficult as a message in code of which half the key has been lost. The process of consciousness has, indeed, a fatal fascination for him, and he perceptibly diminishes the significance of two such splendidly conceived (or observed) characters as Leopold and Marion Bloom by his inability to stop recording their processes of mind. Nevertheless, we must freely admit that "Ulysses" is a magnificent attempt by an extreme subjectivist to overcome the formlessness into which the method must so easily degenerate. The narrative, more or less remotely based upon the Odyssey, is enclosed within the limits of a day in Dublin twenty years ago. All the characters who come into contact with the hero's consciousness have a place in it, and the minds of two of them are submitted to the same exhaustive analysis as his own. But in spite of this considerable degree of objectivity, a complete and satisfying clarity is seldom attained. The objective is chiefly an excuse for another plunge into subjectivity, and we become weary of the effort to follow the processes of three different minds. For us they are exhausted long before Mr. Joyce has done with them. We long to escape from this iron wall of consciousness of which we are everywhere made sensible and to be allowed to trust to the revelation of the object. But we are forbidden. Either the consciousness of Bloom-Ulysses, or of Marion-Penelope, or of Mr. Joyce in his avatar as Stephen Dedalus-Telemachus, or in his apotheosis as the demiurge of the book itself, is ever before us to mist and complicate the thing we desire to see. Mr. Joyce is determined to give us everything, by devious and super-subtle ways: a day of human existence, with all its heritage of the past, its dreams of the future, shall be completely explored.

"Ulysses" is a work of genius; but in spite of its objective moments, it is also a *reductio ad absurdum* of subjectivism. It is the triumph of the desire to discover the truth over the desire to communicate that which is felt as truth. This desire to communicate is, so far as we can see, essential to literature, though not to genius; nor is it by any means necessary that a perceived truth should be communicated. But literature is, almost by definition, a communication of intuitions; and they can only be communicated in terms of a generally perceived reality. It is as though the external world were a common language which the writer speaks with new inflections and accents, giving new life to the old and revealing a hidden significance in the familiar. The writer's duty is to make the approach to his intuitions and sentiments as simple as possible, and he does this by shaping the common reality in accordance with them, so that the reality becomes the symbol of his profoundest certainties.

In this process Mr. Joyce is only casually interested. Rather than sacrifice one atom of his truth of detail, he is arcane and incomprehensible; and it is impossible not to feel he enjoys his own mysteriousness. It gives some kind of fillip to his self-engrossment. "Ulysses" contains many scattered patches of surprising beauty, and at least one sustained passage of metaphysical comedy which justifies our comparing his imaginative powers with those of Goethe and Dostoevsky, but as a whole we must consider it a gigantic aberration, a colossal waste of genius, the last extravagance of Romanticism. Whether the dangers of the Romantic apotheosis of "The Artist," the spiritual outlaw who is glorified by his rejection of all social obligations, even to the last obligation of being comprehensible, needed this ocular demonstration, we cannot tell; but now that we have it we can be grateful for it. The many-minded, the much-wandering Ulysses has ended his voyages, by stranding his ship at the side of the sea. It is not, as some timid spirits seem to fear, a danger to navigation; it is a valuable sea-mark which will warn future voyagers of the futility of no-compromise.

For the art of literature is based upon a compromise. The writer who does not accept the condition may be a man of genius, but he is an imperfect writer. As Goethe said, the writer who writes without the conviction that he will have a million readers has mistaken his vocation. Moreover, it is much easier to be complicated than to be simple, to be mysterious than to be intelligible. The great writer is the man who, without betraying the complexity of his own consciousness, insists on discovering a means of expressing his consciousness in relatively simple terms. It is easy to plunge into the strangest depths of individual sensation:

> sed revocare gradum, superasque evadere ad auras hoc opus, hic labor est. [but to recover the degree, and to turn this sensation to the light of day, here is the toil.]

And this toil, this labor is vital to literature. Only when it has been faced and accomplished does a book possess the mysterious quality in virtue of which we pronounce it a masterpiece, namely, that it gives delight at every level of apprehension. A truly great novel is a tale to the simple, a parable to the wise, and a direct revelation of reality in the light of a unique consciousness to the man who has made it his own.

For this reason it seems that the story is necessary to the novel. It is the means by which the novelist completely projects and embodies his own emotional attitude to life. It is the comprehensible symbol which is the condition of lucidity. Nevertheless, as the complexity of the modern consciousness increases, it is inevitable that the traditional form of story, the simple invented sequence of act and consequence, should appear inadequate to a condition of which a shrinking mistrust of action is one of the most constant elements. The problem that Shakespeare tried to solve when he wrote "Hamlet" still rises before the modern novelist. And there is a further complication which can hardly have been present to Shakespeare's mind. After the nineteenth century it is impossible for the serious writer of fiction to be wholly immune from the influence of a scientific standard of truth. The bold abbreviations of heroic fable are not for him; the comfortable finalities of "a good plot" with its suicides and deaths and unchallengeable felicities are psychologically impossible. He envies the men of old who could invoke their aid with such sublime nonchalance, but he dare not, he cannot imitate them. He is preoccupied with a loyalty to the real, and he satisfies it, as we have seen, either by a surrender to the movement of his own consciousness, or by an insistence upon the moments when the consciousness is scattered by the significant intrusion of the real world.

Thus we have, in advanced modern fiction, the striking antithesis between the big books and the little ones, corresponding to the complete history of a consciousness and its most objective moments. In the big books there are moments which have the vividness of the little ones, because they have the same basis of immediately perceived reality. But in the big books these moments are quickly swallowed up in the analytic subtleties of the narrative as a whole. For hours the mist drags slowly over the mountain-side. Suddenly, there is a burst of blue sky, a streaming sun, and the trees, the valley, the river, and the mountain-tops shine for a moment with miraculous brilliance. Then the mist closes down once more. In the little books we have a sequence of those visions with no intervening mists. But even in them the shining light cannot be steadily maintained; its brilliance depends upon its suddenness, upon an absorption of the whole consciousness by the apparition of reality, a condition which, however frequent in a writer of genius, is a momentary one. He can hardly give us a continuous vision at the same degree of illumination; at most he gives us a sequence of detached visions.

Therefore we may speak, without rhetoric, of the break-up of the novel. We do not have to deplore the disintegration. Obviously, we are in a period of transition, in which new elements are being gathered together for a more perfect artistic realization in the future. New standards of truth, new standards of brilliance and directness in presentation, are being introduced into fiction. When they have been absorbed, the art of the novel will obey its own internal law as an art of literature and evolve towards a new combination of lucidity and comprehensiveness. At present the comprehensiveness is massed on one side and the lucidity upon the other of the small band of important writers of modern fiction. No single writer has been big enough to make the artistic synthesis, so that the only possible synthesis at this moment is the critical one. But we do not doubt that the artistic synthesis will be made. It may be that the divided elements will unite only to divide again into two separate literary achievements. There is a portion of "Ulysses" where Mr. Joyce shows that the strongest part of his talent is magnificently comic.

Satirical Aristophanic comedy is the true satisfaction of exasperation. There never was such an utterly exasperated age as this, in which a universal materialism is opposed by a universal hypersensitiveness. Exasperation is continually manifest as a disturbing influence in the work of such writers of English as Mr. Lawrence, Mr. Pound, Mr. Eliot, Mr. Wyndham Lewis, and, above all, in Mr. Joyce himself; in many of the modern Parisians like Paul Morand and Louis Aragon; in a Russian like Ivan Bunin. Bunin's story, "The Gentleman from San Francisco," comes perhaps nearest to giving it complete artistic expression; but his manner is too minatory and apocalyptic. The liberation of Aristophanic comedy is its ideal expression. These writ-

ers are sometimes on the brink of it. Besides Mr. Joyce the only one who has taken the plunge is M. Morand, who has recently published a remarkable book of stories, "Ouvert la Nuit," in which the comic synthesis is very evident.

We should like to imagine that the exasperation of the modern sensibility will be crystallized out into a new Aristophanism, a new Rabelaisianism, so that an explosive condition might find its proper satisfaction in an explosive art. It would help to clear the ground for the necessary development of the calmer art of the novel, and to clear the minds of those who will have to address themselves to the problem of finding lucid symbols for the complexities they wish to convey. Undoubtedly, there is a means of satisfying the new standards of fidelity to experience without recourse to obscurity and hieroglyphics. The road may not be easy to find, but it must be found. Otherwise the novel will reach the ridiculous position in which all that is interesting is unintelligible and all that is intelligible is uninteresting. That moment, indeed, seems at times to be very near. But we believe the danger is not really serious. Art has a way of surviving the most inevitable disasters. The present unsettlement of the art of fiction is perhaps hardly more than a crisis of indigestion.

Prose fiction is the only vital and comprehensive literary form to-day. After a long period of constraint under the prestige of Flaubert it has had suddenly to accommodate itself to the immense reality of the nineteenth century. For many years the novelist has believed that the nineteenth century was Flaubert and Turgenev; now it turns out to have been Stendhal, Baudelaire, Nietzsche, Dostoevsky, Tolstoi, and Chekhov, and heaven knows what in science besides. We cannot wonder if modern fiction has bad dreams; only if it were not disturbed would there be cause for wonder, and alarm.

Reprinted from *Yale Review,* 12 (1922): 288-304.

Wyndham Lewis

From *Time and Western Man*

I have advanced throughout this essay a carefully constructed body of criticism against various contemporary literary and other modes of thought and methods of expression. I have chosen for discussion for the most part strongly established leaders, of mature talent; and have examined individual work in some detail. This hostile analysis in its entirety has been founded upon those wider considerations that I shall now at least adumbrate.

I will revert to a few of the instances chosen and once more pass them rapidly in review, in the light of this last and more general phase of my argument. Miss Stein I have dealt with at some length, but not because she seems to me a writer of any great importance; rather, living comfortably at the heart of things, and associated with all the main activities of the time, she is a rallying point that it was convenient to take. In her recent pieces her attack upon the logical architecture of words is in its result flat and literally meaningless, I think. Her attempt to use words as though they were sounds purely or "sound-symbols," or as though their symbolism could be distorted or suppressed sufficiently to allow of a "fugue" being made out of a few thousand of them, is a technical mistake, I believe. It is only doing what the musician has been doing for three centuries, but doing it poorly, because the instrument of speech on the one hand, and the verbal symbolism on the other, will not, in the case of words, yield such a purity of effect.

Again, Pound seems in somewhat the same difficulty as Miss Stein—lost half-way between one art and another. Pound's desertion of poetry for music may mean that music is really his native art; and having been misled early in life into the practice of an art in which he had nothing whatever to say, he is now painfully attempting to return to the more fluid abstract medium of musical composition. . . .

The psychology of the different arts—of the visual, static arts, of the art of pure sound, of literature with its apparatus of intellectual symbolism, and so on—has been attended to very little. It may be that as a painter I find it easier to be logical and, at least in writing, to remain technically intact, and do not make allowance enough for the itch, so often found in the writer, to do a little painting in words, or to play the musician. I do not propose to go into that question here. But for our present purposes let us imagine a person so complexly talented that he could with equal effect express himself in musical composition, painting, sculpture or writing— Samuel Butler's ideal person. I think, then, that we should find that that person's writing would show little tendency to divest words of their symbolism, or to distort them, nor to do imitational or "literary" music, nor to tell stories in paint. The rather shallow "revolutionism" that consists in a partial merging of two or more arts would be spared him. He would achieve such a complete revolution every time he dropped from one of his accomplishments into the other, that he would have no incentive to hybrid experiment. He would be the purest possible artist in each of his arts. It is even quite possible to affirm that no artist with only one art in which to express himself, can keep that one art entirely intact and pure.

The powerful impressionism of *Ulysses,* constructed on the most approved "time"-basis—that is, a basis of the fluid material gushing of undisciplined life—I have chosen as in some ways the most important creation so far issued from the "time" mint. The approved "mental" method—dating from the publication of *Matiere de Memoire* or of the earliest psycho-analytic tracts—leads, as it is intended to lead, to a physical disintegration and a formal confusion. A highly personal day-dream, culminating in a phantasmagoria of the pure dream-order, is the result in *Ulysses.* It is a masterpiece of romantic art: and its romance is of the sort imposed by the "time" philosophy. Whimsically, but like much romantic art, it is founded on a framework of classical antiquity—about which its author is very romantic indeed.

....

Before closing this part of my essay I will examine for a moment one aspect of the literary problem that I have neglected; namely, the *politics of style,* as it might be called.

In literature it should always be recalled that what we read is the speech of some person or other, explicit or otherwise. There is a *style* and *tone* in any statement, in any collection of sentences. We can formulate this in the following way: *There is an organic norm to which every form of speech is related. A human individual, living a certain kind of life, to whom the words and style would be appropriate, is implied in all utterance.*

A great many writers to-day are affecting, by their style, to be children. What is implied in much of the writing of Miss Stein, and, of course, of Miss Loos, is the proposition: "I am a child." Another thing that is also very prevalent is a choice of idiom, and of delivery, that is intended to reassure the reader of the mass-democracy that all is well, and that the writer is one of the crowd; a Plain-Man, just another humble cell in the vast democratic body like anybody else; not a detested "highbrow." This is so much the case that occasionally you meet in american papers the remark, in the review of a book, that so and so is "a gentleman writer." This evidently means that a certain absence of slavishness, of gleeful and propitiatory handrubbing, of slang, of a hundred tricks to put the Democracy at its ease, is absent from the work in question. This absence of what is expected of a writer has caused a shock of astonishment in the reviewer. He registers his surprise.

There are as many ways of expressing yourself as there are days in the year; there are all the varieties of stammer and maunder of the idiot, there is all the range of "quaint" naivete of childhood; all the crabbed dialects of toil, the slang of a hundred different "sets" and occupations, the solecisms and parodies of the untaught; there is the pomp of the law and the polish of the aristocratic heyday of european letters. There is the style of the *code Napoleon,* which was Stendhal's model. And in any language there is that most lucid, most logical rendering of the symbols of speech which people employ when they wish to communicate anything as clearly as possible, and are very anxious to be understood. The latter is, after all, the best guarantee you can have that affectation and self-consciousness will be absent from the style in which you are to be addressed. There you get the minimum of fuss or of mannerism. When the mind is most active it is least personal, least mannered.

The psychology at the back of various styles or modes we have been considering is to that extent political, therefore, in the sense that the *child-cult* is a political phenomenon, and without the child-cult men and women of letters would not be expressing themselves in the language and with the peculiarities of infancy. . . .

....

. . . But it is a very curious question indeed to what extent the political atmosphere of the day must modify written speech, or even break it up altogether.

Can language hold out in any degree against politics, when politics are so extremely fluid, and, inevitably, so indifferent to the arts engendered in words? It would be a pity if we were prevented from communicating lucidly and grammatically with each other. There I must leave that question; its applications to the work I have been discussing will be immediately apparent.

For any intelligent European or American the point has certainly been reached where he has to summon whatever resolution he may possess and make a fundamental decision. He has to acquaint himself first of all with the theory of, and then decide what is to be his attitude towards, the time-cult, which is the master-concept of our day. This essay may, I hope, provide him with an adequate conspectus of the positions and source of the issues involved; and it has the initial advantage of not being an arbitrary or frivolous statement, nor one that can be represented as put forward just in order to be "contrary," since it embodies the practical reactions of a worker in one of the great intellectual fields, threatened by the ascendancy of such a cult.

Reprinted from *Time and Western Man* (London: Chatto & Windus, 1927), pp. 131-135.

Elizabeth A. Drew

From "A Note on Technique," in her *The Modern Novel: Some Aspects of Contemporary Fiction*

. . . Art lives upon variety of attempt and the shifting of standpoints, and whatever its detractors may say of the contemporary world of letters, no one can deny it its energetic and indefatigable curiosity in exploring fresh possibilities in its own kingdom. And like most young things, it starts by pointing out the disabilities of its parents. In a recently published essay on the technique of novel-writing, *Mr. Bennett and Mrs. Brown,* Virginia Woolf throws down a challenge to the "Edwardian" novelists, and declares the arrival of a new age in England, the neo-Georgian. She explains that the same experience inspires novelists in all ages.

> Some [Mrs.] Brown, Smith or Jones comes before them, and says in the most seductive and charming way in the world, "Come and catch me if you can." And so, led on by this will o' the wisp, they flounder through volume after volume. . . . Few catch the phantom; most have to be content with a scrap of her dress or a wisp of her hair.

Mrs. Woolf then declares that the Edwardians (Bennett, Wells, and Galsworthy) never look directly at human nature—always at its surroundings; that their one idea has been to interpret character through environment, an idea which necessitates failure, since "novels are in the first place about people and only in the second place about the houses they live in." The Georgians, therefore, have felt that they simply cannot let "Mrs. Brown" be interpreted through environment any more, but that she must be rescued and expressed by some way which makes her more living and more real.

The Georgians, then, on their own showing, are aiming at the same thing as their predecessors—the creation of complete human character. They have no obscure and enigmatical goal which the average reader cannot understand, and they themselves challenge comparison with the older generation in the same field and on the same terms. On equal terms means, of course, that the critic must accustom himself to whatever is unfamiliar in their methods; must be receptive towards a new line of vision, and eager to recognize an extension of his own human and artistic experience through contact with a new human and artistic creation. On these terms, then, let us consider some of Mrs. Brown's new champions and their achievements.

....

. . . This new technique of presenting characters from oblique angles with nothing but the play of glancing lights and shadows upon its half tones, does convey, however, a particular flavour of life on the emotional palate, which is most significant of the present day. It transmits a sense of great intensity to detached moments of experience; it emphasizes the sudden, revealing emotional and intellectual stroke; it probes with searching perception into fugitive and flickering mood, and reminds the reader on every page that as matter is made up of invisible individual electrons, so is experience made up of the silt of unremembered fleeting instants of passing consciousness. It is peculiar in stressing the importance of those individual instants *in themselves* to the almost total neglect of the importance they may have in relation to a general survey of human life—hence the effect of inconsequence which all this kind of writing leaves. Can we interpret this insistence on the "discontinuousness" of experience, as we interpret most of the characteristics, social and literary, of the present-day intelligentsia, by its renunciation of a definite point of view, by its dislike of embodying any activity, cosmic or human, within the bounds of a fixed outline? Is this technique a literary parallel to those painters who attempt to suggest energy by breaking up figures and projecting their parts on to different planes so as to give an impression of movement; who strive to suggest the infinity of design by leaving patterns incomplete; whose ideal is abstract form? The aim of such writers is, presumably, to give an impression of the ceaseless activity of life, while at the same time suggesting the sense of its inconclusive character—its inexorable habit of merely adding day to day instead of building itself into the convenient symmetry of a plot. . . .

....

The craftsmanship of these novels embodies to perfection all the sharp, shifting sense of the disconnection, the irrelevance in the facts and experiences of life, in the emotions and thoughts of man's heart and mind, and the uncontrolled impulses of his unconscious being, on which there is so obvious an emphasis to-day. Its interpretation of this vision of existence is elaborate and striking, but with all its brilliance of workmanship, its sensitive use of word and cadence, its feeling for the shapely structure of language, and the exquisite keenness of

its human and intellectual comment and criticism, I wonder if it will ever catch a very solid and substantial "Mrs. Brown" in its delicate cobwebs.

Reprinted from *The Modern Novel: Some Aspects of Contemporary Fiction* (New York: Harcourt, Brace, 1926), pp. 243-262.

John D. Beresford

From "Experiment in the Novel," in his *Tradition and Experiment in Present-Day Literature:*
Addresses Delivered at the City Literary Institute

. . . Let us come now to that development of ultra-realism. The tradition of the English novel has always been realistic in the main, and by realistic I intend the mode that inclines to portray the real rather than the ideal, that takes its body from life rather than from imagination. . . .

. . . .
. . . the principle implicit in this [ultra-realism] is to eliminate the more marked incidents of human life, just those incidents, such as love and marriage, that have always been the favourite subject for fiction. Let us call those outstanding and inferentially more interesting episodes the "high spots," and come to the consideration of novels that seek to tell a story without reference to these sporadic crises in our history. Virginia Wolff's [sic] *The Voyage Out* may be taken as an early example, but the theory has been developed in what I may perhaps describe as its utmost purity by Miss Dorothy Richardson.

She is one of those inspired and yet deliberate experimenters who have founded a School. So able and famous a writer as Miss May Sinclair openly avowed discipleship in her novel, *Mary Olivier*. And the fact that that School has not flourished is probably due to the strong current that ever since the end of the War has been setting back so strongly in the direction of romance.

Miss Richardson sat down to write the story of her own life, in the person of Miriam Henderson, with the clearest possible conception of what she intended to do. She claimed, for example, that what I have referred to as the "high spots" (a definition I have borrowed from her own conversation) were only so by reason of the emphasis that have been

laid upon them by the novelists; and that in the adventure of the personality, which should be the true subject for the novelist, the "high spots" are of an entirely different order. To demonstrate this contention Miss Richardson invented a new method. Many other novelists before her had told their stories through the consciousness of one of their characters, but Miss Richardson's liaison with the consciousness of Miriam Henderson is so close that we see nothing, hear nothing, feel nothing except through Miriam's senses.

Now as a logical consequence of this—and Miss Richardson is essentially logical in the development of her method—there must be a different record of movement in space and time. The consciousness is not always attentive to its present circumstances. . . . In the series of books—nine of them have now been published—dealing with the experiences of Miriam Henderson, the personality of Miss Richardson, the writer, is entirely absorbed into that of Miss Richardson the experiencer. She cannot, therefore, come out and join up her account of incidents and emotions as all other novelists do by a few words or lines of condensed explanation; for to do that would be momentarily to forsake the consciousness of Miriam Henderson. Thus whereas the orthodox novelist would explain that his heroine left the house, went out by the garden gate, walked across two or three fields and entered the wood; Miss Richardson either skips all account of the transition, or if some emotion experienced in the transit be necessary to her unfolding of Miriam, we suffer it subjectively. We begin, for example, in the house, then suffer some reaction at the sight of a field of daffodils, and thereafter without further copula find ourselves responding to the influences of the Spring wood.

This is certainly the most daring and far-reaching experiment that has up to this point engaged our attention. We may find some precedent for it in the work of Marcel Proust, and I shall presently come to another just recognizably similar experiment in James Joyce's *Ulysses*. But Miss Richardson's work is, nevertheless, unique in fiction (none of her disciples has ever dared the full implications of her theory) and has a metaphysical value that is absent in Proust or Joyce.

For neither of these writers is inspired by the mystical quality that is peculiar to Miss Richardson. Joyce and Proust are objective in their methods more often than not. We are constantly aware of the person of the recorder as opposed to that of the experiencer. Dorothy Richardson has assumed the existence of a soul to which the consciousness has much the same relation that the intelligence has to the consciousness. In *Pointed Roofs*—the first of the Miriam Henderson series—and in all the subsequent volumes, the ebb and flow of Miriam's consciousness, touched now and again to vivid response, at other times somewhat drearily aware of the limitations of physical experience, is the sole agent of the author's expression.

As a consequence the "high spots" of our earlier illustration differ completely in kind from those deemed most interesting for a physical record. The great moments of Miriam's experience are not found in moving adventure nor in moments of physical stress, but at those times when she is most keenly aware of herself in relation to the spirit that moves beneath and animates every phenomenon of the great phantasmagoria we know as life and matter. I am willing to maintain that the realistic method can go no farther than this, for reality is not a term that we can define, and the view of it differs with every individual. If, therefore, we wish to present an aspect of reality, we can do it consistently only by assuming its presentation through the consciousness of a single individual.

....

I have already touched upon this metaphysical aspect of the novelist's relation to his material in speaking of the works of Dorothy Richardson, and now, in conclusion, I want to suggest to you that this great diversity of realities lies at the very heart of our subject.

I have in this lecture dealt exclusively with realist fiction. The romantics seldom, and the classicists never, enter the ranks of the experimenters. If

I sit down to tell you a story out of my head, I shall choose inevitably an accepted, traditional form for the telling of it. By that means my task will be made easier and you will more quickly understand. That road has been well laid and hedged, and why should we not follow it? But if I want to give you a nearer and nearer transcript of life as I have seen it, I find that it cannot be done by following the old signposts. And the more ardent the realism, the greater the necessity to experiment with new methods—until, as I think you will agree, a few modern writers have cast aside the last restrictions of classical form.

And with that gesture of liberation has gone also certain other restrictions, most prominently that of morals. . . . But in the twentieth century our experimenters . . . meant to portray life as they saw it rather than as the moralists insist that it ought to be. And these two declarations of liberty, one for freedom of form and the other for freedom of material, lie behind all the experiments of recent fiction.

And, to get back to my metaphysical thesis, the diverse shapes these experiments have taken are due to the fact that we all have different conceptions of reality. This has always been true, of course. No two people can ever see the same rainbow, and no two people have precisely the same impression of life. But in such an age as the Victorian, there is a greater tendency to merge the individual concept in the group. . . .

With the turn of the century and still more markedly as a result of the effects of the Great War, this group thinking has been broken up. There has been a manifest tendency in life and letters to pull down the old images. Society, government, religion are regarded as relatively unstable. There is an increasing body of people who are losing their faith in the old Institutions. And this scepticism has inevitably had its effect upon the novel. In the stable days of Queen Victoria, a Dickens, a Thackeray, or a Trollope could sit down to his desk with a comfortable sense of assurance that he knew the public for which he was writing and was himself a member of it. He might be an exceptional member, he might have gifts of eloquence, of observation, of insight, that raised him to a platform above the shoulders of the crowd he was addressing. But in the main their beliefs were his also, their reality and his own held enough points of likeness to permit freedom of communication. Also for public purposes, at least, there was but one morality.

Now that comfortable sense of assurance no longer exists for us, and the sincere novelist who writes because he, or she, wishes to express a personal relation to experience, must write as an individual and not as a member of a group. There is no longer the least assurance that the novelist's reality is the same as that of a sufficiently large body of people to ensure popularity. . . .

Reprinted from *Tradition and Experiment in Present-Day Literature: Addresses Delivered at the City Literary Institute* (London: Oxford University Press, 1929), pp. 23-53.

Joseph Warren Beach

"The Modernists," in his *The Twentieth Century Novel: Studies in Technique*

When we speak of the new men, we must start with Conrad, who began writing in the eighteen-nineties, before James was through and before Dreiser had begun. For Conrad was the great experimentalist of his day. He was as ill content with ready-made ways of putting a story together as with ready-made ways of interpreting character. And he did more than any one else to limber up the stiff machine of fiction. And then we must take into account the solitary figure of Lawrence, who, being a painter, brought to fiction some of the subtleties of pictorial art, and, wrestling with the mysteries of sex psychology, stumbled on a technique suited to that elusive subject. These writers are transitional; and as such it will be most convenient to regard Dorothy Richardson, though she was so radical in some of her methods. It is most convenient to consider these three writers together and apart from those who came in with Joyce, whom I call expressionists. But in characterizing the modernists as a whole, in brief anticipation, and in broad contrast to the school of James, it is possible to lump together these transitional writers with those who followed them.

The new men are naturally affected by the new psychology. Modern psychology does not conceive the soul as something which can be adequately rendered in terms of a single dramatic action with a highly simplified issue. It is not something to be caught in the net of neat intellectual definition. The soul is not that simple entity offered to us in most works of fiction. It is a vast fluid, or even vaporous, mass, wide-spreading far beyond the feeble village lights of our conventional reading of character, deep-sounding into our nervous and animal organization, into childhood, heredity. It runs out and down far beyond thought, beyond memory and consciousness. It is not uniform and homogeneous, but varying and full of a great diversity of tinctures and infusions. There are all sorts of debris and

driftwood floating on the surface, and huge water-soaked logs lurking far below. At the bottom is mud, and in the depths are octopuses and starfish and all kinds of undreamed-of monsters. The soul is not one identity but many identities grouped about many centers and often at war with one another, or indifferent and unaware of one another's existence.

For the most part it is no identity at all, but a kind of dreaming welter of sensations and reactions so instantaneous and spontaneous that we never become conscious of them. In many aspects the soul is not individualized as belonging to this or that ego, but is a mere jet of the vitality common to our race or sex or social group. Our consciousness, which is a small part of our soul, does not proceed logically or coherently except at certain times and for certain periods under the pressure of some urgent practical need. For the most part it follows an association of ideas so freakish—though natural—that we cannot chart its progress, running off constantly into what seem irrelevancies as judged by reference to any recognized dominant interest. The soul is supremely indifferent to past and future, near and far. It is a highly specialized faculty of our rational mind that has devised these conventions, these instruments for controlling material things and guiding conduct. Each soul is attached to an individual physical organism; but through the imagination, through the infinite nervous connections between organism and organism, souls have a large capacity for interpenetration. A large part of the life of the soul may be regarded in the light of group actions and reactions.

In short, it becomes more and more awkward and queer to use the term "soul" to cover the phenomena in question. We might try the word "psyche," which is not quite so heavily weighted with discordant connotations.

The new writers are as much concerned as the

old ones with the psyche as the focus of life experience. Only, with their modern conception of the psyche, they grow more and more impatient of the quaint little patterns into which the old psychological novelists had tried to force this protean creature, and their disposition to ignore all sorts of things that go to make up human personality. And the new writers have felt the need to break up these conventional patterns. They have wanted new technical devices, new procedures, for rendering the psyche. In general the new features of their technique are expressions of what is called the romantic as opposed to the classic spirit in art.

Instead of regularity of form, they show a tendency to what at first blush appears a freakish changefulness and unpredictability. Analysis will show that, for the most part, form is not with them so freakish as it seems, perhaps not freakish at all. Only, their principles of form are not those which have been traditional for the novel. They are not determined by the plot, as with Fielding or Trollope; neither are they determined, generally, by that simple dramatic issue which is the form taken by plot in the well-made novel. So that, in their reaction from the particular rigid form favored by their predecessors, we may speak, provisionally, of their tendency to *deformalization*.

Instead of uniformity and simplicity, they tend to diversity and complexity. In this respect they show a superficial resemblance to the earlier Victorian novelists, with their abundance and colorful variety of material. And yet the spirit and technique and dominant preoccupations of the new men are so different from those of the Victorians that no one would dream of comparing the two schools.

Instead of concentration around a limited issue, they show an eccentric tendency, a tendency to fly off in many different directions.

Instead of continuity of action, they show a tendency to discontinuity. A continuous action seems to them too unlike ordinary experience, with its freakish, accidental interruptions, its overleapings of time and circumstance. They feel that the sense of life is often best rendered by an abrupt passing from one series of events, one group of characters, one center of consciousness, to another.

Moreover, they don't particularly care about neatly finishing off a given action, following it through to the fall of the curtain. As the eye, from a line of spaced dots and dashes, has the faculty of supplying what is not there and tracing an uninterrupted line, they know the imagination has the faculty of filling up the gaps in an action presented in fragments, of getting the impression of an entire life from a mere hinting indication of the high moments. Again, they feel that the imagination is stimulated and rendered more active, is actually exhilarated, by broken bits of information, as the nerves are stimulated by the discontinuity of an electric current.

Want of continuity, yes—but not of a sort of rhythm, a sense of movement, of wave-like progress. This rhythm is not metrical like that of verse, but is constituted by repetition, by recurrence of themes, by a kind of lyrical agitation of the stream of consciousness. The word "rhythm" is here used in the sense in which it is applied to the similar quality of well-constructed pictures, especially the abstract paintings which are called post-impressionistic.

Instead of dramatic effect, these men go in for something more like lyricism.

They show a tendency to throw overboard terms intellectual, logical, sentimental. They rely more on impressions of the senses—on a mere succession of sensations—for rendering the psyche. Their idea is perhaps to make the effect at the same time more real and less sharply defined. There are two ways in which this greater reality is brought about by the exploitation of sensations. So largely, by this means, one gets rid of the author's intellectual formulation of the thought-process, which is likely to interfere with directness of presentation and throw its conventional film over everything. And then this method conforms to the actual thought-process, which is chiefly made up of items of sensation, rather than being a connected chain of logical reasoning.

The new men do not represent a sharp and complete break with tradition. In particular, some of them have learned a great deal from the well-made novel. But it will be seen how much they were in reaction against most of its main tendencies. And in general their motive has been to give new life to a form which, in the hands of the writers of that school, had become so impoverished and anemic.

Reprinted from *The Twentieth Century Novel: Studies in Technique* (New York: Appleton-Century-Crofts, 1932), pp. 332-336.

Mary Colum

From "The Revolt," in her *From These Roots: The Ideas That Have Made Modern Literature*

1

In the inner courts of literature, for over fifty years there has been a struggle against the doctrine, the technique, the content, and the language of realism. It began in France, for it was there that the doctrine and the practice had ripened fastest, and the revolt was in full blast before the original doctrine had reached some of the other literatures. The revolters made little headway as far as the novel and drama went, for it was to the interest, not only of the real writers in these forms, but especially of a large group of the new trade writers, to hold the novel and the drama bound to the fact, the document, the observation of external and everyday life. Realism had such sanction that any sort of novel or drama that people could recognize as a transcript of life at first hand was regarded as superior in literary merit to romance and adventure writing of any kind. . . . The Goncourts' term for non-realistic literature, "anodyne," used by them in 1865, became current in America sixty years later as "escapist" literature and was used in the same disparaging sense with regard to any literature of the imagination. A poem like Lindsay's "The Chinese Nightingale," a novel like Thornton Wilder's *The Bridge of San Luis Rey,* were attacked because the authors did not come "to grips with life," and did not deal with strikes, modern industrial life, with economic struggle. . . . As the radical middle-class intelligentsia, interested in political and social reforms, increased in every country, realistic writing became more and more popular and profitable, for it could be made to reflect the special problems of the moment, and be a sort of history of the day.

There was, as has already been noted, a school of poetry, the Parnassian, which corresponded in a manner to the higher realism in prose. The leader of this school, Théophile Gautier, who called himself "a man for whom the exterior world exists," made an effort to translate into poetry the exterior world that he observed and knew, without injecting into it his own personality. Trained in painting, he tried to reproduce in language the effects of painting; his observations he translated into precise images and words, for he prided himself on the exactitude of his imagery and his vocabulary. He and the other Parnassians tried to produce a poetry that was hard, clear and impersonal. The bulk of the Parnassian theories, mixed with a few theories from the Symbolists, was taken over between 1910 and 1920 by a short-lived school of English and American poets who called themselves "Imagists."

2

The first clear indication of a strong revolt against realism was given in poetry. Of the two who began the revolt, Paul Verlaine and Arthur Rimbaud, both were in descent from Baudelaire, though they started with a leaning towards the Parnassians. . . .

. . . .

. . .Rimbaud and Verlaine were the last great French poets; there have been distinguished poets since, but no really great ones. When Rimbaud vanished from the literary scene, leaving his small bulk of work behind him, his admirers said that he had left with Verlaine the secret of the poetry of the future.

If a writer of great genius had then appeared, who could have taken over "the secret," who was capable of making a new synthesis of the exterior and the interior life, of the dream life and the everyday life, another new creative age might have been inaugurated. But the men who took it over, the Symbolists, were not able to use it in a way to render any powerful service to literature. The turning away from the exterior and the concentration on the interior world became, in their case, as exaggerated as the concentration of the realists on the physical world. If the realists de-valued the life of the spirit, the bulk of the Symbolists rejected physical and everyday life as matter for literature in a manner which was destined to be not only limiting but even sterilizing. They were, in the main, accomplished and subtle men of letters, with a gift for poetry, a great flair for theorizing, and an excited interest in anything that seemed to lead to literary reform, such as the verse-forms of Whitman and the poetry and criticism of Edgar Allan Poe.

3

While the Symbolists were the most interesting literary group of the late nineteenth century, interesting for their theories and for their attempts to

343

put them into practice, their chief doctrines did not originate with them, and the ones that did, the minor doctrines, were too esoteric and even eccentric to have vigorous life. . . . What the Symbolists accomplished separately is, in the case of most of them, not of so much importance as the general influence that emanated from the group. They were deliberately in revolt against realism and Parnassianism, more deliberately than were Rimbaud and Verlaine, though the core of their ideas came from these two predecessors. They also believed that inner reality is the only reality, and that the world from which a poet draws his poetry is a transcendent world, outside the everyday world. The whole art of poetry needed to be renewed, and the poetry of the future would be different from the poetry of the past, which had been made—and especially in French—with the same language and according to the same grammatical rules as prose. For the making of *this* poetry, the poetry of the future, the common, logical language, created for practical everyday usage, was no longer suitable; the very words that made up the language were conditioned by everyday employment and were incapable of encompassing ideas from the other world, the transcendent world of dream and poetry. Mallarmé, like Rimbaud, conceived of this language as weighing down poetry with the weight of lead.

What then was to be done with language so that it could be made a fitting vehicle for poetic expression? In the past, every initiator of a literary form had, first of all, to do something with language when it had begun to lose tone and color through being used too long in a particular way. The old way of renewing the literary language was to refresh it from popular speech. This was all very well when Dante took over what he called "the illustrious vernacular," or when Luther took over the language of the housewife and the artisan, or when Wordsworth advocated the language of the common Englishman, the rustic. But in the latter part of the nineteenth century, as in our own time, the spread of popular education meant that "the illustrious vernacular" was disappearing, for the popular language was becoming merely a degeneration of the written one. Faced with the problem of language, Mallarmé advanced a number of ideas, which he himself put into practice and some of which have been upheld by poets and writers ever since. Words, he said, should be deprived of their too obvious meaning; the poet should use words in an evocative and a suggestive instead of a literal and logical sense; the mood, the idea, the emotion should be evoked instead of described. This, it will be remem-

bered, was what Edgar Allan Poe had succeeded in doing, both in verse and prose, and Mallarmé even more than Baudelaire was under the spell of Poe. . . .

....

But what was original with the Symbolists was their attempt to unite these theories with the new philosophies of the unconscious that were then coming in, chiefly the philosophy of Hartmann, but also that of Schopenhauer, which tended to show that intelligence was a by-product of other life-forces and that reason and logic were more or less irrelevant. This gave some of the Symbolists a more metaphysical and cerebral attitude than their predecessors towards the content and structure of a poem. Mallarmé was metaphysical where Novalis was mystical, where Rimbaud was sensuous and ardent, and Verlaine emotional. With Mallarmé, a phase of the interior life of the mind, what he called the transcendent reality, would be translated into an idea, and this idea would then be transposed into a symbol, or several symbols, that would evoke or suggest it, and would contain it as "a plant contains a flower without resembling it." From this came the Symbolist formula, or one of the Symbolist formulas: a work of art is a thought inscribed in a symbol.

....

Towards his last phase [Mallarmé] got to the point where he conceived that poetry should actually be written as music is written, the theme orchestrated instead of developed, the words used like notes in music, grouped in some lines, isolated in others, the whole printed so as to give obscurely the effect of a sheet of music. At this stage he had fallen under the influence of Wagner and Debussy in music, and had reached that old heresy, or old illusion, that a synthesis of all the arts could be achieved and a single art evolved which would convey visual effects and sound effects, suggest plastic effects and color effects, as well as transmit a verbal meaning. The idea of inventing a language which would convey this ensemble occurred to him and to some of his followers; this notion has, in actual fact, been put into practice in our own time by James Joyce, in his strange *Work in Progress*.

4

The poet, sometimes assumed to belong to the Symbolist group, who has had the most influence on writers of our time is Jules Laforgue. While drawing on the ideas of the Symbolists, he can hardly be regarded as one of them, for he was against their favorite doctrine that the interior life represented the only reality, and he considered that they had beaten too complete a retreat from everyday life. He himself evolved a sophisticated realistic poetry in which the two psychic streams, the conscious and the unconscious, were subtly revealed and intermingled. In poems, written in ordinary conversational language, about flirtations, railway stations, pianos playing in the suburbs, the little miseries of winter, or in poems built around the refrains of old songs, he accomplished, in the 'eighties of the last century, almost everything in verse which we consider to be the special expression of this modern, post-war, disintegrated age. He sunk himself in the study of philosophy, and especially in the philosophy of the sub-conscious as, in his pre-Freudian day, it was explained by the German philosopher Hartmann. If he did not succeed in revealing it as Joyce and Proust have done, Laforgue managed to convey, in verse arranged, not logically but according to the association of ideas and with a subtle use of symbolism (not the deliberate symbolism of Mallarmé but a symbolism springing naturally from the subject), the mystery that lies behind the most trivial happenings.

Laforgue's aim was to express in poetry the *homme moyen* of modern civilization, the man who in each country possesses the same sort of apartment, the same sort of piano—in our day it would be a radio—who wears the same sort of clothes, who has fought with the same sort of weapons in the same war. This personage was given by Laforgue a variety of cultivated, sophisticated emotions and ideas, and enough music, art and literature at the back of his mind to color or give a sort of refrain to his experiences of life. Laforgue's influence has been very great, and there have been choruses and choirs of Laforguians in every modern literature. . . .

....

Even more than the official Symbolists Laforgue broke up the logically arranged lines in verse which were an imposition from all previous literatures. Even in the most romantic English poetry, which at times provided a pattern for the Symbolists, it was the poet's design to develop his theme logically, in logically arranged lines. . . .

The influence of Laforgue in breaking up the old logic, the old unity of poetry, was greater than Mallarmé's, and the content and form of his verse, in addition, exercised a considerable influence on the technique of the novel. This was true, however, of all those modern poets who broke off from the older traditions. Baudelaire's peculiar realism, in which he expressed his own personal conflicts with life and the conflict of the interior life with the

exterior world, was one of the influences which made for the modern autobiographic, semi-realistic novel, with a strong strain of lyricism running through it. Another persistent and lasting influence towards this kind of fiction was Goethe's *Wilhelm Meister,* which still holds its glamour for most young men and women, and for all young writers.

Among the other forces acting on the technique of the novel was the Symbolist formula: a writer should not describe a scene or a character or an emotion—he must evoke them. This—with Henry James's "minimum of architecture" and his later device of presenting his characters and his story "through the opportunity and the sensibility of some more or less detached, some not strictly involved, though thoroughly interested and intelligent witness or reporter," his habit of dealing with barely ponderable motives—is responsible for the bulk of modern technical reforms in fiction. The idea of giving us the scene, not as Flaubert did, completely objectively, with the novelist like God in the universe the ideal spectator present everywhere, but simply as one or two persons involved see it, was first carried out by Stendhal, who, in his famous account of the battle of Waterloo, describes only so much of it as was apparent to Fabrizio; similarly, in *Ulysses,* when James Joyce is describing a funeral, his method differs fundamentally from that of Flaubert. In the account of the funeral in *Madame Bovary,* we have every significant detail realistically described—the funeral procession, the graveclothes of Emma, the three coffins, the chanting choristers, the lighted candles, the priest, the lowering of the coffin into the open grave. Through nine or ten pages we have nothing but the funeral. James Joyce takes about thirty pages to present his funeral, but instead of Flaubert's objective description, he presents the streets of Dublin and some people passing along, as they appear, in occasional views through the shaded windows, to the occupants of one of the mourning-carriages. We have the aimless gossip, on all sorts of topics, by the men in the carriage—the half-conscious and subconscious thoughts of the chief character, Leopold Bloom. Similarly, when Virginia Woolf is presenting, in *Jacob's Room,* a party, there is no objective description; she puts the party before us by giving us the conversation of people meeting and passing each other in the ballroom, by remarks thrown out as the partners dance past each other; and the effect, in both cases, of the inconsequent actuality of the conversation is most memorable in bringing to us the funeral and the dance; the reader feels as if he were participating in the events. However, this sort of technique is sometimes bewildering to those accustomed to the realistic, semi-realistic, or romantic novel, for it is often only when the reader has got the impression of a whole chapter in his mind that he knows what is taking place, or where it is taking place.

5

But the great, the overwhelming influences on all literary transformations—on technique, on content, on language—were the new discoveries in psychology, the new knowledge of the mind, arrived at in the last quarter of the nineteenth century and the beginning of the twentieth. When all the old conventions were being shaken to pieces, it was discovered that the universally accepted figure, the conscious man, the man that all laws, governments, civilizations, had been built around, was also a convention. Man was only conscious to a limited degree: the greater part of him was unconscious. This fact had peeped in and out of philosophy for a long time, but as it was very disturbing, the bulk of mankind preferred to ignore it. Hartmann expressed the discovery first, for the Germans, and when his work was translated into French it greatly stirred the writers in reaction against realism, for it seemed then as if this new philosophy would be a pillar of support to those who believed the interior life, the life beyond everyday life, to be the only reality. In the 'eighties, Charcot and Ribot demonstrated the discoveries for the French; and in America, at about the same time, William James, experimenting in psychology, got himself employed as a census-assistant so as to have the opportunity to meet and study a wide variety of human beings. After his census experience he declared, "We all have a subliminal self—that is, a self below the threshold of consciousness, which may at any time make an eruption into our ordinary life. At its lowest, this is only a deposit of forgotten memories; at its highest, we do not know what it is at all." It was James, too, who was responsible for the famous simile of the iceberg—that the conscious mind is comparable to the smaller part that is above water, the unconscious to the greater bulk that is submerged.

Théodule Ribot showed the existence, in us, of unconscious memory. Pierre Janet, Charcot's pupil, who lectured recently at the Harvard Tercentenary, demonstrated how several personalities could exist at the same time in one individual, each now and again breaking through to the other. Freud, a while later, developed the technique by which, he said, the subconscious personality and the hidden memory could be brought to the surface, or partly to the surface. After the conscious man and the unified personality were shown to be conventions, the philosopher, Henri Bergson, came along and said that what we call time is a convention; real time was not hours as measured by a clock, or in days or weeks on a calendar; it, too, was something inward, duration experienced; every moment in life represents our entire past shaping itself into a new creative movement; nothing was fixed or finished; everything was in a state of becoming. For Bergson, also, the unconscious was the source from which flowed, in a thin stream for some, in a wider stream for others, our conscious life.

All the literary philosophies relating to the revelation of life having reached a dead end, the writers had to turn to the experimental and speculative philosophies. Such discoveries as had come through them were eagerly seized upon by that type of mind which initiates new literary modes and ideas. Now the first problem was: Could this subconscious part of man, this part that was now described as the moving force of his being, be expressed in literature? As in poetry the first attempt had been made, in the 'eighties, so now in prose the first attempt also was made, and made by a curiously talented novelist of very limited range, who was a follower of one of the Symbolist groups, Edouard Dujardin, still alive. He attempted to express the undercurrent of the mind of his character by "the interior monologue." Now, what is the interior monologue, which is being so identified with our most advanced novelists, though, like almost every other modern literary device, it dates back to the nineteenth century? I know no better definition of it than Dujardin's own: "The interior monologue is the discourse without auditor, unspoken, by which a person expresses his inmost thought, the thought nearest the unconscious, anterior to any logical organization, by means of sentences with a minimum of syntax. It is done so as to give the impression that it is poured out, and is a slice of the interior life without explanation or commentary."

Dujardin himself had not sufficient clue to the technique to be employed in rendering "the thought nearest the unconscious." But in the interim between him and the writer who took the next step forward, James Joyce, there came all the discoveries of Freud and Freud's technique for getting a patient to pour out his unconscious life. That the interior monologue, which was one of the most discussed features of *Ulysses* on its publication, was managed so successfully was because Freud had actually discovered a method of revealing the subconscious and the twilight stage between the conscious and the unconscious. Freud made the subject lie on a couch while he himself took up a position where he could not be seen, and induced the subject to talk, following step by step anything that came into his mind, one idea leading to another, one memory suggesting another, one association dragging another to the surface of the mind, until the world below consciousness was revealed either wholly or in part. This is really the process followed by Joyce in the celebrated monologue of Marion Bloom with which *Ulysses* ends.

For purposes of illustration, I give a short quotation from this monologue, which is a widely imitated device in recent novels:

> they all write about some woman in their poetry well I suppose he won't find many like me where softly sighs of love the light guitar where poetry is in the air the blue sea and the moon shining so beautifully coming back on the night-boat from Tarifa the light-house at Europa point the guitar that fellow played was so expressive will I never go back there again all new faces two glancing eyes a lattice hid I'll sing that for him they're my eyes as if he has anything of a poet two eyes as darkly bright as love's own star aren't those beautiful words as love's young star it'll be a change the Lord knows to have an intelligent person to talk to about yourself not always listening to him and Billy Prescott's ad and Keyses' ad and Tom the Divil's ad then if anything goes wrong in their business we have to suffer.

Is this actually the way the mind works anterior to consciousness? An extraordinary light was recently thrown on the authenticity of the procedure by the case of a criminal dying in New York. Detectives attached to the criminal bureaus in our large cities are, like writers and doctors, students of psychology, and one of them had the idea of taking down a stenographic report of the utterance of a gangster, Dutch Schultz, while in that state of mind, as the result of a wound, when he was incapable of imposing any logic on what he was saying. The whole stenographic report, not more than a couple of newspaper columns, was a real revelation of the content of the man's mind. Compare the quotation from the novel with the following, from this particular report. Whereas the Joyce extract runs on without punctuation marks, the stenographer has put them into this extract:

> Don't put any one near this check; you might have—please do it for me. Let me get up, heh? In the olden days they waited and they waited. Please give me shot. It is from the factory. Sure, that is bad—well, oh good ahead that happens for trying. I don't want harmony. Oh, mamma, mamma! Who give it to him? Who give it to him? Let me in the district—fire—factory that he was nowhere near. It smoldered.

On the publication of *Ulysses,* it was considered by many that it was not possible in literature to carry the expression of the unconscious further and have it keep any intelligible pattern. However, Joyce's new puzzling book, *Work in Progress,* is an attempt to carry the revelation of the unconscious life many stages further than in *Ulysses* and much further than any other writer has dreamed of bringing it. Proust said of the opening chapter of *A la Recherche du Temps Perdu,* "I have tried to envelope my first chapter in the half-waking impressions of sleep." But Joyce, in this latest work, tries to depict the whole night-life of the mind, and the result, I am afraid, will be intelligible to a very limited number of readers. In *Work in Progress* he is influenced by Novalis's and Mallarmé's theories of the sounds of words, and the work has, in its best-known passage, reproduced so effectively, through the sonority of his words and sentences, the effects of falling night and fluttering river-water that, without the words being even intelligible, the reader can know what the passage is about if it is read aloud and falls on the ear as music does. There are specific points in technique in which it is difficult to believe that any writer can go beyond Joyce. One is the skill with which he evokes a scene, an atmosphere, a personage, a group, without ever once describing them or giving a hint as to who they are or where the scene takes place. He is a master of the evocative method, and if the reader compares the opening of *Ulysses* with the opening of Sinclair Lewis's *It Can't Happen Here,* he will observe immediately and inevitably the difference between the two methods, the evocative and the descriptive. Joyce's mastery of the interior monologue is the second point in his technique in which he is likely to remain unsurpassed, and for this mastery he undoubtedly owes a great deal to Freud.

6

There are a few points in common between James Joyce and the other outstanding modern innovator, Marcel Proust. For Proust, also, the great reality is in the unconscious; he also has an interest in sleep as its great manifestation; for both writers no happening, no event is complete, everything is in a state of becoming. The work of both represents a reaction against realism, and is at the same time a development of it. Again it should be noted that, in literature, the age that is coming to birth is not only a reaction against the age that is dying but also an outgrowth of it. Both Joyce and Proust subscribe to the fundamental dogma of realism—that literature should be about everyday life; the work of each illustrates certain of the realistic doctrines. Joyce began definitely under the influence of Flaubert, which is patent in the stories in *Dubliners,* and though in the meantime, as can be seen in *Portrait of the Artist,* he was affected by the technique of Henry James, the influence of Flaubert is still traceable in *Ulysses,* especially the pre-realistic Flaubert of *La Tentation de Saint Antoine.* His characters are on the same level as Flaubert's and he has always held to the Flaubertian veto as to the author's commenting on his personages. He has, however, a whole battery of technical devices to reveal what is passing in their minds and what rises up in their memories, of which the interior monologue is but one. Others are the use of scenes parallel with scenes from the Odyssey, of paraphrases of myths and legends, and of parodies of writing representing stages in the development of language. The technique is infinitely more complex than Proust's, the interior life revealed very much less so; in fact, it is comparatively simple, comparatively ordinary, and does not embrace a wide variety of experiences.

....

Both Joyce and Proust give the same impression, that they have penetrated into reaches of the inner life of men and presented them with far more actuality than has been done before. Yet we feel that this very same impression was given in their day by the creators of Emma Bovary and Anna Karenina, and it is probably the impression given by all innovators in literature. In both *Ulysses* and *À la Recherche du Temps Perdu,* the author is a character in his own work; this is perhaps always necessary in the literature which may be described as the literature of memory, in which the author invokes Time lived through.

This is true of the American writer whose work, likewise, might be described as Remembrance of Things Past and is also made up of Time, myths, legends, history, language—Thomas Wolfe too introduces Time into his titles, and has named one of his books *Of Time and the River.* Like Proust he tells us of his struggles with Time-elements, and has, in addition to the two Time-elements of Proust, the Present and the Past, brought in a third which he calls Time Immutable, the time of rivers, mountains, oceans and the earth. Like Proust he discourses on the powers of his memory to bring back odors, sounds, colors, shapes; like Joyce he has struggled with the mystery of myths and legends; like many modern writers, Aldous Huxley and D.H. Lawrence, he has expressed the conviction that all serious creative work must at bottom be autobiographical, a conviction with which it is not necessary to agree, but which is undoubtedly true of all those forms of literature in which Time and Memory are the sources of inspiration. . . .

Reprinted from *From These Roots: The Ideas That Have Made Modern Literature* (New York: Columbia University Press, 1937), pp. 312-357.

Supplementary Reading List

Aldridge, John W., ed. *Critiques and Essays on Modern Fiction: 1920-1951.* New York: Ronald, 1952.

Baker, Ernest A. *The History of the English Novel,* volume 10. New York: Barnes & Noble, 1939.

Beach, Joseph Warren. *The Twentieth-Century Novel: Studies in Technique.* New York: Appleton, 1932.

Beebe, Maurice. "Introduction: What Modernism Was." *Journal of Modern Literature,* 3 (1974): 1065-1084.

Beebe. *Ivory Towers and Sacred Founts: The Artist as Hero in Fiction from Goethe to Joyce.* New York: New York University Press, 1964.

Beja, Maurice. *Epiphany in the Modern Novel.* Seattle: University of Washington Press, 1971.

Bell, Clive. *Old Friends; Personal Recollections.* New York: Harcourt, Brace, 1957.

Bell, Quentin. *Bloomsbury.* New York: Basic Books, 1968.

Bentley, Eric, ed. *The Importance of "Scrutiny": Selections from "Scrutiny": A Quarterly Review, 1932-1948.* New York: Stewart, 1948.

Bergonzi, Bernard. *Heroes' Twilight: A Study of the Literature of the Great War.* New York: Coward-McCann, 1965.

Bergonzi. *The Situation of the Novel.* Pittsburgh: University of Pittsburgh Press, 1970.

Bergonzi. *The Turn of the Century: Essays on Victorian and Modern English Literature.* New York: Barnes & Noble, 1973.

Bradbury, Malcolm. *Possibilities: Essays on the State of the Novel.* New York: Oxford University Press, 1973.

Brewster, Dorothy, and Angus Burrell. *Modern Fiction.* New York: Columbia University Press, 1934.

Bridgwater, Patrick. *Nietzsche in Anglosaxony: A Study of Nietzsche's Impact on English and American Literature.* Leicester: Leicester University Press, 1972.

Brown, Edward K. *Rhythm in the Novel.* Toronto: University of Toronto Press, 1950.

Bufkin, E. C. *The Twentieth-Century Novel in English: A Checklist.* Athens: University of Georgia Press, 1967.

Burgum, Edwin B. *The Novel and the World's Dilemma.* New York: Oxford University Press, 1947.

Chapple, J. A. V. *Documentary and Imaginative Literature, 1880-1920.* New York: Barnes & Noble, 1970.

Chevalley, Abel. *The Modern English Novel,* translated by B. R. Redman. New York: Knopf, 1927.

Chiari, Joseph. *The Aesthetics of Modernism.* London: Vision, 1970.

Church, Margaret. *Time and Reality: Studies in Contemporary Fiction.* Chapel Hill: University of North Carolina Press, 1963.

Colum, Mary. *From These Roots: The Ideas That Have Made Modern Literature.* New York: Columbia University Press, 1937.

Coveney, Peter. *The Image of Childhood, The Individual and Society: A Study of the Theme in English Literature,* revised edition. Baltimore: Penguin, 1967.

Cox, C. B. *The Free Spirit: A Study of Liberal Humanism in the Novels of George Eliot, E. M. Forster, Virginia Woolf, Angus Wilson.* London: Oxford University Press, 1963.

Cunliffe, J. W. *English Literature in the Twentieth Century.* New York: Macmillan, 1934.

Daiches, David. *The Novel and the Modern World.* Chicago: University of Chicago Press, 1939; revised, 1960.

Davie, Donald, ed. *Russian Literature and Modern English Fiction: A Collection of Critical Essays.* Chicago: University of Chicago Press, 1965.

Drew, Elizabeth A. *The Modern Novel: Some Aspects of Contemporary Fiction.* New York: Harcourt, Brace, 1926.

Drew. *The Novel: A Modern Guide to Fifteen English Masterpieces.* New York: Dell, 1967.

Dyson, A. E., ed. *The English Novel: Select Bibliographical Guides.* London: Oxford University Press, 1974.

Eagleton, Terry. *Exiles and Emigres: Studies in Modern Literature.* New York: Schocken, 1970.

Edel, Leon. *The Psychological Novel: 1900-1950.* Philadelphia: Lippincott, 1955. Republished as *The Modern Psychological Novel.* New York: Grove, 1959.

Ellis, Geoffrey U. *Twilight on Parnassus: A Survey of Post-War Fiction and Pre-War Criticism.* London: Joseph, 1939.

Evans, B. Ifor. *English Literature between the Wars.* London: Methuen, 1948.

Fleishman, Avrom. *The English Historical Novel: Walter Scott to Virginia Woolf.* Baltimore: Johns Hopkins University Press, 1971.

Ford, Boris, ed. *The Modern Age.* Harmondsworth: Penguin, 1961.

Forster, E. M. *Aspects of the Novel.* London: Arnold, 1927.

Fraser, G. S. *The Modern Writer and His World,* revised edition. London: Deutsch, 1964.

Friedman, Alan W. *The Turn of the Novel.* New York: Oxford University Press, 1966.

Friedman, ed. *Forms of Modern British Fiction.* Austin: University of Texas Press, 1975.

Friedman, Melvin J. *Stream of Consciousness: A Study in Literary Method.* New Haven: Yale University Press, 1955.

Friedman, Melvin J., and John B. Vickery, eds. *The Shaken Realist: Essays in Honor of Frederick J. Hoffman.* Baton Rouge: Louisiana State University Press, 1970.

Frierson, William C. *The English Novel in Transition, 1885-1940.* Norman: University of Oklahoma Press, 1942.

Gadd, David. *The Loving Friends: A Portrait of Bloomsbury*. New York: Harcourt Brace Jovanovich, 1974.

Garrett, Peter K. *Scene and Symbol from George Eliot to James Joyce: Studies in Changing Fictional Mode*. New Haven: Yale University Press, 1969.

Gaunt, William. *The March of the Moderns*. London: Cape, 1949.

Gill, Richard. *Happy Rural Seat: The English Country House and the Literary Imagination*. New Haven: Yale University Press, 1972.

Gillie, Christopher. *Movements in English Literature, 1900-1940*. Cambridge: Cambridge University Press, 1975.

Gindin, James. *Harvest of a Quiet Eye: The Novel of Compassion*. Bloomington: Indiana University Press, 1971.

Glicksberg, Charles I. *Modern Literary Perspectivism*. Dallas: Southern Methodist University Press, 1970.

Glicksberg. *The Sexual Revolution in Modern English Literature*. The Hague: Nijhoff, 1973.

Gregory, Horace. *Spirit of Time and Place: Collected Essays*. New York: Norton, 1973.

Hampshire, Stuart N. *Modern Writers and Others: Essays*. New York: Knopf, 1970.

Hardy, Barbara. *The Appropriate Form: An Essay on the Novel*. London: University of London Press, 1964.

Hardy, John Edward. *Man in the Modern Novel*. Seattle: University of Washington Press, 1964.

Harper, Howard M., and Charles Edge, eds. *The Classic British Novel*. Athens: University of Georgia Press, 1972.

Heilbrun, Carolyn G. "The Bloomsbury Group," in her *Towards Androgyny: Aspects of Male and Female in Literature*. London: Gollancz, 1973, pp. 115-167.

Hoare, Dorothy M. *Some Studies in the Modern Novel*. London: Chatto & Windus, 1938.

Hochman, Baruch. *The Test of Character from the Victorian Novel to the Modern*. Cranbury, N.J.: Fairleigh Dickinson University Press, 1983.

Hoffman, Frederick J. *Freudianism and the Literary Mind*. Baton Rouge: Louisiana State University Press, 1945.

Hoffman. *The Mortal No: Death and the Modern Imagination*. Princeton: Princeton University Press, 1964.

Holroyd, Michael. *Lytton Strachey and the Bloomsbury Group: His Work, Their Influence*. Baltimore: Penguin, 1971.

Hough, Graham. *Image and Experience: Studies in a Literary Revolution*. Lincoln: University of Nebraska Press, 1960.

Howarth, Herbert. *The Irish Writers, 1880-1940: Literature Under Parnell's Star*. London: Rockliff, 1958.

Humphrey, Robert. *Stream of Consciousness in the Modern Novel*. Berkeley & Los Angeles: University of California Press, 1954.

Hynes, Samuel. *Edwardian Occasions: Essays on English Writing in the Early Twentieth Century.* London: Routledge, 1972.

Hynes. *The Edwardian Turn of Mind.* Princeton: Princeton University Press, 1968.

Jackson, Holbrook. *The Eighteen Nineties: A Review of Art and Ideas at the Close of the Nineteenth Century.* London: Richards, 1913.

Jameson, Storm. *The Georgian Novel and Mr. Robinson.* London: Heinemann, 1929.

Johnstone, J. K. *The Bloomsbury Group: A Study of E. M. Forster, Lytton Strachey, Virginia Woolf, and Their Circle.* New York: Noonday, 1954.

Josipovici, Gabriel. *The World and the Book: A Study of Modern Fiction.* Stanford: Stanford University Press, 1971.

Josipovici, ed. *The Modern English Novel: The Reader, the Writer, and the Work.* New York: Harper & Row, 1976.

Kaplan, Harold J. *The Passive Voice: An Approach to Modern Fiction.* Athens: Ohio University Press, 1966.

Kaplan, Sydney Janet. *Feminine Consciousness in the Modern Novel.* Urbana: University of Illinois Press, 1975.

Kenner, Hugh. *Gnomon: Essays on Contemporary Literature.* New York: McDowell, Obolensky, 1958.

Kermode, Frank. "The English Novel, circa 1907," in *Twentieth-Century Literature in Retrospect,* edited by Reuben A. Brower. Cambridge: Harvard University Press, 1971, pp. 45-64.

Kettle, Arnold. *An Introduction to the English Novel,* volume 2, *Henry James to the Present.* London: Hutchinson, 1951.

Krieger, Murray. *The Tragic Vision: Variations on a Theme in Literary Interpretation.* Chicago: University of Chicago Press, 1966.

Kumar, Shiv K. *Bergson and the Stream of Consciousness Novel.* New York: New York University Press, 1963.

Lauterbach, Edward S., and W. Eugene Davies. *The Transitional Age in British Literature, 1880-1920.* Troy, N.Y.: Whitston, 1973.

Leavis, F. R. *The Common Pursuit.* New York: Stewart, 1952.

Leavis, ed. *A Selection from "Scrutiny,"* 2 volumes. Cambridge: Cambridge University Press, 1968.

Leavis, Q. D. *Fiction and the Reading Public.* London: Chatto & Windus, 1932.

Lehmann, John, ed. *The Craft of Letters in England: A Symposium.* London: Crescent, 1956.

Lesser, Simon O. *Fiction and the Unconscious.* Boston: Beacon, 1957.

Lovett, Robert M., and Helen S. Hughes. *The History of the Novel in England.* Boston: Houghton Mifflin, 1932.

Lubbock, Percy. *The Craft of Fiction.* London: Cape, 1921.

Markovic, Vida E. *The Changing Face: Disintegration of Personality in the Twentieth-Century British Novel, 1900-1950.* Carbondale: Southern Illinois University Press, 1970.

Maurois, André. *Prophets and Poets*, translated by Hamish Miles. New York: Harper, 1935.

McCormick, John. *Catastrophe and Imagination: An Interpretation of the Recent English and American Novel.* London: Longmans, Green, 1957.

Melchiori, Giorgio. *The Tightrope Walkers: Studies of Mannerism in Modern English Literature.* London: Routledge, 1956.

Mendilow, A. A. *Time and the Novel.* New York: Humanities Press, 1952.

Muir, Edwin. *The Structure of the Novel.* London: Hogarth Press, 1928.

Nicholson, Norman. *Man and Literature.* London: Macmillan, 1943.

O'Connor, William Van. "Toward a History of Bloomsbury." *Southwest Review,* 40 (1955): 36-52.

O'Connor, ed. *Forms of Modern Fiction: Essays Collected in Honor of Joseph Warren Beach.* Minneapolis: University of Minnesota Press, 1948.

O'Faolain, Sean. *The Vanishing Hero: Studies in Novelists of the Twenties.* London: Eyre & Spottiswoode, 1956.

Paterson, John. *The Novel as Faith: The Gospel According to James, Hardy, Conrad, Joyce, Lawrence and Virginia Woolf.* Boston: Gambit, 1973.

Pendry, E. D. *The New Feminism of English Fiction: A Study in Contemporary Women-Novelists.* Tokyo: Kenkyusha, 1956.

Phelps, Gilbert. *The Russian Novel in English Fiction.* London: Hutchinson, 1956.

Pritchett, V. S. *The Living Novel and Later Appreciations.* New York: Random House, 1964.

Ray, Paul C. *The Surrealist Movement in England.* Ithaca: Cornell University Press, 1971.

Rice, Thomas Jackson. *English Fiction, 1900-1950*, 2 volumes. Detroit: Gale Research, 1979, 1983.

Rosenbaum, Stanford P., ed. *The Bloomsbury Group: A Collection of Memoirs, Commentary, and Criticism.* Toronto: University of Toronto Press, 1975.

Rosenbaum, ed. *English Literature and British Philosophy: A Collection of Essays.* Chicago: University of Chicago Press, 1971.

Savage, Derek S. *The Withered Branch: Six Studies in the Modern Novel.* London: Eyre & Spottiswoode, 1950.

Schorer, Mark. "Technique as Discovery." *Hudson Review,* 1 (Spring 1948): 67-87.

Schorer, ed. *Modern British Fiction.* New York: Oxford University Press, 1961.

Scott-James, Rolfe A. *Fifty Years of English Literature, 1900-1950; With a Postscript, 1951-1955.* London: Longmans, Green, 1956.

Shapiro, Charles, ed. *Twelve Original Essays on Great English Novels.* Detroit: Wayne State University Press, 1960.

Spencer, Sharon. *Space, Time and Structure in the Modern Novel.* Chicago: Swallow, 1971.

Stade, George, ed. *Six Modern British Novelists*. New York: Columbia University Press, 1974.

Starkie, Enid. *From Gautier to Eliot: The Influence of France on English Literature, 1851-1939*. London: Hutchinson, 1960.

Steinburg, Edwin R., ed. *Stream of Consciousness Technique in the Modern Novel*. Port Washington, N.Y.: Associated Faculty Press, 1979.

Stewart, Douglas H. *The Ark of God: Studies in Five Modern Novelists*. London: Carey Kingsgate Press, 1961.

Stewart, J. I. M. *Eight Modern Writers*. Oxford: Clarendon Press, 1963.

Swinnerton, Frank. *The Georgian Scene: A Panorama*. New York: Farrar & Rinehart, 1934.

Taylor, Estella R. *The Modern Irish Writers*. Lawrence: University of Kansas Press, 1954.

Temple, Ruth Z., and Martin Tucker. *Twentieth Century British Literature: A Reference Guide and Bibliography*. New York: Ungar, 1968.

Tillyard, E. M. W. *The Epic Strain in the English Novel*. London: Chatto & Windus, 1963.

Tindall, William York. *Forces in Modern British Literature, 1885-1956*. New York: Knopf, 1956.

Troy, William. *Selected Essays*. Edited by Stanley Edgar Hyman. New Brunswick: Rutgers University Press, 1967.

Unterecker, John, ed. *Approaches to the Twentieth Century Novel*. New York: Crowell, 1965.

Van Ghent, Dorothy. *The English Novel: Form and Function*. New York: Rinehart, 1953.

Verschoyle, Derek, ed. *The English Novelists: A Survey of the Novel by Twenty Contemporary Novelists*. London: Chatto & Windus, 1936.

Vickery, John B. *The Literary Impact of the Golden Bough*. Princeton: Princeton University Press, 1973.

Wagenknecht, Edward. *Cavalcade of the English Novel*. New York: Holt, 1954.

Ward, Alfred C. *The Nineteen-Twenties: Literature and Ideas in the Post-War Decade*. London: Methuen, 1930.

Ward. *Twentieth-Century English Literature, 1900-1960*. London: Methuen, 1964.

Watt, Ian. *The Rise of the Novel*. Berkeley & Los Angeles: University of California Press, 1957.

West, Paul. *The Modern Novel*, volume 1, revised edition. London: Hutchinson, 1965.

Wiley, Paul L. *The British Novel: Conrad to the Present*. Northbrook, Ill.: AHM, 1973.

Williams, Raymond. *The English Novel from Dickens to Lawrence*. London: Chatto & Windus, 1970.

Wilson, Colin. *The Strength to Dream: Literature and the Imagination*. Boston: Houghton Mifflin, 1962.

Wilson, Edmund. *Classics and Commercials: A Literary Chronicle of the Forties*. New York: Farrar, Straus, 1950.

Wilson. *The Shores of Light: A Literary Chronicle of the Twenties and Thirties*. New York: Farrar, Straus & Young, 1952.

Contributors

Bernard Benstock.. *University of Tulsa*
Shari Benstock... *University of Tulsa*
Barbara Brothers...*Youngstown State University*
Charles Burkhart... *Temple University*
Jerry W. Carlson .... *De Paul University*
Douglas M. Catron ....*Iowa State University*
Dido Davies .... *Cambridge, England*
Philip B. Dematteis...*Columbia, South Carolina*
Paul A. Doyle ....*Nassau College, State University of New York*
Kitti Carriker Eastman ....*University of Notre Dame*
David Farmer .... *University of Texas*
Daniel Farson .... *Appledore, England*
Gloria G. Fromm...*University of Illinois at Chicago*
J. V. Guerinot...*University of Wisconsin*
Kenneth Hopkins ....*Norfolk, England*
Rhonda Keith .... *University of Tulsa*
Charles Kemnitz.. *University of Tulsa*
Harry Keyishian ....*Fairleigh Dickinson University*
Margaret B. McDowell.. *University of Iowa*
Mary A. O'Toole .... *University of Tulsa*
Scott Simpkins... *University of Tulsa*
Thomas F. Staley... *University of Tulsa*
Wesley D. Sweetser.................................*State University of New York College at Oswego*
Clark Thayer .... *Tulsa, Oklahoma*
Kingsley Widmer...*San Diego State University*
J. J. Wilson ....*Sonoma State University*

Cumulative Index

Dictionary of Literary Biography, Volumes 1-36
Dictionary of Literary Biography Yearbook, 1980-1983
Dictionary of Literary Biography Documentary Series, Volumes 1-4